Leadership

Enhancing the Lessons of Experience   Sixth Edition

Richard L. Hughes
Robert C. Ginnett
Gordon J. Curphy

McGraw-Hill
Irwin

Boston   Burr Ridge, IL   Dubuque, IA   New York   San Francisco   St. Louis
Bangkok   Bogotá   Caracas   Kuala Lumpur   Lisbon   London   Madrid   Mexico City
Milan   Montreal   New Delhi   Santiago   Seoul   Singapore   Sydney   Taipei   Toronto

McGraw-Hill Irwin

LEADERSHIP: ENHANCING THE LESSONS OF EXPERIENCE

Published by McGraw-Hill/Irwin, a business unit of The McGraw-Hill Companies, Inc., 1221 Avenue of the Americas, New York, NY, 10020. Copyright © 2009, 2006, 2002, 1999, 1996, 1993 by The McGraw-Hill Companies, Inc. All rights reserved. No part of this publication may be reproduced or distributed in any form or by any means, or stored in a database or retrieval system, without the prior written consent of The McGraw-Hill Companies, Inc., including, but not limited to, in any network or other electronic storage or transmission, or broadcast for distance learning.

Some ancillaries, including electronic and print components, may not be available to customers outside the United States.

This book is printed on acid-free paper.

1 2 3 4 5 6 7 8 9 0 DOC/DOC 0 9 8

ISBN 978-0-07-340504-9

MHID 0-07-340504-3

Editorial director: *Brent Gordon*
Publisher: *Paul Ducham*
Managing developmental editor: *Laura Hurst Spell*
Editorial assistant: *Sara Knox Hunter*
Associate marketing manager: *Kelly Odom*
Project manager: *Jim Labeots*
Lead production supervisor: *Carol A. Bielski*
Design coordinator: *Joanne Mennemeier*
Senior media project manager: *Susan Lombardi*
Cover design: *Joanne Mennemeier*
Typeface: *10/12 Palatino*
Compositor: *Laserwords Private Limited*
Printer: *R. R. Donnelley*

Library of Congress Cataloging-in-Publication Data

Hughes, Richard L.
    Leadership : enhancing the lessons of experience / Richard L. Hughes, Robert C. Ginnett,
Gordon J. Curphy.—6th ed.
        p. cm.
    Includes index.
    ISBN-13: 978-0-07-340504-9 (alk. paper)
    ISBN-10: 0-07-340504-3 (alk. paper)
    1. Leadership. I. Ginnett, Robert C. II. Curphy, Gordon J. III. Title.
HM1261.H84 2009
303.3'4—dc22

                                                                        2007041995

www.mhhe.com

About the Authors

Rich Hughes is the Transformation Chair at the U.S. Air Force Academy. In that role he works with other senior leaders to help transform the Academy's culture and practices in the academic, military, and athletic arenas in support of the Academy's mission to develop leaders of character. He served for the past 12 years at the Center for Creative Leadership, an international organization devoted to behavioral science research and leadership education, where he worked primarily with senior executives in the areas of strategic leadership and organizational culture change. Rich also served at the Air Force Academy earlier in his career, including a decade as Head of its Department of Behavioral Sciences and Leadership. He is a clinical psychologist, and a graduate of the U.S. Air Force Academy. He has an MA from the University of Texas and a PhD from the University of Wyoming.

Robert Ginnett is a Partner with Impact, a leadership consulting organization. He also worked for many years at the Center for Creative Leadership, where he conducted research on high-performance teams and organizations and also taught in the Leadership at the Peak course. He has worked with hundreds of organizations including General Motors, Novartis, FMC, Prudential, Masterfoods, GlaxoSmithKlein, Daimler Benz, NASA, the Central Intelligence Agency, United Airlines, and Delta Airlines. He also served earlier in his career as a tenured professor at the U.S. Air Force Academy and as its Director of Leadership and Counseling. He also served in numerous line and staff positions in the Air Force, including leadership of an 875-man combat force during the Vietnam War. Robert is an organizational psychologist whose education includes master of business administration, master of arts, and master of philosophy degrees, and a PhD from Yale University.

Gordy Curphy is the President of C3, a human resource consulting firm that helps public and private sector clients achieve better results through people. Gordy has over 25 years of leadership and technical expertise in job analysis and competency modeling; hourly staffing systems; multi-rater feedback systems; performance management design and implementation; leadership development design, delivery, and evaluation; survey construction, administration, and analysis; assessment center methodology; executive coaching, training, and team building; succession planning; team and organizational effectiveness; and strategic and business planning. Prior to forming his own consulting firm, Gordy spent 10 years as a Vice President of Institutional Leadership at The Blandin Foundation and as a Vice President and General Manager at Personnel Decisions International. He is an industrial/organizational psychologist and a graduate of the U.S. Air Force Academy. He has an MA from the University of St. Mary's and a PhD in industrial/organizational psychology from the University of Minnesota.

Foreword

Often the only difference between chaos and a smoothly functioning operation is leadership; this book is about that difference.

The authors are psychologists; therefore the book has a distinctly psychological tone. You, as a reader, are going to be asked to think about leadership the way psychologists do. There is much here about psychological tests and surveys, about studies done in psychological laboratories, and about psychological analyses of good (and poor) leadership. You will often run across common psychological concepts in these pages, such as personality, values, attitudes, perceptions, and self-esteem, plus some not-so-common "jargon-y" phrases like double-loop learning, expectancy theory, and perceived inequity. This is not the same kind of book that would be written by coaches, sales managers, economists, political scientists, or generals.

Be not dismayed. Because these authors are also teachers with a good eye and ear for what students find interesting, they write clearly and cleanly, and they have also included a host of entertaining, stimulating snapshots on leadership: cartoons, quotes, anecdotal highlights, and personal glimpses from a wide range of intriguing people, each offered as an illustration of some scholarly point.

Also, because the authors are, or have been at one time or another, together or singly, not only psychologists and teachers but also children, students, Boy Scouts, parents, professors (at the U.S. Air Force Academy), Air Force officers, pilots, church members, athletes, administrators, insatiable readers, and convivial raconteurs, their stories and examples are drawn from a wide range of personal sources, and their anecdotes ring true.

As psychologists and scholars, they have reviewed here a wide range of psychological studies, other scientific inquiries, personal reflections of leaders, and philosophic writings on the topic of leadership. In distilling this material, they have drawn many practical conclusions useful for current and potential leaders. There are suggestions here for goal setting, for running meetings, for negotiating, for managing conflict within groups, and for handling your own personal stress, to mention just a few.

All leaders, no matter what their age and station, can find some useful tips here, ranging over subjects such as body language, keeping a journal, and how to relax under tension.

In several ways the authors have tried to help you, the reader, feel what it would be like "to be in charge." For example, they have posed quandaries such as the following: You are in a leadership position with a budget provided by an outside funding source. You believe strongly in, say, Topic A, and have taken a strong, visible public stance on that topic. The head of your funding source takes you aside and says, "We disagree with your stance on Topic A. Please tone down your public statements, or we will have to take another look at your budget for next year."

What would you do? Quit? Speak up and lose your budget? Tone down your public statements and feel dishonest? There's no easy answer, and it's not an unusual situation for a leader to be in. Sooner or later, all leaders have to confront just how much outside interference they will tolerate in order to be able to carry out programs they believe in.

The authors emphasize the value of experience in leadership development, a conclusion I thoroughly agree with. Virtually every leader who makes it to the top of whatever pyramid he or she happens to be climbing does so by building on earlier experiences. The successful leaders are those who learn from these earlier experiences, by reflecting on and analyzing them to help solve larger future challenges. In this vein, let me make a suggestion. Actually, let me assign you some homework. (I know, I know, this is a peculiar approach in a book foreword but stay with me, I have a point.)

YOUR ASSIGNMENT: To gain some useful leadership experience, persuade eight people to do some notable activity together for at least two hours that they would not otherwise do without your intervention. Your only restriction is that you cannot tell them why you are doing this.

It can be any eight people: friends, family, teammates, club members, neighbors, students, working colleagues. It can be any activity, except that it should be something more substantial than watching television, eating, going to a movie, or just sitting around talking. It could be a roller-skating party, an organized debate, a songfest, a long hike, a visit to a museum, or volunteer work such as picking up litter or visiting a nursing home. If you will take it upon yourself to make something happen in the world that would not have otherwise happened without you, you will be engaging in an act of leadership with all of its attendant barriers, burdens, and pleasures, and you will quickly learn the relevance of many of the topics that the authors discuss in this book. If you try the eight-person-two-hour experience first and read this book later, you will have a much better understanding of how complicated an act of leadership can be. You will learn about the difficulties of developing a vision ("Now that we are together, what are we going to do?"), of motivating others, of setting agendas and timetables, of securing resources, of the need for follow-through. You may even learn about "loneliness at the top." However, if you are successful, you will also experience the thrill that comes from successful leadership. One person *can* make a difference by enriching the lives of others, if only for a few hours. And for all of the frustrations and complexities of leadership, the tingling satisfaction that comes from success can become almost addictive. The capacity for making things happen can become its own motivation. With an early success, even if it is only with eight people for two hours, you may well be on your way to a leadership future.

The authors believe that leadership development involves reflecting on one's own experiences. Reading this book in the context of your own leadership experience can aid in that process. Their book is comprehensive, scholarly, stimulating, entertaining, and relevant for anyone who wishes to better understand the dynamics of leadership, and to improve her or his own personal performance.

David P. Campbell

Preface

There have been several different kinds of enhancements for this sixth edition of *Leadership: Enhancing the Lessons of Experience.* Two rather major improvements in formatting will be visible even with relatively light scanning through the contents: (1) We have changed the manner of documentation to chapter end notes rather than the parenthetical documentation used in every previous edition in order to enhance the text's readability; and (2) the material on Leadership Skills has been organized differently so that it might be better integrated into the logical flow of the chapters rather than being presented en masse at the end of the book. In this sixth edition there is a set of skills at the end of Part 2 ("Focus on the Leader"), another at the end of Part 3 ("Focus on the Followers"), and a final set at the end of Part 4 ("Focus on the Situation"). This will make it easier for both instructors and students to link Skills readings and assignments to the respective parts of our leadership framework.

Another major change in this edition involves change from the "3 Leaders" feature in the last several editions to a different manner of highlighting specific leaders in each chapter. We believe that it will enhance the applicability of concepts in the text to include even more illustrations of actual leaders in this sixth edition, and we have done that by adding a new feature to every chapter called "Profiles in Leadership." In each chapter there will be several "Profiles" which feature individuals whose leadership exemplifies some interesting aspect of the chapter's content (e.g., Steve Jobs, Oprah Winfrey, Gandhi, etc.). Also more generally, the Highlights in each chapter have been reviewed and updated (i.e., some deleted and others added).

Finally, the sixth edition involves updates or other changes to content in virtually every chapter. Some chapters, of course, received more extensive revision than others based on both input from users and developing knowledge in the respective content areas of the chapters. The chapter on "Assessing Leadership and Measuring Its Effects" (Chapter 4) has been substantially revised to make this difficult material both more accessible and important to students. This includes a completely new introduction to the chapter involving the personal experiences of one of the authors in the collision of two airliners while on a runway as well as a new and provocative section on managerial incompetence. The chapter on "Groups, Teams, and Their Leadership" (Chapter 10) has been substantially revised with the usage of the Team Leadership Model, a major refinement of the model used in previous editions. The chapter on "Leadership and Values" (Chapter 6) includes a new section on positive forms of leadership, including servant leadership and authentic leadership. It also includes newer work on generational differences in values, and we have reintroduced material on moral reasoning which was included in earlier editions. Chapter 2 has a new section on the ideas of Ron Heifetz concerning adaptive leadership.

As with every preceding edition, we are indebted to the superb editorial staff at McGraw-Hill/Irwin including Laura Spell, Sara Hunter, and Jim Labeots who have been thoroughly professional, helpful, and pleasant to work with on this edition. We are also indebted to those individuals whose evaluations and constructive suggestions about the previous edition provided the foundations for many of our revisions. We are grateful for the scholarly and insightful comments from all of our reviewers:

Charles D. White
The University of Alabama

Edward Jernigan
University of North Carolina at Charlotte

Ross L. Mecham III
Virginia Tech

Brooke Quigg
Peirce College

Donna Willis Cline
Cabarrus College of Health Sciences

Jon S. Sager
University of Southern California

James B. Shaffer
University of Southern Maine School of Business

Richard L. Hughes

Robert C. Ginnett

Gordon J. Curphy

We dedicate this book to the leaders of the past from whom we have learned, the leaders of today whose behaviors and actions shape our ever-changing world, and the leaders of tomorrow who will hopefully benefit from the lessons of this book as they face the challenges of globalization in an increasingly interconnected world.

Contents

Leadership Is a Process, Not a Position

If any single idea is central to this book, it is that leadership is a process, not a position. The entire first part of the book explores that idea. One is not a leader—except perhaps in name only—merely because one holds a title or position. Leadership involves something happening as a result of the interaction between a leader and followers.

In Chapter 1 we define leadership and explore its relationship to concepts such as management and followership. We also suggest that better leadership is something for which everyone shares responsibility. In Chapter 2 we discuss how leadership involves complex interactions between the leader, the followers, and the situation they are in. We also present an interactional framework for conceptualizing leadership which becomes an integrating theme throughout the rest of the book. Chapter 3 looks at how we can become better leaders by profiting more fully from our experiences, which is not to say that either the study or the practice of leadership is simple. Part I concludes with a chapter examining basic concepts and methods used in the scientific study of leaders and leadership.

1

Leadership Is Everyone's Business

Introduction

In the spring of 1972, an airplane flew across the Andes mountains carrying its crew and 40 passengers. Most of the passengers were members of an amateur Uruguayan rugby team en route to a game in Chile. The plane never arrived. It crashed in snow-covered mountains, breaking into several pieces on impact. The main part of the fuselage slid like a toboggan down a steep valley, finally coming to rest in waist-deep snow. Although a number of people died immediately or within a day of the impact, the picture for the 28 survivors was not much better. The fuselage initially offered little protection from the extreme cold, food supplies were scant, and a number of passengers had serious injuries from the crash. Over the next few days, several of the passengers became psychotic and several others died from their injuries. Those passengers who were relatively uninjured set out to do what they could to improve their chances of survival.

Several worked on "weatherproofing" the wreckage, others found ways to get water, and those with medical training took care of the injured. Although shaken from the crash, the survivors initially were confident they would be found. These feelings gradually gave way to despair, as search and rescue teams failed to find the wreckage. With the passing of several weeks and no sign of rescue in sight, the remaining passengers decided to mount several expeditions to determine the best way to escape. The most physically fit were chosen to go on the expeditions, as the thin mountain air and the deep snow made the trips extremely taxing. The results of the trips were both frustrating and demoralizing; the expeditionaries determined they were in the middle of the Andes mountains, and walking out to find help was believed to be impossible. Just when the survivors thought nothing worse could possibly happen, an avalanche hit the wreckage and killed several more of them.

The remaining survivors concluded they would not be rescued and their only hope was for someone to leave the wreckage and find help. Three of the fittest passengers were chosen for the final expedition, and everyone else's work was directed toward improving the expedition's chances of success. The three expeditionaries were given more food and were exempted from routine survival activities; the rest spent most of their energies securing supplies for the trip. Two months after the plane crash, the expeditionaries set out on their final attempt to find help. After hiking for 10 days through some of the most rugged terrain in the world, the expeditionaries stumbled across a group of Chilean peasants tending cattle. One of the expeditionaries stated, "I come from a plane that fell in the mountains. I am Uruguayan . . ." Eventually, 14 other survivors were rescued.

When the full account of their survival became known, it was not without controversy. It had required extreme and unsettling measures; the survivors had lived only by eating the flesh of their deceased comrades. Nonetheless, their story is one of the most moving survival dramas of all time, magnificently told by Piers Paul Read in *Alive*.[1] It is a story of tragedy and courage, and it is a story of leadership.

Perhaps a story of survival in the Andes is so far removed from everyday experience that it does not seem to hold any relevant lessons about leadership for you personally. But consider for a moment some of the basic issues the Andes survivors faced: tension between individual and group goals, dealing with the different needs and personalities of group members, and keeping hope alive in the face of adversity. These issues are not so very different from those facing many groups we're a part of. We can also look at the Andes experience for examples of the emergence of informal leaders in groups. Before the flight, a boy named Parrado was awkward and shy, a "second-stringer" both athletically and socially. Nonetheless, this unlikely hero became the best loved and most respected among the survivors for his courage, optimism, fairness, and emotional support. Persuasiveness in group decision making also was an important part of leadership among the Andes survivors. During the difficult discussions preceding the agonizing decision to survive on the flesh of their deceased comrades, one of the rugby players made his reasoning clear: "I know that if my dead body could help you stay alive, then I would want you to use it. In fact, if I do die and you don't eat me, then I'll come back from wherever I am and give you a good kick in the ass."[2]

The Purpose of This Book

Few of us will ever be confronted with a leadership challenge as dramatic as that faced by the Andes survivors. We may frequently face, however, opportunities for leadership that involve group dynamics which are just as complex. The purpose of this book is to help you be more effective in leadership situations by helping you better understand the complex challenges of leadership.

More specifically, we hope this book will serve as a sort of guide for interpreting leadership theory and research. The book describes and critically evaluates a number of leadership theories and research articles, and also offers practical advice on how to be a better leader. This book is designed to fill the gap between books that provide excellent summaries of leadership research but little practical advice on how to be a better leader and those that are not based on theory or research but primarily offer just one person's views on how to be a better leader (e.g., "how to" books, memoirs).

Lives of great men all remind us
We can make our lives sublime
And, departing, leave behind us
Footprints on the sands of time.
Henry Wadsworth Longfellow

What Is Leadership?

The halls of fame are open wide and they are always full. Some go in by the door called "push" and some by the door called "pull."
Stanley Baldwin, British prime minister in the 1930s

The Andes story and the experiences of many other leaders we'll introduce to you in a series of Profiles sprinkled throughout the chapters provide numerous examples of leadership. But just what *is* leadership? People who do research on leadership actually disagree more than you might think about what leadership really is. Most of this disagreement stems from the fact that **leadership** is a complex phenomenon involving the leader, the followers, and the situation. Some leadership researchers have focused on the personality, physical traits, or behaviors of the leader; others have studied the relationships between leaders and followers; still others have studied how aspects of the situation affect the ways leaders act. Some have extended the latter viewpoint so far as to suggest there is no such thing as leadership; they argue that organizational successes and failures often get falsely attributed to the leader, but the situation may have a much greater impact on how the organization functions than does any individual, including the leader.[3]

Remember the difference between a boss and a leader: a boss says, "Go!"—a leader says, "Let's go!"
E. M. Kelly

Perhaps the best way for you to begin to understand the complexities of leadership is to see some of the ways leadership has been defined. Leadership researchers have defined leadership in many different ways:

- The process by which an agent induces a subordinate to behave in a desired manner.[4]
- Directing and coordinating the work of group members.[5]
- An interpersonal relation in which others comply because they want to, not because they have to.[6]
- The process of influencing an organized group toward accomplishing its goals.[7]
- Actions that focus resources to create desirable opportunities.[8]
- The leader's job is to create conditions for the team to be effective.[9]
- The *ends* of leadership involve getting results through others, and the *means* of leadership involve the ability to build cohesive, goal-oriented

Peter Jackson

PROFILES IN LEADERSHIP 1.1 —*Film Director*

When Peter Jackson read *The Lord of the Rings* trilogy at the age of 18, he couldn't wait until it was made into a movie; 20 years later he made it himself. In 2004 *The Lord of the Rings: The Return of the King* took home 11 Academy Awards, winning the Oscar in every category for which it was nominated. This tied the record for the most Oscars ever earned by one motion picture. Such an achievement might seem unlikely for a producer/director whose film debut was titled *Bad Taste,* which it and subsequent works exemplified in spades. Peter Jackson made horror movies so grisly and revolting that his fans nicknamed him the "Sultan of Splatter." Nonetheless, his talent was evident to discerning eyes—at least among horror film aficionados. *Bad Taste* was hailed as a cult classic at the Cannes Film Festival, and horror fans tabbed Jackson as a talent to follow.

When screenwriter Costa Botes heard that *The Lord of the Rings* would be made into a live action film, he thought those responsible were crazy. Prevailing wisdom was that the fantastic and complex trilogy simply could not be believably translated onto the screen. But he also believed that "there was no other director on earth who could do it justice"

(Botes, 2004). And do it justice he obviously did. What was it about the "Sultan of Splatter's" leadership that gave others such confidence in his ability to make one of the biggest and best movies of all time? What gave *him* the confidence to even try it? And what made others want to *share* in his vision?

Peter Jackson's effectiveness as a leader has been due in large part to a unique combination of personal qualities and talents. One associate, for example, called him "one of the smartest people I know," as well as a maverick willing to buck the establishment. Jackson is also a tireless worker whose early successes were due in no small part to the combination of his ambition and dogged perseverance (Botes, 2004). His initial success was driven largely by his budding genius in making films on a low budget and with virtually no other staff. In reading others' comments who worked with him on the *LOTR* project, however, it's clear that his leadership continued to develop over the years. It was his ability to communicate a shared vision and inspire such extraordinary work out of the incredibly large staff that made *LOTR* so spectacularly successful.

Source: Adapted from Costa Botes, *Made in New Zealand: The Cinema of Peter Jackson,* NZEDGE.com, May 2002.

teams. Good leaders are those who build teams to get results across a variety of situations.[10]

- Leadership represents a complex form of social problem solving.[11]

As you can see, these definitions differ in many ways, and these differences have resulted in various researchers exploring very different aspects of leadership. For example, if we were to apply these definitions to the Andes survival scenario described earlier, researchers adopting Munson's definition would focus on the behaviors Parrado used to keep up the morale of the survivors. Researchers who define leadership as influencing an organized group toward accomplishing its goals would examine how Parrado managed to convince the group to stage and support the final expedition. One's definition of leadership might also influence just *who* is considered an appropriate leader for study. Thus, each group of researchers might focus on a different aspect of leadership, and each would tell a different story regarding the leader, the followers, and the situation.

Although having a large number of leadership definitions may seem confusing, it is important to understand that there is no single correct definition. The various definitions can help us appreciate the multitude of factors that affect leadership, as well as different perspectives from which to view it. For example, in the first definition above, the word *subordinate* seems to confine leadership to downward influence in hierarchical relationships; it seems to exclude informal leadership. The second definition emphasizes the directing and controlling aspects of leadership, and thereby may deemphasize emotional aspects of leadership. The emphasis placed in the third definition on subordinates' "wanting to" comply with a leader's wishes seems to exclude coercion of any kind as a leadership tool. Further, it becomes problematic to identify ways in which a leader's actions are really leadership if subordinates voluntarily comply when a leader with considerable potential coercive power merely asks others to do something without explicitly threatening them. Similarly, a key reason behind using the phrase *desirable opportunities* in one of the definitions was precisely to distinguish between leadership and tyranny. And partly because there are many different definitions of leadership, there is also a wide range of individuals we consider leaders. In addition to stories about leaders and leadership we will sprinkle through the book, there will be several in each chapter that we will highlight in a series of Profiles in Leadership. The first of these is Profiles in Leadership 1.1, which highlights Peter Jackson.

All considered, we find that defining leadership as "the process of influencing an organized group toward accomplishing its goals" to be fairly comprehensive and helpful. There are several implications of this definition which are worth further examination.

Leadership Is Both a Science and an Art

Saying leadership is both a science and an art emphasizes the subject of leadership as a field of scholarly inquiry, as well as certain aspects of the practice of leadership. The scope of the science of leadership is reflected in the number of studies—approximately 8,000—cited in an authoritative reference work, *Bass & Stogdill's Handbook of Leadership: Theory, Research & Managerial Applications.*[12] However, being an expert on leadership research is neither a necessary nor a sufficient condition for being a good leader. Some managers may be effective leaders without ever having taken a course or training program in leadership, and some scholars in the field of leadership may be relatively poor leaders themselves.

This is not to say that knowing something about leadership research is irrelevant to leadership effectiveness. Scholarship may not be a prerequisite for leadership effectiveness, but understanding some of the major research findings can help individuals better analyze situations using a variety of perspectives. That, in turn, can give leaders insight about how to be more effective. Even so, because the skill in analyzing and responding to situations varies greatly across leaders, leadership will always remain partly an art as well as a science.

Leadership Is Both Rational and Emotional

Leadership involves both the rational and emotional sides of human experience. Leadership includes actions and influences based on reason and logic as well as those based on inspiration and passion. We do not want to cultivate merely intellectualized leaders who only respond with logical predictability. Because people differ in their thoughts and feelings, hopes and dreams, needs and fears, goals and ambitions, and strengths and weaknesses, leadership situations can be very complex. Because people are both rational and emotional, leaders can use rational techniques and/or emotional appeals in order to influence followers, but they must also weigh the rational and emotional consequences of their actions.

A full appreciation of leadership involves looking at both these sides of human nature. Good leadership is more than just calculation and planning, or following a "checklist," even though rational analysis can enhance good leadership. Good leadership also involves touching others' feelings; emotions play an important role in leadership too. Just one example of this is the civil rights movement of the 1960s. It was a movement based on emotions as well as on principles. Dr. Martin Luther King, Jr., *inspired* many people to action; he touched people's hearts as well as their heads.

Aroused feelings, however, can be used either positively or negatively, constructively or destructively. Some leaders have been able to inspire others to deeds of great purpose and courage. On the other hand, as images of Adolf Hitler's mass rallies or present-day angry mobs attest, group frenzy can readily become group mindlessness. As another example, emotional appeals by the Reverend Jim Jones resulted in approximately 800 of his followers volitionally committing suicide.

The mere presence of a group (even without heightened emotional levels) can also cause people to act differently than when they are alone. For example, in airline cockpit crews, there are clear lines of authority from the captain down to the first officer (second in command) and so on. So strong are the norms surrounding the authority of the captain that some first officers will not take control of the airplane from the captain even in the event of impending disaster. Foushee[13] reported a study wherein airline captains in simulator training intentionally feigned incapacitation so that the response of the rest of the crew could be observed. The feigned incapacitations occurred at a predetermined point during the plane's final approach in landing, and the simulation involved conditions of poor weather and visibility. Approximately 25 percent of the first officers in these simulated flights allowed the plane to crash. For some reason, the first officers did not take control even when it was clear the captain was allowing the aircraft to deviate from the parameters of a safe approach. This example demonstrates how group dynamics can influence the behavior of group members

Any fool can keep a rule. God gave him a brain to know when to break the rule.

General Willard W. Scott

A democracy cannot follow a leader unless he is dramatized. A man to be a hero must not content himself with heroic virtues and anonymous action. He must talk and explain as he acts—drama.

William Allen White, American writer and editor, *Emporia Gazette*

even when emotional levels are *not* high. (Believe it or not, airline crews are so well trained, this is *not* an emotional situation.) In sum, it should be apparent that leadership involves followers' feelings and nonrational behavior as well as rational behavior. Leaders need to consider *both* the rational and the emotional consequences of their actions.

Leadership and Management

In trying to answer "What is leadership?" it is natural to look at the relationship between leadership and management. To many, the word **management** suggests words like *efficiency, planning, paperwork, procedures, regulations, control,* and *consistency.* Leadership is often more associated with words like *risk taking, dynamic, creativity, change,* and *vision.* Some say leadership is fundamentally a value-choosing, and thus a value-laden, activity, whereas management is not. Leaders are thought to *do the right things,* whereas managers are thought to *do things right.*[14][15] Here are some other distinctions between managers and leaders:[16]

- Managers administer; leaders innovate.
- Managers maintain; leaders develop.
- Managers control; leaders inspire.
- Managers have a short-term view; leaders, a long-term view.
- Managers ask how and when; leaders ask what and why.
- Managers imitate; leaders originate.
- Managers accept the status quo; leaders challenge it.

If you want some ham, you gotta go into the smokehouse.

Huey Long, governor of Louisiana 1928–1932

Zaleznik[17] goes so far as to say these differences reflect fundamentally different personality types, that leaders and managers are basically different kinds of people. He says some people are managers *by nature;* other people are leaders *by nature.* This is not at all to say one is better than the other, only that they are different. Their differences, in fact, can be quite useful, since organizations typically need both functions performed well in order to be successful. For example, consider again the U.S. civil rights movement in the 1960s. Dr. Martin Luther King, Jr., gave life and direction to the civil rights movement in America. He gave dignity and hope of freer participation in national life to people who before had little reason to expect it. He inspired the world with his vision and eloquence, and changed the way we live together. America is a different nation today because of him. Was Dr. Martin Luther King, Jr., a leader? Of course. Was he a manager? Somehow that does not seem to fit, and the civil rights movement might have failed if it had not been for the managerial talents of his supporting staff. Leadership and management complement each other, and both are vital to organizational success.

With regard to the issue of leadership versus management, we take a middle-of-the-road position. We think of leadership and management as

The Response of Leadership to a Natural Disaster

HIGHLIGHT 1.1

Much has been written about the inadequate response of local, state, and federal agencies to Hurricane Katrina. It may be instructive to compare the response of government agencies to a natural disaster on a different coast a century earlier: the San Francisco earthquake and fire of 1906.

While the precipitant disaster was the earthquake itself, much of the eventual destruction resulted from the consequent fire, one disaster aggravating the impact of the other. Because of the earthquake, utility poles throughout the city fell, taking the high-tension wires they were carrying with them. Gas pipes broke; chimneys fell, dropping hot coals into thousands of gallons of gas spilled by broken fuel tanks; stoves and heaters in homes toppled over; and in moments fires erupted across the city. And because the earthquake's first tremors broke water pipes throughout the city as well, street-corner fire hydrants everywhere suddenly went bone dry, making fighting the fires virtually impossible. In objective terms, the disaster is estimated to have killed as many as 3,000 people, rendered more than 200,000 homeless, and by some measures caused $195 billion in property loss as measured by today's dollars.

How did authorities respond to the crisis then, at a time when there were far fewer agencies with presumed response plans to combat disasters, and when high-tech communication methods were unheard of? Consider these two examples:

- The ranking officer assigned to an Army post in San Francisco was away when the earthquake struck, so it was up to his deputy to help organize the Army's and federal government's response.

The deputy immediately cabled Washington, D.C., requesting tents, rations, and medicine. The secretary of war (William Howard Taft, who would become the next U.S. president) responded by immediately dispatching 200,000 rations from Washington State. In a matter of days, every tent in the U.S. Army had been sent to San Francisco, and the longest hospital train in history was dispatched from Virginia.

- Perhaps the most impressive example of leadership initiative in the face of the 1906 disaster should go to the U.S. Post Office. It recovered its ability to function in very short order without losing one single item that was being handled when the earthquake struck. And since the earthquake had effectively destroyed the city's telegraphic connection (telegrams inside the city were temporarily being delivered by the post office), a critical question arose as to how people struck by the disaster could communicate with their families elsewhere. The city postmaster immediately announced his intent that all citizens of San Francisco should be able to use the post office to inform their families and loved ones of their condition and needs. He further stipulated that for outgoing private letters *it would not matter whether the envelope bore a stamp or no.* It was what was needed: Circumstances demanded that people be able to communicate with friends and family whether they could pay for a stamp or not, the "illegality" of mailing an unstamped letter notwithstanding.

Source: Adapted from S. Winchester, *A Crack in the Edge of the World: America and the Great California Earthquake of 1906.* New York: Harper Perennial, 2006.

closely related but distinguishable functions. Our view of the relationship is depicted in Figure 1.1. It shows leadership and management as two overlapping functions. Although some of the functions performed by leaders and managers may be unique, there is also an area of overlap. In reading Highlight 1.1, do you see more good management in the response to the San Francisco earthquake, more good leadership, or both?

FIGURE 1.1
Leadership and management overlap.

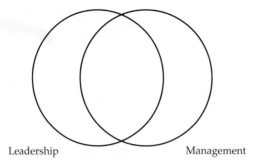

Leadership   Management

Leadership and Followership

One aspect of our text's definition of leadership is particularly worth noting: Leadership is a social influence process shared among *all* members of a group. Leadership is not restricted to the influence exerted by someone in a particular position or role; followers are part of the leadership process, too. In recent years, both practitioners and scholars have emphasized the relatedness of leadership and **followership.** As Burns[18] observed, the idea of "one-man leadership" is a contradiction in terms.

Thus, the question *What is leadership?* cannot be separated from the question *What is followership?* There is no simple line dividing them; they merge. The relationship between leadership and followership can be represented by borrowing a concept from topographical mathematics: the Möbius strip. You are probably familiar with the curious properties of the Möbius strip: When a strip of paper is twisted and connected in the manner depicted in Figure 1.2, it proves to have only one side. You can prove this to yourself by putting a pencil to any point on the strip and tracing continuously. Your pencil will cover the entire strip (i.e., both "sides"), eventually returning to the point at which you started. In order to demonstrate the relevance of this curiosity to leadership, cut a strip of paper. On one side write *leadership,* and on the other side write *followership.* Then twist the strip and connect the two ends in the manner of the figure. You will have created a leadership/followership Möbius strip wherein the two concepts merge one into the other, just as leadership and followership can become indistinguishable in organizations.[19]

This does not mean leadership and followership are the same thing. When top-level executives were asked to list qualities they most look for and admire in leaders and followers, the lists were similar but not identical.[20] Ideal leaders were characterized as honest, competent, forward-looking, and inspiring; ideal followers were described as honest, competent, independent, and cooperative. The differences could become critical in certain situations, as when a forward-looking and inspiring

Leadership and Followership are NOT the same thing.

subordinate perceives a significant conflict between his own goals or ethics and those of his superiors. Such a situation could become a crisis for the individual and the organization, demanding choice between leading and following.

FIGURE 1.2

The leadership/
followership
Möbius strip.

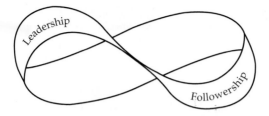

Leadership on Stages Large and Small

Great leaders sometimes seem larger than life. Charles de Gaulle, a leader of France during and after World War II, was such a figure (see Profiles in Leadership 1.2). Not all good leaders are famous or powerful, however, and we believe leadership can be best understood if we study a broad range of leaders, some famous and some not so famous. Most leaders, after all, are not known outside their own particular sphere or activity, nor should they be. Here are a few examples of leadership on the small stage, where individuals influenced and helped their respective groups attain their goals.

- An elderly woman led an entire community's effort to organize an advocacy and support group for parents of mentally ill adult children and provide sheltered living arrangements for these people. She helped these families while also serving an invaluable role in educating state legislators and social agencies about the needs of this neglected constituency. There had been numerous parents with mentally ill children in this community before, but none had had the idea or took the initiative to organize among themselves. As a result of this woman's leadership, many adults live and work in more humane conditions than they did before.

- A seasoned air force sergeant took two young, "green" enlistees under her wing after they both coincidentally reported for duty on the same day. She taught them the ropes at work and took pride as they matured. One of them performed so well that he went on to be commissioned as an officer. Unfortunately, the sergeant discovered the other pilfering cash from the unit gift fund. Though it pained her to do so, the sergeant took action for the enlistee to be discharged from the service. Leadership involves significant intrinsic rewards such as seeing others blossom under your tutelage, but with its rewards also goes the responsibility to enforce standards of conduct.

- The office manager for a large advertising agency directed its entire administrative staff, most of whom worked in the reception area. His engaging personality and concern for others made everyone feel important. Morale in the office was high, and many important customers credit their positive "first impression" of the whole agency to the congeniality and

The Stateliness of Charles de Gaulle

PROFILES IN LEADERSHIP 1.2

Certain men have, one might almost say from birth, the quality of exuding authority, as though it were a liquid, though it is impossible to say precisely of what it consists. In his fascinating book *Leaders,* former U.S. president Richard Nixon described the former French president Charles de Gaulle as one of the great leaders he had met. Following are several aspects of de Gaulle's leadership based on Nixon's observations.

- *He conveyed stately dignity.* De Gaulle had a resolute bearing that conveyed distance and superiority to others. He was at ease with other heads of state but never informal with anyone, even close friends. His tall stature and imperious manner conveyed the message he was not a common man.
- *He was a masterful public speaker.* He had a deep, serene voice and a calm, self-assured manner. He used the French language grandly and eloquently. According to Nixon, "He spoke so articulately and with such precision that his message seemed to resonate apart from his words" (p. 59).
- *He played the part.* De Gaulle understood the role of theater in politics, and his meetings with the press (a thousand at a time!) were like audiences with royalty. He staged them in great and ornate halls, and he deftly crafted public statements that would be understood differently by different groups. In one sense, perhaps, this could be seen as a sort of falseness, but that may be too narrow a view. Nixon reflected on this aspect of de Gaulle's leadership: "General de Gaulle was a facade, but not a false one. Behind it was a man of incandescent intellect and a phenomenal discipline. The facade was like the ornamentation on a great cathedral, rather than the flimsy pretense of a Hollywood prop with nothing behind it" (p. 60).

Source: R. Nixon, *Leaders.* New York: Warner Books, 1982.

positive climate among the office staff. Leaders set the tone for the organization, and followers often model the behaviors displayed by the leader. This leader helped create an office mood of optimism and supportiveness that reached outward to everyone who visited.

These examples are representative of the opportunities every one of us has to be a leader. To paraphrase John Fitzgerald Kennedy, we all can make a difference and each of us should try. However, this book is more than an exhortation for each of us to play a more active leadership role on the various stages of our lives. It is a review of what is known about leadership from available research, a review we hope is presented in a way that will foster leadership development. We are all more likely to make the kind of difference we want if we understand what leadership is and what it is not, how you get it, and what improves it (see Highlight 1.2 for a contrasting view of how much of a difference leaders really make). Toward that end, we will look at leaders on both the large and the small stages of life throughout the book. We will look at leaders on the world stage like film director Peter Jackson, Howard Schultz (the man who made Starbucks what it is today), and former French president Charles de Gaulle;

The Romance of Leadership

HIGHLIGHT 1.2

This text is predicated on the idea that leaders can make a difference. Interestingly, though, while people in the business world generally agree, not all scholars do.

People in the business world attribute much of a company's success or failure to its leadership. One study counted the number of articles appearing in *The Wall Street Journal* that dealt with leadership and found nearly 10 percent of the articles about representative target companies addressed that company's leadership. Furthermore, there was a significant positive relationship between company performance and the number of articles about its leadership; the more a company's leadership was emphasized in *The Wall Street Journal,* the better the company was doing. This might mean the more a company takes leadership seriously (as

reflected by the emphasis in *The Wall Street Journal*), the better it does.

However, the authors were skeptical about the real utility of leadership as a concept. They suggested leadership is merely a romanticized notion, an obsession people want and need to believe in. Belief in the potency of leadership may be a sort of cultural myth, which has utility primarily insofar as it affects how people create meaning about causal events in complex social systems. The behavior of leaders, the authors contend, does not account for very much of the variance in an organization's performance. Nonetheless, people seem strongly committed to a sort of basic faith that individual leaders shape organizational destiny for good or ill.

Source: J. R. Meindl, S. B. Ehrlich, and J. M. Dukerich, "The Romance of Leadership." *Administrative Science Quarterly* 30 (1985), pp 78–102.

and we will look at leaders on those smaller stages closer to home like principals, coaches, and managers at the local store. You also might want to see Highlight 1.3 for a listing of women leaders throughout history from many different stages.

Myths That Hinder Leadership Development

Few things pose a greater obstacle to leadership development than certain unsubstantiated and self-limiting beliefs about leadership. Therefore, before we begin examining what leadership and leadership development are in more detail, we will consider what they are not. We will examine several beliefs (we call them myths) that stand in the way of fully understanding and developing leadership.

Myth: Good Leadership Is All Common Sense

At face value, this myth says one needs only common sense to be a good leader. It also implies, however, that most if not all of the studies of leadership reported in scholarly journals and books only confirm what anyone with common sense already knows.

The problem, of course, is with the ambiguous term *common sense.* It implies a common body of practical knowledge about life that virtually any reasonable person with moderate experience has acquired. A simple

Women and Leadership: A Few Women Leaders throughout History

HIGHLIGHT 1.3

1429   Joan of Arc is finally granted an audience with Charles, the Dauphin of France, and subsequently captains the army at the siege of Orleans.

1492   Queen Isabella of Spain finances Columbus's voyage to the New World.

1638   Religious dissident Anne Hutchinson leads a schismatic group from the Massachusetts Bay Colony into a wilderness and establishes Rhode Island.

1803–1806   Sacajawea leads the Lewis and Clark expedition.

1837   Educator Mary Lyons founds Mount Holyoke Female Seminary (later Mount Holyoke College), the first American college exclusively for women.

1843   Dorothea Dix reports to the Massachusetts legislature on the treatment of the criminally insane, resulting in a significant reform of American mental institutions.

1849   Harriet Tubman escapes from slavery and becomes one of the most successful "conductors" on the Underground Railroad. She helps more than 300 slaves to freedom.

1854   Florence Nightingale, the founder of modern nursing, organizes a unit of women nurses to serve in the Crimean War.

1869   Susan B. Anthony is elected president of the National American Woman Suffrage Association.

1919   Mary Pickford becomes the first top-level female executive of a major film studio.

1940   Margaret Chase Smith is the first woman elected to the U.S. Congress.

1966   The National Organization of Women (NOW) is founded by Betty Friedan.

1969   Golda Meir is elected prime minister of Israel.

1979   Mother Teresa receives the Nobel Prize for her three decades of work leading the Congregation of Missions of Charity in Calcutta, India.

1979   Margaret Thatcher becomes the United Kingdom's first female prime minister.

1981   Sandra Day O'Connor is the first woman appointed to the U.S. Supreme Court.

1988   Benazir Bhutto is elected first female prime minister of Pakistan.

1991   Aung San Suu Kyi wins the Nobel Prize for Peace.

1996   Madeleine Albright is appointed U.S. Secretary of State.

2005   Condaleeza Rice is appointed U.S. Secretary of State.

2007   Nancy Pelosi is elected Speaker of the U.S. House of Representatives, third in line of succession to the presidency.

Source: Originally adapted from the *Colorado Education Association Journal*, February–March 1991. Based on original work by the Arts and Entertainment Network.

experiment, however, may convince you that common sense may be less common than you think. Ask a few friends or acquaintances whether the old folk wisdom "Absence makes the heart grow fonder" is true or false. Most will say it is true. After that ask a different group whether the old folk wisdom "Out of sight, out of mind" is true or false. Most of that group will answer true as well, even though the two proverbs are contradictory.

A similar thing sometimes happens when people hear about the results of studies concerning human behavior. On hearing the results, people may say, "Who needed a study to learn that? I knew it all the time." However, several experiments[21][22] showed that events were much more surprising when subjects had to guess the outcome of an experiment than when subjects were told the outcome. What seems obvious after you know the results and what you (or anyone else) would have predicted beforehand are not the same thing. Hindsight is always 20/20.

The point might become clearer with a specific example you may now try. Read the following paragraph:

> After World War II, the U.S. Army spent enormous sums of money on studies only to reach conclusions that, many believed, should have been apparent at the outset. One, for example, was that southern soldiers were better able to stand the climate in the hot South Sea islands than northern soldiers were.

This sounds reasonable, but there is just one problem; the statement above is exactly contrary to the actual findings. Southerners were no better than northerners in adapting to tropical climates.[23] Common sense can often play tricks on us.

Put a little differently, one of the challenges of understanding leadership may well be to know when common sense applies and when it does not. Do leaders need to act confidently? Of course. But they also need to be humble enough to recognize that others' views are useful, too. Do leaders need to persevere when times get tough? Yes. But they also need to recognize when times change and a new direction is called for. If leadership were nothing more than common sense, then there should be few, if any, problems in the workplace. However, we venture to guess you have noticed more than a few problems between leaders and followers. Effective leadership must be something more than just common sense.

Myth: Leaders Are Born, Not Made — *Leaders are born and made*

Some people believe being a leader is either in one's genes or not; others believe that life experiences mold the individual, that no one is born a leader. Which view is right? In a sense, both and neither. Both views are right in the sense that innate factors as well as formative experiences influence many sorts of behavior, including leadership. Yet both views are wrong to the extent they imply leadership is *either* innate *or* acquired; what matters more is how these factors *interact*. It does not seem useful, we believe, to think of the world as composed of two mutually exclusive types of people, leaders and nonleaders. It is more useful to address the ways in which each person can make the most of leadership opportunities he or she faces.

It may be easier to see the pointlessness of asking whether leaders are born or made by looking at an alternative question of far less popular interest: Are *college professors* born or made? Conceptually, the issues are the

If you miss seven balls out of ten, you're batting three hundred and that's good enough for the Hall of Fame. You can't score if you keep the bat on your shoulder.

Walter B. Wriston, chairman of Citicorp, 1970–1984

same, and here, too, the answer is that every college professor is both born *and* made. It seems clear enough that college professors are partly "born" since (among other factors) there is a genetic component to intelligence, and intelligence surely plays some part in becoming a college professor (well, at least a *minor* part!). But every college professor is also partly "made." One obvious way is that college professors must have advanced education in specialized fields; even with the right genes one could not become a college professor without certain requisite experiences. Becoming a college professor depends partly on what one is "born with" and partly on how that inheritance is shaped through experience. The same is true of leadership.

More specifically, research indicates that many cognitive abilities and personality traits are at least partly innate.[24] Thus, natural talents or characteristics may offer certain advantages or disadvantages to a leader. Take physical characteristics: A man's above-average height may increase others' tendency to think of him as a leader; it may also boost his own self-confidence. But it doesn't "make" him a leader. The same holds true for psychological characteristics which seem related to leadership. The very stability of certain characteristics over long periods of time (e.g., at school reunions people seem to have kept the same personalities we remember them as having years earlier) may reinforce the impression that our basic natures are fixed, but different environments nonetheless may nurture or suppress different leadership qualities.

Never reveal all of yourself to other people; hold back something in reserve so that people are never quite sure if they really know you.
**Michael Korda,
author, editor**

Myth: The Only School You Learn Leadership from Is the School of Hard Knocks

Some people skeptically question whether leadership can develop through formal study, believing instead it can only be acquired through actual experience. It is a mistake, however, to think of formal study and learning from experience as mutually exclusive or antagonistic. In fact, they complement each other. Rather than ask whether leadership develops from formal study or from real-life experience, it is better to ask what kind of study will help students learn to discern critical lessons about leadership from their own experience. Approaching the issue in such a way recognizes the critical role of experience in leadership development, but it also admits that certain kinds of study and training can improve a person's ability to discern critical lessons about leadership from experience. It can, in other words, help accelerate the process of learning from experience.

Progress always involves risks. You can't steal second base and keep your foot on first.
Frederick B. Wilcox

We would argue that one of the advantages of formally studying leadership is that formal study provides students with a variety of ways of examining a particular leadership situation. By studying the different ways researchers have defined and examined leadership, students can use these definitions and theories to better understand what is going on in

Howard Schultz

PROFILES IN LEADERSHIP 1.3

Starbucks began in 1971 as a very different company then than we know it as today. The difference is due in large part to the way its former CEO, Howard Schultz, reframed the kind of business Starbucks should be in. Schultz joined Starbucks in 1981 to head its marketing and retail store operations. While on a trip to Italy in 1983, Schultz was amazed by the number and variety of espresso bars there—1500 in the city of Turin alone. He concluded that the Starbucks stores in Seattle had

missed the point; *Starbucks should not be just a store but an experience—a gathering place.*

Everything looks clearer in hindsight, of course, but the Starbucks owners resisted Schultz's vision; Starbucks was a retailer, they insisted, not a restaurant or bar. Schultz's strategic reframing of the Starbucks opportunity was ultimately vindicated when—after having departed Starbucks to pursue the same idea with another company—Schultz had the opportunity to purchase the whole Starbucks operation in Seattle, including its name.

[handwritten margin note: Chairman and Chief Global Strategist]

any leadership situation. For example, earlier in this chapter we used three different leadership definitions as a framework for describing or analyzing the situation facing Parrado and the remaining survivors of the plane crash, and each definition focused on a different aspect of leadership. These frameworks can similarly be applied to better understand the experiences one has as both a leader and a follower. We think it is very difficult for leaders, particularly novice leaders, to examine leadership situations from multiple perspectives, but we also believe developing this skill can help you become a better leader. Being able to analyze your experiences from multiple perspectives may be the greatest single contribution a formal course in leadership can give you. Maybe you can reflect on your own leadership over a cup of coffee in Starbucks, as you read about the origins of that company in Profiles in Leadership 1.3.

An Overview of This Book

Nurture your mind with great thoughts. To believe in the heroic makes heroes.

Benjamin Disraeli, British prime minister, 1874–1880

In order to fill the gaps between leadership research and practice, this book will critically review the major theories of leadership as well as provide practical advice about improving leadership. As our first steps in that journey, the next three chapters of the book describe how: (*a*) leadership is an interaction between the leader, the followers, and the situation; (*b*) leadership develops through experience; and (*c*) leadership can be assessed and studied. The remainder of the book uses the leader–follower–situation interaction model described in Chapter 2 as a framework for organizing and discussing various theories and research findings related to leadership. The chapters in Part II focus on the leader, beginning with an examination of the issues of power and influence,

[handwritten margin note: Part I]

then of ethics, values, and attitudes. Other chapters look at theories and research concerning the leader: how good and bad leaders differ in personality, intelligence, creativity, and behavior. Part II concludes by looking at charismatic leadership. Part III primarily focuses on the followers; it summarizes the research and provides practical advice on such topics as motivating subordinates and using delegation. Part IV examines how the situation affects the leadership process.

Part V – Explores several specific leadership skills, including practical advice about handling specific leadership challenges.

Summary

Although many definitions of leadership exist, we define leadership as the process of influencing others toward achieving group goals. The chapter also looks at the idea that leadership is both a science and an art. Because leadership is an immature science, researchers are still struggling to find out what the important questions in leadership are; we are far from finding conclusive answers to them. Even those individuals with extensive knowledge of the leadership research may be poor leaders. Knowing what to do is not the same as knowing when, where, and how to do it. The art of leadership concerns the skill of understanding leadership situations and influencing others to accomplish group goals. Formal leadership education may give individuals the skills to better understand leadership situations, and mentorships and experience may give individuals the skills to better influence others. Leaders must also weigh both rational and emotional considerations when attempting to influence others. Leadership sometimes can be accomplished through relatively rational, explicit, rule-based methods of assessing situations and determining actions. Nevertheless, there is also an emotional side of human nature that must be acknowledged. Leaders are often most effective when they affect people at both the emotional level and the rational level. The idea of leadership as a whole-person process can also be applied to the distinction often made between leaders and managers. Although leadership and management can be distinguished as separate functions, a more comprehensive picture of supervisory positions could be made by examining the overlapping functions of leaders and managers. Leadership does not occur without followers, and followership is an easily neglected component of the leadership process. Leadership is everyone's business and everyone's responsibility. Finally, learning certain conceptual frameworks for thinking about leadership can be helpful in making your own on-the-job experiences a particularly valuable part of your leadership development. Thinking about leadership can help you become a better leader than you are right now.

Key Terms

leadership, 4   management, 8   followership, 10

Questions

1. We say leadership involves influencing organized groups toward goals. Do you see any disadvantages to restricting the definition to organized groups?
2. How would you define *leadership*?
3. Are some people the "leader type" and others not the "leader type"? If so, what in your judgment distinguishes them?
4. Identify several "commonsense" notions about leadership that, to you, are patently self-evident.
5. Does every successful leader have a valid theory of leadership?
6. Would you consider it a greater compliment for someone to call you a good manager or a good leader? Why? Do you believe you can be both?
7. Do you believe leadership can be studied scientifically? Why or why not?
8. To the extent leadership is an art, what methods come to mind for improving one's "art of leadership"?

Activity

Describe the best leader you have personally known, or a favorite leader from history, a novel, or a movie.

Minicase

"Richard Branson Shoots for the Moon"

The Virgin Group is the umbrella for a variety of business ventures ranging from air travel to entertainment. With close to 200 companies in over 30 countries, it is one of the largest companies in the world. At the head of this huge organization is Richard Branson. Branson founded Virgin over 30 years ago and has built the organization from a small student magazine to the multibillion-dollar enterprise it is today.

Branson is not your typical CEO. Branson's dyslexia made school a struggle and sabotaged his performance on standard IQ tests. His teachers and tests had no way of measuring his greatest strengths—his uncanny knack for uncovering lucrative business ideas and his ability to energize the ambitions of others so that they, like he, could rise to the level of their dreams.

Richard Branson's true talents began to show themselves in his late teens. While a student at Stowe School in England in 1968, Branson decided to start his own magazine, *Student*. Branson was inspired by the student activism on his campus in the sixties and decided to try something different. *Student* differed from most college newspapers or magazines; it focused on the students and their interests. Branson sold advertising to major corporations to support his magazine. He included articles by Ministers of Parliament, rock stars, intellectuals, and celebrities. *Student* grew to become a commercial success.

In 1970 Branson saw an opportunity for *Student* to offer records cheaply by running ads for mail-order delivery. The subscribers to *Student* flooded the magazine with so many orders that his spin-off discount music venture proved more lucrative than the magazine subscriptions. Branson recruited the staff of *Student* for his discount music business. He built a small recording studio and signed his first artist. Mike Oldfield recorded "Tubular Bells" at Virgin in 1973; the album sold 5 million copies. Virgin Records and the Virgin brand name were born. Branson has gone on to start his own airline (Virgin Atlantic Airlines was launched in 1984), build hotels (Virgin Hotels started in 1988), get into the personal finance business (Virgin Direct Personal Finance Services was launched in 1995), and even enter the cola wars (Virgin Cola was introduced in 1994). And those are just a few of the highlights of the Virgin Group—all this while Branson has attempted to break world speed records for crossing the Atlantic Ocean by boat and by hot air balloon.

As you might guess, Branson's approach is nontraditional—he has no giant corporate office or staff and few if any board meetings. Instead, he keeps each enterprise small and relies on his skills of empowering people's ideas to fuel success. When a flight attendant from Virgin Airlines approached him with her vision of a wedding business, Richard told her to go do it. He even put on a wedding dress himself to help launch the publicity. Virgin Brides was born. Branson relies heavily on the creativity of his staff; he is more a supporter of new ideas than a creator of them. He encourages searches for new business ideas everywhere he goes and even has a spot on the Virgin Web site called "Got a Big Idea?"

In December 1999, Richard Branson was awarded a knighthood in the Queen's Millennium New Year's Honours List for "services to entrepreneurship." What's next on Branson's list? He recently announced that Virgin was investing money in "trying to make sure that, in the not too distant future, people from around the world will be able to go into space." Not everyone is convinced that space tourism can become a fully fledged part of the travel industry, but with Branson behind the idea it just may fly.

1. Would you classify Richard Branson as a manager or a leader? What qualities distinguish him as one over the other?

2. As mentioned earlier in this chapter, followers are part of the leadership process. Describe the relationship between Branson and his followers.

3. Identify the myths of leadership development that Richard Branson's success helps to disprove.

Sources: http://www.johnshepler.com/articles/branson.html;
http://www.wma.com/ richard_branson/summary/;
http://www.virgin.com/aboutvirgin/allaboutvirgin/thewholestory/;
http://www.virgin.com/aboutvirgin/allaboutvirgin/whosrichardbranson/;
http://www.qksrv.net/ click-310374-35140;
http://www.guardian.co.uk/space/article/0,14493,1235926,00.html

Chapter Notes

1. Read, P. P. *Alive.* New York: J. B. Lippincott, 1974.
2. Ibid., p. 77.
3. Meindl, J. R., and S. B. Ehrlich. "The Romance of Leadership and the Evaluation of Organizational Performance." *Academy of Management Journal* 30 (1987), pp. 90–109.
4. Bennis, W. G. "Leadership Theory and Administrative Behavior: The Problem of Authority." *Administrative Science Quarterly* 4 (1959), pp. 259–60.
5. Fiedler, F. *A Theory of Leadership Effectiveness.* New York: McGraw-Hill, 1967.
6. Merton, R. K. *Social Theory and Social Structure.* New York: Free Press, 1957.
7. Roach, C. F., and O. Behling. "Functionalism: Basis for an Alternate Approach to the Study of Leadership." In *Leaders and Managers: International Perspectives on Managerial Behavior and Leadership.* Eds. J. G. Hunt, D. M. Hosking, C. A. Schriesheim, and R. Stewar. Elmsford, NY: Pergamon, 1984.
8. Campbell, D. P. *Campbell Leadership Index Manual.* Minneapolis, MN: National Computer Systems, 1991.
9. Ginnett, R. C. "Team Effectiveness Leadership Model: Identifying Leverage Points for Change." *Proceedings of the 1996 National Leadership Institute Conference.* College Park, MD: National Leadership Institute, 1996.
10. Hogan, R. T., G. J. Curphy, and J. Hogan. "What Do We Know about Personality: Leadership and Effectiveness?" *American Psychologist* 49 (1994), pp. 493–504.
11. Mumford, M.D., S. J. Zaccaro, F. D. Harding, T. O. Jacobs, and E. A. Fleishman. "Leadership Skills for a Changing World." *Leadership Quarterly* 11(1), 2000, pp. 11–35.
12. Bass, B. M. *Bass and Stogdill's Handbook of Leadership*, 3rd ed. New York: Free Press, 1990.
13. Foushee, H. C. "Dyads and Triads at 35,000 Feet: Factors Affecting Group Process and Aircrew Performance." *American Psychologist* 39 (1984), pp. 885–93.
14. Bennis, W. G., and B. Nanus. *Leaders: The Strategies for Taking Charge.* New York: Harper & Row, 1985.
15. Zaleznik, A. "The Leadership Gap." *Washington Quarterly* 6, no. 1 (1983), pp. 32–39.
16. Bennis, W. G. *On Becoming a Leader.* Reading, MA: Addison-Wesley, 1989.
17. Zaleznik, A. "The Leadership Gap." *Washington Quarterly* 6, no. 1 (1983), pp. 32–39.
18. Burns, J. M. *Leadership.* New York: Harper & Row, 1978.

19. Adapted from Macrorie, K. *Twenty Teachers*. Oxford: Oxford University Press, 1984.

20. Kouzes, J. M., and B. Z. Posner. *The Leadership Challenge: How to Get Extraordinary Things Done in Organizations*. San Francisco: Jossey-Bass, 1987.

21. Slovic, P., and B. Fischoff. "On the Psychology of Experimental Surprises." *Journal of Experimental Social Psychology* 22 (1977), pp. 544–51.

22. Wood, G. "The Knew-It-All-Along Effect." *Journal of Experimental Psychology: Human Perception and Performance* 4 (1979), pp. 345–53.

23. Lazarsfeld, P. E. "The American Soldier: An Expository Review." *Public Opinion Quarterly* 13 (1949), pp. 377–404.

24. For example, Tellegen, A., D. T. Lykken, T. J. Bouchard, K. J. Wilcox, N. L. Segal, and S. Rich. "Personality Similarity in Twins Reared Apart and Together." *Journal of Personality and Social Psychology* 54 (1988), pp. 1031–39.

Chapter 2

Leadership Involves an Interaction between the Leader, the Followers, and the Situation

Introduction

In Chapter 1, we defined leadership as the process of influencing an organized group toward accomplishing its goals. In this chapter, we will expand on this definition by introducing and describing a three-factor framework of the leadership process. We find this framework to be a useful heuristic both for analyzing various leadership situations and for organizing various leadership theories and supporting research. Therefore, the remainder of this chapter is devoted to providing an overview of the framework, and many of the remaining chapters of this book are devoted to describing the components of the framework in more detail.

Looking at Leadership through Several Lenses

In attempting to understand leadership, scholars understandably have spent much of their energy studying successful and unsuccessful leaders in government, business, athletics, and the military. Sometimes scholars have done this systematically by studying good leaders as a group,[1][2] and sometimes they have done this more subjectively, drawing lessons about leadership from the behavior or character of an individual leader such as Martin Luther King, Jr., Bill Gates, or Hillary Clinton. The latter approach is similar to drawing conclusions about leadership from observing individuals in one's own life, whether it be a high school coach, a mother or

*A leader is best
When people barely
know that he exists
Not so good when peo-
ple obey and acclaim
him,Worst of all when
they despise him.
"Fail to honor people,
They fail to honor you;"
But of a good leader,
who talks little,
When his work is done,
his aim fulfilled,
They will all say, "We
did this ourselves."*

Lao-tzu

father, or one's boss. It may seem that studying the characteristics of effective leaders is the best way to learn about leadership, but such an approach tells only part of the story.

Consider an example. Suppose a senior minister was told by one of his church's wealthiest and consistently most generous members that he should not preach any more prochoice sermons on abortion. The wealthy man's contributions were a big reason a special mission project for the city's disadvantaged youth had been funded, and we might wonder whether the minister would be influenced by this outside pressure. Would he be a bad leader if he succumbed to this pressure and did not advocate what his conscience dictated? Would the minister be a bad leader if his continued public stand on abortion caused the wealthy man to leave the church and withdraw support for the youth program?

Although we can learn much about leadership by looking at leaders themselves, the preceding example suggests that studying only leaders provides just a partial view of the leadership process. Would we really know all we wanted to about the preceding example if we knew everything possible about the minister himself? His personality, his intelligence, his interpersonal skills, his theological training, his motivation? Is it not also relevant to understand a bit more, for example, about the community, his parishioners, the businessman, and so on? This points out how leadership depends on several factors, including the situation and the followers, not just the leader's qualities or characteristics. Leadership is more than just the kind of person the leader is or the things the leader does. Leadership is the process of influencing others toward the achievement of group goals; it is not just a person or a position.

If we use only leaders as the lens for understanding leadership, then we get a very limited view of the leadership process. We can expand our view of the leadership process by adding two other complementary lenses: the followers and the situation. However, using only the followers or the situation as a lens also would give us an equally limited view of the leadership process. In other words, the clearest picture of the leadership process occurs only when we use all three lenses to understand it.

The Interactional Framework for Analyzing Leadership

Perhaps the first researcher formally to recognize the importance of the leader, follower, and situation in the leadership process was Fred Fiedler.[3] Fiedler used these three components to develop his contingency model of leadership, a theory of leadership that will be discussed in more detail in Chapter 12. Although we recognize Fiedler's contributions, we owe perhaps even more to Hollander's transactional approach to leadership. We call our approach the **interactional framework.**

There are several aspects of this derivative of Hollander's approach that are worthy of additional comment. First, as seen in Figure 2.1, the

FIGURE 2.1

An interactional framework for analyzing leadership.

Source: Adapted from E. P. Hollander, *Leadership Dynamics: A Practical Guide to Effective Relationships.* New York: Free Press, 1978.

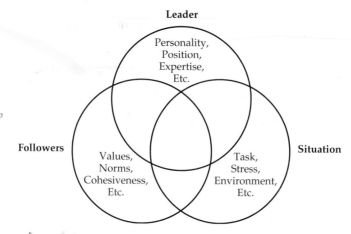

framework depicts leadership as a function of three elements—the **leader,** the **followers,** and the **situation.** Second, a particular leadership scenario can be examined using each level of analysis separately. Although this is a useful way to understand the leadership process, we can have an even better understanding of the process if we also examine the interactions among the three elements, or lenses, represented by the overlapping areas in the figure. For example, we can better understand the leadership process if we not only look at the leaders and the followers but also examine how leaders and followers affect each other in the leadership process. Similarly, we can examine the leader and the situation separately, but we can gain even further understanding of the leadership process by looking at how the situation can constrain or facilitate a leader's actions and how the leader can change different aspects of the situation in order to be more effective. Thus, a final important aspect of the framework is that leadership is the result of a complex set of interactions among the leader, the followers, and the situation. These complex interactions may be why broad generalizations about leadership are problematic; there are many factors that influence the leadership process (see Highlight 2.1).

   An example of one such complex interaction between leaders and followers is evident in what has been called in-groups and out-groups. Sometimes there is a high degree of mutual influence and attraction between the leader and a few subordinates. These subordinates belong to the **in-group** and can be distinguished by their high degree of loyalty, commitment, and trust felt toward the leader. Other subordinates belong to the **out-group.** Leaders have considerably more influence with in-group followers than with out-group followers. However, this greater degree of influence also has a price. If leaders rely primarily on their formal authority to influence their followers (especially if they punish them), then leaders risk losing the

Followership Styles

HIGHLIGHT 2.1

The concept of different styles of leadership is reasonably familiar, but the idea of different styles of followership is relatively new. The very word *follower* has a negative connotation to many, evoking ideas of people who behave like sheep and need to be told what to do. Robert Kelley, however, believes that followers, rather than representing the antithesis of leadership, are best viewed as collaborators with leaders in the work of organizations.

Kelley believes that different types of followers can be described in terms of two broad dimensions. One of them ranges from **independent, critical thinking** at one end to **dependent, uncritical thinking** on the other end. According to Kelley, the best followers think for themselves and offer constructive advice or even creative solutions. The worst followers need to be told what to do. Kelley's other dimension ranges from whether people are **active followers** or **passive followers** in the extent to which they are engaged in work. According to Kelley, the best followers are self-starters who take initiative for themselves, whereas the worst followers are passive, may even dodge responsibility, and need constant supervision.

Using these two dimensions, Kelley has suggested five basic styles of followership:

1. *Alienated followers* habitually point out all the negative aspects of the organization to others. While alienated followers may see themselves as mavericks who have a healthy skepticism of the organization, leaders often see them as cynical, negative, and adversarial.

2. *Conformist followers* are the "yes people" of organizations. While very active at doing the organization's work, they can be dangerous if their orders contradict societal standards of behavior or organizational policy. Often this style is the result of either the demanding and authoritarian style of the leader or the overly rigid structure of the organization.

3. *Pragmatist followers* are rarely committed to their group's work goals, but they have learned not to make waves. Because they do not like to stick out, pragmatists tend to be mediocre performers who can clog the arteries of many organizations. Because it can be difficult to discern just where they stand on issues, they present an ambiguous image with both positive and negative characteristics. In organizational settings, pragmatists may become experts in mastering the bureaucratic rules which can be used to protect them.

4. *Passive followers* display none of the characteristics of the exemplary follower (discussed next). They rely on the leader to do all the thinking. Furthermore, their work lacks enthusiasm. Lacking initiative and a sense of responsibility, passive followers require constant direction. Leaders may see them as lazy, incompetent, or even stupid. Sometimes, however, passive followers adopt this style to help them cope with a leader who expects followers to behave that way.

5. *Exemplary followers* present a consistent picture to both leaders and coworkers of being independent, innovative, and willing to stand up to superiors. They apply their talents for the benefit of the organization even when confronted with bureaucratic stumbling blocks or passive or pragmatist coworkers. Effective leaders appreciate the value of exemplary followers. When one of the authors was serving in a follower role in a staff position, he was introduced by his leader to a conference as "my favorite subordinate because he's a loyal 'No-Man.' "

Exemplary followers—high on both critical dimensions of followership—are essential to organizational success. Leaders, therefore, would be well advised to select people who have these characteristics and, perhaps even more importantly, *create the conditions that encourage these behaviors.*

Source: Adapted from R. Kelley, *The Power of Followership.* New York: Doubleday Currency, 1992.

high levels of loyalty and commitment followers feel toward them. There is even a theory of leadership called **Leader–Member Exchange Theory** that describes these two kinds of relationships and how they affect the types of power and influence tactics leaders use.[5]

Originally, Leader–Member Exchange Theory, or LMX theory, was developed to describe two kinds of relationships that occur among leaders and followers, and how these relationships affect the types of power used by a leader. One type of relationship is characterized by a high degree of mutual influence and attraction between the leader and a limited number of subordinates. These subordinates belong to the in-group and can be distinguished by the high degree of loyalty, commitment, and trust they feel toward the leader. The other subordinates belong to the out-group, and leaders typically use different forms of power and influence in interacting with in-group or out-group members.[5a]

Over time, LMX theory has broadened to include the entire continuum of relationships that leaders may have with members (for the purposes of this text, followers) rather than just in terms of the dichotomy between in-groups and out-groups. Here are a few of the kinds of questions that are used in LMX theory to assess the nature and quality of relationships between leaders and members (parallel versions are written from the leader's point of view):

The crowd will follow a leader who marches twenty steps in advance; but if he is a thousand steps in front of them, they do not see and do not follow him.

Georg Brandes

- Do you know where you stand with your leader?
- How well does your leader understand your job problems and needs?
- How well does your leader recognize your potential?

The unique contribution of LMX theory is that it looks beyond just the personal characteristics of the leader, or the characteristics of the situation, or an interaction between the two, by looking at the nature of the relationship between the leader and his or her members (followers).[5b]

We will now examine each of the three main elements of the interactional framework in turn.

The Leader

This element primarily examines what the leader brings *as an individual* to the leadership equation. This can include unique personal history, interests, character traits, and motivation.

Leaders are *not* all alike, but they do tend to share many common characteristics. Research has shown that leaders differ from their followers, and effective leaders differ from ineffective leaders, on various personality traits, cognitive abilities, skills, and values.[6,7,8,9,10,11] Another way personality can affect leadership is through temperament, by which we mean whether the leader is generally calm or is instead prone to emotional

BIZARRO   by DAN PIRARO

OH, ALRIGHT, YOU WIN! WE'LL ADOPT A FAIR PATERNITY LEAVE PROGRAM AND OFFER ON-SIGHT DAY CARE FACILITIES!!

Source: The "Bizarro" cartoon by Dan Piraro is reprinted courtesy Chronicle
Features, San Francisco, California. All rights reserved. Copyright © Dan Piraro
2007, Bizarro.

outbursts. Leaders who have calm dispositions and do not attack or belittle others for bringing bad news are more likely to get complete and timely information from subordinates than are bosses who have explosive tempers and a reputation for killing the messenger.

Another important aspect of the leader is how he or she achieved leader status. Leaders who are appointed by superiors may have less credibility with subordinates and get less loyalty from them than leaders who are elected or emerge by consensus from the ranks of followers. Often, emergent or elected officials are better able to influence a group toward goal achievement because of the power conferred on them by their followers. However, both elected and emergent leaders need to be sensitive to their constituencies if they wish to remain in power.

More generally, a leader's experience or history in a particular organization is usually important to her or his effectiveness. For example, leaders

I'll be blunt, coach. I'm having a problem with this 'take a lap' thing of yours . . ."

promoted from within an organization, by virtue of being familiar with its culture and policies, may be ready to "hit the job running." In addition, leaders selected from within an organization are typically better known by others in the organization than are leaders selected from the outside. That is likely to affect, for better or worse, the latitude others in the organization are willing to give the leader; if the leader is widely respected for a history of accomplishment, then she may be given more latitude than a newcomer whose track record is less well known. On the other hand, many people tend to give new leaders a fair chance to succeed, and newcomers to an organization often take time to learn the organization's informal rules, norms, and "ropes" before they make any radical or potentially controversial decisions.

A leader's legitimacy also may be affected by the extent to which followers participated in the leader's selection. When followers have had a say in the selection or election of a leader, they tend to have a heightened sense of psychological identification with her, but they also may have higher expectations and make more demands on her.[11a] We also might wonder what kind of support a leader has from his own boss. If followers sense their boss has a lot of influence with the higher-ups, then subordinates may be reluctant to take their complaints to higher levels. On the other hand, if the boss has little influence with higher-ups, subordinates may be more likely to make complaints to these levels.

The foregoing examples highlight the sorts of insights we can gain about leadership by focusing on the individual leader as a level of analysis. Even if we were to examine the individual leader completely, however, our understanding of the leadership process would be incomplete.

The Followers

Followers are a critical part of the leadership equation, but their role has not always been appreciated. For example, we can look at history and be struck by the contributions of extraordinary individual leaders. Does the relative inattention to their followers mean the latter made no contributions themselves to the leadership process? Wasn't Mr. Spock's logic an important counterbalance to Captain Kirk's intuition on Star Trek? Wasn't the Lone Ranger daring partly because he knew he could count on Tonto to rescue him from impossible situations.[12]

Even the major reviews of leadership literature show that early researchers paid relatively little attention to the roles followers play in the leadership process.[13,14,15] However, we know that the followers' expectations, personality traits, maturity levels, levels of competence, and motivation affect the leadership process too.[16,17,18,19,20]

The nature of followers' motivation to do their work is also important. Workers who share a leader's goals and values, and who feel intrinsically rewarded for performing a job well, might be more likely to work extra hours on a time-critical project than those whose motivation is solely monetary.

Even the number of followers reporting to a leader can have significant implications. For example, a store manager having three clerks working for him can spend more time with each of them (or on other things) than

Paul Revere

PROFILES IN LEADERSHIP 2.1

One of the fabled stories of American history is of Paul Revere's ride through the countryside surrounding Boston, warning towns that the "British are coming" so that local militia could be ready to meet them. As a result, when the British did march toward Lexington on the following day, they faced unexpectedly fierce resistance. At Concord the British were beaten by a ragtag group of locals, and so began the American Revolutionary War.

It has been taken for granted by generations of Americans that the success of Paul Revere's ride lay in his heroism *and* in the self-evident importance of the news itself. A little known fact, however, is that Paul Revere was not the only rider that night. A fellow revolutionary by the name of William Dawes had the same mission: to ride simultaneously through a separate set of towns surrounding Boston to warn *them* that the British were coming. He did so, carrying the news through just as many towns as Revere did. But his ride was not successful; those local militia leaders weren't aroused and did not rise up to confront the British. If they had been, Dawes would be as famous today as Paul Revere.

Why was Revere's ride successful when Dawes's ride was not? Paul Revere started a word-of-mouth epidemic, and Dawes did not, *because of differing kinds of relationships the two men had with others.* It wasn't, after all, the nature of the news itself that proved ultimately important so much as the nature of the men who carried it. Paul Revere was a highly gregarious and social person, what Malcolm Gladwell calls a *connector.* Gladwell writes that Revere was "a fisherman and a hunter, a cardplayer and a theater-lover, a frequenter of pubs and a successful businessman. He was active in the local Masonic Lodge and was a member of several select social clubs." He was a man with a knack for always being at the center of things. So when he began his ride that night, it was Revere's nature to stop and share the news with anyone he saw on the road, and he would have known who the key players were in each town to notify.

Dawes was not by nature so gregarious as Revere, and did not have Revere's extended social network. It's likely he *wouldn't* have known who to share the news with in each town, whose door to knock on. Dawes did notify some people, but not enough to tip the scales enough to create the kind of impact that Revere did. Another way of saying that is simply to note that the people Dawes notified didn't know *him* the way that Revere was known by those *he* notified.

It isn't just the information or the ideas you have as a leader that make a difference. It's also who you know, and how many you know—and what they know about you.

Source: Adapted from Malcolm Gladwell, *The Tipping Point.* New York: Little, Brown and Company, 2002.

can a manager responsible for eight clerks and a separate delivery service; chairing a task force with five members is a different leadership activity than chairing a task force with 18 members. Still other relevant variables include followers' trust in the leader and their confidence (or not) that he or she is interested in their well-being. Another aspect of followers' relations to a leader is described in Profiles in Leadership 2.1.

Changing Roles for Followers

The preceding examples illustrate just a few ways in which followers compose an important and complementary level of analysis for understanding leadership. Such examples should point out how leadership must be understood in the context of a particular group of followers as well as in terms of an individual leader. Now, more than ever before, understanding followers is central to understanding leadership.

That is because the leader–follower relationship is in a period of dynamic change.[21,22,23] One reason for this changing relationship is an increasing pressure on all kinds of organizations to function with reduced resources. Reduced resources and company downsizing have reduced the number of managers and increased their span of control, which in turn leaves followers to pick up many of the functions traditionally performed by leaders. Another reason is a trend toward greater power sharing and decentralized authority in organizations, which in turn creates greater interdependence among organizational subunits and increased need for collaboration among them. Furthermore, the nature of problems faced by many organizations is becoming so complex and the changes are becoming so rapid that more and more people are required to solve them.

These trends suggest several different ways in which followers can take on new leadership roles and responsibilities in the future. For one thing, followers can become much more proactive in their stance toward organizational problems. When facing the discrepancy between the way things are in an organization and the way they could or should be, followers can play an active and constructive role collaborating with leaders in solving problems. In general, making organizations better is a task that needs to be "owned" by followers as well as by leaders. With these changing roles for followers, it should not be surprising to find that qualities of good followership are statistically correlated with qualities typically associated with good leadership. One recent study found positive correlations between the followership qualities of active engagement and independent thinking and the leadership qualities of dominance, sociability, achievement orientation, and steadiness.[24]

In addition to helping solve organizational problems, followers can better contribute to the leadership process by becoming better skilled at "influencing upward." Because followers are often at the level where many organizational problems occur, they can provide leaders with relevant information so that good solutions are implemented. Although it is true that some leaders need to become better listeners, it is also true that many followers need training in expressing ideas to superiors more clearly and positively. Still another way followers can assume a greater share of the leadership challenge in the future is by staying flexible and open to opportunities. The future portends more change, not less, and followers who face change with positive anticipation and an openness to self-development will be particularly valued and rewarded.[25]

Thus, to an ever increasing degree, leadership must be understood in terms of both leader variables and follower variables, as well as the

If you act like an ass, don't get insulted if people ride you.

Yiddish proverb

Aung San Suu Kyi

PROFILES IN LEADERSHIP 2.2

In 1991 Aung San Suu Kyi already had spent two years under house arrest in Burma for "endangering the state." That same year she won the Nobel Prize for Peace. Like Nelson Mandela, Suu Kyi stands as an international symbol of heroic and peaceful resistance to government oppression.

Until the age of 43, Suu Kyi led a relatively quiet existence in England as a professional working mother. Her life changed dramatically in 1988 when she returned to her native country of Burma to visit her sick mother. That visit occurred during a time of considerable political unrest in Burma. Riot police had recently shot to death hundreds of demonstrators in the capital city of Rangoon (the demonstrators had been protesting government repression!). Over the next several months, police killed nearly 3,000 people who had been protesting government policies.

When hundreds of thousands of pro-democracy demonstrators staged a protest rally at a prominent pagoda in Rangoon, Suu Kyi spoke to the crowd. Overnight she became the leading voice for freedom and democracy in Burma. Today she is the most popular and influential leader in her country even though she's never held political office.

What prepared this woman whose life was once relatively simple and contented to risk her life by challenging an oppressive government? What made her such a magnet for popular support? Impressive as Aung San Suu Kyi is as a populist leader, it is impossible to understand her effectiveness purely in terms of her own personal characteristics. It is impossible to understand it independent of her followers—the people of Burma. Her rapid rise to prominence as the leading voice for democracy and freedom in Burma must be understood in terms of the living link she represented to the country's greatest modern hero—her father. He was something of a George Washington figure in that he founded the Burmese Army in 1941 and later made a successful transition from military leadership to political leadership. At the height of his influence, when he was the universal choice to be Burma's first president, he was assassinated. Suu Kyi was two years old. Stories about his life and principles indelibly shaped Suu Kyi's own life, but his life and memory also created a readiness among Suu Kyi's countrymen for her to take up his mantle of leadership.

interactions among them. But even that is not enough. In addition to understanding the leader and the followers, we must also understand the particular situations in which leaders and followers find themselves.

The Situation

You've got to give loyalty down, if you want loyalty up.
Donald T. Regan, former CEO and White House chief of staff

The situation is the third critical part of the leadership equation. Even if we knew all we could know about a given leader and a given set of followers, leadership often makes sense only in the context of how the leader and followers interact in a particular situation (see Profiles in Leadership 2.2).

The situation may be the most ambiguous aspect of the leadership framework since it can refer to anything from the specific task a group is engaged in all the way to broad situational contexts such as the remote predicament of the Andes survivors.

Are Good Women Leaders Hard to Find?

One important case in point of the complex interactions among leaders, followers, and the situation involves women in leadership roles. In this section we'll examine the extent to which women are taking on greater leadership responsibility than ever before, whether there are differences in the effectiveness of men and women in leadership roles, and what explanations have been offered to explain differences between men and women in being selected for and succeeding in positions of leadership. This is an area of considerable academic research and popular polemics, as evident in many recent articles in the popular press that claim a distinct advantage for women in leadership roles.[26]

It is clear that women are taking on leadership roles in greater numbers than ever before. That's certainly true in government. In the U.S. Senate, for example, 42 percent of the women who have ever served there were holding office in 2003.[27] Around the world, 43 of the 59 women ever to serve as presidents or prime ministers have come into office since 1990.[28][29] The increasing proportion of women in leadership is evident outside of government as well. In 1972 women held 18 percent of managerial and administrative positions in the United States, but by 2002 the figure had risen to 46 percent.[30][31]

While these statistics are important and promising, the fact is that problems still exist which constrain the opportunity for capable women to rise to the highest leadership roles in organizations (see Highlight 2.2). Many studies have been done considering this problem, a few of which we'll examine here.

In a classic study of sex roles, Schein[32][33] demonstrated how bias in sex role stereotypes created problems for women moving up through these managerial roles. Schein asked male and female middle managers to complete a survey on which they rated various items on a five-point scale in terms of how characteristic they were of (*a*) men in general, (*b*) women in general, or (*c*) successful managers. Schein found a high correlation between the ways both male and female respondents perceived "males" and "managers," but no correlation between the ways the respondents perceived "females" and "managers." It was as though being a manager was defined by attributes thought of as masculine. Furthermore, it does not appear that the situation has changed much over the past two decades. In 1990, management students in the United States, Germany, and Great Britain, for example, still perceived successful middle managers in terms of characteristics more commonly ascribed to men than to women.[34] One area where views *do* seem to have changed over time involves women's perceptions of their own roles. In contrast to the earlier studies, women today see as much similarity between "female" and "manager" as between "male" and "manager."[35] To women, at least, being a woman and being a manager are not a contradiction in terms.

Insights of a Woman Who Broke the Glass Ceiling

HIGHLIGHT 2.2

Kim Campbell distinguished herself in many ways. She was Canada's first female prime minister, and she now chairs the Council of Women World Leaders. In 2002 she was interviewed about the challenges and opportunities for women rising into senior leadership positions in organizations, and here are two brief excerpts of what she said:

You've held many positions that are traditionally filled by men. What's the greatest obstacle you've encountered?

There is a deeply rooted belief that women are not competent and can't lead. That's because there's an overlap in people's minds between the qualities that we associate with leadership and the qualities that we associate with masculinity—decisiveness, aggressiveness, competence. There is much less overlap between leadership qualities and those we associate with being feminine—an inclination toward consensus-building, to be communal, expressive, nurturing. That's why for many people it was rather disturbing that I was prime minister. A woman wasn't supposed to be prime minister. I wasn't entitled to be there.

You've said that having women in leadership is more important now than ever. Why now?

We're living in a time when we see the frightening limitations of masculine cultures. Cultures that are totally masculine can give rise to fundamentalisms—they can be intolerant, narrow, violent, corrupt, antidemocratic. That's at a state level. At a corporate level, a macho culture made Enron possible.

Source: Excerpted from *Harvard Business Review,* 2002, pp. 20–21.

There also have been many other studies of the role of women in management. In one of these, *Breaking the Glass Ceiling,*[36] researchers documented the lives and careers of 78 of the highest-level women in corporate America. A few years later the researchers followed up with a small sample of those women to discuss any changes that had taken place in their leadership paths. The researchers were struck by the fact that the women were much like the senior men they had worked with in other studies. Qualitatively, they had the same fears: They wanted the best for themselves and for their families. They wanted their company to succeed. And, not surprisingly, they still had a drive to succeed. In some cases (also true for the men) they were beginning to ask questions about life balance—was all the sacrifice and hard work worth it? Were 60-hour workweeks worth the cost to family and self?

Looking more quantitatively, however, the researchers expected to find significant differences between the women who had broken the glass ceiling and the men who were already there. After all, the popular literature and some social scientific literature had conditioned them to expect that there is a feminine versus a masculine style of leadership, the feminine style being an outgrowth of a consensus/team-oriented leadership approach. Women, in this view, are depicted as leaders who, when compared to men, are better listeners, more empathic, less analytical, more people-oriented, and less aggressive in pursuit of goals.

In examining women in leadership positions, the researchers collected behavioral data, including ratings by both self and others, assessment center data (gathered from leadership development programs at the Center for Creative Leadership), and their scores on the California Psychological Inventory. Contrary to the stereotypes and popular views, however, there were no statistically significant differences between men's and women's leadership styles. Women and men were equally analytical, people-oriented, forceful, goal-oriented, empathic, and skilled at listening. There were other differences between the men and women, however, beyond the question of leadership styles. The researchers did find (and these results must be interpreted cautiously because of the relatively small numbers involved) that women had significantly lower well-being scores, their commitment to the organizations they worked for was more guarded than that of their male counterparts, and the women were much more likely to be willing to take career risks associated with going to new or unfamiliar areas of the company where women had not been before.

Research shows

Continued work with women in corporate leadership positions has both reinforced and somewhat clarified these findings. For example, the lower scores for women with regard to their ratings of general well-being may reflect the inadequacy of their support system for dealing with day-to-day issues of living. This is tied to the reality for many women that in addition to having roles in their companies they remain chief caretakers for their families. Further, there may be additional pressures of being visibly identified as proof that the organization has women at the top.

Other types of differences—particularly those around "people issues"—are still not evident. In fact, the hypothesis is that such supposed differences may hinder the opportunities for leadership development of women in the future. For example, turning around a business that is in trouble or starting a new business are two of the most exciting opportunities a developing leader has to test her leadership abilities. If we apply the "women are different" hypothesis, then the type of leadership skills needed for successful completion of either of these assignments may well leave women off the list of candidates. However, if we accept the hypothesis that women and men are more alike as leaders than they are different, then women will be found in equal numbers on the candidate list.

Research on second-generation managerial women suggest many of them appear to be succeeding *because of* characteristics heretofore considered too feminine for effective leadership.[37] Survey research by Judith Rosener identified several differences in how men and women described their leadership experiences. Men tended to describe themselves in somewhat transactional terms, viewing leadership as an exchange with subordinates for services rendered. They influenced others primarily through their organizational position and authority. The women, on the other hand, tended to describe themselves in transformational terms. They helped subordinates develop commitment for broader goals than their own self-interest, and described their influence more in terms of personal characteristics like charisma and interpersonal skill than mere organizational position.

According to Rosener, such women leaders encouraged participation and shared power and information, but went far beyond what is commonly thought of as participative management. She called it **interactive leadership.** Their leadership self-descriptions reflected an approach based on enhancing others' self-worth and believing that the best performance results when people are excited about their work and feel good about themselves.

How did this interactive leadership style develop? Rosener concluded it was due to these women's socialization experiences and career paths. As we indicated above, the social role expected of women has emphasized they be cooperative, supportive, understanding, gentle, and service-oriented. As they entered the business world, they still found themselves in roles emphasizing these same behaviors. They found themselves in staff, rather than line, positions, and in roles lacking formal authority over others such that they had to accomplish their work without reliance on formal

"That's what they all say, honey."

power. What they had to do, in other words, was employ their socially acceptable behavioral repertoire in order to survive organizationally.

Neither shall you allege the example of the many as an excuse for doing wrong.

Exodus 23.2

What came easily to women turned out to be a survival tactic. Although leaders often begin their careers doing what comes naturally and what fits within the constraints of the job, they also develop their skills and styles over time. The women's use of interactive leadership has its roots in socialization, and the women interviewees firmly believe that it benefits their organizations. Through the course of their careers, they have gained conviction that their style is effective. In fact, for some it was their own success that caused them to formulate their philosophies about what motivates people, how to make good decisions, and what it takes to maximize business performance.[37a]

Rosener called for organizations to expand their definitions of effective leadership—to create a *wider* band of acceptable behavior so that both men and women will be freer to lead in ways which take advantage of their true talents. The extent of the problem is suggested by data from a study looking at how CEOs, almost all male, and senior female executives explained the paucity of women in corporate leadership roles. Figure 2.2 compares the percentages of CEOs versus female executives who endorsed various possible explanations of the situation. It is clear that the CEOs attributed it primarily to inadequacies in the quantity and quality of experience of potential women candidates for the top spots, while the females themselves attributed it to various forms of stereotyping and bias.

FIGURE 2.2

What prevents women from advancing to corporate leadership?

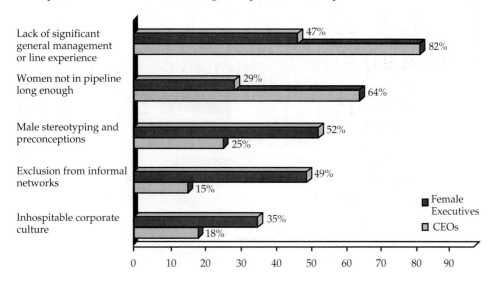

A more recent study sheds additional light on factors that impact the rise of women in leadership positions.[38] It identifies four general factors that explain the shift toward more women leaders.

The first of these is that *women themselves have changed.* That's evident in the ways women's aspirations and attitudes have become more similar to those of men over time. That's illustrated in findings about the career aspirations of female university students,[39] women's self-reports of traits such as assertiveness, dominance, and masculinity,[40][41] and the value that women place on characteristics of work such as freedom, challenge, leadership, prestige, and power.[42] The second factor is that *leadership roles have changed*, particularly with regard to a trend toward less stereotypically masculine characterizations of leadership. Third, *organizational practices have changed*. A large part of this can be attributed to legislation prohibiting gender-based discrimination at work, as well as changes in organizational norms that put a higher priority on results than an "old boy" network. Finally, the *culture has changed.* This is evident, for example, in the symbolic message often intended by appointment of women to important leadership positions, one representing a departure from past practices and signaling commitment to progressive change.

Leadership and Management Revisited

In Chapter 1 we looked at the relationship between leadership and management, and between leaders and managers. While these terms are not mutually exclusive, they do refer to a person's distinctive *style* and *approach.* Even in a particular role, two people may approach it differently; one more like a leader, the other more like a manager. The governor of one state, for example, may function more as a leader, whereas the governor of another state may function more as a manager (and not because there's anything different about the two states). It will be helpful to revisit those concepts in the context of the interactional framework.

Let's begin by reviewing some of the distinctions Bennis makes between leaders and managers as described in Chapter 1.

Leaders *emphasize "Change"*	Managers *emphasize "Stability"*
Innovate	Administer
Develop	Maintain
Inspire	Control
Long-term view	Short-term view
Ask what and why	Ask how and when
Originate	Initiate
Challenge the status quo	Accept the status quo
Do the right things	Do things right

Bennis is hardly alone in contrasting leaders and managers. Numerous other scholars echo the idea of a basic distinction between leadership and management. Kotter,[43] for example, described management in terms of coping with complexity, and leadership in terms of coping with change. Kotter noted how managerial practices and procedures can be traced to the 20th-century phenomenon of large organizations and the need to bring order and consistency to their functioning. Renewed interest in leadership, on the other hand, springs from the challenge of maintaining organizational success in an increasingly dynamic world. He said most U.S. corporations today, for example, are overmanaged and underled, but that "strong leadership with weak management is no better."[44] Fairholm[45] emphasized still other differences between leadership and management when he wrote that

> leadership and management are different in purpose, knowledge base, required skills, and goals. We distinguish leaders as more personal in their orientation to group members than managers. They are more global in their thinking. Leaders, we suggest, focus on values, expectations, and context. Managers, on the other hand, focus on control and results. Leaders impact followers and constituent groups in a way that allows volitional activity of followers, not through formal authority mechanisms . . . Managers give clear direction, make solitary assignments, and work hard for cooperation. The leader communicates indirectly, gives overlapping and ambiguous assignments, and sometimes sets employees up for internecine strife—to test loyalty and the leader's personal strength. Leaders value cooperation, not just coordination. They foster ideas of unity, equality, justice, and fairness in addition to efficiency and effectiveness, the bastions of management value.

Such differences are just what our framework is all about—**interactions.** In other words, the differences between leaders and managers, or between leadership and management, involve more than just differences between types of individuals. The differences extend to how such individuals *interact with* their followers and the situations they confront. Let's explore how these distinctions affect the other two elements of the framework.

Leader–Follower–Situation Interactions

Leaders create environments within which followers' innovations and creative contributions are welcome. Followers feel a stake in *shaping* something new, not just maintaining a status quo. Leaders also encourage growth and development in their followers in ways broader than what we might call mere job training (e.g., encouraging a follower to take on something really new, something that would stretch the follower but may involve failure on the task, or to take on a developmental experience not directly tied to the follower's present job requirements). Leaders generally are more interested in the big picture of followers' work, and tend to

more than managers.

assess their followers' performance less formally and less in terms of specific criteria than managers, and more in terms of holistic, personal, idiosyncratic, or intuitive criteria. Leaders motivate followers more personally and through more personal and intangible factors (e.g., through inspiration or the reward of just being able to work with the leader or on a particular project). Leaders redefine the parameters of tasks and responsibilities, both for individual followers and for the entire group. In that sense, leaders actively *change* the situations they're in rather than just optimize their group's adaptation to it. They are forever "moving outside the constraints of structure."[46] Such redefinitions also may occur through taking a long-term rather than a short-term perspective, through accentuating critical values or ends, or by marshaling energy to cope with some new threat.

Manager–Follower–Situation Interactions

Managers are more likely to emphasize routinization and control of followers' behavior. This might be expressed in terms of greater emphasis on making sure followers conform to policies or procedures ("doing it the way we've always done it") or in a tendency to assign narrower rather than broader tasks for followers to perform. It might be expressed in lesser degrees of decision-making discretion or autonomy given to followers, as in a manager's tendency to review *details* of work for them. Managers tend to assess their followers' performance in terms of explicit, fairly specific job descriptions. Managers motivate followers more with extrinsic, even contractual consequences, both positive and negative. Managers tend to accept the definitions of situations presented to them. They might be unlikely, for example, to reorient a group's task or mission in a whole new direction, or to change the whole culture of an organization. When managers do change things, they would be more likely to effect change officially, through control tactics such as developing new policies or procedures.

In reading the preceding paragraphs, it may seem to you that it's better to be a leader than a manager (or, perhaps, vice versa). But such a conclusion would ignore important characteristics of the followers. In some situations leaders are successful and managers are not, but in other situations the opposite is true. Consider, for example, one of Bennis's prototypical leaders: an inspiring individual having a vision of major institutional change that can be achieved only through the energy and creativity of committed followers. Such an inspiring individual may be thwarted, nonetheless, unless her followers share her value-based vision. If they are motivated primarily by economic incentives and are satisfied with their present lot, then the leader may fail to achieve her vision. The whole idea of *interaction* is that the effectiveness of any particular leader approach can be understood only in the context of certain follower and situational conditions. To return to Bennis's distinctions, managers emphasize *stability* whereas leaders emphasize *change.* Managers emphasize consistency and predictability in follower behavior (doing what's expected, doing things right), whereas leaders emphasize *changing* followers. That may mean transforming them or getting them to do more than they thought they could or thought they would. We'll see a similar distinction in Chapter 13 when we contrast transactional and transformational leadership.

Leadership and Management as Solutions to Different Kinds of Problems

We've already seen several approaches to distinguishing between leadership and management. But whereas these often focus on how one or the other tends to flow from the leader or manager's personal style, Ron Heifetz says that it's more helpful to think of management and leadership as representing different kinds of activities—as solutions to quite different kinds of problems.

Heifetz says that often we face problems or challenges for which the problem-solving resources already exist. In general, you can think of these resources as having two aspects: specialized methods and specialized expertise. There are many technical problems that we can solve by applying widely known though specialized methods for solution. A simple example might be determining the gas mileage your car gets on a cross-country trip. The rules are simple to follow and they always work if you follow the rules correctly. At other times we may not know the answers, but it may be relatively easy to find the people who do. Maybe we can't fix the rattle coming from the car engine, but we believe that the mechanic *can* do so. We may not know how to fix our ailment, but we believe the physician will know what to do. We may not know how to use a new software system, but we believe that we can master it with assistance from an expert. Problems like these are what Heifetz calls **technical problems.** Even though they may be complex, there are expert solutions to them, and experts who know how to solve them even if we don't.[47]

But not all problems are like that. Some problems, by their nature, defy even expert solution. Some problems cannot be solved using currently existing resources and ways of thinking. In fact, it's the nature of such problems that *it can be quite difficult even reaching a common definition of what the problem really is.* Solving such problems requires that the systems facing them make fundamental changes of some kind. Heifetz calls these **adaptive problems.** Whereas technical problems can be solved without changing the nature of the social system itself within which they occur, *adaptive problems can only be solved by changing the system itself.*

At work, the most critical issue in addressing technical problems is making sure they get to someone with the authority to manage the solution. According to Heifetz, however, most social problems turn out to be

All men have some weak points and the more vigorous and brilliant a person may be, the more strongly these weak points stand out. It is highly desirable, even essential, therefore, for the more influential members of a general's staff not to be too much like the general.

Major General Hugo Baron von Freytag-Loringhoven, anti-Hitler conspirator

adaptive in nature. Almost by definition, then, significant organizational change is at least in part an adaptive challenge. Even a seemingly simpler leadership challenge at work, like getting someone else to take more seriously some constructive feedback, is actually an adaptive challenge rather than a technical one. But here is where the distinction between technical problems and adaptive problems can become blurred. Go back to our earlier example of seeing a physician because of a medical problem—but let's assume it's your elderly parent rather than yourself who is the patient. Let's further assume that the physician correctly solves the technical problem and provides the correct technical solution—a particular medication which has a noticeable but tolerable side effect. Getting your parent to take the medicine if they don't want to turns this seemingly simple technical problem into a challenging adaptive one.

How do you know when a challenge is mostly a technical challenge or mostly an adaptive challenge? It's an adaptive challenge either wholly or mostly:

- When people's hearts and minds need to change, and not just their standard or habitual behaviors.
- By a process of elimination—If every technical solution you can think of has failed to improve the situation, then it is more likely to be an adaptive challenge.
- If there is continuing conflict among people struggling with the challenge.
- In a crisis, which may be a reflection of an underlying or unrecognized adaptive problem.

The relevance of all this for our discussion of the relationship between leadership and management is simply that, while effective management practices can solve technical problems, only leadership can solve adaptive problems. That's because <u>adaptive problems involve people's *values*</u>, and finding solutions to problems which involve others' values requires the active engagement of *their* <u>hearts and minds not just the leader's</u>. This is what Heifetz calls **adaptive leadership.**

To summarize, Table 2.1 shows the relationship between whether a problem or a challenge is mostly technical or adaptive in nature, the kind of work required to effectively address the challenge, and who should be thought of as the "problem solver."[48]

TABLE 2.1

	What's the work?	Who does the work?
Technical	Applying current know-how	Authorities
Adaptive	Discovering new ways	The people facing the challenge

A Final Word

Fairholm[49] argued that organizations may need *two different kinds of people at the helm:* good leaders *and* good managers. He wrote, "We need competent, dedicated managers to provide continuity of process, to insure program productivity, and to control and schedule the materials needed for production or service delivery. We also need people who can infuse the organization with common values that define the organization, determine its character, link it to the larger society, and ensure its long-term survival." But do examples like this prove that leaders and managers represent inherently different sorts of talents and interests? We think Kotter[50] is on solid ground when he advises organizations preparing people for executive jobs to "ignore the recent literature that says people cannot manage and lead." He said they should try to develop leader–managers. In other words, it may be useful to distinguish between the functions of leadership and management but still *develop* those complementary functions in the same individuals.

This point may be particularly important with regard to developing the talents of *younger* leader–managers. It would seem inappropriately narrow and limiting for a young person to define himself or herself as "the manager type" or "the leader type." Premature self-definitions of being a leader *or* manager present such *reductio ad absurdum* eventualities as foreclosing real developmental opportunities (e.g., "I guess I shouldn't seek that student body position since it's a leadership role, and I'm really more the management type") or as inappropriate reactions to the sorts of job responsibilities typical for a person early in her career (e.g., "Boss, you've been giving me too many management-type tasks, and I see myself more as a leader around here"). It seems prudent to note the commonalities—as shown in Figure 1.1—between leadership and management and not focus exclusively on the differences between them, *especially in the early stages of a person's professional development.*

There Is No Simple Recipe for Effective Leadership

As noted previously, it is important to understand how the three domains of leadership interact—how the leader, the followers, and the situation are all part of the leadership process. Understanding their interaction is necessary before you can draw valid conclusions from the leadership you observe around you. When you see a leader's behavior (even when it may appear obviously effective or ineffective to you), you should not automatically conclude something good or bad about the leader, or what is the right way or wrong way leaders should act. You need to think about the effectiveness of that behavior in *that* context with *those* followers.

Little things affect little minds.
  Benjamin Disraeli

As obvious as the above sounds, we often ignore it. Too frequently, we just look at the leader's behavior and conclude that he or she is a good leader or a bad leader apart from the context. For example, suppose you observe a leader soliciting advice from subordinates. Obviously, it seems unreasonable to conclude that good leaders always ask for advice or that leaders who do not frequently ask for advice are not such good leaders. The appropriateness of seeking input from subordinates depends on many factors, such as the nature of the problem or the subordinates' familiarity with the problem. It may be that the subordinates have a lot more experience with this particular problem, and soliciting their input is the correct action to take in this situation.

Consider another example. Suppose you hear that a leader did not approve a subordinate's request to take time off to attend to family matters. Was this bad leadership because the leader did not appear to be "taking care of her people"? Was it good leadership because she did not let personal matters interfere with the mission? Again, you cannot make an intelligent decision about the leader's actions by just looking at the behavior itself. You must always assess leadership in the context of the leader, the followers, and the situation.

The following statements about leaders, followers, and the situation make the above points a bit more systematically.

- A leader may need to respond to various followers differently in the same situation.
- A leader may need to respond to the same follower differently in different situations.
- Followers may respond to various leaders quite differently.
- Followers may respond to each other differently with different leaders.
- Two leaders may have different perceptions of the same followers or situations.

Conclusion: Drawing Lessons from Experience

All of the above leads to one conclusion: The right behavior in one situation is not necessarily the right behavior in another situation. It does *not* follow, however, that any behavior is appropriate in any situation. Although we may not be able to agree on the one best behavior in a given situation, we often can agree on some clearly inappropriate behaviors. Saying that the right behavior for a leader depends on the situation is not the same thing as saying it does not matter what the leader does. It merely recognizes the complexity among leaders, followers, and situations. This recognition is a helpful first step in drawing meaningful lessons about leadership from experience.

Summary   Leadership is a process in which leaders and followers interact dynamically in a particular situation or environment. Leadership is a broader concept than that of leaders, and the study of leadership must involve more than just the study of leaders as individuals. The study of leadership must also include two other areas: the followers and the situation. In addition, the interactive nature of these three domains has become increasingly important in recent years and can help us to better understand the changing nature of leader–follower relationships and the increasingly greater complexity of situations leaders and followers face. Because of this complexity, now, more than ever before, effective leadership cannot be boiled down to a simple and constant recipe. It is still true, however, that good leadership makes a difference, and it can be enhanced through greater awareness of the important factors influencing the leadership process.

Key Terms

interactional framework, 25
leader, 26
followers, 26
situation, 26
in-group, 26
out-group, 26

independent, critical thinking, 27
dependent, uncritical thinking, 27
active followers, 27
passive followers, 27
Leader–Member

Exchange Theory, 28
interactive leadership, 38
interactions, 41
technical problems, 43
adaptive problems, 43
adaptive leadership, 44

Questions

1. According to the interactional framework, effective leader behavior depends on many variables. It follows there is no simple prescription for effective leader behavior. Does this mean effective leadership is merely a matter of opinion or subjective preference?
2. Generally, leaders get most of the credit for a group's or an organization's success. Do you believe this is warranted or fair?
3. What are some of the other characteristics of leaders, followers, and situations you could add to those listed in Figure 2.1?

Activity

In this activity you will explore connotations to the words *leadership* and *management*. Divide yourselves into small groups and have each group brainstorm different word associations to the terms *leader* and *leadership* or *manager* and *management*. In addition, each group should discuss whether they would prefer to work for a manager or for a leader, and why. Then the whole group should discuss similarities and differences among the respective perceptions and feelings about the two concepts.

Minicase

"Can Disney Save Disney?"

The Disney name identifies an institution whose $22 billion in annual sales make it the world's largest media company. It was Walt Disney's creative leadership that established the Disney company as one of the leaders in

American business. Walt Disney and his brother Roy started Disney Brothers Studio in Hollywood in 1923. Artistically, the 1930s were Disney's best years. Walt Disney embraced new advances in color and sound, and pushed his team of enthusiastic young artists to pursue the most sophisticated techniques of the day. Disney risked everything on his first feature film, *Snow White and the Seven Dwarfs*, released in 1937. Audiences loved it. His focus on the positive and the life-affirming themes he incorporated into all his work provided much-needed smiles and laughter for audiences during the depths of the Great Depression.

Roy Disney became chairman after Walt died of lung cancer in 1966. In 1971 Roy died and his son, Roy E. Disney, became the company's principal individual shareholder. In 1984 new CEO Michael Eisner and president Frank Wells ushered in an era of innovation and prosperity. They instituted marathon meetings for generating creative ideas, forcing everyone to work grueling hours. The approach worked, and for the first 10 years of his tenure, Eisner was considered a genius. He revived Disney's historic animation unit, invested in the theme parks, led the expansion into Europe, and breathed new life into the company by partnering with cutting-edge companies like Pixar and Miramax. Eisner built Disney into a formidable media powerhouse, boosting its profits sixfold and sending its share price soaring almost 6,000 percent.

But more recent years have been challenging for Eisner and the Disney company. Eisner's initial magical effect has lost its shine and his more recent actions and decisions have had less-than-desirable effects on the company. Roy Disney, the last of the founding family to work at the company, quit the board in 2003 and began a campaign to try and oust Eisner. In his letter of resignation Disney asserted that Eisner has become an ineffective leader, claiming that Eisner consistently "micro-manages" everyone, resulting in loss of morale. He saw Eisner's cost-conscious decisions to shut down an Orlando animation studio and cut costs at theme parks as resulting in "creative brain drain" and creating the perception that the company is looking for "quick buck" solutions rather than long-term value. Disney also cited Eisner's inability to maintain successful relationships with creative partners like Pixar and Miramax (both contracts with these studios were not renewed) and his lack of a succession plan as dangerous to the future of the company.

Eisner ultimately lost his bid to retain his position as CEO and was forced to resign in 2005, one year before his contract as CEO expired.

1. Consider Walt Disney's effectiveness in terms of the three domains of leadership—the leader, the followers, and the situation. For each domain name factors that contributed to Disney's success.
2. Now think about Michael Eisner's leadership effectiveness. Name factors within the three domains of leadership that might be responsible for controversy surrounding Eisner's success and then ultimate failure and removal as Disney CEO.

Sources: R. Grover, *The Disney Touch* (Burr Ridge: Irwin, 1997); BBC News Online business reporter Friday, 13 February, 2004, 08:03 GMT; http://www.usatoday.com/money/media/2004-01-19-disneyoutlook_x.htm; http://www.savedisney.com; R. A. Heifetz, *Leadership without Easy Answers.* Cambridge, MA: Belknap, 1988; U.S. Bureau of Labor Statistics; *Labor Force Statistics Derived From the Current Population Survey: A Databook* (Vol. 1: Bulletin 2096, 1982). Washington, D.C.: U.S. Department of Labor, 1982; U.S. Bureau of Labor Statistics, *Household Data: Monthly Household Data (Table A-19: Employed persons by occupation, sex and age)*, 2002. Retrieved November 24, 2002, from ftp://ftp.bls.gov/pub/auppl/empsit.cpseea19.txt.

Chapter Notes

1. Bennis, W. G., and B. Nanus. *Leaders: The Strategies for Taking Charge.* New York: Harper & Row, 1985.
2. Astin, H. S., and C. Leland. *Women of Influence, Women of Vision.* San Francisco: Jossey-Bass, 1991.
3. Fiedler, F. *A Theory of Leadership Effectiveness.* New York: McGraw-Hill, 1967.
4. Hollander, E. P. *Leadership Dynamics: A Practical Guide to Effective Relationships.* New York: Free Press, 1978.
5. Graen, G. B., and J. F. Cashman. "A Role-Making Model of Leadership in Formal Organizations: A Developmental Approach." In *Leadership Frontiers.* Eds. J. G. Hunt and L. L. Larson. Kent, OH: Kent State University Press, 1975.
5a. Ibid.
5b. Gerstner, C. R., and D. V. Day. "Meta-analytic Review of Leader–Member Exchange Theory: Correlates and Construct Issues." *Journal of Applied Psychology* 82 (1997) (6), pp. 827–44.
6. Stogdill, R. M. "Personal Factors Associated with Leadership: A Review of the Literature." *Journal of Psychology* 25 (1948), pp. 35–71.
7. Stogdill, R. M. *Handbook of Leadership.* New York: Free Press, 1974.
8. Hogan, R. T., G. J. Curphy, and J. Hogan. "What We Know about Personality: Leadership and Effectiveness." *American Psychologist* 49 (1994), pp. 493–504.
9. Lord, R. G., C. L. DeVader, and G. M. Allinger. "A Meta-Analysis of the Relationship between Personality Traits and Leadership Perceptions: An Application of Validity Generalization Procedures." *Journal of Applied Psychology* 71 (1986), pp. 402–10.
10. Kanter, R. M. *The Change Masters.* New York: Simon & Schuster, 1983.
11. Baltzell, E. D. *Puritan Boston and Quaker Philadelphia.* New York: Free Press, 1980.
11a. Hollander and Offerman, 1990.
12. Jones, 2003.
13. Bass, 1981.
14. Bass, B. M. *Bass and Stogdill's Handbook of Leadership.* 3rd ed. New York: Free Press, 1990.
15. Stogdill, 1974.
16. Sutton, C. D., and R. W. Woodman. "Pygmalion Goes to Work: The Effects of Supervisor Expectations in the Retail Setting." *Journal of Applied Psychology* 74 (1989), pp. 943–50.
17. Burke, 1965.

18. Moore, L. I. "The FMI: Dimensions of Follower Maturity." *Group and Organizational Studies* 1 (1976), pp. 203–22.

19. Scandura, T. A, G. B. Graen, and M. A. Novak. "When Managers Decide Not to Decide Autocratically: An Investigation of Leader–Member Exchange and Decision Influence." *Journal of Applied Psychology* 52 (1986), pp. 135–47.

20. Sales, C. A., E. Levanoni, and D. H. Saleh. "Satisfaction and Stress as a Function of Job Orientation, Style of Supervision, and the Nature of the Task." *Engineering Management International* 2 (1984), pp. 145–53.

21. Lippitt, R. "The Changing Leader–Follower Relationships of the 1980s." *Journal of Applied Behavioral Science* 18 (1982), pp. 395–403.

22. Block, P. *Stewardship.* San Francisco: Berrett-Koehler, 1992.

23. Hollander, 1994.

24. Tanoff, G. F., and Barlow, C. B. "Leadership and Followership: Same Animal, Different Spots?" *Consulting Psychology Journal: Practice and Research,* Summer 2002, pp. 157–65.

25. Senge 1990, or 94 (5th discipline).

26. For example, Conlin, M. "The New Gender Gap. From Kindergarten to Grad School, Boys Are Becoming the Second Sex." *BusinessWeek,* May 26, 2003.

27. White House Project, 2002.

28. Adler, N. J. "Global Leaders: Women of Influence." In *Handbook of Gender & Work.* Ed. G. N. Powell. Thousand Oaks, CA: Sage, 1999.

29. De Zarate, R. O. "Women World Leaders: 1945–2003," 2003, retrieved from http://www.terra.es/personal2/monolith/00women.htm.

30. U.S. Bureau of Labor Statistics. *Labor Force Statistics Derived from the Current Population Survey: A Databook* (Vol. 1: Bulletin 2096). Washington, DC: U.S. Department of Labor, 1982.

31. U.S. Bureau of Labor Statistics, "Household Data: Monthly Household Data (Table A-19: Employed persons by occupation, sex and age)," 2002, retrieved November 24, 2002, from ftp://ftp.bls.gov/pub/auppl/empsit.cpseea19.txt.

32. Schein, V. 1973.

33. Schein, V. 1975.

34. Schein & Mueller, 1990.

35. Brenner, O. C., J. Tomkiewicz, and V. E. Schein. "The Relationship Between Sex Role Stereotypes and Requisite Management Characteristics Revisited." *Academy of Management Journal* 32 (1989), pp. 662–69.

36. Morrison, A. M., R. P. White, and E. Van Velsor. *Breaking the Glass Ceiling.* Reading, MA: Addison-Wesley, 1987.

37. Rosener, J. B. "Ways Women Lead." *Harvard Business Review* 68 (1990), pp. 119–25.

37a. Ibid, p. 124.

38. Eagly, A. H., and L. L. Carli. "The Female Leadership Advantage: An Evaluation of the Evidence." *The Leadership Quarterly* 14 (2003), pp. 807–34.

39. Astin, A. W., S. A. Parrott, W. S. Korn, and L. J. Sax. *The American Freshman: Thirty Year Trends.* Los Angeles: Higher Education Research Institute, University of California, 1997.

40. Twenge, J. M. "Changes in Masculine and Feminine Traits over Time: A Meta-analysis." *Sex Roles* 36 (1997), pp. 305–25.

41. Twenge, J. M. "Changes in Women's Assertiveness in Response to Status and Roles: A Cross-Temporal Meta-analysis, 1931–1993." *Journal of Personality and Social Psychology* 81, (2001), pp. 133–45.

42. Konrad, A. M., J. E. Ritchie, Jr., P. Lieb, and E. Corrigall. "Sex Differences and Similarities in Job Attribute Preferences: A Meta-analysis." *Psychological Bulletin* 126, (2000), pp. 593–641.

43. Kotter, J. "What Leaders Really Do." *Harvard Business Review,* May–June 1990, pp. 103–11.

44. Ibid.

45. Fairholm, G. W. *Values Leadership.* Praeger: New York, 1991, p. 40.

46. Ibid.

47. Heifetz, Ronald A. *Leadership without Easy Answers.* Cambridge, MA: Belknap, 1998.

48. Heifetz, Ronald A., and Marty Linsky. *Leadership on the Line: Staying Alive through the Dangers of Leading.* Harvard Business School Press, 2002.

49. Fairholm, G. W. *Values Leadership.* Praeger: New York, 1991, p. 41.

50. Kotter, J. "What Leaders Really Do." *Harvard Business Review,* May–June 1990, p. 104.

Chapter 3

Leadership Is Developed through Education and Experience

Introduction

Leadership and learning are indispensable to each other.

John F. Kennedy

In Chapter 1, we discussed the importance of using multiple perspectives to analyze various leadership situations. Moreover, we argued that it is relatively difficult for leaders to develop this method of analysis on their own and that formal education is one of the best ways to develop multiple perspectives on leadership. Given the importance of formal education and experience in leadership development, this chapter reviews some of the ways you can better learn about leadership. As an overview, we begin this chapter by presenting a general model that describes how we learn from experience. Next, we describe how perceptions can affect a leader's interpretation of, and actions in response to, a particular leadership situation and why reflection is important to leadership development. In addition, this chapter reveals how the people you work with and the task itself can help you become a better leader, and reviews some of the typical content and pedagogy found in many formal leadership education programs. Finally, we discuss how to evaluate and choose between the many different kinds of leadership programs available. A fitting place to begin the chapter might be to look at Highlight 3.1, which identifies the most critical skills leaders will need to be successful in the years ahead.

The Action-Observation-Reflection Model

Consider for a moment what a young person might learn from spending a year working in two very different environments: as a staff assistant in the

What Skills Will the Successful Leader Need in 2010?

HIGHLIGHT 3.1

The Conference Board is a not-for-profit organization that conducts research, assesses trends, and makes forecasts about management to help businesses strengthen their performance and better serve society. In 2002 it identified critical skills leaders will need to be successful in the year 2010. Here's its list:

- Cognitive ability—both raw "intellectual horse-power" and mental agility.
- Strategic thinking, especially with regard to global competition.
- Analytical ability, especially the ability to sort through diverse sources of information and sort out what's most important.

- The ability to make sound decisions in an environment of ambiguity and uncertainty.
- Personal and organizational communication skills.
- The ability to be influential and persuasive with different groups.
- The ability to manage in an environment of diversity—managing people from different cultures, genders, generations, etc.
- The ability to delegate effectively.
- The ability to identify, attract, develop, and retain talented people.
- The ability to learn from experience.

Source: A. Barrett, and J. Beeson, "*Developing Business Leaders for 2010.*" New York: The Conference Board, 2002.

U.S. Congress or as a carpenter on a house construction crew. Each activity has a rich store of leadership lessons there for the taking. Working in Congress, for example, would provide opportunities to observe political leaders both onstage in the public eye and backstage in more private moments. It would provide opportunities to see members of Congress interacting with different constituencies, to see them in political defeat and political victory, and to see a range of leadership styles. A young person could also learn a lot by working on a building crew as it turned plans and materials into the reality of a finished house: watching the coordination with subcontractors, watching skilled craftspeople train younger ones, watching the leader's reactions to problems and delays, watching the leader set standards and assure quality work. At the same time, a person could work in either environment and *not* grow much if he or she were not disposed to. Making the most of experience is key to developing one's leadership ability. In other words, leadership development depends not just on the kinds of experiences one has but also on how one uses them to foster growth. A study of successful executives found that one key quality that characterized them was an "extraordinary tenacity in extracting something worthwhile from their experience and in seeking experiences rich in opportunities for growth."[1]

But how does one do that? Is someone really more likely to get the lessons of experience by looking for them? Why is it not enough just to be there? Experiential learning theorists, such as Kolb,[2] believe people learn more from their experiences when they spend time thinking about them.

FIGURE 3.1
The spiral of
experience.

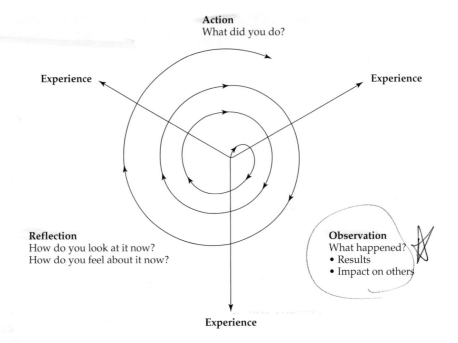

Action
What did you do?

Experience

Experience

Reflection
How do you look at it now?
How do you feel about it now?

Observation
What happened?
• Results
• Impact on others

Experience

These ideas are extended to leadership in the **action-observation-reflection (A-O-R) model,** depicted in Figure 3.1, which shows that leadership development is enhanced when the experience involves three different processes: action, observation, and reflection. If a person acts but does not observe the consequences of her actions or reflect on their significance and meaning, then it makes little sense to say she has learned from an experience. Because some people neither observe the consequences of their actions nor reflect on how they could change their actions to become better leaders, leadership development through experience may be better understood as the growth resulting from repeated movements through all three phases rather than merely in terms of some objective dimension like time (e.g., how long one has been on the job). We believe the most productive way to develop as a leader is to travel along the **spiral of experience** depicted in Figure 3.1.

Perhaps an example from Colin Powell's life will clarify how the spiral of experience pertains to leadership development. Powell held positions at the highest levels of U.S. military and civilian leadership as Chairman of the Joint Chiefs of Staff and U.S. Secretary of State, but in 1963 he was a 26-year-old officer who had just returned to the United States from a combat tour in Vietnam. His next assignment would be to attend a month-long advanced airborne Ranger course. Near the end of the course, he was to parachute with other troops from a helicopter. As the senior officer on the helicopter, Powell had responsibility for assuring it went well. Early in the flight he hollered for everyone to make sure their static lines were secure, the cables which automatically pull the chutes open when you jump.

Nearing the jump site, he yelled for the men to check their hookups one more time. Here are his words describing what happened next:

> Then, like a fussy old woman, I started checking each line myself, pushing my way through the crowded bodies, running my hand along the cable and up to each man's chute. To my alarm, one hook belonging to a sergeant was loose. I shoved the dangling line in his face, and he gasped . . . This man would have stepped out of the door of the helo and dropped like a rock.[3]

So what did Powell learn from this experience? Again, in his own words:

> Moments of stress, confusion, and fatigue are exactly when mistakes happen. And when everyone else's mind is dulled or distracted the leader must be doubly vigilant. "Always check small things" was becoming another one of my rules.[4]

We shall not cease from exploration
And the end of all our exploring
Will be to arrive where we started
And know the place for the first time.

T. S. Eliot

Let us now examine this incident in light of the A-O-R model. *Action* refers to Powell's multiple calls for the parachutists to check their lines. We might speculate from his self-description ("like a fussy old woman") that Powell might have felt slightly uncomfortable with such repeated emphasis on checking the lines, even though he persisted in the behavior. Perhaps you, too, sometimes have acted in a certain manner (or were forced to by your parents!) despite feeling a little embarrassed about it, and then, if it was successful, felt more comfortable the next time acting the same way. That seems to be just what happened with Powell here. The *observation* phase refers to Powell's shocked realization of the potentially fatal accident that would have occurred had he *not* double-checked the static lines. And the *reflection* phase refers to the lesson Powell drew from the experience: "Always check the small things." Even though it was obviously not a totally new insight, its importance was strongly reinforced by this experience. In a very real sense, Powell was "spiraling" through a lesson he'd learned from other experiences too, but embracing it even more this time, making it part of his style.

We also should note Powell himself described his learning in a manner consistent with our interactional framework. He emphasized the situational importance of the leader's attention to detail, especially during moments of stress, confusion, and fatigue, when mistakes may be most likely to happen. Finally, it's worth noting that throughout Powell's autobiography he discusses many lessons he learned from experience. One of the keys to his success was his ability to keep learning throughout his career.

The Key Role of Perception in the Spiral of Experience

Experience is not just a matter of what events happen to you; it also depends on how you perceive those events. Perception affects all three phases of the action-observation-reflection model and thus plays a very important role in what anyone will extract from a leadership course or from any leadership situation. Human beings are not passive recorders of experiences that happen to them; rather, people actively shape and construct their experiences. In order to better understand how perception affects experience, we will examine its role in each part of the action-observation-reflection model. We will begin with the stage that seems to correspond most directly with perception—the observation phase.

Perception and Observation

Observation and perception both deal with attending to events around us. Both seem to take place spontaneously and effortlessly, so it is easy to regard them as passive processes. Our common mental images of the perceptual process reflect this implicit view. For example, it is a common misconception that the eye operates essentially like the film in a continuously running camera. The fallacy of this passive view of perception is that it assumes we attend to all aspects of a situation equally. However, we do not see everything that happens in a particular leadership situation, nor do we hear everything. Instead, we are selective in what we attend to and what we, in turn, perceive. One phenomenon that demonstrates this selectivity is called **perceptual set.** Perceptual sets can influence any of our senses, and they are the tendency or bias to perceive one thing and not another. Many factors can trigger a perceptual set, such as feelings, needs, prior experience, and expectations. Its role in distorting what one hears proved a costly lesson when a sympathetic airline pilot told his depressed copilot, "Cheer up!" The copilot thought the pilot had said, "Gear up," and raised the wheels while the plane was still on the ground.[5] Try your own ability to overcome perceptual set with the following exercise. Read through the narrative passage below several times:

> FINISHED FILES ARE THE RESULT
> OF YEARS OF SCIENTIFIC STUDY
> COMBINED WITH THE
> EXPERIENCE OF MANY YEARS.

Make sure you have read it to yourself several times *before going any further.* Now, go back to the text and count the number of times the letter *F* appears.

How many did you count? Three? Four? Five? Six? Most people do not get the correct answer (six) the first time. The most frequent count is three; perhaps that was how many you saw. If you did not find six, go back and try it again. The most common error in this seemingly trivial task is overlooking the three times the word *of* appears. People easily overlook it because the word *of* has a *v* sound, not an *f* sound. Most people unconsciously make the task an auditory search task and listen for the sound of *F* rather than look for the shape of *F*; hence, they find three *F*s rather than six. Listening for the sound constitutes a counterproductive perceptual set for this task, and having read the passage through several times before counting the *F*s only exaggerates this tendency. Another reason people overlook the word *of* in this passage is that the first task was to *read* the passage several times. Because most of us are fairly accomplished readers, we tend to ignore little words like *of*. It disappears from our perceptual set. Then, when we are asked to count the number of *F*s, we have already defined the passage as a reading task, so the word *of* is really not there for us to count.

There are strong parallels between the example of perceptual set above and the perceptual sets that come into play when we are enrolled in a leadership course or observe a leadership situation. For example, your instructor for this class may dress unstylishly, and you may be prejudiced in thinking that poor dressers generally do not make good leaders. Because of your biases, you may discount or not attend to some things your instructor has to say about leadership. This is unfortunate, as your instructor's taste in clothes has little to do with his or her ability to teach (which is, after all, a kind of leadership).

A similar phenomenon takes place when one expects to find mostly negative things about another person (e.g., a problem employee). Such an expectation becomes a perceptual set to look for the negative and look past the positive things in the process. Stereotypes about gender, race, etc., represent powerful impediments to learning since they function as filters which distort one's observational abilities. For example, if you do not believe women and/or minorities are as successful as white males in influencing others, then you may be biased to identify or remember only those instances where a woman or minority leader failed, and discount or forget those instances where women or minority members succeeded as leaders. Unfortunately, we all have similar biases, although we are usually unaware of them. Often, we only become aware of our perceptual sets when we spend time reflecting about the content of a leadership training program or a particular leadership situation. Still another factor affecting the role observation plays in our ability to learn from experience is described in Highlight 3.2.

It's not what we don't know that hurts, it's what we know that ain't so.

Will Rogers

Perception and Reflection

Perceptual sets influence what we attend to or do not attend to, what we observe or do not observe. In addition, perception also influences the next stage of the spiral of experience—reflection—since reflection deals with how we interpret our observations. Perception is inherently an interpretive, or a meaning-making, activity. One important aspect of this deals with a process called **attribution.**

Attributions are the explanations we develop for the behaviors or actions we attend to. For example, if you see Julie fail in an attempt to get others to form a study group, you are likely to attribute the cause of the failure to dispositional factors within Julie. In other words, you are likely to attribute the failure to form a study group to Julie's intelligence, personality, physical appearance, or some other factor even though factors beyond her control could have played a major part. This tendency to

On Being Observant, Lucky, and Learning from Experience

HIGHLIGHT 3.2

It's often said that some people have all the luck. Do you think that's true—are some people luckier than others? Richard Wiseman, a professor at the University of Hertfordshire, has written a book about just that question, and his findings are very relevant to the role observation plays in our spiral of experience.

In one of his experiments, Wiseman placed advertisements in national newspapers asking for people to contact him who either felt consistently lucky or consistently unlucky. In one experiment, he gave both self-described lucky and unlucky people a newspaper to read, and asked them to look it over and tell him how many photographs were inside. Halfway through the paper he'd put a half-page message with two-inch lettering saying, "Tell the experimenter you have seen this and win $250."

The advertisement was staring everyone in the face, but the unlucky people tended to miss it whereas the lucky people tended to notice it. One reason may be related to the fact that Wiseman claims unlucky people are somewhat more anxious than lucky people, and that might disrupt their ability to notice things that are unexpected.

Source: Adapted from Richard Wiseman, *The Luck Factor.* New York: Miramax Books, 2003.

overestimate the dispositional causes of behavior and underestimate the environmental causes when others fail is called the **fundamental attribution error.**[6] People prefer to explain others' behavior on the basis of personal attributions, even when obvious situational factors may fully account for the behavior.

On the other hand, if *you* attempted to get others to form a study group and failed, you would be more likely to blame factors in the situation for the failure (e.g., there was not enough time, or the others were not interested, or they would not be good to study with). This reflects a **self-serving bias**[7], the tendency to make external attributions (i.e., blame the situation) for one's own failures, yet make internal attributions (i.e., take credit) for one's successes. A third factor which affects the attribution process is called the **actor/observer difference.**[8] It refers to the fact that people who are observing an action are much more likely than the actor to make the fundamental attribution error. Consider, for example, a student who gets a bad score on an exam. The person sitting *next* to her (i.e., an observer) would tend to attribute the bad score to *internal* characteristics (e.g., not very bright, weak in this subject) whereas the student herself would be more likely to attribute the bad score to *external* factors (e.g., the professor graded unfairly). Putting all these factors together, each of us tends to see our own success as due to our intelligence, personality, or physical abilities, but others' success as more attributable to situational factors or to luck.

Common sense is the collection of prejudices acquired by age 18.

Albert Einstein

We hasten to note in concluding this section that reflection also involves higher functions like evaluation and judgment, not just perception and attribution. We will address these broader aspects of reflection, which are crucial to learning from experience, just ahead.

"Just don't make any personal appearances until after the election."

Source: Reprinted from *The Saturday Evening Post Magazine* © 1964. *The Saturday Evening Post Society.*

Perception and Action

We have seen ways perception influences both the observation and reflection stages in the spiral of experience. It also affects the actions we take. For example, Mitchell and his associates[9,10,11] have examined how perceptions and biases affect supervisors' actions in response to poorly performing subordinates. In general, these researchers found that supervisors were biased toward making dispositional attributions about a subordinate's substandard performance and, as a result of these attributions, often recommended that punishment be used to remedy the performance deficit.

Another perceptual variable that can affect our actions is the **self-fulfilling prophecy.** The self-fulfilling prophecy occurs when our expectations or predictions play a causal role in bringing about the events we predict. It is not difficult to see how certain large-scale social phenomena may be effected this way. For example, economists' predictions of an economic downturn may, via the consequent decreased investor confidence, precipitate an economic crisis. But the self-fulfilling prophecy occurs at the interpersonal level, too. A person's expectations about another may influence how he acts toward her, and in reaction to his behavior she may act in a way that confirms his expectations.[12] An illustrative interaction sequence is shown in Figure 3.2.

FIGURE 3.2

The role of expectations in social interaction.

Source: Abstracted with permission from E. E. Jones, "Interpreting Interpersonal Behavior: The Effects of Expectancies," *Science* 234, (3) (October 1986), p. 43. Copyright 1986, American Association for the Advancement of Science. Reprinted with permission.

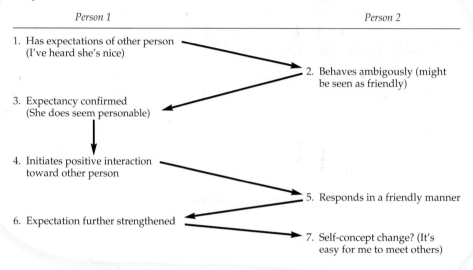

Some of the best evidence to support the effects of the self-fulfilling prophecy on leadership training was collected by Eden and Shani in the context of military boot camp.[13] They conducted a field experiment where they told leadership instructors their students had either unknown, regular, or high command potential. However, the students' actual command potential was never assessed, and unbeknownst to the instructors, the students were actually randomly assigned to the unknown, regular, or high command potential conditions. Nevertheless, students in the high-potential condition had significantly better objective test scores and attitudes than the students in the unknown- or regular-potential conditions, even though instructors simultaneously taught all three types of students. Somehow the students picked up on their instructor's expectations and responded accordingly. Thus, just having expectations (positive or negative) about others can subtly influence our actions, and these actions can, in turn, affect the way others behave.

Reflection and Leadership Development

Perhaps the most important yet most neglected component of the action-observation-reflection model is reflection. Reflection is important because it can provide leaders with a variety of insights into how to frame problems differently, look at situations from multiple perspectives, or better understand subordinates. However, most managers spend relatively little time on this activity, even though the time spent reflecting about leadership can be quite fruitful.

One reason the reflection component is often neglected may be time pressure at work. Leaders are usually very busy people working in pressure-filled situations and often do not have time to ponder all the possible consequences of their actions or reflect on how they could have accomplished a particular action better. Sometimes it takes an out-of-the-ordinary experience to focus one's attention on developmental challenges (see Highlight 3.3). In addition, some leaders may not be aware of the value of reflection in leadership development. Intentional reflection might even prompt one to see potential benefits in experience not initially considered relevant to leadership in organizational settings (see Highlight 3.4). Hopefully, this section will clarify the value of reflection and, in so doing, can complement the emphasis, throughout the remainder of the book, on looking at leadership from different perspectives.

Single- and Double-Loop Learning

It is difficult for leaders to fundamentally change their leadership style without engaging in some kind of reflection. Along these lines, Argyris[14] described an intensive effort with a group of highly successful chief executive officers who became even better leaders through increased self-awareness. His model for conceptualizing this growth is applicable to any level of leader and is worth considering in more detail.

Argyris said that most people interact with others and the environment on the basis of a belief system geared to manipulate or control others, and to minimize one's own emotionality and the negative feelings elicited from others. This belief system also tends to create defensive interpersonal relationships and limits risk taking. People "programmed" with this view of life (as most of us are, according to Argyris) produce group and organizational dynamics characterized by avoidance of conflict, mistrust, conformity, intergroup rivalry, misperceptions of and miscommunications with others, ineffective problem solving, and poor decision making. Most important for our purposes here, it generates a certain kind of learning that Argyris called **single-loop learning.**

Single-loop learning describes a kind of learning between the individual and the environment in which learners seek relatively little feedback that may significantly confront their fundamental ideas or actions. There is relatively little public testing of ideas against valid information. Consequently, an actor's belief system becomes self-sealing and self-fulfilling, and little time is spent reflecting about the beliefs. Argyris used the term *single-loop learning* because it operates somewhat like a thermostat; individuals learn only about subjects within the "comfort zone" of their belief systems. They might, for example, learn how well they are achieving a designated goal. They are far less likely, however, to question the validity

Leadership Development Dilemmas for Women

HIGHLIGHT 3.3

The Women's Leadership Program, offered by the Center for Creative Leadership (CCL), emphasizes receiving feedback, improving self-awareness, and setting leadership and life goals. Members of the CCL staff conducted a series of interviews with 60 executive women who had attended the program, and identified several salient issues these women were struggling with. Four particular themes stood out:

WHOLENESS AND AUTHENTICITY

These executive women desired to have a whole and full life. They felt job demands had forced their lives to become one-dimensional. Often they felt they had given up an important part of themselves: a creative self, friendly self, musical self, athletic self, and so forth. Sometimes they felt their organizations required them to ignore or suppress some part of their true selves in order to succeed.

CLARITY

After the program, many women developed great clarity about their own strengths, weaknesses, values, needs, priorities, and goals as leaders.

CONNECTION

Many women expressed concerns that they did not have the degree of interpersonal connectedness with others they would have preferred. They expressed a desire for closer friendships and family ties. Many said they felt isolated in their organizations, with few confidants of either gender.

CONTROL

One of the strongest themes identified in the interviews was the need to feel more in control. This need was manifested in a number of different ways, including the need to feel more comfortable exercising authority and a need to deal differently with organizational situations that made them feel helpless. Many women also expressed a desire to become more politically sophisticated.

To reflect upon the overall findings of the study, it is encouraging that virtually all of these executive women believed they were continuing to grow both personally and professionally. The experiences of this group of executive women certainly support the view that development persists throughout life.

Source: Adapted from P. Ohlott, "Change and Leadership Development: The Experience of Executive Women," *Leadership in Action* 19, no. 5 (1999), pp. 8–12.

of the goal or the values implicit in the situation, just as a thermostat does not question its temperature setting. That kind of self-confrontation would involve **double-loop learning.**

Double-loop learning involves a willingness to confront one's own views and an invitation to others to do so, too. It springs from an appreciation that openness to information and power sharing with others can lead to better recognition and definition of problems, improved communication, and increased decision-making effectiveness. Mastering double-loop learning can be thought of as learning how to learn. With considerable collective work, including the difficult task of working through personal blind spots, Argyris's group of leaders did move to this stage. In other words, through reflection they learned how to change their leadership styles by questioning their assumptions about others, their roles in the organization, and their underlying assumptions about the importance of their own goals and those of the organization.

The Relevance of Women's Personal Experiences to Their Leadership Effectiveness

HIGHLIGHT 3.4

Record numbers of women are active in the managerial workforce. Not surprisingly, a widespread perception has arisen that the relationship between work and nonwork domains of women's lives is almost inherently one of conflict. Managerial women are described as constantly torn between the demands of their managerial and personal roles. Less attention has been paid to the question of possible benefits of combining employment and personal roles.

Psychologists at the Center for Creative Leadership studied how the roles women play in their personal lives can impact their effectiveness at work. In telephone interviews with women managers, they asked this question (among others): *Are there any dimensions or aspects of your personal life that enhance your professional life?* Six themes characterized the women's responses:

- *Opportunities to enrich interpersonal skills* like motivating, respecting, and developing others—honed at home in raising children—are transferable to motivating, developing, and directing employees.

- *Psychological benefits* from overcoming obstacles, taking risks, and succeeding in personal arenas bolster esteem, self-confidence, energy, and courage.

- *Emotional support and advice* from friends and family who act as sounding boards and motivators, and allow one to vent feelings in a safe environment.

- *Handling multiple tasks* such as planning and juggling a busy family's schedules develops administrative skills such as prioritizing and planning.

- *Personal interests and background* provide skills and helpful perspectives for understanding and connecting with people at work.

- *Leadership opportunities* in volunteer, community organization, or family settings provide leadership lessons and increase comfort in authority roles.

Source: Adapted from: M. N. Ruderman, Patricia J. Ohlott, K. Panzer, & Sara N. King, "Benefits of Multiple Roles for Managerial Women." *Academy of Management Journal* 45 (2) (2002), pp. 369–86.

Leadership Development through Experience

Good flutists learn from experience; unfortunately, so do bad flutists.
Anonymous

Although using the action-observation-reflection model will help you make the most of your leadership experiences and mature into a better leader, it is also important to realize that some situations are developmentally richer than others. In many ways, these developmentally rich situations can be thought of as "crucibles" of experience, recalling the vessels that were used by medieval alchemists in trying to turn base metals into gold.[15] Some of the developmental experiences of one very well-known woman leader are described in Profiles in Leadership 3.1. Two other well-known people are featured in Profiles in Leadership 3.2 and 3.3.

In this section, we will review two developmental factors that make any given experience potent in fostering managerial growth: the people you work with and the characteristics of the task itself.[16,17] These factors

Oprah Winfrey

PROFILES IN LEADERSHIP 3.1

In January 2007, doors opened for the first class of girls at the Oprah Winfrey Leadership Academy near Johannesburg, South Africa. The first admissions included about 150 seventh and eighth grade girls, with plans to expand to more than 400 girls in the seventh through twelfth grades by 2011. Winfrey's vision is that the Academy will help develop the future women leaders of South Africa. One more accomplishment for a woman who has her own television show, publishes two different magazines, was nominated for an Academy Award for acting in *The Color Purple,* made Dr. Phil famous, and whose recommendation can virtually guarantee a book's commercial success. She may be the most influential woman in the world.

No one would have predicted this from the poor and troubled family conditions she was born into. Her Grandmother Hattie Mae, however, who raised Oprah during her first six years, saw something special in her from the beginning. She taught Oprah to read before the age of three, and at church Oprah was known as "The Preacher" because of her ability to recite Bible verses. As a teenager in school she was voted "Most Popular Girl," and she placed second in a national competition for dramatic interpretation. At 18 she won the Miss Black Tennessee beauty pageant.

Even from an early age there were glimpses of the direction Oprah's life would take. As a child she played games "interviewing" everything from her corncob doll to crows on the fence, but her true start in broadcasting came at the age of 17 when she worked part time at a local radio station while attending college. She became the youngest news anchor and the first black female news anchor at WLAC-TV in Nashville. In 1976 she moved to anchor the news in Baltimore, and in 1978 she became cohost of a local TV talk show. She moved to Chicago to host a talk show there, first airing in 1984; months later it was renamed *The Oprah Winfrey Show.* Its first national broadcast was in 1986, and the rest, as they say, is history. Except that Oprah is still *making* history, not only in virtually every facet of media but also in her philanthropic efforts to develop a generation of women leaders in South Africa.

Source: Adapted from Wikipedia.

are important because they provide opportunities for a leader or a leader-to-be to apply the action-observation-reflection model and reflect on how to be a better leader.

One important point to understand is that people who become leaders in any field tend to first stand out by virtue of their technical proficiency. Typically, leaders emerge or are selected for initial supervisory, managerial, or leadership roles on the basis of their competence or proficiency in their primary role requirements. For example, if you got an engineering degree in college, then your success in your first job—if you were lucky enough to get a job in your chosen field—is very likely to depend upon your expertise as an engineer. If and when you are promoted to a role of managing other engineers, however, what becomes more important for your success (and your organization's) is not so much your individual proficiency as an engineer (or chemist, accountant, salesperson, or football player) but rather your effectiveness in getting the best out of other engineers (or chemists, accountants, salespeople, football players, etc.). This is depicted in Figure 3.3.

Steve Jobs

PROFILES IN LEADERSHIP 3.2

Steve Jobs is one of the most famous and successful business leaders in the world, even if also known as having a temperamental, aggressive, and demanding style with others. At the age of twenty, with partner Steve Wozniak, he helped launch the personal computer revolution with Apple Computer, and ultimately through its premier PC, the Macintosh. After leaving Apple, he founded another company, NeXT Computer, and in 1986 bought a computer animation company called Pixar. The company's first film, *Toy Story,* made history by being the first entirely computer-animated feature film. Now back at Apple, Jobs has created even further revolutions in consumer technology products with the iPod and iPhone.

In 2005 Jobs delivered the commencement address at Stanford. In that address he talked about one of the most difficult and yet most valuable experiences of his life: getting fired from Apple, the company that he had helped found. He and Wozniak had started Apple, he said, in 1970 in his parents'

garage. In ten years it had grown into a $2 billion company. He could not believe it, amid that success, when he was fired by Apple's board of directors. "How can you get fired from a company you started? What had been the focus of my entire adult life was gone, and it was devastating." Yet now, reflecting on the opportunities that he was able to take advantage of for having left Apple, Jobs said to the graduating class that, "I didn't see it then, but it turned out that getting fired from Apple was the best thing that ever could have happened to me."

Steve Jobs on Leadership:

> *The only way to be truly satisfied is to do what you believe is great work. And the only way to do great work is to love what you do.*
>
> *Be a yardstick of quality. Some people aren't used to an environment where excellence is expected.*
>
> *Innovation distinguishes between a leader and a follower.*

Source: Adapted from Wikipedia.

The People You Work With

The people you associate with can stimulate development in many ways. Kouzes and Posner[18] noted the diverse ways others nurture our growth:

> Other people have always been essential sources of guidance. We all remember the parent we looked to for advice and support; the special teacher who filled us with curiosity for our favorite subject; the neighbor who always let us watch, even take part in, the tinkering in the garage; the coach who believed that we had promise and inspired us to give our best; the counselor who gave us valuable feedback about our behavior and its impact; the master artisan who instructed us in the fundamentals of a craft; or the first boss who taught us the ropes to skip and the hoops to jump.

Others play an especially important role in personal and professional development at work, so we will focus attention there.

A boss, especially a very good or very bad one, can be a powerful catalyst for growth. Exceptional bosses are vivid examples of how to (or how not to) put values into action. However, bosses are not the only people who contribute to growth and development at work. Working with others who have different backgrounds, perspectives, or agendas can often be a growth experience. Working with problem subordinates can stimulate

Al Gore

PROFILES IN LEADERSHIP 3.3

At the beginning of the film about global warming, *An Inconvenient Truth,* Al Gore introduces himself as the man who used to be known as "the next president of the United States." It's curious that the man who won the popular vote in the 2000 election but lost the presidency may have become even more influential and warmly received for his work on global warming than for his decades of holding political high office, including as vice president of the United States. Perhaps in some ways, after a life of public leadership, he's just now truly "finding his groove." It's interesting to look back to where he started.

Al Gore's exposure to Washington politics began at an early age despite coming from a rural part of Tennessee known as Possum Hollow (it's near such villages and hamlets as Difficult and Defeated). His father was himself a United States senator, and a man whom Gore described as "the greatest man I ever knew in my life." Both parents conveyed high expectations to him, and Gore remembers taking an intense pride in achievement from an early age. He traces it back to an experience in his first week in the one-room schoolhouse in Possum Hollow when

the teacher praised him for learning the alphabet in just five days. Gore says he hungered for that sensation again and again in his life.

In addition to his motivation to achieve, the young Gore also seemed motivated by a desire to conform closely to his elders' expectations of him: in many ways he made himself into the son that his parents wanted, the very model of an upper-class prep school boy. Maybe his time as a youngster in Washington, D.C., when he tried to convey an image of being serious and earnest, contributed some to the stiffness that Gore has had a reputation for throughout his public life. Interestingly, he appeared noticeably more relaxed and at ease in *An Inconvenient Truth.* There may have been early signs of this other side of Gore as well, hidden as it was from most of us. A more carefree and relaxed side of Gore was more evident when he was back home in Tennessee. For example, as soon as he got his learner's permit at age 14 he developed a reputation for reckless driving ("He was constantly running us into hog feeders and running us off the road," said a friend). And when he would go water skiing on a local lake, he is said to have loved standing on his head on the outboard motor.

Source: Adapted from Wikipedia.

managerial growth, *so can peers* but so can the need to influence others over whom you have no direct authority or control. You may work on a project and report to a superior other than your own boss, or you may head a team of peers; such situations are particularly helpful in developing negotiation and other informal influence skills. Finally, different management skills are called on when you must make major changes to a group or project such as downsizing it, restructuring it, or starting it from scratch.[19]

You can learn about effective and ineffective leadership by paying attention to the positive and negative models around you beyond your immediate boss. Watching others in leadership roles may suggest what to do as well as what not to do. Peers, especially, can be a great resource for developing one's effectiveness as a leader. In one program of peer coaching, school principals observed each other interacting in feedback conferences with their respective teachers and then met together afterward to share ideas about how well the conferences went.[20] Such principal-to-principal interaction is especially valuable in that it is rare for any supervisor to get feedback on his or her skill in providing feedback to subordinates. The

FIGURE 3.3

Changing requirements for success.

Source: Adapted from *Twenty-Two Ways to Develop Leadership in Staff Managers,* Robert W. Eichinger and Michael M. Lombardo. Copyright © 1990 Center for Creative Leadership. Reprinted with permission.

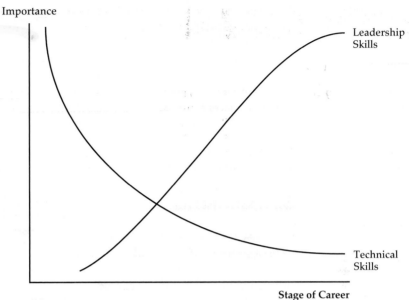

principals praised their peer coaching as an extremely effective mechanism for enhancing their effectiveness as supervisors.

In an organization, you also can gain valuable perspectives and insights through close association with an experienced person willing to take you under his wing. Such an individual is often called a **mentor,** after the character in Greek mythology whom Odysseus trusted to run his household and see to his son's education when Odysseus went off to fight the Trojans. Now, 3,000 years later, Mentor's name is used to describe the process by which an older and more experienced person helps to socialize and encourage younger organizational colleagues.[21]

Generally, mentors are highly placed, powerful individuals who develop relatively long-lasting relationships with younger colleagues whose professional careers are influenced and furthered as a result.[22] Typically, the mentoring relationship is informal, though its value has encouraged some to recommend its use formally and systematically in organizations.[23] In terms of value, both mentors and mentorees benefit from having this relationship. Mentors benefit by the greater influence they accrue by having former mentorees in various positions across the organization. Mentors also benefit by having a younger replacement ready to fill their position if they are promoted.[24] The mentoree benefits from this relationship by gaining an influential ally and by learning through the mentor's tutoring about the subtler aspects of organizational ethics, influence, and leadership. Having a mentor can also result in more career opportunities for the mentoree,[25,26] and the lack of mentors for women has been cited as one reason there are relatively few women in executive positions.[27] Although some may advocate systematizing mentorship programs to improve the career opportunities for all employees, it remains to be seen whether a formalized program would preserve the essence and qualities of more informal, self-selected mentoring relationships.[28]

An idea somewhat related to mentoring is that of **executive coaching.** Increasingly, executive coaching is seen as a general responsibility of all executives toward managers who report to them. It is an investment that can help change counterproductive behavior, often interpersonal, that threatens to derail an otherwise valued manager.

The Task Itself

In addition to the various sorts of relationships with other people, certain kinds of work-related tasks can also be particularly developmental. Developmental tasks are often more complex and ambiguous than those one has faced before. In addition, leadership development can be enhanced if the environment one works in is changing, dynamic, uncontrollable, and unpredictable. The nature of the task may require new and creative solutions; old answers may not work anymore. Projects involving strategic planning and projections into an uncertain future can be quite challenging intellectually and can contribute to a leader's development.[29]

Although we have emphasized the importance of applying the action-observation-reflection model to enhance one's learning from experience, the developmental value of the challenging tasks themselves cannot be denied. The best developmental opportunities are those that stretch individuals and allow them to test themselves against new and difficult tasks.[30] Of course, the difficulty level of tasks and how much one will be stretched by doing them is meaningful mostly in the context of a given individual's maturity and experience. The following are the words of one college student who was in charge of the flag section of her school's marching band:

> I have 30 people under me broken into four sections. I am responsible for conducting our rehearsals, teaching flag routines, taking care of any problems, recruiting new members, and motivating my people. I do some of this through my four section leaders, so I have to make sure they are doing their jobs properly. The biggest challenge of all this is keeping motivation high and making sure that everyone learns what they are supposed to and performs it well. It is really giving me a lot of experience in interacting with people.

Another student described his own best leadership experience in terms of his unique background as an instructor on his collegiate parachute team:

> During this period I learned a lot about what it takes to teach a person to jump out of an airplane successfully and injury free. The foremost concern and responsibility is the welfare of the student, so I had to be certain that they learned the procedures correctly, and be thoroughly convinced that they would be safe once out the door no matter what situation may arise. I was responsible for someone else's life. I had to be very patient and understanding many times when they would not grasp an idea or a procedure properly, spending a lot of time in certain areas until they were proficient.

I took a great deal o' pains with his education, sir; let him run the streets when he was very young, and shift for his-self. It's the only way to make a boy sharp, sir.

Charles Dickens,
Pickwick Papers

Other times I had to be stern and strict to emphasize certain emergency procedures and safety hazards in order to be sure they were aware of the seriousness of the situation. During this period I experienced everything that goes into leadership. I had to work with many people. Many of them were my peers, which makes things more difficult in some cases.

Feeling responsible for someone else's life certainly increases one's personal pressure, and it was partly this pressure that made this student-instructor's role such a valuable leadership experience. Whether or not a particular task is perceived as developmentally challenging and generates a high level of personal pressure depends on several factors. The most commonly cited developmental challenge mentioned by managers was a task where both success and failure were possible and would be obvious to others. The risk of possible failure is a strong incentive for managers to learn. Managers also mentioned deadlines, travel requirements, and longer hours as factors that, while adding to personal pressure, also contributed to professional growth.[31]

One last aspect of leadership-developing tasks should be mentioned. Just as mentoring relationships fail to develop for all members, organizations may not provide the same developmental opportunities for all their members. In particular, there is a striking difference between large and small organizations in the opportunities they offer. This is apparent, for example, in the chances of having a significant responsibility in the school play in schools with either large or small student bodies. In small schools, virtually anyone who wants to have a significant part in putting on the play will be able to do so. In large schools, though, the number of students far exceeds the number of important functions; many motivated students will miss out on the chance to participate and grow from the experience. As John Gardner has pointed out,[32] the sheer size and impersonalness of some of our organizations does not provide the soil in which a young person's leadership can grow.

Making the Most of Your Leadership Experiences: Learning to Learn from Experience

This section builds on the ideas previously introduced in this chapter by providing leadership practitioners with a few suggestions to enhance learning from experience (see Highlight 3.5 for a description of some executives who apparently did not learn enough from experience). For well over a decade, researchers at the Center for Creative Leadership have been studying the role of learning from experience as an important developmental behavior for people in executive positions. While this research has contributed a great deal to *what* people need to learn to be successful (see Highlight 3.6 for a comparison of lessons men and women managers learn from experience), less is known about the process of learning or *how* we learn to be successful.

Bunker and Webb[33] asked successful executives to list adjectives describing how they felt while working through powerful learning events

Executive Derailment: Knocking Yourself Off the Track to Success

HIGHLIGHT 3.5

Some executives on an apparently clear track to the top never make it. They become derailed. For more than a decade, researchers at the Center for Creative Leadership have studied executives who had fallen short of the levels of success predicted of them earlier in their careers. Typically, their derailments were the result of several factors, though insensitivity to others was the most frequent problem. Sometimes styles that served them well earlier became liabilities in new circumstances, and sometimes long-standing liabilities, previously outweighed by other aspects, eventually took their career toll. A 1996 study expanded the work and included samples of European as well as North American executives. In general, the derailment themes in Europe and North America were consistent:

Characteristics of Successful Leaders

Ability to develop or adapt.

Ability to establish collaborative relations.

Ability to build and lead a team.

Nonauthoritarian.

Consistent exceptional performance.

Ambitious.

Characteristics of Derailed Leaders

Inability to develop or adapt.

Poor working relations.

Inability to build and lead a team.

Authoritarian.

Poor performance.

Too ambitious.

How would you interpret these executives' derailments in terms of the action-observation-reflection model? Do you think the problem was in their actions? their observation or awareness of the consequences of their actions? or something else?

Source: Adapted from J. B. Leslie and E. Van Velsor, *A Look at Derailment Today: North America and Europe.* Greensboro, NC: Center for Creative Leadership, 1996.

and potent developmental experiences. Their typical responses were a combination of both positive and negative feelings.

What would a man be wise; let him drink of the river
That bears on its bosom the record of time;
A message to him every wave can deliver.
To teach him to creep till he knows how to climb.
John Boyle O'Reilly

Negatives	Positives
Pained	Challenged
Fearful	Successful
Frustrated	Proud
Stressed	Capable
Anxious	Growing
Overwhelmed	Exhilarated
Uncertain	Talented
Angry	Resourceful
Hurt	Learning

This pattern strongly supports the long-hypothesized notion of a meaningful link between stress and learning.[34] The learning events and developmental experiences that punctuate one's life are usually, perhaps always, stressful.[35,36,37,38]

What Do Men and Women Managers Learn from Experience?

HIGHLIGHT 3.6

For a quarter century or so, significant numbers of women have been represented in the management ranks of companies. During that period companies have promoted large pools of high-potential women, but relatively few of them have achieved truly top-level positions. Several factors probably account for this, but one possibility is that men and women learn differently from their work experiences. Researchers at the Center for Creative Leadership have studied how male and female executives describe the important lessons they've learned from their career experiences, and there are some interesting differences between the genders as well as significant overlap.

Most Frequent Lessons for Men and Women

Directing and motivating employees.

Self-confidence.

Basic management values.

How to work with executives.

Understanding other people's perspective.

Dealing with people over whom you have no authority.

Handling political situations.

For Men Only

Technical/professional skills.

All about the business.

Coping with ambiguous situations.

Shouldering full responsibility.

Persevering through adversity.

For Women Only

Personal limits and blind spots.

Taking charge of career.

Recognizing and seizing opportunities.

Coping with situations beyond your control.

Knowing what excites you.

Why would there be any learning differences between the genders? One hypothesis is that men and women managers tend to have somewhat different career patterns. For example, there is some evidence that women receive fewer truly challenging developmental opportunities.

Source: Adapted from E. Van Velsor and M. W. Hughes, *Gender Differences in the Development of Managers: How Women Managers Learn from Experience* (Technical Report No. 145). Greensboro, NC: Center for Creative Leadership, 1990.

Bunker and Webb note that executives try to be successful without experiencing stress. They are most comfortable when they can draw upon a proven repertoire of operating skills to tackle a challenge they have conquered in the past. Combined with the organizational pressure to have "proven performers" in important positions, there is a tremendous initial pressure to "continue to do what we've always done." In stressful situations, this tendency may become even more powerful. What results is one of the great Catch-22s of adult development: The times when people most need to break out of the mold created by past learning patterns are the times when they are most unwilling to do so. Being able to *go against the grain* of one's personal historical success requires an unwavering commitment to learning and a relentless willingness to let go of the fear of failure and the unknown.

Figure 3.4 depicts the Center for Creative Leadership's work on the process of "learning to learn from experience." Bunker and Webb describe the figure as a segment of life containing a series of learning opportunities. The circled segment represents a stressful episode of life—a potentially

FIGURE 3.4

Anatomy of a learning experience.

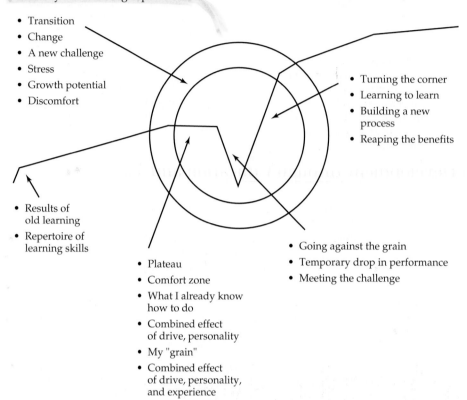

- Transition
- Change
- A new challenge
- Stress
- Growth potential
- Discomfort

- Turning the corner
- Learning to learn
- Building a new process
- Reaping the benefits

- Results of old learning
- Repertoire of learning skills

- Going against the grain
- Temporary drop in performance
- Meeting the challenge

- Plateau
- Comfort zone
- What I already know how to do
- Combined effect of drive, personality
- My "grain"
- Combined effect of drive, personality, and experience

Teach a highly educated person that it is not a disgrace to fail and that he must analyze every failure to find its cause. He must learn how to fail intelligently, for failing is one of the greatest arts in the world.

Charles F. Kettering, inventor, automotive pioneer, and corporate leader

dramatic learning-to-learn event. The left side of the curve represents the growth and development that was stimulated by prior learning experiences. Also represented is a flattening out of learned skill value that often occurs; over time, new skills often become mere routinized habits. People operating in this stabilizing period, called the comfort zone, must overcome the caution generated by ongoing success and the fear of challenging what they already know how to do. The smaller concentric circle represents the tension created by the appearance of a new learning challenge—often arising out of a transition or a stressful experience that requires a response. The sharp dip in success depicts the performance regression that generally accompanies attempts at learning a new set of responses and strategies. One gets through this period (and thus performs at a higher level with broader skills) by coping with the stress or letting go of short-term expectations in favor of more long-term learning. Of course, if one is not willing to go against the grain and tolerate a small dip in performance, then the learning curve becomes flat—no learning.

To be successful, learning must continue throughout life, beyond the completion of one's formal education.

The end of extrinsically applied education should be the start of an education that is motivated intrinsically. At that point the goal of studying is no longer to make the grade, earn a diploma, and find a good job. Rather, it is to understand what is happening around one, to develop a personally meaningful sense of what one's experience is all about.[39]

And that applies to the specific challenge of *becoming* and *remaining* an effective leader, too. People who lead in modern organizations need to be engaged in a never-ending learning process.[40]

Leadership Development through Education and Training

Although we believe experience plays a large role in leadership development, we believe formal education can play an important role, too. For example, many sets of researchers have found that education level or academic performance in college was positively related to future managerial success.[41,42,43] Furthermore, in a major review of the effectiveness of managerial training programs, Burke and Day found that educational programs generally had a positive effect on leadership development.[44] Thus, formal education and training programs can help one become a better leader. However, it is important to note that these programs vary substantially in both content and pedagogy, and not all programs are appropriate for all leaders. The content of different leadership programs varies considerably, depending on the target audience; university-level courses generally provide a survey of the major leadership findings, programs for first-level supervisors often focus on how to train subordinates and give them feedback about their progress, and programs for senior executives often focus on strategic planning and public relations. In this regard, it's helpful to distinguish between leadership development and leadership education, the latter being a component of the former.[45] Programs also vary in the extent to which they are based on well-established and professionally accepted practices and standards. Some leadership training programs represent little more than fads or popularized pseudoscience. In the following pages, we will review some of the more common educational and training techniques used to teach and develop leadership.

Leadership Education is a componet of Leadership Development.

University Courses in Leadership

Today, many hundreds of colleges or universities offer some type of leadership training program. Often these programs consist of extracurricular leadership activities run out of the student development office or are courses much like the one for which you are using this book. The extracurricular activities can vary greatly, but the leadership courses often

and formal courses.

WHAT DO CHILDREN BELIEVE ABOUT LEADERSHIP? "WUT DO LDRS DO?"

HIGHLIGHT 3.7

A five-year-old girl wrote and illustrated an unprompted "book" for her grandfather, a friend of the authors. We've included a few of the pages here. They convey what at least some young children believe are important qualities of leaders. You might ask yourself how valid this characterization is . . . and in what ways it is likely to be shaped by experiences between kindergarten and adulthood. Oh yes—the words are written entirely with a five-year-old's phonetic spelling, so you'll need to be creative in interpreting the qualities!

A

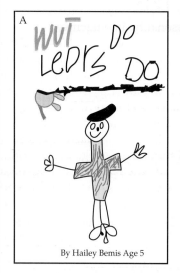

By Hailey Bemis Age 5

B

C

D

E

Translation: What do leaders do; They call 911 if someone gets hurt; They get people excited to learn; They be nice to people; They help people.

have a high degree of overlap in both content and pedagogy. In terms of content, the topics covered in most leadership courses are similar to the subjects addressed in this book and include how personality traits, cognitive abilities, values, behaviors, motivation, group dynamics, communication, situational factors, and different theories of leadership can all be used to describe the leadership process. In addition, many universities offer specialized courses that focus primarily on historical, business, minority, or female leaders.

An educated man can experience more in a day than an uneducated man in a lifetime.

Seneca, Roman statesman, 1st century A.D.

The techniques, or pedagogy, used to impart these different leadership concepts to students can vary greatly. Many courses use the standard lecture method, which has been shown to be an effective way of imparting knowledge about leadership.[46] Some courses also provide **individualized feedback** to students in the form of personality, intelligence, values, or interests test scores or leadership behavior ratings. **Case studies** consist of descriptions of various leadership situations and are used as a vehicle for leadership discussions. **Role playing** is also a popular methodology. In role playing, participants are assigned parts to play (e.g., a supervisor and an unmotivated subordinate) in a job-related scenario. Role playing has the advantage of letting trainees actually practice relevant skills and thus has greater transferability to the workplace than do didactic lectures or abstract discussions about leadership. **Simulations** and **games** are other methods of training. These are relatively structured activities designed to mirror some of the challenges or decisions commonly faced in the work environment. One of the better-known leadership simulations is the Center for Creative Leadership's "Looking Glass," in which participants play different leadership roles in a glass manufacturing plant.[47] A newer approach to leadership development puts participants in relatively unfamiliar territory (e.g., outdoors rather than offices) and presents them physical, emotionally arousing, and often team-oriented challenges.

Leadership Training Programs

There are numerous leadership training programs aimed particularly toward leaders and supervisors in industry or public service. In many ways, these have strong parallels to both the content and techniques used in university-level courses on leadership. However, these programs are usually much shorter (typically less than a week), and the content tends to be more focused than that of a university course. The content of these programs also depends on the organizational level of the recipients; programs for first-level supervisors focus on developing supervisory skills such as training, monitoring, giving feedback, and conducting performance reviews with subordinates. Generally, these programs use lectures, case studies, and role-playing exercises to improve leadership skills.

The programs for mid-level managers often focus on improving interpersonal, oral-communication, and written-communication skills, as well as giving tips on time management, planning, and goal setting. These programs rely more heavily on individualized feedback, case studies, presentations, role playing, simulations, **in-basket exercises,** and **leaderless group discussions** as techniques to help leaders develop. In in-basket exercises, participants are given a limited amount of time to prioritize and respond to a number of notes, letters, and phone messages from a fictitious manager's in-basket. This technique is particularly useful in assessing and improving a manager's planning and time management skills. In leaderless group discussions, facilitators and observers rate participants on the degree of persuasiveness, leadership, followership, or conflict each member manifests in a group that has no appointed leader. These ratings are used to provide managers with feedback about their interpersonal and oral-communication skills.

In reviewing the general field of leadership development and training, Conger offered this assessment: "Leadership programs can work, and work well, if they use a multi-tiered approach. Effective training depends on the combined use of four different teaching methods which I call personal growth, skill building, feedback, and conceptual awareness."[48] Some programs seek to stimulate leadership development by means of oftentimes emotionally intense personal growth experiences such as river rafting, wilderness survival, and so forth. Leadership development through skill building involves structured activities focusing upon the sorts of leadership skills featured in the final section of this book. Some approaches to leadership development emphasize individualized feedback about each person's strengths and weaknesses, typically based upon standardized assessment methods. Feedback-based approaches can help identify "blind spots" an individual may be unaware of, as well as help prioritize which aspects of leadership development represent the highest priorities for development focus. Still other sorts of programs develop leadership by emphasizing its conceptual or intellectual components. An example of this approach would be an emphasis on theory and the use of case studies, common in many MBA programs. There are merits in each of these approaches, but Conger was on solid ground when he emphasized the value of combining elements of each.

In a related vein, others have emphasized that leadership development in the 21st century must occur in more lifelike situations and contexts.[49] Toward that end, they have advocated creating better practice fields for leadership development analogous to the practice fields whereon skills in competitive sports are honed, or practice sessions analogous to those in music training wherein those skills are sharpened. Increasingly, leadership development is occurring in the context of work itself.[50]

Leadership programs for senior executives and CEOs tend to focus on strategic planning, public relations, and interpersonal skills. Many times, the entire senior leadership of a company will go through a leadership program at the same time. One goal of such a group might be to learn how to develop a strategic plan for their organization. In order to improve public relations skills, some programs have CEOs undergo simulated,

All rising to a great place is by a winding stair.
Francis Bacon, philosopher

Tell me and I'll forget; show me and I may remember; involve me and I'll understand.
Chinese proverb

unannounced interviews with television reporters and receive feedback on how they could have done better.

Here's one final thought about *choosing* a program of leadership training. Although a number of leadership training programs are based on sound theory and research, some other programs have no basis in science and should be considered speculative at best. Still others are based on unwarranted and simplistic extensions of scientific findings. Perhaps the best way to guarantee that a leadership program will be useful to you or your organization is to adopt a systematic approach to leadership training. There is value in being an informed consumer, and this is just as true in investing one's time, energy, and money in leadership programs as it is in other products and services.

Building Your Leadership Self-Image

This chapter has explored how leadership develops through experience and formal education. Before concluding, however, we should acknowledge that not everyone wants to be a leader or believes he can be. John Gardner has argued that many of our best and brightest young people actually have been immunized against, and dissuaded from, seeking leadership opportunities and responsibilities.[51] Other young people, even if they want to be leaders, may not believe they have what it takes. Both groups, we believe, are selling themselves short. — *Avoid selling yourself short.*

For those who merely want to avoid the responsibilities of leadership, we encourage an openness of mind about leadership's importance and pervasiveness. We hope this book offers ways of thinking about leadership that make it at once more immediate, more relevant, and more interesting than it may have seemed before. For others, we encourage flexibility in self-image. Do not stay out of the leadership arena based on *Avoid* — some global and self-defeating generalization such as "I am not the leader type." Experiment and take a few risks with different leadership roles. This will help you appreciate new facets of yourself as well as broaden your leadership self-image.

| Summary | This chapter reviews several major points regarding how leadership can be developed through both formal education and experience. One way to get more out of your leadership courses and experiences is through the application of the action-observation-reflection model. This model provides a framework for better understanding of leadership situations. In addition, being aware of the role perception plays in leadership development is also important, as it affects what you observe, how you interpret your observations, and what actions you take as a leader. Finally, it is important to remember that both education and experience can contribute to your development as a leader by enhancing your ability to reflect on |

and analyze leadership situations. Exposure to formal leadership education programs can help you to develop multiple perspectives to analyze leadership situations, and the people you work with and the task itself can also provide you with insights on how to be a better leader. However, what you gain from any leadership program or experience is a function of what you make of it. Successful leaders are those who have "an extraordinary tenacity in extracting something worthwhile from their experience and in seeking experiences rich in opportunities for growth."[52] If you want to become a better leader, then you must seek challenges and try to get all you can from any leadership situation or opportunity.

Key Terms

action-observation-reflection model, *54*
spiral of experience, *54*
perceptual set, *56*
attribution, *57*
fundamental attribution error, *58*
self-serving bias, *58*
actor/observer

difference, *58*
self-fulfilling prophecy, *59*
single-loop learning, *61*
double-loop learning, *62*
mentor, *67*
executive coaching, *68*
individualized

feedback, *75*
case studies, *75*
role playing, *75*
simulations, *75*
games, *75*
in-basket exercises, *76*
leaderless group discussions, *76*

Questions

1. Not all effective leaders seem to be reflective by nature. How do you reconcile that with the concept of the spiral of experience and its role in leadership development?

2. Explain how you can use knowledge about each of the following to enrich the benefits of your own present leadership experiences:

   a. The action-observation-reflection model.

   b. The people you interact and work with.

   c. The activities you're involved in.

3. Using the role of teacher as a specific instance of leadership, discuss how a teacher's perceptual set, expectations of students, and attributions may affect student motivation and performance. Do you think some teachers could become more effective by becoming more aware of these processes? Would that be true for leaders in general?

4. If you were to design the perfect leadership development experience for yourself, how would you do so and what would it include? How would you know it was effective?

5. Do you think people have a need for growth and development?

6. One important aspect of learning from experience is observing the consequences of one's actions. Sometimes, however, the most significant

consequences of a leader's actions do not occur for several years (e.g., the ultimate impact of certain personnel decisions or a strategic decision to change a product line). If that is so, then is there any way individuals can learn from the consequences of those actions in a way to modify their behavior? If consequences are so delayed, is there a danger they might draw the wrong lessons from their experiences?

Activity

Divide yourselves into groups and in each group contrast what attributions you might make about the leadership style of two different individuals. All you know about either of them is the following:

	Person A	Person B
Favorite TV show	*60 Minutes*	*Survivor*
Car	Ford Mustang	Volkswagen Beetle
Favorite sport	American football	Mountain biking
Political affiliation	Republican	Democrat
Favorite music	Country & Western	New Age

Minicase

"Developing Leaders at UPS"

UPS is the nation's fourth largest employer with 357,000 employees worldwide and operations in more than 200 countries. UPS is consistently recognized as one of the "top companies to work for" and was recently recognized by *Fortune* as one of the 50 best companies for minorities. A major reason for UPS's success is the company's commitment to its employees. UPS understands the importance of providing both education and experience for its next generation of leaders—spending $300 million dollars annually on education programs for employees and encouraging promotion from within. All employees are offered equal opportunities to build the skills and knowledge they need to succeed. A perfect example of this is Jovita Carranza.

   Jovita Carranza joined UPS in 1976 as a part-time clerk in Los Angeles. Carranza demonstrated a strong work ethic and a commitment to UPS, and UPS rewarded her with opportunities—opportunities Carranza was not shy about taking advantage of. By 1985 Carranza was the workforce planning manager in metro LA. By 1987 she was district human resources manager based in Central Texas. By 1990 she had accepted a move to district human resources manager in Illinois. She received her first operations assignment, as division manager for hub, package, and feeder operations, in Illinois in 1991. Two years later, she said yes to becoming district operations manager in Miami. In 1996 she accepted the same role in Wisconsin. By 1999 Carranza's progressive successes led UPS to promote her to president of the Americas Region. From there she moved into her current position as vice president of UPS Air Operations, based in Louisville, Kentucky.

The $1.1 billion air hub she currently oversees sprawls across the equivalent of more than 80 football fields. It can handle 304,000 packages an hour, its computers process nearly 1 million transactions a minute, and it serves as the lynchpin for the $33 billion business that has become the world's largest package-delivery company.

Carranza attributes much of her success to her eagerness to take on new challenges: "The one error that people make early on in their careers is that they're very selective about opportunities so they avoid some, prefer others," she says. "I always accepted all opportunities that presented themselves because from each one you can learn something, and they serve as a platform for future endeavors."

It has also been important, she says, to surround herself with capable, skilled employees who are loyal to the company and committed to results. After nearly 30 years with UPS, it is teamwork, interaction, and staff development that Carranza says is one of the achievements of which she is proudest: "Because that takes focus, determination, and sincerity to perpetuate the UPS culture and enhance it through people."

Carranza's corporate achievements, determination, drive, innovation, and leadership in business have earned her the distinction of being named *Hispanic Business Magazine*'s Woman of the Year. She credits her parents, both of Mexican descent, with teaching her "the importance of being committed, of working hard, and doing so with a positive outlook," principles she says continue to guide her personal and professional life. The principles mirror those of the company whose corporate ladder she has climbed nonstop, an organization she says that values diversity, encourages quality, integrity, commitment, fairness, loyalty, and social responsibility, among other values.

Among Carranza's words of wisdom: ". . . sit back and listen and observe," she says. "You learn more by not speaking. Intelligent people learn from their own experiences; with wisdom, you learn from other people's mistakes. I'm very methodical about that."

1. What are the major skills Jovita Carranza has demonstrated in her career at UPS that have made her a successful leader?

2. Consider the spiral of experience that Jovita Carranza has traveled. How has her experience affected her ability as a leader?

3. Take a look at the characteristics of successful leaders in Highlight 3.5. How many of these are demonstrated by Jovita Carranza?

Sources: http://www.ups.com; http://www.hispaniconline.com/vista/febhisp.htm; http://www.hispanicbusiness.com/news/newsbyid.asp?id=15535&page=3; http://www.socialfunds.com/csr/profile.cgi/1841.html

Chapter Notes

1. McCall, M. W., Jr., M. M. Lombardo, and A. M. Morrison. *The Lessons of Experience: How Successful Executives Develop on the Job.* Lexington, MA: Lexington Books, 1988, p. 122.

2. Kolb, D. *Experiential Learning: Experience as the Source of Learning and Development.* Englewood Cliffs, NJ: Prentice-Hall, 1983.

3. Powell, C., with Joe Pirsico. *My American Journey.* New York: Random House, 1995, p. 109.

4. Ibid.

5. Reason, J., and K. Mycielska. *Absent-Minded? The Psychology of Mental Lapses and Everyday Errors.* Englewood Cliffs, NJ: Prentice Hall, 1982, p. 183.

6. Ross, L. "The Intuitive Psychologist and His Shortcomings: Distortions in the Attribution Process." In *Advances in Experimental Social Psychology*, Vol. 10. Ed. L. Berkowitz. New York: Academic Press, 1977, pp. 173–220.

7. Miller, D. T., and M. Ross. "Self-Serving Biases in the Attribution of Causality: Fact or Fiction?" *Psychological Bulletin* 82 (1975), pp. 213–25.

8. Jones, E. E., and R. E. Nisbett. "The Actor and the Observer: Divergent Perceptions of the Causes of Behavior." In *Attribution: Perceiving the Causes of Behavior.* Eds. E. E. Jones, D. E. Kanouse, H. H. Kelley, R. E. Nisbett, S. Valins, and B. Weiner. Morristown, NJ: General Learning Press, 1972.

9. Green, S. G., and T. R. Mitchell. "Attributional Processes of Leaders in Leader–Member Interactions." *Organizational Behavior and Human Performances* 23 (1979), pp. 429–58.

10. Mitchell, T. R., S. G. Green, and R. E. Wood. "An Attributional Model of Leadership and the Poor Performing Subordinate: Development and Validation." In *Research in Organizational Behavior.* Eds. B. M. Staw and L. L. Cummings. Greenwich, CN: JAI 1981, pp. 197–234.

11. Mitchell, T. R., and R. E. Wood. "Supervisors' Responses to Subordinate Poor Performance: A Test of an Attributional Model." *Organizational Behavior and Human Performance* 25 (1980), pp. 123–38.

12. Jones, E. E. "Interpreting Interpersonal Behavior: The Effects of Expectancies." *Science* 234 (3) (October 1986), pp. 41–46.

13. Eden, D., and A. B. Shani. "Pygmalion Goes to Boot Camp: Expectancy, Leadership, and Trainee Performance." *Journal of Applied Psychology* 67 (1982), pp. 194–99.

14. Argyris, C. *Increasing Leadership Effectiveness.* New York: John Wiley, 1976.

15. Bennis, W. G., and R. J. Thomas. "Crucibles of Leadership." *Harvard Business Review,* September 2002, pp. 39–45.

16. Kouzes, J. M., and B. Z. Posner. *The Leadership Challenge: How to Get Extraordinary Things Done in Organizations.* San Francisco: Jossey-Bass, 1987.

17. Lombardo, M. M., and R. W. Eichinger. *Eighty-eight Assignments for Development in Place: Enhancing the Developmental Challenge of Existing Jobs.* Greensboro, NC: Center for Creative Leadership, 1989.

18. Kouzes, J. M., and B. Z. Posner, *The Leadership Challenge: How to Get Extraordinary Things Done in Organizations.* San Francisco: Jossey-Bass, 1987, p. 286.

19. Lombardo, M. M., and R. W. Eichinger, *Eighty-eight Assignments for Development in Place: Enhancing the Developmental Challenge of Existing Jobs.* Greensboro, NC: Center for Creative Leadership, 1989.

20. Gibble, J. L., and J. D. Lawrence. "Peer Coaching for Principals." *Educational Leadership* 45 (1987), pp. 72–73.

21. Wilson, J. A., and N. S. Elman. "Organizational Benefits of Mentoring." *Academy of Management Executive* 4 (1990), pp. 88–93.

22. Uecker, M. E., and B. L. Dilla. "Mentoring as a Leadership Development Tool in the United States Air Force." *Proceedings of the 26th Annual Meeting of the Military Testing Association,* Munich, Germany, 1985, pp. 423–28.

23. Clutterbuck, D. "How Much Does Success Depend upon a Helping Hand from Above?" *International Management* 37 (1982), pp. 17–19.

24. Bass, B. M. *Bass and Stogdill's Handbook of Leadership.* 3rd ed. New York: Free Press, 1990.

25. Whitely, W., T. W. Dougherty, and G. F. Dreher. "The Relationship of Mentoring and Socioeconomic Origin to Managers' and Professionals' Early Career Progress." *Proceedings of the Academy of Management.* Anaheim, CA, 1988, pp. 58–62.

26. Zey, M. G. *The Mentor Connection.* Homewood, IL: Dow Jones-Irwin, 1984.

27. Astin, H. S., and C. Leland. *Women of Influence, Women of Vision.* San Francisco: Jossey-Bass, 1991.

28. Rosenbach, W. E. "Mentoring: A Gateway to Leader Development." In *Contemporary Issues in Leadership.* 2nd ed. Eds. W. E. Rosenbach and R. L. Taylor. Boulder, CO: Westview, 1989, pp. 139–48.

29. Lombardo, M. M., and R. W. Eichinger, *Eighty-eight Assignments for Development in Place: Enhancing the Developmental Challenge of Existing Jobs.* Greensboro, NC: Center for Creative Leadership, 1989.

30. Kouzes, J. M., and B. Z. Posner, *The Leadership Challenge: How to Get Extraordinary Things Done in Organizations.* San Francisco: Jossey-Bass, 1987, p. 286.

31. Lombardo, M. M., and R. W. Eichinger, *Eighty-eight Assignments for Development in Place: Enhancing the Developmental Challenge of Existing Jobs.* Greensboro, NC: Center for Creative Leadership, 1989.

32. Gardner, J. W. *On Leadership.* New York: Free Press, 1990.

33. Bunker, K. A., and A. Webb. *Learning How to Learn from Experience: Impact of Stress and Coping.* Report No. 154. Greensboro, NC: Center for Creative Leadership, 1992.

34. Janis, I. L. *Stress and Frustration.* New York: Harcourt Brace Jovanovich, 1971.

35. Grey, R. J., and G. G. Gordon. "Risk-Taking Managers: Who Gets the Top Jobs?" *Management Review* 67 (1978), pp. 8–13.

36. Hambrick, D. C. "Environment, Strategy and Power within Top Management Teams." *Administrative Science Quarterly* 26 (1981), pp. 253–75.

37. Jennings, G. *The Mobile Manager.* New York: McGraw-Hill, 1971.

38. Schein, E. *Career Dynamics: Matching Individual and Organizational Needs.* Reading, MA: Addison-Wesley, 1978.

39. Csikszentmihalyi, M. *Flow: The Psychology of Optimal Experience.* New York: Harper & Row, 1990, p. 142.

40. Hogan, R. T., and R. Warrenfelz. "Educating the Modern Manager." *Academy of Management Learning and Education* 2 (1) (2003), pp. 74–84.

41. Bray, D. W., R. J. Campbell, and D. L. Grant. *Formative Years in Business: A Long-term AT&T Study of Managerial Lives.* New York: Wiley-Interscience, 1974.

42. Howard, A. "College Experiences and Managerial Performance." *Journal of Applied Psychology* 71 (1986), pp. 530–52.

43. Wakabayashi, M., and G. B. Graen. "The Japanese Career Progress Study: A Seven-Year Follow-Up." *Journal of Applied Psychology* 69 (1984), pp. 603–14.

44. Burke, M. J., and R. R. Day. " A Cumulative Study of the Effectiveness of Managerial Training." *Journal of Applied Psychology* 71 (1986), pp. 242–45.

45. Brungardt, C. "Benchmarking Employee Attitudes." *Training and Development,* June 1992, pp. 49–53.

46. Burke, M. J., and R. R. Day. " A Cumulative Study of the Effectiveness of Managerial Training." *Journal of Applied Psychology* 71 (1986), pp. 242–45.

47. McCall, M. W., Jr., and M. M. Lombardo. "Using Simulation for Leadership and Management Research: Through the Looking Glass." *Management Science* 28 (1982), pp. 533–49.

48. Conger, J. "Can We Really Train Leadership?" *Strategy, Management, Competition,* Winter 1996, pp. 52–65.

49. Nevins, M., and S. Stumpf. "21st-Century Leadership: Redefining Management Education. *Strategy, Management, Competition,* 3rd quarter 1999, pp. 41–51.

50. Hernez-Broome, G., and R. L. Hughes. "Leadership Development: Past, Present and Future." *Human Resource Planning* 27 (1) (2004), pp. 24–32.

51. Gardner, J. W. "The Antileadership Vaccine." Essay in the Carnegie Corporation of New York annual report, 1965.

52. McCall, M. W., Jr. M. M. Lombardo, and A. M. Morrison, *The Lessons of Experience: How Successful Executives Develop on the Job.* Lexington, MA: Lexington Books, 1988.

Chapter

4

Assessing Leadership and Measuring Its Effects

Introduction

Back in May 2005 one of the authors of this book was on a flight from Columbus, OH, to Minneapolis, MN. Northwest Airlines flight 1495 had a fairly heavy passenger load and a crew of two pilots and three flight attendants. The two-hour flight seemed routine but upon landing the author noticed the runway was lined with ambulances and fire trucks. The plane taxied off the runway and stopped some distance short of the gate. After waiting five minutes, one of the pilots finally got on the intercom and announced, "The plane has experienced a systems malfunction." The pilots and flight attendants did not say anything more and about five minutes later the DC-9 began moving again.

The DC-9 had been traveling about 10 seconds when suddenly a loud boom filled the cabin and the plane came to an abrupt stop. Passengers were thrown violently forward in their seats, but luckily everyone was still wearing their seatbelts. The author and other passengers had assumed the plane was taxiing to its gate but after looking out the window it was clear that the DC-9 had collided with another aircraft. Apparently the pilots of the DC-9 had left the engines running and the plane had experienced a hydraulics failure, which caused it to lose all steering and braking capabilities. The DC-9 collided with a Northwest Airlines A-319 that was being pushed back from its gate, and the wing of the A-319 peeled back the first 10 feet of the roof of the DC-9 during the collision.

After the plane had stopped, the lead flight attendant unbuckled her seat belt and started running up and down the aisle yelling, "Assume the

© PhotoLink/Photodisc/Getty Images/dal

crash position! Assume the crash position!" The author (and many of the passengers) were wondering how putting our heads between our knees was going to help since the plane had already come to a stop, but we dutifully complied with the flight attendant's request. After two to three minutes of running up and down the aisle and barking orders, the lead flight attendant hyperventilated and collapsed in a heap behind the first-class bulkhead. The two remaining flight attendants then got out of their seats to check on the lead flight attendant.

Most of the passengers started easing out of the crash position and began looking to the other flight attendants for guidance on what to do, but none was forthcoming. The author then got up and went to the cockpit door, as he could tell that the wing of the A-319 had come in through the cockpit and he was concerned about the pilots. He asked the pilots whether they needed any help, and one of them meekly replied that they needed medical attention. The author then proceeded to try to open the door, but the door reinforcements added after 9/11 made it impossible to get in.

As the author was yanking on the cockpit door handle, he could overhear the two flight attendants having a discussion on whether they should deplane the aircraft. One attendant would ask, "Should we keep them on or get them off?" The other attendant would reply, "I don't know, what do you think?" This conversation went on for three to four minutes, with the lead flight attendant still whispering in the background, "Assume the crash position. Assume the crash position." During this time one of the flight attendants came up to the cockpit door and asked the pilots what to do, but there was no response. She then went back to attend to the lead flight attendant.

At this time the author noticed that jet fuel from the wing of the A-319 had leaked into the cockpit of the DC-9 and had seeped into the first-class cabin. He realized that his shoes and pants were covered in jet fuel and an errant spark would light up two planes full of people. He then turned and yelled at the flight attendants, "I am standing in jet fuel. Get everyone off the plane. NOW!" The two coherent flight attendants got up and proceeded to hustle everyone off the plane using the DC-9's rear exit. Being up at the cockpit door, the author was the last in line to get off the plane. You can imagine how happy he was to see passengers at the rear of the aircraft taking the time to open the overhead bins and retrieve their luggage while he was standing in jet fuel. The flight attendants did not intervene more than giving some mild reminders to passengers to just exit the aircraft and leave the luggage behind.

The good news is that all the passengers from both aircraft escaped with only a few minor injuries. The flight attendants were okay; the two DC-9 pilots needed some medical attention but were released the next day. The bad news is that this incident provides several vivid examples of failures in leadership. The pilots failed to sound the Klaxon to warn the passengers of the impeding collision, nor did they use the thrust reversers to stop the plane. The lead flight attendant's instructions to assume the crash position after the plane was at a complete stop and then collapsing two to three minutes later did not instill a whole lot of confidence. The other two flight attendants needed to step into a leadership role and take over the situation but were unable to make a decision nor tell passengers what to do. Northwest Airlines failed by having Standard Operating Procedures (SOPs) that instructed pilots to leave the engines running in the event of an aircraft hydraulics failure. Instead the SOP should have instructed pilots to shut down the engines and have the plane towed to a gate. The company also failed when the author called in several times offering to describe the incident in order to improve training and was ignored. Later he also found out the company formally rewarded the two pilots and three flight attendants for their outstanding actions during the emergency.

This chapter is about assessing leadership and measuring its impact. Although the story above seems to be a straightforward example of leadership effectiveness, clearly the author and Northwest Airlines had very different ideas on how to evaluate leadership effectiveness. The same holds true for other leaders in different situations. For example, how do you evaluate the leadership effectiveness of athletic coaches, church leaders, junior officers in the military, shift supervisors at fast-food restaurants, heads of volunteer groups, college deans, CEOs, etc.? And more importantly, is it possible to predict who will be the most effective in each of these roles? Wouldn't it be better if Northwest Airlines could predict which pilots and flight attendants would be effective leaders in an emergency *before* an emergency actually took place? Similarly, wouldn't it be good to know who would be a more effective U.S. president, state governor, mayor, church leader, business leader, or military officer before people are voted or promoted into one of these roles?

Delta Airlines used to have a marketing slogan that said, "We love to fly, and it shows!" Given my experiences with the airlines, my travel slogan now is, "I hate to fly, and it shows!"

Gordy Curphy, C3

"Only 8% of fortune 1000 executive directors rate their leadership capacity as excellent while 47% rated their leadership capacity as fair to poor"

— The Conference Board

As you will read later in this chapter, there are many ways to evaluate the effectiveness of leaders and predict who is more likely to be an effective or ineffective leader. None of these techniques are infallible and all have their advantages and disadvantages. Because many of you are either currently in or will eventually occupy a leadership position, it is important to understand how private and public sector organizations go about hiring, evaluating, and promoting people into leadership positions. It is also important to understand that many of the best techniques for predicting leadership success or evaluating leadership effectiveness are often those least used by organizations. This gap between what researchers know about predicting and evaluating leadership effectiveness and the techniques actually used by organizations to hire, evaluate, and promote leaders is known as the **practice-research gap.** More about the practice-research gap can be found later in this chapter, but suffice it to say this gap has a profound impact on the quality of people in leadership positions today. And as you will read below, the results are not pretty.

As an overview, this chapter begins with a discussion of managerial incompetence. Most people in positions of authority have difficulty either getting results or building teams; consequently most organizations are not as profitable or effective as they could be. The best way to reduce managerial incompetence is through the adoption of good leadership talent management practices, which is the next subject of this chapter. We then cover the specific techniques used to predict future leadership effectiveness and measure the effectiveness of people currently occupying leadership positions. The chapter ends with an overview of the methodologies used to study leadership and the differences between maxims and theories of leadership.

Managerial Incompetence

If you put on a blindfold and threw a dart at a map of the world, then there is a 70 percent chance that whatever country the dart lands on is run by some form of dictatorship.

RT Hogan, Hogan Assessment Systems

Although it may appear a bit self-serving, in our minds leadership is the most important topic in the world today. Leadership determines whether countries are democracies or dictatorships or are at peace or war, businesses are good investments or kleptocracies, teams win or lose, health care and education reforms fail or succeed, and rural communities thrive or merely survive. Leadership plays a role in determining where you live, what schools you get into, what laws and rules you must obey, what occupations you enter, whether you have a successful career, and how your children are raised. It plays such a pervasive part in our lives that it is easy to overlook what impact it has on our day-to-day behaviors. Because of the profound ways in which leadership affects us all, it would be nice if the people in positions of authority were good at it. But the **base rate of managerial incompetence** may be somewhere between 50–75 percent.[1,2] In other words, a majority of people in leadership positions may not be

Despite the pervasive role of leadership

The Government's Response to Hurricane Katrina

HIGHLIGHT 4.1

In August 2005 Hurricane Katrina caused massive devastation along the north-central Gulf Coast of the United States. The costliest storm in U.S. history, storm repairs are estimated to cost in excess of $80 billion. But the storm was also costly in terms of human lives, with approximately 2,000 deaths attributed to Hurricane Katrina. A review of local, state, and federal government's performance during and after the storm shows that some of these financial and human costs could have been avoided had key leadership positions been filled by competent leaders. In terms of local government, New Orleans Mayor Ray Nagin failed when he delayed issuing a mandatory evacuation order for the city. His leadership also fell short in failing to arrange enough transportation for evacuees (hundreds of buses sat idle and were eventually flooded by the storm) and properly securing the Superdome, the shelter of last resort for those who could not leave. Louisiana Governor Kathleen Blanco appeared to take all the right steps in securing disaster relief for New Orleans, but she did have problems with coordinating the Louisiana National Guard's disaster relief

efforts with the federal government. By all accounts it appears that the bulk of the blame for the poor response to Hurricane Katrina falls on the federal government. The federal agency in charge of responding to national emergencies is the Federal Emergency Management Agency (FEMA). At the time of the hurricane FEMA was headed by Michael Brown, a lawyer and political appointee with no prior emergency management experience. Brown's incompetent leadership only made a bad situation worse: He failed to send enough adequately trained emergency, medical, or security personnel to substantially help the citizens of New Orleans; too many of the wrong supplies and not enough of the right supplies were delivered to the wrong places; disaster relief efforts were completely uncoordinated and disorganized; disaster relief funds were not getting to the people who needed them; and fraud, waste, and abuse seemed to run rampant through the relief efforts. After considerable public outcry, Michael Brown eventually resigned from FEMA.

Source: Adapted from http://en.wikipedia.org/wiki/Michael_D._Brown; http://en.wikipedia.org/Ray_Nagin; http://www.nrawstory.com/news/2005; http://encyclopedia.thefreedictionary.com/Hurricane+Katrina.

Brownie, you are doing a heck of a job.

**George W. Bush,
U.S. president**

particularly effective at influencing an organized group toward accomplishing its goals.

At first blush it would appear that the base rate of managerial incompetence could not be this high—too many countries, businesses, government and other nonprofit organizations, or volunteer organizations would simply fail if riddled with such a high percentage of incompetent leaders. But consider the following facts:

- Most countries are run by some form of dictatorship. Most ordinary citizens in Saudi Arabia, Egypt, Libya, Jordan, Chad, Zimbabwe, Iran, Turkmenistan, China, and Russia don't have much say over who is in charge, what laws are made, and so on. Although the leaders of these countries do have a following among a minority of people, the majority have little input in who leads them.

- Fifty percent of Fortune 500 CEOs will be dismissed for poor performance over the next three years.[3,4,5]

- In employee satisfaction surveys more than 75 percent of all respondents indicate that the most stressful part of their job is their immediate boss.[2] This finding holds true across countries and industries.

- A study published in *Harvard Business Review* reported that only 30 percent of businesses had "healthy and respectful" work climates. A majority of organizations had dysfunctional and unhealthy work climates.[6]

- At any one time the 800,000 employees at the United States Postal Service have filed 150,000 grievances against their supervisors.[2]

- U.S. Army surveys indicate the record number of mid-level officers resigning from the military is due to a lack of confidence in senior Army leadership. Many mid-level officers indicated that their senior leaders would quickly throw more junior officers under a bus if it would help get them promoted.[7]

- Research shows that somewhere between 50–90 percent of all new businesses fail within five years. This finding seems consistent across all business types and countries. Most of the failures can be attributed to managerial incompetence.[8,9,10,11]

- Research also shows that 67 percent of all IT projects either fail to deliver promised functionality, be delivered on time, or stay within budgeted costs. This IT project failure rate has not improved much over the past 10 years, and U.S. businesses are now spending over $55 billion annually on poorly scoped or executed IT projects.[12]

- The root cause of most major industrial accidents and incidents, such as the Bhopal, India, chemical spill, the Exxon Valdez disaster, or Texas City refinery explosion can be traced back to poor management oversight or management cost-cutting initiatives.[13]

- Over 70 percent of all mergers and acquisitions fail to yield projected improvements in profitability and synergies. Examples might include ATT's acquisition of NCR or Daimler's ill-fated acquisition of Chrysler.[14]

- A majority of large-scale organizational change initiatives fail to achieve their intended results.[15]

Iraq is clearly hubris carried to the point of insanity—it's damn hard to convince people that you are killing them for their own good.

Molly Ivins, writer

As damning as these statistics may be, these examples may seem out of the realm of most readers. So let's make the concept of managerial incompetence a little more personal. One easy way to determine the level of incompetence among persons in positions of authority is to do the **Dr. Gordy test.**[1] To do the test, begin by counting up the total number of people you have been led by in the past. This total should include past bosses, athletic coaches, team captains, choir directors, camp directors, and so on. In other words, it should include anyone for whom you played a more formal followership role. Once you have arrived at a total, you should then count the number of people in this group that you would willingly play, sing, or work for again. How many of these people would you play a followership role for again if given a choice? Now calculate the percentage of competent leaders out of the total group of leaders. When health care, education, business, military, and community leaders are asked the same question, most only need the digits on a single hand to count the number of leaders they would willingly work for again. The percentage of competent leaders people would willingly work for again varies dramatically across individuals, but the percentage seems to hover between 25–40 percent. This means that most people would not work for a majority of leaders they have been exposed to.

A definition of managerial incompetence might help people to better understand the concept. If you remember back in Chapter 1, we defined leadership as the process of influencing an organized group toward accomplishing its goals. If we extend this definition a bit, then effective leaders are individuals who are good at building teams and getting results. Most people in leadership positions get paid to get results, and they get results by building teams.[1,2,17] As seen in Figure 4.1, **Competent Managers** are good at building teams and getting results through others. Although they are the types of leaders most people aspire toward, most people in positions of authority fall into one of the other three categories. **Results Only Managers** are good at achieving results, such as financial targets or win-loss records, but they tend to treat followers so poorly that these results tend to be short-lived. Vivid examples of Results Only Managers might be the typical applicant on *The Apprentice*—just about every applicant is only focused on getting results and would gladly trash any teammate if it would help them get promoted. Like Donald Trump, superiors like Results Only Managers because they do get results and often promote these managers before the consequences of their poor team-building skills become evident. Results Only Managers also have impressive track records, which make them very likely to be hired away by other organizations.

FIGURE 4.1

The two dimensions of managerial incompetence.

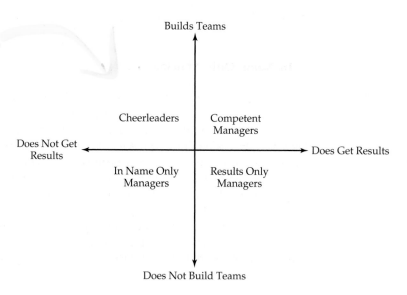

The Moronization of Management

HIGHLIGHT 4.2

Carl Icahn is a multibillionaire who made his fortune buying up companies that were poorly managed, straightening out their operations and finances, and then reselling them for a profit. Senior managers dislike Icahn as they often lose their jobs when he buys their companies, but many would argue that, if they were doing their jobs the company performance would be so good, Icahn would not see an opportunity to buy the company and flip it to make a profit. Icahn has a theory about U.S. businesses which says that many senior executives are the "guys you knew in college, the fraternity president—not too bright, back slapping, but a survivor, politically astute, a nice guy." According to Icahn, to be a chief executive people need to know how not to tread on anyone's toes on the way up. Eventually, a person becomes the number two in the company and they have to be just a little worse than number one in order to survive. When the number two gets promoted to be the CEO, he in turn promotes someone a little less capable than him as the second-in-command. "It is survival of the unfittest—eventually we are all going to be run by morons." Icahn calls this phenomenon of promoting people slightly less capable than the incumbent leader the **moronization of management.**

Source: Adapted from *The Economist,* Feb. 11, 2006, p. 42.

Cheerleaders are those persons in positions of authority who are very people-centered and make it a point of getting along with everyone (think Paula Abdul on *American Idol*). With their focus on making the workplace warm and fun, most people like working for Cheerleaders. The problem is Cheerleaders spend so much time making the workplace enjoyable that they forget why they are paid to be in a leadership position, which is to get results. They also tend to have a difficult time doing anything that could potentially erode their relationships with followers, which includes dealing with conflict or confronting performance problems. Nevertheless, because they are dutiful, highly complimentary of superiors, never make waves, and are well-liked by followers, Cheerleaders often get promoted into senior positions in organizations.

In Name Only Managers have difficulties with both building teams and getting results. They may not be complete failures at either of these two endeavors, but they could be a lot better at building teams or getting results. Many times In Name Only Managers occupy a position of authority and do just enough to stay out of trouble and avoid the spotlight. The last thing In Name Only Managers want is attention, as this might raise superiors' expectations for their performance. Thus high-performing followers can get very frustrated and leave organizations when they find out they are working for an In Name Only Manager.

One might wonder how organizations can succeed with such a high percentage of incompetent managers. Although many small businesses, IT projects, mergers, and organizational change efforts fail, many other businesses make money. Similarly the U.S. military is capable of waging wars, children continue to get educated, and most people receive high

Half of all chief executives are dismissed from office, but those who can deliver results are in greater demand.

Booz Allen Hamilton Consulting

quality health care when they need it. The good news is that organizations may not need every person in a position of authority to be a Competent Manager in order to be successful. The keys to success is for organizations to make sure they have a higher percentage of Competent Managers than their competitors and to make sure Competent Managers are in pivotal leadership roles. Research shows that organizations that have higher percentages of Competent Managers who occupy critical positions are more successful than those with fewer Competent Managers who are not well placed.[18,19] The purpose of this chapter and book is to help increase the odds that you become a Competent Manager and are able to secure positions where you can have an impact on the success of your organization.

Leadership Talent Management

By and large, executives make poor promotion and staffing decisions. By all accounts, their batting average is no better than .333. At most, one-third of such decisions turn out right; one-third are minimally effective; and one-third are outright failures. In no other area would we put up with such miserable performance; indeed, we need not and should not. Managers making people decisions will never be perfect, of course, but they should come pretty close to batting 1.000.

Peter Drucker, management consultant

The number one worry of top leaders, regardless of country or organization, is the lack of high-quality leadership talent. For example, companies in China and India are having no trouble finding laborers (there are literally millions available) but have tremendous difficulty finding people who can effectively manage these people.[20] The three critical ingredients most companies are looking for from people in positions of authority seem to be the ability to solve problems and make sound decisions, local/functional know-how (understanding finance, operations, logistics, sales, or how things work in different countries), and the ability to get things done through others. But finding all three of these qualities in new or existing managers is proving difficult.

There are several factors contributing to this shortfall in managerial competence. One is demographics; because of the Baby Boom approximately 50 percent of the top leaders in many private and public sector organizations are slated to retire in the next five years. Although some of these leaders are incompetent, many have impressive track records of building teams and getting results, and their experiences will be sorely missed. Another demographic issue is that some countries are experiencing very low birth rates. For example, the number of people of the ages 15–64 in Germany, Italy, and Japan is expected to shrink 7–14 percent over the next 10 years, which reduces the number of people in the managerial talent pool.[20]

A second factor organizations must cope with is a lack of employee loyalty. Because of numerous rounds of buyouts, mergers, restructurings, and downsizings, many people have lost faith in their organization's ability to keep them gainfully employed. As a result, at any one time up to 33 percent of employees are actively talking to other organizations about job opportunities.[20] It is difficult to retain competent managers when many are unwilling to wait for a promotion and will transfer to another company as soon as an opportunity appears.[21]

Talented people need organizations less than organizations need talented people.
**Daniel Pink,
Pink, Inc.**

A third factor is lack of good systems for identifying and developing leadership talent. As seen later in this chapter, most organizations use crude and ineffective measures to assess leadership potential and their leadership development efforts are poorly designed and executed.[1,22]

Although organizations spend billions on identifying and developing managerial talent, the return on investment for this money is generally low.[1,2,18,21,23] Many of the wrong people get hired or promoted into positions of authority, the wrong skills get developed, or the leadership training and development programs do not change targeted behavior. Thus many people in positions of authority are seen as Cheerleaders or Results Only or In Name Only Managers.

A fourth and final factor contributing to a shortfall in effective leadership talent is technology. The advent of the personal computer, Internet, and sophisticated software packages has made it possible for people to do things at home that were not possible just 20 years ago. In the past people joined organizations because it was where the technology was located; now people can start up fairly sophisticated businesses for the price of a personal computer, a printer, Internet access, and a Microsoft or Apple productivity suite. As described earlier in this chapter, many of these small businesses fail, but many people would rather work for themselves than for incompetent managers. Employers wishing to tap into this talent pool need to ensure that they have a high percentage of competent managers in place and have a good employee value proposition, such as opportunities to work with competent bosses and teammates, work on exciting projects, or develop new skills, in order to attract high-quality candidates.[20]

It should be clear by now that there are many people who are ineffective in management positions, and demographic, loyalty, development, and technological factors may be making this problem worse rather than better. The way to turn around this sad state of affairs is to get organizations to adopt an effective leadership talent management system. A **leadership talent management system** consists of those processes and procedures organizations use to hire, develop, evaluate, reward, promote, and retain their leaders; research has shown that good talent management systems can have a profound impact on organizational effectiveness and success.[4,19] Some companies, such as General Electric, Proctor & Gamble, Target, Waste Management, Johnson & Johnson, and PepsiCo believe that leadership talent is a critically important competitive advantage, and they put a tremendous amount of emphasis on identifying (i.e., assessing), developing, promoting, and retaining the right leaders. One of the reasons why so many General Electric, PepsiCo, and Proctor & Gamble managers and executives are recruited by other companies is because of their emphasis on leadership talent management.

So what do organizations need to do to have an effective leadership talent management system? The first place to start is to clarify the organization's strategy for the next 5–10 years. Who will be the organization's

The best executive is one who has enough sense to pick good men to do what he wants done, and the self-restraint to keep from meddling while they do it.
**Theodore
Roosevelt, U.S.
president**

Segolene Royal versus Nicolas Sarkozy

PROFILES IN LEADERSHIP 4.1

In many ways elections represent a form of leadership talent management. Voters develop their own implicit competency models for ideal candidates—these models consist of the skills, knowledge, and attributes that the ideal candidate should possess as well as the positions the candidates should have on issues important to voters. Voters then take a look at the slate of candidates and choose the person who comes closest to their ideal. Several major elections will have occurred across the world in the next few years—the United Kingdom has a new prime minister as of 2007, Gordon Brown, and voters in Russia and the United States will have chosen a new president in 2008. Also in 2007 the citizens in France had a choice between the left-wing candidate Segolene Royal and the right-wing candidate Nicolas Sarkozy to replace Jacques Chirac as president. Sarkozy is generally recognized as a highly skilled politician and brilliant orator. He comes across as a charismatic politician willing to make a dramatic break with past traditions, take tough positions on law and order and immigration, and depart from traditional French social and economic principles in favor of American-style economic reforms. Royal is a highly telegenic and popular politician who is trying to become France's first female president. She believes in the sanctity of the 35-hour workweek, raising the minimum wage and unemployment benefits, eliminating poverty, and reducing the level of violence on children's television shows. France has strong labor unions and relatively high levels of unemployment, particularly for people under 25. Dissaffected Muslim youths in Paris caused riots in the summer of 2005 and the national economy has been in the doldrums for the past five years. Given these two choices, the voters in France decided that Sarkozy had "the right stuff" to lead the country.

Source: *The Economist,* Feb 17, 2007, p. 51; http://en.wikipedia.org/wiki/Nicolas_Sarkozy; http://en.wikipedia.org/wiki/Segolene_Royal

customers, competitors, suppliers, and so on, and what will the organization try to accomplish over the next 5 years? Getting clarity on the future of the organization is important, as it takes some time to hire and develop leadership talent. The second step is to identify what are or will be the **critical leadership positions** in the organization.[18] Often times the most critical leadership positions are not the most senior—for example, for big box retailers such as Wal-Mart, Lowe's, or Best Buy the critical leadership positions are store managers, not the executives in charge of merchandise or IT. The store managers are critical leadership positions in these organizations because they are both close to the employees interacting with customers and have the biggest influence on their organization's profitability. Likewise, the critical leadership positions for school systems would be school principals, department heads for hospitals and colleges, and platoon leaders for the U.S. Army or Marine Corps.

The third step would be to develop a competency model for the critical leadership positions. A **competency model** consists of those skills, knowledge, abilities, or other attributes that are relevant to successful performance in a particular job. In other words, what are the skills, types of knowledge, or qualities associated with the most effective store managers? Platoon leaders? School principals? Although some skills and qualities are likely to be similar, there will also be major differences in the skills and types of knowledge needed to be effective in these positions. Developing good competency models for critical leadership positions is extremely important, as they become the framework around which all human resource systems (recruiting, selection, development, succession planning, compensation and benefits, performance management, and retention) are aligned.

The fourth step in a good leadership talent management system is to ensure the organization's recruiting and selection processes are identifying and hiring candidates with the right skills and that the organization's other human resource processes are developing, rewarding, and promoting these skills. Basically this step says that effective leadership talent management systems hire candidates with the right stuff, develop those skills that candidates lack when they join the organization, and reward and promote those individuals who are getting results and demonstrating the right behaviors. As simple as this might sound, most organizations have lousy leadership talent management systems. For example, only 2 percent of 230 professionals in charge of leadership talent management systems reported that their organizations were doing a good job managing leadership talent; one-third indicated their leadership talent management systems needed a lot of work.[24]

The fifth and final step in a good leadership talent management system is to adopt valid and well-researched processes for hiring, developing, and promoting leadership talent. As you will read later in this chapter, some techniques for identifying leadership potential or evaluating current performance are much better than others. But for various reasons organizations shy away from many of these best practices and instead adopt hiring, selection, development, or promotion processes that result in high levels of managerial incompetence.

Assessing Leadership Potential

Assessing leadership potential is fundamentally concerned with *predicting* who will or will not be an effective leader before they have been placed into a position. Accurately predicting managerial effectiveness is critically important but not at all straightforward. Although many people falsely believe that they are good judges of leadership potential, research shows that human judgment is fraught with error, and poor hiring and promotion decisions are leading causes of managerial incompetence.[1] Just how inconsistent these judgments can be is illustrated nicely using some research done by one of the authors. The research in this case deals with leadership in commercial airline crews. Many airline crews consist of two positions with very distinct responsibilities. The aircraft captain is the final authority for all decisions regarding the aircraft and is ultimately

Succession Planning and the Nine-Cell Matrix

HIGHLIGHT 4.3

Succession planning is the process by which organizations evaluate and promote leadership talent. In some organizations, such as family-owned businesses, this process consists of nothing more than the "lucky sperm club." Family members, often sons and daughters, are promoted into critical leadership positions because of their familial relationships with the owners rather than on the basis of their leadership skills. In some privately held companies, such as Saudi Aramco, Anheuser-Busch, Marriott, and Carlson Companies, this process of having successive generations of family members take over multibillion-dollar family businesses has worked quite well. On the other hand, Bill Ford's takeover of Ford Motor Company several years ago has been nothing short of disastrous.

One of the best practice techniques organizations can use for succession planning is the **nine-cell matrix.** As seen below, a nine-cell matrix has two major dimensions. The **leadership potential** dimension assesses the extent to which candidates are capable of assuming greater responsibility and are likely to be successful if promoted one or two

levels up in the organization. Organizations use a number of techniques for assessing leadership potential and these are described in more detail later in this chapter. Those with low leadership potential are assigned a 1, those with moderate potential a 2, and those with high potential a 3. The **leadership performance** dimension assesses the extent to which candidates are achieving results. Those who are not achieving results are assigned a 1, those getting some but not all results a 2, and those exceeding all their goals are assigned a 3. Candidates are then placed on a nine-cell matrix based on the intersection of their potential and performance ratings. The highest potential and best performing candidates can be found in the upper right cell; those with the least potential and who are underperforming can be found in the lower left cell. Discussions about the placement of candidates on nine-cell matrices can be very heated and intense, but these conversations help leaders get more accurate and consistent with their assessment of talent. Organizations use nine-cell matrices to determine possible successors for critical leadership positions, design customized development and retention programs for people in different cells, and revamp recruiting and selection systems.

Nine-Cell Matrix

Potential		Performance	
H	Cassio	Jones Campbell Hogan	Roberts Primavera Nilsen
M	Wilson-Smith	Hudson	Ross Ribbens
L	Krile Marx Kecker Borneman	Hellerman	Melby Byron
	L	**M**	**H**

Source: R. Charan, "Ending the CEO Succession Crisis." *Harvard Business Review,* February 2005, pp. 72–81; K. Cabrera-Suarez, "Leadership Transfer and the Successor's Development in the Family Firm." *The Leadership Quarterly* 16 (2005), pp. 71–96.

Succession Planning and Failure at the Top

HIGHLIGHT 4.4

For better or worse, investors hold chief executive officers (CEOs) responsible for company performance. CEOs have big, complex jobs—those leading Fortune 500 companies often head up organizations having tens of thousands of employees that generate billions of dollars of revenue every year. These top executives decide what businesses their companies will pursue, the overall strategies for these businesses, how much to invest in the businesses, when to sell or acquire new businesses, and so on. They are also among the best compensated individuals in the world, often making $1 million to $200 million in salary and stock options each year. Given the scope, responsibilities, and rewards associated with the CEO position, it seems natural that these individuals should be held accountable for company performance.

Each year over the past 10 years somewhere between 20–33 percent of the CEOs in North American, European, and Asian-Pacific firms are asked to leave for poor performance. And the high visibility scandals at Enron, WorldCom, Parmalat, Xerox, Adelphia, Royal Dutch Shell, Arthur Andersen, and Boeing indicate that boards of directors and shareholders may be even less likely to tolerate mediocre or poor performing CEOs than they have in the past. But when CEOs are finally asked to leave, their companies are often teetering on the brink of bankruptcy. (Nevertheless, dismissed CEOs are almost always given multimillion-dollar severance packages as a reward

for their less than stellar performance, which probably says more about boards of directors' judgment and intestinal fortitude than it does about CEO incompetence.)

But should the successor for the CEO position come from inside or outside the company? Many companies on the brink of disaster look for an external charismatic leader to return the organization to financial health. But research indicates that outside CEOs do no better than internal successors. And because outside CEOs lack organizational and industry-specific knowledge and tend to want to change everything about those organizations they are leading, these leaders often create even more problems than their predecessors. Being an insider was once an important factor in CEO succession: Back in 1980 only 7 percent of CEOs came from outside the company. Now approximately 50 percent of new CEOs come from the outside. This shift in the percentage of CEOs coming from the outside indicates that many organizations may be losing the War for Talent, in that their leadership talent management processes have failed to produce the most important leaders for the organizations.

Sources: E. L. Biggs, "CEO Succession Planning: An Emerging Challenge for Boards of Directors." *Academy of Management Executive* 18 (1) (2004), pp 105–10; R. Khurana, "The Curse of the Superstar CEO." *Harvard Business Review,* September 2002, pp. 60–67; J. A. Sonnenfeld, and R. Khurana, "Fishing for CEOs in Your Own Backyard." *The Wall Street Journal,* July 30, 2002, p. B2; D. Woodruff, "Europe Shows More CEOs the Door." *The Wall Street Journal,* July 31, 2002, p. A11.

responsible for the safety of the passengers and crew. The copilot helps the captain fly the aircraft and is also responsible for the aircraft's preflight inspections and operation of systems (e.g., electrical, hydraulic, fuel, communication). Since airline crews must work together as a coordinated team to successfully complete a flight, the author studied factors affecting crew coordination.[25] As a part of this project he flew with a number of different airline crews and recorded conversations between crew members. The following is an excerpt of an interview between a copilot and the researcher:

Researcher:	Are all the captains you fly with pretty much the same?
Aircrew member:	Oh, no. Some guys are the greatest guys in the world to fly with. I mean they may not have the greatest hands in the world but that doesn't matter. When you fly with them, you feel like you can work together to get the job done. You really want to do a good job for them. Some other captains are just the opposite . . . you just can't stand to work with them. That doesn't mean you'll do anything that's unsafe or dangerous but you won't go out of your way to keep him or her out of trouble either. So you'll just sit back and do what you have to and just hope he or she screws up.
Researcher:	How can you tell which kind of captain you're working with?
Aircrew member:	Oh, you can tell.
Researcher:	How?
Aircrew member:	I don't know how you tell but it doesn't take very long. Just a couple of minutes and you'll know.

The above conversation details some of the difficulties in assessing leadership potential. Although it was the airline pilot's personal opinion that it was relatively easy to recognize good captains, personal opinions about leadership effectiveness can vary substantially across individuals. Thus the copilot may feel that the captain may not be a good leader, but the flight attendants and ground crews might think this captain is very effective. Who is right or whose opinion carries more weight in this situation? Moreover, the copilot thought he could tell good from bad leaders once they were on the job, but many organizations want to know this information *before* they make a hiring decision. As the high-profile cases with Enron, Parmalat, Worldcom, Vivendi, Health South, and Tyco have pointed out, putting the wrong people into key leadership positions can literally cost stockholders billions of dollars and lead to organizational ruin.[1,2,26] There are a number of ways to improve the odds of making good leadership hiring decisions, and some hiring techniques are much more effective than others in predicting leadership success. How do we know this? We know this because researchers have systematically determined which leadership assessment techniques yield more valid and accurate predictions than other techniques. Because the identification of leadership talent is so important to organizations these days, many of them have capitalized on these research findings to create practical tools and processes for assessing the leadership capabilities of potential first-line supervisors through CEOs.[27-34]

Another practical example might help to illuminate the various techniques organizations use to assess leadership. Suppose the president of your college left to head up a large university, and you were asked to head up the search committee that was responsible for picking your next college president. The former president left the school in tough shape—the

When doctors make a poor diagnosis, their patients die and they don't have to deal with it anymore. When lawyers fail to present a good case, their clients go to jail and they don't have to deal with it anymore. But when hiring managers make a mistake, they have to say "Good morning" to it every day.

Pete Ramstad, Toro

school's budget is a mess because of reductions in state funding and alumni donations over the past two years. The janitorial and administrative staffs are threatening a boycott over low wages, and many of the college's best professors have been recruited away by other universities. Because of budget cuts and the hemorrhaging of talent, faculty morale is poor. Students are unhappy with the quality of the teaching assistants and steep tuition increases over the past three years. Finally, the athletic department has just been penalized for several NCAA recruiting violations and the basketball team will be ineligible for postseason play for the next two years. You advertised nationally, and over 50 people have formally applied for the position by the application cutoff date. So what would you do to pick the best candidate from this pool of 50 applicants?

If you didn't know anything about hiring college presidents, then you would probably do what most other organizations do when hiring new leaders. You would begin the process of hiring a college president by reviewing the résumés of the 50 candidates. You would use the results of this résumé screening to identify who you believe are the top 5 to 10 candidates. You would bring this narrower pool of candidates in for one or more interviews and perhaps narrow the pool down to the top two candidates. At this point you would probably call the references of the top two candidates and make a final hiring decision based on the candidate who seemed to have the best "chemistry" or "job fit." Although this hiring process appears to make perfect sense, it is very unlikely that you would pick a college president who will be able to successfully achieve a balanced budget, recruit and retain top faculty, and keep students and staff happy. It may be that the odds of picking a good college president through this process are not much better than picking one of the 50 applicants at random. But how do we know this? As seen in Table 4.1, we know this because leadership research shows that application blanks, unstructured interviews, and reference checks are very poor predictors of leadership effectiveness. Yet these techniques are among the most frequently used by organizations making leadership hiring decisions. That the most frequently used leadership hiring techniques are also the least valid shows how wide the practice-research gap truly is (see Highlights 4.1, 4.2, and 4.4 for more information about the negative consequences of using poor leadership potential assessment techniques).

Best Practices in Assessing Leadership Potential

If you don't know where you are going, you'll probably end up somewhere else.

David Campbell, Center for Creative Leadership

So what should you do if you want to improve the odds of hiring the right college president? Research has shown that the best place to start is to clearly define what you are looking for in a prospective college president. To do this, you would first need to build a competency model for the college president position. In this situation the competency model for a college president might consist of the following: problem-solving and decision-making skills, visioning skills, planning and coordinating skills, fund-raising skills, budgeting skills, delegation skills, organizational change skills,

TABLE 4.1

Typical Correlations between Different Assessment Techniques and Job Performance in the United States

Assessment Technique	Correlation	U.S. Companies Using This Technique (percent)
Work sample/skill test	.54	1–20%
Assessment center/job simulation	.50	1–20
Job knowledge test	.48	20–30
Personality test	.48	1–20
Job tryout	.44	1–20
Biographical questionnaire	.40	1–20
Structured interview*	.40	unknown
Mental abilities test	.24	1–20
Unstructured interview	.20	90+
Reference check	.14	80+
Application blank	.10	90+

*Although interviews are among the most popular assessment techniques, it is uncertain how many are structured versus unstructured interviews.

Sources: K. Pearlman, "Validity Generalization: From Theory to Application" (paper presented at the Center for Human Resources Programs, Institute of Industrial Relations, University of California–Berkeley, 1985); T. A. Judge, "The Impact of I/O Psychology." *The Industrial and Organizational Psychologist* 35 (1997), pp. 108–10; A. M. Ryan, L. McFarland, H. Baron, and R. Page, "An International Look at Selection Practices: Nation and Culture as Explanations for Variability in Practices." *Personnel Psychology* 52, no. 2 (1999), pp. 359–92; American Management Association, *Job Skill Testing and Psychological Measurement*, June 2000; T. A. Judge, A. E. Colbert, & R. Ilies, "Intelligence and Leadership: A Quantitative Review and Test of Theoretical Propositions." *Journal of Applied Psychology* 89, no. 3, pp. 542–52.

coaching skills, performance management skills, the ability to create high-performing teams, conflict management skills, the ability to build relationships with and earn the trust of key internal and external stakeholders, communication skills, the ability to motivate others, honesty and integrity, the ability to cope with high levels of stress, and in-depth knowledge of the higher education system and various educational techniques. The best candidate would be the person who possessed most if not all of these skills and attributes. How would you go about determining how many of these skills and attributes each of the 50 applicants possessed? And wouldn't it be even more important to know how well developed these skills and attributes are in each candidate? Fortunately, researchers have collected a wealth of data that provide answers to these two questions. (See Figure 4.2 for an example of a mid-level leader competency model.)

Once the competency model for college presidents had been finalized, research shows that a **multiple hurdles approach** would be the most cost-effective and valid way to identify the best candidate from the applicant talent pool.[33,36,37] In a multiple hurdles approach, applicants are put through a series of leadership potential assessment techniques and only the applicants who "pass" one assessment are allowed to move on to the next, and so forth. Typically the most inexpensive leadership potential assessment techniques are used first, with the most expensive (and often most valid) techniques used as the last hurdles in the hiring process (see Figure 4.3).

FIGURE 4.2
Example of a mid-level leadership competency model.

Source: K. Louiselle, S. Bridges, and G. J. Curphy, "Talent Assessment Overview," working paper, 2003.

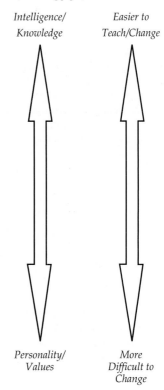

Leading the Business

- Analyzing Problems and Making Decisions
- Thinking Strategically
- Financial and Technical Savvy
- Planning and Organizing
- Managing Execution

Leading People

- Inspiring Shared Purpose
- Driving Change
- Building the Talent Base
- Fostering Teamwork

Building and Sustaining Relationships

- Creating Open Communications
- Building Relationships
- Customer Focus
- Credibility

Adaptive Capacity

- Personal Drive
- Adaptability
- Learning Approach

*Intelligence/
Knowledge*

*Easier to
Teach/Change*

*Personality/
Values*

*More
Difficult to
Change*

Women have for centuries been recognized as talented listeners, nurturers, motivators, and excellent communicators. These very qualities that were once told were unbusinesslike are precisely the qualities that businesses need most to tap human potential.

**Mary Cunningham
Agee**

We would begin the multiple hurdles approach for our candidates by having the pool of 50 applicants take various **Internet or paper-and-pencil measures** of leadership potential.[4,38–40] As shown in Table 4.1, research has found that biographical questionnaires, personality inventories, mental abilities tests, and interest inventories can do a very good job predicting future leadership effectiveness. Moreover, these measures are inexpensive and relatively easy to administer. In the case of identifying the right college president, we would begin the hiring process by having all 50 candidates fill out a biographical questionnaire.[41,42] This questionnaire would ask candidates to identify what they had done in the past that was related to the college president competencies, such as solving problems, making decisions, managing budgets, raising funds, and so forth. The responses to the questionnaire would be scored and only the top 10 scoring candidates would be allowed to proceed to the next hurdle.

The Glass Ceiling Effect

HIGHLIGHT 4.5

Although females represent 50 percent of the workforce, there are significantly fewer women than men in the top leadership positions in corporate America. As recently as 2000 almost 50 percent of the Fortune 1000 had no women in top executive positions, and currently only 10 percent of the executive positions in Fortune 1000 companies are held by women. Of these executive positions, only 2 percent of women hold one of the top five jobs in these organizations. Many Fortune 1000 companies still have no women in any of their top positions and the percentage of women in top leadership positions is no better in Japan, where only 9 percent of middle-level managers are women. This under-representation of women at the executive level is known as the **glass ceiling effect.** Given current trends, some researchers predict that the percentage of women in top leadership positions will not get much better over the next 10 years.

Other research has consistently shown that there are few practical differences in leadership potential and performance between men and women. So, if there are few leadership potential and performance differences between men and women, then why aren't a higher percentage of females filling executive positions? It may well be that top executives hire people in their own image, and if that image is one of a white male, then it is likely white males will be chosen to become their successors. Given the ever-increasing shortfall of high-quality leadership talent and the finding that males and females have the same potential to assume executive positions, perhaps the most effective way to improve the percentage of competent managers in executive positions is for organizations to implement best-practice leadership potential assessment systems.

Sources: J. R. Renshaw, *Kimono in the Boardroom: The Invisible Revolution of Japanese Women Managers.* New York: Oxford University Press, 1999; S. Gebelein, "As Leaders, Women Rule." *BusinessWeek,* November 24, 2000, p. 74; E. A. Powell, "Women Hit a 'Glass Wall'" *Denver Post,* November 12, 1999, p. C-1; "Helping Women get to the Top." *The Economist,* July 23, 2005; "The Conundrum of the Glass Ceiling", *The Economist,* July 23, pp. 63–65; S. A. Hewlett and C. B. Luce, "Off-Ramps and On-Ramps: Keeping Talented Women on the Road to Success." *Harvard Business Review,* March 2005, pp. 43–51; C. E. Helfat, D. Harris, and P. J. Wolfson, "The Pipeline to the Top: Women and Men in the Top Executive Ranks of U.S. Corporations." *The Academy of Management Perspectives* 20 (4) (2006), pp. 42–64.

The next step in the multiple hurdles approach would be to interview the remaining talent pool. In **structured interviews,** the interviewer asks the leader a predetermined set of questions; in **unstructured interviews** the interviewer does not follow a predetermined set of questions.[43–45] In an unstructured format, the interviewer has the latitude to allow the interview to proceed in whatever direction seems appropriate. The conversation between the researcher and aircrew member earlier in this chapter is an excerpt from an unstructured interview. Although unstructured interviews can provide interesting insights into the leadership process, it is difficult to compare the results of interviews from different leaders. Structured interviews, with their common set of questions and rating scales, usually make it much easier to compare different leaders' attributes and skills. To use structured interviews for hiring a new college president, you would begin by asking each candidate the same set of questions. These questions would ask participants to describe situations in the past where they had to exhibit the skills and attributes identified in the college

Facebook, MySpace, and Online Personas

HIGHLIGHT 4.6

The good news is that social networking sites, such as Facebook and MySpace, have made it much easier for people to make connections with others. In an effort to attract attention, many entries on these sites contain highly personal information about sexual practices, drug and alcohol use, philosophies toward life and work, and so on. Some of this information may be true or false and some just hyperbole, but all of it is in the public domain. The bad news is that companies are now searching these same sites and eliminating applicants based on their online personas. An interesting exercise is to identify a critical

leadership position and define the competencies needed to do this position. Then pick out four or five random online personas from MySpace and see if you would hire any of these individuals if they had applied for the position. Then look at your own online persona (if you have one). Would you get hired if an organization was looking for a competent manager to fill this position? What should carry more weight in determining a person's leadership potential, their résumé or online persona?

Source: Adapted from Alan Finder, "For Some, Online Persona Undermines Résumé." *New York Times,* June 11, 2006.

FIGURE 4.3
Multiple hurdles approach.

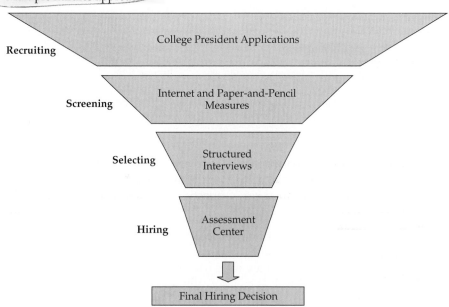

- Recruiting — College President Applications
- Screening — Internet and Paper-and-Pencil Measures
- Selecting — Structured Interviews
- Hiring — Assessment Center

Final Hiring Decision

president competency model. The answers to the questions would then be evaluated using common rating scales. Selection practices in different countries are summarized in Table 4.2. Examples of some structured and unstructured interview questions and examples of what not to do in an interview can be found in Highlight 4.7.

TABLE 4.2
Selection Practices in Europe, Africa, Asia, and Australia

Americans alone cannot be blamed for making poor leadership selection decisions. People all over the world seem to make many of the same leadership selection mistakes. For example, consider the popularity of the assessment techniques used by the following countries:

Assessment Technique	Percent Usage							
	Australia	China	France	Germany	Hong Kong	Japan	South Africa	Sweden
Work sample/skill test	>5%	?	>5%	>5%	>5%	0%	>5%	>5%
Mental abilities test	20–50	?	20–50	1–20	1–20	0	50–80	20–50
Assessment center/ job simulation	1–20	2%	1–20	1–20	1–20	0	20–50	1–20
Personality test	20–50	72%	50–80	1–20	20–50	0	50–80	50–80
Job tryout	1–20	?	20–50	1–20	1–20	0	20–50	1–20
Biographical form	1–20	?	1–20	20–50	1–20	1–20	1–20	1–20
One-on-one interviews	50–80	95%	80–100	80–100	50–80	50–80	80–100	80–100
Reference check	80–100	16	50–80	20–50	50–80	50–80	80–100	80–100
Application blank	50–80	68	80–100	50–80	80–100	80–100	80–100	1–20
Graphology (handwriting analysis)	>5	?	50–80	>5	>5	0	1–20	1–20
Foreign language test	>5	?	20–50	1–20	20–50	0	1–20	20–50

This table provides a nice overview of the process a person would likely go through if hired for a leadership position in another country; those of you with poor handwriting may not want to apply for a leadership position in France. Although French companies seem to believe that graphology can be used to accurately predict leadership potential, there has yet to be a single shred of evidence to support this notion.

Sources: A. M. Ryan, L. McFarland, H. Baron, and R. Page, "An International Look at Selection Practices: Nation and Culture as Explanations for Variability in Practices." *Personnel Psychology* 52, no. 2 (1999), pp. 359–92; S. Ju, Y. and M. Liang, "The Application of Modern Human Resources Assessment Techniques in the Chinese Enterprises." Retrieved July 6 from http://www.pecc.net/HRD/SUYonghva.doc.

The last step in the multiple hurdles approach would be to put the top three candidates through a college president assessment center. **Assessment centers** probably represent the most sophisticated and expensive method for assessing leadership potential. The historical underpinnings of assessment centers lie in Europe where they were used in the 1920s to select officers for the German military as well as civil servants and Foreign Service officers for the British government.[46,47] In the United States, assessment centers were first used to select special agents and spies for the Office of Strategic Services, now known as the Central Intelligence Agency.[48] The purpose of modern-day assessment centers is to assess, identify, and develop leadership potential, and well over 200 institutions utilize this process.[49–54]

Interviewing: The Good, the Bad, and the Ugly

HIGHLIGHT 4.7

The Good: Structured Interviews

Managers make much better hiring decisions if they use structured interviews. Structured interviews use the same set of questions to ask prospective candidates about situations where they have had to demonstrate targeted skills and behaviors in the recent past. Some of the questions for a college president applicant might include:

1. *Driving Change:* Describe the biggest, most complex change you had to make at a college or university. What were the circumstances surrounding the need to change, what did you specifically do to make the change happen, and what were the outcomes?
2. *Labor Relations:* What have been the most difficult labor relations issues you have had to deal with? What was the situation, what did you do, and how did the negotiations turn out?
3. *Talent Management:* Specifically describe what you have done to recruit, develop, and retain top faculty. What happened as a result of these efforts?

You can see that these questions are very job related, ask about specific behavior and outcomes, and make it much easier to compare candidates.

The Bad: Unstructured Interviews

With unstructured interviews candidates are asked whatever questions the interviewer deems necessary. Although this is probably the most popular leadership selection technique, it is also one of the least valid ways to hire effective leaders. At best, many of the questions in unstructured job interviews lack job relevance; at worst they are just plain offensive, illegal, or easy to fake answers to. Many hiring managers use this technique because they suffer from judgment of character bias or are unfamiliar with the research surrounding structured versus unstructured interviews. Typical unstructured interview questions for a college president applicant might include:

1. What is your personal motto?
2. If you could go out to dinner with anyone, who would it be and why?
3. Do you plan on having any more children?

The Ugly: Examples of Stupid Interviewing Tricks

One would think that most candidates are motivated to paint the rosiest picture possible during an interview. But as the examples below all too amply demonstrate, some candidates apparently never learned this lesson:

1. The candidate interrupted the interview so that he could phone his therapist for advice on answering the questions.
2. During the interview he took off his right shoe and sock and sprinkled medicated foot powder on his foot. While he was putting his shoe back on, he mentioned that he had to use foot powder four times a day, and this was one of those times.
3. She wore a Walkman and said she could listen to the interviewer and the music at the same time.

Sources: T. Janz, L. W. Hellervik, and D. C. Gilmore, *Behavior Description Interviewing.* Boston: Allyn and Bacon, 1986; V. Arnold, "Management and Executive Assessment" (paper presented at Personnel Decisions International, Denver, September 1997); B. Byham, *Landing the Job You Want: How to Have the Best Job Interview of Your Life.* Pittsburgh: DDI Press, 1997; L. Littlewood, "First Impression: Honesty, Attitude Turn Interviews into Jobs." *Denver Post,* May 24, 1998, p. E-3; A. N. Garman and T. Lesowitz, "Interviewing Candidates for Leadership Roles." *Journal of Consulting Psychology* 57 (4) (2005), pp. 266–73; T. J. Maurer and J. M. Solamon, "The Science and Practice of a Structured Employment Interview Coaching Program." *Personnel Psychology* 59 (2006), pp. 433–56.

The three rules of hiring are:
1. If you don't know what you are looking for, then you are not likely to find it.
2. If you don't know how to find it, then you are not likely to find it.
3. The best predictor of future behavior is past behavior in similar circumstances.

Pete Hudson, Dell

Making Sense of the Process

The three candidates attending an assessment center would go through a "virtual reality" experience specifically designed for college presidents. They would begin the process by completing personality inventories and mental abilities tests while attending the assessment center. They would also spend one to two days in a simulated college setting where they would be put in a number of difficult, complex situations and their behaviors recorded by highly trained observers. Some of the simulations used in an assessment center include in-basket exercises and role-play simulations. An in-basket exercise is a work simulation that requires candidates to read an overview of a fictitious college and its budgets, enrollments, departments, and organizational charts. The candidates are then given two hours to indicate how they would handle various articles, e-mails, letters, voice mails, and memos in a typical college president's in-basket. Candidates would then participate in a series of role-play simulations of work, some of which might include a 30-minute meeting with a department head who is having performance problems, a mock interview with a TV reporter, a meeting with a group of angry janitorial and administrative staff, and a presentation to the board of trustees on budget issues. The actors in the role-play simulations are trained assessors who observe and rate the performance of each candidate on the competencies embedded in each simulation. The assessors would then look across all of the instruments and simulations to create overall competency scores for each candidate, which would then be summarized in a written report. You and the rest of the search committee would then review the report and make a final hiring decision.

It is to be hoped that the process makes sense: first defining what you want in a leader, using job-relevant paper-and-pencil measures as an initial screen for leadership candidates, and then using structured interviews and high-fidelity work simulations to identify those candidates with the most potential for a leadership position. The first step in improving the bench strength of the leaders within an organization is to hire or promote the right people to begin with, and the multiple hurdles approach provides a road map for doing just that. Not only will organizations see an increase in their leadership bench strength, but also improved organizational performance by using these leadership assessment processes.[1,2,19,33,36,38,50,55,56] This does not mean that organizations need to adopt all of these steps in the multiple hurdles process to hire and promote people with good leadership potential. Many times having a clearly defined competency model, a biographical form, and structured interview questions linked to the model will do a fairly good job of improving the odds of hiring good leaders. This is particularly true when hiring lower-level leaders. However, research has shown that adding mental abilities tests and personality inventories can substantially improve the odds of hiring effective front-line leaders to CEOs. These assessments often get at abilities and behavioral tendencies that can be difficult to assess using biographical questionnaires and structured interviews alone.[1,4,29,38,39,57]

With respect to work simulations, we know they do a good job predicting leadership performance if used by themselves, but still do not know if in-basket exercises or role-plays simulations help to predict leadership performance over and above biographical questionnaires, mental ability tests, personality inventories, and structured interviews. In other words, once we assess candidates using these cheaper, easier-to-administer methods, we do not know whether the benefits of putting candidates through in-basket and role-play simulations outweigh the costs. And work simulations are quite expensive. Many paper-and-pencil measures cost less than $50 per assessment, whereas assessment centers can cost between $2,000–10,000 per candidate. It is clear that the work simulations do provide good developmental feedback for candidates, however.

Men wanted for hazardous journey, small wages, bitter cold, long months of complete darkness—constant danger, safe return doubtful—honor and recognition in case of success.

Sir Ernest Shackleton, Antarctic explorer

Although there are important organizational benefits to hiring the right leaders, perhaps the most important point to be made about the preceding section is that there would be little to write about if it weren't for the efforts of leadership and organizational researchers. Research is the only way we know which assessment techniques are the most valid for which leadership positions. Researchers have conducted thousands of studies to determine how well various assessment techniques work for predicting future leadership effectiveness. Not only has this research helped companies to hire the right leaders, it has also leveled the playing field for candidates by creating fairer hiring processes. Unfortunately, Tables 4.1, 4.2, and Highlights 4.4 and 4.5 show that most of this research continues to be ignored by the people making leadership hiring decisions. Organizations will continue to experience a shortfall in leadership talent as long as they continue to use assessment techniques that essentially result in little more than random selection (see Highlight 4.8).

Measuring the Effects of Leadership

The fundamental question for this section is whether leaders *actually achieve results*? As obvious as this question may seem, measuring the *impact* of a leader is not as straightforward as it might appear. For example, after investing time, energy, and money to hire the right candidate, how would you determine the impact of the new college president? After one year on the job, have the relationships between the college president and department heads and the administrative and janitorial staff improved? Has the president been able to achieve a balanced budget by cutting costs and/or securing more funding? Have the skills of teaching assistants improved and are students happier with their college experiences? Has the president been able to recruit and retain key faculty? What information would you need to collect in order to evaluate the performance of the college president on these issues? And if there are any changes in these performance indicators, are they the direct result of, in spite of, or completely

The Impact of Best-Practice Leadership Talent Management Techniques

HIGHLIGHT 4.8

A very large manufacturer acquired two other large manufacturing firms. The top leaders of the combined organization were faced with several key leadership dilemmas. The first was to determine which individuals would fill the top leadership positions in the combined company, as there was no particularly good information about the leadership talent in any of the three organizations. The second was to create a new culture for the combined organization that emphasized financial acumen, customer service, global perspective, the attraction and development of talent, and a new business strategy that focused on services rather than production. Working against this new culture was the frequent emphasis of the three heritage organizations on technical excellence to the exclusion of profitability and customer service. The third was that many of the top 300 leaders in all three organizations were due to retire in the next three years, and top leadership was uncertain how it could start to identify and build its leadership talent to fill these gaps.

To address these three needs, the combined organization started by having the top 250 executives go through a two-day customized assessment center. The results of the center were used to place people in key leadership positions, identify strengths and weaknesses of individual leaders and leadership teams, and help executives understand the demands, challenges, and expectations of leaders in the new organizational culture. The next 750 leaders in the combined organization then went through another customized assessment center in order to identify and build replacement leaders for those executives who would soon be retiring.

The results of the assessment center process on some of the key unit performance indices of the company have been nothing short of remarkable. In the year after the assessment center was used to identify and deploy the top 250 executives in the company:

- Sales increased from $35 to $38 billion.
- Earnings improved from $277 million to $1.902 billion.
- On-time deliveries improved from 48 percent to 100 percent.
- Stock price increased 27 percent.

Sources: D. Heine, "Using I/O Psychology to Turn Around a Business," in *The Role of I/O Psychology in Executive Assessment and Development.* G. J. Curphy (chair). (symposium at the 15th Annual Conference of the Society for Industrial and Organizational Psychology, New Orleans, LA, 2000).

independent of the efforts of the new college president? Similarly, how would you evaluate the performance of the captain of a cruise ship, the head nurse of an outpatient clinic, a radio station manager, or the leader of a homeless shelter? Just as various techniques are used to assess leaders, there also are various ways to measure the *effects* of leaders on subordinates and organizations. But what do we mean by "effects on subordinates and organizations"? A useful way to think about this is in terms of the ways that we typically define leadership success. We usually do not differentiate between successful and unsuccessful leaders by the behaviors they exhibit or the attributes they possess; rather, we are more likely to consider whether their followers are productive or satisfied or their organization is more profitable. For example, we could make judgments about the success of a leader by looking at the college president's ability to raise funds, a coach's win-loss record, a college professor's end-of-course student ratings, or the production or quality rates for a production manager's work unit. Although the leader's behavior or personality traits will probably play a key role in these indices, when making judgments about the relative success of a leader we are examining the *consequences* or *impact* of these behaviors and not the behaviors per se. The material in this section describes how researchers typically measure leadership impact and the methods' respective strengths and limitations.

Common Measures of Successful and Unsuccessful Leadership

Half of the CEOs in the world are below average.
**David Campbell,
Center for Creative
Leadership**

In reality, there are a vast number of measures available to judge successful and unsuccessful leaders (see, for example, Table 4.3). Some of the more commonly used measures include a superior's effectiveness or promotion ratings, subordinates' ratings of their job satisfaction and morale or of their leader's effectiveness, and various work-unit performance indices. We will use the college president example to discuss each of these in further detail below.

Superiors' Effectiveness and Performance Ratings

One way to judge the effectiveness of a leader is to examine his or her performance appraisal ratings. Most **superiors' performance ratings** are determined by a leader's superior and include ratings of performance on several relevant dimensions as well as a recommendation (or not) for promotion. For example, one group of researchers used superiors' overall performance ratings and promotion recommendations as criteria for judging the leadership effectiveness of navy surface fleet officers.[58]

Because almost all organizations use some type of performance appraisal system, it may be worthwhile to briefly describe a typical performance appraisal form. The better performance appraisal forms typically include several features. First, superiors use some type of scale to rate how well a target leader accomplished several key objectives. Superiors

TABLE 4.3
Common Measures of Successful and Unsuccessful Leadership

Measure	Advantages	Disadvantages
Superiors' ratings	Frequently used	Superiors' biases
		Raters unaware of true performance
		Raters' unwillingness to provide tough feedback
Subordinates' ratings	Subject of leaders' behaviors	Unmotivated subordinates
	Multiple raters	Subordinates' biases
		May be no links between ratings and unit performance
Unit performance indices	Actual results	Results due to factors beyond leaders' control

also rate the leader on several key dimensions the organization believes are important, such as integrity, leadership, administrative skills, communication impact, and so forth. Finally, superiors then rate the overall performance and/or the promotability of the leader.[59,60]

In our college president example, you would rate the college president on *what* he or she actually accomplished over the past year. In other words, how successful was the college president in balancing the budget, resolving staff conflict, building relationships with faculty and alumni, increasing student satisfaction, or making decisions about new economic programs? You would also rate *how* the college president went about accomplishing these objectives. This usually involves rating each of the college president competencies, such as the ability to solve problems and make decisions, meet budgets, coach others, create high-performing teams, manage conflict, and build relationships with and earn the trust of key internal and external stakeholders. These *what* and *how* ratings would then be combined to provide an overall rating of the college president's performance over the past year.

If you were on the college's board of trustees, you would probably want to complete a performance appraisal on the college president. Although you would think that accurate ratings of a leader's performance are pretty much a given, more often than not these rating are fraught with error. Sometimes superiors simply do not take the time to provide accurate and comprehensive performance appraisal ratings; at other times superiors may be largely unaware or unfamiliar with a target leader's performance. This latter phenomenon is becoming more prevalent as organizations move toward virtual teams or increase the number of people any one superior may supervise. Some leaders are so good at strategic sucking up that they convince superiors they are doing a much better job than reality would dictate—examples here might include Michael Brown of Hurricane Katrina fame or former U.S. Attorney General Alberto Gonzales. Other superiors have difficulty dealing with conflict and would rather give average ratings than deal with the emotions and distress associated with unflattering ratings. In addition, friendships, perceptual sets, and attribution errors can bias superiors' ratings of a leader's true performance. Some performance appraisal systems do such a poor job measuring a leader's true impact that superiors find them to be virtually useless when making promotion or compensation decisions. Inaccurate performance appraisal ratings are a major factor contributing to the high base rate of managerial incompetence. Oftentimes Competent Managers are given lower performance appraisal ratings because superiors do not want them to get promoted (due to jealousy or because they don't want to lose them from the work unit); Cheerleaders and In Name Only and Results Only Managers get higher ratings because of their ability to please others, get results, or not make waves. As a result many of the wrong people get promoted into positions of increasing responsibility.

Subordinates' Ratings of Satisfaction, Organizational Climate, Morale, Motivation, and Leadership Effectiveness

If leadership is defined partly in the eyes of followers, then perhaps a better way to judge the college president's success is through **subordinates' ratings of effectiveness.** In this method subordinates would be asked to rate their level of satisfaction or the effectiveness of the college president. Subordinates may be relatively satisfied or dissatisfied, may be motivated or unmotivated, may feel relatively committed or uncommitted to the organization, or may believe their leader is relatively effective or ineffective. Fostering a sense of motivation, cohesiveness, cooperation, and morale among unit members is a goal toward which most leaders will strive, yet several cautions may be in order when using subordinates' motivation or cohesiveness ratings to judge a leader's effectiveness.[61,62] For one thing, some subordinates may be relatively unmotivated toward work no matter what the leader does. For example, it may be relatively difficult for the college president to motivate a highly unionized janitorial or administrative staff or a group of tenured professors. For another, success in instilling a strong sense of motivation and cohesiveness in subordinates does not guarantee effective performance. It often is also necessary, for example, to ensure that subordinates are adequately trained and have the necessary equipment and resources to do the job. Without training and equipment, subordinates' performance still might be relatively low even if the subordinates are motivated. In addition, subordinates may be performing at a low level yet rate their leader as being relatively effective because he or she does not make them work very hard (In Name Only Manager or Cheerleader). Conversely, some subordinates may rate a Competent Manager as relatively ineffective if he or she does make them work hard. Thus, the links between subordinates' ratings and the performance of the college president may be unclear or affected by various factors beyond the president's control.[61–63]

Despite these cautions, there are two reasons why followers' ratings may be a more accurate reflection of a leader's impact than superiors' ratings of performance. First, followers are often in a better position to make these judgments. They usually are the direct recipients of their boss's day-to-day leadership behaviors. Second, although subordinates' ratings can also suffer from distortion or bias, such effects tend to cancel each other out when multiple raters are used.[64,65] In our example, you could collect this information by asking direct reports to rate the college president on the college president competencies. These ratings would be averaged and used as another source of information for evaluating the performance of the college president.

Unit Performance Indices

Rather than use ratings to judge a leader's effectiveness, we could use **unit performance indices** to examine what impact leaders have on the "bottom lines" of their organizations. In other words, we could make judgments about leadership success by examining store sales, profit margins, the number of defective products returned, the number of on-time deliveries, crime rates, high school graduation rates, the dollar amount of charitable contributions collected, win-loss records, or days lost due to accidents. Like the two other sets of measures described earlier, none of these measures is perfect. The biggest qualification to remember in these measures of leadership is that they are often affected by factors beyond a leader's control. For example, Lee Raymond, the former CEO of Exxon Mobil, received a retirement package worth $400 million. Most of this package was based on a dramatic rise in the price of oil, which in turn boosted the price of Exxon Mobil stock. At the time of his retirement oil was at $70 per barrel, a historically high price. Yet Raymond had little if anything to do with the price of oil—the Chinese and Indian economies had driven up demand, and the Iraq War, conflicts in Nigeria, and disagreements between the United States and Venezuela had tightened up supplies. Raymond was handsomely rewarded for boosting Exxon Mobil's stock price, yet in reality he had little to do with the global price of oil.

Similarly, external factors can affect college budgets. These can include economic conditions, alumni fund-raising efforts, school scandals, state legislative efforts, drops in student enrollment, changing demographics, and so on. Conceivably, the college president could do "all the right things," yet still not balance the budget from one year to the next, primarily due to circumstances beyond his or her control. Conversely, the president may make a number of mistakes but may work in a city that sees an economic uptick due to the arrival of several new companies. These companies could provide hundreds of new jobs, which in turn would increase tax revenues and student enrollments. Leadership practitioners need to remember that unit performance indices are often affected by several factors, some of which have more impact than anything a leader might do.[66] It is important to estimate how much a leader's behavior might affect a particular unit performance index before using that index to judge the leader's effectiveness. It is also important to remember that many Cheerleaders, In Name Only Managers, and Results Only Managers will often take credit for results they had little if anything to do with, which affects the base rate of managerial incompetence.

Best Practices in Measuring Leadership Success

If you can't measure it, then you can't manage it.
Peter Drucker, management consultant

So what should a person do with respect to measuring a leader's impact or ability to get results? Ratings by superiors and subordinates have their inherent problems, as do unit performance indices. Despite such problems, these measures generally yield useful information about a leader's effectiveness. Moreover, these measures get at different aspects of effectiveness. It is entirely possible for a leader to get strong ratings from his or her superiors but poor ratings from subordinates. This may be the case if a leader was brought in to turn around a poorly performing college or if a leader has spent a considerable amount of time engaging in "strategic sucking up" with the board of trustees. On the other hand, leaders could have poor relationships with their boss and great relationships with their subordinates, and such relationships would be reflected in the ratings they get from these two groups. Practitioners need to understand the advantages and problems associated with the different measures, and that multiple measures often yield the best information about leadership success.[64]

Practitioners also need to think critically about how their behavior affects the measures used to judge leadership success. Leaders may perform relatively poorly on several unit performance indices yet also realize that performance on these indices is both relatively insensitive to their behavior and largely a function of, say, local economic conditions or inadequate resources. Leaders instead may choose to focus on improving their effectiveness in terms of criteria more sensitive to their actions, such as improving subordinates' perceptions of motivation, climate, or satisfaction (see Highlight 4.8 and 4.10).

Another concern for leadership practitioners might be the degree to which leadership success measures are biased. Research shows that women receive less pay for the same job as their male counterparts in the United States[67,68] and minority female managers make only 57 percent of the earnings of their white male counterparts in the United States.[69] These results imply that females may receive lower performance appraisal ratings across most jobs in the United States. Because males make up the majority of managers in the United States, it may be some time before both genders receive the same level of effectiveness and performance ratings from their superiors (see Highlight 4.5). It is important to remember, however, that not all male managers automatically give all female subordinates lower performance appraisal ratings. The research cited above represents overall trends; individual male managers may or may not give female subordinates lower performance or effectiveness ratings. Yet the trends result in a triple whammy—females get lower pay and are promoted less frequently than their male counterparts and organizations have fewer Competent Managers in positions of authority.

Getting back to our discussion of managerial incompetence from the beginning of the chapter, when all is said and done the best measures of effectiveness may be those that assess a leader's ability to build a team (subordinates' ratings) and get results (unit performance indices).[4,61,62] In general, Competent Managers may be those who achieve higher subordinates' ratings and consistently achieve results that are better than those achieved by other teams or organizations. Cheerleaders may get good ratings from subordinates but will have unit performance indices that fall short. Results Only Managers will achieve just the opposite, and In Name Only Managers will have middling results for both sets of indicators.

Jimmy LaValley

PROFILES IN LEADERSHIP 4.2

Jimmy LaValley recently retired as the Senior Vice President of Human Resources for Waste Management. When Jimmy joined Waste Management, the company was just emerging from a series of poorly executed acquisitions; Wall Street also had questions about the accuracy of the company's financial statements and potential Mafia connections. A new CEO, Maury Myers, was brought in to reduce costs, improve operations and safety, get the company back on sound financial footing, and improve the public reputation of Waste Management. After five years Myers had successfully turned around the company but decided he was not the person to get Waste Management to the next level of growth. LaValley played an instrumental role in helping Waste Management's board define the competencies needed by the next CEO and arranged for the three internal candidates to go through a CEO-level assessment center. LaValley helped the board select the new CEO, Steiner. LaValley worked with David Steiner to define a comprehensive business strategy for Waste Management that was clearly understood and bought into by all 5,000 leaders in the company. He then developed a set of company-wide leadership competencies and implemented comprehensive recruiting, leadership development, succession planning, performance management, and compensation systems in order to systematically upgrade the company's leadership talent. Under LaValley's leadership the company's stock price dramatically improved, and its reputation changed from a bunch of "garbage haulers" to "Think Green" and environmental stewardship. The company's integrated talent management system helped to hire and promote individuals with stronger leadership potential and dismiss those who had difficulty building teams or getting results.

Methodologies Used to Study Leadership

The color of leadership is bright orange. The color of leadership research is slate gray.

Jerry Hunt, Texas Tech University

So far we have discussed the techniques used to assess a person's potential for leadership. We have also gone over the measures commonly used to evaluate a leader's effectiveness. What we have not discussed is how researchers determine whether there is a *relationship* between a leader's personality traits, behaviors, or values and their win-loss records, sales results, percentage of on-time takeoffs, subordinates' level of satisfaction, and so forth. Do leaders who handle stress well, are more outgoing, or are better problem solvers have happier subordinates or achieve better results? The nature and strength of the relationships between various leadership attributes and performance or effectiveness measures is of primary importance to researchers and practitioners alike. If there is little or no relationship between a leader's personality traits or behaviors and unit performance indices, then organizations would be wasting their time and money to assess these values and traits as part of their hiring or promotion processes. However, a large body of research shows that certain leadership attributes can be reliably assessed and are related to a number of positive leadership outcomes. So how do leadership researchers systematically determine whether there is a relationship between leadership potential and effectiveness measures? The techniques used by researchers to determine these relationships can generally be grouped into either qualitative or quantitative approaches.

The Qualitative Approach

The most common qualitative approach is the case study. **Case studies** are an in-depth analysis of a leader's activities; biographies are common examples of case studies. Biographies usually provide detailed descriptions of the various situations facing the leader, the actions taken in response to these situations, and the results of the leader's actions. Case studies can provide leadership practitioners with valuable ideas on what to do in different leadership situations, particularly if the situations facing the practitioner are similar to those described in a biography. However, there is no objective way to determine whether the actions taken actually caused the results described in a case study. Often factors beyond the leader's actions have a greater role in determining outcomes. Because of these problems, caution should always be used when trying to apply lessons discerned from a case study or biography; they may not fit your particular leadership style or apply to your leadership situation. Nevertheless, case studies often provide interesting and valuable reading, and offer leadership practitioners alternative perspectives for analyzing leadership situations. Case studies can also provide researchers with hypotheses to test further, using more precise quantitative methods.[70]

Quantitative Approaches

The two major quantitative approaches include correlational studies and experiments both of which fall into the academic tradition described in Highlight 4.9. **Correlational studies** are used to determine the statistical relationship between leaders' traits, mental abilities, or behaviors and various measures of leadership effectiveness such as subordinates' satisfaction or climate ratings. An example of a correlational study would be to identify a group of leaders (e.g., police chiefs in 100 midsized cities), collect their scores on some type of paper-and-pencil test (a mental abilities test), and also collect satisfaction ratings from their respective subordinates. A **correlation coefficient** would then be calculated between the intelligence test scores and subordinates' satisfaction ratings. A correlation coefficient is a statistical index of the strength of the relationship between two variables and can range between −1.00 and +1.00. Correlation coefficients close to +1.00 would indicate a strong, positive relationship, those close to 0 would indicate no relationship, and those close to −1.00 would indicate a strong inverse relationship between mental ability scores and subordinates' satisfaction ratings. In other words, a positive correlation would indicate that smarter police chiefs had happier departments; a negative correlation would indicate that dumber police chiefs had happier departments. A real example of a correlational study showed

The Academic and Troubadour Traditions of Leadership Research

HIGHLIGHT 4.9

On a practical level, leadership is a topic that almost everyone is interested in at one time or another. People have a vested interest in who is running their government, schools, company, or church, and because of this interest thousands of books and articles have been written about the topic of leadership. Curphy and Hogan believe these manuscripts can be divided into two major camps. The **academic tradition** consists of articles that use data and statistical techniques to make inferences about effective leadership. Because the academic tradition is research based, for the most part these findings are written for other leadership researchers and are virtually uninterpretable to leadership *practitioners.* As such, leadership practitioners are often unfamiliar with the research findings of the academic tradition.

The second camp of leadership literature is the **troubadour tradition.** These books and articles often consist of nothing more than the opinions or score-settling reminiscences of former leaders. Books in the troubadour tradition, such as *Who Moved My Cheese?, What the CEO Wants You to Know, Winning, Lead Like Jesus: Lessons from the Greatest Leadership Role Model of all Time,* are wildly popular, but it is difficult to separate fact from fiction or determine whether these opinions translate to other settings. People who are unfamiliar with the findings of the academic tradition and the limitations of the troubadour tradition find it extremely difficult to differentiate research findings from opinion.

Perhaps the biggest challenge to improving the practice of leadership is to provide practitioners with timely, easily digestible, research-grounded advice on how to effectively lead others. The knowledge accumulated from 90 years of leadership research is of tremendous value, yet scientists have paid little attention to the ultimate consumers of their work—leaders and leaders-to-be. Leadership practitioners often want fast answers about how to be more effective or successful and understandably turn to popular books and articles that *appear* to provide timely answers to their practical concerns. Unfortunately, however, the claims in the popular or "trade" literature are rarely based on sound research; they oversimplify the complexities of the leadership process; and many times they actually offer bad advice. Relatively little weight is given to well-researched leadership studies, primarily because the arcane requirements of publishing articles in scholarly journals make their content virtually unreadable (and certainly uninteresting) to actual leadership practitioners. One of the primary objectives of this book is to make the results of leadership research more usable to leaders and leaders-to-be.

Sources: G. J. Curphy, M. J. Benson, A. Baldrica, and R. T. Hogan, *Managerial Incompetence.* Unpublished manuscript, 2007; G. J. Curphy, *"What We Really Know about Leadership (But Seem Unwilling to Implement.)"* Presentation given to the Minnesota Professionals for Psychology and Applied Work, Minneapolis, MN, January 2004; R. T. Hogan, *Personality and the Fate of Organizations.* Mahwah, NJ: Lawrence Erlbaum Associates, 2007.

that people who scored higher on personality traits associated with stress tolerance, ambition, extraversion, and conscientiousness were more effective leaders than people who scored lower on these traits (all correlations were in the .3–.4 range).[71]

Correlational studies are among the most common methods used to study leadership. Both the ease of data collection and the ability of correlational studies to illuminate relationships between leader potential and effectiveness measures are major advantages of these studies. However, they do have one major drawback. It is usually difficult (though it is often tempting) to make **causal inferences** based on correlational data. A causal inference occurs when leadership researchers can definitely say that certain leadership behaviors or attributes *cause* various kinds of leadership outcomes. Although correlational studies help researchers to determine the relationship between leadership attributes and outcomes, they cannot be used to make causal inferences. For example, in the study described in the previous paragraph we cannot tell if a leader's supportive behaviors cause their subordinates to be more satisfied or if more satisfied subordinates cause their leaders to exhibit more supportive leadership behaviors. Indeed, some of the most common erroneous reasoning from research results involves inferring causal relationships between variables when only a correlational relationship has been established (see Highlight 4.10).

Experiments allow researchers to make causal inferences about leadership, and experimental designs are often based on the results of earlier case and correlational studies. Experiments generally consist of both independent and dependent variables. The **independent variable** is what the researcher manipulates or varies to test the hypothesis; it causes change in the dependent variable. In leadership research, the independent variable is often some type of leadership behavior and the **dependent variable** is usually some measure of leadership effectiveness, such as work-unit performance or subordinates' satisfaction ratings.

A description of a "laboratory" experiment on leadership may help make the distinction between independent and dependent variables a bit clearer. Two researchers were interested in determining whether charismatic leaders caused subordinates to perform at a higher level than supportive or directive leaders. These researchers trained two actresses to manifest charismatic, directive, or supportive leadership styles. Thus, the style of leadership exhibited by the actress-leader for different groups of subordinates was the independent variable in this experiment; with some groups the actress-leaders exhibited only charismatic behaviors, while with others they exhibited only supportive or directive behaviors. The dependent variable was subordinates' performance, which in this case was measured by the number of memos subordinates successfully completed during a 45-minute in-basket exercise. The researchers manipulated or changed the independent variable (the actresses' leadership styles varied across different groups of subordinates), but they merely recorded the subordinates' performance on the dependent variable (the number of memos successfully completed) at the end of each 45-minute session. The researchers reported that subordinates' performance levels were highest when leaders exhibited charismatic behaviors and as a result concluded that these leadership behaviors caused subordinates to perform at the highest levels.

Although experiments allow us to make causal inferences about leadership, experiments have drawbacks of their own. One is that the effects obtained in many laboratory experiments are stronger than the effects obtained when the same experiments are conducted out in the field (i.e., in organizations). This is primarily due to the tightly controlled conditions

Global Leadership

HIGHLIGHT 4.10

There is no doubt about it, the world is getting smaller. Globalization has allowed goods and services to be manufactured, traded, and delivered in places no one thought possible just 10 or 20 years ago. World business leaders, such as Jeffery Immelt of General Electric, Carlos Ghosn of Renault and Nissan Motors, and Steve Ballmer of Microsoft all believe these global trends are irreversible and gaining momentum. But what are the implications of globalization for leadership? It is clear that the ways in which leaders get results through others and build cohesive, goal-oriented teams will vary somewhat from one country to the next. For example, Malaysian leadership culture inhibits assertive, confrontational behavior and puts a premium on maintaining harmony. Effective leaders are expected to show compassion while demonstrating more of an autocratic than participatory leadership style. German leadership culture does not value compassion, and interpersonal relationships are rather straightforward and stern. Effective leaders in Germany generally value autonomy and participation, but have a low team orientation.

So how does one lead in a global economy? Certainly appreciating what different cultures value and how things get done in different countries is an important first step. But do leaders need to do fundamentally different things in order to build teams or get results through others in India, Zimbabwe, or Estonia? Will the leaders of the future need to speak multiple languages or actually live in other countries in order to be effective? The answers to these questions will depend to some extent on the global orientation of the organization. Some organizations, such as Waste Management or ServiceMaster, primarily operate in Canada and the United States and probably will not need to have leaders who have lived in other countries or speak multiple languages. Other organizations, such as 3M, Hewlett-Packard, Pfizer, BP, Levono, Nike, Toyota, or the British military have significant manufacturing, marketing, sales, or operations in multiple countries. These organizations often use a global competency model to outline the expectations for leaders in all countries, and these models tend to vary more by company than by country (see Figure 4.2 for an example of a competency model).

It does seem likely that leaders who have spent time in other countries, have applied the action-observation-reflection model to maximize the lessons learned from their expatriot experiences, and can speak multiple languages would be better able to lead international organizations. But currently this is conjecture, as more research is needed before we can definitively say whether international experience matters, how much and what kind of experience is needed, what the key lessons to be learned from these experiences are, and how we should select and develop leaders to successfully lead international organizations. The good news here is that a group of 150 social scientists working on the GLOBE (Global Leadership and Organizational Behavior Effectiveness) project are actively seeking the answers to these questions and will soon be publishing their findings.

Sources: S. Green, F. Hassan, J. Immelt, M. Marks, and D. Meiland. "In Search of Global Leaders." *Harvard Business Review,* August 2003, pp. 38–45; J. C. Kennedy, "Leadership in Malaysia: Traditional Values, International Outlook." *The Academy of Management Executive,* 16 (3) (2002), pp. 15–24; F. Brodbeck, M. Frese, M. Javidan, and F. G. Kroll, "Leadership Made in Germany: Low on Compassion, High in Performance." *The Academy of Management Executive* 16 (1) (2002), pp. 16–30; GLOBE program: http://mgmt3.ucalgary.ca/web/globe.nsf/index.

under which laboratory experiments are run, whereas experiments in organizations cannot be so tightly controlled. Extraneous influences often minimize or distort the effects of the independent variable on the dependent variable when the experiment is conducted in an organizational setting. Another problem concerns the subjects used in many laboratory experiments. Many times, college undergraduates are used as subjects in

TABLE 4.4
Some Common and Uncommon Variations of Leadership Studies

Feature	Common	Uncommon
Research method	Surveys	Experiments
Time frame	Static	Longitudinal
Research objective	Replication	Explore new issues
Locus of leadership	Heroic individual	Shared/distributed
Causality	Unidirectional	Reciprocal
Data sources	Single	Multiple
Level of leader	Supervisor	Executive

Source: G. Yukl, *Reflections and Directions in Leadership Research* (presentation made at the 14th Annual Conference of the Society of Industrial and Organizational Psychologists, Atlanta, May 1999).

leadership experiments, and these individuals may have little leadership or followership experience. For such reasons it becomes legitimate to ask how much the results of any particular laboratory experiment can be generalized to actual organizations.

Literally thousands of qualitative and quantitative studies have looked at what leaders do and how their actions affect important team or organizational outcomes. Organizations that have capitalized on this accumulation of knowledge and successfully bridged the practice-research gap have been able to design better hiring, performance management, training and development, and succession planning systems for their leaders. These systems almost always result in stronger leadership bench strength and in turn better organizational performance (see Highlight 4.8). Nevertheless, there are a number of important leadership questions that still need to be answered. Gary Yukl, one of the world's premier leadership researchers, maintained that although there is much we still need to learn about leadership, a great deal of the leadership research being conducted these days misses the mark. Leadership researchers appear to be too obsessed with surveys, too ready to replicate previous research, think only of leadership as a one-way relationship, or use the same quantitative designs too frequently for this research to be of much use (see Table 4.4). Yukl maintained that the yield rate of current research is only 11 percent; this is the percentage of studies that actually add something over and above what we already know about leadership.[73] And as stated earlier, much of this leadership research provides little if any useful advice to leadership practitioners. So if the leadership research is not adding to our body of scientific knowledge and practitioners cannot use any of the findings, then what is truly driving leadership research? Unfortunately, it appears that the requirements for tenure are resulting in leadership research that is of little use to anyone.

Maxims and Theories of Leadership

Most of what people read about leadership amounts to little more than someone else's opinion about it. Often, such material is both anecdotal and prescriptive: anecdotal in the sense it reflects just one leader's views,

TABLE 4.5
Jack Welch's Eight Rules

1. Leaders relentlessly upgrade their team, using every encounter as an opportunity to evaluate, coach, and build self-confidence.
2. Leaders make sure people not only see vision, they live and breathe it.
3. Leaders get into everyone's skin, exuding positive energy and optimism.
4. Leaders establish trust with candor, transparency, and credit.
5. Leaders have the courage to make unpopular decisions and gut calls.
6. Leaders probe and push with a curiosity that borders on skepticism, making sure their questions are answered with action.
7. Leaders inspire risk taking and learning by setting an example.
8. Leaders celebrate.

Source: J. Welch and S. Welch, *Winning.* New York: HarperBusiness, 2005.

Death has a tendency to encourage a depressing view of war.
Donald Rumsfeld, former U.S. Secretary of Defense

and prescriptive in advising others how to be more effective. For example, although Jack Welch is commonly acknowledged as one of the best business leaders of recent times, it is nonetheless uncertain whether his maxims would apply equally well for very different leaders in very different situations (see Table 4.5). Maxims are personal opinions that can give leaders valuable advice about leadership. It is important to be mindful of the difference between this kind of literature about leadership and more scientific or empirical approaches to understanding it. The latter are represented by data-based studies and theories reported in this book. Although both approaches have legitimate purposes, it is vital to understand the differences between them.

The scientific alternative to leadership maxims is leadership theory. A leadership **theory** is a framework for conceptualizing relationships between variables and guiding research toward a fuller understanding of phenomena. With a theory a researcher makes public predictions about how certain leadership attributes or behaviors will systematically impact certain leadership effectiveness measures. Then the researcher collects the leadership assessment and effectiveness data prescribed by the theory, and conducts statistical analyses to determine whether his or her predictions are supported or refuted.[75,76] For example, suppose a researcher predicted that the personality traits of dominance (wanting to be in charge of others) and dependability (being a reliable, trustworthy, and hard-working employee) were positively related to sales results in the computer retail industry. The researcher could use a paper-and-pencil measure of personality to assess store managers' standings on the traits of dominance and dependability. The researcher could then collect annual sales results for each store and conduct a correlational study to determine the nature and strength of the relationships between these three variables. The researcher might then publish the results of his or her findings in a scientific journal so that other researchers can gather more information that would support or refute the original theory and findings.

Everything you do at work counts.
Mike Watkins, Western Area Power Administration

The Top Five Critical Thinking Questions Practitioners Should Ask When Reading about Leadership

HIGHLIGHT 4.11

1. *Who is in the sample?*
- How big is the sample?
- Is the sample representative of most leaders?
- How similar are the leaders to you?

2. *What is the situation?*
- What challenges and opportunities do the leaders face?
- If reading about an experiment, how generalizable are the conditions to the "real world"?
- What situational factors could affect the results of the experiment?
- Is the situation similar to the one you currently face?

3. *What leadership qualities, characteristics, or behaviors are being assessed?*
- Are the right attributes being assessed?

- Are the best assessment techniques being used?

4. *How is leadership success being determined?*
- By means of superiors' ratings, subordinates' ratings, or unit performance indices?
- Are the best measures being used, or would alternative measures paint a different picture?
- How might these measures be affected by factors beyond the leader's control?

5. *How do the writers link leadership assessment to success?*
- By means of case studies, correlational studies, or experiments?
- Are the right conclusions being drawn?
- Are there any other plausible alternative explanations?
- Did the writers acknowledge these alternative explanations?

The public predictions of how leadership variables are interrelated, the systematic gathering and analysis of data, and the peer review of results are what make theories so central to scientific research. Theories are often modified to take new findings into account as researchers collect, analyze, and publish their findings about the theory. For example, other researchers may find that store managers' intelligence levels also are related to store performance. The original theory would then need to be modified so that dominance, dependability, and intelligence could all be used to predict sales managers' success. These findings could in turn be used to develop a competency model and selection system for future store managers in the computer retail industry.

The essence of theories of leadership, then, is to provide a reasonably coherent conceptual structure of how critical variables interact, involving ideas that can be put to the test and revised as new data accumulate. Simply put, theories of leadership involve testable ideas, whereas prescriptive ~~Maxims~~ approaches to leadership involve no such intended testability. Although both leadership maxims and theories are useful for understanding leadership situations, in general only leadership theories add to the body of knowledge concerning the science of leadership and help in the development of universal laws of leadership. It is also important to understand that theory building is hard, painstaking work. It is fairly easy to state one's opinions on how one should act as a leader; it is an entirely different matter to design a study, collect data, analyze, and finally publish the results.

Despite all of the advantages of conducting systematic research around the topic of leadership, there remains the question of why case studies and maxims are so popular with leadership practitioners. Perhaps the more central question, however, is why research-based articles in leadership and management journals are not more popular themselves. One reason is that the very format of research articles, with their emphasis on statistical results and so forth, is fairly dull and inaccessible to anyone but university professors and graduate students. However, we also suspect that leadership researchers themselves sometimes forget that other academicians should not be their only important audience. Leadership researchers need to do a better job of making the findings from their studies more relevant and accessible to practicing managers and leaders.

Summary

This chapter begins with the premise that leadership is the most important topic in the world today. Leadership affects virtually every aspect of our lives, including work, travel, religion, health care, education, local and national politics, volunteer activities, community events, and so on. Although everyone plays a leadership role at one time or another, research indicates that only a minority of people can consistently build teams and get results. More likely than not your boss, doctor, college president, athletic coach, rabbi, mayor, and national leaders have difficulties in getting a group of people to work effectively together in order to achieve tangible results. As bad as the current state of leadership appears to be, things could get worse before they get better. Demographic trends, the loss of employee loyalty, poor talent management practices, and technology will make it even more difficult for organizations to identify, develop, and retain effective leaders.

One way for organizations to minimize this crisis in leadership is to adopt a leadership talent management system. A leadership talent management system begins with a clear definition of the organization's strategy—what customers does the organization serve, what goals is it trying to achieve, what products and services is it selling to meet customer needs, and so on. Once an organization has a clear picture of the future, the next step in a leadership talent management system is to identify the critical leadership positions. These positions are those that are vitally important to the organization's success. These might include product development leaders for gaming companies, plant managers for power companies, or ship captains for the U.S. Navy. The third step is to develop a competency model, a description of the skills, behaviors, and attributes needed by incumbents in these critical leadership positions. Organizations then must align their recruiting, selection, development, evaluation, compensation, and retention programs around the competency model. The fifth and final step in an effective talent management system is one that adopts well-researched and valid techniques for identifying leadership potential and performance. Good talent management systems basically identify, develop, reward, and retain candidates with "the right stuff," and research has shown that companies with these systems are more effective than those who have adopted poor talent management practices. Poor talent management practices are also a leading cause of managerial incompetence.

Various techniques exist.

This chapter then describes some of the techniques organizations use to assess leadership potential and performance. Some of those used to predict the future performance of leaders include résumés, interviews, online tests, and work simulations. One reason for the high base rate of managerial incompetence is that the most accurate and valid techniques for predicting future leadership success are typically those that are the least used by organizations. Another reason why so many people are ineffective leaders has to do with the ways in which their current performance is measured. Superiors' ratings, subordinates' ratings, and unit performance measures can many times paint different pictures about the relative success of a leader. All three types of measures have advantages and disadvantages: Some are more sensitive to leaders' efforts, and some may be more strongly influenced by factors beyond their control. Because effective leadership involves building teams and getting results, we recommend that organizations adopt a combination of subordinates' ratings and unit performance indices when evaluating the performance of leaders.

Qualitative: - Case Studies

Readers also should know that there are three methods commonly used to study the linkages between leadership potential and performance measures. Case studies have the advantage of helping practitioners better understand the context in which a leader acts. However, they usually only describe the actions of one leader in one situation, and the generalizability of their findings to the reader may be questionable. Correlational studies have the advantage of using larger sample sizes and describe the statistical relationships between the results of different assessment techniques and success measures. These studies cannot tell us much about cause and effect relationships, however. Leadership experiments do yield valuable information about the cause-and-effect relationships between independent and dependent variables. Thus, experiments can tell us how different leadership behaviors affect group performance, subordinates' satisfaction levels, and so forth. But experiments are hard to conduct in field settings, and most laboratory experiments of leadership use college students as subjects; the generalizability of the findings for the latter experiments is always questionable. Finally, leadership practitioners should understand the difference between maxims and theories of leadership. Maxims may represent valid advice, but they are ultimately no more than personal opinion. Since they amount to little more than personal opinion, different maxims sometimes give conflicting advice, and by their very nature there is no systematic way to "test" maxims. Theories, on the other hand, are a collection

Quantitative: - Correlational Studies

of testable predictions about the relationships between certain variables. Theories are developed on the basis of observations, and their corresponding hypotheses are tested and refined by means of correlational and experimental studies. Theories are useful in that they guide research and make predictions about how different variables interact. Theories add to our collective leadership knowledge, whereas maxims do not. Because we will describe a number of different leadership theories throughout this book, practitioners need to be able to think critically about leadership theories and determine how these theories can help them be better leaders.

Key Terms

practice-research gap, *87*
base rate of managerial incompetence, *87*
Dr. Gordy test, *89*
Competent Managers, *90*
Results Only Managers, *90*
Cheerleaders, *91*
In Name Only Managers, *91*
moronization of management, *91*
management system, *93*
critical leadership positions, *94*
competency model, *94*
succession planning, *96*

nine-cell matrix, *96*
leadership potential, *96*
leadership performance, *96*
glass ceiling effect, *102*
multiple hurdles approach, *100*
Internet or paper-and-pencil measures, *101*
structured interviews, *102*
unstructured interviews, *102*
assessment centers, *104*
superiors' performance ratings, *109*
subordinates' ratings of effectiveness, *111*

unit performance indices, *111*
case studies, *115*
academic tradition, *116*
troubadour tradition, *116*
correlational studies, *115*
correlation coefficient, *115*
causal inferences, *117*
experiments, *117*
independent variable, *117*
dependent variable, *117*
maxims, *120*
theory, *120*

Questions

1. The base rate of managerial incompetence is estimated to be between 50–75 percent. This means that a majority of people in positions of authority have difficulties getting a group of people to work effectively together or get results. What do you think about this percentage of incompetent managers? Is it too high or low, for example?

2. How do you react to the phrase *assessing leadership potential*? What positive and negative connotations does it have for you?

3. Some organizations are using graphology, or handwriting analysis, to assess leadership potential. What do you think about this technique?

4. What are the critical leadership positions for a fast-food restaurant chain? What competencies are needed for people to succeed in these positions?

How would you determine whether external candidates had the potential to succeed in these positions?

5. What are some of the measures you could use to judge the performance of a coach? A teacher? A student? What are the advantages and disadvantages with each of these measures? How much impact would the leader's behaviors have on each of these measures?

6. How could you design a correlational study or an experiment to test one of Jack Welch's Eight Rules in Table 4.5?

7. What is the single best work you have ever read about leadership or being a leader? What would the answers be to the top five critical thinking questions listed in Highlight 4.11 for this work?

Activities

1. Ask students to count how many leaders they have worked, played, or performed for in the past. This number should include anyone for which they were in a followership role. Once students have a total ask them to count how many of these leaders they would willingly work, play, or perform for again. Have students calculate the ratio of effective managers/total managers. Of this total, who were the worst and best leaders they have worked for and what did they do to make them effective or ineffective leaders?

2. Assign groups of students the task of identifying various criteria by which any one of the following leaders (or any others) might be evaluated: an assistant coach, a teacher, a minister, an army general. Then each group should try to achieve consensus about the prioritization of these different criteria. The class as a whole can share views about each group's prioritization, as well as the extent to which there are unique or similar criteria across the different roles or the extent to which the various criteria are measurable.

3. Assign groups of students the task of determining which measures of leadership they would use to evaluate the performance of Peter Jackson (*The Lord of the Rings*), George W. Bush, and Steven Jobs. Who would be the key groups to rate the effectiveness of these leaders, and would they provide different ratings? Which group would provide the "best" ratings of leadership effectiveness, and why? What would the appropriate unit performance indicators be for these three leaders?

Minicase

"McDonald's Strategies for Success"

McDonald's is one of the most well-known and valuable brands in the world. It is the world's leading food service retailer, with more than 30,000 restaurants in 119 countries serving 47 million customers each day. With the biggest franchise system in the world and a cash flow that is the envy of just about any industry, the role of the CEO is a complex one—especially during times of change.

The changes at McDonald's began when Jim Cantalupo (a longtime executive of the company) came out of retirement in late 2003. McDonald's business was sagging and Cantalupo faced numerous challenges, including market saturation, increased competition, and changing tastes in the U.S. fast-food market. Cantalupo recognized these problems and quickly instituted an ambitious three-year turnaround plan: The first phase involved putting money back into existing stores in the United States rather than opening new franchises—cleaning them up and speeding up service and getting back to the core concepts that McDonald's was built on. The second phase would be to revitalize foreign restaurants in much the same way.

Turning around a large global company plagued by years of mismanagement is an enormous challenge and generally takes years to accomplish, yet in less than a year McDonald's had made tremendous progress—profits and stock prices were up and the company appeared to have built real momentum. The first phase was paying off.

Then in the spring of 2004 Jim Cantalupo died suddenly of a heart attack. The McDonald's board had to act swiftly. They called on the company's chief operating officer, Charlie Bell (another veteran of the McDonald's corporation), as Cantalupo's replacement. Franchisees, in the midst of the company's stunning turnaround, rallied behind Bell, and the company didn't miss a beat. Bell took Cantalupo's turnaround plan and ran with it. Good news for employees and investors who saw continued growth. The succession was a success . . . the company would now begin the second phase of the turnaround plan—focusing on the international component of the company. Sadly, within two weeks of his appointment, Bell disclosed that he had been diagnosed with colon cancer. With the death of Cantalupo and Bell's promotion to CEO, the position of chief operations officer—typically number two in a succession plan—was left open. A new succession plan became imperative.

1. What are some measurable factors of the success of Jim Cantalupo's turnaround plan?
2. What are some of the critical components of a competency model for a new CEO for the McDonald's corporation?
3. Consider the profile of the current CEO, Charlie Bell: Bell previously served as president and chief operating officer, and was responsible for the company's more than 30,000 restaurants in 119 countries. He began his career at age 15 as a part-time crew member at the Kingsford restaurant in Sydney, Australia. Bell progressed quickly through the ranks, becoming Australia's youngest store manager at age 19. Bell's career included working for the McDonald's Europe development company in

operations across Europe. He has held the positions of operations director and regional manager, vice president of marketing, and managing director, McDonald's Australia. Bell also served as president of McDonald's Europe, as well as president of Asia/Pacific, Middle East, and Africa Group. What trends do you see in the career of this executive that has likely contributed to his success at the McDonalds' corporation?

Sources: http://www.chicagotribune.com/business/printedition/chi-0407160286jul16,1,7963282.column; http://www.fool.com/news/commentary/2003/commentary031017wt.htm?source=mppromo; http://www.phillyburbs.com/pb-dyn/news/24-05072004-296442.html; http://www.mcdonalds.com; 'McDonald's Keeps Right on Cookin,' Fortune, May 17, 2004, p. 174.

Chapter Notes

1. Curphy, G. J., M. J. Benson, A. Baldrica, and R. T. Hogan. *Managerial Incompetence.* Unpublished manuscript, 2007.

2. Hogan, R. T. *Personality and the Fate of Organizations.* Mahwah, NJ: Lawrence Erlbaum Associates, 2007.

3. Nadler, D. A. "The CEO's Second Act." *Harvard Business Review,* January 2007, pp. 66–75.

4. Lucier, C., P. Kocourek, and R. Habbel. "CEO Succession 2005: The Crest of the Wave." *Strategy + Business* 43 (2006), pp. 40–50.

5. Bossidy, L., and R. Charan. *Execution: The Discipline of Getting Things Done.* New York: Crown Business, 2002.

6. Neilson, G. L., B. A. Pasternack, and K. E. Van Nuys. " The Passive-Aggressive Organization." *Harvard Business Review,* October 2005, pp. 82–95.

7. Pace Communication, Inc. *Hemispheres Magazine,* November 1994, p. 155.

8. Klein, K. E. "What's Behind High Small-Biz Failure Rates." *Frontier Advice and Columns,* September 30, 1999. http://www.businessweek.com/smallbiz/news/coladvice/ask/sa990930.htm.

9. Denbow, C. "Small Business Failure." http://www.elib.org/articles/292/small-business.

10. Tushabomwe-Kazooba, C. "Causes of Small Business Failure in Uganda: A Case Study from Bushenyi and Mbarara. *African Studies Quarterly* 8 (4) (2006), pp. 1–12.

11. Ward, S. "Part 4: Avoiding Business Failure." *Small Business: Canada,* 1997. http://sbinfrocanada.about.com/cs/startup/a/startownbiz.

12. The Standish Group. *Latest Standish Group CHAOS Report Shows Project Success Rates Have Improved 50%.* March 25, 2003. www.standishgroup.com/press/article.

13. Johnson, C. *Visualizing the Relationship between Human Error and Organizational Failure.* 1998. http://www.dcs.gla.ac.uk/~johnson/papers/fault_trees/organizational_error.

14. Warden, J. A., and L. A. Russell. *Winning in Fast Time.* Montgomery, AL: Venturist Publishing, 2002.

15. Kotter, J. P. *Leading Change.* Boston: Harvard Business School Press, 1996.

16. Roach, C. F., and O. Behling. "Functionalism: Basis for an Alternative Approach to the Study of Leadership." In *Leaders and Managers: International Perspectives on Managerial Behavior and Leadership.* Eds. J. G. Hunt, D. M. Hosking, C. A. Schriesheim, and R. Stewar. Elmsford, NY: Pergamon, 1984.

17. Hogan, R. T., G. J. Curphy, and J. Hogan. "What Do We Know about Personality: Leadership and Effectiveness?" *American Psychologist* 49 (1994), pp. 493–504.

18. Huselid, M. A., R. W. Beatty, and B. E. Becker. "'A Players' or 'A Positions'? The Strategic Logic of Workforce Management." *Harvard Business Review,* December 2005, pp. 110–21.

19. Dowdy, J., S. Dorgan, T. Rippen, J. Van Reenen, and N. Bloom. *Management Matters.* London: McKinsey & Company, 2005.

20. "The Search for Talent." *Economist,* October 7, 2005, p. 11.

21. Church, A. *"Talent Management." The Industrial-Organizational Psychologist* 44 (1) (2006), pp. 33–36.

22. Curphy, G. J. "The 3 Rules for Hiring 'A' Players." *Job Dig's HR Forum,* June 19–26, 2006, p. 28.

23. Cohn, J. M., R. Khurana, and L. Reeves. "Growing Talent as if Your Business Depended on It." *Harvard Business Review,* October 2005, pp. 63–70.

24. "SIOP Hits 'Home Run' With Leading Edge Consortium." *The Industrial-Organizational Psychologist* 44 (3) (2006), pp. 119–22.

25. Ginnett, R. C. "Cockpit Crew Effectiveness from the Inside Out: A Microanalysis Leading to Macro Considerations." *Proceedings of the Eleventh Psychology in the Department of Defense Symposium.* Colorado Springs, CO, 1988.

26. Leib, J. "Poor Management Blamed on Most New-Airline Failures." *Denver Post,* July 1, 1998, p. 10C.

27. Bunker, K. A., K. E. Kram, and S. Ting. "The Young and the Clueless." *Harvard Business Review,* December 2002, pp. 80–88.

28. Conger, J. A., and R. M. Fulmer. "Developing Your Leadership Pipeline." *Harvard Business Review,* December 2003, pp. 76–85.

29. Curphy, G. J. and R. T. Hogan. "Managerial Incompetence: Is There a Dead Skunk on the Table?" Working paper, 2004.

30. Curphy, G. J. "Leadership Transitions and Succession Planning." In *Developing and Implementing Succession Planning Programs.* J. Lock (chair), Symposium conducted at the 19th Annual Conference for the Society of Industrial and Organizational Psychology, Chicago, IL, April, 2004.

31. Menkes, J. "Hiring for Smarts." *Harvard Business Review,* November 2005, pp. 100–11.

32. Morgeson, F. P, M. H. Reider, and M. A. Campion. "Selecting Individuals in Team Settings: The Importance of Social Skills, Personality Characteristics, and Teamwork Knowledge." *Personnel Psychology* 58 (2005), pp. 583–611.

33. Curphy, G. J. "Early Leadership Talent Identification and Development." Paper presented at the Conference for Executives of Saudi Aramco, Dhahran, Saudi Arabia, October 2001.

34. Curphy, G. J. "Comments on the State of Leadership Prediction." In *Predicting Leadership: The Good, The Bad, the Indifferent, and the Unnecessary.* J. P. Campbell and M. J. Benson (chairs), Symposium conducted at the

22nd Annual Conference for the Society of Industrial and Organizational Psychology, New York, April 2007.

35. Saal, F. E., and P. A. Knight. *Industrial Organizational Psychology: Science and Practice.* Belmont, CA: Brooks/Cole, 1988.

36. Curphy, G. J. "Concluding Remarks on Executive Assessment and Development." In *The Role of I/O Psychology in Executive Assessment and Development.* G. J. Curphy (chair). Symposium presented at the 15th Annual Conference of the Society for Industrial and Organizational Psychology, New Orleans, LA, 2000.

37. Curphy, G. J. "In-Depth Assessments, 360-Degree Feedback, and Development: Key Research Results and Recommended Next Steps." Presentation at the Annual Conference for HR Managers at US West Communications, Denver, CO.

38. Curphy, G. J. "Executive Integrity and 360-Degree Feedback." In *Assessing Executive Failure: The Underside of Performance.* R. T. Hogan (chair). Symposium presented at the 18th Annual Conference of the Society of Industrial and Organizational Psychology, Orlando, FL, 2003.

39. Curphy, G. J. "Leadership Transitions and Teams." Presentation given at the Hogan Assessment Systems International Users Conference, Istanbul, September 2003b.

40. Naglieri, J. A., F. Drasgow, M. Schmitt, L. Handler, A. Prifitera, A. Margolis, and R. Velasquez. "Psychological Testing on the Internet: New Problems, Old Issues." *American Psychologist* 59 (3) (2004), pp. 150–62.

41. McElreath, J., and A. R. Bass. *Development of a Biodata Measure of Leadership Effectiveness: A Life History Essay Approach.* Paper Presented at the 14th Annual Conference of the Society for Industrial and Organizational Psychology, Atlanta, GA, May 1999.

42. Oswald, F. L., N. Schmitt, B. H. Kim, L. J. Ramsay, and M. A. Gillespie. "Developing a Biodata Measure and Situational Judgment Inventory as Predictors of College Student Performance." *Journal of Applied Psychology* 89 (2) (2004), pp. 187–207.

43. Muir, C. "Managing the Initial Job Interview: Smile, Schmooze, and Get Hired?" *Academy of Management Executive* 19 (1) (2005), pp. 14–16.

44. Garman, A. N., and T. Lesowitz. "Interviewing Candidates for Leadership Roles." *Consulting Psychologist Journal* 57 (4), pp. 266–73.

45. Maurer, T. J., and J. M. Solamon. "The Science and Practice of a Structured Employment Interview Coaching Program. *Personnel Psychology* 59 (2006), pp. 433–56.

46. Simoneit, M. *Grundriss der charakterologischen Diagnostik.* Leipzig: Teubner, 1944.

47. Garforth, F. I. de la P. "War Office Selection Boards." *Occupational Psychology* 19 (1945), pp. 97–108.

48. Murray, H. A., and D. W. MacKinnon. "Assessment of OSS Personnel." *Journal of Consulting Psychology* 10 (1946), pp. 76–80.

49. Sorcher, M., and J. Brant. "Are You Picking the Right Leaders?" *Harvard Business Review,* February 2002, pp. 78–86.

50. Byham, B. C., A. B. Smith, and M. J. Pease. *Grow Your Own Leaders: How to Identify, Develop, and Retain Leadership Talent.* New York: Financial Times/Prentice Hall, 2002.

51. Kwaske, I. H. "Individual Assessments for Personnel Selection: An Update on a Rarely Researched But Avidly Practiced Practice." *Consulting Psychology Journal* 56 (3) (2004), pp. 186–95.

52. Anderson, N., F. Lievens, K. Van Dam, and M. Born. "A Construct-Driven Investigation of Gender Differences in a Leadership-Role Assessment Center." *Journal of Applied Psychology* 91 (2006), pp. 555–66.

53. McFarland, L. A., G. Yun, C. M. Harold, L. Viera, Jr., L. G. Moore. "An Examination of Impression Management Use and Effectiveness Across Assessment Center Exercises: The Role of Competency Demands." *Personnel Psychology* 58, (2005), pp. 949–80.

54. *The Evolution of Assessment over the Past Three Decades.* Minneapolis, MN: Personnel Decisions International., 2001.

55. Heine, D. "Using I/O Psychology to Turn Around a Business." In *The Role of I/O Psychology in Executive Assessment and Development.* G. J. Curphy (chair). Symposium presented at the 15th Annual Conference of the Society for Industrial and Organizational Psychology, New Orleans, LA, 2000.

56. Hogan, R. H., and J. Hogan. "Assessing Leadership: A View from the Dark Side." *International Journal of Selection and Assessment* 9 (1/2) (2001), pp. 40–51.

57. Louiselle, K., S. Bridges, and G. J. Curphy. "Talent Assessment Overview." Working paper, 2003.

58. Bass, B. M., and F. J. Yammarino. *Long-term Forecasting of Transformational Leadership and Its Effects among Naval Officers: Some Preliminary Findings.* Technical Report No. ONR-TR-2. Arlington, VA: Office of Naval Research, 1988.

59. Arvey, R. D., and K. R. Murphy. "Performance Evaluation in Work Settings." *Annual Review of Psychology* 49 (1998), pp. 141–68.

60. Marentette, D. *SHRM/PDI 2000 Performance Management Survey.* Minneapolis, MN: Personnel Decisions International, 2000.

61. Kaiser, R. B. and R. T. Hogan. "Leadership and the Fate of Organizations." Paper presented at the 20th Annual Conference of the Society for Industrial and Organizational Psychology, Los Angeles, CA, April 2005.

62. Kaiser, R .B., and S. G. Ferrell. "Leadership and the Fate of Organizations: On the Measurement of Effectiveness." In *Making Reseach More Relevant*, R. B. Kaiser (chair). Symposium presented at the 20th Annual Conference of the Society for Industrial and Organizational Psychology, Los Angeles, CA, April 2005.

63. Ittner, C. D., and D. F. Larcker. "Coming Up Short on Nonfinancial Performance Measurement." *Harvard Business Review,* November 2003, pp. 88–95.

64. Greguras, G. J., C. Robie, D. J. Schleicher, and M. Goff III. "A Field Study of the Effects of Rating Purpose on the Quality of Multisource Ratings." *Personnel Psychology* 56 (1) (2003), pp. 1–22.

65. Craig, S. B., and K. Hannum. "360-Degree Performance Assessment." *Consulting Psychology Journal,* 58 (2) (2006), pp. 117–22.

66. Phelps, J. L., and M. F. Addonizio. *How Much Do Schools and Districts Matter? A Production Function Approach to School Accountability.* Working paper, Wayne State University, 2002.

67. *Male-Female Income Disparity in the United States.* 2007. http://en.wikipedia.org/wiki/Male-Female_income_disparity_in_the_USA.

68. Fitzpatrick, D. "Nonprofits Pay Men More than Women." *Pittsburgh Post-Gazette*, January 27, 2007. http://www.post-gazette.com/pg/07027/757292-28.stm.

69. Gruenberg. "Male-Female Pay Gap Static Over 20 Years, Wider for Minority Women." *Press Associates News Service*, March 26, 2004.

70. Bryman, A. "Qualitative Research on Leadership: A Critical But Appreciative Review." *The Leadership Quarterly* 15 (6), pp. 729–69.

71. Hogan, J., and B. Holland. "Using Theory to Evaluate Personality and Job-Performance Relations: A Socio-analytic Perspective." *Journal of Applied Psychology* 88 (1) (2003), pp. 100–12.

72. Howell, J. M., and P. Frost. "A Laboratory Study of Charismatic Leadership." *Organizational Behavior and Human Decision Processes* 43 (1988), pp. 243–69.

73. Yukl, G. A. "Reflections and Directions in Leadership Research." Paper presented at the 14th Annual Conference of the Society of Industrial and Organizational Psychologists, Atlanta, GA, May 1999.

74. Hogan, R. T., and G. J. Curphy. "Leadership Matters: Values and Dysfunctional Dispositions." Working paper, 2004.

75. Klimoski, R. "There is Nothing as Dangerous as a Bad Theory." *Academy of Management Learning and Education* 4 (1) (2005), p. 74.

76. Ghoshal, S. "Bad Management Theories Are Destroying Good Management Practices." *Academy of Management Learning and Education* 4 (1) (2005), p. 75–91.

Focus on the Leader

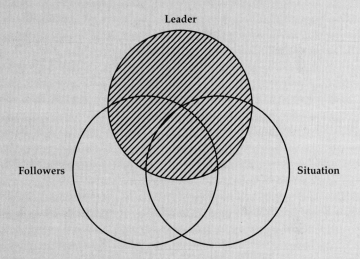

Part II focuses on the leader. The effectiveness of leadership, good or bad, is typically attributed to the leader much more than to the other elements of the framework. Sometimes the leader is the only element of leadership we even think of. One great leader's views were clear enough about the relative importance of leaders and followers:

> Men are nothing; it is the man who is everything . . . It was not the Roman army that conquered Gaul, but Caesar; it was not the Carthaginian army that made Rome tremble in her gates, but Hannibal; it was not the Macedonian army that reached the Indus, but Alexander.

Napoleon

Because the leader plays such an important role in the leadership process, the next four chapters of this book review research related to the characteristics of leaders and what makes leaders effective. Part II begins with a chapter on power and influence since those concepts provide the most fundamental way to understand the process of leadership. Chapter 6 then looks at the closely related issues of leadership and values. In Chapter 7 we consider what aspects of personality are related to leadership, and in Chapter 8 we examine how all these preceding variables are manifested in effective or ineffective leader behavior.

Chapter 5

Power and Influence

Introduction

We begin this part, called "Focus on the Leader," by examining the phenomenon of power. Some of history's earliest characterizations of leaders concerned their use of power. Shakespeare's plays were concerned with the acquisition and failing of power,[1] and Machiavelli's *The Prince* has been described as the "classic handbook on power politics."[2] Current scholars have also emphasized the need to conceptualize leadership as a power phenomenon.[3,4] Power may be the single most important concept in all the social sciences,[5] though scholars today disagree on precisely how to define power or influence. But it's not just scholars who have different ideas about power. The concept of power is so pervasive and complex that each one of us probably thinks about it a little differently.

What comes to *your* mind when *you* think about power? Do you think of a person wielding enormous authority over others? Do you think of high office? Do you think of making others do things against their will? Is power ethically neutral, or is it inherently dangerous as Lord Acton said? ("Power corrupts, and absolute power corrupts absolutely.") Do you think a leader's real power is always obvious to others? What sorts of things might enhance or detract from a leader's power? What are the pros and cons of different ways of trying to influence people? These are the kinds of issues we will explore in this chapter.

Some Important Distinctions

Power has been defined as the capacity to produce effects on others,[6] or the potential to influence others.[7] While we usually think of power belonging to the leader, it is actually a function of the leader, the followers, and the situation. Leaders have the potential to influence their followers' behaviors and attitudes. However, followers also can affect the leader's behavior and attitudes. Even the situation itself can affect a leader's capacity to influence his followers (and vice versa). For example, leaders who can reward and punish followers may have a greater capacity to influence followers than those leaders who cannot use rewards or punishments. Similarly, follower or situational characteristics may diminish a leader's potential to influence followers, as when the latter belong to a strong, active union.

Several other aspects of power also are worth noting. Gardner made an important point about the exercise of power and its effects.[8] He stated that "power does not need to be exercised in order to have its effect—as any hold-up man can tell you."[9] Thus, merely having the capacity to exert influence can often bring about intended effects, even though the leader may not take any action to influence his or her followers. For example, some months after the end of his term, Eisenhower was asked if leaving the White House had affected his golf game. "Yes," he replied, "a lot more people beat me now." Alternatively, power represents an inference or attribution made on the basis of an agent's observable acts of influence.[10] Power is never directly observed but rather attributed to others on the basis and frequency of influence tactics they use and on their outcomes.

Many people use the terms *power, influence,* and *influence tactics* synonymously,[11] but it is useful to distinguish between them. **Influence** can be defined as the change in a target agent's attitudes, values, beliefs, or behaviors as the result of influence tactics. **Influence tactics** refer to one person's actual behaviors designed to change another person's attitudes, beliefs, values, or behaviors. Although these concepts are typically examined from the leader's perspective (e.g., how a leader influences followers), we should remember that followers can also wield power and influence over leaders as well as over each other. Leadership practitioners can improve their effectiveness by reflecting on the types of power they and their followers have and the types of influence tactics that they may use or that may be used *on* them.

Whereas power is the *capacity* to cause change, influence is the degree of actual change in a target person's attitudes, values, beliefs, or behaviors. Influence can be measured by the behaviors or attitudes manifested by followers as the result of a leader's *influence tactics.* For example, a leader may ask a follower to accomplish a particular task, and whether or not the task is accomplished is partly a function of the leader's request. (The follower's ability and skill as well as access to the necessary equipment and resources are also important factors.) Such things as subordinates' satisfaction or motivation, group cohesiveness and climate, or unit performance indices can be used to measure the effectiveness of leaders' influence attempts. The degree to which leaders can change the level of satisfaction, motivation, or cohesiveness among followers is a function of the amount of power available to both leaders and followers. On the one hand, leaders with relatively high amounts of power can cause fairly

The true leader must submerge himself in the fountain of the people.

V. I. Lenin

substantial changes in subordinates' attitudes and behaviors; for example, a new and respected leader who uses rewards and punishments judiciously may cause a dramatic change in followers' perceptions about organizational climate and the amount of time followers spend on work-related behaviors. On the other hand, the amount of power followers have in work situations can also vary dramatically, and in some situations particular followers may exert relatively more influence over the rest of the group than the leader does. For example, a follower with a high level of knowledge and experience may have more influence on the attitudes, opinions, and behaviors of the rest of the followers than a brand-new leader. Thus, the amount of change in the attitudes or behaviors of the targets of influence is a function of the agent's capacity to exert influence and the targets' capacity to resist this influence.

Leaders and followers typically use a variety of tactics to influence each other's attitudes or behaviors (see Highlight 5.1 for a description of some nonverbal power cues common to humans). Influence tactics are the overt behaviors exhibited by one person to influence another. They range from emotional appeals, to the exchange of favors, to threats. The particular tactic used in a leadership situation is probably a function of the power possessed by both parties. Individuals with a relatively large amount of power may successfully employ a wider variety of influence tactics than individuals with little power. For example, a well-respected leader could make an emotional appeal, a rational appeal, a personal appeal, a legitimate request, or a threat to try to modify a follower's behavior. The follower in this situation may only be able to use ingratiation or personal appeals in order to change the leader's attitude or behavior.

At the same time, because the formal leader is not always the person who possesses the most power in a leadership situation, followers often can use a wider variety of influence tactics than the leader to modify the attitudes and behaviors of others. This would be the case if a new leader were brought into an organization in which one of his or her subordinates was extremely well liked and respected. In this situation, the subordinate may be able to make personal appeals, emotional appeals, or even threats to change the attitudes or behaviors of the leader, whereas the new leader may be limited to making only legitimate requests to change the attitudes and behaviors of the followers.

Power and Leadership

And when we think we lead, we are most led.
Lord Byron

We began this chapter by noting how an understanding of power has long been seen as an integral part of leadership. Several perspectives and theories have been developed to explain the acquisition and exercise of power. In this section we will first examine various *sources* of power. Then we will look at how individuals vary in their personal *need* for power.

Gestures of Power and Dominance

HIGHLIGHT 5.1

We can often get clues about relative power just by paying attention to behaviors between two people. There are a number of nonverbal cues we might want to pay attention to.

The phrase **pecking order** refers to the status differential between members of a group. It reminds us that many aspects of human social organization have roots, or at least parallels, in the behavior of other species. The animal kingdom presents diverse and fascinating examples of stylized behaviors by which one member of a species shows its relative dominance or submissiveness to another. There is adaptive significance to such behavioral mechanisms since they tend to minimize actual physical struggle and maintain a stable social order. For example, lower-ranking baboons step aside to let a higher-status male pass; they become nervous if he stares at them. The highest-status male can choose where he wants to sleep and whom he wants to mate with. Baboons "know their place." As with humans, rank has its privileges.

Our own stylized power rituals are usually so second-nature we aren't conscious of them. Yet there is a "dance" of power relations among humans just as among other animals. The following are some of the ways power is expressed nonverbally in humans.

Staring. In American society, it is disrespectful for a person of lower status to stare at a superior, though superiors are not bound by a similar restriction. Children, for example, are taught not to stare at parents. And it's an interesting comment on the power relationship between sexes that women are more likely to avert their gaze from men than vice versa.

Pointing. Children are also taught it's not nice to point. However, adults rarely correct each other for pointing because, more than mere etiquette, pointing seems to be a behavior that is acceptable for high-status figures or those attempting to assert dominance. An angry boss may point an index finger accusingly at an employee; few employees who wanted to keep their jobs would respond in kind. The same restrictions apply to frowning.

Touching. Invading another person's space by touching the person without invitation is acceptable when one is of superior status but not when one is of subordinate status. It's acceptable, for example, for bosses or teachers to put a hand on an employee's or a student's shoulder, respectively, but not vice versa. The disparity also applies to socioeconomic status; someone with higher socioeconomic status is more likely to touch a person of lower socioeconomic status than vice versa.

Interrupting. Virtually all of us have interrupted others, and we have all been interrupted ourselves. Again, however, the issue is who was interrupting whom? Higher-power or -status persons interrupt; lower-power or -status persons are interrupted. A vast difference in frequency of behaviors also exists between the sexes in American society. Men interrupt much more frequently than women do.

Source: D. A. Karp and W. C. Yoels, *Symbols, Selves, and Society.* New York: Lippincott, 1979.

Sources of Leader Power

Where does a leader's power come from? Do leaders *have* it, or do followers *give* it to them? As we shall see, the answer may be both . . . and more.

Something as seemingly trivial as the arrangement of furniture in an office can affect perceptions of another person's power. One vivid example comes from John Ehrlichman's book, *Witness to Power.*[12] Ehrlichman described his first visit to J. Edgar Hoover's office at the Department of

Justice. The legendary director of the FBI had long been one of the most powerful men in Washington, D.C., and as Ehrlichman's impressions reveal, Hoover took every opportunity to reinforce that image. Ehrlichman was first led through double doors into a room replete with plaques, citations, trophies, medals, and certificates jamming every wall. He was then led through a second room, similarly decorated, then into a third trophy room, and finally to a large but bare desk backed by several flags and still no J. Edgar Hoover. The guide opened a door behind the desk, and Ehrlichman went into a smaller office, which Hoover dominated from an impressive chair and desk that stood on a dais about six inches high. Erhlichman was instructed to take a seat on a lower couch, and Hoover peered down on Ehrlichman from his own loftier and intimidating place.

On a more mundane level, many people have experienced a time when they were called in to talk to a boss and left standing while the boss sat behind the desk. Probably few people in that situation misunderstand the power messages there. In addition to the factors just described, other aspects of office arrangements also can affect a leader's or follower's power. One factor is the shape of the table used for meetings. Individuals sitting at the ends of rectangular tables often wield more power, whereas circular tables facilitate communication and minimize status differentials. However, specific seating arrangements even at circular tables can affect participants' interactions; often individuals belonging to the same cliques and coalitions will sit next to each other. By sitting next to each other, members of the same coalition may exert more power as a collective group than they would sitting apart from each other. Also, having a private or more open office may not only *reflect* but also *affect* power differentials between people. Individuals with private offices can dictate to a greater degree when they want to interact with others by opening or closing their doors or by giving instructions about interruptions. Individuals with more open offices have much less power to control access to them. By being aware of dynamics like these, leaders can somewhat influence others' perceptions of their power relationship.

Prominently displaying symbols like diplomas, awards, and titles also can increase one's power. This was shown in an experiment in a college setting where a guest lecturer to several different classes was introduced in a different way to each. To one group he was introduced as a student; to other groups he was introduced as a lecturer, senior lecturer, or professor, respectively. After the presentation, when he was no longer in the room, the class estimated his height. Interestingly, the same man was perceived by different groups as increasingly taller with each increase in academic status. The "professor" was remembered as being several inches taller than the "student."[13]

This finding demonstrates the generalized impact a seemingly minor matter like one's title can have on others. Another study points out more dramatically how dangerous it can be when followers are overly responsive to the *appearances* of title and authority. This study took place in a medical setting and arose from concern among medical staff that nurses were responding mechanically to doctors' orders. A researcher made telephone calls to nurses' stations in numerous different medical wards. In each, he identified himself as a hospital physician and directed the nurse answering the phone to prescribe a particular medication for a patient in that ward. Many nurses complied with the request despite the fact it was against hospital policy to transmit prescriptions by phone. Many did so despite never even having talked to the particular "physician" before the call—and despite the fact that the prescribed medication was dangerously excessive, not to mention unauthorized. In fact, 95 percent of the nurses complied with the request made by the most easily falsifiable symbol of authority, a bare title.[14] (See also Highlight 5.2.)

Even choice of clothing can affect one's power and influence. Uniforms and other specialized clothing have long been associated with authority and status, including their use by the military, police, hospital staffs, clergy, and so on. In one experiment, people walking along a city sidewalk were stopped by someone dressed either in regular clothes or in the uniform of a security guard and told this: "You see that guy over there by the meter? He's overparked but doesn't have any change. Give him a dime!" Whereas fewer than half complied when the requestor was dressed in regular clothes, over 90 percent did when he was in uniform.[15]

He who has great power should use it lightly.
Seneca

This same rationale is given for having personnel in certain occupations (e.g., airline crew members) wear uniforms. Besides more easily identifying them to others, the uniforms increase the likelihood that in emergency situations their instructions will be followed. Similarly, even the presence of something as trivial as tattoos can affect the amount of power wielded in a group. One of the authors of this text had a friend named Del who was a manager in an international book-publishing company. Del was a former merchant marine whose forearms were adorned with tattoos. Del would often take off his suit coat and roll up his sleeves when meetings were not going his way, and he often exerted considerably more influence by merely exposing his tattoos to the rest of the group.

A final situational factor that can affect one's potential to influence others is the presence or absence of a crisis. Leaders usually can exert more power during a crisis than during periods of relative calm. Perhaps this is because during a crisis leaders are willing to draw on bases of power they normally forgo. For example, a leader who has developed close interpersonal relationships with followers generally uses her referent power to influence them. During crises or emergency situations, however, leaders may be more apt to draw on their legitimate and coercive bases of power to influence subordinates. That was precisely the finding in a study of bank managers' actions; the bank managers were more apt to use legitimate and coercive power during crises

The Milgram Studies

HIGHLIGHT 5.2

One intriguing way to understand power, influence, and influence tactics is to read a synopsis of Stanley Milgram's classic work on obedience and to think about how this work relates to the concepts and theories discussed in the present chapter. Milgram's research explored how far people will go when directed by an authority figure to do something that might injure another person. More specifically, Milgram wanted to know what happens when the dictates of authority and the dictates of one's conscience seem incompatible.

The participants were men from the communities surrounding Yale University. They were led to believe they were helping in a study concerning the effect of punishment on learning; the study's legitimacy was certainly enhanced by being conducted on the Yale campus itself. Two subjects at a time participated in the study, one as a teacher and the other as learner. The roles apparently were assigned randomly. The teacher's task was to help the learner memorize a set of word pairs by providing electric shocks whenever the learner (who would be in an adjacent room) made a mistake.

A stern experimenter described procedures and showed participants the equipment for administering punishment. This "shock generator" looked ominous, with rows of switches, lights, and warnings labeled in 15-volt increments all the way to 450 volts. Various points along the array were marked with increasingly dire warnings such as *extreme intensity* and *danger: severe.* The switch at the highest level of shock simply was marked *XXX*.

Every time the learner made a mistake, the teacher was ordered by the experimenter to administer the next-higher level of electric shock.

In actuality, there was only one true subject in the experiment—the teacher. The learner was really a confederate of the experimenter. The supposed random assignment of participants to teacher and learner conditions had been rigged in advance. The real purpose of the experiment was to assess how much electric shock the teachers would administer to the learners in the face of the latter's increasingly adamant protestations to stop. This included numerous realistic cries of agony and complaints of a heart condition—all standardized, predetermined, tape-recorded messages delivered via the intercom from the learner's to the teacher's room. If the subject (i.e., the teacher) refused to deliver any further shocks, the experimenter prodded him with comments such as "The experiment requires that you go on" and "You have no other choice; you must go on."

Before Milgram conducted his experiment, he asked mental health professionals what proportion of the subjects would administer apparently dangerous levels of shock. The consensus was that only a negligible percentage would do so, perhaps 1 or 2 percent of the population. Milgram's actual results were dramatically inconsistent with what any of the experts had predicted. Fully 70 percent of the subjects carried through with their orders, albeit sometimes with great personal anguish, and delivered the maximum shock possible—450 volts!

Source: S. Milgram, "Behavioral Study of Obedience." *Journal of Abnormal and Social Psychology* 67 (1963), pp. 371–78.

than during noncrisis situations.[16] This same phenomenon is observable in many dramatizations. In the television series *Star Trek, the Next Generation,* for example, Captain Picard normally uses his referent and expert power to influence subordinates. During emergencies, however, he will often rely on his legitimate and coercive power. Another factor may be that during crises followers are more willing to accept greater direction, control, and structure from leaders, whatever power base may be involved.

FIGURE 5.1
Sources of leader
power in the
leader–follower–
situation framework.

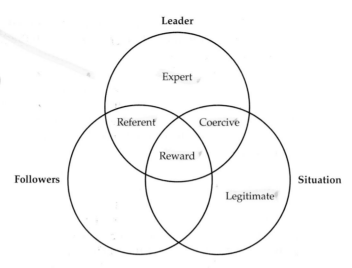

Leader

Expert

Referent

Coercive

Reward

Followers

Situation

Legitimate

A Taxonomy of Social Power

French and Raven identified five sources, or bases, of power by which an individual can potentially influence others.[17] As seen in Figure 5.1, these five sources include one that is primarily a function of the leader; one that is a function of the relationship between leaders and followers; one that is primarily a function of the leader and the situation; one that is primarily a function of the situation; and finally, one that involves aspects of all three elements. Understanding these bases of power can give leadership practitioners greater insight about the predictable effects—positive or negative—of various sorts of influence attempts. Following is a more detailed discussion of French and Raven's five bases of social power.[18]

Expert Power

Expert power is the power of knowledge. Some people are able to influence others through their relative expertise in particular areas. A surgeon may wield considerable influence in a hospital because others depend on her knowledge, skill, and judgment, even though she may not have any formal authority over them. A mechanic may be influential among his peers because he is widely recognized as the best in the city. A longtime employee may be influential because his corporate memory provides a useful historical perspective to newer personnel. Legislators who are experts in the intricacies of parliamentary procedure, athletes who have played in championship games, and soldiers who have been in combat before are valued for the lessons learned and wisdom they can share with others.

Because expert power is a function of the amount of knowledge one possesses relative to the rest of the members of the group, it is possible for followers to have considerably more expert power than leaders in certain situations. For example, new leaders often possess less knowledge of the jobs and tasks performed in a particular work unit than the followers do, and in this case the followers can potentially wield considerable influence when decisions are made regarding work procedures, new equipment, or the hiring of additional workers. Probably the best advice for leaders in this situation is to ask a lot of questions and perhaps seek additional training to help fill this knowledge gap. So long as different followers have considerably greater amounts of expert power, it will be difficult for a leader to influence the work unit on the basis of expert power alone.

Referent Power

One way to counteract the problems stemming from a lack of expertise is to build strong interpersonal ties with subordinates. **Referent power** refers to the potential influence one has due to the strength of the relationship between the leader and the followers. When people admire a leader and see her as a role model, we say she has referent power. For example, students may respond positively to advice or requests from teachers who are well liked and respected, while the same students might be unresponsive to less popular teachers. This relative degree of responsiveness is primarily a function of the strength of the relationship between the students and the different teachers. We knew one young lieutenant who had enormous referent power with the military security guards working for him due to his selfless concern for them, evident in such habits as bringing them hot chocolate and homemade cookies on their late-night shifts. The guards, sometimes taken for granted by other superiors, understood and valued the extra effort and sacrifice this young supervisor put forth for them. When Buddy Ryan was fired as head coach of the Philadelphia Eagles football team, many of the players expressed fierce loyalty to him. One said, "We'd do things for Buddy that we wouldn't do for another coach. I'd sell my body for Buddy."[19] That is referent power.

Power in an organization is the capacity generated by relationships.
Margaret A. Wheatley, futurist

Another way to look at referent power is in terms of the role friendships play in making things happen. It is frequently said, for example, that many people get jobs based on who they know, not what they know. The fact is there is some truth to that. But we think the best perspective on this issue was offered by David Campbell, who said, "It's not who you know that counts. It's what who you know *knows about you* that counts!" (personal communication).

Referent power often takes time to develop. Furthermore, it can have a downside in that a desire to *maintain* referent power may limit a leader's actions in particular situations. For example, a leader who has developed a strong relationship with a follower may be reluctant to discipline the follower for poor work or chronic tardiness, as these actions could disrupt the nature of the relationship between the leader and the follower. Thus, referent power is a two-way street; the stronger the relationship, the more influence leaders and followers exert over each other. Moreover, just as it

Michael Dell

PROFILES IN LEADERSHIP 5.1

The problem of having power you didn't know you had and might not even want.

It's hard to imagine anyone not recognizing the name Michael Dell. As founder of the computer company Dell, Inc., he created one of the most profitable computer companies in the world, with annual sales of up to $50 billion. Michael Dell has also become one of the wealthiest people in the world with a fourth place listing on the *Forbes* rich Americans list in 2005 with an estimated worth of $18 billion. In July 2007, *USA Today* published their ranking of the 25 most influential business leaders in the last 25 years. Number 17 on their list was Michael Dell.

With just $1000 in his pocket, Dell started PC's Limited in 1984. From his university dorm room Dell started building and selling personal computers from stock computer parts. In 1988 PC's Limited had a name change to Dell Computer Corporation and had an initial public offering (IPO) that valued the company at roughly $80 million. By 1992 Dell Computer Corporation was listed on the Fortune 500 list of the five hundred largest companies in the world, making Dell the youngest ever CEO to head a Fortune 500 company.

One of this book's authors worked with Michael Dell in the early 1990s (and wishes he had bought stock—but that's another story). I was chatting with Michael and describing the problems that can happen in large organizations when the leader has a lot of personal or referent power. Michael said, "Oh, I'm learning about that. We've even got a name for that problem. We call them, 'Michael saids.'"

Here's an example of a "Michael said." One afternoon, Michael was walking around the plant and stopped to ask one of the assembly employees how things were going and what could be done to make things better. The assembler said that things were great but that occasionally there was some confusion with a particular electronic component (let's call it a resistor). Sometimes the resistors were red and sometimes they were green, and the red ones looked like another component. The assembler suggested that this problem could be eliminated if this particular resistor only came in green. Michael said that seemed like a reasonable solution and passed that information along to the people who bought resistors from the suppliers.

Six months later, Michael was having a meeting in his office when someone knocked on the door. It was a rather frazzled looking person who said he was terribly sorry to interrupt but there was a crisis down in manufacturing and production was about to grind to a halt. "Why?" asked Michael. The messenger said that the supplier of green resistors had a problem and the only resistors they could get were red and they couldn't use the red resistors. "Why not?" asked Michael. The messenger looked sheepishly at his feet and passed along the bad news. They couldn't use the red ones because "Michael said we could only use green resistors."

While referent and expert power may be the best to use, as Dell and others have found out, there can be a potential downside of which you might not even be aware.

is possible for leaders to develop strong relationships with followers and, in turn, acquire more referent power, it is also possible for followers to develop strong relationships with other followers and acquire more referent power. Followers with relatively more referent power than their peers are often the spokespersons for their work units and generally have more latitude to deviate from work-unit norms. Followers with little referent power have little opportunity to deviate from group norms. For example, in an episode of the television show *The Simpsons,* Homer Simpson was fired for wearing a pink shirt to work (everybody else at the Springfield nuclear power plant had always worn white shirts). Homer was fired partly because he "was not popular enough to be different."

Legitimate Power

Legitimate power depends on a person's organizational role. It can be thought of as one's formal or official authority. Some people make things happen because they have the power or authority to do so. The boss can assign projects; the coach can decide who plays; the colonel can order compliance with uniform standards; the teacher assigns the homework and awards the grades. Individuals with legitimate power exert influence through requests or demands deemed appropriate by virtue of their role and position. In other words, legitimate power means a leader has authority because he or she has been assigned a particular role in an organization. Note that the leader has this authority only as long as he or she occupies that position and operates within the proper bounds of that role (see Profiles in Leadership 5.2 for an illustration of the egregious abuse of legitimate power).

It is important to note that legitimate authority and leadership are not the same thing. Holding a position and being a leader are not synonymous, despite the relatively common practice of calling position holders in bureaucracies the leaders. The head of an organization may be a true leader, but he also may not be. Effective leaders often intuitively realize they need more than legitimate power to be successful. Before he became president, Dwight Eisenhower commanded all Allied troops in Europe during World War II. In a meeting with his staff before the Normandy invasion, Eisenhower pulled a string across a table to make a point about leadership. He was demonstrating that just as you can pull a string, not push it, officers must lead soldiers and not push them from the rear.

It is also possible for followers to use their legitimate power to influence leaders. In these cases, followers can actively resist a leader's influence attempt by only doing work specifically prescribed in job descriptions, bureaucratic rules, or union policies. For example, many organizations have job descriptions that limit both the time spent at work and the types of tasks and activities performed. Similarly, bureaucratic rules and union policies can be invoked by followers to resist a leader's influence attempts. Often the leader will need to change the nature of his or her request or find another way to resolve the problem if these rules and policies are invoked by followers. If this is the case, then the followers will have successfully used legitimate power to influence their leader.

Reward Power

Reward power involves the potential to influence others due to one's control over desired resources. This can include the power to give raises, bonuses, and promotions; to grant tenure; to select people for special

Mike Nifong

PROFILES IN LEADERSHIP 5.2

On March 14, 2006, a 28-year-old dancer told Durham, N.C., police she was raped by three men after performing at a party in a house rented by Duke University lacrosse team members. Durham County District Attorney Mike Nifong charged Reade Seligmann, Collin Finnerty, and David Evans, white students at the university, with kidnapping and raping the black exotic dancer. Nifong quickly propelled himself into the headlines by giving interviews in which he called the players "hooligans" and said he would not allow Durham to become known as home to "a bunch of lacrosse players from Duke raping a black girl."

The case played out on the national stage as a morality tale of class, race, and sex. Nifong's actions brought an avalanche of actions against the accused students and their associates. The media rushed to judgment. Civil rights leaders held rallies charging racism. The Duke president, Richard Brodhead, in an abandonment of normal jurisprudence, canceled the lacrosse season and fired the coach. After all this and more, the truth began to emerge.

It turns out that Nifong had grossly abused the power of his office. Apparently more concerned about an upcoming election than justice, Nifong lied to a judge and withheld details of DNA evidence from defense attorneys that indicated none of the players' genetic material was found on their accuser. Evidence later showed that two of the three accused students were not even present at the time of the attack.

The *Orlando Sentinel,* in an editorial, stated the following: "The unraveling of the sexual assault case against three Duke lacrosse players is a sobering reflection of how ego and bravado trumped the pursuit of justice. The blame falls squarely on Durham County District Attorney Mike Nifong, whose ethical standards were so out of whack that he is now facing violations that could get him disbarred. Another prosecutor who took over the case concluded not only that the evidence was insufficient, but that no attack took place. There was much more than wholesome entertainment going on in March of 2006 when exotic dancers visited a team party. To accuse young men of bad judgment is one thing. But to spin it into rape, kidnapping, and sexual-offense charges without sufficient evidence is disgraceful."

Charges against the men were dropped in April 2007. North Carolina Attorney General Roy Cooper declared the men "innocent" victims of a "rogue prosecutor" making a "tragic rush to accuse." But the problems for Nifong are far from over. Shortly before publication of this textbook edition, Nifong was stripped of his law license after a disciplinary committee found him guilty of multiple ethical violations when he prosecuted three Duke University lacrosse players on rape charges ultimately found to be false.

When legitimate power is abused, not only does it have an adverse impact on the person engaging in the abuse, but on the entire system granting the legitimate power in the first place. Such was the concern of the North Carolina Bar Association.

"There is no discipline short of disbarment that would be appropriate in this case," Lane Williamson, chairman of the North Carolina State Bar Disciplinary Hearing Commission, said in announcing Nifong's disbarment. "His judgment was so clouded by his own selfishness that he wandered off the path of justice . . . " According to Douglas Brocker, an attorney for the North Carolina Bar Association, "Mr. Nifong engaged in a systematic abuse of prosecutorial trust, power, and discretion."

assignments or desirable activities; to distribute desired resources like computers, offices, parking places, or travel money; to intercede positively on another's behalf; to recognize with awards and praise; and so on. Many corporations use rewards extensively to motivate employees. At

McDonald's, for example, there is great status accorded the All-American Hamburger Maker, the cook who makes the fastest, highest-quality hamburgers in the country. At individual fast-food restaurants, managers may reward salespeople who handle the most customers during rush periods. Tupperware holds rallies for its salespeople. Almost everyone wins something, ranging from pins and badges to lucrative prizes for top performers.[20] Schools pick teachers of the year, and professional athletes are rewarded by selection to all-star teams for their superior performance.

The potential to influence others through the ability to administer rewards is a joint function of the leader, the followers, and the situation. Leaders vary considerably in the types and frequency in which they mete out rewards, but the position they fill also helps to determine the frequency and types of rewards administered. For example, employees of the month at Kentucky Fried Chicken are not given new cars; the managers of these franchises do not have the resources to offer such awards. Similarly, leaders in other organizations are limited to some extent in the types of awards they can administer and the frequency with which they can do so. Nevertheless, leadership practitioners can enhance their reward power by spending some time reflecting on the followers and the situation. Often a number of alternative or innovative rewards can be created, and these rewards, along with ample doses of praise, can help a leader overcome the constraints his or her position puts on reward power.

Although using the power to administer rewards can be an effective way to change the attitudes and behaviors of others, there are several situations where a leader's use of reward power can be problematic. For example, the perception that a company's monetary bonus policy is handled equitably may be as important in motivating good work (or avoiding morale problems) as the amount of the bonus itself. Moreover, a superior may mistakenly assume that a particular reward is valued when it is not. This would be the case if a particular subordinate were publicly recognized for her good work when she actually dislikes public recognition. Leadership practitioners can avoid the latter problem by developing good relationships with subordinates and administering rewards that they, not the leader, value. Another potential problem with reward power is that it may produce compliance but not other desirable outcomes like commitment.[21] In other words, subordinates may perform only at the level necessary to receive a reward and may not be willing to put forth the extra effort needed to make the organization better. An overemphasis on rewards as payoff for performance may also lead to resentment and feelings by workers of being manipulated, especially if it occurs in the context of relatively cold and distant superior–subordinate relationships. Extrinsic rewards like praise, compensation, promotion, privileges, and time off may not have the same effects on behavior as intrinsic rewards such as feelings of accomplishment, personal growth, and development. There is evidence that under some conditions extrinsic

> *Unreviewable power is the most likely to self-indulge itself and the least likely to engage in dispassionate self-analysis.*
>
> **Warren E. Burger, U.S. Supreme Court, Chief Justice, 1969–1986**

rewards can decrease intrinsic motivation toward a task and make the desired behavior less likely to persist when extrinsic rewards are not available.[22,23] Overemphasis on extrinsic rewards may instill an essentially contractual or economic relationship between superiors and subordinates, diluting important aspects of the relationship like mutual loyalty or shared commitment to higher ideals.[24]

All these cautions about reward power should not cloud its usefulness and effectiveness, which is very real. As noted previously, top organizations make extensive use of both tangible and symbolic rewards in motivating their workers. Furthermore, some of the most important rewards are readily available to all leaders—sincere praise and thanks to others for their loyalty and work. The bottom line is that leadership practitioners can enhance their ability to influence others based on reward power if they (*a*) determine what rewards are available, (*b*) determine what rewards are valued by their subordinates, and (*c*) establish clear policies for the equitable and consistent administration of rewards for good performance.

Finally, because reward power is partly determined by one's position in the organization, some people may believe followers have little, if any, reward power. This may not be the case. If followers have control over scarce resources, then they may use the administration of these resources as a way of getting leaders to act in the manner they want. Moreover, followers may reward their leader by putting out a high level of effort when they feel their leader is doing a good job, and they may put forth less effort when they feel their leader is doing a poor job. By modifying their level of effort, followers may in turn modify a leader's attitudes and behaviors. And when followers compliment their leader (e.g., for running a constructive meeting), it is no less an example of reward power than when a leader compliments a follower. Thus, leadership practitioners should be aware that followers can also use reward power to influence leaders.

You do not lead by hitting people over the head—that's assault, not leadership.
       Dwight D. Eisenhower

Coercive Power

Coercive power, the opposite of reward power, is the potential to influence others through the administration of negative sanctions or the removal of positive events. In other words, it is the ability to control others through the fear of punishment or the loss of valued outcomes. Like reward power, coercive power is partly a function of the leader, but the situation often limits the coercive actions a leader can take. Examples of coercive power include police giving tickets for speeding, the army court-martialing AWOL soldiers, a teacher detaining disruptive students after school, employers firing lazy workers, and parents spanking children.[25] Even presidents resort to their coercive powers. Historian Arthur Schlesinger, Jr., for example, described Lyndon Johnson as having a

BEETLE BAILEY © King Features Syndicate.

"devastating instinct for the weaknesses of others." Lyndon Johnson was familiar and comfortable with the use of coercion; he once told a White House staff member, "Just you remember this. There's only two kinds at the White House. There's elephants and there's ants. And I'm the only elephant."[26]

Coercive power, like reward power, can be used appropriately or inappropriately. It is carried to its extreme in harsh and repressive totalitarian societies. One of the most tragic instances of coercive power was in the cult led by Jim Jones, which tragically and unbelievably self-exterminated in an incident known as the Jonestown massacre.[27] Virtually all of the 912 who died there drank, at Jones's direction, from large vats of a flavored drink containing cyanide. The submissiveness and suicidal obedience of Jones's followers during the massacre were due largely to the long history of rule by fear Jones had practiced. For example, teenagers caught holding hands were beaten, and adults judged slacking in their work were forced to box for hours in marathon public matches against as many as three or four bigger and stronger opponents. Jim Jones ruled by fear, and his followers became self-destructively compliant.

Perhaps the preceding example is so extreme that we can dismiss its relevance to our own lives and leadership activities. On the other hand, it does provide a dramatic reminder that reliance on coercive power has inherent limitations and drawbacks. This is not to say the willingness to use disciplinary sanctions is never necessary. Sometimes it is. Informal coercion, as opposed to the threat of formal punishment, can also be used to change the attitudes and behaviors of others. Informal coercion is usually expressed implicitly, and often nonverbally, rather than explicitly. It may be the pressure employees feel to donate to the boss's favorite charity, or it may be his glare when they bring up an unpopular idea. One of the most common forms of coercion is simply a superior's temperamental outbursts. The intimidation caused by a leader's poorly controlled anger is usually, in its long-term effects, a dysfunctional style of behavior for leaders.

It is also possible for followers to use coercive power to influence their leader's behavior. For example, a leader may be hesitant to take disciplinary action against a large, emotionally unstable follower. Followers can threaten leaders with physical assaults, industrial sabotage, or work slowdowns and strikes, and these threats can serve to modify a leader's behavior. In all likelihood, followers will be more likely to use coercive power to change their leader's behavior if they have a relatively high amount of referent power with their fellow co-workers. This may be particularly true if threats of work slowdowns or strikes are used to influence a leader's behavior.

Concluding Thoughts about French and Raven's Power Taxonomy

On the basis of all this, can we reach any conclusions about what base of power is best for a leader to use? As you might have anticipated, we must say that's an unanswerable question without knowing more facts about a particular situation. For example, consider the single factor of whether or not a group is facing a crisis. This might affect the leader's exercise of power simply because leaders usually can exert *more* power during crises than during periods of relative calm. Perhaps this is because during a crisis leaders are willing to draw on bases of power they normally forgo. For example, a leader who has developed close interpersonal relationships with followers generally uses her referent power to influence them, but during crises or emergency situations leaders may be more apt to draw on their legitimate and coercive bases of power to influence subordinates. That was precisely the finding in a study of bank managers' actions; the bank managers were more apt to use legitimate and coercive power during crises than during noncrisis situations.[28] Furthermore, it may be that during crises followers are more *eager* to receive direction and control from leaders.

But can't we make *any* generalizations about using various sources of power? Actually, there has been considerable research looking at French and Raven's ideas, and generally the findings indicate that leaders who relied primarily on referent and expert power had subordinates who were more motivated and satisfied, were absent less, and performed better.[29] However, Yukl[30] and Podsakoff and Schriesheim[31] have criticized these findings, and much of their criticism centers on the instrument used to assess a leader's bases of power. Hinkin and Schriesheim[32] developed an instrument that overcomes many of the criticisms, and future research should more clearly delineate the relationship between the five bases of power and various leadership effectiveness criteria.

Even though much of the research to date about the five bases of power may be flawed, four generalizations about power and influence still seem warranted. First, effective leaders typically take advantage of *all* their sources of power. Effective leaders understand the relative advantages and disadvantages of different sources of power, and they selectively emphasize one or another depending on their particular objectives in a given situation. Second, whereas leaders in well-functioning organizations have strong influence over their subordinates, *they are also open to being influenced by them.* High degrees of reciprocal influence between leaders and followers characterize the most effective organizations.[33] Third, leaders vary in the extent to which they share power with subordinates. Some leaders seem to view their power as a fixed resource that, when shared with others (like cutting a pie into pieces), reduces their own portion. They see power in zero-sum terms. Other leaders see power as an expandable pie. They see the possibility of increasing a subordinate's power without reducing their own. Needless to say, which view a leader subscribes to can have a major impact on the leader's support for power-sharing activities like delegation and participative management. A leader's support for power-sharing activities (or, in today's popular language, *empowerment*) is also affected by the practice of holding leaders responsible for subordinates' decisions and actions as well as their own. It is, after all, the coach or manager who often gets fired when the team loses.[34,35] Fourth, effective leaders generally work to increase their various power bases (i.e., whether expert, referent, reward, or legitimate) or become more willing to use their coercive power.

Leader Motives

Thus far we have been looking at how different *sources* of power can affect others, but that's only one perspective. Another way of looking at the relationship between power and leadership involves focusing on the individual leader's personality. We will look most closely at the role personality plays in leadership in an upcoming chapter, but it will be nonetheless useful now to briefly examine how all people (including leaders) vary in their personal motivation to have or wield power.

People vary in their motivation to influence or control others. McClelland[36] called this the **need for power,** and individuals with a high need for power derive psychological satisfaction from influencing others. They seek positions where they can influence others, and they are often involved concurrently in influencing people in many different organizations or decision-making bodies. In such activities they readily offer ideas, suggestions, and opinions, and also seek information they can use in influencing others. They are often astute at building trusting relationships and assessing power networks, though they can also be quite outspoken and forceful. They value the tangible signs of their authority and status as well as the more intangible indications of others' deference to them. Two different ways of expressing the need for power have been identified: **personalized power** and **socialized power.** Individuals who have a high need for personalized power are relatively selfish, impulsive, uninhibited, and lacking in self-control. These individuals exercise power for their own self-centered needs, not for the good of the group or the organization. Socialized power, on the other hand, implies a more emotionally mature expression of the motive. Socialized power is exercised in the service of higher goals to others or organizations and often involves self-sacrifice toward those ends. It often involves an empowering, rather than an autocratic, style of management and leadership.

Although the need for power has been measured using questionnaires and more traditional personality inventories, McClelland and his associates have used the Thematic Apperception Test (TAT) to assess need for power. The TAT is a **projective personality test** consisting of pictures such as a woman staring out a window or a boy holding a violin. Subjects are asked to make up a story about each picture, and the stories are then interpreted in terms of the strengths of various needs imputed to the characters, one of which is the need for power. Since the pictures are somewhat ambiguous, the sorts of needs projected onto the characters are presumed to reflect needs (perhaps at an unconscious level) of the storyteller. Stories concerned with influencing or controlling others would receive high scores for the need for power.

The need for power has been found to be positively related to various leadership effectiveness criteria. For example, McClelland and Boyatzis[37] found the need for power to be positively related to success for nontechnical managers at AT&T, and Stahl[38] found that the need for power was positively related to managers' performance ratings and promotion rates. In addition, Fodor[39] reported that small groups of ROTC students were more likely to successfully solve a subarctic survival situation if their leader had a strong need for power. Although these findings appear promising, several cautions should be kept in mind. First, McClelland and Boyatzis[40] also reported that the need for power was unrelated to the success of technical managers at AT&T. Apparently, the level of knowledge (i.e., expert power) played a more important role in the success of the technical managers versus the nontechnical managers. Second, McClelland[41] concluded that, although some need for power was necessary for leadership potential, successful leaders also have the ability to inhibit their manifestation of this need. Leaders who are relatively uninhibited in their need for power will act like a dictator; such individuals use power impulsively, to manipulate or control others, or to achieve at another's expense. Leaders with a high need for power but low activity inhibition may be successful in the short term, but their followers, as well as the remainder of the organization, may pay high costs for this success. Some of these costs may include perceptions by fellow members of the organization that they are untrustworthy, uncooperative, overly competitive, and looking out primarily for themselves. Finally, it may be worth pointing out that some followers have a high need for power too. This can lead to tension between leader and follower when a follower with a high need for power is directed to do something.

[handwritten margin note: May create hazards for the longterm.]

Individuals vary in their motivation to manage, just as in their need for power. Miner[42] described **motivation to manage** in terms of six composites:

- Maintaining good relationships with authority figures.
- Wanting to compete for recognition and advancement.
- Being active and assertive.
- Wanting to exercise influence over subordinates.
- Being visibly different from followers.
- Being willing to do routine administrative tasks.

Like McClelland, Miner also used a projective test to measure a person's motivation to manage. Miner's Sentence Completion Scale (MSCS) consists of a series of incomplete sentences dealing with the six components described above (e.g., "My relationship with my boss . . . "). Respondents are asked to complete the sentences, which are then scored according to established criteria. The overall composite MSCS score (though not component scores) has consistently been found to predict leadership success in hierarchical or bureaucratic organizations.[43] Thus, individuals who maintained respect for authority figures, wanted to be recognized, acted assertively, actively influenced subordinates, maintained "psychological distance" between themselves and their followers, and readily took on routine administrative tasks were more apt to be successful in bureaucratic organizations. However, Miner also claimed that different qualities were needed in flatter, nonbureaucratic organizations, and his[44] review of the MSCS supports this view. Findings concerning both the need for power and the motivation to manage have several implications for leadership practitioners. First, not all individuals like being leaders. One reason may be that some have a relatively low need for power or motivation to manage. Because these scores are relatively stable and fairly difficult to change, leaders who do not enjoy their role may want to seek positions where they have fewer supervisory responsibilities.

Second, a high need for power or motivation to manage does not guarantee leadership success. The situation can play a crucial role in determining whether the need for power or the motivation to manage is related to leadership success. For example, McClelland and Boyatzis[45] found the need for power to be related to leadership success for nontechnical managers only, and Miner[46] found motivation to manage was related to leadership success only in hierarchical or bureaucratic organizations.

Third, in order to be successful in the long term, leaders may have to have both a high need for socialized power and a high level of activity inhibition. Leaders who impulsively exercise power merely to satisfy their own selfish needs will probably be ineffective in the long term. Finally, it is important to remember that followers, as well as leaders, differ in the need for power, activity inhibition, and motivation to manage. Certain followers may have stronger needs or motives in this area. Leaders may need to behave differently toward these followers than they might toward followers having a low need for power or motivation to manage.

Influence Tactics

Whereas power is the capacity or potential to influence others, influence tactics are the actual behaviors used by an agent to change the attitudes, opinions, or behaviors of a target person. Kipnis and his associates accomplished much of the early work on the types of influence tactics one person uses to influence another.[47] Various instruments have been developed to study influence tactics, but the Influence Behavior Questionnaire, or IBQ,[48] seems to be the most promising. Here is a detailed discussion of the different influence tactics assessed by the IBQ.

Types of Influence Tactics

The IBQ is designed to assess nine types of influence tactics, and its scales provide us with a convenient overview of various methods of influencing others. **Rational persuasion** occurs when an agent uses logical arguments or factual evidence to influence others. An example of rational persuasion would be when a politician's advisor explains how demographic changes in the politician's district make it important for the politician to spend relatively more time in the district seeing constituents than she has needed to in the recent past. Agents make **inspirational appeals** when they make a request or proposal designed to arouse enthusiasm or emotions in targets. An example here might be when a minister makes an impassioned plea to members of his congregation about the good works which could be accomplished if a proposed addition to the church were built. **Consultation** occurs when agents ask targets to participate in planning an activity. An example of consultation would be if the minister in the preceding example established a committee of church members to help plan the layout and uses of that new church addition. In this case the consultative work might not only lead to a better building plan but also *strengthen member commitment* to the very idea of a new addition. **Ingratiation** occurs when the agent attempts to get you in a good mood before making a request. A familiar example here would be a salesperson's good-natured or flattering banter with you before you make a decision about purchasing a product. Agents use **personal appeals** when they ask another to do a favor out of friendship. A sentence that opens with, "Bill, we've known each other a long time and I've never asked anything of you before" represents the beginning of a personal appeal, whereas influencing a target through the exchange of favors is labeled **exchange.** If two politicians agree to vote for each other's pet legislation despite minor misgivings about each other's bills, that is exchange. **Coalition tactics** are different from consultation in that they are used when agents seek the aid or support of others to influence the target. A dramatic example of coalition tactics occurs when several key significant people in an alcoholic's life (e.g., spouse, children, employer, neighbor) agree to confront the alcoholic in unison about the many dimensions of his problem. Threats or persistent reminders used to influence targets are known as **pressure tactics.** A judge who gives a convicted prisoner a suspended sentence but tells him to consider the suspension a "sword hanging over your head" if he breaks the law again is using pressure tactics. Finally, **legitimizing tactics** occur when agents make requests based on their position or authority. A principal may ask a teacher to be on the school's curriculum committee, and the teacher may accede to the request despite reservations just because it is the principal's prerogative to appoint any teacher to that role. In practice, of course, actual tactics often reflect combinations of these different approaches. Rarely, for example, is an effective appeal purely inspirational, without any rational elements at all.

Influence Tactics and Power

As alluded to throughout this chapter, a strong relationship exists between the relative power of agents and targets and the types of influence tactics used. Because leaders with relatively high amounts of referent power have built up close relationships with followers, they may be more able to use a wide variety of influence tactics to modify the attitudes and behaviors of their followers. For example, leaders with a lot of referent power could use inspirational appeals, consultations, ingratiation, personal appeals, exchanges, and even coalition tactics to increase the amount of time a particular follower spends doing work-related activities. Note, however, that leaders with high referent power generally do not use legitimizing or pressure tactics to influence followers since, by threatening followers, leaders risk some loss of referent power. Leaders who have only coercive or legitimate power may be able to use only coalition, legitimizing, or pressure tactics to influence followers.

Other factors also can affect the choice of influence tactics.[49] People typically use hard tactics (i.e., legitimizing or pressure tactics) when an influencer has the upper hand, when she anticipates resistance, or when the other person's behavior violates important norms. People typically use soft tactics (e.g., ingratiation) when they are at a disadvantage, when they expect resistance, or when they will personally benefit if the attempt is successful. People typically use rational tactics (i.e., the exchange and rational appeal) when parties are relatively equal in power, when resistance is not anticipated, and when the benefits are organizational as well as personal. Other studies, too, have shown that influence attempts based on factual, logical analyses are the most frequently reported method by which middle managers exert lateral influence[50] and upward influence.[51] Other important components of successful influence of one's superiors include thoroughly preparing beforehand, involving others for support (i.e., coalition tactics), and persisting through a combination of approaches.[52]

Findings about who uses different tactics, and when, provide interesting insights into the influence process. It is clear that one's influence tactic of choice depends on many factors, including intended outcomes and one's power relative to the target person. Whereas it may not be very surprising that people select influence tactics as a function of their power relationship with another person, it is striking that the relationship holds true so universally across different social domains. The relationship holds true for business executives, for parents and children, and for spouses. There is a strong tendency for people to resort to hard tactics whenever they have an advantage in clout if other tactics fail to get results.[53] As the bank robber Willie Sutton once said, "A gun and a smile are more effective than a smile by itself." This sentiment is apparently familiar to bank managers, too. The latter reported greater satisfaction in handling subordinates' poor performance when they were relatively more punishing.[54] Highlight 5.3 offers thoughts on how men and women managers sometimes use different techniques in "managing upward."

Don't threaten. I know it's done by some of our people, but I don't go for it. If people are running scared, they're not going to make the right decisions. They'll make decisions to please the boss rather than recommend what has to be done.

Charles Pilliod

(i.e., "legitimizing or pressure tactics")

Gender Differences in Managing Upward: How Male and Female Managers Get Their Way

HIGHLIGHT 5.3

Both male and female managers in a Fortune 100 company were interviewed and completed surveys about how they influence upward—how they influence their own bosses. The results generally supported the idea that female managers' influence attempts showed greater concern for others, while male managers' influence attempts showed greater concern for self. Female managers were more likely to act with the organization's broad interests in mind, consider how others felt about the influence attempt, involve others in planning, and focus on both the task and interpersonal aspects of the situation. Male managers, on the other hand, were more likely to act out of self-interest, show less consideration for how others might feel about the influence attempt, work alone in developing their strategy, and focus primarily on the task alone.

One of the most surprising findings of the study was that, contrary to prediction, female managers were less likely than male managers to compromise or negotiate during their influence attempts. The female managers were actually more likely to persist in trying to persuade their superiors, even to the point of open opposition. At first this may seem inconsistent with the idea that the female managers'

influence style involved greater concern for their relatedness to others. However, it does seem consistent with the higher value placed by the women managers on involvement. Perhaps female managers demonstrate more commitment to their issue, and greater self-confidence that they are doing the "right thing," precisely because they have interacted with others in the organization more already and know they have others' support.

While male and female managers emphasized different influence techniques, it is important to note neither group overall was more effective than the other. Nonetheless, there may be significant implications of the various techniques for a manager's career advancement. At increasingly higher management levels in an organization, effectiveness may be defined primarily by its fit with the organization's own norms and values. Managers whose style matches most closely that of their superior's may have an advantage in evaluations and promotion decisions. This may be a significant factor for women, given the highly skewed representation of males in the most senior executive ranks.

Source: K. E. Lauterbach and B. J. Weiner, "Dynamics of Upward Influence: How Male and Female Managers Get Their Way." *Leadership Quarterly* 7, no. 1 (1996), pp. 87–107.

It is not power that corrupts, but fear. Fear of losing power corrupts those who wield it and fear of the scourge of power corrupts those who are subject to it.

Aung San Suu Kyi

Although hard tactics can be effective, relying on them can change the way we see others. This was demonstrated in an experiment wherein leaders' perceptions and evaluations of subordinates were assessed after they exercised different sorts of authority over the subordinates.[55] Several hundred business students acted as managers of small work groups assembling model cars. Some of the students were told to act in an authoritarian manner, exercising complete control over the group's work; others were told to act as democratic leaders, letting group members participate fully in decisions about the work. As expected, authoritarian leaders used more hard tactics, whereas democratic leaders influenced subordinates more through rational methods. More interesting was the finding that subordinates were evaluated by the two types of leaders in dramatically different ways even though the subordinates of both types did equally good work. Authoritarian leaders judged their subordinates as less motivated, less skilled, and less suited for promotion. Apparently, bosses who use hard tactics to control others' behavior tend not to attribute any resultant good performance to the subordinates themselves. Ironically, the act of using hard tactics leads to negative attributions about others, which, in turn, tend to corroborate the use of hard tactics in the first place.

All forms of tampering with human beings, getting at them, shaping them against their will to your own pattern, all thought control and conditioning, is, therefore, a denial of that in men which makes them men and their values ultimate.

**A. A. Berle, Jr.,
writer on
corporations**

Finally, we should remember that using influence tactics can be thought of as a social skill. Choosing the right tactic to use may not always be enough to ensure good results; the behavior must be *skillfully executed.* We are not encouraging deviousness or a manipulative attitude toward others, merely recognizing the obvious fact that clumsy attempts to influence do often come across as phoney. They may be counterproductive in the end. See Highlight 5.4 for some interesting ways skills are applied in the political arena.

A Concluding Thought about Influence Tactics

In the above discussion, an implicit lesson for leaders is the value of being conscious of what influence tactics one uses and what effects are typically associated with each tactic. Knowledge of such effects can help a leader make better decisions about her manner of influencing others. It might also be helpful for leaders to think more carefully about why they (pay attention to)

To Be or Not to Be . . . a Porcupine

HIGHLIGHT 5.4

We said before that there are no simple recipes for leadership. This is perfectly evident in the various ways power and influence are exercised in the halls of the U.S. Congress. In *The Power Game,* author Hedrick Smith offers numerous examples of how Washington, D.C., actually works. For example, it is true that interpersonal relationships play a key part in one's effectiveness, but there are many paths to interpersonal power and influence in government, as the following anecdotes point out.

Barney Frank, a Democratic congressman from Massachusetts, likens success in the House of Representatives to high school. Nobody in the House can give any other member an order, not even the speaker of the house. Neither can anyone be fired except by his or her own constituencies. That means, therefore, that those in Congress become influential by persuading people and having others

respect but not resent them. In that sense it's like high school. Sometimes, however, it may pay to be *unlikable,* at least in some situations. Former senator (and later secretary of state) Ed Muskie had a reputation for being a "porcupine," for being difficult in the conference committees where final versions of legislation were hammered out. A former staff member said Muskie was the best porcupine of them all because nobody wanted to tangle with him. Muskie will "be gross. He'll smoke a god-awful cigar. He'll just be difficult, cantankerous." One of the reasons Muskie was so successful as a legislator was precisely that he could be nearly impossible to deal with. People would rather ignore him, try to avoid fights or confrontations with his notorious temper. Muskie knew how to be a porcupine, and he used that behavior to advantage in authoring critical legislation.

Source: H. Smith, *The Power Game.* New York: Random House, 1988.

believe a particular influence tactic might be effective. Research indicates that some reasons for selecting among various possible influence tactics lead to successful outcomes more frequently than others. More specifically, thinking an act would improve an employee's self-esteem or morale was frequently associated with successful influence attempts. On the other hand, choosing an influence tactic because it followed company policy and choosing one because it was a way to put a subordinate in his place were frequently mentioned as reasons for unsuccessful influence attempts.[56] In a nutshell, these results suggest that leaders should pay attention not only to the actual influence tactics they use—to *how* they are influencing others—but also to *why* they believe such methods are called for. It is perhaps an obvious but nonetheless important conclusion to reach from these results that influence efforts intended to build others up more frequently lead to positive outcomes than influence efforts intended to put others down.

Summary	This chapter has defined power as the capacity or potential to exert influence, influence tactics as the behaviors used by one person to modify the attitudes and behaviors of another, and influence as the degree of change in a person's attitudes, values, or behaviors as the result of another's influence tactic. Because power, influence, and influence tactics play such important roles in the leadership process, this chapter provides ideas to help leaders improve their effectiveness. By reflecting on their different bases of power, leaders may better understand how they can affect followers and even expand their power. The five bases of power also offer clues as to why subordinates are able to influence leaders and successfully resist leaders' influence attempts.

Leaders also may gain insight into why they may not enjoy certain aspects of their responsibilities by reflecting on their own need for power or motivation to manage; they may also better understand why some leaders exercise power selfishly by considering McClelland's concepts of personalized power and activity inhibition. Leaders can improve their effectiveness by finding ways to enhance their idiosyncratic credit and not permitting in-group and out-group rivalries to develop in the work unit.

Although power is an extremely important concept, having power is relatively meaningless unless a leader is willing to exercise it. The exercise of power occurs primarily through the influence tactics leaders and followers use to modify the attitudes and behaviors of each other. The type of influence tactics used seems to depend on the amount of different types of power possessed, the degree of resistance expected, and the rationale behind the different influence tactics. Because influence tactics designed to build up others are generally more successful than those that tear down others, leadership practitioners should always consider why they are using a particular influence attempt before they actually |

use it. By carefully considering the rationale behind the tactic, leaders may be able to avoid using pressure and legitimizing tactics and to find ways to influence followers that build them up rather than tear them down. Being able to use influence tactics that modify followers' attitudes and behaviors in the desired direction at the same time they build up followers' self-esteem and self-confidence should be a skill all leaders strive to master.

Key Terms

power, *135*
influence, *136*
influence tactics, *136*
pecking order, *138*
expert power, *142*
referent power, *143*
legitimate power, *145*
reward power, *145*
coercive power, *148*

need for power, *152*
personalized power, *152*
socialized power, *152*
projective personality test, *152*
motivation to manage, *153*
rational persuasion, *155*

inspirational appeals, *155*
consultation, *155*
ingratiation, *155*
personal appeals, *155*
exchange, *155*
coalition tactics, *155*
pressure tactics, *155*
legitimizing tactics, *155*

Questions

1. The following questions all pertain to the Milgram studies (Highlight 5.2).
   a. What bases of power were available to the experimenter, and what bases of power were available to the subjects?
   b. Do you think subjects with a low need for power would act differently from those subjects with a high need for power? What about subjects with differing levels of the motivation to manage?
   c. What situational factors contributed to the experimenter's power?
   d. What influence tactics did the experimenter use to change the behavior of the subjects, and how were these tactics related to the experimenter's power base?
   e. What actually was influenced? In other words, if influence is the change in another's attitudes, values, or behaviors as the result of an influence tactic, then what changes occurred in the subject as the result of the experimenter's influence tactics?
   f. Many people have criticized the Milgram study on ethical grounds. Assuming that some socially useful information was gained from the studies, do you believe this experiment could or should be replicated today?

2. Some definitions of leadership exclude reliance on formal authority or coercion (i.e., certain actions by a person in authority may work but should not be considered leadership). What are the pros and cons of such a view?

3. Does power, as Lord Acton suggested, tend to "corrupt" the power holder? If so, what are some of the ways it happens? Is it also possible subordinates are corrupted by a superior's power? How? Or is it even possible that superiors can be corrupted by a subordinate's power?

4. Some people say it dilutes a leader's authority if subordinates are allowed to give feedback to the leader concerning their perceptions of the leader's performance. Do you agree?

5. Is leadership just another word for influence? Can you think of some examples of influence that you would *not* consider leadership?

Activity

This activity will demonstrate how the five bases of power are manifest in behavior. Write down the five bases of power on the board or put them on an overhead. Break students into five groups, and give each group a 3 × 5 card that lists one of the five bases of power. Give the group 10 minutes to plan and practice a 1-minute skit which will be presented to the rest of the class. The skit should demonstrate the base of power listed on the 3 × 5 card. After the skit is presented, the remaining groups should guess which base of power is being used in the skit. As an alternative, you might choose a project for out-of-class work. Another variation is to assign the groups the task of finding a 3–4 minute segment from a movie or video representing a base of power and bring that in to the class.

Minicase

"The Prime Minister's Powerful Better Half"

Ho Ching's power has been recognized by many. As chief executive officer of Temasek Holdings, she ranked number 18 on a list of Asia's Most Powerful Business People and number 24 on Forbes's list of the World's Most Powerful Women. How does a shy, Stanford-educated electrical engineer end up with this kind of power? Ho was a government scholar who started off in civil service and ended up working for the Defense Ministry in Singapore. There she met and married Lee Hsien Loong, Singapore's current prime minister and the son of Lee Kwan Yew—one of modern Singapore's founding fathers. Ho's experience, education, and connections led to her appointment as chief executive of Temasek where she oversees a portfolio worth over $50 billion and influences many of Singapore's leading companies.

Temasek Holdings was established in 1974 in an attempt by the Singapore government to drive industrialization. Through Temasek Holdings the Singapore government took stakes in a wide range of companies including the city-state's best-known companies: Singapore Airlines, Singapore Telecommunications, DBS Bank, Neptune Orient Lines, and Keppel Corp. The company's Web site describes Temasek's "humble roots during a turbulent and uncertain time" and its commitment "to building a vibrant future [for Singapore] through successful enterprise." Ho's appointment to Temasek in May 2002 caused some controversy; as prime minister her husband has a supervisory role over the firm. Ho denies any conflict of interest:

> The issue of conflict does not arise because there are no vested interests. Our goal is to do what makes sense for Singapore, I don't always agree with him (Mr. Lee) and he doesn't always agree with me. We have a healthy debate on issues.

In her role as CEO, Ho is pushing for a more open policy and an aggressive drive into the Asian market. Under Ho's leadership Temasek has decided to publicly disclose its annual report with details of its performance—details that have formerly remained private and been known only to Temasek executives.

Ho is concentrating on broadening Temasek's focus beyond Singapore, most recently opening an office in India. At a recent conference of top Indian companies, Ho appealed to investors to look to India for opportunities for Asian growth:

> Since the Asian Financial Crisis in 1997, the word *Asia* had lost a bit of its sparkle. But that sparkle is beginning to return. In the '60s and '70s, the Asia economic miracle referred to East Asia, specifically Japan. The '70s and '80s saw the emergence of the four Asian Tigers of Korea, Taiwan, Hong Kong, and Singapore.

> Now is India's turn to stir, standing at an inflexion point, after 10 years of market liberalisation and corporate restructuring. Since 1997, Singapore's trade with India grew by 50 percent, or a respectable CAGR of about 7.5 percent. Confidence is brimming in India, and Indian companies began to reach out boldly to the world over the last five years.

> All these waves of development have shown that Asia, with a combined population of 3 billion, has been resilient. If Asia continues to work hard and work smart, honing her competitive strengths and leveraging on her complementary capabilities across borders, the outlook in the next decade or two looks very promising indeed.

1. We have described *power* as the capacity to cause change and *influence* as the degree of actual change in a target's behaviors. Ho Ching's power as a leader has been recognized by many, but would you describe Ho Ching as an influential leader? Why?
2. Based on the excerpt from Ho Ching's speech, what type of tactics does she use to influence the behavior of others?
3. Ho Ching has been named one of the most powerful leaders in Asia. What are her major sources of power?

Sources: http://www.fastcompany.com/online/13/womenofpr.html;
http://www.forbes.com/finance/lists/11/2004/LIR.jhtml?passListId=11&passYear=2004&

passListType=Person&uniqueId=OO5O&datatype=Person;
http://www.businessweek.com/magazine/content/02_36/b3798161.htm;
http://www.laksamana.net/vnews.cfm?ncat=31&news_id=5292;
http://in.rediff.com/money/2004/apr/03spec.htm; http://www.theaustralian.news.com.au/
common/story_page/0%2C5744%2C10427548%255E2703%2C00.html;
http://in.news.yahoo.com/040812/137/2fgoc.html

Chapter Notes

1. Hill, N. "Self-Esteem: The Key to Effective Leadership." *Administrative Management* 40, no. 9 (1985), pp. 71–76.

2. Donno, D. "Introduction." In *The Prince and Selected Discourses: Machiavelli.* Ed. and trans. D. Dunno. New York: Bantam, 1966.

3. Gardner, J. W. *On Leadership.* New York: Free Press, 1990. ———. The Tasks of Leadership. Leadership paper no. 2. Washington, DC: Independent Sector, 1986.

4. Hinkin, T. R., and C. A. Schriesheim. "Development and Application of New Scales to Measure the French and Raven (1959) Bases of Social Power." *Journal of Applied Psychology* 74 (1989), pp. 561–67.

5. Burns, J. M. *Leadership.* New York: Harper & Row, 1978.

6. House, R. J. "Power in Organizations: A Social Psychological Perspective." Unpublished manuscript, University of Toronto, 1984.

7. Bass, B. M. *Bass and Stogdill's Handbook of Leadership.* 3rd ed. New York: Free Press, 1990.

8. Gardner, J. W. *On Leadership.* New York: Free Press, 1990. ———. The Tasks of Leadership. Leadership paper no. 2. Washington, DC: Independent Sector, 1986.

9. Gardner, J. W. *On Leadership.* New York: Free Press, 1990. ———. The Tasks of Leadership. Leadership paper no. 2. Washington, DC: Independent Sector, 1986.

10. Schriesheim, C. A., and T. R. Hinkin. "Influence Tactics Used by Subordinates: A Theoretical and Empirical Analysis and Refinement of the Kipnis, Schmidt, and Wilkinson Subscales." *Journal of Applied Psychology* 75 (1990), pp. 246–57.

11. Bass, B. M. *Bass and Stogdill's Handbook of Leadership.* 3rd ed. New York: Free Press, 1990.

12. Ehrlichman, J. *Witness to Power.* New York: Simon & Schuster, 1982.

13. Wilson, P. R. "The Perceptual Distortion of Height as a Function of Ascribed Academic Status." *Journal of Social Psychology* 74 (1968), pp. 97–102.

14. Cialdini, R. B. *Influence.* New York: William Morrow, 1984.

15. Bickman, L. "The Social Power of a Uniform." *Journal of Applied Social Psychology* (1974), pp. 47–61.

16. Mulder, M., R. D. de Jong, L. Koppelar, and J. Verhage. "Power, Situation, and Leaders' Effectiveness: An Organizational Study." *Journal of Applied Psychology* 71 (1986), pp. 566–70.

17. French, J., and B. H. Raven. "The Bases of Social Power." In *Studies of Social Power.* Ed. D. Cartwright. Ann Arbor, MI: Institute for Social Research, 1959.

18. French, J., and B. H. Raven. "The Bases of Social Power." In *Studies of Social Power.* Ed. D. Cartwright. Ann Arbor, MI: Institute for Social Research, 1959.

19. Associated Press, January 9, 1991.

20. Peters, T. J., and R. H. Waterman. *In Search of Excellence.* New York: Harper & Row, 1982.

21. Yukl, G. *Leadership in Organizations.* 2nd ed. Englewood Cliffs, NJ: Prentice Hall, 1989.

22. Deci, E. L. "Effects of Contingent and Noncontingent Rewards and Controls on Intrinsic Motivation." *Organizational Behavior and Human Performance* 22 (1972), pp. 113–20.

23. Ryan, E. M., V. Mims, and R. Koestner. "Relation of Reward Contingency and Interpersonal Context to Intrinsic Motivation: A Review and Test Using Cognitive Evaluation Theory." *Journal of Personality and Social Psychology* 45 (1983), pp. 736–50.

24. Wakin, M. M. "Ethics of Leadership." In *Military Leadership.* Eds. J. H. Buck and L. J. Korb. Beverly Hills, CA: Sage, 1981.

25. Klein, S. B. *Learning.* 2nd ed. New York: McGraw-Hill, 1991.

26. Barnes, F. "Mistakes New Presidents Make." *Reader's Digest,* January 1989, p. 43.

27. Conway, F., and J. Siegelman. *Snapping.* New York: Delta, 1979.

28. Mulder, M., R. D. de Jong, L. Koppelar, and J. Verhage. "Power, Situation, and Leaders' Effectiveness: An Organizational Study." *Journal of Applied Psychology* 71 (1986), pp. 566–70.

29. Yukl, G. A. *Leadership in Organizations.* 1st ed. Englewood Cliffs, NJ: Prentice Hall, 1981.

30. Ibid.

31. Podsakoff, P. M., and C. A. Schriesheim. "Field Studies of French and Raven's Bases of Power: Critique, Reanalysis, and Suggestions for Future Research." *Psychological Bulletin* 97 (1985), pp. 387–411.

32. Hinkin, T. R., and C. A. Schriesheim. "Development and Application of New Scales to Measure the French and Raven (1959) Bases of Social Power." *Journal of Applied Psychology* 74 (1989), pp. 561–67.

33. Yukl, G. *Leadership in Organizations.* 2nd ed. Englewood Cliffs, NJ: Prentice Hall, 1989.

34. Hollander, E. P., and L. R. Offermann. "Power and Leadership in Organizations." *American Psychologist* 45 (1990), pp. 179–89.

35. Pfeffer, J. "The Ambiguity of Leadership." In *Leadership: Where Else Can We Go?,* Eds. M. W. McCall, Jr., and M. M. Lombardo. Durham, NC: Duke University Press, 1977.

36. McClelland, D. C. *Power: The Inner Experience.* New York: Irvington, 1975.

37. McClelland, D. C., and R. E. Boyatzis. "Leadership Motive Pattern and Long-Term Success in Management." *Journal of Applied Psychology* 67 (1982), pp. 737–43.

38. Stahl, M. J. "Achievement, Power, and Managerial Motivation: Selecting Managerial Talent with the Job Choice Exercise." *Personnel Psychology* 36 (1983), pp. 775–89.

39. Fodor, E. "Motive Pattern as an Influence on Leadership in Small Groups." Paper presented at the meeting of the American Psychological Association, New York, August 1987.

40. McClelland, D. C., and R. E. Boyatzis. "Leadership Motive Pattern and Long-Term Success in Management." *Journal of Applied Psychology* 67 (1982), pp. 737–43.

41. McClelland, D. C. *Human Motivation.* Glenview, IL: Scott Foresman, 1985.

42. Miner, J. B. "Student Attitudes toward Bureaucratic Role Prescriptions and the Prospects for Managerial Shortages." *Personnel Psychology* 27 (1974), pp. 605–13.

43. Miner, J. B. "Twenty Years of Research on Role Motivation Theory of Managerial Effectiveness." *Personnel Psychology* 31 (1978), pp. 739–60.

44. Miner, J. B. "Twenty Years of Research on Role Motivation Theory of Managerial Effectiveness." *Personnel Psychology* 31 (1978), pp. 739–60.

45. McClelland, D. C., and R. E. Boyatzis. "Leadership Motive Pattern and Long-Term Success in Management." *Journal of Applied Psychology* 67 (1982), pp. 737–43.

46. Miner, J. B. "Twenty Years of Research on Role Motivation Theory of Managerial Effectiveness." *Personnel Psychology* 31 (1978), pp. 739–60.

47. Kipnis, D., and S. M. Schmidt. *Profiles of Organizational Strategies.* Form M. San Diego, CA: University Associates, 1982.

48. Yukl, G. A., R. Lepsinger, and T. Lucia. "Preliminary Report on the Development and Validation of the Influence Behavior Questionnaire." In *Impact of Leadership.* Eds. K. E. Clark, M. B. Clark, and D. P. Campbell. Greensboro, NC: Center for Creative Leadership, 1992.

49. Kipnis, D., and S. M. Schmidt. "The Language of Persuasion." *Psychology Today* 19, no. 4 (1985), pp. 40–46.

50. Keys, B., T. Case, T. Miller, K. E. Curran, and C. Jones. "Lateral Influence Tactics in Organizations." *International Journal of Management* 4 (1987), pp. 425–37.

51. Case, T., L. Dosier, G. Murkison, and B. Keys. "How Managers Influence Superiors: A Study of Upward Influence Tactics." *Leadership and Organization Development Journal* 9, no. 4 (1988), pp. 4, 25–31.

52. Case, T., L. Dosier, G. Murkison, and B. Keys. "How Managers Influence Superiors: A Study of Upward Influence Tactics." *Leadership and Organization Development Journal* 9, no. 4 (1988), pp. 4, 25–31.

53. Kipnis, D., and S. M. Schmidt. "The Language of Persuasion." *Psychology Today* 19, no. 4 (1985), pp. 40–46.

54. Green, S. G., G. T. Fairhurst, and B. K. Snavely. "Chains of Poor Performance and Supervisory Control." *Organizational Behavior and Human Decision Processes* 38 (1986), pp. 7–27.

55. Kipnis, D. "Technology, Power, and Control." *Research in the Sociology of Organizations* 3 (1984a), pp. 125–56.

56. Dosier, L., T. Case, and B. Keys. "How Managers Influence Subordinates: An Empirical Study of Downward Influence Tactics." *Leadership and Organization Development Journal* 9, no. 5 (1988), pp. 22–31.

Chapter 6

Leadership and Values

Introduction

In the previous chapter, we examined many different facets of power and its use in leadership. The topics in this chapter go hand in hand with understanding the role of power in leadership. That is because leaders can use power for good or ill, and the leader's personal values may be one of the most important determinants of how power is exercised or constrained. For example, a political leader may be able to stir a group into a frenzy (and become even more popular) by identifying a scapegoat to blame for a community's or nation's problems, but would it be right? Is it *ever* right for a political leader to stir a populace into a frenzy? And what standards should govern the application of such power? Or, a person may be promoted to leadership positions of ever-greater responsibility and reward, but at a cost of broken relationships in his family life; would *you* choose that trade-off?

The mere possession of power, of any kind, leads inevitably to ethical questions about how that power should and should not be used. The challenge of leadership becomes even more complex when we consider how *in a* individuals of different backgrounds, cultures, and nationalities may hold *divers* quite different values yet be thrown into increasingly closer interaction *and* with each other as our world becomes both smaller and more diverse. This *glo ba* chapter will explore these fascinating and important aspects of leadership. *environm*

Leadership and "Doing the Right Things"

In Chapter 1, we referred to a distinction between leaders and managers that says leaders do the right things whereas managers do things right. But just what does the "right things" mean? Does it mean the "morally right" things? The "ethically right" things? The "right things" for the company to be successful? And who's to say what the "right things" are?

Leaders face dilemmas that require choices between competing sets of values and priorities, and the best leaders recognize and face them with a commitment to doing what is right, not just what is expedient. Of course, the phrase *doing what is right* sounds deceptively simple. Sometimes it will take great moral courage to do what is right, even when the right action seems clear. At other times, though, leaders face complex challenges that lack simple black-and-white answers. Whichever the case, leaders set a moral example to others that becomes the model for an entire group or organization, for good or bad. Leaders who themselves do not honor truth do not inspire it in others. Leaders mostly concerned with their own advancement do not inspire selflessness in others. Leaders should internalize a strong set of **ethics**, principles of right conduct or a system of moral values.

Both Gardner[1] and Burns[2] have stressed the centrality and importance of the moral dimension of leadership. Gardner said leaders ultimately must be judged on the basis of a framework of values, not just in terms of their effectiveness. He put the question of a leader's relations with his or her followers or constituents on the moral plane, arguing (with the philosopher Immanuel Kant) that leaders should always treat others as ends in themselves, not as objects or mere means to the leader's ends (which, however, does not necessarily imply that leaders need to be gentle in interpersonal demeanor or "democratic" in style). Burns took an even more extreme view regarding the moral dimension of leadership, maintaining that leaders who do not behave ethically do not demonstrate true leadership.

Whatever "true leadership" means, most people would agree that at a minimum it would be characterized by a high degree of trust between leader and followers. Bennis and Goldsmith[3] describe four qualities of leadership that engender trust. These qualities are vision, empathy, consistency, and integrity. First, we tend to trust leaders who create a compelling *vision:* who pull people together on the basis of shared beliefs and a common sense of organizational purpose and belonging. Second, we tend to trust leaders who demonstrate *empathy* with us—who show they understand the world as we see and experience it. Third, we trust leaders who are *consistent.* This does not mean that we only trust leaders whose positions never change, but that changes are understood as a process of evolution in light of relevant new evidence. Fourth, we tend to trust leaders whose *integrity* is strong, who demonstrate their commitment to higher principles through their actions.

Another important factor impacting the degree of trust between leaders and followers involves fundamental assumptions people make about human nature. Several decades ago, Douglas McGregor[4] explained different styles of managerial behavior on the basis of people's implicit attitudes about human nature, and his work remains quite influential today.

Leadership cannot just go along to get along . . . Leadership must meet the moral challenge of the day.

Jesse Jackson

McGregor identified two contrasting sets of assumptions people make about human nature, calling these **Theory X** and **Theory Y**.

In the simplest sense, Theory X reflects a more pessimistic view of others. Managers with this orientation rely heavily on coercive, external-control methods to motivate workers such as pay, disciplinary techniques, punishments, and threats. They assume people are not naturally industrious or motivated to work. Hence, it is the manager's job to minimize the harmful effects of workers' natural laziness and irresponsibility by closely overseeing their work and creating external incentives to do well and disincentives to avoid slacking off. Theory Y, on the other hand, reflects a view that most people are intrinsically motivated by their work. Rather than needing to be coaxed or coerced to work productively, such people value a sense of achievement, personal growth, pride in contributing to their organization, and respect for a job well done. Peter Jackson, the director of the *Lord of the Rings* film trilogy, seems to exemplify a Theory Y view of human nature. When asked, "How do you stand up to executives?" Jackson answered, "Well, I just find that most people appreciate honesty. I find that if you try not to have any pretensions and you tell the truth, you talk to them and you treat them as collaborators, I find that studio people are usually very supportive."

But are there practical advantages to holding a Theory X or Theory Y view? Evidently there are. There is evidence that success more frequently comes to leaders who share a positive view of human nature. Hall and Donnell[5] reported findings of five separate studies involving over 12,000 managers that explored the relationship between managerial achievement and attitudes toward subordinates. Overall, they found that managers who strongly subscribed to Theory X beliefs were far more likely to be in their lower-achieving group.

One behavior common to many good leaders is that they tend to align the values of their followers with those of the organization or movement; they make the links between the two sets more explicit. But just what are values? How do values and ethical behavior develop? Is one person's set of standards better or higher than another's? These are the sorts of questions we will address in this section.

What Are Values?

Values are "constructs representing generalized behaviors or states of affairs that are considered by the individual to be important."[6] When Patrick Henry said, "Give me liberty, or give me death," he was expressing the value he placed upon political freedom. The opportunity to constantly study and learn may be the fundamental value or "state of affairs" leading a person to pursue a career in academia. Someone who values personal integrity may be forced to resign from an unethical company. Thus, values play a fairly central role in one's overall psychological makeup and can affect behavior in a variety of situations. In work settings, values can affect decisions about joining an organization, organizational commitment, relationships with co-workers, and decisions about leaving an organization.[7] It is important for leaders to realize that individuals in the same work unit can have considerably different values, especially since we cannot see values directly. We can only make inferences about people's values based on their behavior.

Some of the major values that may be considered important by individuals in an organization are listed in Table 6.1. The instrumental values found in Table 6.1 refer to modes of behavior, and the terminal values refer to desired end states.[8] For example, some individuals value equality, freedom, and a comfortable life above all else; others may believe that family security and salvation are important goals to strive for. In terms of instrumental values, such individuals may think that it is important always to act in an ambitious, capable, and honest manner, whereas others may think it is important only to be ambitious and capable. We should add that the instrumental and terminal values in Table 6.1 are only a few of those Rokeach has identified.

Are There Generational Differences in Values?

Various researchers have said that the pervasive influence of broad forces like major historical events and trends, technological changes, and economic conditions tend to create common value systems among people growing up at a particular time that distinguish them from people who grow up at different times.[9–11] They attribute much of the misunderstanding that may exist between older leaders and younger followers to the fact that their basic value systems were formulated during quite different social and cultural conditions, and these analyses offer a helpful perspective for understanding how differences in values can add tension to the interaction between some leaders and followers.

Zemke is another researcher who has looked at differences in values across generations, and how those value differences impact their approaches to work and leadership.[12] Following is his delineation of four generations of workers, each one molded by distinctive experiences during their critical developmental periods.

TABLE 6.1
People Vary in the Relative Importance They Place on Values Like the Following

Source: Adapted from M. Rokeach, *The Nature of Human Values.* New York: Free Press, 1973.

Terminal Values	Instrumental Values
An exciting life	Being courageous
A sense of accomplishment	Being helpful
Family security	Being honest
Inner harmony	Being imaginative
Social recognition	Being logical
Friendship	Being responsible

The Veterans (1922–1943): Veterans came of age during the Great Depression and World War II, and represent a wealth of lore and wisdom. They've been a stabilizing force in organizations for decades, even if they are prone to digressions about "the good old days."

The Baby Boomers (1942–1960): These were the postwar babies who came of age during violent social protests, experimentation with new lifestyles, and pervasive questioning of establishment values. But they're graying now, and don't like to think of themselves as "the problem" in the workplace even though they frequently are. Boomers still have passion about bringing participation, spirit, heart, and humanity to the workplace and office. They're also concerned about creating a level playing field for all, but they hold far too many meetings for the typical Gen Xer.

The Gen Xers (1960–1980): Gen Xers grew up during the era of the Watergate scandal, the energy crisis, higher divorce rates, MTV, and corporate downsizing; many were latchkey kids. As a group they tend to be technologically savvy, independent, and skeptical of institutions and hierarchy. They are entrepreneurial and they embrace change. Having seen so many of their parents work long and loyally for one company only to lose their job to downsizing, Xers don't believe much in job security; to an Xer, job security comes from having the kinds of skills that make you attractive to an organization. Hence, they tend to be more committed to their vocation than to any specific organization. In fact, the free-agency concept born in professional sports also applies to Xers, who are disposed to stay with an organization until a better offer comes along. Among the challenges they present at work is how to meet their need for feedback despite their dislike of close supervision. Xers also seek balance in their lives more than preceding generations; they work to live rather than live to work. (Also see Highlight 6.1.)

The Nexters (1980): This is *your* generation, so any generalizations we make here are particularly risky. In general, however, Nexters share an optimism born, perhaps, from having been raised by parents devoted to the task of bringing their generation to adulthood; they are the children of soccer moms and Little League dads. They doubt the wisdom of traditional racial and sexual categorizing, perhaps not unexpected from a generation rich with opportunities like having Internet pen pals in Asia whom they can interact with any time of the day or night.

Researchers at the *Center for Creative Leadership* have also been interested in Gen Xers and how their values impact the leadership process at work. One clear finding from this research involved the distinctively different view of authority held by Xers than previous generations. "While past generations might have at least acknowledged positional authority, this new generation has little respect for and less interest in leaders who are unable to demonstrate that they can personally produce. In other words, this generation doesn't define leading as sitting in meetings and making profound vision statements, but instead as eliminating obstacles and giving employees what they need to work well and comfortably."[13] Gen Xers expect managers to "earn their stripes," and not be rewarded with leadership responsibilities merely because of seniority. Often that attitude is interpreted as an indication of disrespect toward elders in general, and bosses in particular. It may be more accurate, however, to characterize the attitude as one of skepticism rather than disrespect. Such skepticism could have arisen from the fact that Generation X grew up during a time when there were relatively few heroes or leaders it could call its own. It also might have arisen from growing up in an environment of such pervasive marketing that anything smacking of "hype" is met with suspicion.[14] That skepticism is also evident in the fact that 53 percent of them believe that the soap opera *General Hospital* will be around longer than Medicare, and that a majority of them are more likely to believe in UFOs than that Social Security will last until their retirement.[15]

Question authority, but raise your hand first.
Bob Thaues

Lest we overemphasize the significance of intergenerational differences, however, we should consider the results of a scientific sampling of over 1,000 people living in the United States which found *little* evidence of a generation gap in basic values.

Indeed, the director of one of the largest polling organizations in the world called the results some of the most powerful he had seen in 30 years of public-opinion research. They showed, he said, that even though young people have different tastes, they do *not* buy into a different set of values than their elders.[16] Considering the weight of scholarly research on value differences across generations, it's been said that the idea of a generational gap in values may be more popular culture than good social science.[17]

A relatively new approach to generational differences is based on the idea that it's not just external events per se (e.g., war, depression) that shape a generation's attitudes and values, but also what phase of life a particular generation is in when those events occur.[18] Events will impact generations differently depending not only on the nature of the event itself but also whether those events impact a generation during its youth, young adulthood, midlife, or elderhood. From this perspective, a generation isn't like the generation that raised it so much as like the one that *shaped the generation that raised them.* This pattern has been revealed in research showing that certain generational archetypes recur with striking regularity in American history, and in other societies around the world as well. The four recurring generational archetypes are:

Prophet generations, born *after* a great war or other crisis when there is rejuvenated community life and consensus around a new societal order.

Nomad generations, born *during* a cultural renewal, when social idealism and spiritual agendas among the young foster a revolt against the established institutional order.

Main Events in the Lives of Gen Xers

HIGHLIGHT 6.1

A number of historical events over the past three and a half decades have had significant impacts on the lives and worldviews of today's emerging leaders.

GENERAL

1968 Martin Luther King, Jr., assassinated

1969 U.S. lands on the moon

1973 Watergate scandal begins

1975 Vietnam war ends

1976 Energy crisis

1979 Iran hostage crisis

1981 Center for Disease Control's first published report on AIDS

1981 Reagan assassination attempt

1984 Ozone depletion detected

1984 Extensive corporate downsizing begins

1986 Space shuttle disaster

1986 Chernobyl disaster

1989 Berlin Wall falls

1990 Persian Gulf War

1991 USSR dissolves

2001 Terrorist attacks on World Trade Center

2003 Enron and other corporate scandals

TECHNOLOGICAL

1971 Intel's first chip developed

1972 First e-mail management program

1974 Videocassette recorder introduced on the consumer market

1975 Microsoft founded

1975 Personal computer introduced on the consumer market

1979 First commercial cellular telephone system

1980 CNN begins 24-hour broadcasting

1981 MTV launched

1983 C Shugs@holly.colostate.eduompact discs mass marketed

1991 World Wide Web launched

Source: Adapted from B. Baldwin and S. Trovas, *Leadership in Action* 21 (6), January/February 2002, p. 17.

Hero generations are born *after* a spiritual awakening, leading to a time of individual pragmatism, self-reliance, laissez-faire, and national (or sectional or ethnic) chauvinism.

Artist generations are born *during* a great war or other crisis, when worldly dangers force a relatively simple focus on essentials, and public consensus and personal sacrifice prevail.

Here's a specific illustration of how different generational archetypes interact with each other: Boomers in middle age (a prophet generation focused on values, individualism, and inner life) have been raising Nexters (a hero generation, focused on actions, community, and institutional life). Based on the experience of Boomers and Xers, it's sometimes been assumed that each generation of young adults will be more alienated and risk prone than the one before. However, according to this model, many Nexters will instead want to correct for the impracticality of Boomers and the lack of discipline among Xers. Here are some other predictions for what the Nexter generation might look like as its members move through their twenties:

Nexters

- They will revive the ideal of the common man, whose virtue is defined less by self than by a collegial center of gravity.
- They will develop community norms based on rules, standards, and personal responsibility.
- Their lives will become more mannerly, structured, and civic-minded.
- In college, they will return to spirited affirmation of their campus and broader community, favoring social rituals and community building over personal and more individualized and private spirituality.
- They will create new ways of thinking about public cyberspace, using information to empower groups. They'll be engaged in essentially continuous interaction with peers using new informational capabilities to create new ways of social networking.

Moral Reasoning

Up to this point the discussion has focused on the *content* of a person's values. Equally important, however, is the question of how one *thinks about* value-laden issues or ethical dilemmas. **Moral reasoning** refers to the process leaders use to make decisions about ethical and unethical behaviors. Moral reasoning does not refer to the morality of individuals per se, or their espoused values, but rather to the *manner by which they solve moral problems*. Values play a key role in the moral reasoning process since value differences among individuals often result in different judgments regarding ethical and unethical behavior. Kohlberg theorized that people progress through a series of developmental stages in their moral reasoning.[19] Each stage reflects a more cognitively complex way of analyzing moral situations than the preceding one, and the sequence of stages is fixed, or invariant. Moral reasoning is assessed using ethical dilemmas such as whether a man would be morally justified in stealing an overpriced drug to save his dying wife, and an individual's stage of moral reasoning is based on the *way the answer is explained* rather than the particular answer given. Two individuals, for example, may each argue that the husband was morally wrong to steal the drug—even in those extenuating circumstances—yet offer qualititatively different kinds of reasons as to why the action was wrong. Similarly, two individuals may each argue the husband was morally justified in stealing the drug, yet offer different reasons as to why it was justifiable. The focus is on the reasoning process rather than on the decision per se.

That distinction may be clearer by looking in greater detail at different ways of evaluating the husband's behavior. The table on page 174 outlines Kohlberg's six stages of moral development, as well as how a person at each stage might evaluate the husband's behavior. Note that the six stages themselves are organized into three higher-order levels: the **preconventional level**, in which a person's criteria for moral behavior are based primarily on *self-interest* such as avoiding punishment or being

Developmental Levels and Stages of Moral Reasoning

Source: Adapted from L. Kohlberg, *The Psychology of Moral Development: Essays on Moral Development.* Vol. 2. San Francisco: Harper & Row, 1984.

Descriptions of Stages	Examples of Moral Reasoning in Support of Stealing the Drug	Examples of Moral Reasoning Against Stealing the Drug
Preconventional Level *Stage 1*: "Bad" behavior is that which is punished.	"If you let your wife die, you will get in trouble."	"If you steal the drug, you will get in trouble."
Stage 2: "Good" behavior is that which is concretely rewarded.	"If you do happen to get caught, you could give the drug back and not get much of a sentence."	"Even if you were caught and didn't get much of a sentence, your wife would probably die while you were in jail and it wouldn't do you much good."
Conventional Level *Stage 3*: "Good" behavior is that which is approved by others; "bad" behavior is that which is disapproved by others.	"If you don't steal the drug, you'll never be able to look anyone in the face again."	"Everyone would know you are a thief."
Stage 4: "Good" behavior conforms to standards set by social institutions; transgressions lead to feelings of guilt or dishonor.	"If you have any sense of honor, you'd do your duty as a husband and steal the drug."	"If you stole the drug, however desperate you felt, you'd never be able to look at yourself in the mirror again."
Postconventional Level *Stage 5*: "Good" behavior conforms to community standards set through democratic participation; concern with maintaining self-respect and the respect of equals.	"If you don't steal the drug you'd lose your own respect and everyone else's too."	"We've all agreed to live by common rules, and any form of stealing breaks that bond."
Stage 6: "Good" behavior is a matter of individual conscience based on responsibly chosen commitments to ethical principles.	"If you didn't steal it, you might have satisfied the letter of the law, but you wouldn't have lived up to your own standards of conscience."	"Maybe others would have approved of your behavior, but stealing the drug would still have violated your own conscience and standards of honesty."

rewarded; the **conventional level**, in which the criteria for moral behavior are based primarily on *gaining others' approval* and *behaving* (as the name implies) *conventionally*; and the **postconventional level**, in which the criteria are based on *universal, abstract principles* which may even transcend the laws of a particular society. Finally, to say moral development progresses in invariant stages does not imply that all individuals actually achieve the highest stages. Few adults do. How do you think, in that regard, a political leader at the conventional level may differ in behavior (e.g., in the "stands" he or she takes on issues) from one at the postconventional level?

But what is it that actually moves an individual from one level to the next? In summarizing several decades of research on moral judgment, Rest highlighted fundamental, dramatic, and extensive changes which occur in young adulthood (the twenties and thirties) in how people define what is morally right or wrong.[20] Rest noted that formal education is strongly correlated with these, though no specific academic or personal experiences proved pivotal. Moral judgment is part of each person's general personal and social development, and those individuals whose moral judgment develop most are those who "love to learn, seek new challenges, who enjoy intellectually stimulating environments, who are reflective, who make plans and set goals, who take risks, and who take responsibility for themselves in the larger social context of history and institutions, and who take responsibility for themselves and their environs." At the same time, deliberate curricular attempts to affect moral judgment have been shown to be effective.

You may find it interesting to reflect on the moral issues raised in Highlight 6-2. Obviously, different individuals may have quite different points of view on these ethical questions.

Values and Leadership

How Values Impact Leadership

So near is a falsehood to truth that a wise man would do well not to trust himself on the narrow edge.

Cicero

Because values play such a central role in a person's psychological makeup, they have a profound effect on leadership. First and foremost, it is important to understand that values play a key role in the choices made by leaders.[21] Values are a primary determinant in what data are reviewed by leaders and how they define problems. Leaders with strong Commercial values are likely to focus on financial results and shortcomings; those with strong Aesthetic values are more likely to review quality indicators. Values also affect the solutions generated and the decisions made about problems. For example, followers with strong Security values will offer solutions that help ensure a stable and predictable work environment. But if the leader had a strong Recognition value, she might be more likely to choose a riskier solution that would thrust her in the spotlight. In addition, values often influence a leader's perceptions of individual and organizational successes as well as the manner in which these successes are achieved. Leaders with strong Science values will define organizational success differently than those with strong Power values.

What Would You Do?

HIGHLIGHT 6.2

Here are several situations in which values play a large part in determining your response. How would you act in each one, and by what principles or reasoning process do you reach each decision?

- Would you vote for a political candidate who was honest, competent, and agreed with you on most issues if you also knew that person was alcoholic, sexually promiscuous, and twice divorced?

- Assume that as a teenager you smoked marijuana once or twice, but that was years ago. Would you answer truthfully on an employment questionnaire if it asked whether you had ever used marijuana?

- Your military unit has been ambushed by enemy soldiers and suffered heavy casualties. Several of your soldiers have been captured, but you also captured one of the enemy soldiers. Would you torture the captured enemy soldier if that were the only way of saving the lives of your own soldiers?

- Terrorists have captured a planeload of tourists and threatened to kill them unless ransom demands are met. You believe that meeting the ransom demands is likely to lead to the safe release of those passengers, but also likely to inspire future terrorist acts. Would you meet the terrorists' demands (and probably save the hostages) or refuse to meet the terrorists' demands (and reduce the likelihood of future incidents)?

- If you were an elementary school principal, would you feel it was part of your school's responsibility to teach moral values, or only academic subject matter?

- Assume that you have been elected to your state's legislature, and that you are about to cast the deciding vote in determining whether abortions will be legally available to women in your state. What would you do if your own strong personal convictions on this issue were contrary to the views of the majority of the people you represent?

Source: Adapted from G. Stock, *The Book of Questions: Business, Politics, and Ethics.* New York: Workman Publishing, 1991.

Values also help leaders choose right from wrong, and between ethical and unethical behavior. Along these lines, research has shown that leaders with strong Commercial values and weak Altruistic values are often seen as greedy and selfish.[22] Many of these leaders are so obsessed with wealth and material possessions that they think nothing of "cooking the books" in order to make money. Unfortunately, many of the high-visibility examples from Enron, Arthur Andersen, Tyco, WorldCom, Charter Communications, Computer Associates, Parmalat, Ahold NV, Boeing, Royal Dutch Shell, and the investment banking and mutual fund industries seem to confirm the notion that many top-level executives are willing to do whatever it takes in order to make money (see Highlight 6.3). Even those executives with strong Commercial and weak Altruistic values who do not engage in organizationally delinquent behaviors think nothing of cutting thousands of jobs in order to improve "shareholder value." These same executives, who also happen to own a considerable number of shares in their companies, often run their companies into the ground but personally make tens to hundreds of millions of dollars in the process (examples include the Qwest acquisition of US West or the AOL–Time Warner merger).

Values not only affect the choices leaders make about what is and what is not important, they also have an impact on the choices leaders make about direct reports. Leaders tend to like followers with similar values and dislike those with dissimilar values. If you knew nothing about a person except his or her values, and those values were similar to your own, then it would be very likely that you would like this individual. The opposite is also true. Because unstructured interviews are a very common selection technique (see Chapter 4), in most cases these are more valued than competence-based assessments. Although hiring direct reports with similar values will make the decision-making process much easier, in many cases groups with identical values can sometimes miss the forest for the trees. For example, one of the authors worked with the top nine leaders of a billion dollar health care system in the United Kingdom. The system was $50,000,000 in debt, and the nine leaders were likely to get sacked if they did not turn their financial problems around by the end of the year. None of the nine leaders had strong Commercial or Power values, but they all had strong Affiliation and Altruistic values. Their meetings focused entirely on patient care and staff morale and they did little real work to address their budget shortfall. Consequently, many of these leaders were let go at the end of the year. The key point here is that it is important for leaders to surround themselves with followers who possess divergent values. This will likely cause more tension and conflict within the group, but

Ask Yourself These Questions

HIGHLIGHT 6.3

An important foundation of behaving ethically at work is to become more self-conscious of one's own ethical standards and practices. The National Institute of Ethics uses the following questions in its Self-Evaluation to facilitate that kind of self-reflection:

- How do I decide ethical dilemmas?
- Do I have set ethical beliefs or standards?
- If so, do I live by these beliefs or standards?
- How often have I done something that I am ashamed of?
- How often have I done things that I am proud of?
- Do I admit my mistakes?
- What do I do to correct mistakes that I make?

- Do I often put the well-being of others ahead of mine?
- Do I follow the golden rule?
- Am I honest?
- Do people respect my integrity?
- List the three best things that have ever happened to me.
- What is the most dishonest thing I have ever done?
- Did I ever rectify the situation?
- What is the most honest thing that I have ever done?

Source: N. Trautman, *Integrity Leadership.* Longwood, FL: National Institute of Ethics, 1998.

this approach will also make it more likely that a broader variety of problems and solutions will be brought forward for discussion.[23]

What values are most important to the leadership process? There is no definitive answer to that question; many different value schemas have been proposed, and many different instruments to measure values have been developed. For purposes of illustration we'll look at one of these, presented in Table 6.2.

TABLE 6.2
Key Work Values

Source: Adapted from J. Hogan and R. T. Hogan, *Motives, Values and Preferences Inventory Manual.* Tulsa, OK: Hogan Assessment Systems, 1996.

Recognition: Leaders with strong Recognition values, such as politicians, want to stand out and be the center of attention. They value fame, visibility, and publicity, and are motivated by public recognition and seek jobs where they will be noticed.

Power: Leaders with strong Power values enjoy competition and being seen as influential, and drive hard to make an impact. They value achievement and accomplishment and are motivated to work in jobs where they can achieve, get ahead, and succeed.

Hedonism: Leaders with strong Hedonism values like to have fun at work and entertain others. They are motivated by pleasure, variety, and excitement, and can often be found in the entertainment, hospitality, recreation, sports, sales, or travel industries.

Altruistic: Leaders with strong Altruism values, such as health care or educational leaders, believe in actively helping others who are less fortunate. They are motivated to help the needy and powerless and to improve society, and believe in social justice.

Affiliation: Leaders with strong Affiliation values, such as sales leaders, find being around and working with others to be highly motivating. They value meeting new people, networking, and working in team environments.

Tradition: Leaders with strong Tradition values, such as religious or military leaders, believe in family values and codes and conduct, and value moral rules and standards. These individuals are motivated to live a lifestyle that is in accordance with religious or institutional customs and standards of behavior.

Security: Leaders with strong Security values, such as bureaucratic leaders, are motivated to work in stable, predictable, and risk-free environments. They create structure and processes in order to minimize uncertainty and avoid criticism.

Commerce: Leaders with strong Commerce values, such as business leaders, are motivated by financial success. They are constantly on the lookout for new business opportunities and are concerned about wealth and material possessions.

Aesthetics: Leaders with strong Aesthetics values, such as film directors, musical conductors, or marketing leaders, are motivated to work in environments that place a premium on experimentation, artistic expression, and creative problem solving. They place more importance on appearance or quality than on quantity.

Science: Leaders with strong Science values, such as research and development leaders, enjoy learning, digging deeply into problems, and keeping up to date on technology. They enjoy analyzing data to get at the truth.

In looking over the values in Table 6.2, it is important to note that there is nothing right or wrong, or good or bad, about any of these work values per se; some leaders think making money is very important, other leaders believe that their most important responsibility is helping others, and other leaders may believe being in the limelight or living a life according to one's religious beliefs to be very important. Leaders are motivated to act in ways consistent with their values, and they typically spend most of their time engaged in activities that are consistent with their values. Similarly, as individuals, leaders and followers are not particularly motivated to work on activities that are inconsistent with their values.

In most cases leaders possess several key values. The example in Figure 6.1 shows the results of a formal values assessment for a Vice President of Product Development for a leadership consulting firm. This individual is responsible for a team that creates, markets, sells, and delivers various psychological assessment and development products for leaders. Figure 6.1 indicates that she believes that working in a team environment (Affiliation), making a difference and having an impact (Power), and doing creative, high-quality work (Aesthetics) are extremely important. Conversely, having the opportunity to work in a stable and predictable environment (Security), make money (Commerce), or do research (Science) are not nearly as important to or motivating for her. Another aspect of individual values is addressed in Highlight 6.6.

FIGURE 6.1
Leadership values profile.

Source: Adapted from J. Hogan and R. T. Hogan, *Motives, Values and Preferences Inventory.* Tulsa, OK: Hogan Assessment Systems, 2002.

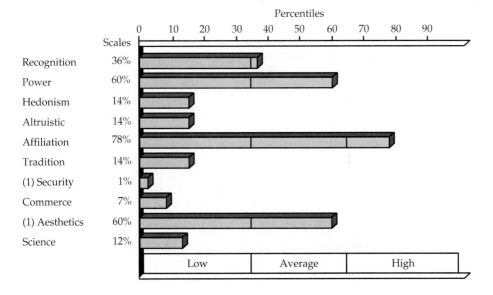

Leadership and Organizational Values

Beware of the man who had no regard for his own reputation, since it is not likely he should have any for yours.

George Shelley

Organizational Culture is affected by top leadership's collective values.

Subordinates cannot be left to speculate as to the values of the organization. Top leadership must give forth clear and explicit signals, lest any confusion or uncertainty exist over what is and is not permissible conduct. To do otherwise allows informal and potentially subversive "codes of conduct" to be transmitted with a wink and a nod, and encourages an inferior ethical system based on "going along to get along" or the notion that "everybody's doing it."

Richard Thornburgh, former U.S. attorney general

Just as individuals possess a set of personal values, so too do organizations possess a set of organizational values. Many times these values are featured prominently in the company's annual report, Web site, and posters. These values represent the principles by which employees are to get work done and treat other employees, customers, and vendors. Whether these stated values truly represent operating principles or so much "spin" for potential investors will depend on the degree of alignment between the organization's stated values and the collective values of top leadership.[24,25] For example, many corporate value statements say very little about making money, but frankly this is the key organizational priority for most business leaders, and as such is a major factor in many company decisions. It is interesting to note, by the way, that there is often a significant gap between a company's stated values and the way it truly operates. Knowing the values of top leadership can sometimes tell you more about how an organization actually operates than the organization's stated values will. Two quite ancient and contrasting sets of values are described in Highlight 6.4.

In any organization, the top leadership's collective values play a significant role in determining organizational culture, just as an individual leader's values play a significant role in determining team climate. Related to the notion of culture and climate is employee "fit." Research has shown that employees with values similar to the organization or team are more satisfied and likely to stay; those with dissimilar values are more likely to leave.[26,27] Thus, one reason why leaders fail is not due to a lack of competence, but rather due to a misalignment between personal and organizational values. This is unfortunate, as leaders with dissimilar values may be exactly what the company needs to drive change and become more effective. A relatively new approach to differences in organizational culture is described in Highlight 6.5.

Finally, values are often a key factor in conflict. Many of the most difficult decisions made by leaders have to do with choices between two values. This is particularly true when the choices represent values in opposition (see Table 6.3). Leaders with strong Commercial and Altruistic values, for example, would probably struggle mightily when having to make a decision about cutting jobs in order to improve profitability. Those leaders who have strong Commercial and weak Altruistic values (or vice versa) would have much less trouble making the same decision. Likewise, some leaders would have difficulties making decisions when friendships may get in the way of making an impact (Affiliation versus Power), or when taking risks to gain visibility runs counter to stability (Recognition versus Security). It is important to note that values also play a key role in conflict between groups. The differences between Bill O'Reilly and Al Franken, the Israelis and Palestinians, the Shiite and Sunni Muslims in Iraq, the Muslims and Hindus in Kashmir, and Christians and Muslims in Kosovo all have to do with values. Because values develop early and are

Ancient Eastern Philosophies and the Board Room

HIGHLIGHT 6.4

Thirty years ago, a best-selling business book called *Theory Z* purported to help Western business leaders apply the art of Japanese management to their own circumstances. Since then other Eastern philosophies have also gained popularity among Western leaders, albeit often in highly simplified forms. One perspective that has become popular in the West is based on the Chinese philosopher Sun Tzu's, whose classic work *The Art of War* was written 2500 years ago. Another is the *Bhagavad Gita,* a sacred Indian text containing the wisdom of Lord Krishna believed to have been written nearly that long ago as well. There are quite different implications for leadership derived from these two classic writings, a few of which are noted here.

	The Art of War	*Bhagavad Gita*
On Material Incentives	People need extrinsic incentives to be motivated. Give your soldiers shares of the booty and conquered territory.	Never act for material rewards only. Focus instead on doing well, and good things will follow.
On Handling Followers	Rule with iron discipline. Maintain your authority over them, knowing that too much kindness toward your followers could make them useless.	Enlightened leaders are selfless and compassionate toward others. Followers who are treated as equals are more motivated to enthusiastically support their leader.
On the Ultimate Goal	Winning, which requires cleverness and sometimes even deception.	Success means satisfying multiple different stakeholders.

Source: Adapted from *BusinessWeek*, October 30, 2006.

difficult to change, it will be extremely difficult to resolve the conflicts between these groups.

It's vital for a leader to set a personal example of values-based leadership, and it is also important for leaders—especially more senior ones—to make sure that clear values guide *everyone's* behavior in the organization. That's only likely to happen, of course, if the leader's behavior sets an example of desired behavior. You might think of it as a necessary but not sufficient condition for principled behavior throughout the organization. That's because if there is indifference or hypocrisy toward values at the highest levels, then it is fairly unlikely that principled behavior will be considered important by others throughout the organization. Bill O'Brien, the former CEO of a major insurance company, likened an organization's poor ethical climate to a bad odor one gets used to:

Stages of Leadership Culture Development

HIGHLIGHT 6.5

Researchers at the Center for Creative Leadership have been studying different kinds of leadership cultures, which they define as the values, beliefs, and often taken-for-granted assumptions about how people work together in an organization, reflecting its collective approach to achieving direction, alignment, and commitment. While virtually all large organizations include aspects of all three types, often one of these cultures will be most dominant. Furthermore, these types of leadership culture are thought to represent successive stages of culture development analogous to the stages of individual leader development discussed in Chapter 3. An important practical purpose of this work is to help organizations transform their cultures in ways better suited to the organization's current and future challenges.

Dependent leadership cultures are characterized by widespread beliefs and practices that it's primarily people in positions of authority who are responsible for leadership. This assumption may lead to organizations that emphasize top-down control and deference to authority. In general, you can think of dependent cultures as "conforming" cultures. Other characteristics often associated with dependent cultures include:

- There may be a command and control mindset.
- Seniority and position levels are important bases of respect.
- There's great emphasis on keeping things running smoothly.
- Most people operate with the philosophy that it's usually safest to check things out with one's boss before taking a new direction.

Independent leadership cultures are characterized by widespread beliefs and practices that leadership emerges as needed from a variety of individuals, based on knowledge and expertise. There's great emphasis upon individual responsibility; decentralized decision making; and the promotion of experts, professionals, and individual contributors into positions of authority. In general, you can think of independent cultures as "achievement-oriented" cultures. Other characteristics associated with independent cultures include:

- The results that leaders achieve, whatever it takes, is an important basis of respect.
- Even during times of stress, there is great pressure not to let performance numbers go down.
- Bold and independent action that gets results is highly prized.
- The organization is successful because of its large number of highly competent and ambitious individuals.

Interdependent leadership cultures are characterized by widespread beliefs and practices that leadership is a collective activity requiring mutual inquiry and learning. There's widespread use of dialogue, collaboration, horizontal networks, valuing of differences, and a focus on learning. In general, you can think of interdependent cultures as "collaborative" cultures. Other characteristics associated with interdependent cultures include:

- Many people wear several hats at once and roles change frequently as the organization continually adapts to changing circumstances.
- People believe it's important to let everyone learn from your experience, even your mistakes.
- There's a widely shared commitment doing what it takes to make the entire organization be successful, not just one's own group.
- Openness, candor, and building trust across departments is valued.

**TABLE 6.3
Values in
Opposition**

Source: Adapted from G. J.
Curphy, *Team Leader Program.*
St. Paul, MN: Author, 2004.

Commercial (making money) vs. Altruistic (helping others)
Affiliation (having friends) vs. Power (making an impact)
Recognition (taking risks) vs. Security (minimizing risks)
Hedonism (having fun) vs. Tradition (adhering to norms)
Aesthetic (appearance) vs. Scientific (the truth)

> Organizations oriented to power, I realized, also have strong smells, and even if people are too inured to notice, that smell has implications. It affects performance, productivity, and innovation. The worst aspect of this environment is that it stunts the growth of personality and character of everyone who works there.[28]

Carried to an extreme, it can lead to the kinds of excesses all too frequently evident during the past decade:

It's important that people know what you stand for. It's equally important that they know what you won't stand for.

Mary Waldrop

> Who knew the swashbuckling economy of the 90s had produced so many buccaneers? You could laugh about the CEOs in handcuffs and the stock analysts who turned out to be fishier than storefront palm readers, but after a while the laughs became hard. Martha Stewart was dented and scuffed [and subsequently convicted]. Tyco was looted by its own executives. Enron and WorldCom turned out to be the twin towers of false promises. They fell. Their stockholders and employees went down with them. So did a large measure of faith in big corporations.

Time Magazine, January 2, 2003

Others, too, are calling attention to the organizational dimensions of ethical behavior. It seems clear that ethical behavior within an organization (or *by* it) is not simply the sum of the collective moralities of its members. Covey, for example, has developed and popularized an approach called **principle-centered leadership**.[29] This approach postulates a fundamental interdependence between the personal, the interpersonal, the managerial, and the organizational levels of leadership. The unique role of each level may be thought of like this:

Personal: The first imperative is to be a trustworthy person, and that depends on both one's character *and* competence. Only if one is trustworthy can one have trusting relationships with others.

Interpersonal: Relationships that lack trust are characterized by self-protective efforts to control and verify each other's behavior.

Managerial: Only in the context of trusting relationships will a manager risk empowering others to make full use of their talents and energies. But even with an empowering style, leading a high-performing group depends on skills such as team building, delegation, communication, negotiation, and self-management.

Organizational: An organization will be most creative and productive when its structure, systems (e.g., training, communication, reward), strategy, and vision are aligned and mutually supportive. Put differently, certain organizational alignments are more likely to nurture and reinforce ethical behavior among its members than others.

Conflicts over values can arise even when an organization has clearly published values that are embraced by everyone. That can happen when employees and leaders have divergent perceptions of whether the leader's behavior embodies important corporate values. At one company, for example, employees concluded that their CEO's behavior had betrayed the very corporate values that he had been instrumental in establishing. As they perceived the CEO's behavior deviating more and more from those values, employees gradually concluded that he had "sold out," and they became disillusioned with his leadership.

That disillusionment was a far cry from the initial perceptions employees had of their CEO. Consider the situation at Maverick when the CEO, John Bryant (both fictionalized names), started the company:

> Bryant located Maverick's offices in an unassuming warehouse district and gave each member of his small staff a festive company shirt with a logo on the back and their name stitched over the front pocket, like shirts mechanics wear. He provided a companywide profit-sharing plan, above-market salaries, and perks like free lunch on Friday, and he encouraged people to head home by six o'clock. He recruited employees whose varied races,

The Average Self-Rating on "Ethical Behavior" Is Way above Average

HIGHLIGHT 6.6

David Campbell, a senior fellow at the Center for Creative Leadership, is one of the most prolific researchers in the world in the field of leadership. Among other things, he has authored numerous widely used surveys to assess various facets of leadership. The following story relates his efforts to develop an ethics scale for the Campbell Leadership Index (CLI).

In preliminary work on the CLI, it seemed obvious that "ethics" was central to the practice of good leadership and, therefore, should be one of the scales on the instrument (the CLI now includes 17 scales, including ambitious, enterprising, considerate, entertaining, organized, and productive). Consequently, in the early versions of the survey Campbell included adjectives such as *ethical, honest, trustworthy,* and *candid,* and negative adjectives

such as *deceptive* and *scheming.* As with other CLI scales, this one was normed so that the average person would receive a score of 50 on the ethics scale; obviously some would get higher scores and some lower scores.

During the CLI testing period, however, a major problem emerged because almost no one wanted to believe that he or she was merely "average" in ethical behavior, let alone "below average." To soften the impact of such feedback, Campbell changed the name of the scale to "trustworthy" in the hope that this would retain the meaning but lessen the adverse reaction. But that change helped little. Eventually Campbell changed the name of the scale to "credible," which is more acceptable and also better captures the reasons why some executives may get low ratings on the scale despite self-perceptions of scrupulous honesty.

backgrounds, and lifestyles broadcast Maverick's commitment to diversity, and on the weekends he let a minority youth organization use the company's offices. He spoke passionately to everyone about Maverick's people-oriented values and promoted them in company posters, client materials, and the employee handbook.

In short, Bryant did everything right. And by all accounts, Maverick in its early years was a great place to work—employees were motivated, loyal, hardworking, and enthusiastically committed to the company and the ideals Bryant promoted.[30]

Then the finger-pointing began. As the small, young company more than doubled in size during the 1990s, a remarkable shift occurred in how employees perceived the company and its leader. They came to see Bryant as a hypocrite, whose behavior violated everything he continued to proclaim the company stood for. As a consequence, employee commitment and creativity declined sharply.

What could account for such an unfortunate turnaround? That's not a simple question to answer, especially when the leader—Bryant himself—continued to see his own behavior in much more positive ways. Part of the answer to this enigma, it seems, involved a pivotal event in the company's history. In 1995 Bryant decided to double the size of the company's staff and operations. To him, this was a way to provide more professional growth and reward opportunities for staff. Employees, however, saw this as an act of greed on Bryant's part that would erode company values by disrupting the small, close-knit family the company had been. They also saw other decisions by him as similarly self-serving. When he decided to give long-term employees shares in the company as a reward for their hard work, for example, other employees perceived this as inconsistent with the company's commitment to equality. All the while this was happening, no one ever let Bryant himself know that perceptions of him had taken a 180-degree turn.

In doing a sort of organizational postmortem of what happened at Maverick, it became clear that over time employees had *implicitly and unconsciously* shaped their understanding of the company's values to correspond more closely with their own. For example, employees came to believe that hierarchies of position and power were inconsistent with Maverick's values. In fact, no one ever had said anything like that. Thus, Bryant's behavior *was* inconsistent with company values *as the employees had come to understand them,* even though it *wasn't* inconsistent with Bryant's understanding of the values on which he'd founded the company.

There's an important lesson for leaders in this story that's hinted at in Bryant's own lack of awareness of the growing negative perceptions of his behavior. It's unlikely that subordinate members of an organization will offer unsolicited negative perceptions to leaders when they think that the latter have violated the values. It's essential, then, for leaders themselves to proactively invite discussion by regularly asking people what they're thinking and feeling. You don't want to be caught blindsided like John Bryant was.

Positive Forms of Leadership

Can you be a good leader without being a good person? Does it make any sense at all to say, for example, that Hitler was an "effective leader" even if he was an evil and bad person? In recent years there has been a rekindling of interest in various positive forms of leadership. Two of the approaches in this movement are described below.

Authentic leadership is grounded in the principle found in the familiar adage from Greek philosophy, "to thine own self be true." Its roots are also in various expressions of the humanistic movement in psychology including Maslow's theory of self-actualization (see Chapter 9) and Carl Rogers' concept of the fully-functioning person.[31] Central to both of these is the idea that individuals can develop to modes of understanding and interacting with their social environments so as to become more truly independent of others' expectations of them (individual, group, and cultural) and guided more by the dictates of universal truths and imperatives. Such individuals manifest congruence between how they feel on the inside and how they act, between what they say and what they do. They have realistic self-perceptions, free from the blind spots and misperceptions of self that are common to most people. At the same time, they are accepting of themselves, their nature, and of others too. To paraphrase the title of a popular book from several decades ago, they feel OK themselves, and believe others are OK too. They have strong ethical convictions which guide their behavior not so much to avoid doing "wrong" things as to always try to do the "right" things including treating others with respect and dignity. They know where they stand on their fundamental values and on key issues. Authentic leaders behave the way they do because of personal conviction rather than to attain status, rewards, or other advantages.

One way to understand authentic leadership is to contrast it with *inauthentic* leadership. If you think of a leader who "plays a role," or puts on a different act with different audiences in order to manage the impression she creates, that is being inauthentic. For example, two detectives playing the roles of "good cop" and "bad cop" when interviewing a suspect are being inauthentic (you may believe that it makes sense for them to do so, but it's inauthentic nonetheless). A boss who exaggerates his anger at an employee's mistake to "teach him a lesson" is being inauthentic. A leader who denies that her feelings were affected by very critical feedback from her direct reports is perhaps being inauthentic.

The study of authentic leadership has gained momentum recently because of beliefs that: (a) enhancing self-awareness can help people in organizations find more meaning and connection at work; (b) promoting transparency and openness in relationships—even between leader and followers—builds trust and commitment; and (c) fostering more inclusive structures and practices in organizations can help build more positive ethical climates.[32]

Servant leadership has been used since 1970 to describe a quite different approach to leadership than that derived from a bureaucratic and mechanistic view of organizations wherein workers were thought of as mere cogs in a machine. In the latter, the leader's primary role may be understood as doing whatever it takes to assure that things run smoothly, that tasks are performed and goals are met. This has commonly involved a very top-down and hierarchical approach to leadership. From the perspective of servant leadership, however, the leader's role, literally, is to serve others.

The modern idea of servant leadership was developed and popularized by Robert Greenleaf after he read a short novel by Herman Hesse called *Journey to the East*.[33,34] It's the mythical story of a group of people on a spiritual quest. Accompanying the party is a servant by the name of Leo, whose nurturing character sustained the group on its journey until one day he disappeared. The group fell apart and abandoned its quest when it realized that it was helpless without its servant. Finally, after many years of continued searching, the story's narrator found the religious order that had sponsored the original quest in the first place. It turned out that Leo, whom the narrator had only known as a servant, was actually the order's revered leader. To Greenleaf, this story meant that true leadership emerges when one's primary motivation is to help others.

The idea of servant leadership, of course, has been around for thousands of years. It stems at least in part from the teachings of Jesus, who instructed his disciples that servanthood is the essence of worthy leadership (e.g., through the example of *him* washing *their* feet). There are ten characteristics which are often associated with servant-leaders. As you'll see, most of them also seem quite in line with the idea of authentic leadership described above:[35]

- *Listening*. While all leaders need to communicate effectively, the focus is often on communicating *to* others; but servant leadership puts the emphasis upon *listening* effectively to others.
- *Empathy*. Servant leaders need to understand others' feelings and perspectives.
- *Healing*. Servant leaders help foster each person's emotional and spiritual health and wholeness.
- *Awareness*. Servant leaders understand their own values and feelings, strengths and weaknesses.
- *Persuasion*. Rather than relying on positional authority, servant leaders influence others through their persuasiveness.
- *Conceptualization*. Servant leaders need to integrate present realities and future possibilities.
- *Foresight*. Servant leaders need to have a well-developed sense of intuition about how the past, present, and future are connected.

- *Stewardship.* Servant leaders are stewards who hold an organization's resources in trust for the greater good.
- *Commitment to others' growth.* The ultimate test of a servant leader's work is whether those served develop toward being more responsible, caring, and competent individuals.
- *Building community.* Such individual growth and development is most likely to happen when one is part of a supportive community. Unfortunately, numerous factors like geographic mobility and the general impersonalism of large organizations has eroded people's sense of community. Thus, it is the servant leader's role to help re-create a sense of community among people.

Not surprisingly, the concept of servant leadership has detractors as well as adherents. The most common criticism is that while the idea of servant leadership has a certain popular appeal in what we might call its "soft" form (e.g., leaders should be *more* concerned about others' well-being and development, should create a *more* developmental climate in their organizations, seek what's good for the whole organization rather than just their own advancement), when taken more literally and extremely the concept seems to suggest that serving others is an end in itself rather than as a means to other organizational goals and purposes. That version strikes many as impractical even if laudable.

A man who embodied some of the most central qualities of both authentic leadership and servant leadership is featured in Profiles in Leadership 6.1.

When Good People Do Bad Things

An important aspect of ethical conduct involves the mental gymnastics by which people can dissociate their moral thinking from their moral acting. One's ability to reason about hypothetical moral issues, after all, does not assure that one will *act* morally. Furthermore, one's moral actions may not always be consistent with one's espoused values. Bandura, in particular, has pointed out several ways people with firm moral principles nonetheless may behave badly without feeling guilt or remorse over their behavior. We should look at each of these. [36,37]

Moral justification involves reinterpreting otherwise immoral behavior in terms of a higher purpose. This is most dramatically revealed in the behavior of combatants in war.

> Moral reconstrual of killing is dramatically illustrated by the case of Sergeant York, one of the phenomenal fighters in the history of modern warfare. Because of his deep religious convictions, Sergeant York registered as a conscientious objector, but his numerous appeals were denied. At camp, his battalion commander quoted chapter and verse from the Bible to persuade him that under appropriate conditions it was Christian to fight

Gandhi

PROFILES IN LEADERSHIP 6.1

Gandhi was one of the great leaders in world history. No less an intellect than Albert Einstein wrote this of him: "Generations to come, it may be, will scarce believe that such a one as this ever in flesh and blood walked upon this earth." Viscount Louis Mountbatten, the last Viceroy of India, compared him to the Buddha and to Christ. As a young journalist, William L. Shirer chronicled Gandhi's rebellion against British colonialism in India and described his first meeting with Gandhi. In reading it, think about what aspects of Gandhi's personality, behavior, vision, and values made him so charismatic a leader.

Gandhi was squatting on the floor in the corner of the verandah, spinning. He greeted me warmly, with a smile that lit up his face and made his lively eyes twinkle. The welcome was so disarming, his manner so friendly and radiant, that my nervousness evaporated before I could say a word . . .

As our talk began I tried to take in not only what Gandhi was saying but how he looked. I had seen many photographs of him but I was nevertheless somewhat surprised at his actual appearance. His face at first glance did not convey at all the stature of the man, his obvious greatness. It was not one you would have especially noticed in a crowd. It struck me as not ugly, as some had said—indeed it radiated a certain beauty—but it was not uncommon either. Age—he was 61—and fasting, and Indian sun and the strain of years in prison, of long, hard, nervous work, had obviously taken their toll, turned the nose down, widened it at the nostrils, sunk in his mouth just a little so that the lower lip protruded, and teeth were missing—I could see only two. His hair was closely cropped, giving an effect of baldness. His large ears spread out, rabbit-like. His gray eyes lit up and sharpened when they peered at you through his steel-rimmed spectacles and then they softened when he lapsed, as he frequently did, into a mood of almost puckish humor. I was almost taken aback by the gaiety in them. This was a man inwardly secure, who, despite the burdens he carried, the hardships he had endured, could chuckle at man's foibles, including his own.

He seemed terribly frail, all skin and bones, though I knew that this appearance was deceptive, for he kept to a frugal but carefully planned diet that kept him fit, and for exercise he walked four or five miles each morning at a pace so brisk, as I would learn later when he invited me to accompany him, that I, at 27 and in fair shape from skiing and hiking in the Alps below Vienna, could scarcely keep up. Over his skin and bones was a loosely wrapped dhoti, and in the chilliness of a north Indian winter he draped a coarsely spun white shawl over his bony shoulders. His skinny legs were bare, his feet in wooden sandals.

As he began to talk, his voice seemed high-pitched, but his words were spoken slowly and deliberately and with emphasis when he seemed intent on stressing a point, and gradually, as he warmed up, the tone lowered. His slightly accented English flowed rhythmically, like a poet's at times, and always, except for an occasional homespun cliché, it was concise, homely, forceful.

For so towering a figure, his humble manner at first almost disconcerted me. Most of the political greats I had brushed up against in Europe and at home had seemed intent on impressing you with the forcefulness of their personalities and the boldness of their minds, not being bashful at all in hiding their immense egos. But here was the most gentle and unassuming of men, speaking softly and kindly, without egotism, without the slightest pretense of trying to impress his rather awed listener.

How could so humble a man, I wondered, spinning away with his nimble fingers on a crude wheel as he talked, have begun almost single-handedly to rock the foundations of the British Empire, aroused a third of a billion people to rebellion against foreign rule, and taught them the technique of a new revolutionary method—nonviolent civil disobedience—against which Western guns and Eastern lathis were proving of not much worth? That was what I had come to India to find out?

Source: W. L. Shirer, *Gandhi.* New York: Simon & Schuster, 1979, pp 27–29. Reprinted with the permission of Simon & Schuster Adult Publishing Group and Don Congdon Associates, Inc. Copyright © 1979 by William L. Shirer.

and kill. A marathon mountainside prayer finally convinced him that he could serve both God and country by becoming a dedicated fighter.[38]

Another way to dissociate behavior from one's espoused moral principles is through **euphemistic labeling**. This involves using "cosmetic" words to defuse or disguise the offensiveness of otherwise morally repugnant or distasteful behavior. Terrorists, for example, may call themselves "freedom fighters," and firing someone may be referred to as "letting him go." **Advantageous comparison** lets one avoid self-contempt for one's behavior by comparing it to even more heinous behavior by others ("If you think *we're* insensitive to subordinates' needs, you should see what it's like working for *Acme*"). Through **displacement of responsibility** people may violate personal moral standards by attributing responsibility to others. Nazi concentration camp guards, for example, attempted to avoid moral responsibility for their behavior by claiming they were merely "carrying out orders."

A related mechanism is **diffusion of responsibility**, whereby reprehensible behavior becomes easier to engage in and live with if others are behaving the same way. When everyone is responsible, it seems, no one is responsible. This way of minimizing individual moral responsibility for collective action can be one negative effect of group decision making. Through **disregard** or **distortion of consequences**, people minimize the harm caused by their behavior. This can be a problem in bureaucracies when decision makers are relatively insulated by their position from directly observing the consequences of their decisions. **Dehumanization** is still another way of avoiding the moral consequences of one's behavior. It is easier to treat others badly when they are dehumanized, as evidenced in epithets like "gooks" or "satan-worshippers." Finally, people sometimes try to justify immoral behavior by claiming it was caused by someone else's actions. This is known as **attribution of blame**.

How widespread are such methods of minimizing personal moral responsibility? When people behave badly, Bandura said, it is *not* typically because of a basic character flaw; rather, it is because they use methods like these to construe their behavior in a self-protective way.[39]

Darley suggested still another way people justify seemingly unethical conduct, and his observations illuminate certain common leadership practices. He said *ethical problems are almost inherent in systems designed to measure performance.*[40]

> The more any quantitative performance measure is used to determine a group's or an individual's rewards and punishments, the more subject it will be to corruption pressures and the more apt it will be to distort and corrupt the action patterns and thoughts of the group or individual it is intended to monitor . . . The criterial control system unleashes enormous human ingenuity. People will maximize the criteria set. However, they may do so in ways that are not anticipated by the criterion setters, in ways that destroy the validity of the criteria. The people "make their numbers" but the numbers no longer mean what you thought they did.[41]

(handwritten margin note: Performance measurement Systems; 3 general problems)

Three general problems can arise when performance measurement systems are put in place. A person might cheat on the measurement system by exploiting its weaknesses either in hopes of advancement or through fear of falling behind. Or, even with the best will in the world, a person might act in a way that optimizes his or her performance measurements without realizing that this outcome was not what the system really intended. Finally, a person may even have the best interests of the system in mind and yet manipulate the performance measurement system to allow continuation of the actions that best fulfill his or her reading of the system goals. One major disadvantage of this particular approach is that it "takes underground" constructive dialogue about system goals or modifications in system measurements.

What, ethically, should one do when one is part of a performance measurement system? Darley suggested "that the time for the individual to raise the moral issue is when he or she feels the pressure to substitute accountability for morality, to act wrongly, because that is what the system requires. And that intervention might then be directed at the system, by honorably protesting its design."[42] For those who are governed by a performance measurement system, a constant moral vigilance is necessary—it is needed most of all by those in leadership positions.

David Halberstam described another organization in which the "numbers game" had a corrupting effect.[43] In this case, it was in Ford Motor Company. In the eyes of those who worked in Ford plants around the country in the 1950s, Detroit "number crunchers" like Robert McNamara (later a Secretary of Defense during the Vietnam War) did not want to know the truth. McNamara and his people in Detroit were the ones who kept making liberal agreements with the unions and at the same time setting higher and higher levels of production while always demanding increased quality. They talked about quality, but they did not give the plant managers the means for quality; what they really wanted was production. So the plant managers were giving them what they wanted, numbers, while playing lip service to quality. Years later in Vietnam, some American officers, knowing McNamara's love of numbers, cleverly juggled the numbers and played games with body counts in order to make a stalemated war look more successful than it was. They did this not because they were dishonest, but because they thought if Washington really wanted the truth it would have sought the truth in an honest way. In doing so they were the spiritual descendants of the Ford factory managers of the 1950s (p. 220).

Only mediocrities rise to the top in a system that won't tolerate wave making.

Lawrence J. Peter,
author of *The Peter*
Principle

Leading across Cultures

A rather common problem for office managers in the United States is controlling the use of the office copier. Frequently, office managers publish policies and procedures to govern use of the machines, and hence control administrative costs. When a U.S. manager of a water resources project in

The Cult of Enron

HIGHLIGHT 6.7

Enron has come to represent the epitome of greed, ethical lapse, and spectacular failure in the business world. Its senior executives like CEO Kenneth Lay and Jeffrey Skilling are blamed (and were prosecuted) for the company's collapse and callous indifference to the welfare of its employees. But the problems at Enron ran deeper than just the shoddy ethics and illegal actions of a few people at the top. A large part of the problem was the Enron culture itself that people *throughout* the company perpetuated.

A root of the problem may be that Enron's culture had many characteristics of a cult. Cults are characterized as having these four qualities:

- charismatic leadership
- a compelling and totalistic vision
- a conversion process
- a common culture

Here are some of the ways that Enron's corporate culture was like a cult. By reading these you can get an idea how corporations as well as religious cults can encourage counterproductive conformity and penalize dissent.

Charismatic Leadership

Enron's leaders created an aura of charisma around themselves through ever more dramatic forms of self-promotion. Skilling, for example, cultivated his image as the Enron version of "Darth Vader," even referring to his traders as "Storm Troopers." The reputations of Skilling and other top executives at Enron were further reinforced by the ways in which they were lionized in respected business publications and by the opulent lifestyles that they enjoyed.

Compelling and Totalistic Vision

Hyperbole was rampant at Enron, as in banners proclaiming its vision to be the "world's leading company." Such exalted self-images easily encourage members to feel a certain sense of privilege and destiny. Employees were bombarded with messages that they were the best and the brightest. Their commitment to organizational success had an almost evangelistic fervor, and workweeks of even eighty hours a week were considered normal.

Conversion and Indoctrination

From an employee's recruitment to Enron onward, communication was one-way: top-down. In the early stages this involved intense and emotionally draining rituals over several days wherein the recruit would hear powerful messages from the leaders. Group dynamics research has shown that such initiation rituals incline people to more strongly exaggerate the benefits of group membership in their minds. In Enron's case the purpose was to ingrain in employees a single-minded personal commitment to continued high rates of corporate growth.

Common Culture

Despite all the effort put into selecting new employees and imbuing them with a sense of privilege, a punitive internal culture was also nurtured through which all the psychic and material benefits of being in Enron could be withdrawn on a managerial whim. Enron was quick to fire any of these "best and brightest" who did not conform; they could be branded, almost overnight, "losers" in others' eyes. This could happen for mere dissent with the corporate line as well as for failing to meet Enron's exceedingly high performance goals.

Source: D. Tourish, and N. Vatcha, "Charismatic Leadership and Corporate Cultism at Enron: The Elimination of Dissent, the Promotion of Conformity and Organizational Collapse." *Leadership* 1 (4) (2005), pp. 455–80.

Indonesia did the same thing, however, an action he considered routine, he was accused of insensitivity to Indonesian ways—in fact, accused not just of unfriendliness but of unethical behavior. After a series of similar incidents, he lost his job. Leading across cultures requires an appreciation of the sometimes profound differences in the value systems of other cultures.

What Is Culture?

A good starting place for understanding differences in cultural value systems is with the concept of culture itself. **Culture** refers to those learned behaviors characterizing the total way of life of members within any given society. Cultures differ from one another just as individuals differ from one another. To outsiders, the most salient aspect of any culture typically involves behavior—the distinctive actions, mannerisms, and gestures characteristic of that culture. Americans visiting Thailand, for example, may find it curious and even bothersome to see male Thais hold hands with each other in public. They may react negatively to such behavior since it is untypical to *them,* and laden with *North American* meaning (e.g., "It's okay for women to hold hands in public, but men just shouldn't do that!"). Salient as such behaviors are, however, they are also just the tip of the iceberg. The "mass" of culture is not so readily visible, just as most of an iceberg lies beneath the water. Hidden from view are the beliefs, values, and myths that provide context to manifest behaviors.[44] A clear implication for business leaders in the global context, therefore, is the need to become aware and respectful of cultural differences and cultural perspectives. Barnum pointed out the importance of being able to look at one's own culture through the eyes of another:

> Consciously or unconsciously they will be using their own beliefs as the yardsticks for judging you, so know how to compare those yardsticks by ferreting out their values and noting where they differ the least and most from yours. For example, if their belief in fatalism outweighs your belief in accountability, there will be conflicts down the road. This is a severe problem in the Middle East, for instance, and affects management styles in companies and even the ability to market life insurance, which is frowned upon in communities where Muslim observances are strong.[45]

A Framework for Understanding Cultural Differences

Thus, it can be helpful to see one's own culture through the eyes of another, just as it also can be helpful to see other cultures through eyes unbiased (or at least less biased) by one's own filters. For decades Hofstede[46] has been studying fundamental dimensions of cultural values and beliefs. He has identified five: individualism versus collectivism, masculinity versus femininity, tolerance versus intolerance of uncertainty, power distance, and long-term versus short-term orientation.

More recently, researchers at the Center for Creative Leadership have developed a conceptual framework for analyzing cultural differences based on seven fundamental dilemmas that people of all cultures face.[47] Let us look at each of these seven dilemmas in greater detail.

Source of Identity: Individual–Collective. This deals with the degree to which individuals should pursue their own interests and goals or contribute to a larger group, whether extended family, ethnic group, or company.

Goals and Means of Achievement: Tough–Tender. This deals with how success is defined in a culture. Is it defined by tangible rewards like financial success and material well-being or by intangible rewards such as good relationships with others or spiritual satisfaction?

Orientation to Authority: Equal–Unequal. How should people of different status, authority, or power behave toward each other—as equals or unequals?

Response to Ambiguity: Dynamic–Stable. To what extent is uncertainty accepted or tolerated? In running an organization, are tight controls and structure imposed to ensure certainty, or is greater tolerance for ambiguity and uncertainty evident via loose or nonexistent control systems?

Means of Knowledge Acquisition: Active–Reflective. Is action or reflection more valued as a means of acquiring information and knowledge?

Perspective on Time: Scarce–Plentiful. Is the sense or experience of time urgent or relaxed?

Outlook on Life: Doing–Being. Which is preferred—mastery over nature or living in harmony with nature? Is the outcome of life more dependent upon human effort or on the expression of divine will?

You probably can see how misunderstandings and slights can occur when people from different cultures are working together, but let us look at two specific applications of this scheme. First, consider the historic U.S. emphasis on individualism (e.g., the focus on *self*-confidence, *self*-control, *self*-concept, *self*-expression, or the way rugged individualists are heroically portrayed in film, television, and literature) and how it might impact work. Given an individualist perspective, certain management practices and expectations seem self-evident, such as the idea of individual accountability for work. When individual accountability is valued, for example, decision-making authority tends to be delegated to individual managers. What's more, those same managers may be inclined to take personal credit when the job is well done. A different norm, however, applies in industrialized Japan. Decision making is often very time-consuming, to assure that everyone who will be impacted by a decision has input on it beforehand. Another "self-evident" principle to the U.S. mind is that individual career progress is desirable and "good." In some other cultures, however, managers resist competing with peers for rewards or promotions so as not to disturb the harmony of the group or appear self-interested.

Another example of potential conflict or misunderstanding can be seen in the case of orientation to authority, how people should handle power and authority relationships with others. The United States is a relatively young and mobile country, populated mostly by immigrants. Relative to other countries, there is little concern with family origin or class background. There is a belief that success should come through an individual's hard work and talent, not by birthright or class standing. This all leads to a relative informality at work, even among individuals of strikingly different position within a company. Subordinates expect their bosses to be accessible, even responsive in some ways to their subordinates. In some other cultures, however, higher status in a company confers nearly unchallengeable authority, and an expectation as well that most decisions will be referred *up* to them (as distinguished from delegated down to others). You can see even from these two examples that the seven dimensions of cultural values create quite an array of possible tensions between people from different cultures working together.

> *I do believe in the spiritual nature of human beings. To some it's a strange or outdated idea, but I believe there is such a thing as a human spirit. There is a spiritual dimension to man which should be nurtured.*
>
> **Aung San Suu Kyi**

The Universality of Leadership Attributes

It is an interesting question whether the attributes of effective leaders are shared universally around the world, or whether different attributes of leadership are valued more in some cultures than in others. A very ambitious project known as the GLOBE research program is addressing that question. Its goal is to develop an empirically based theory of leadership to help predict the effectiveness of leader and organizational practices in

Autocrats, Democrats, and Meritocrats

HIGHLIGHT 6.8

Many people take for granted that very similar attitudes about leadership are shared among business people, at least in Western nations. However, a recent poll of senior executives in the U.K., Germany, and France revealed some striking differences in national attitudes concerning different aspects of leadership. These differences led the researchers to label French business leaders as "autocrats," German business leaders as "democrats," and British business leaders as "meritocrats."

Here are some of the findings that led to those designations:

- While you may assume that no bosses like being challenged about decisions they make, fewer than three in 10 French bosses said they were happy about such challenges compared to half

of German bosses and more than nine out of 10 business leaders in the U.K.

- Nearly two-thirds of French bosses said that one of the three best things about being a leader was "the freedom to make decisions with minimum interference."

- 50 percent of German bosses and 70 percent of British bosses said that the best thing about the job is developing talent in the company. Only 14 percent of French bosses rated it among the top three benefits of leadership.

- French leaders are three times more likely than the British and eight times more likely than German leaders to consider "being in a position of power" one of the best things about the job.

Source: Adapted from Alison Maitland, "Le Patron, der Chef and the Boss." *The Financial Times Limited,* January 9, 2006, *Business Life,* p. 1. Copyright © 2006 The Financial Times Limited. Reprinted with permission.

TABLE 6.4 **Leader Attributes and Behaviors Universally Viewed as Positive**

Source: Adapted from House et al., *Cultural Influences on Leadership and Organizations: Project Globe. Advances in Global Leadership.* Vol. 1. JAI Press Inc., 1999, pp. 171–233.

Trustworthy	Positive	Intelligent
Just	Dynamic	Decisive
Honest	Motive arouser	Effective bargainer
Foresighted	Confidence builder	Win-win problem solver
Plans ahead	Motivational	Administratively skilled
Encouraging	Dependable	Communicative
Informed	Coordinator	Team builder
Excellence oriented		

different countries. The GLOBE program has been going on since 1993, collecting data from over 17,000 middle managers from 92 different countries. So far, the project has identified 22 specific attributes and behaviors that are viewed universally across cultures as contributing to leadership effectiveness.[48] They are listed in Table 6.4. In addition, the project has identified eight characteristics that are universally viewed as impediments to leader effectiveness (see Table 6.5). And GLOBE has identified 35 leader characteristics that are viewed as positive in some cultures but negative in others (see some in Table 6.6).

Implications for Leadership Practitioners

The perspectives and findings presented in this chapter have significant implications for leadership practitioners. Perhaps most important, leadership practitioners should *expect* to face a variety of challenges to their own system of ethics, values, or attitudes during their careers. Additionally, values often are a source of interpersonal conflict. Although we sometimes say two people don't get along because of a personality conflict, often these conflicts are due to differences in value systems, not personality traits. Often, people on either side of an issue see *only* themselves and their own side as morally justifiable. Nonetheless, people holding seemingly antithetical values may still need to work together, and dealing with diverse and divergent values will be an increasingly common challenge for leaders. As noted

TABLE 6.5 **Leader Attributes and Behaviors Universally Viewed as Negative**

Source: Adapted from House et al. *Cultural Influences on Leadership and Organizations: Project Globe. Advances in Global Leadership.* Vol. 1. JAI Press Inc., 1999, pp. 171–233.

Loner	Nonexplicit
Asocial	Egocentric
Noncooperative	Ruthless
Irritable	Dictatorial

TABLE 6.6 **Examples of Leader Behaviors and Attributes That Are Culturally Contingent**

Source: Adapted from House et al. *Cultural Influences on Leadership and Organizations: Project Globe. Advances in Global Leadership*. Vol. 1. JAI Press Inc., 1999, pp. 171–233.

Ambitious	Logical
Cautious	Orderly
Compassionate	Sincere
Domineering	Worldly
Independent	Formal
Individualistic	Sensitive

earlier, interacting with individuals and groups holding divergent and conflicting values will be an <u>inevitable</u> fact of life for future leaders. This does not mean, however, that increased levels of interpersonal conflict are inevitable. Both leaders and followers might be well advised to minimize the conflict and tension often associated with value differences. Leaders in particular have a responsibility <u>not</u> to let their own personal values <u>interfere</u> with professional leader–subordinate relationships unless the conflicts pertain to issues clearly relevant to the work and the organization.

Summary

This chapter reviews evidence regarding the relationships between values and leadership. Values are constructs that represent general sets of behaviors or states of affairs that individuals consider to be important, and they are a central part of a leader's psychological makeup. Values impact leadership through a cultural context within which various attributes and behaviors are regarded differentially—positively or negatively.

Key Terms

ethics, *167*
Theory X, *168*
Theory Y, *168*
values, *168*
Veterans, *170*
Baby Boomers, *170*
Gen Xers, *170*
Nexters, *170*
prophet generations, *171*
nomad generations, *171*
hero generations, *172*
artist generations, *172*

moral reasoning, *173*
preconventional level, *173*
conventional level, *175*
postconventional level, *175*
principle-centered leadership, *183*
authentic leadership, *186*
servant leadership, *187*
moral justification, *188*

euphemistic labeling, *190*
advantageous comparison, *190*
displacement of responsibility, *190*
diffusion of responsibility, *190*
distortion of consequences, *190*
dehumanization, *190*
attribution of blame, *190*
culture, *193*

Questions

1. Do you think it always must be "lonely at the top" (or that if it is not, you are doing something wrong)?
2. How do you believe one's basic philosophy of human nature affects one's approach to leadership?
3. Identify several values you think might be the basis of conflict or misunderstanding between leaders and followers.
4. Can a leader's public and private morality be distinguished? Should they be?
5. Can a bad person be a good leader?
6. Are there any leadership roles men and women should not have equal opportunity to compete for?

Activities

1. Each person should select his or her own 10 most important values from the following list, and then rank-order those 10 from most important (1) to least important (10). Then have an open discussion about how a person's approach to leadership might be influenced by having different "highest priority" values. The values are: Achievement, Activity (keeping busy), Advancement, Adventure, Aesthetics (appreciation of beauty), Affiliation, Affluence, Authority, Autonomy, Balance, Challenge, Change/Variety, Collaboration, Community, Competence, Competition, Courage, Creativity, Economic Security, Enjoyment, Fame, Family, Friendship, Happiness, Helping Others, Humor, Influence, Integrity, Justice, Knowledge, Location, Love, Loyalty, Order, Personal Development, Physical Fitness, Recognition, Reflection, Responsibility, Self-Respect, Spirituality, Status, Wisdom.

2. Explore how the experiences of different generations might have influenced the development of their values. Divide into several groups and assign each group the task of selecting representative popular music from a specific era. One group, for example, might have the 1950s, another the Vietnam War era, and another the 1990s. Using representative music from that era, highlight what seem to be dominant concerns, values, or views of life during that period.

Minicase

"Balancing Priorities at Clif Bar"

Gary Erickson is a man of integrity. In the spring of 2000 Erickson had an offer of more than $100 million from a major food corporation for his company Clif Bar, Inc. He had founded Clif Bar, Inc., in 1990 after a long bike ride. Erickson, an avid cyclist, had finished the 175-mile ride longing for an alternative to the tasteless energy bars he had brought along. "I couldn't make the last one go down, and that's when I had an epiphany—make a product that actually tasted good." He took a look at the list of ingredients on the package and decided he could do better. He called on his experience in his family's bakery and after a year in the kitchen, the Clif Bar—named for Erickson's father—was launched in 1992. Within five years sales had skyrocketed to $20 million. He considered the $100 million offer on the table and what it meant for his company and decided against the deal. He realized that the vision he had for the company would be compromised once he lost control, so he walked away from the $100 million deal.

He has stuck to his vision and values ever since. His commitment to environmental and social issues are evident in everything he does. On the environmental front, his company has a staff ecologist who is charged with working to reduce Clif Bar's ecological footprint on the planet. More than 70 percent of the ingredients in Clif Bars are organic. A change in packaging has saved the company (and the planet) 90,000 pounds of shrink-wrap a year. And the company funds a Sioux wind farm to offset the carbon dioxide emissions from its factories. On the social side, Erickson launched a project called the 2,080 program (2,080 is the total number of hours a full-time employee works in one year). Through the 2,080 program employees are encouraged to do volunteer work on company time. Recently Erickson agreed to support employees who wanted to volunteer in Third World countries with salaries and travel expenses.

Erickson is also committed to his team. He thinks about things like, "What should our company be like for the people who come to work each day?" He sees work as a living situation and strives to make Clif Bar, Inc.'s offices a fun place to be—there are plenty of bikes around; a gym and dance floor; personal trainers; massage and hair salon; a game room; an auditorium for meetings, movies, and music; dog days everyday; and great parties.

As the company grows, however, maintaining such values may not be easy. Clif Bar already has 130 employees, and revenue has been rising by more than 30 percent a year since 1998, according to Erickson. "We're at a point where we have to find a way to maintain this open culture while we may be getting bigger," says Shelley Martin, director of operations. "It's a balancing act."

1. Without knowing Gary Erickson's age, where would you guess he falls in the four generations of workers as delineated by Zemke?
2. Consider the key work values in Table 6.2. Recalling that leaders are motivated to act consistently with their values, what values appear to be most important to Gary Erickson?
3. Clif Bar, Inc., possesses a definite set of organizational values. If you visit the company Web site (www.clifbar.com), you will see evidence of these values: "Fight Global Warming" and "Register to Vote" are just as

prominent as information about the product. Knowing some of the values of Gary Erickson, how closely aligned do you think the organizational values are to the way the company actually operates?

Sources: http://www.fortune.com/fortune/smallbusiness/managing/articles/ 0,15114,487527,00.html; http://www.clifbar.com; *The Costco Connection,* "Marathon Man," July 2004, p. 19.

Chapter Notes

1. Gardner, J. W. *On Leadership.* New York: Free Press, 1990.
2. Burns, J. M. *Leadership.* New York: Harper & Row, 1978.
3. Bennis, W., and J. Goldsmith. *Learning to Lead.* Reading, MA: Perseus Books, 1997.
4. McGregor, D. *Leadership and Motivation.* Cambridge, MA: MIT Press, 1966.
5. Hall, J., and S. M. Donnell. "Managerial Achievement: The Personal Side of Behavioral Theory." *Human Relations* 32 (1979), pp. 77–101.
6. Gordon, L. V. *Measurement of Interpersonal Values.* Chicago: Science Research Associates, 1975, p. 2.
7. Boyatzis, R. E., and F. R. Skelly. "The Impact of Changing Values on Organizational Life." In *Organizational Behavior Readings.* 5th ed. Eds. D. A. Kolb, I. M. Rubin, and J. Osland. Englewood Cliffs, NJ: Prentice Hall, 1991, pp. 1–16.
8. Rokeach, M. *The Nature of Human Values.* New York: Free Press, 1973.
9. Boyatzis, R. E., and F. R. Skelly. "The Impact of Changing Values on Organizational Life." In *Organizational Behavior Readings.* 5th ed. Eds. D. A. Kolb, I. M. Rubin, and J. Osland. Englewood Cliffs, NJ: Prentice Hall, 1991, pp. 1–16.
10. Maccoby, M. "Management: Leadership and the Work Ethic." *Modern Office Procedures* 28, no. 5 (1983), pp. 14, 16, 18.
11. Massey, M. *The People Puzzle: Understanding Yourself and Others.* Reston, VA: Reston, 1979.
12. Zemke, R., C. Raines, and B. Filipczak. *Generations at Work: Managing the Class of Veterans, Boomers, Xers, and Nexters in Your Workplace.* New York: AMA Publications, 2000.
13. Deal, J. J., K. Peterson, and H. Gailor-Loflin. *Emerging Leaders: An Annotated Bibliography.* Greensboro, NC: Center for Creative Leadership, 2001.
14. Deal, J. J., K. Peterson, and H. Gailor-Loflin. *Emerging Leaders: An Annotated Bibliography.* Greensboro, NC: Center for Creative Leadership, 2001.
15. Foley, E., and A. LeFevre. *Understanding Generation X.* Zagnoli McEvoy Foley LLC, 2001. www.zmf.com.
16. Ladd, E. C. "Generation Gap? What Generation Gap?" *The New York Times,* December 9, p. A16.
17. Giancola, F. "The Generation Gap: More Myth Than Reality." *Human Resource Planning* 29, no. 4 (2006), pp. 32–37.
18. Howe, N., and W. Strauss. "The Next 20 Years: How Customer and Workforce Attitudes Will Evolve." *Harvard Business Review,* July–August 2007.
19. Kohlberg, L. *The Psychology of Moral Development: Essays on Moral Development.* Vol. 2. San Francisco: Harper & Row, 1984.

20. Rest, J. "Research on Moral Judgment in College Students." In *Approaches to Moral Development, New Research and Emerging Themes.* Ed. A Garrod. New York: Teachers College Press, Columbia University, 1993, pp. 201–13.

21. England, G. W., and R. Lee. "The Relationship between Managerial Values and Managerial Success in the United States, Japan, India, and Australia." *Journal of Applied Psychology* 59 (1974), pp. 411–19.

22. Hogan, R. T., and G. J. Curphy. "Leadership Matters: Values and Dysfunctional Dispositions." Working paper, 2004.

23. Hogan, R. T., and G. J. Curphy. "Leadership Matters: Values and Dysfunctional Dispositions." Working paper, 2004.

24. Hogan, R. T., J. Hogan, and B. W. Roberts. "Personality Measurement and Employment Decisions: Questions and Answers." *American Psychologist* 51, no. 5 (1996), pp. 469–77.

25. Hogan, R. T., and G. J. Curphy. "Leadership Matters: Values and Dysfunctional Dispositions." Working paper, 2004.

26. Hogan, R. T., J. Hogan, and B. W. Roberts. "Personality Measurement and Employment Decisions: Questions and Answers." *American Psychologist* 51, no. 5 (1996), pp. 469–77.

27. Hogan, R. T., and G. J. Curphy. "Leadership Matters: Values and Dysfunctional Dispositions." Working paper, 2004.

28. O'Brien, B. "Designing an Organization's Governing Ideas." In *The Fifth Discipline Fieldbook.* Eds. P. Senge et al. New York: Doubleday, 1994, p. 306.

29. Covey, S. R. *Principle-Centered Leadership.* New York: Simon & Schuster, 1990.

30. Edmondson, A. C., and S. E. Cha. "When Company Values Backfire." *Harvard Business Review,* November 2002, pp. 18–19.

31. Rogers, C. "Fully functioning person."

32. Avolio, B. J., and W. L. Gardner. "Authentic Leadership Development: Getting to the Root of Positive Forms of Leadership." *The Leadership Quarterly* 16 (2005), pp. 315–38.

33. Spears, L. "Practicing Servant-Leadership." *Leader to Leader* 34 (Fall 2004).

34. Greenleaf, R. K. *Servant Leadership.* New York: Paulist Press, 1977.

35. Spears, L. "Practicing Servant-Leadership." *Leader to Leader* 34 (Fall 2004).

36. Bandura, A. *Social Foundations of Thought and Action.* Englewood Cliffs, NJ: Prentice Hall, 1986.

37. Bandura, A. "Mechanisms of Moral Disengagement." In *Origins of Terrorism: Psychologies, Ideologies, Theologies, States of Mind.* Ed. W. Reich. Cambridge: Cambridge University Press., 1990, pp. 161–91.

38. Bandura, A. "Mechanisms of Moral Disengagement." In *Origins of Terrorism: Psychologies, Ideologies, Theologies, States of Mind.* Ed. W. Reich. Cambridge: Cambridge University Press, 1990, p. 164.

39. Bandura, A. "Self-Efficacy: Toward a Unifying Theory of Behavioral Change." *Psychological Review* 84 (1977), pp. 191–215.

40. Darley, J. "Inadvertent Moral Socialization in Military Simulations: Making Disasters Happen." Keynote address at the Applied Behavioral Sciences Symposium, U.S. Air Force Academy, 1994.

41. Darley, J. "Inadvertent Moral Socialization in Military Simulations: Making Disasters Happen." Keynote address at the Applied Behavioral Sciences Symposium, U.S. Air Force Academy, 1994.

42. Darley, J. "Inadvertent Moral Socialization in Military Simulations: Making Disasters Happen." Keynote address at the Applied Behavioral Sciences Symposium, U.S. Air Force Academy, 1994.

43. Halberstam, D. *The Reckoning.* New York: Avon, 1986.

44. Kohls, L. R. *Survival Kit for Overseas Living.* Intercultural Press, 2001.

45. Barnum, D. F. "Effective Membership in the Global Business Community." In *New Traditions in Business.* Ed. J. Renesch. San Francisco: Berrett-Koehler, 1992, p. 153.

46. Hofstede, G. *Cultural Consequences: Comparing Values, Behaviors, Institutions and Organizations across Nations.* 2nd ed. Thousand Oaks, CA: Sage Publications, 2001.

47. Wilson, M. S., M. H. Hoppe, and L. R. Sayles. *Managing across Cultures: A Learning Framework.* Greensboro, NC: Center for Creative Leadership, 1996.

48. House, R. et al. *Cultural Influences on Leadership and Organizations: Project Globe. Advances in Global Leadership.* Vol. 1. JAI Press Inc., 1999, pp. 171–233.

Chapter 7

Leadership Traits

Introduction

> Successful leaders share three abilities. The first is the ability to get along with others and build teams. Another is the ability to make sound and timely decisions. And the third is the ability to get things done. Unfortunately, only a relatively small percentage of leaders possess all three of these attributes.
>
> *Gordy Curphy, Curphy Consulting Corporation*

In Chapter 1 leadership was defined as "the process of influencing an organized group toward accomplishing its goals." Chapter 4 further refined this definition by illustrating that effective leaders have the ability to build cohesive teams and get results. Given these definitions, one question that leadership researchers have tried to answer over the past 100 years is whether certain personal attributes or characteristics help or hinder the leadership process. In other words, does athletic ability, height, personality, intelligence, or creativity help a leader to build a team, get results, or influence a group? Put in the context of national U.S. presidential elections, are those candidates who win the primaries and eventually go on to become president smarter, more creative, more ambitious, or more outgoing than their less successful counterparts? Do these leaders act in fundamentally different ways than their followers, and are these differences in behavior due to differences in their innate intelligence, certain personality traits, or creative ability? If so, then could these same characteristics also be used to differentiate successful from unsuccessful leaders, executives from first-line supervisors, or leaders from individual contributors? It was questions like these that led to what was perhaps the earliest theory of leadership, the **Great Man theory.**[1]

The roots of the Great Man theory can be traced back to the early 1900s, when many leadership researchers and the popular press maintained that leaders and followers were fundamentally different. This led to hundreds of research studies that looked at whether certain personality traits, physical attributes, intelligence, or personal values differentiated leaders from followers. Ralph Stogdill was the first leadership researcher to summarize the results of these studies, and he came to two major conclusions. First, leaders were not qualitatively different than followers; many followers were just as tall, smart, outgoing, and ambitious as the people who were leading them. Second, some characteristics, such as intelligence, initiative, stress tolerance, responsibility, friendliness, and dominance, were modestly related to leadership success. In other words, people who were smart, hardworking, conscientious, friendly, or willing to take charge were often more successful at building teams and influencing a group to accomplish its goals than people who were less smart, lazy, impulsive, grumpy, or did not like giving orders.[2] Having "the right stuff" in and of itself was no guarantee of leadership success, but it did improve the odds of successfully influencing a group toward the accomplishment of its goals.

Subsequent reviews involving hundreds of more sophisticated studies came to the same two conclusions.[1,3] Although these reviews provided ample evidence that people with the right stuff were more likely to be successful as leaders, many leadership researchers focused solely on the point that leaders were not fundamentally different than followers. They erroneously concluded that personal characteristics could not be used to predict future leadership success; as a result most of the subsequent research shifted toward other leadership phenomena. It was not until the publication of seminal articles published in the 1980s and 1990s that intelligence and personality regained popularity with leadership researchers.[4-6] Because of these articles and subsequent leadership research, we now know a lot about how intelligence and various personality traits help or hinder leaders in their efforts to build teams and get results.[7-10] This research also provided insight on the role that various situational and follower characteristics have in affecting how a leader's intelligence and personality play out in the workplace. The purpose of this chapter is to summarize what we currently know about personality, intelligence, and leadership. As an overview, this chapter defines personality, intelligence, creativity, and emotional intelligence, reviews some of the key research findings for these concepts, and discusses the implications of this research for leadership practitioners.

Personality Traits and Leadership

What Is Personality?

There is an optical illusion about every person we ever meet. In truth, they are all creatures of a given temperament, which will appear in a given character, whose boundaries they will never pass: but we look at them, they seem alive, and we presume there is impulse in them. In the moment, it seems like an impulse, in the year, in the lifetime, it turns out to be a certain uniform tune, which the revolving barrel of the music box must play.

Ralph Waldo Emerson

Despite its common usage, Robert Hogan noted that the term **personality** is fairly ambiguous, and has at least two quite different meanings.[6] One meaning refers to the impression a person makes on others. This view of personality emphasizes a person's *social reputation* and reflects not only a description but also an evaluation of the person in the eyes of others. From the standpoint of leadership, this view of personality addresses two distinct issues: "What kind of leader or person is this?" and "Is this somebody I would like to work for or be associated with?" In a practical sense, this view of personality comes into play whenever you describe the person you work for to a roommate or friend. For example, you might describe him or her as pushy, honest, outgoing, impulsive, decisive, friendly, and independent. Furthermore, whatever impression this leader made on you, chances are others would use many of the same terms of description. In that same vein, many people would probably say that U.S. President George W. Bush is self-confident, friendly, outgoing, conventional, stubborn, loyal, and somewhat close-minded.

The second meaning of personality emphasizes the underlying, unseen structures and processes inside a person that explain why we behave the way we do; why each person's behavior tends to be relatively *similar across different situations*, yet also *different from another person's behavior*. Over the years psychologists have developed many theories to explain how such unseen structures may cause individuals to act in their characteristic manner. For example, Sigmund Freud believed that the intrapsychic tensions among the id, ego, and superego caused one to behave in characteristic ways even if the real motives behind the behaviors were unknown (i.e., unconscious) to the person.[11] Although useful insights about personality have come from many different theories, most of the research addressing the relationship between personality and leadership success has been based on the **trait approach,** and that emphasis is most appropriate here.

Traits refer to recurring regularities or trends in a person's behavior, and the trait approach to personality maintains that people behave the way they do because of the strengths of the traits they possess.[6] Although traits cannot be seen, they can be inferred from consistent patterns of behavior and reliably measured by personality inventories. For example, the personality trait of dependability differentiates leaders who tend to be hardworking and rule abiding from those who tend to be lazy and are more prone to break rules. Leaders getting higher scores on the trait of

Angela Merkel

PROFILES IN LEADERSHIP 7.1

Angela Merkel is commonly acknowledged as one of the most powerful females in the world. Assuming office in November 2005, she is the first female to have been elected as Chancellor of Germany and is the first person from the former German Democratic Republic to lead a unified Germany. She is also only the third female to serve on the G8 council and is currently the President of the European Union. At 53 she is also the youngest chancellor since World War II.

Merkel grew up in a rural community in Eastern Germany and showed an aptitude for math and science at a very early age. A member of the communist youth movement in Eastern Germany, she went on to earn both undergraduate and doctoral degrees in physics, specializing in quantum chemistry. She spent much of the 1970s and 80s in academic positions doing cutting-edge chemical research and publishing her work in such periodicals as *Molecular Physics* and *International Journal of Quantum Chemistry.* Chancellor Merkel did not get involved in politics until the fall of the Berlin Wall in 1989.

In the 1990s she was appointed to several ministerial positions in the Helmet Kohl government and was a young protégé of Chancellor Kohl's. A quick study, she learned the intricacies of national politics and international diplomacy under Kohl's mentorship and used this knowledge to run for and win national elections in Germany in 2005. Merkel currently leads a "grand coalition" of parties representing both the left and right wings of German politics. She is leading efforts to liberalize Germany's economy by allowing employers to increase the workweek from 35 to 40 hours and lay off employees during economic downturns. She also supports extending the life of Germany's nuclear power plants beyond 2020 and is opposed to Turkey becoming a full member of the European Union. Despite strong public outcry, Merkel supported the U.S. invasion of Iraq and believes in strong transatlantic relationships with the United States.

Given her background, what can you discern about Chancellor Merkel's public reputation (i.e., personality traits), values, and intelligence?

Source: http//:en.wikipedia.org/wiki/Angela_Merkel.

dependability on a personality inventory would be more likely to come to work on time, do a thorough job in completing work assignments, and rarely leave work early. We would also infer that leaders getting lower scores on the trait of dependability would be more likely to be late to appointments, make impulsive decisions, or fail to follow through with commitments and achieve results.

Personality traits are useful concepts for explaining why people act fairly consistently from one situation to the next. This cross-situational consistency in behavior may be thought of as analogous to the seasonal weather patterns in different cities.[12,13] We know that it is extremely cold and dry in Minneapolis in January and hot and humid in Hong Kong in August. Therefore, we can do a pretty good job predicting what the weather will generally be like in Minneapolis in January, even though our predictions for any particular day will not be perfect. Although the average temperature in Minneapolis hovers around 20°F, the temperature ranges from $-30°F$ to 30°F on any single day in January. Similarly, knowing how two people differ on a particular personality trait can help us predict more accurately how they will tend to act in a variety of situations.

Just as various climate factors can affect the temperature on any single day, so can external factors affect a leader's behavior in any given situation. The trait approach maintains that a leader's behavior reflects an interaction between his or her personality traits and various situational factors (see, for example, Highlight 7.1). Traits play a particularly important role in determining how people behave in unfamiliar, ambiguous, or what we might call **weak situations.** On the other hand, situations that are governed by clearly specified rules, demands, or organizational policies—**strong situations**—often minimize the effects traits have on behavior.[14–18]

The strength of the relationship between personality traits and leadership effectiveness is often inversely related to the relative strength of the situation (i.e., personality traits are more closely related to leadership effectiveness in weak situations). Given the accelerated pace of change in most organizations today, it is likely that leaders will be facing even more unfamiliar and ambiguous situations in the future. Therefore, personality traits may play an increasingly important role in a leader's behavior. If organizations can accurately identify those personality traits and the individuals who possess them, then they should be able to do a better job promoting the right people into leadership positions. And if the right people are in leadership positions, the odds of achieving organizational success should be dramatically improved. The next section describes some of the efforts researchers have taken to identify those personality traits that help leaders build teams and get results through others.

The Five Factor Model of Personality: The Bright Side of Personality

Although personality traits provide a useful approach to describing distinctive, cross-situational behavioral patterns, one potential problem is the sheer number of traitlike terms available to describe another's stereotypical behaviors. As early as 1936 researchers identified over 18,000 trait-related adjectives in a standard English dictionary.[19] Despite this large number of adjectives, research has shown that most of the traitlike terms people use to describe others' behavioral patterns could be reliably categorized into five broad personality dimensions. Historically, this five-dimension model was first identified as early as 1915 and independently verified in 1934, but over the years a number of researchers using very diverse samples and assessment instruments have noted similar results.[5,20,21] Given the robustness of the findings, there appears to be a compelling body of evidence to support these five dimensions of personality. These dimensions are referred to in the personality literature as the **Five Factor Model (FFM) of personality,** and most modern personality researchers endorse some version of this model.[5,6,8,9,17,22–33]

Personality and the Presidency

HIGHLIGHT 7.1

Traits are unseen dispositions that can affect the way people act. Their existence can be inferred by a leader's consistent pattern of behaviors. One way of examining a leader's standing on the trait of achievement orientation is to examine one's achievements and accomplishments over the life span. Leaders with higher levels of achievement orientation tend to set high personal goals and are persistent in the pursuit of these goals. When considering the following leader's achievements and accomplishments, think about this person's standing on this personality trait, and try to guess who this person might be:

Age 23: lost a job.

Age 23: was defeated in bid for state legislature.

Age 24: failed in business venture.

Age 25: was elected to legislature.

Age 26: sweetheart died.

Age 27: experienced several emotional problems.

Age 27: was defeated in bid to be speaker of the house.

Age 34: was defeated for nomination to Congress.

Age 37: was elected to Congress.

Age 39: lost renomination to Congress.

Age 40: was defeated in bid for land office.

Age 45: was defeated in bid for U.S. Senate.

Age 47: was defeated for nomination to be vice president.

Age 49: was defeated in bid for Senate a second time.

Age 51: was elected president of the United States.

The person was Abraham Lincoln.

Secretary Powell and I agree on every single issue that has ever been before this administration except for those instances where Colin is still learning.

Donald Rumsfeld, former U.S. Secretary of Defense

At its core, the FFM of personality is a categorization scheme. Most, if not all, of the personality traits that you would use to describe someone else could be reliably categorized into one of the FFM personality dimensions. A description of the model can be found in Table 7.1. The five major dimensions include surgency, agreeableness, dependability, adjustment, and intellectance. **Surgency** (also referred to as dominance, self-confidence, the need for power, or dynamic) involves patterns of behavior often exhibited in group settings and generally concerned with getting ahead in life.[17,33–35] Such behavioral patterns often appear when someone is trying to influence or control others, and individuals higher in surgency come across to others as outgoing, competitive, decisive, impactful, and self-confident. Individuals lower in surgency generally prefer to work by themselves and have relatively little interest in influencing or competing with others. Because leaders' decisiveness, competitiveness, and self-confidence can affect their ability to successfully influence a group, build a team, and get results, it is not surprising that leaders often have higher surgency scores than non-leaders.[8,9,17,27,36,37] You can see differences in people's standing on surgency every time a group of people gets together. Some people in a group are going to be outgoing and will try to get the group to do certain things; others are more comfortable going along with rather than arguing over group activities. This strong need to assume leadership positions in groups is often associated with a willingness to take risks and make decisions, and with upward

TABLE 7.1
The Five Factor Model of Personality

Five Factor Dimensions	Hogan Personality Inventory Dimensions	Behaviors/Items
Surgency	Ambition	I like having responsibility for others.
	Sociability	I have a large group of friends.
Agreeableness	Interpersonal sensitivity	I am a sympathetic person.
Dependability	Prudence	I usually make "to do" lists.
		I practice what I preach.
		I rarely get into trouble.
Adjustment	Adjustment	I remain calm in pressure situations.
		I take personal criticism well.
Openness to Experience	Inquisitive	I like traveling to foreign countries.
	Learning Approach	I like staying up to speed on certain topics.

[Handwritten margin notes: "Not the same as Intelligence"; "Intellectance Curiosity"]

mobility. Many of the candidates on the television show *The Apprentice* have higher surgency scores. These candidates are more than willing to make decisions and vociferously argue why they shouldn't be fired when their projects go poorly. Those with lower surgency scores often get "run over" by those with higher scores on their project teams. But as various episodes on this television show demonstrate, being the most decisive and domineering individual in a group does not guarantee project success. Many times those with the highest surgency scores make very poor decisions about their projects and/or fail to get the people on their projects to work together effectively.

Although possessing a high level of surgency is no guarantee for leadership success, people who are decisive and self-confident do seem to be more effective leaders, and as such surgency is a very important measure of leadership potential. It is also associated with the four managerial types described in Chapter 4. Competent and Results Only Managers usually have higher surgency levels, Cheerleaders have moderate levels, and In Name Only Managers typically have lower scores on surgency trait measures.

Another FFM personality dimension is **agreeableness** (also known as empathy, friendliness, interpersonal sensitivity, or the need for affiliation). This personality dimension concerns how one gets along with, as opposed to gets ahead of, others.[17,33,35] Individuals high in agreeableness come across to others as charming, diplomatic, warm, empathetic, approachable, and optimistic; those lower in agreeableness are more apt to appear as insensitive, socially clueless, grumpy, cold, and pessimistic. Differences in agreeableness can easily be seen on the television show *American Idol*. Paula Abdul has a high agreeableness score and never has a harsh word to say about any candidate, no matter how poorly he or she performs. Randy

Thermonuclear coaching sessions can be very effective techniques for getting the attention of pilots.

Anthony Burke, F-16 pilot

Jackson has a moderate agreeableness score and tries to provide both positive and negative feedback to candidates. Simon Cowell has a very low agreeableness score. He could care less if anyone likes him and does not pull any punches when giving feedback to candidates.

Although persons with high agreeableness trait scores tend to be better at building teams than those with lower scores, they can struggle with getting results through others. This is because persons with higher scores have difficulties making unpopular decisions or dealing with conflict and performance issues, which in turn can negatively erode the effectiveness of their teams. Because of these difficulties, research has shown that agreeableness has had mixed results in predicting leadership effectiveness.[8,27,37–39] Agreeableness is related to the four managerial types found in Chapter 4. Competent Managers have moderate levels, Results Only Managers have low levels, and Cheerleaders have extremely high levels of agreeableness. In Name Only Managers seem to have mixed agreeableness scores.

Unlike surgency and agreeableness, **dependability** (also known as conscientiousness or prudence) does not involve interacting with others but rather concerns those behavioral patterns related to people's approach to work. Leaders who are higher in dependability tend to be planful, organized, and earnest, take commitments seriously, and rarely get into trouble. Those who are lower in dependability tend to be more spontaneous, creative, impulsive, rule bending, and less concerned with following through with commitments. The characters Jerry Seinfeld and George Costanza from the television show *Seinfeld* provide a nice illustration of high and low dependability trait scores. Jerry is a cautious neat freak; George is lazy and impulsive and rarely keeps promises. Research shows that individuals with higher dependability scores are more likely to be effective leaders than those with lower scores.[8,9,17,30,37,40,41]

In many ways dependability may be more concerned with management than leadership. That is because people with higher scores are planful, organized, and goal oriented, and prefer structure but are also risk averse, uncreative, somewhat boring, and dislike change. Although the situation will determine how important these tendencies are for building teams and getting results, research has shown that dependability is a good indicator of leadership potential. Like surgency and agreeableness, dependability also has some relationship with the four managerial types described in Chapter 4. In all likelihood Competent Managers have moderate levels whereas Results Only Managers have high levels of dependability. Cheerleaders and In Name Only Managers often have lower dependability trait scores.

Adjustment (also known as neuroticism, emotional stability, or self-control) is concerned with how people react to stress, failure, or personal criticism. Leaders higher in adjustment tend to be thick-skinned, calm, and optimistic, tend not to take mistakes or failures personally, and hide their emotions, whereas those lower in adjustment may become thin-skinned, tense, or anxious, or lose their temper when stressed or criticized. Followers

Persistence. Nothing in the world can take the place of persistence. Talent will not; nothing is more common than unsuccessful men with talent. Genius will not; unrewarded genius is almost a proverb. Education will not; the world is full of educated derelicts. Persistence and determination alone are omnipotent. "Press on" has solved and always will solve the problems of the human race.

Calvin Coolidge, U.S. President

Some people are just more excitable than others.

Cosmo Kramer, *Seinfeld*

Level 5 Leadership

HIGHLIGHT 7.2

Over the past 20 years, some private corporations, such as Coca-Cola, General Electric, British Petroleum, IBM, and Wal-Mart, have performed very well. People who invested $10,000 in these companies would have seen their investments increase four- to tenfold over this time. But there are some companies that outperformed even these high fliers. Jim Collins and his staff examined all the companies that appeared on the Fortune 500 list from 1965 to 1995 and found 11 companies that dramatically beat all the others in terms of returns. One critical component of this tremendous financial success was **Level 5 Leadership.** According to Collins, all of these companies were led by leaders who had a unique combination of humility and will. As Collins says, Abraham Lincoln never let his ego get in the way of his dream of building a great, enduring nation. Similarly, these corporate leaders did not let their egos get in the way of building great companies. These leaders avoided the spotlight (low Sociability scores), but they were very focused on creating a company that delivered outstanding results (high Ambition scores). They also possessed an unbreakable resolve that channeled all of their energy toward the success of their companies, as opposed to the pursuit of ever grander personal titles. All of these leaders were calm in crises, were never boastful and took responsibility for failure

(high Adjustment scores), and were courteous and polite (high Agreeableness). These leaders set the tone for their respective organizations and spent a considerable amount of time surrounding themselves with the right people and building high-performing teams. As a result, these companies returned $471 for every dollar invested in 1965.

It is worth noting that Level 5 Leaders act quite differently from stereotypical corporate executives. Back in the late 1990s senior executives would do all they could to get on television, and many of these charismatic leaders seemed more interested in personal aggrandizement than company success (e.g., Dennis Kozlowski, John Rigas, Jeffrey Skilling, or Bernie Ebbers). Unfortunately, it appears that many boards of directors have not paid attention to the key lessons of Collins's book, as they continue to look for charismatic rather than Level 5 CEOs to run their organizations.

Sources: J. Collins, *Good to Great.* New York: Harper Collins, 2001; R. Khurana, "The Curse of the Superstar CEO." *Harvard Business Review,* September 2002, pp. 60–67; J. A. Sonnenfeld and R. Khurana, "Fishing for CEOs in Your Own Backyard." *The Wall Street Journal,* July 30, 2002, p. B2; R. S. Peterson, D. B. Smith, P. V. Martorana, and P. D. Owens, "The Impact of Chief Executive Officer Personality on Top Management Team Dynamics: One Mechanism by Which Leadership Affects Organizational Performance." *Journal of Applied Psychology* 88 (5) (2003), pp. 795–808.

often mimic a leader's emotions or behaviors under periods of high stress, so leaders who are calm under pressure and thick-skinned can often help a group stay on task and work through difficult issues. Unfortunately, the opposite is also true.

Differences in adjustment can easily be observed in the judges on *American Idol.* Paula Abdul has a low adjustment score and readily laughs or cries on the show; Simon Cowell has a high adjustment score and rarely displays any emotion on the show. Differences in emotional volatility certainly can affect a person's ability to build teams and get results, and research has shown adjustment is another good predictor of leadership potential.[5,8,9,17,29,30,40,41] It is also related to the four managerial types described in Chapter 4. Competent Managers have moderate adjustment scores; Cheerleaders and Results Only Managers tend to have lower

Why do people think artists are so special? It is just another job.
Andy Warhol, artist

adjustment scores. In Name Only Managers often have very high adjustment scores.

Those behavioral patterns dealing with how one approaches problems, learns new information, and reacts to new experiences are related to the personality dimension of **openness to experience** (also known as intellectance, curiosity, inquisitiveness, and learning approach). Leaders higher in openness to experience tend to be imaginative, broad-minded, and curious, and are more strategic, big-picture thinkers; they seek out new experiences through travel, the arts, movies, sports, reading, going to new restaurants, or learning about new cultures. Individuals lower in openness to experience tend to be more practical and have narrower interests; they like doing things the tried-and-true way rather than experimenting with new ways. It is important to note that openness to experience is not the same thing as intelligence—smart people are not necessarily intellectually curious.

Like the other FFM dimensions, research has shown that openness to experience is an important component of leadership effectiveness.[8,17,28,29,30,31,37,41,42] Openness to experience seems particularly important at higher organizational levels or for overseas assignments. For example, people with higher openness to experience scores like to take a more strategic approach to solving problems. These higher scores help business unit leaders and CEOs to keep abreast of market trends, competitive threats, new products, and regulatory changes. And because people with higher openness to experience scores also like new and novel experiences, they often enjoy the challenges associated with living and leading in foreign countries.

Implications of the Five Factor Model

The trait approach and the FFM provide leadership researchers and practitioners with several useful tools and insights. For one, personality traits provide researchers and practitioners with an explanation for leaders' and followers' tendencies to act in consistent ways over time. They help us to understand why some leaders appear to be dominant versus deferent, outspoken versus quiet, planful versus spontaneous, warm versus cold, and so forth. It is also important to note that the behavioral manifestations of personality traits are often exhibited automatically and without much conscious thought. People high in surgency, for example, will often maneuver to influence or lead whatever groups or teams they are a part of without even thinking about it. Although personality traits predispose us to act in certain ways, we can nonetheless learn to modify our behaviors through experience, feedback, and reflection.

As seen in Figure 7.1, personality traits are one of the key components of behavior and are relatively difficult to change. Moreover, because personality traits tend to be stable over the years and the behavioral manifestations of traits occur somewhat automatically, it is extremely important

Personality Types and Leadership

HIGHLIGHT 7.3

The FFM provides a useful framework for describing leaders' behaviors, but it is not the only way to describe personality. An alternative way to describe how leaders and followers differ in their day-to-day behavior patterns is through **types**, or in terms of a **personality typology**. Unlike traits, which assume people fall somewhere along a continuum of low to high scores on any particular bright side personality dimension, personality typology assumes that there are qualitatively different types of people and leaders. The signs of the Zodiac provide an unscientific but popular illustration of personality typology. For example, Leos are assumed to be fundamentally different than Pisces or Aquarians. The same holds true for the Chinese calendar; people born in the year of the Monkey are assumed to be qualitatively different than people born in the year of the Pig or Goat.

Isabel Myers and her colleagues created what would turn out to be a very popular personality typology for working adults. Myers began her career as a writer of detective novels who later became enamored with the idea of personality types. She created a typology loosely based on the research of a famous psychologist, Carl Jung, and created an instrument that categorizes people into one of 16 personality types. This instrument, the **Myers-Briggs Type Indicator (MBTI)**, is perhaps the most popular psychological assessment today and is taken by over 2 million people per year. The MBTI is used in 89 of the Fortune 100 companies and in college-level and adult leadership development courses, career and marriage counseling, child-rearing programs, coaching programs, and team-building interventions.

According to this typology, people differ on four bipolar dimensions, which include **extraversion–introversion, sensing–intuition, thinking–feeling,** and **judging–perceiving.** Scores on each of the four dimensions results in one of the 16 personality types (e.g., an extraversion, intuition, thinking, and judging type, an introversion, sensing, thinking, and judging type, etc.). Although the test publishers have done extensive research and claim that the MBTI is a reliable and valid measure of personality, outside reviewers believe the instrument has at least three major limitations. First, the MBTI has somewhat of a cult-like following and many of its converts can only see the world through MBTI glasses. Personality types can become a perceptual filter by which we perceive others as well as a rationalization for our own or others' behavior. Second, personality types are not stable—research indicates that types will change 50 percent of the time during a retest. Third, the test is relatively easy to fake. Once people gain a basic understanding of the four dimensions, they can easily manipulate their assessment results to be any one of the 16 types. Because of these limitations it is difficult to see how the assessment could be used for selection or development purposes, as types are likely to change from one setting to the next. Despite these limitations, the MBTI is a very popular and potentially useful instrument for understanding the nature of personality and how it plays out in day-to-day behaviors.

Sources: McCarley and Carskadon, 1983, p. 570; Myers, 1976, 1977, 1980, p. 572; Myers and Briggs, 1943/1965, p. 573; Myers and McCaulley, 1985, p. 573; P. B. Myers and K. D. Myers, *The Myers-Briggs Type Indicator Step II (Form Q) Profile.* Palo Alto, CA: Consulting Psychologists Press, 2001, 2003; Quast & Hansen, 1996, p. 577; N. L. Quenk and J. M. Kummerow, *The Myers-Briggs Type Indicator Step II (Form Q) Profile (Form B).* Palo Alto, CA: Consulting Psychologists Press, 2001; Thayer, 1988, p. 584; A. Murphy Hall, *The Cult of Personality.* New York, Free Press, 2005; D. J. Pittinger, "Cautionary Comments Regarding the Myers-Briggs Type Indicator." *Journal of Consulting Psychology* 57 (3) (2005), pp. 210–21; F. W. Gibson and G. J. Curphy, "The MBTI: Skewering A Sacred Cow." Presentation given to the Colorado Organizational Development Network, Denver, CO, 1996.

FIGURE 7.1
The building blocks
of skills.

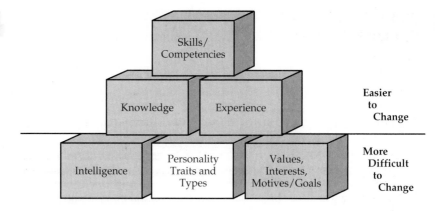

for leaders, and leaders to be, to have insight into their personalities. For example, consider a leader who is relatively low in the trait of adjustment but also is deciding whether to accept a high-stress/high-visibility job. On the basis of his personality trait scores alone, we might predict that this leader could be especially sensitive to criticism and could be moody and prone to emotional outbursts. If the leader understood that he may have issues dealing with stress and criticism, then he could choose not to take the position, modify the situation to reduce the level of stress, or learn techniques for effectively dealing with these issues. A leader who lacked this self-insight would probably make poorer choices and have more difficulties coping with the demands of this position.[43]

The FFM has proved to be very useful in several different ways. It is fairly robust, and most personality researchers currently embrace some form of the Big Five model.[6,8,17,22,23,26,29–31,37,40–45] Furthermore, the model has proved to be a very useful scheme for categorizing the findings of the personality–leadership performance research. Because research has shown personality to be an effective measure of leadership potential, organizations now use the results of FFM personality assessments for hiring new leaders, providing leaders with developmental feedback about various personality traits, and as a key component in succession planning processes to promote leaders.[46]

Another advantage of the FFM is that it is a useful method for profiling leaders. For example, a business unit leader's results on a FFM personality assessment, the Hogan Personality Inventory, can be found in Figure 7.2.[47] According to this profile, this leader will generally come across to others as optimistic, resilient, and calm under pressure (high Adjustment); self-confident, goal oriented, and competitive (high Ambition); outgoing, liking to be the center of attention, but also distractible and a poor listener (high Sociability); diplomatic and charming, but having trouble dealing with performance problems (high Interpersonal Sensitivity); planful and rule abiding (high Prudence); a strategic, big-picture thinker (high Inquisitive);

FIGURE 7.2
Leadership potential profile.

Source: Adapted with permission of Hogan Assessment Systems.

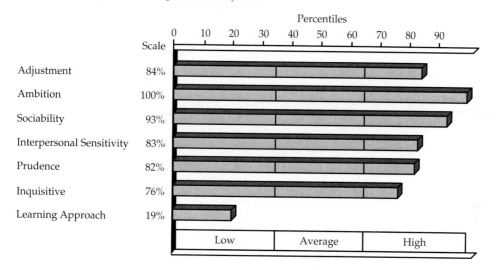

but someone who prefers to learn using a just-in-time, hands-on approach as opposed to sitting in a classroom setting. Other leaders will have different behavioral tendencies, and knowing this type of information *before* someone gets hired or promoted into a leadership position can help improve the odds of organizational success. When aggregated, these individual personality profiles can yield some interesting results. For example, researchers reported that a unique set of personality traits differentiated senior leaders in operational units compared with those in staff functions in the U.S. Army.[48] Other researchers showed that engineers and accountants tended to be lower in the trait of surgency but higher in the trait of dependability.[28,49] On the other hand, marketing and sales place a premium on creativity and on influencing others, and people in these occupations tended to be higher in surgency but lower in dependability. There is a compelling body of evidence showing that surgency, agreeableness, dependability, adjustment, and openness to experience are all positively correlated with leadership success—the higher the scores on one or more of these five FFM dimensions, the more likely an individual will be an effective leader.[5,8,9,17,27,29,33,40,41,46,50–52] Some of this research also showed that surgency is the best predictor of a leadership job offer after an interview and successful completion of an overseas leadership assignment.[53,54] Agreeableness and openness to experience are also key factors in completing overseas leadership assignments and working in tightly confined team situations, such as submarine crews.[39,42] Dependability is related to the amount of time people take to prepare for an interview and their overall job performance and satisfaction; lower scores increase their likelihood of engaging in counterproductive work behaviors.[23,26,32,36,53,55,56] Higher adjustment scores also helped leaders to complete an overseas assignment, successfully cope with change, and report positive earnings per share after an initial public offering.[57,58] Research has shown that FFM traits can reliably predict entrepreneurial status and firm growth and employee productivity, performance, and job satisfaction.[5,6,9,27,29,30,41,56,59,60] In a similar vein, one researcher reported some interesting findings for military cadets who were higher in agreeableness and surgency.[61] His research indicated that higher agreeableness was positively related to performance ratings during the freshman and sophomore years but that higher surgency was more strongly related to performance ratings over the last two years at the U.S. Coast Guard Academy. Apparently getting along with others and developing strong social supports are very important during the first two years of a military cadet's life, but getting ahead becomes more important over the last two years. It may be that it takes a couple of years to develop strong social networks and supports, and once they have been established, other personality traits, such as surgency, become more important.

Another advantage of the Five Factor Model is that it appears universally applicable across cultures.[12,14,16,37,62,63] People from Asian, Western European, Middle Eastern, Eastern European, or South American cultures seem to use the same five personality dimensions to categorize, profile, or describe others. Not only do people from different cultures describe others using the same FFM framework, these dimensions all seem to predict job and leadership performance across cultures. For example, in a comprehensive review of the research, Salgado reported that all five of the FFM dimensions predicted blue collar, professional, and managerial performance in various European countries.[37,63] But the strength of the personality–job performance relationship depends on the particular job. Some jobs, such as sales, put a premium on interpersonal skills and goal orientation (e.g., surgency and agreeableness); whereas manufacturing jobs put more of a premium on planning and abiding by safety and productivity rules (e.g., dependability). Researchers often get much stronger personality–job performance relationships when the personality traits being measured have some degree of job relatedness.[17,18,29]

In summary, there are several things we can say about the bright side of personality. First, people tend to describe others using traitlike terms, and personality traits can be reliably categorized into the five major dimensions of the FFM. Second, personality traits are good measures of leadership potential and as such can be used to make predictions about how effective candidates will be if placed in leadership positions. Third, there is an overwhelming body of research that shows all five of the FFM dimensions are related to leadership success across different cultures. However, the strength of the personality–leadership performance relationships will depend on the particular demands of the situation and the job. Fourth, personality tends to be difficult to change—people are "hard wired" to exhibit

Personality, Values, and Character Development

HIGHLIGHT 7.4

As described in this chapter, personality traits are fairly well ingrained and difficult to change. Once a person reaches their early twenties their scores on surgency, agreeableness, dependability, adjustment, and openness to experience remain relatively unchanged. The same holds true with the core values described in Chapter 6. Once a person reaches their late teens or early twenties they will always be motivated to get results (Power), achieve tenure (Security), make money (Commercial), or help others (Altruism). Thus by the early twenties the die has been cast and an individual's personality traits and core values remain relatively unchanged for the next 50+ years. This does not mean people can't change their behavior to fit the demands of a situation. Through experience, most people learn how their personality and values help or hurt them in different situations and how to modify their behavior accordingly. But a key fact is that who you are now is pretty much who you will be as you approach your late sixties and seventies. Personality and values are essential components of a person's character. **Character** can be defined as a person's fundamental beliefs and public reputation. If you ask about a person's "character," virtually all the responses involve religiosity, ethics, motives, and enduring qualities—i.e., personality traits and core values. Given that core values and personality traits are fairly set by the time a person

is a junior or senior in college, a question that begs asking is whether college-level programs specifically designed to improve character are effective. Some of the most intensive character development training occurs at military academies, where students are constantly taking classes in ethics, law, sexual harassment, substance abuse, honor codes, etc. These institutions have large bureaucracies and spend millions of dollars each year to support these programs, yet incidents of cheating, sexual harassment, and alcohol abuse seem to occur on an all too regular basis. And rest assured that cadets endure even more character development training as soon as one of these instances goes public.

Despite all of this training, situational factors rather than character development programs may be the biggest deterrents of abhorrent cadet behavior. Cadets are constantly reminded of the institution's expectations for their behavior and are punished whenever they are caught deviating from these standards. It is very likely that the academies are getting *compliance* to behavioral standards through the use of sanctions, but it is uncertain whether character development programs achieve cadets' enduring *commitment* to these standards. One cost-effective way to decrease the number of high-visibility incidents of cadet misconduct and increase the odds of graduating cadets with good character would be to use personality and values assessments as part of the cadet selection process.

those behaviors associated with their personality traits. Fifth, all behavior is under conscious control. We may more or less have an automatic response to stress based on our adjustment scores, but we can choose to act differently if we want to. But it does take conscious effort to exhibit nontrait behaviors. Sixth, having insight into one's personality traits can give people information about their leadership potential, strengths, development needs, and how much effort they will have to put forth to overcome these needs. Because personality has been shown to be an effective predictor of leadership potential, more and more organizations are incorporating personality assessment into their hiring and succession planning practices. That being said, it is very likely that you will take some kind of personality assessment as you apply for jobs after graduation.

Why Do Some Leaders Fail? The Dark Side of Personality

Managerial failure may be due more to having undersirable qualities than lacking desirable ones.

Bob and Joyce Hogan, Hogan Assessment System

As described in Chapter 4, the base rate of managerial incompetence may be as high as 75 percent; a majority of people in positions of authority have difficulty building cohesive, goal-oriented teams and achieving superior results.[41,46,64–71] Some people in leadership positions seem able to get results without building a team, but these results are typically very short-term. Others seem more focused on playing the role of a cheerleader and are able to build cohesive teams, but these teams often do not get much accomplished.

There are several reasons for this high level of incompetence, some of which include invalid selection and succession planning systems (see Chapter 4), ill-defined performance expectations (see Chapter 9), and poorly designed leadership development programs (see Chapter 3). But **dark-side personality traits** are some of the other key reasons for the high failure rate of leaders. Dark-side personality traits are irritating, counterproductive behavioral tendencies that interfere with a leader's ability to build cohesive teams and cause followers to exert less effort toward goal accomplishment.[40,41,46,71,72] A listing of 11 common dark-side traits can be found in Table 7.2. Any of these 11 tendencies, if exhibited on a regular basis, will negatively affect the leader's ability to get results through others. And if you thought about some of the worst bosses you ever worked for, chances are these individuals possessed one or more of these 11 dark-side personality traits.

It is probably not an exaggeration to state that if individuals with significant narcissistic characteristics were stripped from the ranks of public figures, the ranks would be perilously thinned.

Jerrold M. Post, political psychologist

There are several aspects of dark-side personality traits that are worth noting. First, everyone has at least one dark-side personality trait. Figure 7.3 shows a graphic output from a typical dark-side personality measure, and indicates that this individual has strong leisurely and diligent tendencies and moderate cautious and dutiful tendencies (scores above the 90th percentile indicate a high risk and within the 70–89th percentiles indicate a moderate risk of dark-side tendencies). These results in Figure 7.3 indicate that when in a crisis this leader will slow down the decision-making process, not follow though on commitments, tend to micro-manage others, and not stand up for his or her followers and get them the resources they need to get tasks accomplished. Second, dark-side traits usually emerge during crises or periods of high stress and are coping mechanisms for dealing with stress. People act differently when under stress and the behaviors associated with dark-side traits help leaders to deal with stress more effectively. The problem is that although these coping behaviors *positively affect leaders'* ability to deal with stress, these same behaviors *negatively affect followers'* motivation and performance. Although yelling and temper tantrums might help leaders to blow off steam (excitable), it makes followers feel like they are walking on eggshells and wondering if they are going to be the next target of their leader's tirades.

Third, dark-side traits have a bigger influence on performance for people in leadership versus followership roles. Individual contributors

TABLE 7.2
Dark-Side
Personality Traits

Excitable	Leaders with these tendencies have difficulties building teams because of their dramatic mood swings, emotional outbursts, and inability to persist on projects.
Skeptical	Leaders with this dark-side trait have an unhealthy mistrust of others, are constantly questioning the motives and challenging the integrity of their followers, and are vigilant for signs of disloyalty.
Cautious	Because these leaders are so fearful of making "dumb" mistakes, they alienate their staffs by not making decisions or taking action on issues.
Reserved	During times of stress these leaders become extremely withdrawn, are uncommunicative, difficult to find, and unconcerned about the welfare of their staffs.
Leisurely	These passive-aggressive leaders will only exert effort in the pursuit of their own agendas and will procrastinate or not follow through with requests that are not in line with their agendas.
Bold	Because of their narcissistic tendencies, these leaders often get quite a bit done. But their feelings of entitlement, inability to share credit for success, tendency to blame their mistakes on others, and inability to learn from experience often result in trails of bruised followers.
Mischievous	These leaders tend to be quite charming but take pleasure in seeing if they can get away with breaking commitments, rules, policies, and laws. When caught, they also believe they can talk their way out of any problem.
Colorful	Leaders with this tendency believe they are "hot" and have an unhealthy need to be the center of attention. They are so preoccupied with being noticed that they are unable to share credit, maintain focus, or get much done.
Imaginative	Followers question the judgment of leaders with this tendency, as these leaders think in eccentric ways, often changing their minds, and make strange or odd decisions.
Diligent	Because of their perfectionistic tendencies, these leaders frustrate and disempower their staffs through micro-management, poor prioritization, and an inability to delegate.
Dutiful	These leaders deal with stress by sucking up to superiors. They lack spines, are unwilling to refuse unrealistic requests, won't stand up for their staffs, and burn them out as a result.

Source: Hogan Assessment Systems, *The Hogan Development Survey.* Tulsa, OK: 2002.

I did not have sexual rela-tions with that woman.
Bill Clinton, U.S. president

might have leisurely or cautious tendencies, but because they do not have to get work done through others these tendencies have less of an impact on their work units than if these same individuals were first-line supervisors or business unit leaders. Let there be no doubt that these individual contributors may not be fun to work with, but their counterproductive tendencies will not be as debilitating to their teams as they would if these

FIGURE 7.3
Leadership challenge profile.

Source: Adapted with permission of Hogan Assessment Systems.

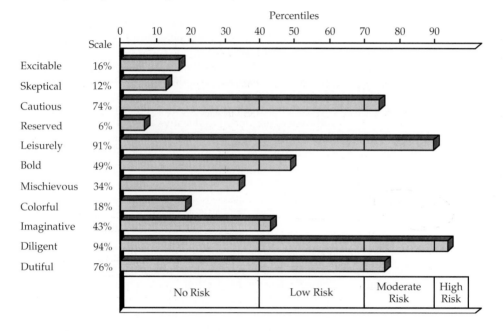

people were leading their teams. Fourth, the dark-side traits are usually only apparent when leaders are not attending to their public image. In other words, people will not see the behaviors associated with dark-side traits when leaders are concerned with how they are coming across to others. These tendencies are much more likely to appear under times of stress, when multitasking or focusing on task accomplishment, during crises, or when leaders feel comfortable enough around others to "let their guard down."[33,40,41,64,70–72] And given the high level of stress, challenge, and complexity associated with most leadership positions, the conditions are ripe for the appearance of dark-side traits.

Fifth, many dark-side traits co-vary with social skills and are difficult to detect in interviews or assessment centers, or with bright-side personality inventories.[5,41,64,68,70–72] In other words, people who possess bold, mischievous, colorful, and imaginative dark-side traits often do well in interviews. And many of these individuals get hired because of their performance in interviews. It is only after these individuals have been on the job for some time that their dark-side tendencies begin to emerge. Sixth, the 11 dark-side personality traits are related to extreme FFM scores. For example, diligent is often associated with extremely high

Ted Haggard

PROFILES IN LEADERSHIP 7.2

Ted Haggard is the founder and former pastor at the New Life Church in Colorado Springs, Colorado. He is also the founder of the Association of Life-Giving Churches and the leader of the 30,000,000-member National Association of Evangelicals from 2003 to 2006. Known as Pastor Ted to his parishioners, Haggard grew up in Indiana and his father was a veterinarian who founded an international charismatic ministry. Born again in 1972, Ted Haggard received an undergraduate degree from Oral Roberts University and got married in 1978. While working in various ministries and raising his five children, Haggard had a vision to build a church in Colorado Springs. Starting in his basement in 1984, Ted Haggard recruited new members and eventually had to rent space in various strip malls in order to accommodate his ever-expanding flock. His membership grew so large that he eventually built the New Life Church in the northern suburbs of Colorado Springs. By late 2006 the New Life Church had 14,000 active members. Based on his success as a minister, *Time* named Ted Haggard one of the top 25 influential evangelicals in the nation. A firm supporter of G. W. Bush, Haggard was credited with rallying evangelicals around the country to vote for President Bush in the 2004 election. As seen in the movie *Jesus Camp*, Haggard is a believer in biblical literalism and has spoken out prominently against homosexuality and same sex marriage. In the fall of 2006 the citizens of Colorado were to vote on a state amendment that defined marriage as a man and a women and Ted Haggard was an active spokesperson for the amendment's passage. Unfortunately for Haggard, a former male prostitute named Mike Jones publicly stated that he had been having sex and doing drugs with Haggard from 2003 to 2006. Haggard initially denied these charges but a later press release stated, "I am guilty of sexual immorality, and take responsibility for the entire problem. I am a deceiver and a liar. There is a part of my life that is so dark that I've been warring against it all of my adult life . . . The accusations that have been leveled against me are not all true, but enough of them are true that I have been appropriately and lovingly removed from ministry."

Haggard was stripped of his ministry in November of 2006 because of these alleged incidents with Mike Jones, but prior to his downfall he was clearly a Competent Manager—he was able to build cohesive teams and these teams were able to consistently achieve results. He was one of the most influential religious leaders in America and his leadership helped get President Bush elected to his second term and create a 14,000-member church. His values and bright-side traits helped him to achieve greatness but his dark-side traits eventually led to his downfall. What bright-side traits do you think contributed to Haggard's success? What dark-side traits do you think led to his downfall?

Sources: http://en.wikipedia.org/wiki/Ted_Haggard. http://www.washingtonpost.com/wp-dyn/content/article/2006/11/02/AR2006

dependability scores, and excitable is associated with extremely low adjustment scores. However, just because a person has an extremely high or low FFM dimension score does not necessarily mean they also possess the corresponding dark-side personality traits. But there are strong relationships between the FFM and the dark-side personality traits.[33,64] Seventh, the behaviors associated with dark-side personality traits can occur at any leadership level, and many times organizations tolerate these behaviors because the leader is smart, experienced, or possesses unique skills (see Profiles in Leadership 7.2, 7.3, and 7.4 and Highlights 7.4 and 7.6). Along these lines, persons with bold tendencies are particularly adept at moving up in organizations. Nothing ever got launched without a healthy dose of narcissism, and leaders with bold tendencies are quick to volunteer for new assignments, take on seemingly impossible challenges, and consistently underestimate the amount of time, money, and effort it will take to get a job accomplished. In some cases these leaders pull off the seemingly impossible and get promoted because of their accomplishments (for example, see Howard Hughes in the movie *The Aviator*). But when things go south (which they often do), these same leaders are quick to blame the situation or others for their failures and as a result never learn from their mistakes.[64,68,70,72,75–79]

The final point to be made about dark-side tendencies is that they are a leading cause of managerial incompetence. Dark-side traits are prevalent (everybody has at least one), they are virtually impossible to detect using the most common selection techniques (interviews and résumés), and they tend to emerge during periods of stress (workloads, workplace stress, and burnout are at all-time highs these days). From Chapter 4, Competent Managers are those who have gained insight into their dark-side traits and have found ways to negate their debilitating effects on followers. Results Only Managers are likely to exhibit excitable, reserved, bold, and diligent tendencies, and Cheerleaders usually suffer from unchecked leisurely, mischievous, colorful, and dutiful tendencies. In Name Only Managers often exhibit the behaviors associated with skeptical, cautious, and imaginative dark-side traits.

So if virtually everyone has dark-side personality tendencies, what can individuals and organizations do about them? First and foremost, leaders and leaders to be need to identify their dark-side personality traits. This can be done by asking trusted others about how one acts under pressure or what behaviors interfere with one's ability to build teams, or by completing a dark-side personality assessment. Once these counterproductive tendencies are identified, leaders then need to understand the situations or conditions in which these tendencies are likely to appear. Again, dark-side traits are most likely to appear during times of stress and heavy workload, so finding ways to better manage stress and workload will help reduce the likelihood of these dark-side tendencies. Just being aware of one's dark-side tendencies and understanding the circumstances in which they appear will go a long way toward controlling the manifestation of counterproductive leadership behaviors. Exercise and other stress reduction techniques and having trusted followers who can tell leaders when they are exhibiting dark-side traits can also help control these tendencies. Finally, having higher scores on the FFM dimension of adjustment also helps with some of these dimensions, as these leaders seem to be better able to cope with stress than those with low scores.

The Negative Consequences of Dark-Side Personality Traits

HIGHLIGHT 7.5

From 1999–2004 the U.S. Navy relieved of duty at least 80 commanding officers for various performance problems. Roughly a third of these dismissals were due to mishaps, such as ship collisions or the death of crew members. But many of the other dismissals were due to inappropriate behavior, such as adultery, inappropriate relationships with subordinates, or alcohol abuse. The good news is that only a small percentage of the people occupying one of the 1,300 command officer positions in the U.S. Navy were dismissed. At first blush this seems like the prevalence of dark-side traits among U.S. Navy officers (or at least the manifestation of these traits) is quite low. But it is important to remember that many of the officers exhibiting dark-side tendencies either failed to get promoted, voluntarily resigned, or were dismissed or discharged before they got a chance to assume a command position. In these cases the U.S. Navy's succession planning system worked, as many of these people were weeded out before assuming a command position. It is also quite likely that some of the officers occupying these command positions are exhibiting dark-side behaviors, but these tendencies in and of themselves may not be problematic enough for dismissal (but will make life hell for subordinates).

The bad news is that the prevalence of dark-side traits among people in significant positions of authority may be even higher in the business world than it is in the U.S. military. From 1978 to 2002 federal regulators initiated 585 investigations of financial misrepresentation by publicly traded companies. These investigations involved 2,310 individuals in 657 firms and resulted in $16.5 billion in fines and civil penalties to individuals and $8.4 billion in fines and damages to the companies they worked for. And these monetary damages were only for those individuals and firms that got caught and were most likely the result of only two dark-side traits— bold and mischievous. The cost associated with lost productivity, poor morale, and high turnover are truly staggering if all the unchecked dark-side traits exhibited by people in positions of authority across all private and public sector organizations is factored in.

Sources: Associated Press, "Navy Assesses Troubling Performance Problems Among Commanding Officers." *Minneapolis Star Tribune,* December 23, 2004, p. A3; K. Cools, "Ebbers Rex." *The Wall Street Journal,* March 22, 2005, p. B2.

Intelligence and Leadership

What Is Intelligence?

Perhaps no concept in the history of psychology has had or continues to have as great an impact on everyday life in the Western world as that of general intelligence.

Sandra Scarr,
researcher

The first formal linkage between intelligence and leadership was established around 1115 B.C. in China, where the dynasties used standardized tests to determine which citizens would play key leadership roles in the institutions they had set up to run the country.[80] Using intelligence tests to identify potential leaders in the United States goes back to World War I, and to a large extent this use of intelligence testing continues today. Over 100 years of very comprehensive and systematic research provides overwhelming evidence to support the notion that general intelligence plays a substantial role in human affairs.[81–90] Still, intelligence and intelligence testing are among the most controversial topics in the social sciences today. There is contentious debate over questions like how heredity and the environment affect intelligence, whether

Dick Cheney

PROFILES IN LEADERSHIP 7.3

By all accounts Dick Cheney is the most powerful Vice President in modern United States history. Starting his academic career at Yale, Cheney dropped out after a few semesters and moved back to Wyoming. Vice President Cheney finished undergraduate and master's degrees in political science at the University of Wyoming but never completed his doctoral degree at the University of Wisconsin. While attending college Cheney received five draft deferments and thus avoided military service during the Vietnam War. When asked about these deferments by a reporter for *The Washington Post,* Cheney replied, "I had other priorities in the 60s than military service."

Cheney's political career took off when he became an intern in the Nixon administration. He attracted the attention of Donald Rumsfeld and held a number of appointed positions while serving under President Nixon. He rose quickly through the ranks and at the age of 34 became President Ford's chief of staff. While in this position, Cheney and Rumsfeld worked together to purge a number of Ford staffers, forcing then Vice President Nelson Rockfeller to find another job, easing William Colby out of the CIA chief role and replacing him with George H. W. Bush, stripping Henry Kissinger of his National Security Advisor role, and replacing then Secretary of Defense James Schlesinger with Donald Rumsfeld.

Cheney served as the campaign manager for Gerald Ford in the 1976 presidential election, but Ford lost the election to then Georgia Governor Jimmy Carter. Cheney moved back to Wyoming where he was elected to the U.S. House of Representatives for five terms. While a congressman, Cheney voted against making Martin Luther King, Jr.'s birthday a national holiday, the creation of the Department of Education, funding Head Start, a nonbinding resolution calling for the release of Nelson Mandela, and economic sanctions against South Africa (which was practicing apartheid at the time). Cheney then served as the Secretary of Defense from 1989–1993 under President George H. W. Bush. During his time in Congress, Cheney became convinced that the CIA was consistently underestimating the Soviet threat and was also extremely skeptical of the CIA's estimates of the Iraqi military capabilities and weapons of mass destruction before Gulf War I. Because of this skepticism, Cheney hired his own intelligence experts to review CIA data and made repeated trips to CIA Headquarters to interrogate CIA analysts. After President George H. W. Bush lost the 1992 election to then Arkansas Governor Bill Clinton, Cheney became the chief executive officer of Halliburton Energy. Under Cheney's tenure the number of Halliburton subsidiaries in offshore tax havens increased from 9 to 44. As the CEO of Halliburton, Cheney lobbied Congress to lift U.S. sanctions against Libya and Iran, saying that sanctions only damaged U.S. interests. While serving as CEO of Halliburton he headed George W. Bush's vice president search committee and somehow became the most logical choice for Vice President.

Vice President Cheney is not only the most powerful person to hold this position over the past 50 years, he is also the most secretive. He repeatedly refuses to tell reporters how many people actually work in his office, let alone tell them what they do. He went to court to keep the membership of the Energy Committee from going public and even the official residence of the vice president has been pixilated out of Google maps. He appears to have played a critical role in the outing of Valerie Plame, an undercover CIA agent who is also the wife of Joseph Wilson, a former U.S. ambassador. In 2002 Wilson went on a trip to determine the veracity of an intelligence lead indicating that Saddam Hussein was buying uranium from Niger. After the trip Wilson published an op/ed piece in *The New York Times* stating that the rumor was false. According to testimony at the Scooter Libby trial, it was only after the publication of this article that Cheney went after Wilson with a vengeance.

He is also one of the few people who still believe that Saddam Hussein possessed weapons of mass destruction before Gulf War II and that there was a link between Saddam Hussein and Al-Qaeda before 9/11. He also heavily lobbied Congress to allow the United States to use torture in the War on Terror and arranged for Halliburton to receive multibillion dollar no-bid contracts for Iraq. In early 2007 Cheney's

continued

Continued

approval rating hovered around 30 percent. It is clear Vice President Cheney possesses a number of personality traits that have allowed him to be incredibly powerful and successful. But it also appears that several dark-side traits and work values have played a

role in some of the decisions he has made in the past. What do you think these traits and values might be?

Sources: http://en.wikipedia.org/wiki/Dick_Cheney; "Lexington: Dick Cheney Under the Microscope," *The Economist.* February 17, 2007, p. 38.

Be willing to make decisions. That's the most important quality of a good leader.

George S. Patton, U.S. Army general

---

intelligence tests should be used in public schools, and whether ethnic groups differ in average intelligence test scores. For the most part, however, we will bypass such controversies here. Our focus will be on the relationship between intelligence and leadership.

We define **intelligence** as a person's all-around effectiveness in activities directed by thought.[81,91] So what does this definition of intelligence have to do with leadership?

Research has shown that more intelligent leaders are faster learners; make better assumptions, deductions, and inferences; are better at creating a compelling vision and developing strategies to make their vision a reality; can develop better solutions to problems; can see more of the primary and secondary implications of their decisions; and are quicker on their feet than leaders who are less intelligent.[4,7,50,66,86–90,92–100] To a large extent people get placed into leadership positions to solve problems, be they customer, financial, operational, interpersonal, performance, political, educational, or social in nature. Therefore, given the behaviors associated with higher intelligence, it is easy to see how a more intelligent leader will oftentimes be more successful in influencing a group to accomplish its goals than a less intelligent leader. Like personality traits, however, intelligence alone is not enough to guarantee leadership success. There are plenty of smart people who make poor leaders just as there are less intelligent people who are great leaders. Nevertheless, many leadership activities do seem to involve some degree of decision-making and problem-solving ability, which means that a leader's intelligence can affect the odds of leadership success in many situations.

As seen in Figure 7.4, intelligence is relatively difficult to change. Like personality, it is also an unseen quality and can only be inferred by observing behavior. Moreover, intelligence does not affect behavior equally across all situations. Some activities, such as following simple routines, put less of a premium on intelligence than others.[89,99] Finally, we should point out that our definition of intelligence does not imply that intelligence is a fixed quantity. Although heredity plays a role, intelligence can be and is modified through education and experience.[81,86–88,91,97,99,101,102]

Managers and executives need to make decisions on how to meet customer needs, develop products, compete, get results, and allocate resources. Each decision is a problem-solving exercise. The history and success of an organization is the cumulative sum of these problem-solving exercises and subsequent decisions.

Bob and Joyce Hogan, Hogan Assessment Systems

The Triarchic Theory of Intelligence

Although there is a positive relationship between intelligence and leadership effectiveness, there is still an ongoing debate about the nature of intelligence. Many psychologists have tried to determine the structure of

FIGURE 7.4
The building blocks
of skills.

Source: © 1991–2000
Personnel Decisions
International Corporation.
Reprinted with permission.

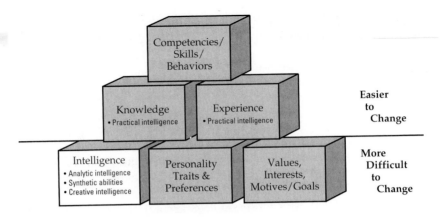

intelligence; is intelligence a unitary ability, or does it involve a collection of related mental abilities?[22,91,94,103] Other psychologists have said that the *process* by which people do complex mental work is much more important than determining the number of mental abilities.[85,88,104] One of the most comprehensive and compelling theories of intelligence developed and tested over the past 20 years is Sternberg's **triarchic theory of intelligence.**[85,86,87,97] It also offers some of the most significant implications for leadership. The triarchic theory focuses on what a leader *does* when solving complex mental problems, such as how information is combined and synthesized when solving problems, what assumptions and errors are made, and the like. According to this theory, there are three basic types of intelligence. **Analytic intelligence** is general problem-solving ability and can be assessed using standardized mental abilities tests. Analytic intelligence is important because leaders and followers who possess higher levels of this type of intelligence tend to be quick learners, do well in school, see connections between issues, and have the ability to make accurate deductions, assumptions, and inferences with relatively unfamiliar information.

There is still much, however, that analytic intelligence does not explain. There are a number of people who do well on standardized tests but not in life.[86,87,97–99,105] At the same time, some people do relatively poorly on standardized intelligence tests but often develop ingenious solutions to practical problems. For example, Sternberg and his associates described a situation where students in a school for the mentally retarded did very poorly on standardized tests yet consistently found ways to defeat the school's elaborate security system. In this situation the students possessed a relatively high level of **practical intelligence,** or "street smarts." People with street smarts know how to adapt to, shape, or select new situations in order to get their needs met better than people lacking street smarts (e.g., think of a stereotypical computer nerd and an inner-city kid both lost in downtown New York). In other words, practical intelligence involves knowing how things get done and how to do them. For leaders,

Leading Clever People

HIGHLIGHT 7.6

Organizations are constantly looking for smart, creative people to develop new product and service ideas, manufacturing or logistical processes, or marketing campaigns. But one thing we do know about followers with these abilities is that they do not like to be led. Researchers Rob Goffee and Gareth Jones conducted over 100 interviews with leaders of clever people and had some interesting findings. One finding is that smart, clever people know that companies need them more than they need companies. These individuals also tend to ignore the corporate hierarchy and expect instant access to top management. They have a low threshold for boredom and are flight risks if their ideas are not respected and they don't get audiences with key decision makers. To manage these individuals, Goffee and Jones suggest that leaders act as "benevolent guardians." Leaders should treat creative, smart types with the respect and recognition they demand, get them the resources they need, protect them from organizational policies and politics, and give them room to be creative and fail.

Source: R. Goffee and G. Jones, "Leading Clever People." *Harvard Business Review,* March 2007, pp. 72–79.

practical intelligence is important because it involves knowing what to do and how to do it when confronted with a particular leadership situation, such as dealing with a poorly performing subordinate, resolving a problem with a customer, or getting a team to work better together.[106]

Everyone is ignorant, only on different subjects.
Will Rogers,
comedian

Because of its potential importance to leadership effectiveness, there are several other aspects of practical intelligence worth noting. First, practical intelligence is much more concerned with knowledge and experience than analytic intelligence (see Figure 7.4). Leaders can build their practical intelligence by building their leadership knowledge and experience. Thus, textbooks such as this one can help you to build your practical intelligence. Getting a variety of leadership experiences, and perhaps more important, reflecting on these experiences, will also help you to build practical intelligence. But you should understand that it will take some time before you will become an "expert" at leadership, as research shows that it takes 10 years to truly master any particular topic.[107]

Second, practical intelligence is *domain specific*. A leader who has a lot of knowledge and experience in leading a pharmaceutical research team may feel like a duck out of water when asked to lead a major fund-raising effort for a charitable institution. As another example, one of the authors worked with a highly successful retail company having over 100,000 employees. All of the key leaders had over 20 years of retail operations and merchandising experience, but they also did very poorly on standardized intelligence tests. The company had successfully expanded in the United States (which capitalized on their practical intelligence), but their attempt to expand to foreign markets was an abysmal failure. This failure was due in part to the leaders' inability to learn, appreciate, or understand the intricacies of other cultures (analytic intelligence), their lack of knowledge and experience in foreign markets (practical intelligence), and in turn their development of inappropriate strategies for running the business in other countries (a combination of analytic and practical intelligence). Thus, practical intelligence is extremely useful when leading in familiar situations, but analytic intelligence may play a more important role when leaders are facing new or novel situations.

We do know with certain knowledge that Osama bin Laden is either in Afghanistan, in some other country, or dead.

Donald Rumsfeld, former U.S. Secretary of Defense

Third, this example points out the importance of having both types of intelligence. Organizations today are looking for leaders and followers who have the necessary knowledge and skills to succeed (practical intelligence) and the ability to learn (analytic intelligence).[86–88,97,99,108,109] Fourth, it may be that high levels of practical intelligence may compensate for lower levels of analytic intelligence. Leaders having lower analytic abilities may still be able to solve complex work problems or make good decisions provided they have plenty of job-relevant knowledge or experience. But leaders with more analytic intelligence, all things being equal, may develop their street smarts more quickly than leaders with less analytic intelligence. Analytic intelligence may play a lesser role once a domain of knowledge is mastered, but a more important role when encountering new situations.

The best way to have a good idea is to have a lot of ideas.

Dr. Linus Pauling, researcher

The third component of the triarchic theory of intelligence is **creative intelligence.** Creative intelligence is the ability to produce work that is both novel and useful.[85,88,110–113] Using *both* criteria (novel and useful) as components of creative intelligence helps to eliminate many of the more outlandish solutions to a potential problem by ensuring that adopted solutions can be realistically implemented or have some type of practical payoff. Several examples might help to clarify the novel and practical components of creative intelligence. The inventor of Velcro got his idea while picking countless thistles out of his socks; he realized that the same principle that produced his frustration might be translated into a useful fastener. The inventor of 3M's Post-it notes was frustrated because bookmarks in his church hymnal were continually sliding out of place, and he saw a solution in a low-tack adhesive discovered by a fellow 3M scientist. The scientists who designed the *Spirit* and *Opportunity* missions to Mars were given a budget that was considerably smaller than that of the previous missions to Mars. Yet the scientists were challenged to develop two spacecraft that had more capabilities than the *Pathfinder* and the *Viking Lander.* Their efforts with *Spirit* and *Opportunity* were a resounding success, due in part to some of the novel solutions used both to land the spacecrafts (an inflatable balloon system) and to explore the surrounding area (both were mobile rovers).

Two of the more interesting questions surrounding creativity concern the role of intelligence and the assessment of creative ability. Research shows that analytic intelligence correlates at about the .5 level with creative intelligence.[112] Thus, the best research available indicates that analytic intelligence and creativity are related, but the relationship is far from perfect. Some level of analytic intelligence seems necessary for creativity,

The Competent Hot Potato

HIGHLIGHT 7.7

What should leaders do when one of their followers is very smart and competent (i.e., has a high level of practical and analytic intelligence) but has difficulties getting along with other team members? Clearly followers with high levels of analytic intelligence and domain knowledge can help their teams make better decisions, but the cost of this knowledge is often strained relationships with or high levels of turnover among teammates. Research shows that when given a choice, team members would prefer to work with a lovable but incompetent fool than an irritable but competent jerk. On the one hand, team performance is likely to suffer if everyone on the team is happy but incompetent. On the other hand, performance is also likely to suffer when a toxic follower is part of a team. It appears that many managers resolve this dilemma by having competent jerks on their teams during the initial phases of projects—when ideas about project direction, possibilities, and solutions are being determined. Once these decisions are made, many managers then arrange to have competent jerks leave their teams. The good news is that the team gets to capitalize on the competent jerk's expertise during the decision-making phase of the project but doesn't have to suffer their dysfunctional behavior during the execution phase. The bad news is that a very common way to get rid of competent jerks is to get them promoted. Many managers would rather see a toxic follower become a toxic leader rather than confront difficult performance issues. Subsequent bosses often repeat the "hot potato" process, helping toxic leaders move into roles with ever-increasing responsibilities.

Although this phenomenon of promoting highly competent individuals with dark-side tendencies contributes to the high base rate of managerial incompetence, many times teammates share some of the blame with bosses for these promotions. When teammates complain to their managers about competent jerks and the manager discusses these issues with the problematic individuals, competent jerks deny all the allegations. And when competent jerks confront their teammates about these allegations, teammates are unwilling to share their complaints. With team members failing to provide feedback, leaders often stand accused of having it out for the competent jerk. Oftentimes the only face-saving way out of this situation is to give the competent jerk a transfer to or promotion in another department.

Sources: J. Sandberg, "Sometimes Colleagues Are Just Too Bad to Not Get Promoted." *The Wall Street Journal,* August 17, 2005, p. A5; J. Casciaro and M. S. Lobo, "Competent Jerks, Lovable Fools, and the Formation of Social Networks." *Harvard Business Review,* June 2006, pp. 92–100.

but having a high level of analytic intelligence is no guarantee that a leader will be creative. And like practical intelligence, creativity seems to be specific to certain fields and subfields: Bill Gates cannot write music and Madonna cannot do math.[86,91,110,112,114–116]

In addition, actually assessing creativity is no simple matter. Tests of creativity, or **divergent thinking,** are very different from tests that assess **convergent thinking.** Tests of convergent thinking usually have a single best answer; good examples here are most intelligence and aptitude tests. Conversely, tests of creativity or divergent thinking have many possible answers.[117] Although Sternberg and his associates all showed that it is possible to reliably judge the relative creativity of different responses, the fact remains that judging creativity is more difficult than scoring convergent tests.[110,112,118] For example, there are no set answers or standards for determining whether a movie, a marketing ad, or a new manufacturing process is truly creative. Another difficulty in assessing creativity is that it may wax and wane over time; many of the most creative people seem to have occasional dry spells or writer's block. This is very different from analytic intelligence, where performance on mental abilities tests remains fairly constant over time.

The Components of Creative Intelligence

So far we have discussed creative intelligence as a unitary ability. However, as seen in Table 7.3, research suggests that creativity appears to be made up of seven components: *synthetic ability, analytic intelligence, practical intelligence, thinking style, personality factors, intrinsic motivation,* and *environmental factors.*[87,97,104,111–113,118–122] **Synthetic ability** is what we traditionally view as creativity; these skills help people see things in new ways or recognize novel patterns or connections. Analytic intelligence helps people to evaluate solutions, and practical intelligence provides the knowledge and experience base from which novel solutions are developed. These first three components are very important to the creative process, and leaders lacking in any one of them will be less creative than those possessing all three.[87,97,112] Thinking style is somewhat related to synthetic ability. Thinking styles are not abilities per se, but rather are the preferred ways for using the abilities one has.[123,124] For example, some people seem to prefer improving or adapting already existing products or processes. A first-line supervisor in a manufacturing facility may be very adept at modifying existing production schedules or equipment in order to better meet customers' needs. Other people seem to prefer developing completely new products. A team leader tasked with developing a new ad campaign for a major brewer might come up with a series of promotional

Most artists have to hack through a tangled thicket of negativity, logic, and procrastination on the way to creating anything. Peter seems to be supernaturally free of any such concerns. This is a guy with a big wide conduit running from the creative, imaginative part of his brain, straight to the place where most of us keep our willpower. That could be a recipe for a monstrously selfish ego. Again, Jackson's ability to chase goals doesn't come with that type of baggage. He's driven, and he's incredibly demanding, but he's always focused on results, never on himself.

**Costa Botes,
screenwriter**

TABLE 7.3
The Components of Creative Intelligence

Synthetic Ability: These skills help people see things in new ways or recognize novel connections between seemingly unrelated issues or concepts.
Analytic Intelligence: This helps to evaluate the usefulness of potential solutions to problems.
Practical Intelligence: Novel solutions to problems are usually based on relevant knowledge and experience.
Thinking Style: People either prefer to modify what already exists or completely start over with new solutions.
Personality Factors: Lower prudence, higher openness to experience, and higher surgency scores are related to creativity.
Intrinsic Motivation: People tend to generate more creative solutions when the problem at hand is personally interesting.
Environmental Factors: Supportive leadership, a lack of time pressure, team stability, and weaker social ties are all related to generating more creative solutions to problems.

ads using novel attention-getting devices, such as cavemen or chameleons. These two examples illustrate the difference between **adaptive** and **innovative thinking styles.** Adaptors prefer to modify or change existing products or processes; innovators prefer to create entirely new processes or products.[125] Adaptors and innovators may have the same level of synthetic ability, but they just seem to use this ability in different ways. It is important to note that U.S. companies seem particularly adept at developing new technology (i.e., innovation), whereas Japanese industries are very good at improving the technology and finding efficient ways to bring it to the marketplace (i.e., adaptation).

Several personality factors also seem to play a role in creativity. More specifically, people having higher levels of self-confidence, independence, and energy (synergy), risk-taking and impulsiveness (dependability), and natural curiosity (openness to experience) seem to be more creative than people who lack self-confidence, are more conforming, and are less open to new and novel experiences.[112,119,126–129] People will also be more creative when they are intrinsically motivated or feel challenged by the subject matter or problem itself or are expected to be creative.[86,119,121,130,131] Creative people are more likely to focus attention on solving the problem at hand, not on the need to meet deadlines, make money, or impress others. Finally, several situational or environmental factors appear related to creativity. People who have more complex or challenging jobs, who have supportive, noncontrolling leaders, and are given ample time seem to be more creative than people in uninteresting jobs who are under tight deadlines and also have highly controlling supervisors.[96,121,129,132–135] Several aspects of work groups also seem to affect creativity. Although the size of the group did not seem to matter, teams that were given clear goals, stayed task focused, and provided mutual support and participation often developed more innovative solutions than teams lacking these qualities.[136,137] Team stability also seems to play a role in creativity. Amabile and Conti studied companies before, during, and after going through a large downsizing, and reported that teams that remained relatively intact during this process were substantially more creative in terms of patent applications than teams that were broken up. These authors also reported that an organization's support for creativity, in terms of time and resources, was a key factor in the creativity of individual employees.[138,139]

Another factor that affects creativity is team cohesiveness. You might think that teams with higher levels of cohesiveness would be more creative than teams that do not get along, but research shows that just the opposite is true. Because highly cohesive teams tend to share the same values, their team members often look at the world in similar ways. Teams having members with dissimilar values will likely have more conflict, but they are also more likely to look at problems from different perspectives. And looking at issues differently is critical to creative problem solving.[137,140–142]

The story of Chester Carlson provides a good example of how some of the seven components play important roles in developing a creative and useful solution to a problem. Chester Carlson invented the photocopy duplicating process, which revolutionized office work. Duplicating machines are relied on so much today that most people probably assume the invention was met with instant acceptance. That was not the case, however. Most people do not realize that it was 22 years from the time Carlson got the idea to the time his product became commercially available—or that refining and "selling" his concept was an uphill battle primarily because of the existence of carbon paper. (With carbon paper, people thought, why would you need anything else?) His solution for making copies of documents was certainly imaginative, but it was also derived from his considerable technical expertise. Moreover, his persistence in developing and persuading others of the potential of his process is a testament to the importance of intrinsic motivation in creativity.

Many if not most inventions were developed by people driven by curiosity or a love of tinkering, in absence of product demand.

Jared Diamond, author

Creative thinking is not an entirely rational or conscious process. Many times we do our most imaginative thinking unconsciously; people often gain sudden insights to an old problem out of the blue. There are interesting anecdotal accounts of how different creative thinkers recognized and even harnessed these unconscious processes. Albert Einstein, for example, once remarked that he got his best ideas in the morning when he was shaving. The great inventor Thomas Edison reportedly developed a technique to awaken himself and capture the typically unusual imagery and mental activity occurring as one falls asleep. These thinkers recognized the mind's fertility during its resting periods. Einstein's and Edison's receptivity to ideas emerging from their nonlogical mental processes was surely an important part of their genius. They were able to harness their unconscious rather than censor it, as many of us may do by suppressing or discounting mental activity that seems purposeless, nonsensical, or threatening.

Implications of the Triarchic Theory of Intelligence

The fastest way to succeed is to double the failure rate.

Thomas Watson, Sr., IBM

Some 200 separate studies have examined the relationship between intelligence test scores and leadership effectiveness or emergence, and these studies have been the topic of major reviews.[1,2,3,4,7,143–147] These reviews provided overwhelming support for the idea that leadership effectiveness or emergence is positively correlated with analytic intelligence. Nonetheless, it is important to recognize that the correlation between analytic intelligence and leadership success is not that strong and is not as strong as previously assumed. It now appears that personality is much more predictive of leadership emergence and effectiveness than analytic intelligence.[7,8] Leadership situations that are relatively routine or unchanging, or require specific in-depth product or process knowledge may place more importance on personality and practical intelligence than analytic intelligence. Having a high level of analytic intelligence seems more important when solving ambiguous, complex problems, such as those encountered by executives at the top levels of an organization. Here leaders must be able to detect themes and patterns in seemingly unrelated information, make accurate assumptions about market conditions, or make wise merger, acquisition, or divestiture decisions. Further evidence that higher levels of analytic intelligence are associated with top leaders can be found in Figure 7.5.

Although a high level of analytic intelligence is usually an asset to a leader, research also suggests that in some situations analytic intelligence may have a *curvilinear* relationship with leadership effectiveness.[1,143] When differences in analytic intelligence between leader and followers are too great, communication can be impaired; a leader's intelligence can become an impediment to being understood by subordinates.[146,148] An alternative explanation for the curvilinear relationship between analytic intelligence and leadership effectiveness may have to do with how stress affects leader–subordinate interactions. Fiedler and his associates found that smart but inexperienced leaders were less effective in stressful situations than less intelligent, experienced leaders.[147,149,150] An example of this finding was clearly demonstrated in the movie *Platoon*. In one frantic scene an American platoon is ambushed by the Vietcong. An inexperienced, college-educated lieutenant calls for artillery support from friendly units. He calls in the wrong coordinates, however, and as a result artillery shells are dropped on his own platoon's position rather than the enemy's position. The situation comes under control only after an experienced

FIGURE 7.5

Average intelligence test scores by management level.

Source: N. Kuncel, "Personality and Cognitive Differences among Management Levels." Unpublished manuscript, Personnel Decisions International, Minneapolis, 1996.

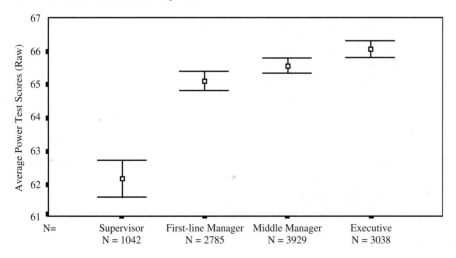

sergeant sizes up the situation and tells the artillery units to cease firing. This example points out the importance of practical intelligence in stressful situations. Leaders revert to well-practiced behaviors under periods of high stress and change, and leaders with high levels of practical intelligence have a relatively broad set of coping and problem-solving behaviors to draw upon in these situations. Because of the level of stress and change associated with many leadership positions today, systematically improving practical leadership skills through education and experience is extremely important for leaders and leaders to be.

With respect to creative intelligence, perhaps the most important point leaders should remember is that their primary role is not so much to be creative themselves as to *build an environment where others can be creative.* This is not to say that leaders should be uncreative, but rather that most innovations have their roots in ideas developed by people closest to a problem or opportunity (i.e., the workers). Leaders can boost the creativity throughout their groups or organizations in many ways, but particularly through selecting creative people in the first place, and providing opportunities for others to develop their creativity, and through broader interventions like making sure the motivation or incentives for others are conducive to creativity and providing at least some guidance or vision about what the creative product or output should look like.[121,122,129,133,135,140,141,151,152]

There are several things leaders can do to improve the group and organizational factors affecting creativity. Leaders should be mindful of the effect various sorts of incentives or rewards can have on creativity; certain types of motivation to work are more conducive to creativity than others. Research has shown that people tend to generate more creative solutions when they are told to focus on their intrinsic motivation for doing so (i.e., the pleasure of solving the task itself) rather than focusing on the extrinsic motivation (i.e., public recognition or pay).[119,120] When they need to foster creativity, leaders may find it more effective to select followers who truly enjoy working on the task at hand (i.e., are intrinsically motivated) rather than relying on rewards (i.e., extrinsic motivation) to foster creativity.

It is also helpful to remember that synthetic abilities can also be hindered if people believe that their ideas will be evaluated. Experiments by Amabile and Zhou showed that students who were told their projects were to be judged by experts produced less creative projects than students who were not told their projects would be judged.[153,154] A similar sort of phenomenon can occur in groups. Even when a group knows its work must ultimately be evaluated, there is a pronounced tendency for members to be evaluative and judgmental too early in the solution-generating process. This tends to reduce the number of creative solutions generated, perhaps because of a generally shared belief in the value of critical thinking (and in some groups the norm seems to be the more criticism, the better) and of subjecting ideas to intense scrutiny and evaluation. When members of a group judge ideas as soon as they are offered, two dysfunctional things can happen. People in the group may censor themselves (i.e., not share all their ideas with the group), as even mild rejection or criticism has a significant dampening effect, or they may prematurely reject others' ideas through negativistic focus on an idea's flaws rather than its possibilities.[155] Given these findings, leaders may want to hold off on evaluating new ideas until they are all on the table, and should also encourage their followers to do the same.

Finally, leaders who need to develop new products and services should try to minimize the level of turnover in their teams and provide them with clear goals. Teams having unclear goals may successfully develop new or novel products, but these products may have low marketability or usefulness. Two examples might help illustrate this point. In the 1980s Texas Instruments (TI) decided to delve into the personal computer business. TI had a reputation for technical excellence, and one of the best managers in the company was asked to head up the project. The manager did not have a clear sense of what customers wanted or what a personal computer should be able to do. This lack of clarity had some fairly dramatic effects. As more and more engineers were added to the project, more and more innovative hardware ideas were added to the computer design. These additions caused the project to take much longer and cost a lot more than planned,

TABLE 7.4 **Creativity Killers:** **How to Squelch the** **Creativity of Direct** **Reports**	The following is a list of things leaders can do if they wish to stifle the creativity of their followers: **Take Away All Discretion and Autonomy:** People like to have some sense of control over their work. Micro-managing staff will help to either create yea-sayers or cause people to mentally disengage from work. **Create Fragmented Work Schedules:** People need large chunks of uninterrupted time to work on novel solutions. Repeated interruptions or scheduling "novel solution generation time" in 15-minute increments around other meetings will disrupt people's ability to be innovative. **Provide Insufficient Resources:** People need proper data, equipment, or money to be creative. Cut these off, and watch creativity go down the tubes. **Focus on Short-Term Goals:** Asking a person to be creative at right this moment is like asking Chris Rock to be funny the first time you meet him. People can be creative and funny if given enough time, but focusing on only short-term outcomes will dampen creativity. **Create Tight Timelines:** The tighter the deadlines, the more likely that innovation will be reduced. **Discourage Collaboration and Coordination:** The best ideas often come from teams having members with very different work experiences and functional backgrounds. By discouraging cross-functional collaboration, leaders can help guarantee that team members will only offer up tried and true solutions to problems. **Keep People Happy:** If you keep workers happy enough, then they will have little motivation to change the status quo.

Source: T. M. Amabile and J. Zhou, in S. F. Dingfelder, "Creativity on the Clock." *Monitor on Psychology,* November 2003, pp. 56–58.

but the TI personal computer ended up winning a number of major engineering awards. Unfortunately, it was also a business disaster, as the product ultimately failed to meet customer needs. Although Compaq computers arose from the ashes of TI's failure, the TI project serves as a good example for a concept called **creeping elegance.** Leaders not having a clear vision of what a final project should look like may end up with something that fails to meet customer needs. Leaders need to provide enough room for creativity to flourish, but enough direction for effort to be focused.[133,140,141]

One industry that places a premium on creativity is the motion picture industry. Because creativity is so important to the commercial success of a movie, it is relatively easy for a movie to succumb to creeping elegance. But how do movie directors successfully avoid creeping elegance when dealing with highly creative people having huge egos? Part of the answer may be in the approach of two of Hollywood's most successful directors. Steven Spielberg and Ron Howard said that before they ever shot a scene they first had a very clear picture of it in their own minds. If they did not have a clear picture, then they sat down with the relevant parties and worked it out. Both situations point out the importance of having a clear vision when managing creativity.

Intelligence and Stress: Cognitive Resources Theory

In the preceding section we noted that intelligence may be a more important quality for leaders in some situations than others. You may be surprised to learn, however, that recent research actually suggests there are times when intelligence may be a disadvantage. A key variable affecting this paradoxical finding seems to be whether or not the leader is in a stressful situation. Recent research suggests that stress plays a key role in determining just how a leader's intelligence affects his or her effectiveness. While it is not surprising that stress affects behavior in various ways, Fiedler and Garcia developed the **cognitive resources theory (CRT)** to explain the interesting relationships between leader intelligence and experience levels, and group performance in stressful versus nonstressful conditions.[156]

As first described in Chapter 4, CRT consists of several key concepts. Certainly one of these is intelligence. Fiedler and Garcia defined intelligence as we have earlier—it is one's all-around effectiveness in activities directed by thought and is typically measured using standardized intelligence tests (i.e., analytic intelligence).[149,156,157] Another key concept is experience, which represents the habitual behavior patterns, overlearned knowledge, and skills acquired for effectively dealing with task-related problems (i.e., practical intelligence). Although experience is often gained under stressful and unpleasant conditions, experience also provides a "crash plan" to revert back to when under stress.[147,149,157] As Fiedler observed, people often act differently when stressed, and the crash plan describes this change in behavior patterns. For most of the CRT studies, experience has been defined as time in the job or organization. A third key concept in

Scott Rudin

PROFILES IN LEADERSHIP 7.4

Few people know who Scott Rudin is, but many have seen his work. Rudin has been a Hollywood movie producer for over 20 years and has produced such movies as *The Addams Family, Sister Act, The Truman Show, A Civil Action, The Firm, Team America: World Police, Zoolander, The School of Rock, The Queen, Notes on a Scandal,* and many others. Rudin also has the reputation of being the most difficult boss to work for in Hollywood; it is estimated that he has fired over 250 assistants over the past five years. His caustic rants, shrieking threats, impulsive firings, and revolving door of assistants are legendary. For example, he allegedly once fired an assistant for bringing in the wrong breakfast muffin. Rudin describes his own leadership style as a cross between Attila the Hun and Miss Jean Brodie and it is rumored that the role of Miranda Priestly in *The Devil Wears Prada* was loosely modeled after Rudin.

An extreme micro-manager, Rudin is involved with every detail of the films he is producing. Because he is producing several films at any one time, it is not unusual for Rudin to make over 400 calls in a single day. Rudin's assistants start their days at 6:00 AM with a 30-page annotated list of phone calls that are to be set up that day. During the day assistants will also do anything from picking up dry cleaning, answering phones, scheduling appointments, arranging travel, buying birthday presents, dropping off kids, etc. You name it, the assistant does it. So why do assistants put up with Rudin? The hours are long but the pay is good—most interns make $70,000–$150,000 per year. More importantly, those aides that do survive get a chance to rub shoulders with A list talent and learn the ins and outs of the movie business. Plus the opportunities for advancement for those who survive are very good— many of Rudin's aides have themselves become movie producers.

Given this background, what bright-side traits help Rubin to produce successful movies? What dark-side traits make him so difficult to work for? Is Rubin a Competent Manager or a Results Only Manager?

Sources: http://en.wikipedia.org/wiki/Scott_Rudin; K. Kelly and M. Marr. "Boss-Zilla!" *The Wall Street Journal,* September 24–25, 2005, p. A1.

CRT is stress. Stress is often defined as the result of conflicts with superiors or the apprehension associated with performance evaluation.[150,157] This interpersonal stress is believed to be emotionally disturbing and can divert attention from problem-solving activities.[158] In other words, people can get so concerned about how their performance is being evaluated that they may fail to perform at an optimal level. In sum, cognitive resources theory provides a conceptual scheme for explaining how leader behavior changes under stress levels to impact group performance.

Cognitive resources theory makes two major predictions with respect to intelligence, experience, stress, and group performance. First, because experienced leaders have a greater repertoire of behaviors to fall back on, leaders with greater experience but lower intelligence are hypothesized to have higher-performing groups under conditions of high stress. Experienced leaders have "been there before" and better know what to do and how to get it done when faced with high-stress situations. Leaders' experience levels can interfere with performance under low-stress conditions, however.

That leads to a second hypothesis. Because experience leads to habitual behavior patterns, leaders with high levels of experience will have a tendency to misapply old solutions to problems when creative solutions are called for.[147,149,157] Experienced leaders overrely on the tried and true when faced with new problems, even when under relatively low periods of stress. Thus, leaders with higher levels of intelligence but less experience are not constrained by previously acquired behavior patterns and should have higher-performing groups under low-stress conditions. In other words, experience is helpful when one is under stress but is often a hindrance to performance in the absence of stress.

These two major predictions of CRT can be readily seen in everyday life. For the most part, it is not the most intelligent but the most experienced members of sporting teams, marching bands, acting troops, or volunteer organizations who are selected to be leaders. These leaders are often chosen because other members recognize their ability to perform well under the high levels of stress associated with sporting events and public performances. In addition, research with combat troops, firefighters, senior executives, and students has provided strong support for the two major tenets of CRT.[7,147,149,150,156,157]

Despite this initial empirical support, one problem with CRT concerns the apparent dichotomy between intelligence and experience. Fiedler and Garcia's initial investigations of CRT did not examine the possibility that leaders could be *both* intelligent and experienced.[156] Subsequent research by Gibson showed not only that many leaders were both intelligent and experienced, but also that these leaders would fall back on their experience in stressful situations and use their intelligence to solve group problems in less-stressful situations.[150]

Another issue with CRT concerns the leader's ability to tolerate stress. As Schonpflug and Zaccaro correctly pointed out, some leaders may be better able to tolerate high levels of stress than others.[159,160] Some leaders have personalities characterized by high adjustment scores, and it may be that such leaders may do well in high-stress situations even when they lack experience because of their inherent ability to handle stress. Further research on this issue seems warranted.

A third issue with CRT concerns stress and dark-side traits. As stated earlier in this chapter, the dysfunctional tendencies associated with dark-side traits are more likely to emerge during times of stress. It may be that more experienced leaders are either better able to tolerate stress or have learned how to limit the emergence of their dark sides during times of high stress. Less experienced leaders may not have learned about their dark sides and how they come out when stressed. The emergence of dark-side traits does not contradict the major tenets of CRT but may provide an explanation for why less experienced leaders do not perform as well under stressful conditions.

In general, there appears to be solid evidence to support the major tenets of CRT. Because of this research, CRT has several important implications for leaders. First, it may be that the best leaders are often smart *and* experienced. Although intelligence tests are good indicators of raw mental horsepower, it is just as important for leaders to broaden their leadership knowledge and experience if they want to be successful in high-stress situations. This latter point may be very important today, where the additional stress of organizational downsizing and "delayering" may cause the performance of leaders to be scrutinized even more closely than in the past. In fact, this additional scrutiny may well cause leaders who were previously successful to perform rather poorly in this high-stress environment.

Second, leaders may not be aware of the degree to which they are causing stress in their followers. If followers perceive that their performance is being closely watched, then they are likely to revert to their crash plans in order to perform. If the situation calls for new and novel solutions to problems, however, the leaders' behavior may be counterproductive. A key point here is that leaders may be unaware of their impact on followers. For example, they may want to review their followers' work more closely in order to be helpful, but followers may not perceive it this way.

Third, the level of stress inherent in the position needs to be understood before selection of leaders. Those doing the selection to fill high-stress leadership positions can either look for experienced leaders or reduce the stress in the situation so that more intelligent leaders can be more successful.[149,161] Another alternative could be to hire more intelligent leaders and put them through some type of stress management program so that the effects of stress are minimized.[149,157] It is also possible that experienced leaders may get bored if placed into low-stress positions.[162]

Emotional Intelligence and Leadership

What Is Emotional Intelligence?

In terms of the building blocks of skills, Chapter 6 described the role values play in leadership. Similarly, this chapter has discussed how bright- and dark-side personality traits and analytic, practical, and creative intelligence are related to leadership effectiveness. In other words, people's core beliefs and how they make decisions, develop plans, interact with others, and react to stress can affect their ability to build teams and get results. But do moods affect a person's ability to build teams and get results through others? Moods and emotions are constantly at play at work, yet most people are hesitant to discuss moods with anybody other than close friends. It also appears that moods can be contagious, in that the moods of leaders often affect followers in both positive and negative ways. And charismatic or transformational leaders use emotions as the catalyst for achieving better than expected results (see Chapter 13). Given the importance and prevalence of emotions in the workplace, it would seem that there would be a wealth of research regarding mood and leadership effectiveness. But this is not

There is no single entity called EQ (emotional intelligence quotient) as people have defined it. One sympathetic interpretation of what journalists were saying is that there were a dozen unrelated things, which collectively might predict more than intelligence, things like warmth, optimism, and empathy. But there was nothing new about that. Instead, the story became this fabulous new variable that is going to outpredict intelligence. There is no rational basis for saying that.

**John Mayer,
EQ researcher**

the case. Researchers have really begun to seriously examine the role of emotions in leadership only over the past 15–20 years.

The relationships between a leader's emotions and their effects on teams and outcomes became popularized by researcher Dan Goleman with the publication of a book, *Emotional Intelligence.*[163] But what is emotional intelligence (EQ), and how is it the same as or different from personality or the three types of intelligence described in this chapter? Unfortunately, there appear to be at least four major definitions of **emotional intelligence.** The term *emotional intelligence* can be attributed to two psychologists, Peter Salovey and John Mayer, who studied why some bright people fail to be successful. Salovey and Mayer discovered that many of them ran into trouble because of their lack of interpersonal sensitivity and skills, and defined emotional intelligence as a group of mental abilities that help people to recognize their own feelings and those of others.[164] Reuven Bar-On believed that emotional intelligence was another way of measuring human effectiveness and defined it as a set of 15 abilities necessary to cope with daily situations and get along in the world.[165] Rick Aberman defined emotional intelligence as the degree to which thoughts, feelings, and actions were aligned. According to Aberman, leaders are more effective and "in the zone" when their thoughts, feelings, and actions are perfectly aligned.[166,167] Daniel Goleman, a science writer for *The New York Times*, substantially broadened these definitions and summarized some of this work in his books *Emotional Intelligence* and *Working with Emotional Intelligence.*[163,168] Goleman argued that success in life is based more on one's self-motivation, persistence in the face of frustration, mood management, ability to adapt, and ability to empathize and get along with others than on one's analytic intelligence or IQ. Table 7.5 provides a comparison between the Salovey and Mayer, Bar-On, and Goleman models of emotional intelligence.

Although these definitions can cause confusion for people interested in learning more about emotional intelligence, it appears that these four definitions of EQ can be broken down into two models: an ability model and a mixed model of emotional intelligence.[169] The ability model focuses on how emotions affect how leaders think, decide, plan, and act. This model defines emotional intelligence as four separate but related abilities, which include: (a) the ability to accurately perceive one's own and others' emotions; (b) the ability to generate emotions to facilitate thought and action; (c) the ability to accurately understand the causes of emotions and the meanings they convey; and (d) the ability to regulate one's emotions. According to Caruso, Mayer, and Salovey, some leaders might be very good at perceiving emotions and leveraging them to get results through others, but have difficulties regulating their own emotions. Or they could be very good at understanding the causes of emotions but not as good at perceiving others' emotions. The ability model is not intended to be an all-encompassing model of leadership, but rather supplements the FFM and triarchic theory of intelligence.[169] Just as leaders differ on adjustment or practical intelligence, so do they differ on their ability to perceive and regulate emotions.

TABLE 7.5 Ability and Mixed Models of Emotional Intelligence

Ability Model	Mixed Models	
Mayer, Salovey, and Caruso	**Goleman et al.**	**Bar-On**

Perceiving Emotions	Self-Awareness
	  Emotional Awareness
	  Accurate Self-Assessment
	  Self-Confidence
		Intrapersonal
		  Self-Regard
		  Emotional Self-Awareness
		  Assertiveness
		  Independence
		  Self-Actualization

Managing Emotions	Self-Regulation
	  Self-Control
	  Trustworthiness
	  Conscientiousness
	  Adaptability
	  Innovation
		Adaptability
		  Reality Testing
		  Flexibility
		  Problem-Solving

Using Emotions	Motivation
	  Achievement
	  Commitment
	  Initiative
	  Optimism
		Stress Management
		  Stress Tolerance
		  Impulse Control

Understanding Emotions	Empathy
	  Understanding Others
	  Developing Others
	  Service Orientation
	  Diversity
	  Political Awareness
	
	Social Skills
	  Influence
	  Communication
	  Conflict Management
	  Leadership
	  Change Catalyst
	  Building Bonds
	  Collaboration/Cooperation
	  Team Capabilities
		Interpersonal
		  Empathy
		  Social Responsibility
		  Interpersonal Relationship
		
		General Mood
		  Optimism
		  Happiness

Sources: R. Bar-On, *Emotional Quotient Inventory.* North Tonawanda, NY: Multi-Health Systems, Inc., 2001; D. Goleman, *Working with Emotional Intelligence.* New York: Bantam Doubleday Dell, 1998; D. R. Caruso, J. D. Mayer, and P. Salovey, "Emotional Intelligence and Emotional Leadership," in R. E. Riggio, S. E. Murphy, and F. J. Pirozzolo (Eds.), *Multiple Intelligences and Leadership.* Mahwah, NJ: Lawrence Erlbaum Associates, 2002, pp. 55–74; online source: http://www. eiconsortium.org.

The ability model of EQ is helpful because it allows researchers to determine if EQ is in fact a separate ability and whether it can predict leadership effectiveness over and above the FFM and cognitive abilities.

The Goleman and Bar-On definitions of EQ fall into the mixed model category. These researchers believe emotional intelligence includes not only the abilities outlined in the previous paragraph but also includes a number of other attributes. As such, the mixed model provides a much broader, more comprehensive definition of emotional intelligence. A quick review of Table 7.5 shows that the attributes of emotional intelligence are qualities that most leaders should have, and Goleman, Boyatzis, and McKee maintain that leaders need more or less all of these attributes to be emotionally intelligent.[168,170,171] Moreover, the mixed model of emotional intelligence has been much more popular with human resource professionals and in the corporate world than the ability model. But does the mixed model really tell us anything different from what we already know? More specifically, is the mixed model any different than the FFM of personality? The fact of the matter is that the mixed model is very, very similar to the FFM. Comprehensive research by Van Rooy and Viswesvaran shows that EQ predicts job performance or other important job outcomes no better than the FFM.[169,172] Goleman and Bar-On should deservedly get credit for popularizing the notion that noncognitive abilities are important predictors of leadership success. But on the negative side, they also maintain that they have discovered something completely new and do not give enough credit to the 100 years of personality research that underlie many of the attributes in the mixed model.

Can Emotional Intelligence Be Measured and Developed?

The publication of *Emotional Intelligence* has sprouted a cottage industry of books, training programs, and assessments related to measurement and development of emotional intelligence. Mayer, Salovey, and Caruso's Emotional Intelligence Test (MSCEIT) is a measure of the ability model of emotional intelligence and asks subjects to recognize the emotions depicted in pictures, what moods might be helpful in certain social situations, and so forth.[173] Bar-On has self, self-other, youth, and organizational measures of emotional intelligence, such as the Bar-On Emotional Quotient—360 or EQi-S.[174]

The Emotional Competence Inventory (ECi) was developed by Goleman and consists of 10 questionnaires. These questionnaires are completed by the individual and nine others; the responses are aggregated and given to the participant in a feedback report. Because these researchers have defined emotional intelligence differently and use a different process to assess EQ, it is not surprising that these instruments often provide leaders with conflicting results.[175] Nevertheless, the U.S. Air Force Recruiting Service has used the EQ-i to screen potential recruiters; it found that candidates scoring higher on the attributes of assertiveness, empathy, happiness, self-awareness, and problem solving were much less likely to turn over prematurely in the position and had a 90 percent chance of meeting their recruiting quotas.[175]

One issue that most EQ researchers do agree upon is that emotional intelligence can be developed. Goleman and Aberman have developed one- to five-day training programs to help leaders improve their emotional intelligence; Bar-On has developed 15 e-learning modules that are available at EQ University.com. One of the big adopters of EQ training has been the sales staff at American Express Financial Advisors (AEFA). Leaders at AEFA discovered that the company had a well-respected set of investment and insurance products for customers, but many sales staff were struggling with how to respond to the emotions exhibited by clients during sales calls. Moreover, the best salespeople seem to be better able to "read" their clients' emotions and respond in a more empathetic manner. Since 1993 more than 5,500 sales staff and 850 sales managers at AEFA have attended a five-day training program to better recognize and respond to the emotions exhibited by clients. AEFA found that sales staff attending this program increased annual sales by an average of 18.1 percent, whereas those who did not attend training only achieved a 16.1 percent increase. However, the sample was very small and the comparison somewhat unfair because the control group did not receive any kind of sales training in lieu of the EQ training.[175] Therefore, it is uncertain whether the EQ training content actually adds value over and above five days of sales training.

Implications of Emotional Intelligence

Aberman maintained that people can be extremely ineffective when their thoughts, feelings, and actions are misaligned—for example, arguing with someone on your cellular phone when driving on the interstate highway.[166,167] It seems likely that leaders who are thinking or feeling one thing and actually doing something else are probably less effective in their ability to influence groups toward the accomplishment of their goals. The EQ literature should also be credited with popularizing the idea that noncognitive abilities, such as stress tolerance, assertiveness, and empathy, can play important roles in leadership success. Today, many organizations are using *both* cognitive and noncognitive measures as part of the process of hiring or promoting leaders. Finally, the EQ literature has also helped to bring emotion back to the workplace. Human emotions are very important aspects of one-on-one interactions and teamwork,[176–179] but too many leadership practitioners and researchers have chosen to ignore the role they play. When recognized and leveraged properly, emotions can be the motivational fuel that help individuals and groups to accomplish their goals. When ignored or discounted, emotions can significantly impede a leader's ability to build teams or influence a group. As discussed in the FFM section of this chapter, leaders who can empathize and get along with others are often more successful than those who cannot.

Some of the more recent research in emotional intelligence indicates that it moderates employees' reactions to job insecurity and their ability to cope with stress when threatened with job loss. Employees with lower EQ reported more negative emotional reactions and used less effective coping strategies when dealing with downsizing than those with higher EQ.[180] Along these lines, other researchers report relationships between leaders' moods and followers' moods, job performance, job satisfaction, and creativity.[177,178,181] And Boyatzis, Stubbs, and Taylor accurately point out that most MBA programs are more focused on cognitive abilities and developing financial skills than on those abilities needed to successfully build teams and get results through others.[182]

Despite these positive contributions, emotional intelligence has several limitations. First, Goleman and his associates and Bar-On have not acknowledged the existence of personality, much less 100 years of personality–leadership effectiveness research. As seen in Table 7.6, Goleman's conceptualization of EQ looks very similar to the FFM found in Table 7.1. At least as conceptualized by these two authors, it is difficult to see how EQ is any different from personality. Second, if the EQ attributes are essentially per-

TABLE 7.6
Comparison between the FFM and Goleman's Model of EQ

Goleman et al.	Likely FFM Correlates
Self-Awareness	
Emotional Awareness	Agreeableness
Accurate Self-Assessment	Adjustment
Self-Confidence	Surges
Self-Regulation	
Self-Control	Adjustment, Dependability
Trustworthiness	Dependability
Conscientiousness	Dependability
Adaptability	Adjustment, Dependability
Innovation	Openness to Experience, Dependability
Motivation	
Achievement	Surgency
Commitment	Surgency
Initiative	Surgency
Optimism	Adjustment
Empathy	
Understanding Others	Agreeableness
Developing Others	Openness to Experience
Service Orientation	Agreeableness
Diversity	Agreeableness
Political Awareness	Agreeableness
Social Skills	
Influence	Surgency, Agreeableness
Communication	Surgency
Conflict Management	Agreeableness
Leadership	Surgency
Change Catalyst	Surgency
Building Bonds	Agreeableness
Collaboration/Cooperation	Agreeableness
Team Capabilities	Surgency, Agreeableness

FIGURE 7.6
Emotional
intelligence and the
building blocks of
skills.

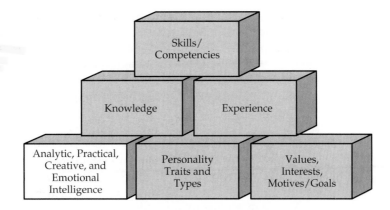

sonality traits, then it is difficult to see how they will change as a result of a training intervention. Personality traits are very difficult to change, and the likelihood of changing 20 to 40 years of day-to-day behavioral patterns as the result of some e-learning modules or a five-day training program seems highly suspect. As we will see in Chapter 8 people can change their behavior, but it takes considerable effort and coaching over the long term to make it happen. Finally, an important question to ask is whether EQ is really something new, or simply a repackaging of old ideas and findings? If EQ is defined as an ability model, such as the one put forth by Mayer, Salovey, and Caruso, then emotional intelligence probably is a unique ability and worthy of additional research (see Figure 7.6). A leader's skills in accurately perceiving, regulating, and leveraging emotions seem vitally important in building cohesive, goal-oriented teams, and measures like the MSCEIT could be used in conjunction with FFM and cognitive abilities measures to hire and develop better leaders. But if EQ is defined as a mixed model, then it is hard to see that Goleman and his associates and Bar-On are really telling us anything new.

Summary

This chapter examined the relationships between personality, intelligence, and emotional intelligence with the ability to build teams and get results. In general, all of these attributes can help a leader to influence a group toward the accomplishment of its goals, but in and of themselves they are no guarantee of leadership success. Oftentimes the situation will dictate which personality traits, components of intelligence, or emotional intelligence attributes will positively affect a leader's ability to build a team or get results through others.

Although the term *personality* has many different meanings, we use the term to describe one's typical or characteristic patterns of behavior. There are several different theories to describe why people act in characteristic ways, but the trait approach to personality has been the most thoroughly researched, and as such plays a key role in the chapter. The adoption of the Five Factor Model (FFM) of personality has helped to clarify the personality–leadership relationships, and researchers have noted that leadership success is positively correlated with the FFM personality dimensions of surgency, dependability, agreeableness, and adjustment.

The FFM comprises the bright side of personality, but there are a number of traits that also constitute the dark side of personality. Dark-side personality traits are irritating, counterproductive behaviors that are exhibited during times of stress and interfere with a leader's ability to build teams or get results through others. Virtually everyone has one or two dark-side traits; some of the keys to being a more successful leader is knowing which dark-side traits you possess, identifying the situations in which they appear, and developing strategies to manage them.

A more recent theory for understanding intelligence divides it into three related components: analytic intelligence, practical intelligence, and creative intelligence. All three components are interrelated. Most research shows that leaders possess higher levels of analytic intelligence than the general population, and that more intelligent leaders often make better leaders. Analytic intelligence appears to confer two primary benefits upon leaders. First, leaders who are smarter seem to be better problem solvers. Second, and perhaps more important, smarter leaders seem to profit more from experience.

The roles of practical and creative intelligence in leadership are receiving increasing attention. Practical intelligence, or one's relevant job knowledge or experience, is proving to be extremely important for leaders. Leaders with higher levels of practical intelligence seem to be better at solving problems under stress. Moreover, practical intelligence seems to be the easiest of the three components to change. This implies that leaders should use techniques such as the action-observation-reflection model, described in Chapter 3, to extract the most learning from their experiences.

Creative intelligence involves developing new and useful products and processes, and creativity is extremely important to the success of many businesses today. Creativity consists of seven components, including synthetic abilities, analytic intelligence, practical intelligence, thinking skills, relevant personality traits, intrinsic motivation, and several environmental factors. Understanding the seven components of creativity is important as the factors can give leaders ideas about how to improve their own and their followers' creativity. It is important that leaders learn how to successfully stimulate and manage creativity, even more than being creative themselves.

In some ways emotional intelligence is a relatively new concept and it is generally concerned with accurately understanding and responding to one's own and others' emotions. Leaders who can better align their thoughts and feelings with their actions may be more effective than leaders who think and feel one way about something but then do something different about it. Although emotional intelligence has helped to point out the role emotions and noncognitive abilities play in leadership success, some of it seems to be nothing more than another label for personality. If this is the case, then emotional intelligence may be a leadership fad that will fade away over time.

Key Terms

Great Man theory, *203*
personality, *205*
trait approach, *205*
traits, *205*
weak situations, *207*
strong situations, *207*
Five Factor Model
(FFM) of personality,
207
surgency, *208*
agreeableness, *209*
dependability, *210*
adjustment, *210*
Level 5 Leadership, *211*
openness to
experience, *212*
types, *213*
personality typology,
213

Myers-Briggs Type
Indicator (MBTI), *213*
extraversion–
introversion, *213*
sensing–intuition, *213*
thinking–feeling, *213*
judging–
perceiving, *213*
character, *217*
dark-side personality
traits, *218*
intelligence, *225*
triarchic theory of
intelligence, *226*
analytic
intelligence, *226*
practical
intelligence, *226*

creative intelligence,
228
divergent thinking, *229*
convergent thinking,
229
synthetic ability, *230*
adaptive thinking
style, *231*
innovative thinking
style, *231*
creeping elegance, *236*
cognitive resources
theory (CRT), *236*
emotional
intelligence, *240*

Questions

1. What FFM and dark-side personality traits do you think would help professional sports players be more or less successful? Would successful coaches need the same or different personality traits and preferences? Would successful players and coaches need different traits for different sports?

2. How would you rank-order the importance of analytic intelligence, practical intelligence, creative intelligence, or emotional intelligence for politicians? Would this ranking be the same for college professors or store managers at a Target or Best Buy store?

3. Think of all the ineffective leaders you have ever worked or played for. What dark-side traits did these leaders possess that caused them to be ineffective?

4. Individuals may well be attracted to, selected for, or successful in leadership roles early in their lives and careers based on their analytic intelligence. But what happens over time and with experience? Do you think *wisdom,* for example, is just another word for intelligence, or is it something else?

5. What role would downsizing play in an organization's overall level of practical intelligence?

6. We usually think of creativity as a characteristic of individuals, but might some organizations be more creative than others? What factors do you think might affect an organization's level of creativity?

7. Can better leaders more accurately perceive and leverage emotions? How could you determine if this was so?

Activities

1. Your instructor has access to a self-scored personality type assessment as well as online FFM and dark-side personality assessments. The online assessments take about 40 minutes to complete and could be given as homework. Once the assessments are completed, you should review the feedback reports and discuss in class.

2. Your instructor could suspend a 30-foot rope approximately 2 feet off the ground. You and the rest of the class would get on one side of the rope. The rope represents an electrified fence, and your task is to get everyone successfully *over* the rope without touching it. You may not touch, lower, raise, or adjust the rope in any manner. You may not let any part of your skin or clothing touch the rope, nor can you drape anything over the rope to protect you from the current. There are two rules you must follow to successfully navigate the rope. First, before starting to cross the fence, everyone in the group must form a line parallel to the rope and hold hands with the people on either side. These links with the other people in the group cannot be broken. Second, a quality error is committed if any group member touches the fence. If the group detects their own error, then only the person currently attempting to navigate the fence needs to start over. If the instructor catches the error but the group does not, then the instructor has the right to have the entire group start over. This is analagous to catching a bad product before it is delivered to a customer instead of delivering defective products to customers. You will have about 25 minutes to plan and execute this exercise. After the exercise your group should discuss the role of bright-side and dark-side personality traits as well as analytic, practical, creative, and emotional intelligence in the exercise.

Minicase

"Lessons on Leadership from Ann Fudge"

How do you rescue one of the largest advertising and media services firms in the world from a downward spiral? That is the question Martin Sorrell faced when his London-based WPP Group acquired Young & Rubicam in 2000. After many years on top, Y&R was starting to lose momentum—and clients. Kentucky Fried Chicken, United Airlines, and Burger King had all decided to take their advertising dollars elsewhere. Sorrell needed to stop the exodus, but how? He decided a fresh face was needed and started a search for a new CEO for Y&R—he wanted a dynamic leader who could revitalize Y&R. He found such a leader in Ann Fudge.

Ann Fudge was formerly president of Kraft Foods. At Kraft she had been responsible for the success of the $5 billion division that included well-known brands such as Maxwell House, Grape Nuts, Shredded Wheat, and General Foods International Coffees. Fudge's reputation as a charismatic leader who listens was a major issue for Sorrell when he went looking for a new CEO for Y&R. Among the talents Fudge had to offer was an ability to interact effectively with all constituencies of a consumer business. Mattel Chairman and CEO Bob Eckert was Fudge's boss when he was president and CEO of Kraft. Of Fudge, Eckert says, "She is equally comfortable with consumers at the ballpark, factory workers on a production line, and executives in the boardroom. She could engage all three constituents in the same day and be comfortable. She is very comfortable with herself, and she's not pretending to be someone else. That's what makes her such an effective leader."

Her commitment to her work and the people she works with is evident in the lessons she offers to other leaders:

1. Be yourself; do not feign behavior that you think will make you "successful."

2. Always remember it's the people, not you. A leader cannot be a leader if he/she has no followers. Be honest with people. Give them feedback. Put the right people in the right jobs. Surround yourself with the smartest people you can find—people who will offer differing perspectives and diversity of experience, age, gender, race.

3. Touch your organization. It's easy to get stuck behind your desk. Fight the burden of paperwork and get out in the field. Don't be a remote leader. You cannot create a dynamic culture if people can't see, hear, touch you. Let them know you as a person.

4. Steer the wheel with a strategic focus, yet maintain a wide peripheral vision. Know when to stop, speed up, slow down, brake quickly, swerve, or even gun it!

Fudge had a difficult decision to make when she was approached by Sorrell about the position at Y&R. She was in the midst of a two-year break—after 24 years working for corporate America, Fudge decided to take some time for herself. She had left her position as president of Kraft Foods in 2001 based not on her dissatisfaction with her job, but on a desire to define herself by more than her career. "It was definitely not satisfaction, it was more about life," says Fudge about her sabbatical. During her two-year break she traveled, cycling around Sardinia and Corsica; she took up yoga; and she wrote a book: *The Artist's Way at Work,* a manual for improving creativity and innovation on the job.

Fudge took on the challenge and has not looked back. In her tenure at Y&R she has worked hard to get Y&R back on top. She has traveled the globe, visiting with Y&R employees around the world, living rule number three of her own leadership rules. She frequently puts in 15-hour days pushing her strategy to focus on clients, encouraging teamwork, and improving creativity. A major undertaking for Fudge is to try and bring together the various business entities under the Y&R umbrella to better meet the needs of clients. She's also trying to institute a Six Sigma method for creativity—looking for ways to increase productivity so employees have more time to be creative. Fudge's hard work is paying off. Y&R has recently added Microsoft and Toys R Us to its list of clients, and, if Fudge has her way, the list will continue to grow until Y&R is back on top.

1. How would Ann Fudge fall into each of the Five Factor Model (FFM) categories?

2. Consider the components of creative intelligence from Table 7.3. Identify the key components that have impacted Ann Fudge's success.

3. Ann Fudge decided to take a sabbatical to focus more on her personal life. Based on her experience, what are some of the benefits to such a break? What might be some of the drawbacks?

Sources: Diane Brady, "Act Two: Ann Fudge's Two-Year Break from Work Changed Her Life. Will Those Lessons Help Her Fix Young & Rubicam?" *BusinessWeek* (March 29, 2004), p. 72; http://www.internet-marketing-branding.com/News/african_american.htm; http://www.brandweek.com/brandweek/search/article_display.jsp?vnu_content_id1000506747; http://www.linkageinc.com/conferences/leadership/gild/

Chapter Notes

1. Stogdill, R. M. *Handbook of Leadership.* New York: Free Press, 1974.

2. Stogdill, R. M. "Personal Factors Associated with Leadership: A Review of the Literature." *Journal of Psychology* 25 (1948), pp. 35–71.

3. Mann, R. D. "A Review of the Relationships between Personality and Performance in Small Groups." *Psychological Bulletin* 56 (1959), pp. 241–70.

4. Lord, R. G., C. L. DeVader, and G. M. Allinger. "A Meta-analysis of the Relationship between Personality Traits and Leadership Perceptions: An Application of Validity Generalization Procedures." *Journal of Applied Psychology* 71 (1986), pp. 402–10.

5. Hogan, R. T., G. J. Curphy, and J. Hogan. "What Do We Know about Personality: Leadership and Effectiveness?" *American Psychologist* 49 (1994), pp. 493–504.

6. Hogan, R. T. "Personality and Personality Measurement." In *Handbook of Industrial and Organizational Psychology* Vol. 2. Eds. M. D. Dunnette and L. M. Hough. Palo Alto, CA: Consulting Psychologists Press, 1991, pp. 873–919.

7. Judge, T. A., A. E. Colbert, and R. Ilies. "Intelligence and Leadership: A Quantitative Review and Test of Theoretical Propositions." *Journal of Applied Psychology* 89 (3), (2004), pp. 542–52.

8. Judge, T. A., J. E. Bono, R. Ilies, and M. W. Gerhardt. "Leadership and Personality: A Qualitative and Quantitative Review." *Journal of Applied Psychology* 87 (4) (2002), pp. 765–80.

9. Zaccaro, S. J. "Trait-Based Perspectives on Leadership." *American Psychologist* 62 (1) (2007), pp. 6–16.

10. Hogan, R. T., J. Hogan, and B. W. Roberts. "Personality Measurement and Employment Decisions: Questions and Answers." *American Psychologist* 51, no. 5 (1996), pp. 469–77.

11. Freud, S. *Group Psychology and the Analysis of the Ego*, trans J. Strachey. 2nd ed. The Standard Edition of the Complete Works of Psychological Works of Sigmund Freud, Vol. 2. London: Hogarth Institute for Psycho-Analysis.

12. Curphy, G. J. *The Consequences of Managerial Incompetence*. Presentation given at the 3rd Hogan Assessment Systems International Users Conference, Prague, Czech Republic, September 2004.

13. Roberts, B. W. "An Alternative Perspective on the Relation between Work and Psychological Functioning: The Reciprocal Model of Person–Environment Interaction." In *Personality and Organizational Behavior*. R. T. Hogan, Chair. Symposium presented at the 104th Annual Meeting of the American Psychological Association, Toronto, Canada, 1996.

14. Curphy, G. J. *Personality, Intelligence, and Leadership*. Presentation given to the Pioneer Leadership Program at Denver University, Denver, CO, 1997.

15. Curphy, G. J. "Personality and Work: Some Food for Thought." In *Personality Applications in the Workplace: Thinking Outside the Dots*. R. T. Hogan (chair). Symposium presented at the 12th Annual Conference of the Society of Industrial and Organizational Psychology, St. Louis, MO, 1997.

16. Curphy, G. J. "New Directions in Personality." In *Personality and Organizational Behavior*. R. T. Hogan (chair). Symposium presented at the 104th Annual Meeting of the American Psychological Association, Toronto, Canada, 1996.

17. Hogan, J., and B. Holland. "Using Theory to Evaluate Personality and Job-Performance Relations: A Socio-analytic Perspective." *Journal of Applied Psychology* 88 (1) (2003), pp. 100–12.

18. Tett, R. P., and D. D. Burnett. "A Personality Trait-Based Interactionist Model of Job Performance." *Journal of Applied Psychology* 88 (3) (2003), pp. 500–17.

19. Allport, G. W., and H. S. Odbert. "Trait-names: A Psycho-Lexical Study." *Psychological Monographs* 47 (1936), pp. 171–220.

20. Deary, J. J. "A (Latent) Big-Five Personality Model in 1915? A Reanalysis of Webb's Data." *Journal of Applied Psychology* 71, no. 5 (1996), pp. 992–1005.

21. Thurstone, L. L. "The Factors of the Mind." *Psychological Review* 41 (1934), pp. 1–32.

22. Azar, B. "Searching for Intelligence Beyond G." *APA Monitor* 26, no. 1 (1995), p. 1.

23. Barrick, M. R., and M. K. Mount. "The Big Five Personality Dimensions and Job Performance: A Meta-analysis." *Personal Psychology* 44 (1991), pp. 1–26.

24. Curphy, G. J. *User's Guide and Interpretive Report for the Leadership Personality Survey*. Minneapolis, MN: Personnel Decisions International, 1998.

25. Costa, P. T., Jr., and R. R. McCrae. "Domains and Facets: Hierarchical Personality Assessment Using the Revised NEO Personality Inventory." *Journal of Personality Assessment* 64 (1995), pp. 21–50.

26. Barrick, M. R. "Answers to Lingering Questions about Personality Research." Paper presented at the 14th Annual Conference of the Society of Industrial and Organizational Psychology, Atlanta, GA, 1999.

27. Thoresen, C. J., J. C. Bradley, P. D. Bliese, and J. D. Thoresen. "The Big Five Personality Traits and Individual Job Growth Trajectories in Maintenance and Transitional Job Stages. *Journal of Applied Psychology* 89 (5) (2004), pp. 835–53.

28. Bono, J. E., and T. A. Judge. "Personality and Transformational and Transactional Leadership." *Journal of Applied Psychology* 89 (5) (2004), pp. 901–10.

29. Davies, S., J. Hogan, J. Foster, and F. Elizondo. "Recombinant Personality Measures for Predicting Leadership Competence." Paper presented at the 20th Annual Conference of the Society of Industrial and Organizational Psychology, Los Angeles, CA, April 2005.

30. Barrick, M. R., L. Parks, and M. K. Mount. "Self Monitoring as a Moderator of the Relationships between Personality Traits and Performance." *Personnel Psychology* 58 (2005), pp. 745–67.

31. Zhau, H., and S. E. Seibert. "The Big Five Personality Dimensions and Entrepreneurial Status: A Meta-analytic Review." *Journal of Applied Psychology* 91 (2) (2006), pp. 259–71.

32. Mount, M., R. Ilies, and E. Johnson. "Relationship between Personality Traits and Counterproductive Work Behaviors: The Mediating Effects of Job Satisfaction." *Personnel Psychology* 59 (2006), pp. 591–622.

33. Curphy, G. J. *Hogan Assessment Systems Certification Workshop Training Manuals.* Tulsa, OK: Hogan Assessment Systems, 2003.

34. Michel, R., and R. T. Hogan. "Personality and Organizational Behavior." In *Personality and Organizational Behavior.* R. T. Hogan (chair). Symposium presented at the 104th Annual Meeting of the American Psychological Association, Toronto, Canada, 1996.

35. Hogan, R. T. "The Role of Big Five Personality Traits in Executive Selection." In *The Role of I/O Psychology in Executive Assessment and Development.* G. J. Curphy (chair). Paper presented at the 15th Annual Conference of the Society of Industrial and Organizational Psychology, New Orleans, LA, 2000.

36. Hurtz, G. M., and J. J. Donovan. "Personality and Job Performance: The Big Five Revisited." *Journal of Applied Psychology* 85, no. 6 (2000), pp. 869–79.

37. Salgado, J. F. "Predicting Job Performance Using FFM and non-FFM Personality Measures." *Journal of Occupational and Organizational Psychology* 76 (3) (2003), pp. 323–46.

38. Curphy, G. J., and K. D. Osten. *Technical Manual for the Leadership Development Survey.* Technical Report No. 93-14. Colorado Springs, CO: U.S. Air Force Academy, 1993.

39. Hogan, R. T., J. Hogan, and R. Warrenfelz. *The Hogan Guide.* Tulsa, OK: Hogan Assessment Systems, 2007.

40. Benson, M. J. "New Explorations in the Field of Leadership Research: A Walk on the Dark Side of Personality & Implications for Leadership (In)Effectiveness." Ph.D dissertation, University of Minnesota, 2006.

41. Hogan, R. T. *Personality and the Fate of Organizations.* Mahwah, NJ: Lawrence Erlbaum, 2007.

42. Lievens, F., M. H. Harris, E. Van Keer, and C. Bisqueret. "Predicting Cross-Cultural Training Performance: The Validity of Personality, Cognitive Ability, and Dimensions Measures by an Assessment Center and a Behavior Description Interview." *Journal of Applied Psychology* 88 (3) (2003), pp. 476–89.

43. Curphy, G. J. "Executive Coaching: How to Achieve Long-Term Behavioral Change." Panel presentation at the 15th Annual Applied Behavioral Sciences Symposium, U.S. Air Force Academy, CO, 1996.

44. Howard, P. J., and J. M. Howard. "Buddy, Can You Paradigm?" *Training & Development,* September 1995, pp. 28–34.

45. Bono, J. E. "Transformational Leadership: What We Know and Why You Should Care!" Presentation delivered to Minnesota Professionals for Psychology Applied to Work, Minneapolis, MN, September 2002.

46. Curphy, G. J. "Comments on the State of Leadership Prediction." In *Predicting Leadership: The Good, The Bad, the Indifferent, and the Unnecessary.* J. P. Campbell and M. J. Benson (chairs). Symposium conducted at the 22nd Annual Conference for the Society of Industrial and Organizational Psychology, New York, April 2007.

47. Hogan, R. T., and J. Hogan. *The Leadership Potential Report*. Tulsa, OK: Hogan Assessment Systems, 2002.

48. Mumford, M. D., S. J. Zaccaro, J. F. Johnson, M. Diana, J. A. Gilbert, and K. V. Threlfall. "Patterns of Leader Characteristics: Implications for Performance and Development." *Leadership Quarterly* 11, no. 1 (2000), pp. 115–36.

49. Heckman, R. J., and B. W. Roberts. "Personality Profiles of Effective Managers across Functions: A Person-Centered Approach." In *Personality Applications in the Workplace: Thinking Outside the Dots.* R. T. Hogan (chair). Symposium presented at the 12th Annual Conference of the Society of Industrial and Organizational Psychology, St. Louis, MO, 1997.

50. Curphy, G. J. "Early Leadership Talent Identification and Development." Paper presented at the Conference for Executives of Saudi Aramco, Dhahran, Saudi Arabia, October 2001.

51. Curphy, G. J. "Leadership Transitions and Succession Planning." In *Developing and Implementing Succession Planning Programs.* J. Lock (chair). Symposium conducted at the 19th Annual Conference for the Society of Industrial and Organizational Psychology, Chicago, April 2004.

52. Quirk, M. P., and P. M. Fandt. *The Second Language of Leadership*. Mahwah, NJ: Erlbaum, 2000.

53. Caldwell, D. F., and J. M. Burger. "Personality Characteristics of Job Applicants and Success in Screening Interviews." *Personnel Psychology* 51, no. 1 (1998), pp. 119–36.

54. Caliguiri, P. M. "The Big Five Personality Characteristics as Predictors of Expatriot's Desire to Terminate the Assignment and Supervisor-Rated Performance." *Personnel Psychology* 53, no. 1 (2000), pp. 67–88.

55. Sarchione, C. D., M. J. Cuttler, P. M. Muchinsky, and R. O. Nelson-Grey. "Prediction of Dysfunctional Job Behaviors among Law Enforcement Officers." *Journal of Applied Psychology* 83, no. 6 (1998), pp. 904–12.

56. Judge, T. A., D. Heller, and M. K. Mount. "Five-Factor Model of Personality and Job Satisfaction." *Journal of Applied Psychology* 87 (2) (2002), pp. 530–41.

57. Judge, T. A., C. A. Higgins, C. J. Thoresen, and M. R. Barrick. "The Big Five Personality Traits, General Mental Ability, and Career Success across the Life Span." *Personnel Psychology* 52, no. 3 (1999), pp. 621–52.

58. Welbourne, T. M., and L. A. Cyr. "The Human Resource Executive Effect in Initial Public Offering Firms." *Academy of Management Journal* 42, no. 6 (1999), pp. 616–29.

59. Erdogan, B., and T. N. Bauer. " Enhancing the Benefits of Employee Proactive Personality: The Role of Fit in Organizations." *Personnel Psychology* 58 (2005), pp. 859–91.

60. Baum, R. J. and E. A. Locke. "The Relationship of Entrepreneurial Traits, Skill, and Motivation to Subsequent Venture Growth." *Journal of Applied Psychology* 89 (4) (2004), pp. 587–98.

61. Blake, R. J. "Relations between Worker Satisfaction and Personality." In *Personality and Organizational Behavior.* R. T. Hogan (chair). Symposium presented at the 104th Annual Meeting of the American Psychological Association, Toronto, Canada, 1996.

62. Schmidt, M. J., J. A. Kihm, and C. Robie. "Development of a Global Measure of Personality." *Personnel Psychology* 53, no. 1 (2000), pp. 153–92.

63. Salgado, J. F. "The Five-Factor Model of Personality and Job Performance in the European Community." *Journal of Applied Psychology* 82, no. 1 (1997), pp. 30–43.

64. Hogan, R. H., and J. Hogan. "Assessing Leadership: A View from the Dark Side." *International Journal of Selection and Assessment* 9 (1/2) (2001), pp. 40–51.

65. Curphy, G. J. "Executive Integrity and 360-Degree Feedback." In *Assessing Executive Failure: The Underside of Performance.* R. T. Hogan (chair). Symposium presented at the 18th Annual Conference of the Society of Industrial and Organizational Psychology, Orlando, FL, 2003.

66. Curphy, G. J. "Leadership Transitions and Teams." Presentation given at the Hogan Assessment Systems International Users Conference, Istanbul, September 2003b.

67. Curphy, G. J. "What We Really Know about Leadership (But Seem Unwilling to Implement)." Presentation given at Minnesota Professionals for Psychology Applied to Work, Minneapolis, MN, January, 2004a.

68. Hogan, R. T., and G. J. Curphy. "Leadership Matters: Values and Dysfunctional Dispositions." Working paper, 2004.

70. Curphy, G. J., and R. T. Hogan. "Managerial Incompetence: Is There a Dead Skunk on the Table?" Working paper, 2004.

71. Curphy, G. J., and R.T. Hogan. "What We Really Know about Leadership (But Seem Unwilling to Implement)." Working paper, 2004.

72. Dotlich, D. L., and P. E. Cairo. *Why CEOs Fail: The 11 Behaviors That Can Derail Your Climb to the Top and How to Manage Them.* New York: Wiley, 2001.

73. Curphy, G. J. "A Commentary on Moral Character Screening." In *Moral Character Screening: Sorting Good and Bad Apples.* W. Sellman (chair). Symposium presented at the 105th Annual Meeting of the American Psychological Association, Chicago, 1997.

74. Curphy, G. J., F. W. Gibson, B. Asiu, J. Horn, and G. Macomber. *The Attaché & Selection Project.* Technical Report No. 94-2. Colorado Springs, CO: U.S. Air Force Academy, 1994.

75. Rosenthal, S. A., and T. L. Pittinsky. "Narcissitic Leadership." *The Leadership Quarterly* 17 (2006), pp. 617–33.

76. *The Economist.* "The Brand of Me," August 12, 2006, p. 51.

77. Judge, T. A., J. A. LePine, and B. L. Rich. "Loving Yourself Abundantly: Relationship of the Narcissistic Personality to Self—and Other Perceptions of Workplace Deviance, Leadership, and Task and Contextual Performance." *Journal of Applied Psychology* 91(4) (2006), pp. 762–76.

78. Spreier, S. W., M. H. Fontaine, and R. L. Malloy. "Leadership Run Amok: The Destructive Potential of Overachievers. *Harvard Business Review*, June 2006, pp. 72–81.

79. Paunonen, S. V., J. E. Lonnqvist, M. Verkasalo, S. Leikas, and V. Nissinen. "Narcissism and Emergent Leadership in Military Cadets." *The Leadership Quarterly* 17 (2006), pp. 475–86.

80. Dubois, P. H. "A Test Dominated Society: China 1115 B.C.–1905." In *Testing Problems in Perspective*. Ed. A. Anastasi. American Council on Education, 1964.

81. Arvey, R. D., et al. "Mainstream Science on Intelligence." *The Wall Street Journal*, December 13, 1994.

82. Riggio, R. E. "Multiple Intelligences and Leadership: An Overview." In *Multiple Intelligences and Leadership*. R. E. Riggio, S. E. Murphy, and F. J. Pirozzolo. Eds. Mahwah, NJ: Lawrence Erlbaum Associates, 2002, pp. 1–7.

83. Schmidt, F. L., and J. E. Hunter. "Development of a Causal Model of Job Performance." *Current Directions in Psychological Science* 1, no. 3 (1992), pp. 89–92.

84. Scarr, S. "Protecting General Intelligence: Constructs and Consequences for Interventions." In *Intelligence: Measurement, Theory, and Public Policy*. Ed. R. L. Linn. Chicago: University of Illinois Press, 1989.

85. Sternberg, R. J. "The Concept of Intelligence: Its Role in Lifelong Learning and Success." *American Psychologist* 52, no. 10 (1997), pp. 1030–37.

86. Sternberg, R. J. "Creativity as a Decision." *American Psychologist*, May 2002, p. 376.

87. Sternberg, R. J. "WICS: A Model of Leadership in Organizations." *Academy of Management: Learning and Education* 2 (4) (2003a), pp. 386–401.

88. Sternberg, R. J. "A Model of Leadership: WICS." *American Psychologist* 62 (1) (2007), pp. 34–42.

89. Salgado, J. F., N. Anderson, S. Moscoso, C. Bertua, F. de Fruyt, and J. P. Rolland. "A Meta-analytic Study of General Mental Ability Validity for Different Occupations in the European Community." *Journal of Applied Psychology* 88 (6) (2003), pp. 1068–81.

90. Menkes, J. "Hiring for Smarts." *Harvard Business Review*, November 2005, pp. 100–11.

91. Cronbach, L. J. *Essentials of Psychological Testing*. 4th ed. San Francisco: Harper & Row, 1984.

92. Herrnstein, R. J., and C. Murray. *The Bell Curve: Intelligence and Class Structure in American Life*. New York: Free Press, 1994.

93. Curphy, G. J. "Concluding Remarks on Executive Assessment and Development." In *The Role of I/O Psychology in Executive Assessment and Development*. G. J. Curphy (chair). Symposium presented at the 15th Annual Conference of the Society for Industrial and Organizational Psychology, New Orleans, LA, 2000.

94. Curphy, G. J. "Early Leadership Talent Identification and Development." Paper presented at the Conference for Executives of Saudi Aramco, Dhahran, Saudi Arabia, October 2001.

95. Curphy, G. J. "What Role Should I/O Psychologists Play in Executive Education?" In *Models of Executive Education*. R. T. Hogan (chair). Presentation given

at the 17th Annual Society for Industrial and Organizational Psychology, Toronto, Canada, April 2002.

96. Curphy, G.J. "Leadership Transitions and Succession Planning." In *Developing and Implementing Succession Planning Programs.* J. Lock (chair). Symposium conducted at the 19th Annual Conference for the Society of Industrial and Organizational Psychology, Chicago, April 2004.

97. Sternberg, R. J. "A Broad View of Intelligence: The Theory of Successful Intelligence." *Journal of Consulting Psychology* 55 (3) (2003b), pp. 139–54.

98. Ferris, G. R., L. A. Witt, and W. A. Hochwarter. "Interaction of Social Skill and General Mental Ability on Job Performance and Salary." *Journal of Applied Psychology* 86 (6) (2001), pp. 1075–82.

99. Hogan, R. T., and J. Hogan. *The Hogan Business Reasoning Inventory.* Tulsa, OK: Hogan Assessment Systems, 2007.

100. Goffee. R., and G. Jones. "Leading Clever People." *Harvard Business Review*, March 2007, pp. 72–79.

101. Brody, N. "Intelligence, Schooling, and Society." *American Psychologist* 52, no. 10 (1997), pp. 1046–50.

102. Humphreys, L. G. "Intelligence: Three Kinds of Instability and Their Consequences for Policy." In *Intelligence: Measurement, Theory, and Public Policy.* Ed. R. L. Linn. Chicago: University of Illinois Press, 1989, pp. 193–216.

103. Gardner, H. *Frames of Mind: The Theory of Multiple Intelligences.* New York: Basic Books, 1983.

104. Sternberg, R. J. *Beyond IQ: A Triarchic Theory of Human Intelligence.* New York: Cambridge University Press, 1985.

105. Sternberg, R. J., R. K. Wagner, W. M. Williams, and J. A. Horvath. "Testing Common Sense." *American Psychologist* 50, no. 11 (1995), pp. 912–27.

106. Hedlund, J., G. B. Forsythe, J. A. Horvath, W. M. Williams, S. Snook, and R. J. Sternberg. "Identifying and Assessing Tacit Knowledge: Understanding the Practical Intelligence of Military Leaders." *The Leadership Quarterly* 14 (2) (2003), pp. 117–40.

107. Sternberg, R. J. *Handbook of Creativity.* New York: Cambridge University Press, 1999.

108. Connelly, M. S., J. A. Gilbert, S. J. Zaccaro, K. V. Threlfell, M. A. Marks, and M. D. Mumford. "Exploring the Relationship of Leadership Skills and Knowledge to Leader Performance." *The Leadership Quarterly* 11 (1) (2000), pp. 65–80.

109. Ireland, D. R., and C. C. Miller. "Decision-Making and Firm Success." *Academy of Management Executive* 18 (4) (2004), pp. 8–12.

110. Sternberg, R. J., and N. K. Dees. "Creativity for the New Millenium." *American Psychologist* 56, no. 4 (2001), p. 332.

111. Kersting, L. M. "What Exactly Is Creativity?" *Monitor on Psychology,* November 2003, pp. 40–41.

112. Sternberg, R. J., and T. I. Lubart. "Investing in Creativity." *American Psychologist* 52, no. 10 (1997), pp. 1046–50.

113. Sternberg, R. J., E. L. Grigorenko, and J. L. Singer. *Creativity: From Potential to Realization.* Washington DC: American Psychological Association Press, 2004.

114. Kaufman, J. C., and J. Baer. "Hawking's Haiku, Madonna's Math: Why It Is Hard to Be Creative in Every Room." In *Creativity: From Potential to Realization*. Eds. R. J. Sternberg, E. L. Grigorenko, and J .L. Singer. Washington DC: American Psychological Association Press, 2004.

115. Lubart, T., and J. H. Guigard. "The Generality-Specificity of Creativity: A Multivariate Approach." In *Creativity: From Potential to Realization*. Eds. R. J. Sternberg, E. L. Grigorenko, and J. L. Singer. Washington DC: American Psychological Association Press, 2004.

116. Feist., G. J. "The Evolved Fluid Specificity of Human Creative Talent." In *Creativity: From Potential to Realization*. Eds. R. J. Sternberg, E. L. Grigorenko, and J. L. Singer. Washington DC: American Psychological Association Press, 2004.

117. Guilford, J. P. *The Nature of Human Intelligence*. New York: McGraw-Hill, 1967.

118. Sternberg, R. J. "What Is the Common Thread of Creativity? Its Dialectical Relationship to Intelligence and Wisdom." *American Psychologist* 56, no. 4 (2001), pp. 360–62.

119. Amabile, T. M. "Beyond Talent: John Irving and the Passionate Craft of Creativity." *American Psychologist* 56, no. 4 (2001), pp. 333–36.

120. Collins, M. A., and T. M. Amabile. "Motivation and Creativity." In *Handbook of Creativity*. Ed. R. J. Sterberg. New York: Cambridge University Press, 1999.

121. Amabile, T. M., E. A. Schatzel, G. B. Moneta, and S. J. Kramer. "Leader Behaviors and the Work Environment for Creativity: Perceived Leader Support." *The Leadership Quarterly* 15 (1) (2004), pp. 5–32.

122. Reiter-Palmon, R., and R. Ilies. "Leadership and Creativity: Understanding Leadership from a Creative Problem Solving Perspective." *The Leadership Quarterly* 15 (1) (2004), pp. 55–77.

123. Sternberg, R. J., and E. L. Grigorenko. "Are Cognitive Styles Still in Style?" *American Psychologist* 51, no. 7 (1996), pp. 677–88.

124. Sternberg, R. J. *Wisdom, Intelligence, and Creativity Synthesized*. New York: Cambridge University Press, 2003.

125. Kirton, M. J. *Test Manual for the Kirton Adaptation-Innovation Inventory*. Hatfield, UK: Occupational Research Centre, 1987.

126. Amabile, T. M., and S. S. Gryskiewicz. *Creativity in the R&D Laboratory*. (Tech Report No. 30). Greensboro, NC: Center for Creative Leadership, 1987.

127. Hogan, R. T., and J. Morrison. "Managing Creativity." In *Create to Be Free: Essays in Honor of Frank Barron*. Ed. A. Montouri. Amsterdam: J. C. Gieben, 1993.

128. Curphy, G. J. "In-Depth Assessments, 360-Degree Feedback, and Development: Key Research Results and Recommended Next Steps." Presentation at the Annual Conference for HR Managers at US West Communications, Denver, CO, January 1998a.

129. Zhou, J. "When the Presence of Creative Co-Workers Is Related to Creativity: Role of Supervisor Close Monitoring, Developmental Feedback, and Creative Personality." *Journal of Applied Psychology* 88 (3) (2003), pp. 413–22.

130. Tierney, P., and S. M. Farmer. "Creative Self-Efficacy: Potential Antecedents and Relationship to Creative Performance." *Academy of Management Journal* 45 (6) (2002), pp. 1137–48.

131. Carmeli, A., and J. Schraubroeck. "The Influence of Leaders' and Other Referents' Normative Expectations on Individual Involvement in Creative Work." *The Leadership Quarterly* 18 (2007), pp. 35–48.

132. Oldham, G. R., and A. Cummings. "Employee Creativity: Personal and Contextual Factors at Work." *Academy of Management Journal* 39 (1996), pp. 607–34.

133. Shalley, C. E., and L. L. Gilson. "What Leaders Need to Know: A Review of the Social and Contextual Factors That Can Foster or Hinder Creativity." *The Leadership Quarterly* 15 (1) (2004), pp. 33–53.

134. Dingfelder, S. F. "Creativity on the Clock." *Monitor on Psychology*, November 2003, p. 58.

135. Basadur, M. "Leading Others to Think Innovatively Together: Creative Leadership." *The Leadership Quarterly* 15 (1) (2004), pp. 103–21.

136. West, M. A., and N. R. Anderson. "Innovation in Top Management Teams." *Journal of Applied Psychology* 81, no. 6 (1996), pp. 680–93.

137. Fischer, B., and A. Boyton. "Virtuoso Teams." *Harvard Business Review*, July–August 2005, pp. 117–23.

138. Amabile, T. M., and R. Conti. "What Downsizing Does to Creativity." *Issues & Observations* 15, no. 3 (1995), pp. 1–6.

139. Kaufman, J. C., and R. J. Sternberg. *The International Handbook of Creativity*. New York: Cambridge University Press, 2006.

140. Florida, R., and J. Goodnight. "Managing for Creativity." *Harvard Business Review*, July–August 2005, pp. 125–31.

141. Florida, R., R. Cushing, and G. Gates. "When Social Capital Stifles Innovation." *Harvard Business Review*, August 2002, p. 20.

142. Perry-Smith, J. E., and C. E. Shalley. "The Social Side of Creativity: A Static and Dynamic Social Network Perspective." *Academy of Management Review* 28 (1) (2003), pp. 89–106.

143. Ghiselli, E. E. "Intelligence and Managerial Success." *Psychological Reports* 12 (1963), p. 89.

144. Bray, D. W., R. J. Campbell, and D. L. Grant. *Formative Years in Business: A Long-term AT&T Study of Managerial Lives*. New York: Wiley-Interscience, 1974.

145. Bray, D. W., and A. Howard. "The AT&T Longitudinal Study of Managers." In *Longitudinal Studies of Adult Psychological Development*. Ed. K. W. Schaiel. New York: Guilford, 1983.

146. Bass, B. M. *Bass and Stogdill's Handbook of Leadership*. 3rd ed. New York: Free Press, 1990.

147. Fiedler, F. E. "The Effect and Meaning of Leadership Experience: A Review of Research and a Preliminary Model." In *Impact of Leadership*. Eds. K. E. Clark, M. B. Clark, and D. P. Campbell. Greensboro, NC: Center for Creative Leadership, 1992.

148. Ferris, G. R., L. A. Witt, and W. A. Hochwarter. "Interaction of Social Skill and General Mental Ability on Job Performance and Salary." *Journal of Applied Psychology* 86 (6) (2001), pp. 1075–82.

149. Fiedler, F. E. "The Curious Role of Cognitive Resources in Leadership." In *Multiple Intelligences and Leadership.* Eds. R. E. Riggio, S. E. Murphy, and F. J. Pirozzolo. Mahwah, NJ: Lawrence Erlbaum Associates, 2002, pp. 91–104.

150. Gibson, F. W. "A Taxonomy of Leader Abilities and Their Influence on Group Performance as a Function of Interpersonal Stress." In *Impact of Leadership.* Eds. K. E. Clark, M. B. Clark, and D. P. Campbell. Greensboro, NC: Center for Creative Leadership, 1992.

151. Mumford, M. D., G. M. Scott, B. Gaddis, and J. M. Strange. "Leading Creative People: Orchestrating Expertise and Relationships." *The Leadership Quarterly* 13 (6) (2002), pp. 705–50.

152. Sternberg, R. J. "WICS: A Model of Leadership in Organizations." *Academy of Management: Learning and Education* 2 (4) (2003a), pp. 386–401.

153. Amabile T. M. "The Motivation to Be Creative." In *Frontiers in Creativity: Beyond the Basics.* Ed. S. Isaksen. Buffalo, NY: Bearly, 1987.

154. Zhou, J. "Feedback Valence, Feedback Style, Task Autonomy, and Achievement Orientation: Interactive Effects on Creative Performance." *Journal of Applied Psychology* 83, no. 2 (1998), pp. 261–76.

155. Prince, G. M. "Creative Meetings through Power Sharing." *Harvard Business Review* 50, no. 4 (1972), pp. 47–54.

156. Fiedler, F. E., and J. E. Garcia. *New Approaches to Leadership: Cognitive Resources and Organizational Performance.* New York: John Wiley, 1987.

157. Fiedler, F. E. "Cognitive Resources and Leadership Performance." *Applied Psychology: An International Review* 44, no. 1 (1995), pp. 5–28.

158. Sarason, I. "Stress, Anxiety, and Cognitive Interference: Reactions to Stress." *Journal of Personality and Social Psychology* 46 (1986), pp. 929–39.

159. Schonpflug, W. "The Noncharismatic Leader-Vulnerable." *Applied Psychology: An International Review* 44, no. 1 (1995), pp. 39–42.

160. Zaccaro, S. J. "Leader Resources and the Nature of Organizational Problems." *Applied Psychology: An International Review* 44, no. 1 (1995), pp. 32–36.

161. Levy-Leboyer, C. "Leadership Performance: Towards a More Complex Model." *Applied Psychology: An International Review* 44, no. 1 (1995), pp. 43–44.

162. Curphy, G. J. "Personality, Intelligence, and Leadership." Presentation given to the Pioneer Leadership Program at Denver University, Denver, CO, 1997.

163. Goleman, D. *Emotional Intelligence.* New York: Bantam Doubleday Dell, 1995.

164. Salovey, P., and J. D. Mayer. "Emotional Intelligence." *Imagination, Cognition, and Personality* 9 (1990), pp. 185–211.

165. Bar-On, R. *The Emotional Quotient Inventory (EQ-i).* Toronto, Canada: Multi-Health Systems, 1996.

166. Aberman, R. "Emotional Intelligence." Paper presented at the Quarterly Meeting of the Minnesota Human Resource Planning Society, Minneapolis, MN, November 2000.

167. Aberman, R. "Emotional Intelligence and Work." Presentation given to the Minnesota Professionals for Psychology Applied to Work, Minneapolis, MN, January, 2007.

168. Goleman, D. *Working with Emotional Intelligence.* New York: Bantam Doubleday Dell, 1998.

169. Caruso, D. R., J. D. Mayer, and P. Salovey. "Emotional Intelligence and Emotional Leadership." In *Multiple Intelligences and Leadership*. Eds. R. E. Riggio, S. E. Murphy, and F. J. Pirozzolo. Mahwah, NJ: Lawrence Erlbaum Associates, 2002, pp. 55–74.

170. Goleman, D., R. Boyatzis, and A. McKee. "Primal Leadership: The Hidden Driver of Great Performance." *Harvard Business Review,* December 2001, pp. 42–53.

171. Goleman, D., R. Boyatzis, and A. McKee. *Primal Leadership: Realizing the Power of Emotional Intelligence.* Boston: Harvard Business School Press, 2002.

172. Antonakis, J. "On Why Emotional Intelligence Will Not Predict Leadership Effectiveness beyond IQ and the Big Five. An Extension and Rejoinder." *Organizational Analysis* 12 (2) (2004), pp. 171–82.

173. Mayer, J. D., D. R. Caruso, and P. Salovey. "Selecting a Measure of Emotional Intelligence: The Case for Ability Testing." In *Handbook of Emotional Intelligence.* Eds. R. Bar-On and J. D. A. Parker. New York: Jossey-Bass, 2000.

174. Bar-On, R. "The Bar-On Emotional Quotient Inventory (EQ-i): Rational, Description, and Summary of Psychometric Properties." In *Measuring Emotional Intelligence: Common Ground and Controversy.* Ed. Glenn Geher, Hauppauge, NY: Nova Science Publishers, 2004, pp. 111–42.

175. Schwartz, T. "How Do You Feel?" *Fast Company,* June 2000, pp. 297–312.

176. Druskat, V. U., and S. B. Wolff. "Building the Emotional Intelligence of Groups." *Harvard Business Review,* March 2001, pp. 80–91.

177. Sy, T., S. Cote, and R. Saavedra. "The Contagious Leader: Impact of the Leader's Mood on the Mood of Group Members, Group Affective Tone, and Group Processes." *Journal of Applied Psychology* 90 (2) (2005), pp. 295–305.

178. Ting Fong, C. "The Effects of Emotional Ambivalence on Creativity." *Academy of Management Journal* 49 (5) (2006), pp. 1016–30.

179. Bradberry, T., and J. Greaves. "Heartless Bosses?" *Harvard Business Review,* December 2005, p. 24.

180. Jordan, P. J., N. M. Ashkanasy, and C. E. J. Hartel. "Emotional Intelligence as a Moderator of Emotional and Behavioral Reactions to Job Security." *Academy of Management Review* 27 (3) (2002), pp. 361–72.

181. Wong, C. S., and K. S. Law. "The Effects of Leader and Follower Emotional Intelligence on Performance and Attitude: An Exploratory Study." *The Leadership Quarterly* 13 (3) (2002), pp. 243–74.

182. Boyatzis, R. E., E. C. Stubbs, and S. N. Taylor. "Learning Cognitive and Emotional Intelligence Competencies through Graduate Management Education." *Academy of Management Learning and Education* 1 (2) (2002), pp. 150–62.

Chapter 8

Leadership Behavior

Introduction

Leadership is action, not position.

Donald H. McGannon, Westinghouse Broadcasting Corporation

Throughout Chapters 4–7 we have been talking about different ways to assess leaders. But when all is said and done, how can we tell "good" leaders from "bad" leaders? One way to differentiate leaders is to look at results; some leaders have a track record of getting good results across a variety of situations whereas others seem to have difficulties getting work done through others. But another key way we distinguish between effective and ineffective leaders is to look at what they do on a day-to-day basis. Some leaders do a good job making decisions, providing direction, creating plans, giving regular feedback, and getting their followers the resources they need to be successful and as a result build cohesive teams. Other leaders have difficulties making decisions, set vague or unclear goals, and ignore followers' requests for equipment and subsequently cannot build teams. Although a leader's values, personality, and intelligence are important, variables like these only have an indirect relationship with leadership effectiveness. Their effect presumably comes from the impact they have on leader behavior, which appears to have a more direct relationship with the leader's ability to build teams and get results through others. One advantage of looking at leaders in terms of behavior instead of, say, personality is that behavior is often easier to measure; leadership behaviors can be observed whereas personality traits, values, or intelligence must be inferred from behavior or measured with tests. Another advantage of looking at leader behavior is that many people are less defensive about, and feel in more control of, specific behaviors than they do about their personalities or intelligence. This point has significant implications for developing leadership skills, a topic we will take up in detail at the end of this book.

261

Leaders with certain traits, values, or attitudes may find it easier to effectively perform some leadership behaviors than others. For example, leaders with higher agreeableness scores (as defined in Chapter 7) may find it relatively easy to show concern and support for followers but may also find it difficult to discipline followers. Likewise, leaders with a low Affiliation value (Chapter 6) and who score low on the personality trait of sociability (Chapter 7) will prefer working by themselves versus with others. Because behavior is under conscious control, we can always choose to change our behavior as leaders if we want to. It is important to remember, however, that the ease in which we exhibit or can change behavior will partly be a function of our values, personality, and intelligence.

Followers and the situation are the two other major factors to keep in mind when evaluating leadership behavior. As described in Chapter 7, strong situational norms can play pervasive roles in leaders' behavior. Similarly, follower and situational factors can help determine whether a particular leadership behavior is "bad" or "good." Say a leader provided a group of followers with extremely detailed instructions on how to get a task accomplished. If the followers were new to the organization or had never done the task before, then this level of detail would probably help the leader get better results through others. But if the followers were very experienced, then this very same leader behavior would likely have detrimental effects. The same would be true if the company were in a financial crisis versus having a very successful year.

This chapter begins with a discussion on why it is important to study leadership behavior. We then review some of the early research on leader behavior, and discuss several ways to categorize or conceptualize different leadership behaviors. Next, we briefly summarize what is currently known about a common leadership behavior assessment technique, the 360-degree, or multirater, feedback questionnaire. The next section describes the research surrounding managerial derailment, a concept closely related to managerial incompetence. The last section provides both a research perspective and some practical advice on behavioral change and includes such topics as development planning, coaching, and mentoring.

Studies of Leadership Behavior

Why Study Leadership Behavior?

Thus far, we have reviewed research on a number of key variables affecting leadership behavior, but we have not directly examined fundamentally what leaders actually do to successfully build a team or get results through others. For example, what behaviors did Shane Aguero and Jerry Swope take in order to influence their platoon in Iraq (see Profiles in Leadership 8.1)? What did Hillary Clinton, John McCain, Rudy

Lieutenant Shane Aguero and SFC Jerry Swope

PROFILES IN LEADERSHIP 8.1

Lt. Shane Aguero and SFC Jerry Swope were among the 21,000 soldiers from First Calvary who were deployed to Iraq in early 2004. Their unit was responsible for patrolling the area known as Sadr City. The unit they were replacing had patrolled Sadr City for the past year and during that time reported only a single incident between the 2,500,000 Shiite residents and the U.S. Army. By all accounts the First Calvary was expecting to have similar relationships with the local population and believed its primary mission would be to provide local security and infrastructure improvement. But intelligence reports indicated that many of the Imams in Sadr City had started calling for the ouster of U.S. forces from Iraq and in late March Paul Bremer, U.S. Administrator of Iraq, closed down the local newspaper, *Al-Hawza,* because it was inciting violence. By early April intelligence reports indicated that "Sadr City was a volcano ready to explode."

Lt. Shane Aguero and the 17 members of Aguero's platoon and an Iraqi interpreter were riding in four Humvees that were escorting three trucks collecting sewage from Sadr City on April 4. The drivers of the sewage trucks were getting more and more nervous as the day went on and at the end of the day quit their jobs—stating that they would be killed as collaborators if they remained. During the day the streets of Sadr City were busy with the normal hustle and bustle of a large city, but as the day came to a close the city streets became deserted. As Aguero's platoon was leaving Sadr City, they encountered a large crowd of people as well as a number of barriers that barred their travel on certain roads. They then came under gunfire. The gunfire started slowly at first, from one or two weapons from shooters who were fairly spread out, but then quickly escalated into a full firefight involving hundreds of enemy solders. Aguero and his platoon were driving as fast as they could down the only street they could travel, a street that was lined with hundreds of members of the Mahdi Army and Sadr militia who were intent on killing everyone in the platoon.

Aguero ordered his platoon to park their four vehicles outside a three-story building and set up a defensive position on the roof. By this time one of his troops had been killed and one wounded. SFC Jerry Swope remained in one of the Humvees in order to maintain radio contact with the Tactical Operations Center and coordinate a rescue. The building rapidly became surrounded by an overwhelming force of enemy soldiers who also had an intimate knowledge of the local terrain. Dozens of enemy shooters were closing in from all directions by taking 5–6 quick shots and then ducking down to advance to better vantage points. While this was happening the locals sent hundreds of men, women, and children down both ends of the alleyway in front of the building in a massive frontal assault. The alley was only wide enough for five or six people, but the enemy arranged the assault so that several rows of children were at the front of the line, several rows of women behind them, and then more rows of men at the rear firing their weapons at the U.S. soldiers.

At the time of the first assault Aguero's platoon had experienced five casualties—four wounded and one killed. SFC Swope and two other soldiers were in the exposed Humvees when the frontal assault took place. Aguero did not want to shoot women and children, but it was abundantly clear the Mahdi Army was using them as human shields. Aguero waited until the last possible moment and then had his troops open fire. His squad likely went through 3,000 rounds of ammunition in 30 seconds and in less than one minute hundreds of Iraqis had died. Aguero and his troops continued to experience high levels of fire from the shooters on other rooftops when the Mahdi Army mounted a second frontal assault. The same tactics were used and it soon became clear that the enemy was using the assaults to exhaust the platoon's ammunition supply. By this time the battle had waged four hours and Aguero's platoon had experienced eight casualties and was dangerously close to "going black" (running out of ammunition). SFC Swope remained at the Humvee to coordinate the rescue efforts even though it had been hit by thousands of

continued

Continued

enemy rounds and its bulletproof glass had been shot out. It took three different rescue attempts before Aguero's troops were finally saved. The fighting was so intense that one of the rescue units alone experienced 47 casualties in an hour.

SFC Jerry Swope received a Silver Star for his actions. His citation reads "[His] actions, more than any single event, led to the overall survival of the platoon." Lt. Shane Aguero has been promoted to Captain and is doing a tour in Afghanistan as part of a reconstruction team.

Source: M. Raddatz, *The Long Road Home.* New York: G. P. Putnam's Sons, 2007.

Giuliani, or Barack Obama do to organize and run for the U.S. presidential election in 2008? What behaviors differentiated those who won their party's nominations versus those who lost in the primaries? What does Jeffrey Immelt, the CEO of GE, do to keep the company profitable? What exactly did Peter Jackson do to get a troupe of actors to commit to seven years of filming a trilogy that many said could not be done? Or to get New Line Productions to invest the $250,000,000 needed to create the *Lord of the Rings* movies? Because of these questions, it is appropriate to turn our attention to leader behavior itself, for if we could identify how successful leaders act compared with unsuccessful leaders, then we could design leadership talent management systems that would allow organizations to hire, develop, and promote the skills necessary for future success. Unfortunately, given the success of the Dilbert comic strip and the explosive growth of management consulting firms, there appears to be a number of persons in positions of authority who either do not know how to build teams or get results through others or do not realize how their behavior is negatively affecting the people who work for them.[1–10]

Before we go into the different ways to categorize what leaders do to build teams or influence a group, it might be good to review what we know so far about leadership skills and behaviors. As seen in Figure 8.1, leadership behaviors (which include skills and competencies) are a function of intelligence, personality traits, emotional intelligence, values, attitudes, interests, knowledge, and experience. The factors in the bottom layer of blocks are relatively difficult to change, and they predispose a leader to act in distinctive ways. As described in Chapter 7, one's personality traits are pervasive and almost automatic, occurring typically without much conscious attention. The same could be said about how values, attitudes, and intelligence affect behaviors. Over time, however, it is hoped that leaders learn and discern which behaviors are more appropriate and effective than others. It is always useful to remember the pivotal roles individual difference and situational variables can play in a leader's actions (see Highlight 8.1).

FIGURE 8.1
The building blocks
of skills.

Initiating Structure & Consideration
Employee & Job-Centered Dimensions
The Leadership Grid
360-Degree Feedback
Managerial Derailment
Self-Defeating Behaviors
Coaching and Mentoring Behaviors

Behavior/
Skills/
Competencies

Knowledge

Experience

Intelligence

Personality
Traits, Types,
and Emotional
Intelligence

Values,
Interests,
Motives/Goals

The Early Studies

If you were asked how to study and identify the behaviors that best differentiated effective from ineffective leaders, how would you do it? As
described in Chapter 4, interviews, behavioral observation, and paper-
and-pencil techniques (e.g., questionnaires) would seem to be the most
likely approaches. You could ask leaders what they do, follow the leaders
around to see how they actually behave, or administer questionnaires to
ask them and those they work with how often the leaders exhibited certain behaviors. These three approaches have been used extensively in past
and present leadership research.

Much of the initial leader behavior research was conducted at Ohio State
University and the University of Michigan. Collectively, the Ohio State University studies developed a series of questionnaires to measure different
leader behaviors in work settings. These researchers began by collecting
over 1,800 questionnaire items that described different types of leadership
behaviors. These items were collapsed into 150 statements, and these statements were then used to develop a questionnaire called the **Leader Behavior Description Questionnaire (LBDQ).**[11,12] In order to obtain information
about a particular leader's behavior, subordinates were asked to rate the
extent to which their leader performed behaviors like the following:

He lets subordinates know when they've done a good job.

He sets clear expectations about performance.

He shows concern for subordinates as individuals.

He makes subordinates feel at ease.

In analyzing the questionnaires from thousands of subordinates, the
statistical pattern of responses to all the different items indicated leaders
could be described in terms of two independent dimensions of behavior

called consideration and initiating structure.[13,14] **Consideration** refers to how much a leader is friendly and supportive toward subordinates. Leaders high in consideration engage in many different behaviors that show supportiveness and concern, such as speaking up for subordinates' interests, caring about their personal situations, and showing appreciation for their work. **Initiating structure** refers to how much a leader emphasizes meeting work goals and accomplishing tasks. Leaders high in initiating structure engage in many different task-related behaviors, such as assigning deadlines, establishing performance standards, and monitoring performance levels.

The LBDQ was not the only leadership questionnaire developed by the Ohio State researchers. They also developed, for example, the Supervisory Descriptive Behavior Questionnaire (SBDQ), which measured the extent to which leaders in industrial settings exhibited consideration and initiating structure behaviors.[15] The Leadership Opinion Questionnaire (LOQ) asked leaders to indicate the extent to which they believed different consideration and initiating behaviors were important to leadership success.[16] The LBDQ-XII was developed to assess 10 other categories of leadership behaviors in addition to consideration and initiating structure.[17] Some of the additional leadership behaviors assessed by the LBDQ-XII included acting as a representative for the group, being able to tolerate uncertainty, emphasizing production, and reconciling conflicting organizational demands.

Rather than trying to describe the variety of behaviors leaders exhibit in work settings, the researchers at the University of Michigan sought to

Behaviors versus Skills

HIGHLIGHT 8.1

Leadership behaviors are somewhat different from leadership skills. A **leadership behavior** concerns a specific action, such as "setting specific performance goals for team members." A **leadership skill** consists of three components, which include a well-defined body of knowledge, a set of related behaviors, and clear criteria of competent performance. Perhaps leadership skills may be better understood by using an analogy from basketball. People differ considerably in their basketball skills; good basketball players know when to pass and when to shoot and are adept at making layups, shots from the field, and free throws. Knowing when to pass and when to shoot is an example of the knowledge component, and hitting layups and free throws are examples of the behavioral component of skills. In addition, shooting percentages can be used as one criterion for evaluating basketball skills. Leadership skills, such as delegating, can be seen much the same way. Good leaders know when and to whom a particular task should be delegated (i.e., knowledge), they effectively communicate their expectations concerning a delegated task (i.e., behavior), and they check to see whether the task was accomplished in a satisfactory manner (i.e., criteria). Thus, a leadership skill is knowing when to act, acting in a manner appropriate to the situation, and acting in such a way that it helps the leader accomplish team goals.

identify leader behaviors that contributed to effective group performance.[18] They concluded that four categories of leadership behaviors are related to effective group performance: leader support, interaction facilitation, goal emphasis, and work facilitation.[19]

Both goal emphasis and work facilitation are **job-centered dimensions** of behavior similar to the initiating structure behaviors described earlier. **Goal emphasis** behaviors are concerned with motivating subordinates to accomplish the task at hand, and **work facilitation** behaviors are concerned with clarifying roles, acquiring and allocating resources, and reconciling organizational conflicts. Leader support and interaction facilitation are **employee-centered dimensions** of behavior similar to the consideration dimension of the various Ohio State questionnaires (see Table 8.1). **Leader support** includes behaviors where the leader shows concern for subordinates; **interaction facilitation** includes those behaviors where leaders act to smooth over and minimize conflicts among followers. Like the researchers at Ohio State, those at the University of Michigan also developed a questionnaire, the Survey of Organizations, to assess the degree to which leaders exhibit these four dimensions of leadership behaviors.[19]

Although the behaviors composing the task-oriented and people-oriented leadership dimensions were similar across the two research programs, there was a fundamental difference in assumption underlying the work at the University of Michigan and that at Ohio State. Researchers at the University of Michigan considered job-centered and employee-centered behaviors to be at *opposite ends of a single continuum of leadership behavior.* Leaders could theoretically manifest either strong employee- *or* job-centered behaviors, but not both. On the other hand, researchers at Ohio State believed that consideration and initiating structure were *independent continuums.* Thus, leaders could be high in both initiating structure and consideration, low in both dimensions, or high in one and low in the other.

The key assumption underlying both research programs was that certain behaviors could be identified that are universally associated with a leader's ability to successfully influence a group toward the accomplishment of its goals. Here are the kinds of questions researchers were interested in:

- From the University of Michigan perspective, who tends to be more effective in helping a group to accomplish its goals, job- or employee-centered leaders?

TABLE 8.1

Ohio State Dimensions	University of Michigan Dimensions
Initiating Structure	Goal Emphasis & Work Facilitation
Consideration	Leader Support & Interaction Facilitation

- From the Ohio State perspective, are leaders who exhibit high levels of *both* task- and people-oriented behaviors more effective than those who exhibit *only* task or people behaviors?
- What role do situational factors play in leadership effectiveness? Are employee-centered leadership behaviors more important in non-profit organizations or downsizing situations, whereas job-centered behaviors are more important in manufacturing organizations or start-up situations?

The answers to these questions have several practical implications. If leaders need to exhibit only job- or employee-centered behaviors, then selection and training systems need to focus only on these behaviors. But if situational factors play a role, then researchers need to identify which variables are the most important, and to train leaders how to modify their behavior accordingly. As you might suspect, the answer to all of these questions is, "It depends." In general, researchers have reported that leaders exhibiting a high level of consideration or employee-centered behaviors had more satisfied subordinates. Leaders who set clear goals, explained what followers were to do and how to get tasks accomplished, and monitored results (i.e., initiating structure or job-centered) often had higher-performing work units if the group faced relatively ambiguous or ill-defined tasks.[20-22] At the same time, however, leaders whose behavior was highly autocratic (an aspect of initiating structure) were more likely to have relatively dissatisfied subordinates.[20] Findings like these suggest that *there is no universal set of leader behaviors always associated with leadership success.* Often the degree to which leaders need to exhibit task- or people-oriented behaviors depends upon the situation, and it is precisely this finding that prompted the research underlying the contingency theories of leadership described in Chapter 12. If you review these theories, you will see strong links to the job- and employee-centered behaviors identified 40 years ago.

Alternative Conceptualizations of Leadership Behaviors

The Ohio State and University of Michigan studies were a good first step in describing what leaders actually do. Other researchers have extended these findings into more user-friendly formats or developed different schemes for categorizing leadership behaviors. Like the earlier research, these alternative conceptualizations are generally concerned with: (*a*) identifying key leadership behaviors, (*b*) determining whether these behaviors have positive relationships with leadership success, and (*c*) developing those behaviors related to leadership success. One popular conceptualization of leadership is really an extension of the findings reported by the University of Michigan and Ohio State leadership researchers. The **Leadership Grid**® profiles leader behavior on two dimensions: **concern for people** and **concern for production**.[23,24] The word *concern* reflects how a leader's underlying assumptions about people at work and the importance of the bottom line affect leadership style. In that sense, then, the Leadership Grid deals with more than just behavior. Nonetheless, it is included in this chapter because it is such a direct descendant of earlier behavioral studies.

As Figure 8.2 shows, leaders can get scores ranging from 1 to 9 on both concern for people and concern for production depending on their responses to a leadership questionnaire. These two scores are then plotted on the Leadership Grid, and the two score combinations represent different leadership orientations. Each orientation reflects a unique set of assumptions for using power and authority to link people to

FIGURE 8.2 The Leadership Grid figure.

Source: Robert R. Blake and Anne Adams McCanse, *Leadership Dilemmas—Grid Solutions.* Houston: Gulf Publishing, 1991, p. 29. Copyright 1991. Reprinted with permission of Grid International.

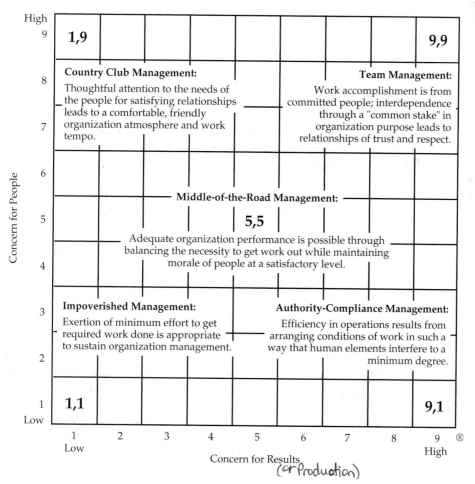

production.[23] Amid the different leadership styles, the most effective leaders are claimed to have both high concern for people and high concern for production, and Leadership Grid training programs are designed to move leaders to a 9,9 leadership style. Whereas this objective seems intuitively appealing, where do you think former U.S. Secretary of Defense Donald Rumsfeld or the current Secretary-General of the United Nations, Ban Ki-Moon, score on these two dimensions? Do both of them show a high concern for production and people? Are there differences between the two leaders, or are both 9,9 leaders?

Although the Leadership Grid can be useful for describing or categorizing different leaders, we should note that the evidence to support the assertion that 9,9 leaders are the most effective comes primarily from Blake, Mouton, and their associates. However, other more recent research might shed some light on whether 9,9 leaders are really the most effective. Robie, Kanter, Nilsen, and Hazucha conducted a study of 1,400 managers in the United States, Germany, Denmark, the United Kingdom, Italy, Spain, France, and Belgium to determine whether the same leadership behaviors were related to effectiveness across countries. They reported that leadership behaviors associated with problem solving and driving for results (initiating structure or 9,1 leadership) were consistently related to successfully building teams, influencing a group to accomplish its goals, and getting results, regardless of country.[25] Similar results about initiating structure and job performance were reported by Judge, Piccolo, and Ilies.[21] Using 800 managers in a U.S. high-tech firm, Goff reported that managers who spent more time building relationships (consideration or 1,9 leadership) also had more satisfied followers (i.e., they were less likely to leave the organization).[26] Likewise, other researchers reported strong support for the notion that higher consideration behavior can reduce employee turnover.[21,22] These results seem to indicate that the most effective leadership style might just depend on the criteria used to judge effectiveness. The context and style of a leader's behavior are also factors that affect their ability to build teams and get results through others (see Highlight 8.2).

So far in this section we have described several ways to categorize leaders or leadership behaviors, but what are the implications of this research for leadership practitioners? Believe it or not, you can see the practical application of this leadership behavior research in just about every Global 1000 company. As first discussed in Chapter 4, competency models describe the behaviors and skills managers need to exhibit if an organization is to be successful.[6,27-34] Just as leaders in different countries may need to exhibit behaviors uniquely appropriate to that setting to be successful, different businesses and industries within any one country often emphasize different leadership behaviors. Therefore, it is not unusual to see different organizations having distinct competency models depending upon the nature and size of the business, its business

I don't do quagmires . . . I don't do diplomacy . . . I don't do foreign policy . . . I don't do predictions . . . I don't do numbers . . .

Donald Rumsfeld, former U.S. Secretary of Defense

The Globe Leadership Project: Culture and Leadership across the World

HIGHLIGHT 8.2

Research conducted at Ohio State and the University of Michigan, and by Blake and his associates, focused on the behaviors exhibited by people in positions of authority. Most if not all of this research was done on samples from the United States, with the vast majority being men. Over the past 11 years Bob House and his associates have been involved with extensive research study involving 17,000 middle managers from 62 different cultures in order to determine whether there are some universal dimensions of leadership that cut across cultures, societies, and countries. House and his associates found that there were six universal dimensions to leadership—factors that seemed to be associated with effective leadership across all cultures. These factors include:

- *Charismatic/Value-Based:* the ability to inspire, motivate, and expect high performance outcomes from others on the basis of firmly held core values.
- *Team Oriented:* the ability to build effective teams and influence them in the pursuit of a common purpose or set of goals.
- *Participative:* the degree to which leaders involve others in the decision-making process.
- *Humane Oriented:* the degree to which leaders demonstrate supportive or considerate leadership.

- *Self-Protective:* the degree to which leaders ensure the safety and security of team members.
- *Autonomous:* refers to independent and individualistic leadership.

These findings indicate that no matter what country or culture a person is in, if he or she exhibits the leadership behaviors associated with these six universal dimensions, then they will have a much easier time building teams and getting results through others. People are in agreement as to what constitutes good leadership and bad leadership—thus, a leader is a leader is a leader, no matter what culture, industry, or profession one is in.

Sources: R. J. House, P. J. Hanges, M. Javidan, P. W. Dorfman, and V. Gupta, *Culture, Leadership, and Organizations: The GLOBE Study of 62 Societies.* Thousand Oaks, CA: Sage Publications, 2004; J. S. Chhokar, F. C. Brodbeck, and R. J. House, *Culture and Leadership across the World: The Globe Book of In-Depth Studies of 25 Societies.* Mahwah, NJ: Lawrence Erlbaum Associates, 2007; M. Javidan, and N. Lynton, "The Changing Face of the Chinese Executive." *Harvard Business Review,* December 2005, pp. 28–29; R. J. House, M. Javidan, P. W. Dorfman, and M. Sully de Luque, "A Failure of Scholarship: Response to George Graen's Critique of GLOBE." *Academy of Management Perspectives* 20 (4) (2006), pp. 102–14; G. Graen, "In the Eye of the Beholder: Cross-Cultural Lessons in Leadership from Project GLOBE: A Response Viewed from the Third Culture Bonding (TCB) Model of Cross-Cultural Leadership." *Academy of Management Perspectives* 20 (4) (2006), pp. 95–101; http://www.grovewell.com/pub-GLOBE-leadership.html.

> *Being global is not just about where you do business.*
>
> **Robert J. House, leadership researcher**

model, the level of globalization, or the role of technology or teams in the business.[6,27,28,30,35,36] Examples of a competency model for the executives working at Waste Management, a $15 billion dollar company in the waste industry, can be found in Figure 8.3.

Many of the best organizations now have competency models for different levels of management. For example, the behaviors and skills needed by department supervisors, store managers, district managers, regional vice presidents, and division presidents at The Home Depot vary considerably, and these differences are reflected in the competency

FIGURE 8.3

Leadership competency model for executives at Waste Management.

PERSONAL CHARACTER

- Lives by company values and holds others to the same standard
- Maintains an optimistic outlook, working constructively under pressure
- Responds resourcefully to change, ambiguity, and setbacks
- Shares credit and visibility, maintains and projects confidence
- Follows through on commitments and inspires trust from others
- Has the courage to make tough decisions and have tough conversations, confronting the cold, hard facts

PEOPLE LEADERSHIP

- Builds and deploys teams that leverage individual and collective capabilities
- Sets clear expectations, accurately evaluates others, provides honest feedback and coaching
- Creates a culture of personal investment, excellence, and accountability
- Works effectively with employees at all levels, actively promotes and models collaboration
- Actively works to increase diversity and inclusion in the workplace and in successor pools

STAKEHOLDER FOCUS

- Develops and leverages a high performance workforce to create competitive advantage
- Understands customer issues and demonstrates a passion for exceeding customer needs
- Ensures that the organization has the trust of the community and general public
- Maintains a focus on short- and long-term protection and improvement of the environment
- Demonstrates a strong commitment to doing what is best for shareholders

PERSONAL LEADERSHIP

- Ensures extensive communication throughout the organization, encouraging open expression of ideas and opinions
- Listens actively, seeking to understand the perspectives and opinions of others
- Communicates own ideas clearly and powerfully, adjusting message to fit the needs of the audience
- Promotes ideas persuasively, shaping others' opinions, and working through conflicts to win/win solutions
- Demonstrates a high level of energy and passion, energizing others to achieve exceptional results
- Projects credibility and poise even in highly visible or adversarial situations, demonstrating professionalism and passion

EXECUTION AND RESULTS

- Applies broad knowledge and seasoned experience when reasoning through relevant information, addresses complex issues, and makes timely and sound decisions
- Knows what it takes to be successful in the organization, and has a thorough knowledge of the industry's history, customers, and competitive environment

continued

Continued

- Uses financial indicators and analysis to manage overall financial performance and evaluate business opportunities
- Links strategy, priorities, people, and assets to drive work efforts ahead and produce desired results
- Sizes up and resourcefully responds to changing market conditions, new business challenges, and new opportunities
- Sets and pursues aggressive individual and team goals with a sense of urgency, demonstrates a passion for beating the competition

STRATEGIC LEADERSHIP

- Works with a perspective that goes beyond the "day-to-day," balancing the big picture with the details
- Uses knowledge of extental trends and the organization's competitive position to identify strategic opportunities and directions
- Develops and implements distinctive strategies to achieve competitive advantage, aligning the organization to support strategic priorities
- Identifies new business opportunities and makes them a reality, championing innovation and risk taking
- Has the courage to make and champion changes that will improve the business, gaining others' support and buy-in

Source: D. Roberts and G. Curphy, "Developing a Leadership Framework for Waste Management." Workshop Conducted with Executives at Waste Management, Banff, Alberta, Canada, July 2006.

models for each management group. These models help to clarify expectations of performance for people in different leadership positions and describe the skills necessary for promotion. They also help human resource professionals to design selection, development, performance management, and succession planning programs so that organizations have a steady supply of leadership talent.[2,5,6,7,28,30,37–42]

According to Hogan and Warrenfelz, the skills and behaviors found in virtually every organizational competency model fall into one of four major categories. **Intrapersonal skills** are those leadership competencies and behaviors having to do with adapting to stress, goal orientation, and adhering to rules. It is important to note that these skills and behaviors do not involve interacting with others and they are among the most difficult to change. **Interpersonal skills** are those that involve direct interaction, such as communicating and building relationships with others. These skills are somewhat easier to develop. **Leadership skills** are those skills and behaviors concerned with building teams and getting results through others, and these are more easily developed than the skills and behaviors associated with the first two categories. Finally, those competencies concerned with analyzing issues, making decisions, financial savvy, and strategic thinking fall into the **business skills** category. These skills and competencies are often the focus of MBA programs and are among the easiest to learn of the four categories. The Hogan and Warrenfelz domain model of leadership competencies is important as it allows people to see connections between seemingly different organizational competency models and makes predictions about how easy or difficult it will be to change various leadership behaviors and skills.[41]

The Hogan and Warrenfelz model is also important as it points out what behaviors leaders need to exhibit in order to build teams and get results through others. Because organizational competency models are more alike than different, the behaviors needed to build teams and get results are fairly universal across organizations. Leaders wanting to build high performing teams need to effectively cope with stress, set high goals, and play by the rules. They also need to communicate and build relationships with others. Effective leaders also get followers involved in decisions, fairly distribute workloads, develop talent, keep abreast of events that could affect the team, and make sound financial and operational decisions. Thus, competency models provide a sort of recipe for leaders wanting to build teams and get results in different organizations. As described in Highlight 8.2 many of these leadership behaviors are universal across cultures and industries, but there may also be some important differences by company and leadership level. Ancona, Malone, Orlikowski, and Senge aptly point out that most leaders don't possess all of the skills listed in many competency models, but effective leaders are those who understand their strengths and have learned how to staff around those areas in which they are less skilled.[43]

Never doubt that a group of thoughtful, committed citizens can change the world. Indeed, it is the only thing that ever has.

Margaret Mead, anthropologist

Although organizational competency models have played a pervasive role in selecting, developing, and promoting government and business leaders, they have not played much of any role in another common form of leadership, which is community leadership. **Community leadership** is the process of building a team of volunteers to accomplish some important community outcome and represents an alternative conceptualization of leadership behavior.[44] Examples of community leadership might include forming a group to raise funds for a new library, gathering volunteers for a blood drive, or organizing a campaign to stop the construction of a Wal-Mart. Thus, community leadership takes place whenever a group of volunteers gets together to make something happen (or not happen) in their local community.

But leading a group of volunteers is very different than being a leader in a publicly traded company, the military, or a government agency. For one thing, community leaders do not have any position power; they cannot discipline followers who do not adhere to organizational norms, get tasks accomplished, or show up to meetings. They also tend to have fewer resources and rewards than most other leaders. And because there is no formal selection or promotion process, anyone can be a community leader. But whether they will be successful in their community change effort will depend on three highly interrelated competencies (see Figure 8.4). Just as you need the three ingredients of oxygen, fuel, and an igniter to

Critical Leadership Behaviors in Wartime

HIGHLIGHT 8.3

It is very likely that the behaviors needed to build teams and get results during peacetime and wartime operations may be different for officers in the U.S. military. A study sponsored by the Commanding General, U.S. Army Training and Doctrine Command, asked researchers to determine the critical behaviors leaders need to exhibit in order to build teams and get results while conducting Operation Iraqi Freedom (OIF). The researchers conducted extensive interviews with and administered surveys to 77 officers who had recently returned from OIF and asked them to identify the most important behaviors leaders need to exhibit when operating in a battlefield environment. Some of the most important behaviors leaders need to exhibit during wartime include:

- Adapts quickly to new situations and requirements.
- Keeps cool under pressure.
- Clearly explains missions, standards, and priorities.
- Sees the big picture; provides context and perspective.

- Sets high standards with a "zero defects" mentality.
- Can handle "bad news."
- Gets out of headquarters and visits the troops.
- Sets a high ethical tone; demands honest reporting.
- Knows how to delegate and not "micromanage."
- Can make tough, sound decisions on time.
- Builds and supports teamwork within staff and among units.
- Is positive, encouraging, and reasonably optimistic.

Having identified these critical leadership behaviors, the U.S. Army is now conducting training to develop these behaviors *before* sending leaders over to Iraq. It is also worth noting that many of these behaviors map on to those found in the GLOBE leadership study (see Highlight 8.2) as well as the Hogan and Warrenfelz domain model.

Source: W. J. Ulmer, Jr, M. D. Shaler, R. C. Bullis, D. F. DiClemente, and T. O. Jacobs, *Leadership Lessons at Division Command Level—2004.* Report prepared under the direction of the United States Army War College, November 2004.

FIGURE 8.4

The components of community leadership.

Source: J. Krile, G. Curphy, and D. Lund, *The Community Leadership Handbook: Framing Ideas, Building Relationships, and Mobilizing Resources.* St. Paul, MN: Fieldstone Alliance, 2006.

The Components of Community Leadership

start a fire, so will you need the three competencies of framing, building social capital, and mobilization to successfully drive community change efforts.

Framing is the leadership competency of helping a group or community recognize and define its opportunities and issues in ways that result in effective action. Framing helps the group or community decide *what* needs to be done, *why* it is important that it be done, and *how* it is to be done, and to communicate that in clear and compelling ways. Any community could take on a myriad of potential projects, but many of these projects never get off the ground because the person "in charge" never framed the project in such a way that others could understand: (*a*) the outcome; (*b*) how they would benefit by the outcome; or (*c*) what they would need to do to achieve the outcome.

Building social capital is the leadership competency of developing and maintaining relationships that allow people to work together in the community across their differences. Just as financial capital allows individuals to make choices about what they can purchase, such as buying a new television, car, or house, so too does social capital allow a community leader to make choices about which community change initiatives or projects are likely to be successful. If you have very little money, your options are severely limited. Likewise, leaders lacking social capital will have a very difficult time getting anything done in their communities, as they will not be able to mobilize the resources necessary to turn their vision into reality. Social capital is the power of relationships shared between individuals, an individual and a group, or between groups. Engaging a critical mass to take action to achieve a specific outcome or set of outcomes is the leadership competency of **mobilization.** Community leaders will have achieved a critical mass when they have enough human and other resources to get done what they want to get done. People, money, equipment, and facilities are often needed to pass bond issues or attract new businesses to a community. Mobilization is about strategic, planned purposeful activity to achieve clearly defined outcomes. Almost anyone can get resources moving, but it takes leadership to get enough of the right resources moving toward the same target.

So how would the community leadership model come into play if you wanted to have a new student union built on your campus? First, you would need to frame the issue in such a way that other students understood what was in it for them and what they would need to do to make a new student union become reality. Second, you would need to reach out and build relationships with all of the current and potential users of the new student union. You would need to identify the formal and informal leaders of the different user groups and meet with them in order to gain and maintain their trust. Third, you would need these different user groups to take action in order to get the new student union built. Some of these actions might include raising funds, making phone calls, canvassing students to sign

Does Humor Matter?

HIGHLIGHT 8.4

Leaders exhibit many kinds of behavior. Some are focused on task accomplishment, whereas others are more related to supporting followers. Some leaders are naturally funny, and others seem stern and humorless. Does a leader's sense of humor affect his or her ability to build teams, influence others, or get results? Researchers have examined this question and discovered the answer is not a simple yes or no. The effectiveness of humor seems to depend on the context, the outcomes leaders are trying to achieve, and the leadership style used. Laissez-faire leaders (1,1) who used humor reported having more satisfied followers, but did not have higher performing work groups. Task-focused leaders (9,1) who used humor actually had less satisfied and lower performing work units. Apparently their use of humor seemed out of sync with their constant focus on goal setting, productivity, and cost-cutting initiatives.

Transformational leaders (9,9) and those leaders with high levels of emotional intelligence who used humor seemed to have higher performing work groups. The key lesson from this research appears to be that the impact of a leader's humor will depend on the leader's style and the context in which it is delivered. Task-focused leaders should be keenly attuned to followers' needs when the company is facing an economic downturn or a difficult organizational dilemma, and also be aware that the use of humor in these situations will probably have just the opposite effect as intended.

Sources: B. J. Avolio, J. M. Howell, and J. J. Sosik, "A Funny Thing Happened on the Way to the Bottom Line: Humor as a Moderator of Leadership Style Effects." *Academy of Management Journal* 42, no. 2 (1999), pp. 219–27; F. Sala, "Laughing All the Way to the Bank," *Harvard Business Review,* September 2003, pp. 16–17; E. J. Romero and K. W. Cruthirds, "The Use of Humor in the Workplace." *Academy of Management Perspectives* 20(2) (2006), pp. 58–69.

petitions, mounting a publicity campaign, and meeting with university and state officials who are the key decision makers about the issue.

It is worth noting that you need to do all three of the community leadership components well if you are to build teams of volunteers and successfully accomplish community outcomes. You might be able to succinctly frame the issue, but if you lacked social capital or could not get a critical mass mobilized, then you would probably not get very far on building the new student union. The same would be true if you had a broad and well-established network of students but did not frame the issue in such a way that followers could take action. It is likely that as many community change efforts fail as succeed, and the reasons for failure often have to do with inadequate framing, social capital, or mobilization. These three components are critical when it comes to building teams of volunteers and achieving community goals.

Assessing Leadership Behaviors: Multirater Feedback Instruments

One way to improve leadership effectiveness is to provide leadership practitioners with feedback regarding the frequency and skill with which they perform various types of leadership behaviors. A $200-million industry has developed over the past two decades to meet this need. This is the

Denise Fleming

PROFILES IN LEADERSHIP 8.2

Denise Fleming is a former group practice and hospital administrator for the University of Michigan. She has 20 years of experience in strategic planning, health care administration, hospital and ambulatory care operations, and health care systems implementation and management. About 10 years ago Denise moved to North Oaks, MN, and decided to switch careers and become a stay-at-home mom. While at home Denise started looking for volunteer organizations where her skills and energy could make a positive contribution and soon took charge of the annual North Oaks Community Fair. Prior to Denise's involvement the community fair was a loosely run, poorly attended event. She canvassed the local citizenry about what they wanted the fair to achieve, organized a group of well-connected volunteers, and then put together an action plan for the fair. The Community Fair is now the most popular event in North Oaks and Denise has been able to use the funds from these events to upgrade the playground equipment at the community beach and two recreation centers.

One of Denise's most impressive community leadership activities was playing a key leadership role in getting the local community to pass a $10 million operating levy for the local school district. Denise has a background in accounting and possesses an MBA and was concerned that the local school district was wasting funds. She is not an advocate of tax increases, but she took the time to attend school board meetings and get educated on the intricacies of school funding and budgets. She

determined that the school board was not wasting money, but the governor's promise of "no new taxes" and a state legislature quick to pass unfunded mandates made it increasingly difficult for schools to meet required educational standards with an ever-decreasing pool of state funds. Denise and the operating levy leadership team started by identifying all the major stakeholders in the school district and then conducting a series of personal outreach activities for these constituencies. The operating levy leadership team also bought mailing lists, designed different marketing campaigns, conducted a series of mailing and literature drop-off campaigns, spoke at city council meetings, etc., in order to raise awareness and gain support for passing the operating levy. The operating team also framed the levy differently depending on the stakeholder group. For example, communities with poor schools often have declining property values, and this finding was marketed to retirees. The impact of large class sizes was marketed to families with preschool age children.

Two complications facing the operating levy leadership team were that 70 percent of the citizens in the school district did not have children attending one of the local schools and voter turnout was going to be very high. But due to the efforts of Denise and the operating levy leadership team, the levy passed by 41 votes (out of 34,000 cast). Where do the concepts of framing, social capital, and mobilization come into play with the community fair and operating levy examples? What kind of skills does Denise possess that help her to build teams and achieve results?

360-degree, or **multirater feedback,** instrument industry, and it is difficult to overestimate the importance it has had on management development both in the United States and overseas. Jack Welch, the former CEO of General Electric, has stated that these tools have been critical to GE's success.[45] Practically all of the Global 1000 companies are using some type of multirater feedback instrument for managers and key individual contributors.[2,6,7,8,46–52] Multi-rater feedback instruments have been translated into 16 different languages and well over five million managers have now received feedback on their leadership skills and behaviors from these instruments.[37] Because of the pervasiveness of multirater feedback in both the public and private sectors, it will be useful to examine some of the issues surrounding these instruments.

Three hundred and sixty degree feedback results show that there are plenty of leaders who are leadership legends in their own minds but are also charismatically challenged in the eyes of others.

**Gordy Curphy,
Curphy Consulting
Corporation**

Many managers and human resource professionals have erroneously assumed that a manager's self-appraisal was the most accurate source of information regarding leadership strengths and weaknesses. This view has changed, however, with the introduction of multirater feedback instruments. These tools show that direct reports, peers, and superiors can have very different perceptions about a target leader's behavior, and these perspectives can paint a more accurate picture of the strengths and development needs of the leader than self-appraisals alone (see Figures 8.5 and 8.6). A manager may think he or she gets along exceptionally well with others, but if 360-degree feedback ratings from peers and direct reports indicate that the manager is very difficult to work with, then the manager should gain new insights on what to do to improve his or her leadership effectiveness. Prior to the introduction of 360-degree instruments, it was difficult for managers to get accurate information about how others perceived their on-the-job behaviors since the feedback they received from others in face-to-face meetings tended to be adulterated or watered down.[2,5,6,34,46,48,49,52–57] Moreover, the higher one goes in an organization, the less likely one is to ask for feedback, which results in bigger discrepancies between self and other perceptions.[6,56,58] And, as described in Chapter 7, many of the most frequent behaviors exhibited by leaders are rooted in personality traits and occur almost automatically and as a result many leaders do not understand or appreciate their impact on others. It was difficult for managers to accurately determine their leadership strengths and development needs until the advent of 360-degree feedback instruments. Today, most organizations use 360-degree tools as an integral part of the training, coaching, succession planning, and/or performance management components of a comprehensive leadership talent management system.[6,34,41,42,48–50,53,59–61]

FIGURE 8.5
Sources for 360-degree feedback.

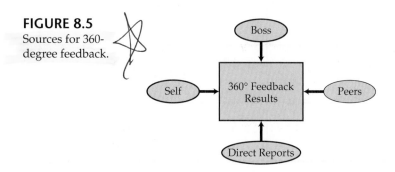

FIGURE 8.6   Example of 360-degree feedback.

Source: K. Louiselle, G. J. Curphy, and S. Bridges. *C3 360–Degree Feedback Report.* Eagan, MN: Advantis Research and Consulting, 2003. Reprinted with permission of Advantis Research and Consulting.

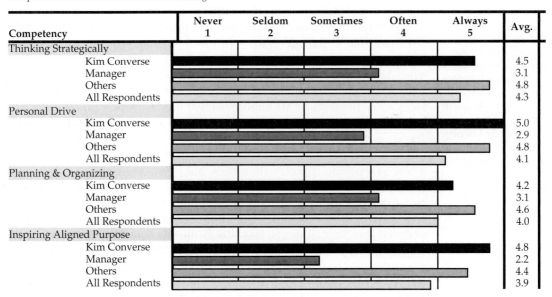

Competency	Never 1	Seldom 2	Sometimes 3	Often 4	Always 5	Avg.
Thinking Strategically						
Kim Converse						4.5
Manager						3.1
Others						4.8
All Respondents						4.3
Personal Drive						
Kim Converse						5.0
Manager						2.9
Others						4.8
All Respondents						4.1
Planning & Organizing						
Kim Converse						4.2
Manager						3.1
Others						4.6
All Respondents						4.0
Inspiring Aligned Purpose						
Kim Converse						4.8
Manager						2.2
Others						4.4
All Respondents						3.9

Inspiring Aligned Purpose

Successfully engages people in the mission, vision, values and direction of the organization; fosters a high level of motivation.

Average Ratings for Each Item and Respondent-Type

Items	Self	Manager	Others	All Respondents
1. Communicates a compelling vision of the future.	5.0	1.0	4.5	3.8
2. Provides a clear sense of purpose and direction for the team.	5.0	3.0	4.3	4.0
3. Sets challenging goals and expectations.	5.0	4.0	4.5	4.4
4. Fosters enthusiasm and buy-in for the direction of the team/organization.	5.0	1.0	4.8	4.0
5. Supports initiatives of upper management through words and actions.	4.0	2.0	4.0	3.2

Given the pervasive role 360-degree feedback plays in many organizations today, it is not surprising that there has been an extensive amount of research on the construction, use, and impact of these tools. Much of this research has explored how to use competency models to build effective 360-degree questionnaires, whether 360-degree feedback even matters, whether self-observer perceptual gaps matter, whether leaders' ratings can improve over time, and whether there are meaningful culture/gender/race issues with 360-degree feedback ratings. With respect to the first issue, researchers have reported that the construction of 360-degree feedback questionnaires is very important. Poorly conceived competency models and ill-designed questionnaire items can lead to spurious feedback results, thus depriving managers of the information they need to perform at a higher level.[6,34,49,50] In terms of whether 360-degree feedback matters, a number of researchers have held that leaders who received 360-degree feedback had higher performing work units than leaders who did not receive this type of feedback. These results indicate that 360-degree feedback ratings do matter.[6,59,62–68] But a study of 750 firms by Watson-Wyatt, a human resource consulting firm, reported that companies that used 360-degree feedback systems had a 10.6 percent decrease in shareholder value.[61] Although this research provides strong evidence that 360-degree feedback may not "work," it is important to note how these systems were being used in these firms. For the most part, Pfau and Kay examined firms using 360-degree feedback for performance appraisal, not development purposes. This distinction is important, as most 360-degree feedback systems are not designed to make comparisons *between* people. Instead, these systems are designed to tell leaders about their own relative strengths and development needs. But because 360-degree feedback tools are data based and provide, good development feedback, many organizations decided to modify the process for performance appraisal purposes. This can be a mistake, as many 360-degree feedback tools used in performance appraisals are poorly constructed and often result in such inflated ratings that the resulting feedback no longer differentiates between high, average, and low level performers. The end result is a costly, time-intensive performance appraisal system that has little if any benefit to the individual or the boss and yields organizational results similar to those reported by Watson-Wyatt. The bottom line is that 360-degree feedback systems can add tremendous value, but only if they are well-conceived and constructed.[5,6,7,48–50,56,59,69,70]

In many cases the only person who is surprised by his or her 360-degree feedback results is the feedback recipient.

**Gordy Curphy,
Curphy Consulting
Corporation**

As stated earlier, one of the advantages of 360-degree feedback is that it provides insight into self-perceptions and others' perceptions of leadership skills. But do self-observer gaps matter? Are leaders more effective if they have a high level of insight (i.e., rate their strengths and weaknesses as a leader the same as others do)? As depicted in Figure 8.6, some level of disagreement is to be expected, as bosses, peers, and direct reports may each have different expectations for a leader. Nevertheless, insight does not seem to matter as far as leadership effectiveness is concerned. Even leaders with large self-observer gaps were effective as long as they had high observer ratings. On the other hand, the least effective leaders were those with high self and low others' ratings. The important lesson here is that leadership is in the eyes of others. And the key to high observer ratings is to develop a broad set of leadership skills that will help groups to accomplish their goals.[52,54,62,63,66,71–75]

Yes

Another line of research has looked at whether 360-degree feedback ratings improve over time. In other words, is it possible to change others' perceptions of a leader's skills? One would hope that this would be the case, given the relationship between others' ratings and leadership effectiveness. Walker and Smither reported that managers who shared their 360-degree feedback results with their followers and worked on an action plan to improve their ratings had a dramatic improvement in others' ratings over a five-year period.[76] Johnson and Johnson looked at 360-degree ratings over a two-year period and reported leadership productivity improvements of 9.5 percent for 515 managers in a manufacturing company.[77] A more recent article reviewed the findings from 24 different studies and concluded that 360-degree feedback ratings do change over time, but the amount of change tends to be small.[51] Other researchers aptly point out that 360-degree feedback alone is not a panacea to improve leadership skills. In addition to gaining insight from 360-degree feedback, leaders must also create a set of development goals and commit to a development plan if they want to see improvement in others' ratings (and, in turn, leadership effectiveness) over time.[2,6,7,70,78,79]

The last line of research has explored whether there are important cultural, racial, or gender issues with 360-degree feedback. In terms of cultural issues, some countries, such as Japan, do not believe that peers or followers should provide leaders with feedback.[80,81] Other countries, such as Saudi Arabia, tend more to avoid conflict and provide only positive feedback to leaders. The latter phenomenon is not limited to other countries, but appears also in the United States where researchers working in small organizations or in rural communities often report similar findings. People seem more hesitant to provide leaders with constructive feedback if they have to deal with the consequences of this feedback both on and off work. These findings provide further support to the notion that 360-degree feedback is not a management panacea; societal or organizational culture plays a key role in the accuracy and utility of the 360-degree feedback process.[2,4,6,32,33,37,47]

Also race and gender play a role in accuracy and utility of the 360° feedback process.

With respect to racial differences, a comprehensive study by Mount, Sytsma, Hazucha, and Holt looked at the pattern of responses from bosses, peers, and subordinates for over 20,000 managers from a variety of U.S. companies. In general, these researchers reported that blacks tended to give higher ratings to other blacks, irrespective of whether they were asked to provide peer, subordinate, or boss ratings. However, the overall

Indra Nooyi

PROFILES IN LEADERSHIP 8.3

As described in Chapter 4, PepsiCo is commonly acknowledged as having one of the best leadership talent management systems in the world. Pepsi's talent management systems make extensive use of competency models, 360-degree feedback tools, personality and intelligence assessments, in-basket simulations, and unit performance indices. One of the people who have benefited from this in-depth assessment and development is Indra Nooyi. Nooyi is currently the chief executive officer of PepsiCo and is ranked by *Forbes* as the fourth most powerful woman in the world and the most powerful businesswoman in the world. Nooyi grew up in India and received an undergraduate degree from Madras Christian College and a postgraduate Diploma in Management from the Indian Institute in Management. She also has a degree from the Yale School of Management. While in college Nooyi fronted an all-female rock band and is refreshingly funny and candid when speaking in public. In May 2005 Nooyi started a controversy when she spoke to graduates of Columbia Business School and said the United States "must be careful that when we extend our arm in either business or political sense, we take pains to assure we are giving a hand . . . not the finger."

Before emigrating to the United States in 1978, Nooyi was a product manager for Johnson and Johnson and the textile firm Mettur Beardsell in India. Her first job after graduating from Yale was to work as a consultant with The Boston Consulting Group. She then took senior leadership positions at

Motorola and Asea Brown Boveri before moving to PepsiCo in 1994. While at Pepsi Nooyi played a vital role in the spin-off of Tricon, which is now known as Yum! Brands Inc. (Taco Bell and Kentucky Fried Chicken are some of the franchises in Yum! Brands Inc.). She also took the lead in Pepsi's acquisition of Tropicana and Quaker Oats in the late 1990s. In 2001 Nooyi was promoted to chief financial officer and to the CEO position in 2006. As the head of PepsiCo, Nooyi heads up a company of 157,000 employees that generate $35 billion dollars in annual revenues through the worldwide sales of products such as Pepsi, Mountain Dew, Tropicana, Gatorade, Aquafina, Dole, Lipton, Doritos, Ruffles, Lays, Quaker Oats, Life cereal, and Rice-A-Roni. Under Nooyi, Pepsi has developed new products and marketing programs through the liberal use of cross-cultural advisory teams.

Given Pepsi's global reach and emphasis on brand management, Nooyi's background seems well-suited for her latest leadership challenge. In 2006 a group of individuals in India claimed that both Coke and Pepsi products were tainted with pesticides. Later investigations disproved these allegations, but the surrounding publicity damaged Pepsi's brand in a large, developing market. Nooyi is now working hard to restore the Indian public's confidence regarding the safety of PepsiCo's products.

Sources: http://www.forbes.com/lists/2006/11/06/women_ Indra-Nooyi; http://www.Pepsico.com/PEP; http://en.wikipedia.org/wiki/Indra_Nooyi; http://www.businessweek.com/investor/content/aug2006/pi20060814; http://www.hoovers.com/pepsico.

size of this effect was rather small. White peers and subordinates generally gave about the same level of ratings for both black and white peers and bosses. This was not the case for white bosses, however, who tended to give significantly higher ratings to whites who reported directly to them. These findings imply that black leaders are likely to advance at a slower pace than their white counterparts, as 80–90 percent of salary, bonus, and promotion decisions are made solely by bosses.[82,83] Later this chapter will describe how these racial differences play out in mentoring programs.

With respect to gender issues, research indicates that there are some gender differences, though these differences tend to be slight. Female managers tend to get higher ratings on the majority of skills, yet their male counterparts are generally perceived as having higher advancement potential. There does not appear to be any same-sex bias in 360-degree feedback ratings, and female managers tend to be lower self-raters. Male managers tend to have less accurate self-insight and a higher number of blind spots when compared to their female counterparts. In summary, male and female 360-degree feedback ratings are very similar and any differences are of little practical significance.[84]

So what should a leadership practitioner take away from all of this 360-degree feedback research? First, given the popularity of the technique, it is likely that you will receive 360-degree feedback sometime in your career. Second, 360-degree feedback should be built around an organization's competency model, which in turn describes the leadership behaviors needed to achieve organizational goals.[5–7,8,35,50] Third, 360-degree feedback may be one of the best sources of "how" feedback for leadership practitioners. Leaders tend to get plenty of "what" feedback—what progress they are making toward group goals, what level of customer service is being achieved, win–loss records, and so on, but they get very little feedback on "how" they should act to get better results. Multirater instruments provide feedback on the kinds of things leaders need to do in order to build cohesive, goal-oriented teams and get better results through others. Fourth, effective leaders seem to have a broad set of well-developed leadership skills—they do not just do one or two things very well and do everything else poorly. Instead, they seem to possess a broad pallet of leadership strengths. Fifth, leaders need to create specific goals and development plans in order to improve leadership skills—360-degree feedback results give leaders ideas on what to improve but may not be enough in and of themselves to affect behavioral change. Sixth, leadership behavior can change over time, but it may take a year or two to acquire new skills and for the changes to be reflected in 360-degree feedback ratings. Finally, there are some cultural, racial, and gender issues associated with 360-degree feedback, and practitioners should be aware of these issues before implementing any 360-degree feedback process.

Managerial Derailment

So far we have talked about what leaders can do in order to improve their ability to build teams and get results through others. The first lesson might be to determine which behaviors are most closely aligned with success, perhaps by identifying key behaviors by means of a competency model. Another lesson might be to get 360-degree feedback on these key behaviors. This feedback helps identify strengths and potential development needs. Not all leaders, however, truly learn such lessons. It might behoove us to look not just at how leaders succeed, but at the complementary question: why do some leaders *fail*? We can learn valuable lessons about what *not* to do as a leader by studying people who have failed to build teams or get results through others.

As described in Chapters 4 and 7, there is a growing body of research that indicates that a majority of people in positions of authority have difficulties building teams or getting results.[2,5–7,9,34,85–87] A concept closely related to managerial incompetence is managerial derailment. Initial research on **managerial derailment**—whereby individuals who at one time were on the fast track but now had their careers derailed—was conducted in the early 1980s by researchers at the Center for Creative Leadership. The researchers went to the human resource departments in a number of Fortune 100 companies seeking lists of their "**high-potential**" **managers.** McCall and Lombardo defined high potentials as those individuals who had been identified as eventually becoming either the CEO/president or one of his or her direct reports sometime in the future. They waited for three years and then returned to these organizations to ask what had happened to the people on the lists. They discovered that roughly a quarter of the high potentials had been promoted to one of the top two levels in the organization and an equal percentage had not yet been promoted but would be as soon as a position became available. Another 25 percent had left the company; some had quit to form their own company and others were given a better offer somewhere else. Finally, about a quarter of the people on the list were no longer being considered for promotion. If they were still with the company, then they had been moved to a less influential and visible position. This last group of individuals represented cases of managerial derailment.[88]

Several other researchers have investigated the managerial derailment phenomenon.[87,89–93] This additional research used much larger samples (one researcher examined over 600 derailed managers), European samples, and more sophisticated assessment tools (i.e., 360-degree feedback instruments). Moreover, a substantially higher percentage of women and minorities were represented in this later research, as the initial high-potential list was dominated by white males. As Van Veslor and Leslie point out, this research focused on identifying those factors which helped derailment candidates initially get identified as high potentials as well as on those factors contributing to their ultimate professional demise.[93] Although these studies varied in many ways, there are many consistent findings across them. Both successful and derailed candidates were smart, ambitious, and willing to do whatever it took to get the job done, and had considerable technical expertise. In other words, all of the high-potential candidates had impressive track records in their organizations.

On the other hand, the derailed candidates exhibited one or more behavioral patterns not evident in the high potentials who succeeded. The

TABLE 8.2
Themes in Derailment Research

Four Enduring Themes	McCall & Lombardo (1983)	Morrison et al. (1987)	Lombardo & McCauley (1988)	United States (1993–94)	Europe (1993–94)
Problems with interpersonal relationships	Insensitive to others; cold, aloof, arrogant; overly ambitious	Poor relationships, too ambitious	Problems with interpersonal relationships, isolates self	Poor working relations	Poor working relations, organizational isolation, authoritarian, too ambitious
Failure to meet business objectives	Betrayal of trust; poor performance	Performance problems	Lack of follow-through	Too ambitious, lack of hard work	Too ambitious, poor performance
Inability to build and lead a team	Failing to staff effectively	Can't manage subordinates	Difficulty molding a staff	Inability to build and lead a team	Inability to build and lead a team
Inability to develop or adapt	Unable to adapt to a boss with a different style, unable to think strategically	Unable to adapt to a boss or culture, not strategic	Strategic differences with management, difficulty making strategic transitions	Unable to develop or adapt to conflict with upper management	Unable to develop or adapt
Emergent themes	—	Too narrow business experience	—	Not prepared for promotion, narrow functional orientation	Not prepared for promotion, narrow functional orientation
Disappearing themes	Overdependent on advocate or mentor	—	Over-dependence	—	—

Source: E. Van Velsor and J. B. Leslie, "Why Executives Derail: Perspectives across Time and Cultures." *Academy of Management Executive* 9, no. 4 (1995), pp. 62–71.

derailment themes can be found in Table 8.2 and are described in more detail below. It is important to note that four of the derailment themes included in Table 8.2 have been consistently reported in the research both in the United States and Europe, and that apparently a new theme is emerging and another is disappearing over time. The first derailment pattern has to do with an **inability to build relationships** with co-workers. The derailed managers exhibiting this pattern of behavior were very insensitive to the needs and plights of their followers and co-workers, and were often overly competitive, demanding, and domineering. They embraced the "my way or the highway" school of management and many would be categorized as Results Only Managers as described in Chapter 4. Many were also extremely arrogant and truly believed no one in their organizations was as good as they were, and they let their co-workers know it every chance they could. Some of these derailed managers also did whatever they felt necessary to get the job done, even if it meant stepping on a few toes in the process. Unfortunately, this is not one of the recommended techniques for winning friends and influencing people. It's better to remember the old adage that you should be careful whom you step on going up the ladder, because you may meet them again on your way down. Many of these managers left a trail of bruised people who were just waiting for the right opportunity to bring these leaders down. Highlight 8.5 illustrates the case of a sales manager with this derailment potential.

The devil that you know is better than the one you do not know.
Old folk saying

According to Van Velsor and Leslie, approximately two-thirds of European and one-third of American derailment candidates fall into this pattern.[93] For example, a female vice president of marketing and sales for a cellular phone company was fired from her $200,000 a year job for exhibiting many of the behaviors just listed. She was very bright, had an excellent technical background (an engineer by training), had already been the CEO for several smaller organizations, and worked very long hours. Her in-depth managerial assessment results (Chapters 4 and 7) indicated that she also had a strong leaderlike personality, with higher scores in surgency and dependability and average scores in agreeableness and adjustment. This assessment also indicated she had extremely high bold scores, and at work this dark-side trait would manifest itself by her talking down to people, quickly identifying and capitalizing on others' faults, constantly commenting on their incompetence, running over her peers when she needed resources or support, promoting infighting among her peers and subordinates, and expecting to be pampered. Interestingly, she had no idea she was having such a debilitating effect on those she worked with until she received her 360-degree feedback. Had she received this feedback sooner, she might have been able to stop her career from derailing.

Charan and Colvin, Dotlich and Cairo, Hogan, and Curphy have all stated that people problems are one of the primary reasons why CEOs fail. However, unlike derailed mid-level managers, most CEOs get along with others in the company. The problem with CEOs is that they get along with some of their direct reports too well and do not take timely action to address problem performers. More specifically, some CEOs fail because they place loyal subordinates into jobs they are incapable of handling, falsely believe they can help poorly performing subordinates to change ineffective behavior, do not want to offend Wall Street or the board by letting popular (but ineffective) executives go, or do not feel comfortable hiring outsiders to fill key executive positions.[6,9,34,85,87]

An Example of a Derailed Leader

HIGHLIGHT 8.5

The following is a story about a sales manager who seems to have derailment potential. See if you can pick out which derailment factors may be at play in this story. In addition, what advice would you give to the writer to "fix" the problem?

I've been working in a medium-sized manufacturing company for the past 20 years. I'm not in sales, but interact with salespeople on a daily basis. Over the past year or so, I have noticed the sales force has been frustrated. After numerous conversations not only with the sales force, but also with other people in all aspects of the company, I have realized that the poison is coming from one person: Mike, the sales manager. Mike has been with the company for over 10 years and has successfully maneuvered his way to the position of sales manager. All of his promotions were given to him because of his own self-promotion. He has an enormous ego. His tactics of bulldog management, double standards, and outright lying are driving his sales force out and are frustrating people all over the company. He is

disliked, even hated, by almost everyone in the company. Amazingly, Mike doesn't realize what people think of him. I believe the owners tolerate Mike's behavior because he has produced decent sales over the years. This year sales are substantially down. I believe the company is going to start to lose good salespeople because of Mike. Here's why: Nobody will confront him because if they do, he threatens them or makes them do some ridiculous assignment. All conversations with Mike are one-sided. If you bring up a concern that involves him, he will change the subject and dismiss you. It's like he is afraid of the truth. He is dishonest and essentially a loose cannon. I believe the owners know the truth about Mike but they continue to let him act this way. I believe Mike will never leave because he knows he could never get away with the things he does here anywhere else. My concern is that if the owners don't fix the "Mike problem" they will start to lose good salespeople. Any advice?

Source: J. Lloyd, "Good Firms Work to Find Out Truth about Bad Managers." *Milwaukee Journal Sentinel,* August 20, 2000, p. 20.

Another derailment pattern identified in Table 8.2 is a **failure to meet business objectives.** Although both successful and derailed managers experience business downturns, the groups handled setbacks quite differently. Successful managers took personal responsibility for their mistakes and sought ways to solve the problem. Derailed managers tended to engage in finger-pointing and blaming others for the downturn. *But as long as things were going well,* it was difficult to differentiate these two groups on this factor. Some of these managers were also untrustworthy. They blatantly lied about business results, cooked the books, or failed to keep promises, commitments, or deadlines. The most common reason for CEO failure is the inability to meet earnings projections. However, this inability to meet financial projections is not the result of a poor business strategy, unwanted products and services, or inadequate distribution channels. Most CEOs have well-above-average analytic and practical intelligence, so they usually do not have a problem developing a vision or strategy for the company, nor do they make poor decisions concerning which markets to pursue and products to develop. In many cases, CEOs fail to get results because of their inability to execute according to the business strategy. They tend to get distracted and lose focus or do not hold their direct reports accountable for getting the results outlined in their business plans.[9,87,94]

The third derailment pattern identified by Van Velsor and Leslie was an **inability to build and lead a team.**[93] Some managers derailed because they hired staff who were just like themselves, which in turn only served to magnify their own strengths and weaknesses. Others wanted to stay in the limelight and hired staff less capable than they were. Still others micro-managed their staffs, even when not expert themselves in the tasks (not that it's ever recommended). These bosses wanted their followers to "check their brains at the door" before coming to work. One factor that often underlies this derailment pattern is the presence of dark-side traits described in Chapter 7. But another key reason why leaders cannot build teams is when they spend too much time doing activities that should be done by direct reports. Mid- or senior-level leaders who spend too much time doing individual contributor or first-line supervisor tasks risk disempowering all the managers who work for them. Because these leaders are making all the decisions that their followers would normally make, followers become disengaged with work and team performance suffers as a result.[6,7,95]

Another derailment profile has to do with a leader's **inability to adapt to new bosses, businesses, cultures, or structures.** As pointed out earlier in this chapter, many business situations require different leadership behaviors and skills, and some derailed managers could not adapt or adjust their styles to changing bosses, followers, and situations. They persisted in acting the same way, even when it was no longer appropriate to new circumstances. When solving problems, they often imposed past solutions that were no longer viable (i.e., high cautious scores from Chapter 7). For example, a first-line supervisor for an electronics firm that built video poker machines was having a very difficult time transitioning from his old job as a missile guidance repairman in the U.S. Air Force. He thought he should lead his subordinates the way he led others in the military: His staff should be willing to work long hours and over the weekends without being told and to travel for extended periods of time with short notice. Their thoughts or opinions on ways to improve work processes did not matter to him and he expected everyone to maintain cool and professional attitudes at work. After half of his staff quit as a direct result of his supervision, he was demoted and replaced by one of his subordinates.

In the past, organizations could afford to take their time in identifying and developing leadership talent. And as described in Chapter 4 many of the best organizations today have strong programs for systematically developing leadership bench strength. However, more and more organizations today are under increasing pressure to find good leaders quickly and they are increasingly asking their own high-potential but inexperienced leadership talent to step up to the plate and fill these key roles. Although these new leaders are bright and motivated, they often have narrow technical backgrounds and lack the leadership breadth and depth necessary for the new positions. The unfortunate result is that many of these leaders leave the organization because of **inadequate preparation for promotion.**

For example, a relatively young woman attorney was promoted to be the vice president of human resources in a large telecommunications firm. Although she was extremely bright and ambitious, it soon became apparent that she lacked much of the necessary skill or knowledge. Although she tried very hard to be successful, she kept acting as a front-line leader instead of a functional leader and failed to earn the respect of her staff. After six months she was given a generous separation package and asked to leave the company. According to Van Velsor and Leslie, this is a relatively new derailment theme. Given the contributing factors, it is also a theme that is likely to be more prevalent in the future.[93]

It is worth noting that most derailed managers manifested several of these themes; the presence of only one of these behavioral patterns was usually not enough for derailment. The only exception to this rule was a failure to meet business objectives. Managers who did not follow through with commitments, broke promises, lied, were unethical, and did not get results did not stay on the high-potential list for long (i.e., high mischievous and bold scores from Chapter 7). Although this research has not identified any unique derailment patterns for minorities, some male–female differences have been noted. Females were more likely to derail because of their inability to deal with broader and more complex organizational issues or to lead people from different technical backgrounds than their own (practical intelligence). Males were more likely to derail because of their arrogance, inflexibility, or abrasive interpersonal style (bold, cautious, or excitable dark-side traits).

One might think that most managers exhibiting derailment behavioral patterns would be aware of the negative impact they have on others. Unfortunately, research shows that in many cases incompetence is bliss, at least for the person demonstrating incompetence. Researchers Dunning and Kruger conducted a series of experiments which asked people to rate the funniness of 65 jokes. They then asked eight professional comedians to do the same and compared the differences between the expert and test subjects' ratings. They found that some participants could not predict what others would find funny, yet they described themselves as excellent judges of humor. Similarly, Nilsen and Campbell reported that managers who consistently overrated their performance on 360-degree feedback instruments tended to overrate their performance on everything they did. Not only did these individuals believe they were good leaders, they also believed they were excellent drivers, mothers and fathers, athletes, dancers, lovers, judges of character, etc., and tended to

The first and paramount responsibility of anyone who purports to manage is to manage the self: one's own integrity, character, ethics, knowledge, wisdom, temperament, words, and acts. It is a complex, unending, incredibly difficult, oft-shunned task. We spend little time and rarely excel at self-management precisely because it is so much more difficult than prescribing and controlling the behavior of others. However, without management of self, people are not fit for authority no matter how much they acquire, for the more authority they acquire, the more dangerous they become. It is management of the self that should occupy 50 percent of our time and the best of our ability. And when we do that, the ethical, moral, and spiritual elements of management are inescapable.

Dee Hock, CEO, Visa

overlook evidence that pointed to the contrary. Given these findings, it is absolutely imperative that people in positions of authority get regular feedback on performance. Ideally this performance information should be in the form of 360-degree feedback, as leadership is more in the eyes of others than of self-perceptions.[96,97]

Managerial Derailment, Managerial Incompetence, and Bad Leadership

HIGHLIGHT 8.6

It might not seem obvious, but there is a big difference between managerial derailment and bad leadership. As described in this chapter, managerial derailment occurs when smart, ambitious, and upwardly mobile people manifest one or more sets of career-limiting behaviors. These dysfunctional tendencies interfere with their ability to build teams, influence others, and/or get results and eventually negatively impact their career prospects. But what happens when leaders with strong team building skills use them to achieve evil or selfish ends? For example, Adolph Hitler was arguably the most impactful leader of the 20th century. He certainly demonstrated an ability to build teams and achieve results, but these results were morally abhorrent. The same could be said about Kim Jong-Il, Fidel Castro, the dictators running most of the countries in Africa and the Middle East, and many of the former Communist leaders of the U.S.S.R. (Joseph Stalin is estimated to have killed 50 million citizens alone through his purges and economic mismanagement). These leaders created enough loyal followers to take over and manage entire countries and those followers who got to share the wealth believed these bad leaders were achieving good results. And as the Enron, WorldCom, and more recent stock option backdating scandals point out, there appear to be a number of business and public sector leaders who are doing exactly the same thing.

Barbara Kellerman accurately points out that the United States has an overly optimistic outlook on leadership. Most of the leadership books written for U.S. consumption have an overly positive tone and generally maintain that leadership is relatively easy to learn. Similarly, many leadership training programs delivered in the United States are built on the erroneous assumption that leaders are inherently good and effective; bad or incompetent leadership is the exception rather than the rule. Yet Jared Diamond's book, *Guns, Germs, and Steel: The Fates of Human Societies,* shows that most societies from the earliest times to those of today are kleptocracies. Some are more legitimized kleptocracies, where kings, queens, and elected officials dictate laws or write rules in order to increase their power or personal wealth. Dictators that emerge after violent overthrows of previous governments seem to benefit greatly from their change in status but rarely if ever improve the lot of commoners (see Profile in Leadership 8.4). Thus **bad leadership** occurs when Competent Managers use their team-building skills in order to achieve results for greedy and selfish results. And as history mournfully suggests, evil, corrupt, greedy, and selfish leadership will likely be around for a long time.

Sources: B. Kellerman, *Bad Leadership: What It Is, How It Happens, Why It Matters (Leadership for the Common Good).* Boston, MA: Harvard Business School Press, 2004; W. Bennis, "The Challenges of Leadership in the Modern World: Introduction to the Special Issue." *American Psychologist* 62 (1) (2007), pp. 2–5; J. Diamond, *Guns, Germs, and Steel: The Fates of Human Societies.* New York: W. W. Horton & Company, 1999; R. T. Hogan, *Personality and the Fate of Organizations.* Mahwah, NJ: Lawrence Erlbaum Associates, 2007.

Robert Mugabe

PROFILES IN LEADERSHIP 8.4

Robert Mugabe was elected president of Zimbabwe at the end of 1987 and has remained in this role for the past 20 years. Mugabe's administration has moved Zimbabwe from impressive success to one of the biggest collapses in the last 100 years. He has attracted international criticism for corruption, economic and land reform mismanagement, deteriorating human rights, antigay crusades, and stifling of all political opposition to his rule. He is widely blamed for driving Zimbabwe's annual inflation rate to such a state that the money needed to buy a brick house with a tennis court and pool in 1990 could not buy a single brick today. Widely despised by his own citizens and the international community, Mugabe is also seen by many as charismatic,

well-educated, and clever. A near vegetarian and a nondrinking workaholic, Mugabe starts each day with a heavy regimen of yoga and exercise before putting in 14 hours of work. Educated as a teacher and currently possessing seven academic degrees, Mugabe also has a self-proclaimed "degree in violence." Rival leaders, members of the opposition, and journalists are either beaten regularly or killed. Many predicted his demise 10 years ago, yet Mugabe's iron rule and ability to constantly reinvent himself makes his position as president seem as safe as ever.

Sources: *The Economist,* "Robert Mugabe. The Man Behind the Fist," March 31, 2007, pp. 27–23. C. Shepherd, "News of the Weird." *Minneapolis Star Tribune,* March 15, 2007, p. E3. http://en/wikipedia.org/wiki/Robert_Mugabe.

Changing Behavior

Why Change Behavior?

Organizations don't change; people change. If you want your organization to do something differently, then you'll have to figure out how to get people to change their behavior.

David B. Peterson, Personnel Decisions International

The material covered so far can help leadership practitioners better understand the key behaviors associated with building cohesive teams and achieving results; how successful leadership behaviors may vary depending on the leadership level, country, culture, or business; what kind of behaviors could get them into trouble; and how to get feedback on these behaviors. But often knowing this information is not enough—sooner or later a person's behavior will need to *change* if they are going to effectively build teams or get results through others. But changing behavior, especially long-standing patterns of behavior, can be quite difficult.

How many times have you asked yourself how you could possibly change your own or another's behavior? <u>Learning how to change your own and others' behaviors is a key leadership skill,</u> given that situations, technology, organizational structure, followers, bosses, products, rules and regulations, and competitors seem to be in a constant state of flux. Moreover, think about the new behaviors and skills you will need to acquire as you move from one organization to another or from individual contributor, front-line supervisor, or mid-level manager to executive roles. Not only will you need to learn how to adapt your behavior to meet the changing demands of the role or situation, you also need to know how to change and modify the behaviors of followers so that they can be more effective team members and better achieve goals. In the next section we discuss research surrounding three common methods of behavioral change: development planning, coaching, and mentoring.

Development Planning

How many times have you made a resolution to change a habit, only to discover two months later that you are still exhibiting the same behaviors? This is often the fate of well-intentioned New Year's resolutions. Most people do not even make such resolutions since the failure rate is so high. Given this track record, you might wonder if it is even possible to change one's behavior, particularly if it has been reinforced over time and is exhibited almost automatically. Fortunately, however, it is possible to change behavior, even long-standing habits. For example, many people permanently quit smoking or drinking without going through any type of formal program. Others may change after they gain insight into how their behavior affects others. Some will need support to maintain a behavioral change over time, while still others seem destined to never change.[10,98–100]

Managers seem to fall into the same categories; some managers change once they gain insight, others change with support, and others may not ever change. But do people just fall into one of these groups by accident? Is there any way to stack the odds in favor of driving behavioral change? Research provides several suggestions that leaders can take to accelerate the development of their own leadership skills and we can use the Development Pipeline described in Chapter 3 as a way to categorize these suggestions.[3,6–8,100–106] The five components in Figure 8.7 lend themselves to five critical behavioral change questions and leaders must provide positive answers to all five questions if they want to maximize the odds of permanent behavior change taking place.

Question 1: Do leaders know what behaviors need to change? Leaders are capable of exhibiting hundreds of different behaviors, but do they precisely

FIGURE 8.7   The PDI Development Pipeline®.

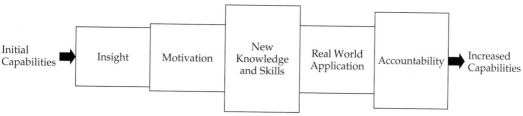

Can People Really Change?

HIGHLIGHT 8.7

When all is said and done, the terms *leadership* and *change* are almost synonymous. Effective leaders are those who are constantly changing their own and followers' behaviors in order to better adapt to the situations they face. Leaders and followers often have to exhibit new behaviors with the launch of new products and services, the introduction of new IT or financial systems, the acquisition or divestiture of companies, or the downsizing of staff. Although there is constant pressure to change, it is important to understand that most people naturally resist change. Some of this resistance stems from difficulty in dealing with ambiguity, some of it comes from a fear of no longer knowing the rules and what it will take to succeed, and some of it is out of competing agendas and a strong fear of failure. Successful leaders are those who can consistently overcome the resistance to change and get people to exhibit the new behaviors needed to achieve team goals.

But how much can people really change? According to Buckingham & Coffman's book, *First, Break All the Rules,* people change very little. These authors believe people are more or less "hard wired" as a result of their values, intelligence, and personality, so leaders would be better off trying to find jobs that leverage followers' natural strengths rather than trying to change their behaviors. Although this book has proved wildly popular over the past five years, some of the advice contained therein is simply wrong. First, there is in fact ample evidence to show that people can and do change. They may not change

that much, but even subtle changes can have large payoffs for people in leadership positions. Second, many leaders simply do not have the luxury of changing jobs to fit their followers' strengths. For example, a typical route manager at Waste Management may supervise 25 drivers of garbage trucks. It would be nice to find 25 different jobs that leveraged each of the drivers' strengths, but at the end of the day the garbage still needs to get picked up. Third, and perhaps most importantly, what may at one time be seen as strengths can easily turn into fatal flaws. Someone who was very planful and detail-oriented as an individual contributor could also be a micro-manager as a mid-level manager. Leaders need to understand where and when to leverage their strengths and when these same behaviors can get them into trouble. On the positive side, Buckingham and Coffman are correct in pointing out that hiring the right people and putting them in the right jobs can go a long way toward achieving team goals.

Sources: M. Buckingham and C. Coffman, *First, Break All The Rules.* New York: Simon & Schuster, 1999; R. Kegan and L. Laskow Lahey, "The Real Reason People Won't Change." *Harvard Business Review,* November 2001, pp. 84–93; P. LaBarre, "Marcus Buckingham Thinks Your Boss Has an Attitude Problem." *Fast Company,* August 2001, pp. 88–98; M. Buckingham, "What Great Leaders Do." *Harvard Business Review,* March 2005, pp. 70–79; L. Morgan Roberts, G. Spreitzer, J. Dutton, R. Quinn, E. Heaphy, and B. Barker. "How to Play to Your Strengths." *Harvard Business Review,* January 2005, pp. 74–81; J. H. Zenger, K. W. Sandholtz, and J. R. Folkman, *Leadership Under the Microscope.* Orem, UT: Extraordinary Performance Group, 2004.

know which behaviors they need to start, stop, or keep doing in order to build effective teams or achieve better results? Thus, the insight component of the Development Pipeline is concerned with providing leaders with accurate feedback on their strengths and development needs and 360-degree feedback can provide very useful information in this regard. Other sources of information about development needs can come from the results of an assessment center, a performance appraisal, or direct feedback from others.

Question 2: Is the leader motivated to change these behaviors? The next step in developing one's own leadership skills is working on development goals that matter. No leader has all of the knowledge and skills necessary to be successful; as a result most leaders have multiple development needs. Leaders need to determine which new skills will have the highest personal and organizational payoffs and build development plans that address these needs. The development plan should be focused on only one or two needs; plans addressing more than this tend to be overwhelming and unachievable. If leaders have more than two development needs, then they should first work to acquire one or two skills before moving on to the next set of development needs.

Question 3: Do leaders have plans in place for changing targeted behaviors? Figure 8.7 indicates that acquiring new knowledge and skills is the next step in the Development Pipeline. For leaders, this means creating a written **development plan** that capitalizes on available books, seminars, college courses, e-learning modules, and so forth, to acquire the knowledge underlying a particular development need (see Figure 8.8). For example, you can either learn how to delegate through the school of hard knocks or take a seminar to learn the best practices of delegation skills. As we will see, knowledge alone is not enough to develop a new skill, but relevant books and courses can accelerate the learning process.[6,8,37,70,106,107] In addition, it is important not to underestimate the power of having a written development plan. Leaders (and followers) who have a written plan seem more likely to keep development on their radar screens and take the actions necessary to acquire new skills.

Question 4: Do leaders have opportunities to practice new skills? Taking courses and reading books are good ways for leaders to acquire foundational knowledge, but new skills will only be acquired when they are practiced on the job. Just as surgeons can read about and watch a surgery but will only perfect a surgical technique through repeated practice, so too will leaders only acquire needed skills if they practice them on the job. Therefore, good development plans capitalize upon on- the-job experiences to hone needed leadership skills. Peterson maintains that most leadership positions offer ample opportunities to develop new skills, provided that leaders leverage all of the experiences available to them. These on-the-job activities are so important to development that 70 to 80 percent of the action steps in a development plan should be job related.[100,103,105]

Question 5: Are leaders held accountable for changing targeted behaviors? The last step in acquiring new skills is accountability and there are several ways to make this happen with a development plan. One way to build in accountability is to have different people provide ongoing feedback on the action steps taken to develop a skill. For example, leaders could ask for feedback from a peer or direct report on their listening skills immediately after staff meetings. Another way to build accountability is to periodically

The more you crash, the more you learn.
David B. Peterson, Personnel Decisions International

The only thing more painful than learning from experience is not learning from experience.
Archibald MacLeish, Librarian of Congress

FIGURE 8.8 Sample individual development plan.

Source: G. J. Curphy, *Personal Insights and Development Planning Training Manual.* North Oaks, MN: Curphy Consulting Corporation, 2007.

Individual Development Plan (IDP)

Name: Mark McMurray   Supervisor: Steve Tolley   Planning Period: Apr–Dec 2008

Development Goals	Action Plans – Developmental Activities & Resources (What, Who & How)	Time Line (Target Dates)	Criteria for Success (What will successful outcomes be?)
• Control reactions in stressful situations.	1. Set up a regular exercise routine (at least 5 times per week).	NLT 30 April 2008	Boss does not receive any reports of emotional outbursts from now until Dec 2008.
	2. Exercise at least 5 times per week for at least 45 minutes.	Review each week until end of year	
	3. Identify triggers and situations most likely to cause me to lose my temper.	NLT 30 April 2008	Higher manager ratings on end of year employee survey.
	4. Work with Steve Tolley to develop strategies to either avoid or cope with stressful situations.	Begin 30 April 2008	
• Develop more patience when dealing with others.	1. Identify those people or situations that cause me to lose patience.	NLT 15 May 2008	Be viewed as approachable and responsive by all staff – Manager, Peers, and Associates.
	2. Develop listening skills through consistent practice. Work with peers and direct reports to practice and demonstrate skills.	Begin 15 May 2008	Have a better understanding of key issues, role responsibilities, and resulting actions. As a result, achieve better results on the job.
	a) Wait my turn in conversation: work on not interrupting conversations.		
	b) Take notes in meetings to capture key messages and refer back to notes later.	Begin 15 May 2008	Higher manager ratings on end of year employee survey.
	c) Practice asking clarifying questions to probe issues and gain full understanding.		
	3. Engage in two-way dialogue on a consistent basis. End conversations with a clear understanding of the purpose, discussion points, and resulting action items.		
• Improve team building skills.	1. Work with key direct reports to develop a common set of assumptions, vision, and goals for the team.	30 May 2008	Team assumptions, vision, and goals submitted to Steve Tolley for approval.
	2. Work with Steve Tolley to review and upgrade team bench strength in light of team goals.	30 June 2008	Team consists of only A and B players as reviewed with Steve Tolley.
	3. Work with team to develop common meeting, communication, decision-making, and accountability norms.	30 July 2008	New norms written up, sent to all team members, and reviewed on a regular basis with the team.
	4. Work with Steve Tolley to develop strategies for motivating team members or acquiring the resources needed to achieve team goals.	30 July 2008	
	5. Review progress on team goals with team members and Steve Tolley.	Monthly	Team results.

review progress on development plans with the boss. This way the boss can look for opportunities to help the leader further practice developing skills and determine when it is time to add new development needs to the plan.

It is important to realize that **development planning** is more than a plan—it is really a process.[6,70,100] Good development plans are constantly being revised as new skills are learned or new opportunities to develop skills become available. Leaders who take the time to write out and execute best-practice development plans usually report the most improvement in later 360-degree feedback ratings. Development planning provides a methodology for leaders to improve their behavior, and much of this development can occur as they go about their daily work activities.

Coaching

Development plans tend to be self-focused; leaders and followers use them as a road map for changing their own behaviors. When trying to change the behavior of followers, however, leaders can often do more than review a follower's development plan, provide ongoing feedback, or review plans periodically with followers. The next step in followers' development often involves coaching. Coaching is a key leadership skill, as it can help leaders to improve the bench strength of the group, which in turn should help the group to accomplish its goals. Because of its role in development, coaching can also help to retain high-quality followers.[108,109] Because of these outcomes, coaching is a popular topic these days, but it is also a frequently misunderstood one. It is hoped that the material in this section will help to clarify what coaching is, and identify some best-coaching practices.

Coaching is the "process of equipping people with the tools, knowledge, and opportunities they need to develop and become more successful."[103] In general, there are two types of coaching, informal and formal coaching. **Informal coaching** takes place whenever a leader helps followers to change their behaviors. According to Peterson and Hicks, the best informal coaching generally consists of five steps[103] (see Table 8.3). In *forging a partnership,* leaders build a trusting relationship with their followers, identify followers' career goals and motivators, and learn how their followers view the organization and their situation. The key question to be answered in this first step of coaching is "development for what?" Where do the followers want to go with their careers? Why do they want to go there? The answers to these questions help to create a target or end goal as well as a personal payoff for development. Nevertheless, if a leader fails to build a relationship based on mutual trust with a follower, then chances are the follower will not heed the leader's guidance and advice. Therefore, it is important that coaches also *determine the level of mutual trust,* and then improve the relationship if necessary before targeting development needs or providing feedback and advice. Too many inexperienced coaches either fail to build trust, or take the relationship for granted, with the long-term end result being little, if any, behavioral change, and a frustrated leader and follower.

Once career goals have been identified and a solid, trusting relationship has been built, leaders then need to *inspire commitment.* In this step, leaders work closely with followers to gather and analyze data to determine development needs. A leader and a follower may review appraisals

TABLE 8.3
The Five Steps of Informal Coaching

Source: D. B. Peterson and M. D. Hicks, *Leader as Coach: Strategies for Coaching and Developing Others.* Minneapolis, MN: Personnel Decisions International, 1996.

Forge a Partnership Coaching only works if there is a trusting relationship between the leader and his or her followers. In this step leaders also determine what drives their followers and where they want to go with their careers.
Inspire Commitment In this step leaders help followers determine which skills or behaviors will have the biggest payoff if developed. Usually this step involves reviewing the results of performance appraisals, 360-degree feedback, values, personality assessment reports, etc.
Grow Skills Leaders work with followers to build development plans that capitalize on on-the-job experiences and create coaching plans to support their followers' development.
Promote Persistence Leaders meet periodically with followers in order to provide feedback, help followers keep development on their radar screens, and provide followers with new tasks or projects to develop needed skills.
Shape the Environment Leaders need to periodically review how they are role-modeling development and what they are doing to foster development in the workplace. Because most people want to be successful, doing this step well will help attract and retain followers to the work group.

Coaching is the quickest, most customized, and most powerful behavior change technique available to a leader.

**David B. Peterson,
Personnel Decisions
International**

of past performance, feedback from peers or former bosses, project reports, 360-degree feedback reports, and any organizational standards that pertain to the follower's career goals. By reviewing this data, the leader and the follower should be able to identify and prioritize those development needs most closely aligned with career goals.

The next step in the coaching process involves *growing skills*. Followers use their prioritized development needs to create a development plan, and leaders in turn develop a **coaching plan** that spells out precisely what they will do to support the followers' development plan. Leaders and followers then review and discuss the development and coaching plans, make necessary adjustments, and execute the plans.

Just because a plan is developed does not mean it will be executed flawlessly. Learning often is a series of fits and starts, and sometimes followers either get distracted by operational requirements or get into developmental ruts. In the step called *promote persistence*, leaders help followers to manage the mundane, day-to-day aspects of development. Leaders can help followers refocus on their development by capitalizing on opportunities to give followers relevant, on-the-spot feedback. Once the new behavior has been practiced a number of times and becomes part of the follower's behavioral repertoire, then leaders help followers to *transfer the skills to new environments* by applying the skills in new settings and revising their development plans. In this step, leaders need to also ask themselves how they are role-modeling development and whether they are creating an environment that fosters individual development.

There are several points about informal coaching worth additional comment. First, the five-step process identified by Peterson and Hicks can be used by leadership practitioners to diagnose why behavioral change is *not*

Tony Dungy

PROFILES IN LEADERSHIP 8.5

Anthony Kevin "Tony" Dungy is currently the head coach of the Indianapolis Colts, the 2007 Super Bowl champions. Dungy grew up in Michigan and played football for the University of Minnesota. Starting as a freshman at the quarterback position, Dungy set a number of school records for passing attempts, completions, passing yards, and passing touchdowns. Upon graduation Dungy played two years as a backup safety for the Pittsburgh Steelers (when they won the 1978 Super Bowl) and a year for the San Francisco 49ers. In his fourth NFL year Dungy was traded and subsequently cut from the New York Giants, when he then took a job at the University of Minnesota as an assistant coach. He returned to the NFL as an assistant coach for the Pittsburgh Steelers. He worked for 13 years as a defensive backs coach and defensive coordinator for the Pittsburgh Steelers, Kansas City Chiefs, and Minnesota Vikings before taking over the head coaching position for the Tampa Bay Buccaneers in 1995. Under Dungy's leadership the Buccaneers went to the National Football League playoffs four times. But offensive woes during the playoffs caused the Buccaneer management to lose faith in Dungy and they eventually let him go in 2001.

In early 2002 Dungy was hired as the head coach of the Indianapolis Colts; a team with a potent offense but poor defense. Dungy spent the next five years retooling the team's defense and as a result his team had one of the best winning records in the NFL for those five years. Like his Tampa Bay team, the Colts were highly successful but regularly faltered in the playoffs until they beat the Chicago Bears 29–17 in Super Bowl XLI.

Dungy's coaching philosophy is quite different than other NFL head coaches'. Rather than getting up early to review game films and leading practices through yelling and intimidation, Dungy believes that good coaches are essentially teachers that do not belittle or scream at players. He also believes that faith and family take priority over football and he is very active in such charitable programs as Big Brothers/Big Sisters, the Boys and Girls Club, and the Prison Ministry. Dungy's religious convictions are so strong that he once considered going into the prison ministry instead of coaching. Not only has Dungy been able to create a football dynasty in Indiana, he has also extended his reach in the NFL by having four of his assistant coaches move into head coaching positions with other NFL teams. As a matter of fact, Lovie Smith, the head coach of the Chicago Bears in Super Bowl XLI, was one of Dungy's former assistant coaches and very much subscribes to the same coaching philosophy.

Source: http://en/wikipedia.org/wiki/Tony_Dungy.

occurring and what can be done about it. For example, followers may not be developing new skills because they do not trust their leader, the skills have not been clearly identified or are not important to them, or they do not have a plan in place to acquire these skills. Second, informal coaching can and does occur anywhere in the organization. Senior executives can use this model to develop their staffs, peers can use it to help each other, and so forth. Third, this process is just as effective for high-performing followers as it is for low-performing followers. Leadership practitioners have a tendency to forget to coach their solid or top followers, yet these individuals are often making the greatest contributions to team or organizational success. Moreover, research has shown that the top performers in a job often produce 20–50 percent more than the average performer, depending on the complexity of the job.[110] So if leaders would focus on moving their solid performers into the highest-performing ranks and making their top performers even better, chances are their teams might be substantially more effective than if they only focused on coaching those doing most poorly (see Figure 8.9).

Fourth, both "remote" coaching of people and coaching of individuals from other cultures can be particularly difficult.[111,112] It is more difficult for leaders to build trusting relationships with followers when they are physically separated by great distances. The same may be true with followers from other cultures—what may be important to, say, a Kenyan follower and how this person views the world may be very different from what his or her Dutch or Singaporean leader believes.

The kinds of behaviors that need to be developed can also vary considerably by culture. For example, one senior executive for a high-tech firm was coaching one of his Japanese direct reports on how to do better presentations to superiors. The follower's style was formal, stiff, and somewhat wooden, and the leader wanted the follower to add some humor and informality to his presentations. However, the follower said that by doing so he would lose the respect of his Japanese colleagues, so his commitment to this change was understandably low. What was agreed upon was that his style was very effective in Japan, but that it needed to change when he was giving presentations in the United States.

Informal coaching can help groups to be successful as well as to reduce turnover among employees, but what does it take to be a good informal

FIGURE 8.9   What were the most useful factors in the coaching you received?

Source: "The Business Leader as Development Coach." *PDI Portfolio,* Winter 1996, p. 6.

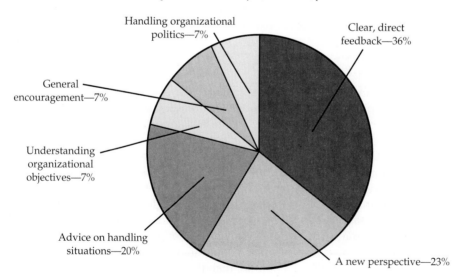

coach? Research by Wenzel showed that the most effective informal coaches had a unique combination of leadership traits and skills. Leaders with higher levels of intelligence, surgency, and agreeableness were often more effective as coaches than those with lower scores. These leadership traits were the foundation for the relationship building, listening, assertiveness, and feedback skills associated with effective informal coaches. Good informal coaches use these traits and skills to build trusting relationships with their followers, build best-practice coaching and development plans, and deliver tough and honest feedback when necessary.[108]

Some Critical Lessons Learned from Formal Coaching

HIGHLIGHT 8.8

1. **The person being coached has got to want to change.** It is very difficult to get someone to change their behavior unless they want to change. Coaches need to ensure that coachees clearly understand the benefits for changing their behavior and the consequences if they do not change. Oftentimes it is much easier to get people to change when coaches link the new behaviors to coachees' values and career goals.

2. **Assessments are important.** Formal assessments involving personality, values, mental abilities, and multirater feedback are essential to understanding what behaviors coachees need to change, what is driving these needed changes, and how easy or difficult it will be to change targeted behaviors.

3. **Some behaviors cannot be changed.** Some behaviors are so ingrained or unethical that the best option may be termination. For example, one of the authors was asked to coach a married vice president who got two of his executive assistants pregnant in less than a year. Given that the coach was not an expert in birth control or Lamaze, the coach turned down the engagement.

4. **Practice is critical.** Good coaches not only discuss what needs to change, but also make coachees practice targeted behaviors. Often the initial practice takes place during coaching sessions, where the coach may play the role of another party and provide the coachee with feedback and suggestions for improvement. These practices are then extended to work, where the coachee must use these newly acquired behaviors in real world situations.

5. **There is no substitute for accountability.** Superiors must be kept in the loop about coachees' progress, and must hold them accountable for on-the-job changes. If coaches are working with potential derailment candidates, then superiors must be willing to let coachees go if they do not make needed changes. Although fear or threats are not the best way to get people to change, some derailment candidates are in so much denial about their problems that it is only by fear of losing their high status jobs that they are motivated to change.

Sources: S. Berglas, "The Very Real Dangers of Executive Coaching." *Harvard Business Review,* June 2002, pp. 86–93; G. J. Curphy, "What Role Should I/O Psychologists Play in Executive Education?" In *Models of Executive Education,* R. T. Hogan (chair), presentation at the 17th Annual Society for Industrial and Organizational Psychology, Toronto, Canada, April 2002.

Most people are familiar with the idea of a personal fitness trainer, a person who helps design a fitness program tailored to a specific individual's needs and goals. **Formal coaching** programs provide a similar kind of service for executives and managers in leadership positions.[5,6,109,112–120] Approximately 65 percent of the Global 1000 companies use some form of formal coaching.[112] Formal coaching programs are quite individualized by their very nature, but several common features deserve mention. There is a one-on-one relationship between the manager and the coach (i.e., an internal or external consultant) which lasts from six months to more than a year. The process usually begins with the manager's completion of an extensive battery of personality, intelligence, interests, value, and 360-degree feedback instruments, as well as with interviews by the coach of other individuals in the manager's world of work. As the result of the assessment phase of this process, both the manager and the coach have a clear picture of development needs and how the different components of the building-block model interact and affect these needs. The coach and the manager then meet regularly (roughly monthly) to review the results of the feedback instruments and work on building skills and practicing target behaviors. Role plays and videotape are used extensively during these sessions, and coaches provide immediate feedback to clients practicing new behaviors in realistic work situations. Another valuable outcome of coaching programs can involve clarification of managers' values, and identification of discrepancies between their espoused values and their actual behaviors and devising strategies to better align their behaviors with their values.

A formal coaching program can cost more than $100,000 and it is reasonable to ask if this money is well-spent. A solid body of research shows that well-designed and well-executed coaching programs do in fact change behavior.[9,91,92,109,112,118–124] Figure 8.10 reveals that some of this research shows that coaching may be even more effective at changing behavior than more traditional learning and training approaches. Moreover, the behavioral changes appear to be in place one year after the termination of a coaching program, indicating permanent behavioral change.[122] Such changes can be particularly important if the person making them—that is, the leader being coached—is in a highly placed or very responsible position. Most coaching candidates have hundreds, if not thousands, of subordinates, and usually oversee multimillion or multibillion dollar budgets. Thus, the money spent on a coaching program can be relatively small in comparison to the budgets and resources the candidates control and as a result turn out to be a very good return on investment.

No man is so foolish but he may sometimes give another good counsel, and no man so wise that he may not easily err if he takes no other counsel than his own. He that is taught only by himself has a fool for a master.

Ben Jonson

Mentoring

Mentoring is a personal relationship in which a more experienced mentor (usually someone two to four levels higher in an organization) acts as a

FIGURE 8.10   The power of coaching.

Source: D. B. Peterson, *Individual Coaching Services: Coaching That Makes a Difference*. Minneapolis, MN: Personnel Decisions International, 1999.

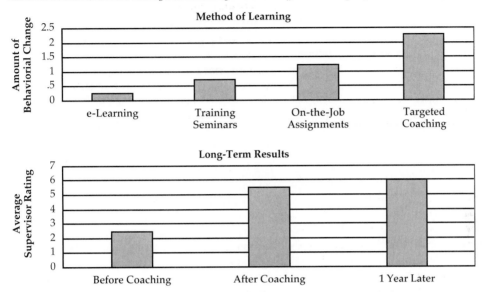

guide, role model, and sponsor of a less experienced protégé. Mentors provide protégés with knowledge, advice, challenge, counsel, and support about career opportunities, organizational strategy and policy, office politics, and so forth.[125–133] Although mentoring has a strong developmental component, it is not the same as coaching. One key difference is that mentoring may not target specific development needs. Protégés often meet with their mentors to get a different perspective of the organization or for advice on potential committee and task force assignments or promotion opportunities. Another difference is that this guidance is not coming from the protégé's immediate supervisor, but rather from someone several leadership levels higher in the organization. Protégés often do receive informal coaching from their boss, but may be more apt to seek career guidance and personal advice from their mentors. Another difference is that the mentor may not even be part of the organization. Some mentors may have retired from the organization, or may have been someone for whom the protégé worked a number of years earlier.

Parents are the first leadership trainers in life.

Bruce Avolio, leadership researcher

As in coaching, there are both formal and informal mentoring programs. *Informal mentoring* occurs when a protégé and mentor build a long-term relationship based on friendship, similar interests, and mutual respect. These relationships often begin with the protégé working in some part of the mentor's organization or on a high-visibility project for the mentor. *Formal mentoring* programs occur when the organization assigns a

The Wild West of Coaching

HIGHLIGHT 8.9

Executive coaching has become a big business. Over 10,000 people in the United States and another 5,000 people around the rest of the world provide coaching services to managers and executives, and these individuals generate over one billion dollars in coaching fees annually. Unlike other professions, such as airline pilots, medical doctors, accountants, or cosmetologists, there are no standards or licensing requirements for executive coaching. That being the case, anyone and everyone seem to be doing executive coaching these days. Some executive coaches are former fighter pilots, professional or Olympic athletes, and business executives; others are business school professors, family therapists, or motivational speakers. Although these individuals routinely charge up to $5,000 per day for their services, few of these individuals possess the knowledge and skills needed to permanently change the behavior of people in positions of authority. Effective coaches possess four different domains of knowledge, which include an in-depth understanding of:

- Business models, operations, structures, functions, processes, metrics, finances.
- Personality, intelligence, values, behavior, and skills.
- Leadership, management, teams, and organizational change.
- Knowledge acquisition, skill development, and behavioral change.

When these four criteria are applied to people providing coaching services, it is easy to see why many coaching interventions are ineffective. Too many coaches lack even a basic understanding of business, personality, leadership, or behavioral change and are unable to help people in authority become Competent Managers.

Perhaps some of the worst coaching advice comes from close friends and family members. These individuals are constantly dispensing guidance on how to deal with complex work issues, handle difficult employees, lead others, or pursue different career opportunities. But friends and family members are not particularly objective and often lack expertise in one or more of the domains described above. Good coaches, on the other hand, are trusted advisors who provide brutally honest, unbiased feedback and sound advice for changing behavior.

Ill-equipped professional coaches, friends, and family members are not the only ones contributing to the high base rate of managerial incompetence. A recent book from the dean of the Yale Leadership Institute urges executives fired for incompetence to deny culpability, shift responsibility for their poor performance onto others, reduce the offensiveness of any inappropriate acts, and offer acceptable motives for questionable behavior. In other words, incompetent executives should make up stories and lie about why they are looking for a new job. With advice like this, is it any wonder that people who have difficulties building teams or getting results continue to move into roles at the top of large organizations?

Sources: G. J. Curphy, "Concluding Remarks on Executive Assessment and Development." In *The Role of Psychology in Executive Assessment and Development*, G. J. Curphy (chair), symposium presented at the 15th Annual Conference of the Society for Industrial and Organizational Psychology, New Orleans, LA, 2000; J. Sandberg, "Our Better Halves Sometimes Expose Our Worst Side." *The Wall Street Journal*, March 25, 2007, p. B1; J. A. Sonnenfeld and A. Ward, *Firing Back: How Great Leaders Rebound after Career Disasters*. Boston, MA: Harvard Business School Press, 2007; R. L. Orenstein, "Measuring Executive Coaching Efficacy? The Answer Was Right Here All the Time?" *Journal of Consulting Psychology* 58 (2) (2006), pp. 106–16; S. Sherman and A. Freas, "The Wild West of Executive Coaching." *Harvard Business Review*, November 2004, pp. 82–93.

Ref mentoring (handwritten margin note)

relatively inexperienced but high-potential leader to one of the top executives in the company. The protégé and mentor get together on a regular basis so that the protégé can gain exposure and learn more about how decisions are made at the top of the organization. Oftentimes organizations implement formal mentoring programs to accelerate the development of female or minority protégés.[126–128,130,131]

Mentoring is quite prevalent in many organizations today. Researchers reported that 74 percent of the noncommissioned officers and officers in the U.S. Army had mentors and 67 percent of all U.S. Navy admirals had mentors sometime in their career. Moreover, many admirals reported having an average of 3.5 mentors by the time they retired.[134,135] Other researchers have reported positive relationships between mentoring, personal learning, career satisfaction, pay, promotions, and retention.[128,129,131–133] But some of this research also found that formal mentoring programs were better than no mentoring programs but less effective than informal mentoring for protégé compensation and promotion.[126,130,131] The reason for these diminished results may be that most formal mentoring programs have a difficult time replicating the strong emotional bonds found in informal programs. In addition, most formal mentoring programs only lasted a year, whereas many informal mentoring relationships can last a lifetime (see Highlight 8.10).

Overview of a Formal Mentoring Program

HIGHLIGHT 8.10

Menttium Corporation specializes in the development and delivery of formal mentoring programs for high-potential females. Most of the protégés have 6–20 years of professional experience and are often in mid-level management roles and are matched with mentors from other organizations at the vice president level or higher. The Menttium 100 program is one year long and begins with a two-day kickoff conference. During this conference mentors and protégés meet each other, get an overview of the program, learn about important leadership and business topics, and network with other mentors and protégés. Over the course of the year mentors and protégés get together at least once a month and protégés attend quarterly business education and networking events. The Menttium 100 program seems to have a very positive impact on both mentors and protégés. For example:

- 75% of protégés said the program helped improve their leadership capabilities.
- 77% of protégés are more likely to stay with their parent companies.
- 80% of protégés believe their companies have benefited by their attending the program.

Although these results are promising, Menttium is currently engaged in a more rigorous, long-term study to assess the overall impact of its program on both mentors and protégés.

Source: Menttium, *Menttium 100: Cross-Company Mentoring for High Potential Women.* Minneapolis, MN: The Menttium Corporation, 2006.

Thomas examined the role mentoring played in the careers of minority leaders. He reported that minority leaders at the top of their organizations often had two key qualities. First, successful minority executives were concerned with getting the right experiences and developing the right foundation of leadership skills when they first joined the organization. Their focus was more on personal growth at each leadership level than with titles and rewards. Second, they had an extensive set of mentors and corporate sponsors who provided guidance and support over their careers. These mentors and sponsors helped the executives to develop the three Cs critical to advancement: confidence, competence, and credibility. Thomas also stated that the most successful white mentor–minority protégé relationships recognized that race was a potential barrier to advancement but were still able to bring up and work through touchy issues. Less successful white mentor–minority protégé relationships engaged in "protective hesitation," in which race or sensitive issues were avoided, ignored, or discounted.[127]

Because of the benefits of informal mentoring, leadership practitioners should look for opportunities to build mentoring relationships with senior leaders whenever possible. However, it is important to realize that protégés cannot make these relationships happen by themselves. In many cases, mentors seek out protégés, or mentors and protégés seek out each other to build relationships. But leaders and leaders to be can do a couple of things to improve the odds of finding a mentor. The first step is to do one's current job extremely well. Mentors are always looking for talent, and they are very unlikely to take someone under their wing who appears unmotivated or incompetent. The second step is to look for opportunities to gain visibility and build social relationships with potential mentors. Working on a key task force, doing presentations for the executive committee, or signing up for community activities sponsored by a top executive are just a few of the pathways one could take to gain the attention of potential mentors.

Summary

Leaders can benefit from the leadership behavior research in several ways. First, the behavioral approach has served the important purpose of directing attention to identifying types of leadership behavior critical to success. Second, the behavioral approach allows leadership practitioners to focus on concrete and specific examples of leader behavior. Third, an outgrowth of the behavioral approach has been the development of competency models and 360-degree feedback instruments. The 360-degree feedback instruments can be used to provide valuable feedback to leadership practitioners and often play important roles in many training, coaching, and succession-planning programs. Research has also helped to identify factors that can cause high-potential managers to fail. This research on managerial derailment has identified "fatal flaws," including such counterproductive leadership behaviors as arrogance, insensitivity, or untrustworthiness.

The chapter also examined the process of behavior change. Research shows that some managers seem to be able to change on their own after gaining insight on how their behavior affects others. This insight is often gained through reflection, in-depth assessments, or 360-degree feedback. Nevertheless, more managers will change if some formal system or process of behavioral change is put into place; these systems include development planning, informal and formal coaching programs, and mentorships. Development planning is the process of pinpointing development needs, creating development plans, implementing plans, and reflecting on and revising plans on a regular basis. Good development plans focus on one or two development needs, capitalize upon on-the-job experiences, and specify sources of feedback. Organizations with formal development systems are likely to realize greater behavioral changes from a greater number of managers than organizations having no system or only an informal one.

Leaders can create development plans for themselves, and they can also help their followers with behavioral change through coaching or mentoring programs. Informal coaching programs often consist of a series of steps designed to create permanent behavioral changes in followers and both leaders and followers play active roles in informal coaching programs. Formal coaching people utilize a formal assessment process and a series of one-on-one coaching sessions over a six- to twelve-month period. These sessions target specific development needs and capitalize on practice and feedback to acquire needed skills. Mentoring programs have many of the same objectives as coaching programs but take place between an individual (the protégé) and a leader several levels higher in the organization (the mentor).

Key Terms

Leader Behavior Description Questionnaire (LBDQ), 265
consideration, 266
initiating structure, 266
leadership behavior, 266
leadership skill, 266
job-centered dimensions, 267
goal emphasis, 267
work facilitation, 267

employee-centered dimensions, 267
leader support, 267
interaction facilitation, 267
Leadership Grid, 268
concern for people, 268
concern for production, 268
intrapersonal skills, 273
interpersonal skills, 273

leadership skills, 273
business skills, 273
community leadership, 274
framing, 276
building social capital, 276
mobilization, 276
360-degree or multirater feedback, 278
managerial derailment, 285

Questions

1. Could you create a competency model for college professors? For college students? If you used these competency models to create 360-degree feedback tools, who would be in the best position to give professors and students feedback?

2. Do you know anyone who has derailed from a leadership position? What did this person do? Use the leader–follower–situation model to better understand why this individual derailed.

3. What would a development plan for student leaders look like? How could you capitalize on school experiences as part of a development plan?

4. What would a leadership coaching or mentoring program for students look like? How could you tell whether the program worked?

Activities

1. Read the Development Planning material in Part 4 of this book. Complete a GAPS analysis and create your own development plan. Share your development plan with someone in class. Your partner should use the Development Planning Checklist found in the Coaching section of Part 4 to critique your plan. Check with your partner in two to four weeks to review progress on your plans.

2. Read the Coaching material in Part 4 of this book. Complete a GAPS analysis for someone you would like to coach. Use the results of the GAPS analysis to create development and coaching plans for this individual.

3. Given the model of community leadership described earlier in this chapter, analyze an ongoing community change initiative. Has the leader framed the issue in such way to make it easy for others to take action? Do they have strong bonds with other groups? Have they created a plan and mobilized a critical mass of people and resources to make the change become reality?

Minicase

"Paying Attention Pays Off for Andra Rush"

Paying attention has been the key for Andra Rush. As a nursing school graduate she was paying attention when other nurses complained about unfair treatment and decided she wanted to do something about it—so she enrolled in the University of Michigan's MBA program so she could do something about how employees were treated. As she completed her business courses and continued to work as a nurse, she was paying attention when a patient described his experience in the transport business. The business sounded intriguing, and so, with minimal experience and minimal resources, Rush took a risk and started her own trucking business. She scraped together the funds to buy three trucks by borrowing money from family and maxxing out her credit cards. She specialized in emergency shipping and accepted every job that came her way, even if it meant driving the trucks herself. She answered phones, balanced her books, and even repaired the trucks. She paid attention to her customers and made a point of exceeding their expectations regardless of the circumstances. When the terrorist attacks of September 11 shut down local bridges, Rush rented a barge to make sure a crucial shipment for DaimlerChrysler made it to its destination on time.

Rush continues to pay attention and credits her listening skills as a major reason for her success. Rush is distinct in the traditionally white male–dominated trucking industry—a woman and a minority (Rush is Native American) who credits her heritage and the "enormous strength" of her Mohawk grandmother for helping her prevail.

"It is entirely possible that my Native spirit, communicated to me by my grandmother and my immediate family, have enabled me to overcome the isolation, historical prejudice, and business environment viewed as a barrier to Native- and woman-owned businesses. The willingness to listen, to understand first, and act directly and honestly with integrity is a lesson and code of conduct my elders have bequeathed to me. Being an entrepreneur has reinforced those lessons again and again."

Her Mohawk heritage is pervasive. Rush's company logo is a war staff with six feathers representing the Six Nations of the Iroquois: Mohawk, Onondaga, Oneida, Cayuga, Tuscarora, and Seneca. She believes in the power of a diverse workforce and as a result more than half of the 390 employees at Rush Trucking are women and half are minorities.

Rush keeps close tabs on her company and its employees. Though the company has grown from its humble three-truck beginning to a fleet of 1,700 trucks, Rush still takes time to ride along with drivers. She has provided educational programs like "The Readers' Edge," a literacy program, to improve the skills and lives of her employees. Rush is actively involved in several organizations that work to improve the position of minorities—she's on the boards of directors of the Michigan Minority Business Development Council, Minority Enterprise Development/Minority Business Development Agency, Minority Business Roundtable, and has served as president of the Native American Business Alliance.

1. As we have discussed, competency models describe the behaviors and skills managers need to exhibit if an organization is to be successful. Consider the general competencies found in Figure 8.3 and apply these to Andra Rush, providing examples of why these competencies apply.

2. Mentoring has played a role in the careers of many successful minorities in leadership positions. Who could be identified as a coach or mentor for Andra Rush?

3. Consider some of the self-defeating behaviors outlined in this chapter that contribute to management derailment. What lessons has Andra Rush obviously learned from the failure of others?

Sources: http://www.inc.com/magazine/20040401/25rush.html; http://www.crainsdetroit.com/cgi-bin/page.pl?pageId=400; http://www.readfaster.com/pr20030912.pdf; http://www.turtle-tracks. org/issue41/i41_3.html; http://www.indiancountry.com/?2224.

Chapter Notes

1. Curphy, G. J. "In-Depth Assessments, 360-Degree Feedback, and Development: Key Research Results and Recommended Next Steps." Presentation at the Annual Conference for HR Managers at US West Communications, Denver, CO, January 1998.

2. Curphy, G. J. "What Role Should I/O Psychologists Play in Executive Education?" In *Models of Executive Education.* R. T. Hogan (chair). Presentation given at the 17th Annual Society for Industrial and Organizational Psychology, Toronto, Canada, April 2002.

3. Curphy, G. J. "Leadership Transitions and Teams." Presentation given at the Hogan Assessment Systems International Users Conference, Istanbul, September 2003.

4. Curphy, G. J. "The Consequences of Managerial Incompetence." Presentation given at the 3rd Hogan Assessment Systems International Users Conference, Prague, Czech Republic, September 2004.

5. Curphy, G. J. "Comments on the State of Leadership Prediction." In *Predicting Leadership: The Good, The Bad, the Indifferent, and the Unnecessary.* J. P. Campbell and M. J. Benson (chairs). Symposium conducted at the 22nd Annual Conference for the Society of Industrial and Organizational Psychology, New York, April 2007.

6. Curphy, G. J., M. J. Benson, A. Baldrica, and R. T. Hogan. *Managerial Incompetence.* Unpublished manuscript, 2007.

7. Curphy, G. J., and R. T. Hogan. "What We Really Know about Leadership (But Seem Unwilling to Implement)." Working paper, 2004.

8. Hogan, R. T., and G. J. Curphy, *Leadership Effectiveness and Managerial Incompetence.* Unpublished manuscript, 2007.

9. Charan, R., and G. Colvin. "Why CEOs Fail." *Fortune,* June 21, 1999, pp. 69–82.

10. Goldsmith, M., and M. Reiter. *What Got You Here Won't Get You There.* New York: Hyperion, 2007.

11. Hemphill, J. K. "The Leader and His Group." *Journal of Educational Research* 28 (1949), pp. 225–29, 245–46.

12. Hemphill, J. K., and A. E. Coons. "Development of the Leader Behavior Description Questionnaire." In *Leader Behavior: Its Description and Measurement.* Eds. R. M. Stogdill and A. E. Coons. Columbus: Ohio State University, Bureau of Business Research, 1957.

13. Fleishman, E. A. "Twenty Years of Consideration and Structure." In *Current Developments in the Study of Leadership.* Eds. E. A. Fleishman and J. G. Hunt. Carbondale: Southern Illinois University Press, 1973.

14. Halpin, A. W., and B. J. Winer. "A Factorial Study of the Leader Behavior Descriptions." In *Leader Behavior: Its Descriptions and Measurement.* Eds. R. M. Stogdill and A. E. Coons. Columbus: Ohio State University, Bureau of Business Research, 1957.

15. Fleishman, E. A. *Examiner's Manual for the Supervisory Behavior Description Questionnaire.* Washington, DC: Management Research Institute, 1972.

16. Fleishman, E. A. *Examiner's Manual for the Leadership Opinion Questionnaire.* Rev. ed. Chicago: Science Research Associates, 1989.

17. Stogdill, R. M. *Individual Behavior and Group Achievement.* New York: Oxford University Press, 1959.

18. Likert, R. *New Patterns of Management.* New York: McGraw-Hill, 1961.

19. Bowers, D. G., and S. E. Seashore. "Predicting Organizational Effectiveness with a Four Factor Theory of Leadership." *Administrative Science Quarterly* 11 (1966), pp. 238–63.

20. Bass, B. M. *Bass and Stogdill's Handbook of Leadership.* 3rd ed. New York: Free Press, 1990.

21. Judge, T. A., R. F. Piccolo, and R. Ilies. "The Forgotten Ones? The Validity of Consideration and Initiating Structure in Leadership Research." *Journal of Applied Psychology* 89 (1) (2004), pp. 36–51.

22. Eisenberger, R., F. Stinglhamber, C. Vandenberghe, I. L. Sucharski, and L. Rhoades. "Perceived Supervisor Support: Contributions to Perceived Organizational Support and Employee Retention." *Journal of Applied Psychology* 87 (3) (2002), pp. 565–73.

23. Blake, R. R., and A. A. McCanse. *Leadership Dilemmas—Grid Solutions.* Houston, TX: Gulf, 1991.

24. Blake, R. R., and J. S. Mouton. *The Managerial Grid.* Houston, TX: Gulf, 1964.

25. Robie, C., K. Kanter, D. L. Nilsen, and J. Hazucha. *The Right Stuff: Understanding Cultural Differences in Leadership Performance.* Minneapolis, MN: Personnel Decisions International, 2001.

26. Goff, M. *Critical Leadership Skills Valued by Every Organization.* Minneapolis, MN: Personnel Decisions International, 2000.

27. Davis, S., J. Volker, R. C. Barnett, P. H. Batz, and P. Germann. *Leadership Matters: 13 Roles of High Performing Leaders.* Minneapolis, MN: MDA Leadership Consulting, 2006.

28. Hollenbeck, G. P., M. W. McCall, and R. F. Silzer. "Leadership Competency Models." *The Leadership Quarterly* 17 (2006), pp. 398–413.

29. Tischler, L. "IBM's Management Makeover." *Fast Company*, November 2004, pp. 112–16.

30. Lievens, P., J. I. Sanchez, and W. DeCorte. "Easing the Inferential Leap in Competency Modeling: The Effects of Task-Related Information and Subject Matter Expertise." *Personnel Psychology* 57 (2004), pp. 881–904.

31. King, A. W., S. W. Fowler, and C. P. Zeithaml. "Managing Organizational Competencies for Competitive Advantage: The Middle-Management Edge." *Academy of Management Executive* 15, no. 2 (2001), pp. 95–106.

32. Curphy, G. J. *The Blandin Education Leadership Program.* Grand Rapids, MN: The Blandin Foundation, 2004f.

33. Curphy, G. J. *The Blandin Health Care Leadership Program.* Grand Rapids, MN: The Blandin Foundation, 2004g.

34. Curphy, G. J., and R. T. Hogan. "Managerial Incompetence: Is There a Dead Skunk on the Table?" Working paper, 2004.

35. Ulrich, D., J. Zenger, and N. Smallwood. *Results-Based Leadership.* Boston: Harvard Business School Press, 1999.

36. Peterson, D. B. "Making the Break from Middle Manager to a Seat at the Top." *The Wall Street Journal*, July 7, 1998.

37. Curphy, G. J. "Early Leadership Talent Identification and Development." Paper presented at the Conference for Executives of Saudi Aramco, Dhahran, Saudi Arabia, October 2001.

38. Louiselle, K., S. Bridges, and G. J. Curphy. "Talent Assessment Overview." Working paper, 2003.

39. Gebelein, S. H. "360-Degree Feedback Goes Strategic." *PDI Portfolio*, Summer 1996, pp. 1–3.

40. Shippmann, J. S., R. A. Ash, M. Battista, L. Carr, L. D. Eyde, B. Hesketh, J. Kehoe, K. Pearlman, E. P. Prien, and J. I. Sanchez. "The Practice of Competency Modeling." *Personnel Psychology* 53, no. 3 (2000), pp. 703–40.

41. Hogan, R. T., and R. Warrenfelz. "Educating the Modern Manager." *Academy of Management Learning and Education* 2 (1) (2003), pp. 74–84.

42. Church, A. H. "Talent Management." *The Industrial-Organizational Psychologist* 44 (1) (2006), pp. 33–36.

43. Ancona, D., T. W. Malone, W. J. Orlikowski, and P. M. Senge. "In Praise of the Incomplete Leader." *Harvard Business Review*, February 2007, pp. 92–103.

44. Krile, J., G. J. Curphy, and D. Lund. *The Community Leadership Handbook: Framing Ideas, Building Relationships and Mobilizing Resources.* St Paul, MN: Fieldstone Alliance, 2005.

45. Tichy, N. M., and E. Cohen. *The Leadership Engine: How Winning Companies Build Leaders at Every Level.* New York: HarperCollins, 1997.

46. Campbell, D. P., G. J. Curphy, and T. Tuggle. *360 Degree Feedback Instruments: Beyond Theory.* Workshop presented at the 10th Annual Conference of the Society for Industrial and Organizational Psychology, Orlando, FL, May 1995.

47. Curphy, G. J. "Executive Integrity and 360-Degree Feedback." In *Assessing Executive Failure: The Underside of Performance.* R. T. Hogan (chair). Symposium presented at the 18th Annual Conference of the Society of Industrial and Organizational Psychology, Orlando, FL, 2003.

48. Toegel, G., and J. A. Conger. "360–Degree Assessment: Time for Reinvention." *Academy of Management Learning and Education* 2 (3), pp. 297–311.

49. Kaiser, R. B., and S. B. Craig. "Building a Better Mousetrap: Item Characteristics Associated with Rating Discrepancies in 360-Degree Feedback." *Consulting Psychology Journal* 57 (4) (2005), pp. 235–245.

50. Morgeson, F., T. V. Mumsford, and M. A. Campion. "Coming Full Circle: Research and Practice to Address 27 Questions about 360-Degree Feedback Programs." *Consulting Psychology Journal* 57 (3) (2005), pp. 196–209.

51. Smither, J. W., M. London, and R. R. Reilly. "Does Performance Improve Following Multisource Feedback? A Theoretical Model, Meta-analysis, and Review of Empirical Findings." *Personnel Psychology* 58 (2005), pp. 33–66.

52. Bono, J. E., and A. E. Colbert. "Understanding Responses to Multi-Source Feedback: The Core of Self-Evaluations." *Personnel Psychology* 58 (2005), pp. 171–203.

53. Bracken, D. W., C. W. Timmreck, and A. H. Church. *The Handbook of Multisource Feedback.* San Francisco: Jossey-Bass, 2000.

54. Atkins, P. W. B., and R. E. Wood. "Self- Versus Others' Ratings as Predictors of Assessment Center Ratings: Validation Evidence for 360-Degree Feedback Programs." *Personnel Psychology* 55 (2002), pp. 871–84.

55. Curphy, G. J. "Some Closing Remarks about the Use of Self- and Other-Ratings of Personality and Behaviors." In *Multirater Assessment Systems: What We've Learned.* M. D. Dunnette, chair. Symposium conducted at the 99th American Psychological Association Convention, San Francisco, August 1991.

56. Jackman, J. M., and M. H. Strober. "Fear of Feedback." *Harvard Business Review,* April 2003, pp. 101–08.

57. Peiperl, M. A. "Getting 360-Degree Feedback Right." *Harvard Business Review,* January 2001, pp. 142–48.

58. Sala, F. "Executive Blind Spots: Discrepancies Between Self- and Other-Ratings." *Consulting Psychology Journal* 55 (4) (2003), pp. 222–29.

59. Craig, S. B., and K. Hannum. "Research Update: 360-Degree Performance Assessment." *Consulting Psychology Journal* 58 (2) (2006), pp. 117–24.

60. Church, A. H., and J. Waclawski. "A Five-Phase Framework for Designing a Successful Multisource Feedback System." *Consulting Psychology Journal* 53, no. 2 (2001), pp. 82–95.

61. Pfau, B., and I. Kay. "Does 360-Degree Feedback Negatively Affect Company Performance?" *HR Magazine,* June 2002, pp. 55–59.

62. Antonioni, D. "360-Degree Feedback for a Competitive Edge." *Industrial Management* (42) (2000), pp. 6–10.

63. Sala, F., and S. A. Dwight. "Predicting Executive Performance with Multirater Surveys: Whom You Ask Makes a Difference." *Consulting Psychology Journal* 55 (3) (2003), pp. 166–72.

64. Curphy, G. J. "An Empirical Investigation of Bass' (1985) Theory of Transformational and Transactional Leadership." PhD dissertation, University of Minnesota, 1991.

65. Curphy, G. J. "The Effects of Transformational and Transactional Leadership on Organizational Climate, Attrition, and Performance." In *Impact of Leadership.*

Ed. K. E. Clark, M. B. Clark, and D. P. Campbell. Greensboro, NC: Center for Creative Leadership, 1992.

66. Church, A. H. "Managerial Self-Awareness in High-Performing Individuals in Organizations." *Journal of Applied Psychology* 82, no. 2 (1997), pp. 281–92.

67. Church, A. H. "Do Higher Performing Managers Actually Receive Better Ratings?" *Consulting Psychology Journal* 52, no. 2 (2000), pp. 99–116.

68. Ghorpade, J. "Managing Six Paradoxes of 360-Degree Feedback." *Academy of Management Executive* 14, no. 1 (2000), pp. 140–50.

69. Greguras, G. J., C. Robie, D. J. Schleicher, and M. Goff III. "A Field Study of the Effects of Rating Purpose on the Quality of Multisource Ratings." *Personnel Psychology* 56 (1) (2003), pp. 1–22.

70. Curphy, G. J. *Afterburner 360 Training Manual.* North Oaks, MN: Curphy Consulting Corporation, 2003.

71. Greguras, G. J., and C. Robie. "A New Look at Within-Source Interrater Reliability of 360-Degree Feedback Ratings." *Journal of Applied Psychology* 83, no. 6 (1998), pp. 960–68.

72. Mount, M. K., T. A. Judge, S. E. Scullen, M. R. Sytsma, and S. A. Hezlett. "Trait, Rater, and Level Effects in 360-Degree Performance Ratings." *Personnel Psychology* 51, no. 3 (1998), pp. 557–77.

73. Ostroff, C., L. E. Atwater, and B. J. Feinberg. "Understanding Self-Other Agreement: A Look at Rater and Ratee Characteristics, Context, and Outcomes." *Personnel Psychology* 57 (2) (2004), pp. 333–76.

74. Atwater, L. E, C. Ostroff, F. J. Yammarino, and J. W. Fleenor. "Self-Other Agreement: Does It Really Matter?" *Personnel Psychology* 51, no. 3 (1998), pp. 577–98.

75. Fleenor, J. W., C. D. McCauley, and S. Brutus. "Self-Other Rating Agreement and Leader Effectiveness." *Leadership Quarterly* 7, no. 4 (1996), pp. 487–506.

76. Walker, A., and J. W. Smither. "A Five-Year Study of Upward Feedback: What Managers Do with Their Results Matters." *Personnel Psychology* 52, no. 2 (1999), pp. 395–423.

77. Johnson, K., and J. Johnson. *Economic Value of Performance Change after 360 Degree Feedback.* Minneapolis, MN: Personnel Decisions International, 2001.

78. Curphy, G. J. *Role of the Supervisor Training Manual.* North Oaks, MN: Curphy Consulting Corporation, 2007.

79. Smither, J. W., M. London, R. Flautt, Y. Vargas, and I. Kucine. "Can Working with an Executive Coach Improve Multisource Feedback Ratings over Time? A Quasi-Experimental Field Study." *Personnel Psychology* 56 (1) (2003), pp. 23–44.

80. Tornow, W. W., and M. London. *Maximizing the Value of 360-Degree Feedback.* San Francisco, CA: Jossey-Bass, 1998.

81. Chhokar, J. S., F. C. Brodbeck, and R. J. House. *Culture and Leadership Across the World: The Globe Book of In-Depth Studies of 25 Societies.* Mahwah, NJ: Lawrence Erlbaum Associates, 2007.

82. Mount, M. K., M. R. Sytsma, J. F. Hazucha, and K. E. Holt. "Rater-Ratee Effects in Development Performance Ratings of Managers." *Personnel Psychology* 50, no. 1 (1997), pp. 51–70.

83. Bernardin, H. J., and R. W. Beatty. *Performance Appraisal: Assessing Human Behavior at Work.* Boston: Kent, 1984.

84. Personnel Decisions International. *PROFILOR® Certification Workshop Manual.* Minneapolis, MN: Author, 2007.

85. Hogan, R. T. *Personality and the Fate of Organizations.* Mahwah, NJ: Lawrence Erlbaum Associates, 2007.

86. Hogan, R. T., G. J. Curphy, and J. Hogan. "What Do We Know about Personality: Leadership and Effectiveness?" *American Psychologist* 49 (1994), pp. 493–504.

87. Dotlich, D. L., and P. E. Cairo. *Why CEOs Fail: The 11 Behaviors That Can Derail Your Climb to the Top and How to Manage Them.* New York: Wiley, 2001.

88. McCall, M. W., Jr., and M. M. Lombardo. "Off the Track: Why and How Successful Executives Get Derailed." Technical Report No. 21. Greensboro, NC: Center for Creative Leadership, 1983.

89. Hazucha, J. F. *PDI Indicator: Competence, Potential, and Jeopardy. What Gets Managers Ahead May Not Keep Them out of Trouble.* Minneapolis, MN: Personnel Decisions, September 1992.

90. Lombardo, M. M., M. N. Ruderman, and C. D. McCauley. "Explorations of Success and Derailment in Upper-Level Management Positions." Paper presented at meeting of the Academy of Management, New York, 1987.

91. Peterson, D. B. *A Psychometric Approach to Evaluating Individual Training Outcomes.* Paper presented at the Eighth Annual Conference of the Society of Industrial and Organizational Psychology. San Francisco, April 1993.

92. Peterson, D. B. "Skill Learning and Behavioral Change in an Individually Tailored Management Coaching and Training Program." Unpublished doctoral dissertation, University of Minnesota, 1993.

93. Van Velsor, E., and J. B. Leslie. "Why Executives Derail: Perspectives across Time and Cultures." *Academy of Management Executive* 9, no. 4 (1995), pp. 62–71.

94. Bossidy, L., and R. Charan. *Execution: The Discipline of Getting Things Done.* New York: Crown Business, 2002.

95. Charan, R., S. Drotter, and J. Noel. *The Leadership Pipeline: How to Build the Leadership-Powered Company.* San Francisco: Jossey-Bass, 2001.

96. Abrahams, M. "Those Who Can't, Don't Know It." *Harvard Business Review,* December 2005, p. 9.

97. Nilsen, D. L. *Using Self and Observers' Rating of Personality to Predict Leadership Performance.* Unpublished doctoral dissertation, University of Minnesota, 1995.

98. Miller, W. R., and S. Rollnick. *Motivational Interviewing: Preparing People to Change Addictive Behavior.* New York: Guilford Press, 1991.

99. Polivy, J., and C. P. Herman. "If at First You Don't Succeed: False Hopes of Self-Change." *American Psychologist* 57 (9) (2002), pp. 677–89.

100. Peterson, M. D., and M. D. Hicks. *Development FIRST: Strategies for Self-Development.* Minneapolis, MN: Personnel Decisions International, 1995.

101. Hazucha, J. F., S. A. Hezlett, and R. J. Schneider. "The Impact of 360-Degree Feedback on Management Skills Development." *Human Resource Management* 32 (1993), pp. 325–51.

102. McCauley, C. D., M. N. Ruderman, P. J. Ohlott, and J. E. Morrow. "Assessing the Developmental Components of Managerial Jobs." *Journal of Applied Psychology* 79, no. 4 (1994), pp. 544–60.

103. Peterson, D. B., and M. D. Hicks. *Leader as Coach: Strategies for Coaching and Developing Others.* Minneapolis, MN: Personnel Decisions International, 1996.

104. Behar, K, D. Arvidson, W. Omilusik, B. Ellsworth, and B. Morrow. *Developing Husky Oil Leaders: A Strategic Investment.* Calgary, Canada: Husky Energy, 2000.

105. Peterson, D. B. *The Science and Art of Self-Development.* Paper presented at the Arabian States Human Resource Management Society Annual Conference, Bahrain, October 2001.

106. Curphy, G. J. "Good Leadership is Hard to Find." *JobDig.* August 21–28, 2006, pp. 23–24.

107. Arthur, W., Jr., W. Bennett Jr., P. S. Edens, and S. T. Bell. "Effectiveness of Training in Organizations: A Meta-analysis of Design and Evaluation Features." *Journal of Applied Psychology* 88 (2) (2003), pp. 234–45.

108. Wenzel, L. H. "Understanding Managerial Coaching: The Role of Manager Attributes and Skills in Effective Coaching." Unpublished doctoral dissertation, Colorado State University, 2000.

109. Wasylyshyn, K. M., B. Gronsky, and J. W. Hass. "Tigers, Stripes, and Behavior Change: Survey Results of a Commissioned Coaching Program." *Consulting Psychology Journal,* 58 (2) (2006), pp. 65–81.

110. Hunter, J. E., F. L. Schmidt, and M. K. Judiesch. "Individual Differences in Output Variability as a Function of Job Complexity." *Journal of Applied Psychology* 74 (1990), pp. 28–42.

111. Curphy, G. J. *The Accelerated Coaching Program Training Manual.* North Oaks, MN: Curphy Consulting Corporation, 2003.

112. Peterson, D. B., and M. D. Hicks. *Professional Coaching: State of the Art, State of the Practice.* Minneapolis, MN: Personnel Decisions International, 1998.

113. Cashman, K., and J. Forem. *Awakening the Leader Within.* Hoboken, NJ: John Wiley & Sons, 2003.

114. Sherman, S., and A. Freas. "The Wild West of Executive Coaching." *Harvard Business Review,* November 2004, pp. 82–93.

115. Kaiser, R. B., and R. B. Kaplan. "The Deeper Work of Executive Development: Outgrowing Sensitivities." *Academy of Management Learning & Education* 5 (4) (2006), pp. 463–83.

116. Kilburg, R. R. "Trudging Toward Dodoville: Conceptual Approaches and Case Studies in Executive Coaching." *Consulting Psychology Journal* 56 (4) (2004), pp. 203–13.

117. Lowman, R. L. "Executive Coaching: The Road to Dodoville Needs Paving with More than Good Assumptions." *Consulting Psychology Journal* 57 (1) (2005), pp. 90–96.

118. Evers, W. J. G., A. Brouwers, and W. Tomic. "A Quasi-Experimental Study on Management Coaching Effectiveness." *Consulting Psychology Journal* 58 (3) (2006), pp. 174–82.

119. Peterson, D. B., and J. Millier. "The Alchemy of Coaching: You're Good, Jennifer, But You Could Be Really Good." *Consulting Psychology Journal* 57 (1) (2005), pp. 14–40.

120. Bowles, S. V., and J. J. Picano. "Dimensions of Coaching Related to Productivity and Quality of Life." *Consulting Psychology Journal* 58 (4) (2006), pp. 232–39.

121. Waldman, D. A. "Does Working with an Executive Coach Enhance the Value of Multisource Performance Feedback?" *Academy of Management Executive* 17 (3) (2003), pp. 146–48.

122. Peterson, D. B. *Individual Coaching Services: Coaching That Makes a Business Difference.* Minneapolis, MN: Personnel Decisions International, 1999.

123. Taylor, P. J., D. F. Russ-Eft, and D. W. L. Chan. "A Meta-analytic Review of Behavioral Modeling Training." *Journal of Applied Psychology* 90 (4) (2005), pp. 692–709.

124. Passmore, J. "An Integrative Model for Executive Coaching." *Consulting Psychology Journal* 59 (1) (2007), pp. 68–78.

125. Ragins, B. R., and J. L. Cotton. "Mentoring Functions and Outcomes: A Comparison of Men and Women in Formal and Informal Mentoring Relationships." *Journal of Applied Psychology* 84, no. 4 (1999), pp. 529–40.

126. Ragins, B. R., J. L. Cotton, and J. S. Miller. "Marginal Mentoring: The Effects of Types of Mentor, Quality of Relationship, and Program Design of Work and Career Attitudes." *Academy of Management Journal* 43, no. 6 (2000), pp. 1177–94.

127. Thomas, D. A. "The Truth about Mentoring Minorities: Race Matters." *Harvard Business Review,* April 2001, pp. 98–111.

128. Menttium. *Menttium 100: Cross-Company Mentoring for High Potential Women.* Minneapolis, MN: The Menttium Corporation, 2007.

129. Allen, T. D., L. T. Eby, M. L. Poteet, E. Lentz, and L. Lima. "Career Benefits Associated with Mentoring for Protégés: A Meta-analysis." *Journal of Applied Psychology* 89 (1) (2004), pp. 127–36.

130. Allen, T. D., L. T. Eby, and E. Lentz. "Mentorship Behaviors and Mentorship Quality Associated with Formal Mentoring Programs: Closing the Gap between Research and Practice." *Journal of Applied Psychology* 91 (3) (2006), pp. 567–78.

131. Allen, T. D., L. T. Eby, and E. Lentz. "The Relationship between Formal Mentoring Program Characteristics and Perceived Program Effectiveness." *Personnel Psychology* 59 (2006), pp. 125–53.

132. Eby, L. T., M. Butts, A. Lockwood, and S. A. Simon. "Protégés' Negative Mentoring Experiences: Construct Development and Nomological Validation." *Personnel Psychology* 57 (2) (2004), pp. 411–48.

133. Abrahams, M. "Making Mentoring Pay." *Harvard Business Review,* June 2006, p. 21.

134. Steinberg, A. G., and D. M. Foley. "Mentoring in the Army: From Buzzword to Practice." *Military Psychology* 11, no. 4 (1999), pp. 365–80.

135. Lall, R. "Mentoring Experiences of Retired Navy Admirals." Paper presented at Personnel Decisions International, Denver, CO, May 6, 1999.

136. De Janasz, S. C., S. E. Sullivan, and V. Whiting. "Mentor Networks and Career Success: Lessons for Turbulent Times." *Academy of Management Executive* 17 (3) (2003), pp. 78–88.

Part 6

Leadership Skills

One reason any person can improve his or her leadership effectiveness is that part of leadership involves skills, and skills can be practiced and developed. A further advantage of looking at leadership skills is that most people are less defensive about deficits in skills (which can be improved) than about suggested deficits in, say, personality. We will present a section on leadership skills following each of the three parts of the book, looking at the respective elements of our interactional framework. In each of those three skill sections we will address a number of leadership skills that are most relevant to that part of our framework. Thus, this first skill section focuses on skills particularly relevant to the leader himself or herself.

List of Part Two Leadership Skills

- Learning from Experience
- Communication
- Listening
- Assertiveness
- Guidelines for Effective Stress Management
- Building Technical Competence
- Building Effective Relationships with Superiors
- Building Effective Relationships with Peers
- Building Credibility

Basic Leadership Skills

Learning from Experience

Creating Opportunities to Get Feedback
Taking a 10 Percent Stretch
Learning from Others
Keeping a Journal
Having a Developmental Plan

Leadership practitioners can enhance the learning value of their experiences by (*a*) creating opportunities to get feedback, (*b*) taking a 10 percent stretch, (*c*) learning from others, (*d*) keeping a journal of daily leadership events, and (*e*) having a developmental plan.

Creating Opportunities to Get Feedback

 It may be difficult for leaders to get relevant feedback, particularly if they occupy powerful positions in an organization. Yet leaders often need feedback more than subordinates do. Leaders may not learn much from their leadership experiences if they get no feedback about how they are doing. Therefore, they may need to create opportunities to get feedback, especially with regard to feedback from those working for them.

First of all, leaders should not assume they have invited feedback merely by saying that they have an open-door policy. A mistake some bosses make is presuming that others perceive them as open to discussing things just because they say they are open to discussing things. How truly open a door is, clearly, is in the eye of the beholder. In that sense, the key to constructive dialogue (i.e., feedback) is not just expressing a policy but also being perceived as approachable and sincere in the offer.

Some of the most helpful information for developing your own leadership can come from asking for feedback from others about their perceptions of your behavior and its impact on your group's overall effectiveness. Leaders who take psychological tests and use periodic surveys or questionnaires will have greater access to feedback than leaders who fail to systematically solicit feedback from their followers. Unless leaders ask for feedback, they may not get it.

Taking a 10 Percent Stretch

Learning always involves stretching. Learning involves taking risks and reaching beyond one's comfort zone. This is true of a toddler's first unsteady steps, a student's first serious confrontation with divergent worlds of thought, and leadership development. The phrase *10 percent stretch* conveys the idea of voluntary but determined efforts to improve leadership skills. It is analogous to physical exercise, though in this context stretching implies extending one's behavior, not muscles, just a bit beyond the comfort zone. Examples could include making a point to converse informally with everyone in the office at least once each day, seeking an opportunity to be chair of a committee, or being quieter than usual at meetings (or more assertive, as the case may be). There is much to be gained from a commitment to such ongoing "exercise" for personal and leadership development.

Several positive outcomes are associated with leaders who regularly practice the 10 percent stretch. First, their apprehension about doing something new or different gradually decreases. Second, leaders will broaden their repertoire of leadership skills. Third, because of this increased repertoire, their effectiveness will likely increase. And finally, leaders regularly taking a 10 percent stretch will model something very valuable to others. Few things will send a better message to others about the importance of their own development than the example of how sincerely a leader takes his or her own development.

One final aspect of the 10 percent stretch is worth mentioning. One reason the phrase is so appealing is that it sounds like a measurable yet manageable change. Many people will not offer serious objection to trying a 10 percent change in some behavior, whereas they might well be resistant (and unsuccessful) if they construe a developmental goal as requiring fundamental change in their personality or interpersonal style.

Despite its nonthreatening connotation, though, an actual 10 percent change in behavior can make an enormous difference in effectiveness. In many kinds of endeavor the difference between average performers and exceptional performers is 10 percent. In baseball, for example, many players hit .275, but only the best hit over .300—a difference of about 10 percent.

Learning from Others

Leaders learn from others, first of all, by recognizing they *can* learn from others and, importantly, from *any* others. That may seem self-evident, but in fact people often limit what and whom they pay attention to, and thus what they may learn from. For example, athletes may pay a lot of attention to how coaches handle leadership situations. However, they may fail to realize they could also learn a lot by watching the director of the school play and the band conductor. Leaders should not limit their learning by narrowly defining the sorts of people they pay attention to.

Similarly, leaders also can learn by asking questions and paying attention to everyday situations. An especially important time to ask questions is when leaders are new to a group or activity and have some responsibility for it. When possible, leaders should talk to the person who previously had the position to benefit from his or her insights, experience, and assessment of the situation. In addition, observant leaders are able to extract meaningful leadership lessons from everyday situations. Something as plain and ordinary as a high school car wash or the activities at a fast-food restaurant may offer an interesting leadership lesson. Leaders can learn a lot by actively observing how others react to and handle different challenges and situations, even very common ones.

Keeping a Journal

Another way leaders can mine experiences for their richness and preserve their learning is by keeping a journal.[1] Journals are similar to diaries, but they are not just accounts of a day's events. A journal should include entries that address some aspect of leaders or leadership. Journal entries may include comments about insightful or interesting quotes, anecdotes, newspaper articles, or even humorous cartoons about leadership. They may also include reflections on personal events, such as interactions with bosses, coaches, teachers, students, employees, players, teammates, roommates, and so on. Such entries can emphasize a good (or bad) way somebody handled something, a problem in the making, the differences between people in their reactions to situations, or people in the news, a book, or a film. Leaders should also use their journals to "think on paper" about leadership readings from textbooks or formal leadership programs or to describe examples from their own experience of a concept presented in a reading.

There are at least three good reasons for keeping a journal. First, the very process of writing increases the likelihood that leaders will be able to look at an event from a different perspective or feel differently about it. Putting an experience into words can be a step toward taking a more objective look at it. Second, leaders can (and should) reread earlier entries. Earlier entries provide an interesting and valuable autobiography of a leader's evolving thinking about leadership and about particular events in his or her life. Third, journal entries provide a repository of ideas that leaders may later want to use more formally for papers, pep talks, or speeches. As seen in Highlight P2.1, good journal entries provide leaders with a wealth of examples that they may use in speeches, presentations, and so on.

Having a Developmental Plan

Leadership development almost certainly occurs in ways and on paths that are not completely anticipated or controlled. That is no reason, however, for leaders to avoid actively directing some aspects of their own development. A systematic plan outlining self-improvement goals and strategies will help leaders take advantage of opportunities they otherwise might overlook. Developing a systematic plan also will help leaders prioritize the importance of different goals so that their efforts can be put into areas with the greatest relative payoffs. Leaders who carefully choose which seminars and conferences to attend may help themselves maximize their contribution to their personal developmental goals. Leaders should look for opportunities on the job or in volunteer work for responsibilities that may further their growth. Leaders should recognize, however, that they may experience conflict—both internal and external—between doing more of what they already do well and stretching developmentally.

The following is an example of such a conflict. Suppose Sheila is an accountant who has just joined the board of a local charity. Because handling financial records is something many people do not enjoy, and because Sheila has a demonstrable knack for and interest in it, others on the board may well ask her to become the treasurer. Almost certainly Sheila would do as good a job as anyone else on the board. But suppose Sheila's personal goals include developing her public speaking skills. In such a case, doing what she does best (and what others want her to do) might stand in the way of growth in another area.

Sheila has several alternatives. She could refuse the job of treasurer because she has had her fill of accounting. Alternatively, she could accept the job of treasurer and look for yet another activity in which to develop her public speaking skills.

Unfortunately, both of these options may present their own problems. Still another alternative would be to negotiate to expand the role of treasurer to allow greater opportunity to blend the role with her own developmental goals. For example, Sheila might choose to make regular oral reports to the board instead of submitting solely written reports. Additionally, she might take on a larger share of speaking at local service clubs

Sample Journal Entries

HIGHLIGHT P2.1

I went skiing this weekend and saw the perfect example of a leader adapting her leadership style to her followers and situation. While putting on my skis, I saw a ski instructor teaching little kids to ski. She did it using the game "red light, green light." The kids loved it and seemed to be doing very well. Later that same day, as I was going to the lodge for lunch, she was teaching adults, and she did more demonstrating than talking. But when she talked she was always sure to encourage them so they did not feel intimidated when some little kid whizzed by. She would say to the adults that it's easier for children, or that smaller skis are easier. She made the children laugh and learn, and made the adults less self-conscious to help them learn too . . .

Today may not exactly be a topic on leadership, but I thought it would be interesting to discuss. I attended the football game this afternoon and could not help but notice our cheerleaders. I was just thinking of their name in general, and found them to be a good example (of leadership). Everyone gets rowdy at a football game, but without the direction of the cheerleaders there would be mayhem. They do a good job of getting the crowd organized and the adrenaline pumping (though of course the game is most important in that too!). It's just amazing to see them generate so much interest that all of the crowd gets into the cheering. We even chant their stupid-sounding cheers! You might not know any of them personally, but their enthusiasm invites you to try to be even louder than them. I must give the cheerleaders a round of applause . . .

I've been thinking about how I used to view/understand leadership, trying to find out how my present attitudes were developed. It's hard to remember past freshman year, even harder to go past high school. Overall, I think my father has been the single most important influence on my leadership development—long before I even realized it. Dad is a strong "Type A" person. He drives himself hard and demands a great deal from everyone around him, especially his family and especially his only son and oldest child. He was always pushing me to study, practice whatever sport I was involved in at the time, get ahead of everybody else in every way possible.

for the purpose of public education about the charity and her own expert view of its needs with regard to fund-raising and financial support. The point here is that leaders simply need to be deliberate in seeking opportunities to put their personal development plans into action. Leaders should exercise control over events to the extent they can; they should not let events exercise a counterproductive control over them.

A leader's first step in exercising control over his personal development is to identify what his goals actually are. The example above presumed Sheila already had identified public speaking as a skill she wanted to improve. But what if a leader is uncertain about what he or she needs to improve? As described earlier, leaders should systematically collect information from a number of different sources. One place a leader can get information about where to improve is through a review of current job performance, if that is applicable. Ideally, leaders will have had feedback sessions with their own superiors, which should help them identify areas of relative strength and weakness. Leaders should treat this feedback as a helpful perspective on their developmental needs. Leaders also should look at their interactions with peers as a source of ideas about what they might work on. Leaders should especially take notice if the same kind of problem comes up in their interactions with different individuals in separate situations. Leaders need to look at their own role in such instances as objectively as they can; there might be clues about what behavioral changes might facilitate better working relationships with others. Still another way to identify developmental objectives is to look ahead to what new skills are needed to function effectively at a higher level in the organization, or in a different role than the leader now has. Finally, leaders can use formal psychological tests and questionnaires to determine what their relative strengths and weaknesses as a leader may be.

On a concluding note, there is one activity leaders should put in their developmental plans whatever else might be included in them: a program of personal reading to broaden their perspectives on leadership. This reading can include the classics as well as contemporary fiction, biographies and autobiographies of successful leaders, essays on ethics and social responsibility, and assorted self-improvement books on various leadership and management issues. A vital part of leadership development is intellectual stimulation and reflection, and an active reading program is indispensable to that. Leaders might even want to join (or form) a discussion group that regularly meets to exchange ideas about a book everyone has read. Bass[2] defined communication effectiveness as the degree to which someone tells others something and ensures they understand what was said. In an even more general sense, **effective communication** involves the ability to transmit and receive information with a high probability that the intended message is passed from sender to receiver. Few skills are more vital to leadership. Studies show that good leaders communicate feelings and ideas, actively solicit new ideas from others, and effectively articulate arguments, advocate positions, and persuade others.[3–5] It seems likely the same can be said of good followers, though far less study has gone into that question. Moreover, the quality of a leader's communication is positively correlated with subordinate satisfaction[6] as well as with productivity and quality of services rendered.[7] Effective communication skills are also important because they provide leaders and followers with greater access to information relevant to important organizational decisions.[8]

Communication

Know What Your Purpose Is

Choose an Appropriate Context and Medium

Send Clear Signals

Actively Ensure That Others Understand the Message

A systems view of communication is depicted in Figure P2.1. Communication is best understood as a process beginning with an intention to exchange certain information with others. That intention eventually takes form in some particular expression, which may or may not adequately convey what was intended. The next stage is reception. Just as with a weak or garbled radio signal or malfunctioning antenna, what is received is not always what was sent. Reception is followed by interpretation. If a driver asks, "Do I turn here?" and a passenger answers, "Right," did the passenger mean *yes* or *turn right*? Finally, it is not enough merely to receive and interpret information; others' interpretations may or may not be consistent with what was intended at the outset. Therefore, it always helps to have a feedback loop to assess any communication's overall effectiveness.

We also can use the scheme in Figure P2.1 to think about the knowledge, behaviors, and criteria used to evaluate communication skills. According to this model, the knowledge component of communication skills concerns the intentions of the leader, knowing what medium is most effective, and knowing whether the message was heard and understood. The behavioral component of communication skills concerns the behaviors associated with communicating verbally and nonverbally. Feedback concerning whether or not the message was understood by the receiver constitutes the evaluative component of communication skills. An important aspect regarding feedback is that it is an outcome of the previous steps in the communication process. In reality, the effectiveness of the communication process depends on the successful integration of all of the steps in the communication process. Effectiveness in just one step (e.g., speaking ability) is not enough. Successful communication needs to be judged in terms of the effective operation of the whole system.

The model also suggests a number of reasons why communication breakdowns might occur. For example, communication breakdowns can occur because the purpose of the message was unclear, the leader's or follower's verbal and nonverbal behaviors were inconsistent, the message was not heard by the receiver, or because someone may have misinterpreted another's message. Most people see themselves as effective communicators, and senders and receivers of messages often seem disposed to believe communication breakdowns are the other person's fault. Communication breakdowns often lead to blaming someone else for the problem, or "finger pointing" (see Figure P2.2). One way to avoid the finger pointing associated with communication breakdowns is to think of communication as a process, not as a set of discrete individual acts (i.e., giving instructions to someone). By using the communication model, leadership practitioners can minimize the conflict typically associated with communication breakdowns.

The model in Figure P2.1 can provide leadership practitioners with many ideas about how to improve communication skills. They can do so

FIGURE P2.1
A systems view of communication.

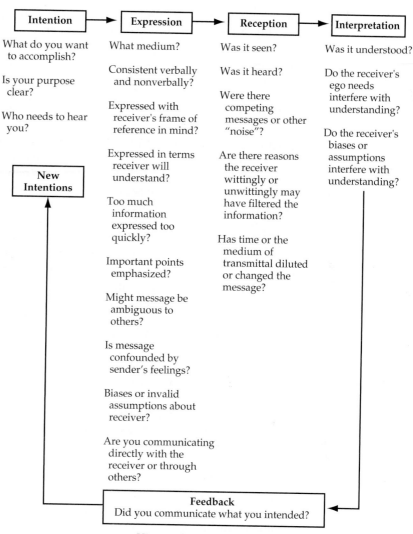

| Intention | Expression | Reception | Interpretation |

Intention

What do you want to accomplish?

Is your purpose clear?

Who needs to hear you?

Expression

What medium?

Consistent verbally and nonverbally?

Expressed with receiver's frame of reference in mind?

Expressed in terms receiver will understand?

Too much information expressed too quickly?

Important points emphasized?

Might message be ambiguous to others?

Is message confounded by sender's feelings?

Biases or invalid assumptions about receiver?

Are you communicating directly with the receiver or through others?

Reception

Was it seen?

Was it heard?

Were there competing messages or other "noise"?

Are there reasons the receiver wittingly or unwittingly may have filtered the information?

Has time or the medium of transmittal diluted or changed the message?

Interpretation

Was it understood?

Do the receiver's ego needs interfere with understanding?

Do the receiver's biases or assumptions interfere with understanding?

New Intentions

Feedback
Did you communicate what you intended?

History of prior communications
Context of relationships and common practices
Concurrent events

FIGURE P2.2 Breakdowns in communication sometimes lead to finger pointing.

Person A

"You weren't listening!"
"That isn't what I said."
"You didn't follow directions."
"That isn't what you were supposed to do."

Person B

"I only did what you told me to."
"Why didn't you say so?"
"But you didn't seem serious."

by (*a*) determining the purpose of their communication before speaking, (*b*) choosing an appropriate context and medium for the message, (*c*) sending clear signals, and (*d*) actively ensuring that others understand the message. The following is a more detailed discussion of some of the different ways in which leaders can improve their communication skills.

Know What Your Purpose Is

One will communicate more effectively with others if one is clear about what one intends to communicate. By knowing purpose, a leader or follower can better decide whether to communicate publicly or privately, orally or in writing, and so on. These decisions may seem trivial, but often the specific content of a message will be enhanced or diminished by how and where it is communicated.

Choose an Appropriate Context and Medium

There is a rule of thumb that says leaders should praise followers in public and punish them in private. It points out the importance of selecting physical and social settings that will enhance the effectiveness of any communication. If the leader has an office, for example, then how much communication with subordinates should occur in her office and how much in the followers' workplace?

Sometimes, of course, an office is the best place to talk. Even that decision, however, is not all a leader needs to consider. The arrangement of office furniture can enhance or interfere with effective communication. Informal, personal communications are enhanced when two people sit at a 90-degree angle and are relatively close to each other; more formal communication is enhanced when the follower remains standing when the leader is sitting or if the leader communicates across his desk to followers.

Additionally, a leader's communications often take place in a whole organizational context involving broader existing practices, policies, and procedures. Leaders need to take care that their words and deeds do not inadvertently undercut or contradict such broader organizational communications, including their own bosses'. Organizational factors also help determine whether any particular communication is most appropriately expressed orally or in writing. Oral communication is the most immediate, the most personal, the most dynamic, and often the most impactive; it is ideal when communication needs to be two-way or when the personalized aspect is especially important. At the other extreme, a more permanent modality is probably most appropriate when the leader needs a record of the communication or when something needs to be expressed in a particular way to different people, at different times, in different settings.

Send Clear Signals

Leaders and followers can enhance the clarity of their communications in several ways. First, it is helpful to be mindful of others' level of expertise, values, experiences, and expectations and how these characteristics affect their **frames of reference.** For example, the leader may brief followers on a new organizational policy, and they may come up with different interpretations of this policy based on different values and expectations. By being sensitive to followers' frames of reference and modifying messages accordingly, leaders can minimize communication breakdowns. Another way to clarify messages is to create a common frame of reference for followers before communicating a message. For example, consider the following passage:

> With hocked gems financing him, our hero bravely defied all scornful laughter that tried to prevent his scheme. "Your eyes deceive," he had said. "An egg, not a table, correctly typifies this unexplored planet." Now, three sisters sought sturdy proof.

> Forging along, sometimes through calm vastness, yet more often over turbulent peaks and valleys, days became weeks as many doubters spread fearful rumors about the edge. At last, welcome winged creatures appeared signifying momentous success.[9]

Many are slow to recognize that the passage is about Christopher Columbus. Once the correct frame of reference is known, however, the previously confusing elements become sensible. Followers more readily understand new or ambiguous material when leaders paint a common frame of reference prior to introducing new material.

Another way to send clear signals is to use familiar terms, jargon, and concepts. This can serve to clarify and abbreviate messages when receivers are familiar with the terms. However, messages containing jargon can also be confusing to receivers unfamiliar with those terms. For example, a freshman cadet at the United States Air Force Academy might say to another, "I hope we get an ONP this weekend, because after three GRs, a PCE, and a SAMI, I'll need it." Because the second cadet understands this organizational jargon, he or she would have no difficulty understanding what was said. However, a person unfamiliar with the Air Force Academy would not have the slightest idea what this conversation meant. Leaders should make sure followers understand any jargon they use—especially if the followers are relatively inexperienced. (In case you were wondering, the cadet said, "I hope we get a pass to go downtown this weekend, because after three academic tests, a military test, and a room inspection, I'll need it.")

Two other ways to improve the clarity of messages are to use unambiguous, concrete terms and to send congruent verbal and nonverbal signals. For example, a leader who tells a follower, "Your monthly sales were down 22 percent last month" will more effectively communicate her concerns and cause less follower defensiveness than a leader who states, "Your performance has been poor." Thus, the more specific the message, the less likely receivers will be confused over what it means. In addition, leaders will be more effective communicators if their nonverbal signals match the content of the message. Followers, like everyone, can get confused, and tend to believe nonverbal signals when leaders send mixed verbal and nonverbal messages.[10] Similarly, followers may send mixed messages to leaders; communication goes both ways.

One particularly destructive form of incongruent verbal and nonverbal signals is sarcasm. It is not the anger of the message per se but rather the implicit message conveyed by dishonest words that drives a wedge in the trust between leaders and followers. It is not a wise idea for leaders to always share their transitory feelings with subordinates, but if the leader is going to share his or her feelings, it is important to do so in a congruent manner. Similarly, it can be just as unwise for followers to share transitory feelings with leaders; but if it's done, it's important for verbal and nonverbal behaviors to be congruent.

Actively Ensure That Others Understand the Message

Leaders and followers can ensure that others understand their messages by practicing two-way communication and by paying attention to the others' emotional responses. Effective leaders and followers tend to actively engage in two-way communication (though this usually is more under the control of the leader than the follower). They can do so in many ways: by seeking feedback, by mingling in each other's work areas, and, in the case of leaders, by being sincere about having an open-door policy.[11]

Although such steps appear to be straightforward, leaders typically believe they utilize two-way communication more frequently than their followers perceive them to be using it.[12] Leaders can get clues about the clarity of their messages by paying attention to the nonverbal signals sent by their followers. When followers' verbal and nonverbal messages seem to be incongruent, it may be because the message sent to them was unclear. For example, followers may look confused when they verbally acknowledge that they understand a particular task. In this case, leaders may find it useful to address the mixed signals directly in order to clear up such confusion.

Listening

Demonstrate Nonverbally That You Are Listening
Actively Interpret the Sender's Message
Attend to the Sender's Nonverbal Behavior
Avoid Becoming Defensive

Our systems view of communication emphasized that effectiveness depends upon both *transmitting and receiving* information. It may seem inconsistent, therefore, to distinguish the topic of listening from the more general topic of communication. Isn't listening *part* of communication, you may ask? Of course, and we do not intend to imply it's not. Our separate treatment of listening is simply for emphasis. It seems to us most discussions of communication emphasize the transmission side and neglect the receiving side. Good leaders and followers recognize the value of two-way communication. Listening to others is just as important as expressing oneself clearly to them. People in leadership roles are only as good as the information they have, and much of their information comes from watching and listening to what goes on around them.

At first, it may seem strange to describe listening as a skill. Listening may seem like an automatic response to things being said, not something one practices to improve, like free throws. However, the best listeners are **active listeners,** not passive listeners.[13] In passive listening, someone may be speaking but the receiver is not focused on understanding the speaker. Instead, the receiver may be thinking about the next thing he will say or how bored he is in listening to the speaker. In either case, the receiver is not paying attention to what the sender is saying. To truly get the fullest meaning out of what someone else says, one needs to practice active listening. Individuals who are listening actively exhibit a certain pattern of nonverbal behaviors, do not disrupt the sender's message, try to put the sender's message into their own words, and scan the sender for various nonverbal signals. Knowing what nonverbal signals to send and correctly interpreting the sender's nonverbal signals are the knowledge component of listening skills. One's nonverbal signals are the behavioral component, and how well one can paraphrase a sender's message makes up the evaluative component of listening skills.

In addition to helping one understand others better, active listening is a way to visibly demonstrate that one respects others. People, particularly those with high self-monitoring scores, can often sense when others are not truly paying attention to what they are saying. Followers will quickly decide it is not worth their time to give their leader information if they perceive they are not being listened to. Leaders may do the same. To avoid turning off others, leaders and followers can improve their active listening skills in a number of ways. Some of these tips include learning to (*a*) model nonverbal signals associated with active listening, (*b*) actively interpret the sender's message, (*c*) be aware of the sender's nonverbal behaviors, and (*d*) avoid becoming defensive. The following is a more detailed discussion of these four ways to improve active listening skills.

Demonstrate Nonverbally That You Are Listening

Make sure your nonverbal behaviors show that you have turned your attention entirely to the speaker. Many people mistakenly assume that listening is a one-way process. Although it seems plausible to think of information flowing only from the sender to the receiver, the essence of active listening is to see all communication, even listening, as a two-way process. Listeners show they are paying attention to the speaker with their own body movements. They put aside, both mentally and physically, other work they may have been engaged in. Individuals who are actively listening establish eye contact with the speaker, and they do not doodle, shoot rubber bands, or look away at other things. They show they are genuinely interested in what the speaker has to say.

Actively Interpret the Sender's Message

The essence of active listening is trying to understand what the sender truly means. It is not enough merely to be (even if you could) a perfect human tape recorder. One must look for the meaning behind someone else's words. In the first place, this means one needs to keep one's mind open to the sender's ideas. This, in turn, implies not interrupting the speaker and not planning what to say while the speaker is delivering the message. In addition, good listeners withhold judgment about the sender's ideas until they have heard the entire message. This way, they avoid sending the message that their mind is made up and avoid jumping to conclusions about what the sender is going to say. Another reason to avoid sending a closed-minded message is that it may lead others to *not* bring up things one definitely needs to hear.

Another valuable way to actively interpret what the sender is saying is to **paraphrase** the sender's message. By putting the speaker's thoughts into their own words, leaders can better ensure that they fully understand what their followers are saying, and vice versa. The value of paraphrasing even a simple idea is apparent in the following dialogue:

Sarah: "Jim should never have become a teacher."

Fred: "You mean he doesn't like working with kids? Do you think he's too impatient?"

Sarah: "No, neither of those things. I just think his tastes are so expensive he's frustrated with a teacher's salary."

In this example, Fred indicated what he thought Sarah meant, which prompted her to clarify her meaning. If he had merely said, "I know what you mean," Fred and Sarah mistakenly would have concluded they agreed when their ideas were really far apart. Paraphrasing also actively communicates your interest in what the other person is saying. Highlight P2.2 offers various "communication leads" that may help in paraphrasing others' messages to improve your listening skills.

Attend to the Sender's Nonverbal Behavior

People should use all the tools at their disposal to understand what someone else is saying. This includes paraphrasing senders' messages, and being astute at picking up on senders' nonverbal signals. Much of the social meaning in messages is conveyed nonverbally, and when verbal and nonverbal signals conflict, people often tend to trust the nonverbal

Communication Leads for Paraphrasing and Assuring Mutual Understanding

HIGHLIGHT P2.2

From your point of view . . .

It seems you . . .

As you see it . . .

You think . . .

What I hear you saying is . . .

Do you mean . . . ?

I'm not sure I understand what you mean; is it . . . ?

I get the impression . . .

You appear to be feeling . . .

Correct me if I'm wrong, but . . .

signals. Thus, no one can be an effective listener without paying attention to nonverbal signals. This requires listening to more than just the speaker's words themselves; it requires listening for feelings expressed via the speaker's loudness, tone of voice, and pace of speech as well as watching the speaker's facial expressions, posture, gestures, and so on. These behaviors convey a wealth of information that is immensely richer in meaning than the purely verbal content of a message, just as it is richer to watch actors in a stage play rather than merely read their script.[14] Although there may not be any simple codebook of nonverbal cues with which one can decipher what a sender "really" feels, listeners should explore what a sender is trying to say whenever they sense mixed signals between the sender's verbal and nonverbal behaviors.

Avoid Becoming Defensive

Defensive behavior is most likely to occur when someone feels threatened.[15] Although it may seem natural to become defensive when criticized, defensiveness lessens a person's ability to constructively make use of the information. Acting defensively may also decrease followers' subsequent willingness to pass additional unpleasant information on to the leader or other followers, or even the leader's willingness to give feedback to followers. Defensiveness on the part of the leader can also hurt the entire team or organization, as it includes a tendency to place blame, categorize others as morally good or bad, and generally question others' motives. Such behaviors on a leader's part hardly build a positive work or team climate.

Leaders can reduce their defensiveness when listening to complaints by trying to put themselves in the other person's shoes. Leaders have an advantage if they can empathize with how they and their policies are seen by others; they can better change their behaviors and policies if they know how others perceive them. Leaders need to avoid the temptation to explain how the other person is wrong and should instead just try to understand how he perceives things. A useful warning sign that a leader may be behaving defensively (or perhaps closed-mindedly) is if he begins a conversation saying, "Yes, but . . . "

Assertiveness

Use "I" Statements

Speak Up for What You Need

Learn to Say No

Monitor Your Inner Dialogue

Be Persistent

What is **assertive behavior,** and what are assertiveness skills? Basically, individuals exhibiting assertive behavior are able to stand up for their own rights (or their group's rights) in a way that also recognizes the concurrent right of others to do the same (see Highlight P2.3). Like the skills already discussed, assertiveness skills also have knowledge, behavioral, and evaluative components. The behavioral component of assertiveness skills was mentioned already—it involves standing up for one's own or the group's rights in a constructive, nonhostile way. The knowledge component of assertiveness skills concerns knowing where and when not to behave assertively. People who are overly assertive may be perceived as aggressive and often may "win the battle but lose the war." Finally, the evaluative component comes into play when individuals are successful (or unsuccessful) in standing up for their own or their group's rights and continually working in an effective manner with others.

Perhaps the best way to understand assertiveness is to distinguish it from two other styles people have for dealing with conflict: acquiescence (nonassertiveness) and aggression.[16] **Acquiescence** is avoiding interpersonal conflict entirely either by giving up and giving in or by expressing one's needs in an apologetic, self-effacing way. Acquiescence is not synonymous with politeness or helpfulness, though it is sometimes rationalized as such. People who are acquiescent, or nonassertive, back down easily when challenged. By not speaking up for themselves, they abdicate power to others and, in the process, get trampled on. Besides the practical outcome of not attaining one's goals, an acquiescent style typically leads to many negative feelings such as guilt, resentment, and self-blame, as well as a low self-image. Sometimes people justify their nonassertiveness to themselves with the idea that acquiescing to others is being polite or helpful, but this often is just a rationalization.

Aggression, on the other hand, is an effort to attain objectives by attacking or hurting others. Aggressive people trample on others, and their aggressiveness can take such direct forms as threats, verbal attacks, physical intimidation, emotional outbursts, explosiveness, bullying, and hostility—and such indirect forms as nagging, passive-aggressive uncooperativeness, guilt arousal, and other behaviors that undermine an adversary's autonomy. It is important to understand that aggressiveness is not just an emotionally strong form of assertiveness. Aggressiveness tends to be reactive, and it tends to spring from feelings of vulnerability and a lack of self-confidence. Aggressive people inwardly doubt their ability to resolve issues constructively through the give-and-take of direct confrontation between mutually respecting equals. Aggressiveness is a form of interpersonal manipulation in which one tries to put oneself in a "top dog" role and others in a "bottom dog" role.[17] Additionally, aggressive people have difficulty expressing positive feelings.

Assertiveness is different from both acquiescence and aggression; it is not merely a compromise between them or a midpoint on a continuum. Assertiveness involves direct and frank statements of one's own goals and feelings, and a willingness to address the interests of others in the spirit of mutual problem solving and a belief that openness is preferable to secretiveness and hidden agendas. Assertiveness is the behavioral opposite of both acquiescence and aggression, as depicted in Figure P2.3. The qualitative differences between these three styles are like the differences between fleeing (acquiescence), fighting (aggression), and problem solving (assertiveness).

It may seem axiomatic that leaders need to behave assertively with subordinates. Sometimes, however, leaders also need to be assertive with their own bosses. Followers often need to be assertive with other followers and even with their leaders sometimes. For example, middle-level supervisors need to communicate performance expectations clearly and directly to subordinates, and they need to be strong advocates for their subordinates'

Assertiveness Questionnaire

HIGHLIGHT P2.3

Do you let someone know when you think he or she is being unfair to you?

Can you criticize someone else's ideas openly?

Are you able to speak up in a meeting?

Can you ask others for small favors or help?

Is it easy for you to compliment others?

Can you tell someone else you don't like what he or she is doing?

When you are complimented, do you really accept the compliment without inwardly discounting it in your own mind?

Can you look others in the eye when you talk to them?

If you could answer most of these questions affirmatively for most situations, then you do behave assertively.

Source: Adapted from R. E. Alberti and M. L. Emmons, *Your Perfect Right.* San Luis Obispo, CA: Impact, 1974.

interests with senior supervisors. Likewise, leaders sometimes need to give their own superiors bad news, and it is best to do so directly rather than hesitantly and guardedly. Followers may sometimes need to be assertive with a peer whose poor work habits are adversely impacting the work group. In addition, leaders sometimes need to be assertive with representatives of other power-holding or special-interest groups. For example, the leader of a community group seeking a new elementary school in a residential area may need to take a very assertive stand with local school board officials.

It is important to note that sometimes the hardest people to be assertive with are friends, family, and peers. Leaders who fail to be assertive with friends and peers run the risk of becoming victims of the Abilene paradox (see Highlight P2.4).

The **Abilene paradox**[18] occurs when someone suggests that the group engage in a particular activity or course of action, and no one in the group really wants to do the activity (including the person who made the suggestion). However, because of the false belief that everyone else in the group wants to do the activity, no one behaves assertively and voices an honest opinion about it. Only after the activity is over does anyone voice an opinion (and it is usually negative). For example, someone in your group of friends may suggest that the group go to a particular movie on a Friday night. No one in the group really wants to go, yet because of the false belief everyone else is interested, no one points out the movie is not supposed to be very good and the group should do something else instead. If group members' true opinions surface only *after* the movie, then the group has fallen victim to the Abilene paradox. Leaders can avoid the Abilene paradox by being assertive when suggestions about group decisions and activities are first made.

There are several things everyone can do to help themselves behave more assertively. These things include (*a*) using "I" statements, (*b*) speaking up for what you need, (*c*) learning to say no, (*d*) monitoring your inner dialogue, and (*e*) being persistent. The following is a more detailed discussion of these assertiveness tips.

FIGURE P2.3

Relationships between assertiveness, acquiescence, and aggression.

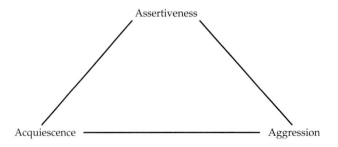

The Abilene Paradox

HIGHLIGHT P2.4

That July afternoon in Coleman, Texas (population 5,607), was particularly hot—104 degrees according to the Rexall's thermometer. In addition, the wind was blowing fine-grained West Texas topsoil through the house. But the afternoon was still tolerable—even potentially enjoyable. A fan was stirring the air on the back porch; there was cold lemonade; and finally, there was entertainment. Dominoes. Perfect for the conditions. The game requires little more physical exertion than an occasional mumbled comment, "Shuffle 'em," and an unhurried movement of the arm to place the tiles in their appropriate positions on the table. All in all, it had the makings of an agreeable Sunday afternoon in Coleman. That is, until my father-in-law suddenly said, "Let's get in the car and go to Abilene and have dinner at the cafeteria."

I thought, "What, go to Abilene? Fifty-three miles? In this dust storm and heat? And in an unair-conditioned 1958 Buick?"

But my wife chimed in with, "Sounds like a great idea. I'd like to go. How about you, Jerry?" Since my own preferences were obviously out of step with the rest, I replied, "Sounds good to me," and added, "I just hope your mother wants to go."

"Of course I want to go," said my mother-in-law. "I haven't been to Abilene in a long time."

So into the car and off to Abilene we went. My predictions were fulfilled. The heat was brutal. Perspiration had cemented a fine layer of dust to our skin by the time we arrived. The cafeteria's food could serve as a first-rate prop in an antacid commercial.

Some four hours and 106 miles later, we returned to Coleman, hot and exhausted. We silently sat in front of the fan for a long time. Then, to be sociable and to break the silence, I dishonestly said, "It was a great trip, wasn't it?"

No one spoke.

Finally, my mother-in-law said, with some irritation, "Well, to tell the truth, I really didn't enjoy it much and would rather have stayed here. I just went along because the three of you were so enthusiastic about going. I wouldn't have gone if you all hadn't pressured me into it."

I couldn't believe it. "What do you mean 'you all'?" I said. "Don't put me in the 'you all' group. I was delighted to be doing what we were doing. I didn't want to go. I only went to satisfy the rest of you. You're the culprits."

My wife looked shocked. "Don't call me a culprit. You and Daddy and Mama were the ones who wanted to go. I just went along to keep you happy. I would have had to be crazy to want to go out in heat like that."

Her father entered the conversation with one word. "Shee-it." He then expanded on what was already absolutely clear: "Listen, I never wanted to go to Abilene. I just thought you might be bored. You visit so seldom I wanted to be sure you enjoyed it. I would have preferred to play another game of dominoes and eat the leftovers in the icebox."

After the outburst of recrimination, we all sat back in silence. Here we were, four reasonably sensible people who—of our own volition—had just taken a 106-mile trip across a godforsaken desert in furnace-like heat and a dust storm to eat unpalatable food at a hole-in-the-wall cafeteria in Abilene, when none of us had really wanted to go. To be concise, we'd done just the opposite of what we wanted to do. The whole situation simply didn't make sense.

At least it didn't make sense at the time. But since that day in Coleman, I have observed, consulted with, and been a part of more than one organization that has been caught in the same situation. As a result, the organizations have either taken side trips or, occasionally, terminal journeys to Abilene, when Dallas or Houston or Tokyo was where they really wanted to go. And for most of those organizations, the negative consequences of such trips, measured in terms of both human misery and economic loss, have been much greater than for our little Abilene group.

I now call the tendency for groups to embark on excursions that no group member wants "the Abilene paradox." Stated simply, when organizations
continued

Continued

blunder into the Abilene paradox, they take actions in contradiction to what they really want to do and therefore defeat the very purpose they are trying to achieve. Business theorists typically believe that managing conflict is one of the greatest challenges faced by an organization, but a corollary of the Abilene paradox states that the inability to manage agreement may be the major source of organization dysfunction.

Source: Jerry B. Harvey, "The Abilene Paradox: The Management of Agreement." *Organizational Dynamics,* Summer 1974. Copyright 1974, Reprinted with permission from Elsevier.

Use "I" Statements

Assertive people take responsibility for what they say. They are clear in their own minds and with others about what they believe and what they want. One of the easiest ways to do this is to use first-person pronouns when you speak. Highlight P2.5 provides examples of how to be more assertive by using first-person pronouns.

Speak Up for What You Need

No one has all of the skills, knowledge, time, or resources needed to do all of the tasks assigned to their work group. Virtually everyone will need to ask superiors, peers, or subordinates for help at some time. Both effective leaders and effective followers ask for help from others when they need it. Highlight P2.5 also provides guidelines when making requests for help.

Learn to Say No

No one can be all things to all people, but it takes assertiveness to say no to others. Leaders, for example, may need to say no to their own superiors at times to stand up for their subordinates' or organization's rights and to keep from spreading themselves too thin and detracting from other priorities. Additionally, people who cannot (i.e., who *do not*) say no often build up a reservoir of negative emotions, such as those associated with the feeling of being taken advantage of. Tips for assertively refusing to do something also can be found in Highlight P2.5.

Monitor Your Inner Dialogue

Most of us talk to ourselves, though not out loud. Such self-talk is natural and common, though not everyone is aware of how much it occurs or how powerful an influence on behavior it can be. Assertive people have self-talk that is positive and affirming. Nonassertive people have self-talk that is negative, doubtful, and questioning. Learning to say no is a good example of the role self-talk plays in assertiveness. Suppose that someone was asked to serve on a volunteer committee he simply does not have time for and that he *wants* to say no. In order to behave assertively, the person would need to talk to himself positively. He would need to

Tips for Being Assertive

HIGHLIGHT P2.5

Examples of Good and Bad "I" Statements

Bad: Some people may not like having to maintain those new forms.

Good: I don't think these new forms are any good. I don't think they're worth the effort.

Bad: Maybe that candidate doesn't have all the qualifications we're looking for.

Good: I think his academic record looks fine, but we agreed only to consider candidates with at least five years' experience. I think we should keep looking.

Tips for Speaking up for What You Need

Do not apologize too much or justify yourself for needing help or assistance (e.g., "I just hate to ask you, and I normally wouldn't need to, but . . . ").

At the same time, giving a brief reason for your request often helps.

Be direct. Do not beat around the bush, hinting at what you need and hoping others get the message.

Do not play on someone's friendship.

Do not take a refusal personally.

Tips for Saying No

Keep your reply short and polite. Avoid a long, rambling justification.

Do not invent excuses.

Do not go overboard in apologizing because you cannot do it.

Be up-front about your limitations and about options you could support.

Ask for time to consider it if you need to.

Source: Adapted from K. Back and K. Back, *Assertiveness at Work.* New York: McGraw-Hill, 1982.

---

ensure that he is not defeated by his own self-talk. It would hardly help the person's resolve, for example, to have an inner dialogue that says, "They'll think I'm selfish if I don't say yes," or "If they can make time for this committee, I should be able to make time for it, too." In learning to behave more assertively, therefore, it is necessary for leaders to become more aware of their own counterproductive self-talk, confront it, and change it.

Be Persistent

Assertive individuals stick to their guns without becoming irritated, angry, or loud. They persistently seek their objectives, even in the face of another person's excuses or objections. Exchanging merchandise can provide a good occasion for assertive persistence. Suppose someone had purchased a shirt at a department store, had worn it once, and then noticed the seam was poorly sewn. A person acting assertively might have an exchange much like that found in Highlight P2.6. An assertive person is similarly persistent in standing up for his own or his group's rights.

Example Exchange between a Buyer and a Clerk

HIGHLIGHT P2.6

Buyer: "I bought this shirt last week, and it's poorly made."

Clerk: "It looks like you've worn it. We don't exchange garments that already have been worn."

Buyer: "I understand that is your policy, but it's not that I don't like the shirt. It is obviously defective. I didn't know it had these defects when I wore it."

Clerk: "Maybe this seam came loose because of the way you wore it."

Buyer: "I didn't do anything unusual. It is defective. I want it exchanged."

Clerk: "I'm sorry, but you should have returned it earlier. We can't take it back now."

Buyer: "I understand your point, but I didn't get what I paid for. You need to return my money or give me a new shirt."

Clerk: "It's beyond my authority to do that. I don't make the policies. I just have to follow them."

Buyer: "I understand you don't think you have the authority to change the policy. But your boss does. Please tell her I'd like to see her right now."

Guidelines for Effective Stress Management

> Monitor Your Own and Your Followers' Stress Levels
> Identify What Is Causing the Stress
> Practice a Healthy Lifestyle
> Learn How to Relax
> Develop Supportive Relationships
> Keep Things in Perspective
> The A-B-C Model

People use the term *stress* in a number of different ways. Sometimes people use the term to describe particular sorts of events or *environmental conditions.* For example, fans might speculate that a professional football coach's heart attack was caused by the *pressures* of his profession. Other examples might include receiving a failing grade on a physics exam, or arriving noticeably late to an important meeting, or playing a sudden-death overtime in hockey. We would acknowledge, for example, that walking in late to a meeting could be very embarrassing (i.e., stressful). Likewise for working at the service counter of a major department store on the day after Christmas; it's a *stressful job.* In each of these instances, stress refers to *characteristics of the environment.* But people also use the term in a quite different way. Sometimes it refers to the *effects* of those environments. The phrase "I'm feeling a lot of stress" might refer to various *symptoms* a person is experiencing, such as muscular tension or difficulty concentrating.

Before we proceed further, therefore, it will be useful to agree upon some conventions of terminology.

We will define stress as the process by which we perceive and respond to situations that challenge or threaten us. These responses usually include increased levels of emotional arousal and changes in physiological symptoms, such as increases in perspiration and heart rates, cholesterol levels, or blood pressure. Stress often occurs in situations that are overly complex, demanding, or unclear. Stressors are those specific characteristics in individuals, tasks, organizations, or the environment that pose some degree of threat or challenge to people (see Highlight P2.7). Although all the factors in Highlight P2.7 probably have an adverse impact on people, the degree of stress associated with each of them depends on one's overall level of stress tolerance and previous experience with the stressor in question.[19] Similarly, it is important to realize that stress is in the eye of the beholder— what one person may see as challenging and potentially rewarding, another may see as threatening and distressful.[20,21]

Who do you think typically experiences greater stress—leaders or followers? In one sense, the answer is the same as that for much psychological research: It depends. The role of leader certainly can be quite stressful. Leaders face at least one major stressful event at least once a month.[22] Followers' stress levels, on the other hand, often depend on their leaders. Leaders can help followers cope with stress or, alternatively, actually increase their followers' stress levels. Many leaders recognize when followers are under a lot of stress and will give them time off, try to reduce their workload, or take other actions to help followers cope. On the other hand, about two out of three workers say their bosses play a bigger part in creating their stress than any other personal, organizational, or environmental factor.[23,24] Others have reported that working for a tyrannical boss was the most frequently cited source of stress among workers. It is clear that leaders play a substantial role in how stressful their followers' work experience is, for good or ill.[25]

Stress can either facilitate or inhibit performance, depending on the situation. Too much stress can take a toll on individuals and organizations that includes decreased health and emotional well-being, reduced job performance, and decreased organizational effectiveness (see Highlight P2.8 for an example of how too much stress impaired one person's performance).

In order to understand the effects of stress, an analogy might be helpful. Kites need an optimal amount of wind to fly; they will not fly on windless days, and the string may break on a day that is too windy. You can think of stress as like the wind for a kite: There is a certain level that is optimal, neither too little nor too much. Another analogy is your car. Just as an automobile engine operates optimally within a certain range of revolutions per minute (RPM), most people function best at certain levels of stress. A certain amount of stress or arousal is helpful in increasing motivation and performance, but too much stress can be counterproductive. For example, it is common and probably helpful to feel a little anxiety before giving a speech, but being too nervous can destroy one's effectiveness.

Stress Symptoms

HIGHLIGHT P2.7

Are you behaving "unlike" yourself?

Has your mood become negative, hostile, or depressed?

Do you have difficulty sleeping?

Are you defensive or touchy?

Are your relationships suffering?

Have you made more mistakes or bad decisions lately?

Have you lost interest in normally enjoyable activities?

Are you using alcohol or other drugs?

Do you seem to have little energy?

Do you worry a lot?

Are you nervous much of the time?

Have you been undereating or overeating?

Have you had an increase in headaches or back pains?

This checklist can also be used to help determine the level of stress in followers.

The optimal level of stress depends on a number of factors. One is the level of physical activity actually demanded by the task. Another is the perceived difficulty of the task. Performance often suffers when difficult tasks are performed under stressful situations. For example, think how one's performance might differ when learning to first drive a car with an instructor who is quiet and reserved rather than one who yells a lot. Chances are performance will be much better with the first instructor than with the second.

It is important to note that task difficulty is generally a function of experience; the more experience one has with a task, the less difficult it becomes. Thus, the more driving experience one has, the easier the task becomes. Moreover, not only do people cope with stress more readily when performing easier tasks, people often need higher levels of stress for performing them optimally. One underlying purpose behind any type of practice, be it football, marching band, soccer, or drama, is to reduce task difficulty and help members or players to perform at an even higher level when faced with the stress of key performances and games.

Although stress can have positive effects, research has focused on the negative implications of too much stress on health and work. In terms of health, stress has been linked to heart disease,[26] immune system deficiencies[27] and the growth rates of tumors.[28] In terms of work behaviors, various studies have reported that work-related stress has caused a dramatic increase in drug and alcohol use in the workplace[29,30] and that stress was positively related to absenteeism, intentions to quit, and turnover.[31] There were estimates even back in the 1980s that the economic impact of stress to companies in the United States ranged between $70 billion and $150 billion annually—in 1980 dollars, many times that today.[32,33] Stress can also affect the decision-making process. Although leaders need to act decisively in stressful situations (i.e., crises), they may not make good decisions under stress.[34–36] Some have suggested that people make poor decisions when under stress because they revert to their intuition rather than think rationally about problems.[37,38]

As we have noted, too much stress can take a toll on individuals and their organizations. For individuals, the toll can be in terms of their health, mental and emotional well-being, job performance, or interpersonal relationships. For organizations, the toll includes decreased productivity and increased employee absenteeism, turnover, and medical costs. It stands to reason, then, that leaders in any activity should know something about stress. Leaders should understand the nature of stress because the leadership role itself can be stressful and because leaders' stress can impair the performance and well-being of followers. To prevent stress from becoming so excessive that it takes a toll in some important dimension of your own or your followers' lives, the following guidelines for effective stress management are provided.

Stress on a TV Game Show

HIGHLIGHT P2.8

The television game show *Wheel of Fortune* pits contestants against each other in trying to identify common sayings. By spinning a wheel, contestants determine varying dollar amounts to be added to their potential winnings.

The game is similar to the game of "Hangman" you may have played as a child. It begins with spaces indicating the number of words in a saying and the number of letters in each word. One player spins the wheel, which determines prize money, and then guesses a letter. If the letter appears somewhere in the saying, then the player spins the wheel again, guesses another letter, and so on. The letters are "filled in" as they are correctly identified. A player may try to guess the saying after naming a correct letter.

If a player names a letter which does not appear in the saying, then that prize money is not added to the contestant's potential winnings and play moves on to another contestant.

One day a contestant was playing for over $50,000 to solve the puzzle below. Perhaps because of the stress of being on television and playing for so much money, the contestant could not accurately name a letter for one of the four remaining spaces. Most people, not experiencing such stress, easily solve the problem. Can you? For the answer, see the bottom of the box.

```
T  H  E     T  H  R  I  __  __  __
O  F     __  I  __  T  O  R  Y
      A  N  D     T  H  E
   A  G  O  N  Y     O  F
      D  E  F  E  A  T
```

Answer: The Thrill of Victory and the Agony of Defeat.

Monitor Your Own and Your Followers' Stress Levels

One of the most important steps in managing stress is to *monitor your own and your followers' stress levels.* Although this seems straightforward, a seemingly paradoxical fact about stress is that it often takes a toll without one's conscious awareness. A person experiencing excessive stress might manifest various symptoms apparent to everyone but him or her. For that reason, it is useful to develop the habit of regularly attending to some of the warning signs that your stress level may be getting too high. Some of the warning signs of stress are in Highlight P2.7. If you answered yes to any of these questions, then your own or your followers' stress levels may be getting too high and it would probably be a good idea to put some of the following stress management strategies into practice right away. On the other hand, answering some of the questions affirmatively does not necessarily mean your stress level is too high. There could, for example, be some other physiological explanation.

Identify What Is Causing the Stress

Monitoring your stress will reduce the chances that it will build to an unhealthy level before you take action, but monitoring is not enough. Leaders also need to *identify what is causing the stress.* It may seem at first that the causes of stress always will be obvious, but that is not true. Sometimes the problems are clear enough even if the solutions are not (e.g., family finances or working in a job with a high workload and lots of deadlines). At other times, however, it may be difficult to identify the root problem. For example, a coach may attribute his anger to the losing record of his team, not recognizing that a bigger cause of his emotional distress may be the problems he is having at home with his teenage son. A worker may feel frustrated because her boss overloads her with work, not realizing that her own unassertiveness keeps her from expressing her feelings to her boss. Problem solving can be applied constructively to managing stress, but only if the problem is identified properly in the first place. Once the problem is identified, then a plan for minimizing stress or the effects of the stressor can be developed.

Practice a Healthy Lifestyle

Practicing a healthy lifestyle is one of the best ways to minimize stress. There are no substitutes for balanced nutrition, regular exercise, adequate sleep, abstention from tobacco products, and drinking only moderate amounts of alcohol (if at all) as keys to a healthy life. A long-term study of the lifestyles of nearly 7,000 adults confirmed these as independent factors contributing to wellness and the absence of stress symptoms.[39] Insufficient sleep saps energy, interferes with alertness and judgment, increases irritability, and lowers resistance to illness. Exercise, besides being a valuable part of any long-term health strategy, is also an excellent way to reduce tension.

Learn How to Relax

Believe it or not, some people just do not know how to relax. Although physical exercise is a good relaxation technique, sometimes you will need to relax but not have an opportunity to get a workout. Having practiced other relaxation techniques will come in handy when the situation prevents strenuous exercise. Also, of course, some people simply prefer alternative relaxation techniques to exercise. *Deep-breathing techniques, progressive muscle relaxation, and thinking of calming words and images* can be powerful on-the-spot calming techniques to reduce arousal level. They are applicable in stressful situations ranging from job interviews to sports. The effectiveness of these techniques is somewhat a matter of personal preference, and no single one is best for all purposes or all people.

Develop Supportive Relationships

Another powerful antidote to stress is having a *network of close and supportive relationships* with others.[40] People who have close ties to others through marriage, church membership, or other groups tend to be healthier than those with weaker social ties. Also, social supports of various kinds (e.g., the supportiveness of one's spouse, co-workers, or boss) can buffer the impact of job stress,[41,42] and unit cohesion is believed to be a critical element of soldiers' ability to withstand even the extreme physical and psychological stresses of combat.[43] Leaders can play a constructive role in developing mutual supportiveness and cohesiveness among subordinates, and their own open and frank communication with subordinates is especially important when a situation is ambiguous as well as stressful.

Keep Things in Perspective

As we noted earlier, the stressfulness of any event depends partly on the way one interprets it, not just on the event itself. For example, a poor grade on an examination may be more stressful for one student than for another, just as a rebuke from a boss may be more stressful for one worker than for another. This is partly due, of course, to the fact individuals invest themselves in activities to different degrees because they value different things. A problem in an area of heavy personal investment is more stressful than one in an area of little personal investment. It goes deeper than that, however. Managing stress effectively depends on *keeping things in perspective.* This is difficult for some people because they have a style of interpreting events that aggravates their felt stress.

Individuals who have relatively complex self-concepts, as measured by the number of different ways they describe or see themselves, are less susceptible to common stress-related complaints than are people with lesser degrees of "self-complexity."[44] Take, for example, someone who has suffered a setback at work, such as having lost out to a colleague for a desired promotion. Someone low in self-complexity (e.g., a person whose self-concept is defined solely in terms of professional success) could be devastated by the event. Low self-complexity implies a lack of resilience to threats to one's ego. Consider, on the other hand, someone with high self-complexity facing the same setback. The person could understandably feel disappointed and perhaps dejected about work, but if she were high in self-complexity, then the event's impact would be buffered by the existence of relatively uncontaminated areas of positive self-image. For example, she might base her feelings of professional success on more criteria than just getting (or not getting) a promotion. Other criteria, such as being highly respected by peers, may be even more important bases for her feelings of professional success. Furthermore, other dimensions of her life (e.g., her leadership in the local Democratic Party, support to her family) may provide more areas of positive self-image.

The A-B-C Model

Unfortunately, because there are no shortcuts to developing self-complexity, it is not really a viable stress management strategy. There are other cognitive approaches to stress management, however, that can produce more immediate results. These approaches have the common goal of changing a person's self-talk about stressful events. One of the simplest of these to apply is called the A-B-C model.[45,46]

To appreciate the usefulness of the A-B-C model, it is helpful to consider the chain of events that precedes feelings of stress. Sometimes people think of this as a two-step sequence. Something external happens (i.e., a stressful event), and then something *internal* follows (i.e., symptoms of stress). We can depict the sequence like this:

A. Triggering Event (e.g., knocking your boss's coffee onto his lap)
C. Feelings and Behaviors (e.g., anxiety, fear, embarrassment, perspiration)

In other words, many people think their feelings and behaviors result directly from external events. Such a view, however, leaves out the critical role played by our thoughts, or self-talk. The actual sequence looks like this:

A. Triggering Event (knocking your boss's coffee onto his lap)
B. Your Thinking ("He must think I'm a real jerk.")
C. Feelings and Behaviors (anxiety, fear, embarrassment, perspiration)

From this perspective you can see the causal role played by inner dialogue, or self-talk, in contributing to feelings of stress. Such inner dialogue can be rational or irrational, constructive or destructive—and which it will be is under the individual's control. People gain considerable freedom from stress when they realize that, by changing their own self-talk, they can control their emotional responses to events around them. Consider a different sequence for our scenario:

A. Triggering Event (knocking your boss's coffee onto his lap)
B. Your Thinking ("Darn it! But it was just an accident.")
C. Feelings and Behavior (apologizing and helping clean up)

Thus, a particular incident can be interpreted in several different ways, some likely to increase feelings of stress and distress, and others likely to maintain self-esteem and positive coping. You will become better at coping with stress as you practice listening to your inner dialogue and changing destructive self-talk to constructive self-talk. Even this is not a simple change to make, however. Changing self-talk is more difficult than you might think, especially in emotionalized situations. Because self-talk is covert, spontaneous, fleeting, and reflexive,[47] like any bad habit it can be difficult to change. Nevertheless, precisely because self-talk is just a habit, you can change it.

Finally, leaders need to recognize their role in their followers' stress levels. A leader in a stressful situation who is visibly manifesting some of the symptoms found in Highlight P2.7 is not going to set much of an example for followers. On the contrary, because followers look to leaders for guidance and support, these behaviors and symptoms could become contagious and may serve to increase followers' stress levels. Leaders need to recognize the importance of role modeling in reducing (or increasing) followers' stress levels. Leaders also need to make sure their style of interacting with subordinates does not make the leaders "stress carriers."

Building Technical Competence

Determining How the Job Contributes to the Overall Mission
Becoming an Expert in the Job
Seeking Opportunities to Broaden Experiences

Technical competence concerns the knowledge and repertoire of behaviors one can bring to bear to successfully complete a task. For example, a highly skilled surgeon possesses vast knowledge of human anatomy and surgical techniques and can perform an extensive set of highly practiced surgical procedures; a highly skilled volleyball player has a thorough understanding of the rules, tactics, and strategies of volleyball and can set, block, and serve effectively. Individuals usually acquire technical competence through formal education or training in specialized topics (i.e., law, medicine, accounting, welding, carpentry), on-the-job training, or experience,[48] and many studies have documented the importance of technical competence to a person's success and effectiveness as both a leader and a follower. This section describes why technical competence is important to followers and leaders; it also provides readers with ideas about how to increase their own technical competence.

There are many reasons why followers need to have a high level of technical competence. First, performance is often a function of technical competence.[49,50] Relatedly, research has shown that technical expertise plays a key role in supervisors' performance appraisal ratings of subordinates.[51,52] Second, followers with high levels of technical competence have a lot of expert power, and at times can wield more influence in their groups than the leader does.[53,54] Third, individuals with high levels of technical competence may be more likely to be a member of a leader's in-group.[55] Relatedly, followers with high levels of technical competence are more likely to be delegated tasks and asked to participate in the decision-making process. Conversely, supervisors are more likely to use a close, directive leadership style when interacting with subordinates with poor technical skills.[56–59] Similarly, Blau[60] noted that organizations with relatively high numbers of technically competent members tended to have a flatter organizational structure; organizations with relatively fewer qualified members tended to be more centralized and autocratic. Thus, if followers wish to earn greater rewards, exert more influence in their groups, and have greater say in the decision-making process, then they should do all they can to enhance their technical competence.

There are also many reasons why it benefits leaders to have high levels of technical competence. First, technical competence has been found to be consistently related to managerial promotion rates. Managers having higher levels of technical competence were much more likely to rise to the top managerial levels at AT&T than managers with lower levels of technical competence.[61,62] Second, having a high level of technical competence is important because many leaders, particularly first-line supervisors, often spend considerable time training followers.[63] Perhaps nowhere is the importance of technical competence in training more readily apparent than in coaching; little is as frustrating as having a coach who knows less about the game than the team members. Third, leaders with high levels of technical competence seem to be able to reduce the level of role ambiguity and conflict in their groups,[64,65] and followers are generally more satisfied with leaders who have high rather than average levels of technical competence.[66,67] Finally, leaders who have a high level of technical competence may be able to stimulate followers to think about problems and issues in new ways, which in turn has been found to be strongly related to organizational climate ratings and followers' motivation to succeed.[68,69] Given these findings for both leaders and followers, below is some practical advice for improving technical competence.

Determining How the Job Contributes to the Overall Mission

The first step in building technical competence is to determine how one's job contributes to the overall success of the organization. By taking this step, individuals can better determine what technical knowledge and which behaviors are most strongly related to job and organizational success. Next, people should evaluate their current level of technical skills by seeking verbal feedback from peers and superiors, reviewing past performance appraisal results, or reviewing objective performance data (e.g., golf scores, team statistics, the number of products rejected for poor quality). These actions will help individuals get a better handle on their own strengths and weaknesses, and in turn can help people be certain that any formal education or training program they pursue is best suited to meet their needs.

Becoming an Expert in the Job

Becoming an expert in one's primary field is often the springboard for further developmental opportunities. There are a number of ways in which individuals can become experts in their field, and these include enrolling in formalized education and training programs, watching others, asking questions, and teaching others. Attending pertinent education and training courses is one way to acquire technical skills, and many companies often pay the tuition and fees associated with these courses. Another way to increase expertise in one's field is by being a keen observer of human behavior. Individuals can learn a lot by observing how others handle work-coordination problems, achieve production goals, discipline team members, or develop team members with poor skills. However, merely observing how others do things is not nearly as effective as observing and reflecting about how others do things. One method of reflection is trying to explain others' behaviors in terms of the concepts or theories described in this book. Observers should look for concepts that cast light on both variations and regularities in how others act and think about the reasons why a person might have acted a certain way. Additionally, observers can develop by trying to think of as many different criteria as possible for evaluating another person's actions.

It is also important to ask questions. Because everyone makes inferences regarding the motives, expectations, values, or rationale underlying another person's actions, it is vital to ask questions and seek information likely to verify the accuracy of one's inferences. By asking questions, observers can better understand why team practices are conducted in a particular way, what work procedures have been implemented in the past, or what really caused someone to quit a volunteer organization. Finally, perhaps nothing can help a person become a technical expert more than having to teach someone else about the equipment, procedures, strategies, problems, resources, and contacts associated with a job, club, sport, or activity. Teachers must have a thorough understanding of the job or position in order to effectively teach someone else. By seeking opportunities to teach others, individuals enhance their own technical expertise as well as that of others.

Seeking Opportunities to Broaden Experiences

Individuals can improve their technical competence by seeking opportunities to broaden their experiences. Just as a person should try to play a variety of positions in order to better appreciate the contributions of other team members, so should a person try to perform the tasks associated with the other positions in his or her work group in order to better appreciate how the work contributes to organizational success. Similarly, people should visit other parts of the organization in order to gain an understanding of its whole operation. Moreover, by working on team projects, people get a chance to interact with members of other work units and often get the opportunity to develop new skills. Additionally, volunteering to support school, political, or community activities is another way to increase one's organization and planning, public speaking, fundraising, and public relations skills, all of which may be important aspects of technical competence for certain jobs.

Building Effective Relationships with Superiors

Understanding the Superior's World
Adapting to the Superior's Style

As defined here, superiors are those individuals with relatively more power and authority than the other members of the group. Thus, superiors could be teachers, band directors, coaches, team captains, heads of committees, or first-line supervisors. Needless to say, there are a number of advantages to having a good working relationship with superiors. First, superiors and followers sharing the same values, approaches, and attitudes will experience less conflict, provide higher levels of mutual support, and be more satisfied with superior–follower relationships than superiors and followers having poor working relationships.[70,71] Relatedly, individuals having good superior–follower relationships are often in the superior's in-group and thus are more likely to have a say in the decision-making process, be delegated interesting tasks, and have the superior's support for career advancement.[72] Second, followers are often less satisfied with their supervisor and receive lower performance appraisal ratings when superior–follower relationships are poor.[73,74]

Although the advantages of having a good working relationship with superiors seem clear, one might mistakenly think that followers have little, if any, say in the quality of the relationship. In other words, followers might believe their relationships with superiors are a matter of luck; either the follower has a good superior or a bad one, or the superior just happens to like or dislike the follower, and there is little if anything the follower can do about it. However, the quality of a working relationship is not determined solely by the superior, and effective subordinates do not limit themselves to a passive stance toward superiors. Effective subordinates have learned how to take active steps to strengthen the relationship and enhance the support they provide their superior and the organization.[75,76]

Wherever a person is positioned in an organization, an important aspect of that person's work is to help his superior be successful, just as an important part of the superior's work is to help followers be successful. This does not mean that followers should become apple-polishers, play politics, or distort information just to make superiors look good. It does mean, however, that followers should think of their own and their superior's success as interdependent. It means that followers are players on their superior's team and should be evaluated on the basis of the team's success, not just their own. If the team succeeds, then both the coach and the team members should benefit; if the team fails, then the blame should fall on both the coach and the team members. Because team, club, or organizational outcomes depend to some extent on good superior–follower relationships, understanding how superiors view the world and adapting to superiors' styles are two things followers can do to increase the likelihood their actions will have positive results for themselves, their superiors, and their organizations.[77]

Understanding the Superior's World

There are a number of things followers can do to better understand their superior's world. First, they should try to get a handle on their superior's personal and organizational objectives. Loyalty and support are a two-way street, and just as a superior can help subordinates attain their personal goals most readily by knowing what they are, so can subordinates support their superior if they understand the superior's goals and objectives. Relatedly, knowing a superior's values, preferences, and personality can help followers better understand why superiors act the way they do and can give followers insights into how they might strengthen relationships with superiors.

Second, followers need to realize that superiors are not supermen or superwomen; superiors do not have all the answers, and they have both strengths and weaknesses. Subordinates can make a great contribution to the overall success of a team by recognizing and complementing a superior's weaknesses, and understanding his constraints and limitations. For example, a highly successful management consultant might spend over 200 days a year conducting executive development workshops, providing organizational feedback to clients, or giving speeches at various public events. This same consultant, however, might not be skilled in designing and making effective visual aids for presentations, or she might dislike having to make her own travel and accommodation arrangements. A follower could make both the consultant and the consulting firm more successful through his own good organization and planning, attention to detail, computer graphics skills, and understanding that the consultant is most effective when she has at least a one-day break between engagements. A similar process can take place in other contexts, as when subordinates help orient and educate a newly assigned superior whose expertise and prior experience may have been in a different field or activity.

In an even more general sense, subordinates can enhance superior–follower relationships by keeping superiors informed about various activities in the work group or new developments or opportunities in the field. Few superiors like surprises, and any news should come from the person with responsibility for a particular area—especially if the news is potentially bad or concerns unfavorable developments. Followers wishing to develop good superior–follower relationships should never put their superior in the embarrassing situation of having someone else know more about her terrain than she does (her own boss, for instance). As Kelley[78] maintained, the best followers think critically and play an active role in their organizations, which means that followers should keep their superiors informed about critical information and pertinent opinions concerning organizational issues.

Adapting to the Superior's Style

Research has shown that some executives fail to get promoted (i.e., are derailed) because they are unable or unwilling to adapt to superiors with leadership styles different from their own.[79] Followers need to keep in mind that it is their responsibility to adapt to their superior's style, not vice versa. For example, followers might prefer to interact with superiors face-to-face, but if their superior appreciates written memos, then written memos it should be. Similarly, a follower might be accustomed to informal interactions with superiors, but a new superior might prefer a more businesslike and formal style. Followers need to be flexible in adapting to their superiors' decision-making styles, problem-solving strategies, modes of communication, styles of interaction, and so on.

One way followers can better adapt to a superior's style is to clarify expectations about their role on the team, committee, or work group. Young workers often do not appreciate the difference between a job description and one's role in a job. A job description is a formalized statement of tasks and activities; a role describes the personal signature an incumbent gives to a job. For example, the job description of a high school athletic coach might specify such responsibilities as selecting and training a team or making decisions about lineups. Two different coaches, however, might accomplish those basic responsibilities in quite different ways. One might emphasize player development in the broadest sense, getting to know her players personally and using sports as a vehicle for their individual growth; another might see his role simply to produce the most winning team possible. Therefore, just because followers know what their job is does not mean their role is clear.

Although some superiors take the initiative to explicitly spell out the roles they expect subordinates to play, most do not. Usually it is the subordinate's task to discern his or her role. One way followers can do this is to make a list of major responsibilities and use it to guide a discussion with the superior about different ways the tasks might be accomplished and the relative priorities of the tasks. Relatedly, followers will also find it helpful to talk to others who have worked with a particular superior before.

Finally, followers interested in developing effective relationships with superiors need to be honest and dependable. Whatever other qualities or talents a subordinate might have, a lack of integrity is an absolutely fatal flaw. No one—superior, peer, or subordinate—wants to work with someone who is untrustworthy. After integrity, superiors value dependability. Superiors value workers who have reliable work habits, accomplish assigned tasks at the right time in the right order, and do what they promise.[80]

Building Effective Relationships with Peers

> Recognizing Common Interests and Goals
> Understanding Peers' Tasks, Problems, and Rewards
> Practicing a Theory Y Attitude

The phrase *influence without authority*[81] captures a key element of the work life of increasing numbers of individuals. More and more people are finding that their jobs require them to influence others despite having no formal authority over them. No man is an island, it is said, and perhaps no worker in today's organizations can survive alone. Virtually everyone needs a co-worker's assistance or resources at one time or another. Along these lines, some researchers have maintained that one of the fundamental requirements of leadership effectiveness is the ability to build strong alliances with others, and groups of peers generally wield more influence (and can get more things done) than individuals working separately.[82] Similarly, investing the time and effort to develop effective relationships with peers not only has immediate dividends but also can have long-term benefits if a peer ends up in a position of power in the future. Many times, leaders are selected from among the members of a group, committee, club, or team and, having previously spent time developing a friendly rather than an antagonistic relationship with other work group members, leaders will lay the groundwork for building effective relationships with superiors and becoming a member of superiors' in-groups. Given the benefits of strong relationships with peers, the following are a few ideas about how to establish and maintain good peer relationships.

Recognizing Common Interests and Goals

Although Chapters 5 through 8 described a variety of ways people vary, one of the best ways to establish effective working relationships with peers is to acknowledge shared interests, values, goals, and expectations.[83] In order to acknowledge shared aspirations and interests, however, one must know what peers' goals, values, and interests actually are. Establishing informal communication links is one of the best ways to discover common interests and values. To do so, one needs to be open and honest in communicating one's own needs, values, and goals, as well as being willing to acknowledge others' needs, aspirations, and interests. Little can destroy a relationship with peers more quickly than a person who is overly willing to share his own problems and beliefs but unwilling to listen to others' ideas about the same issues. Moreover, although some people believe that participating in social gatherings, parties, committee meetings, lunches, company sport teams, or community activities can be a waste of time, peers with considerable referent power often see such activities as opportunities to establish and improve relationships with others. Thus, an effective way to establish relationships with other members of a team, committee, or organization is to meet with them in contexts outside of normal working relationships.

Understanding Peers' Tasks, Problems, and Rewards

Few things reinforce respect between co-workers better than understanding the nature of each other's work. Building a cooperative relationship with others depends, therefore, on knowing the sorts of tasks others perform in the organization. It also depends on understanding what their problems and rewards are. With the former, one of the best ways to establish strong relationships is by lending a hand whenever peers face personal or organizational problems. With the latter, it is especially important to remember that people tend to repeat those behaviors that are rewarded and are less likely to repeat behaviors that go unrewarded. A person's counterproductive or negative behaviors may be due less to his personal characteristics (e.g., "He is just uncooperative") than to the way his rewards are structured. For example, a teacher may be less likely to share successful classroom exercises with others if teachers are awarded merit pay on the basis of classroom effectiveness. To secure cooperation from others, it helps to know which situational factors reinforce both positive and negative behaviors in others.[84] By better understanding the situation facing others, people can determine whether their own positive feedback (or lack thereof) is contributing to, or hindering the establishment of, effective relationships with peers. People should not underestimate the power of their own sincere encouragement, thanks, and compliments in positively influencing the behavior of their colleagues.

Practicing a Theory Y Attitude

Another way to build effective working relationships with peers is to view them from a Theory Y perspective (see Chapter 6). When a person assumes that others are competent, trustworthy, willing to cooperate if they can, and proud of their work, peers will view that person in the same light. Even if one practices a Theory Y attitude, however, it may still be difficult to get along with a few co-workers. In such cases, it is easy to become preoccupied with the qualities one dislikes. This should be resisted as much as possible. A vicious cycle can develop in which people become enemies, putting more and more energy into criticizing each other or making the other person look bad than into doing constructive work on the task at hand. The costs of severely strained relationships also can extend beyond the individual parties involved. Cliques, or sides, can develop among other co-workers as well, which can impair the larger group's effectiveness. The point here is not to overlook interpersonal problems, but rather to not let the problems get out of hand.

Practicing Theory Y does *not* mean looking at the world through rose-colored glasses, but it *does* mean recognizing someone else's strengths as well as weaknesses. Nevertheless, sometimes peers will be assigned to work on a task together when they don't get along with each other, and the advice "Practice a Theory Y attitude" may seem too idealistic. At such times, it is important to decide whether to focus energy first on improving the relationship (before addressing the task) or to focus it solely on the task (essentially ignoring the problem in the relationship).

Cohen and Bradford[85] suggested several guidelines for resolving this problem. They said it is best to work on the task if there is little animosity between the parties, if success can be achieved despite existing animosities, if group norms inhibit openness, if success on the task will improve the feelings between the parties, if the other person handles directness poorly, or if you handle directness poorly. Conversely, they said it is best to work on the relationship if there is great animosity between the parties, if negative feelings make task success unlikely, if group norms favor openness, if feelings between the parties are not likely to improve even with success on the task, if the other person handles directness well, *and* if you handle directness well.

Building Credibility

The Two Components of Credibility
Building Expertise
Building Trust
Expertise × Trust

Interviews with thousands of followers as well as the results of over half a million 360-degree feedback reports indicate that credibility may be one of the most important components of leadership success and effectiveness.[86,87] Employees working for leaders they thought were credible were willing to work longer hours, felt more of a sense of ownership in the company, felt more personally involved in work, and were less likely to leave the company over the next two years.[88] Given the difficulties companies are having finding and retaining talented leaders and workers and the role intellectual capital and bench strength play in organizational success, it would appear that credibility could have a strong bottom-line impact on many organizations. Credibility is a little like leadership in that many people have ideas of what credibility is (or is not), but there may not be a lot of consensus on one "true" definition of credibility. This section will define what we believe credibility is, present the two components of credibility, and explore what leadership practitioners can do (and avoid doing) if they want to build their credibility.

The Two Components of Credibility

Credibility can be defined as the ability to engender trust in others. Leaders with high levels of credibility are seen as trustworthy; they have a strong sense of right and wrong, stand up and speak up for what they believe in, protect confidential information, encourage ethical discussions of business or work issues, and follow through with commitments. Sometimes dishonest leaders, personalized charismatic leaders, or power wielders can initially be seen by followers to be credible, but their selfish and self-serving interests usually come to light over time. Credibility is made up of two components, which include expertise and trust. Followers will not trust leaders if they feel their leaders do not know what they are talking about. Similarly, followers will not trust leaders if they feel confidential information will be leaked, if their leaders are unwilling to take stands on moral issues, or if their leaders do not follow through with their promises. Much about these two components of credibility have already been discussed in the sections on "Building Technical Competence," "Building Effective Relationships with Superiors," and "Building Effective Relationships with Peers." What follows is a brief overview of these three skills as well as some additional considerations that can help leadership practitioners build their credibility.

Building Expertise

Expertise consists of technical competence as well as organizational and industry knowledge, so building expertise means increasing your knowledge and skills in these three areas. Building technical competence, described earlier in this section, concerns increasing the knowledge and repertoire of behaviors one can bring to bear to successfully complete a task. To build technical competence, leadership practitioners must determine how their job contributes to the overall mission of the company or organization, become an expert in the job through formal training or teaching others, and seek opportunities to broaden their technical expertise.

Nonetheless, building expertise takes more than just technical competence. Leaders also need to understand the company and the industry they are in. Many followers are not only looking for leaders to coach them on their skills, they are also looking to their leaders to provide some context for organizational, industry, and market events. Building one's organizational or industry knowledge may be just as important as building technical competence. However, the ways in which leadership practitioners build these two knowledge bases is somewhat different from building technical competence. Building technical competence often takes more of a hands-on approach to development, but it is hard to do this when building organizational or industry knowledge. One way to build your organizational or industry knowledge is by regularly reading industry-related journals, annual reports, *The Wall Street Journal, Fortune, Inc.,* or various Web sites. Many leaders spend 5–10 hours a week building their industry and organizational knowledge bases using this approach. Getting a mentor or being coached by your boss is another way to build these knowledge bases. Other leadership practitioners have taken stretch assignments where they work on special projects with senior executives. Often these assignments allow them to work closely with executives, and through this contact they better understand the competitive landscape, the organization's history and business strategies, and organizational politics. The bottom line is that your learning is not over once you have obtained your degree. In many ways, it will have just started.

Finally, it is important to remember that expertise is more than experience. As noted previously, some leaders get one year's worth of experience out of five years' work, whereas others get five years' worth of experience after one year's work. Leaders who get the most from their experience regularly discuss what they have been learning with a partner, and they frequently update their development plans as a result of these discussions.

Building Trust

The second component of credibility is building trust, which can be broken down into clarifying and communicating your values, and building relationships with others. In many ways leadership is a moral exercise. For example, one of the key differences between charismatic and transformational leaders is that the latter base their vision on their own and their followers' values, whereas the former base their vision on their own possibly selfish needs. Having a strong values system is an important component both in the building blocks model of skills and in leadership success. Because of the importance of values and relationships in building trust, the remainder of this section explores these two topics in more depth.

Chapter 6 defined values as generalized behaviors or states of affairs that an individual considers to be important. Provided that leaders make ethical decisions and abide by organizational rules, however, differences in values among leaders and followers may be difficult to discern. Since people do not come to work with their values tattooed to their foreheads, others typically make inferences about a leader's values based on their day-to-day behaviors (or, just as importantly, their absence of certain day-to-day behaviors). Unfortunately, in many cases leaders' day-to-day behaviors are misaligned with their personal values; they are not living their life (at work, at least) in a manner consistent with their values.

An example of a leader not living life according to his values might be illustrative. An executive with an oil and gas firm was responsible for all exploration (i.e., drilling) operations in western Canada. Because he felt the discovery of new oil and gas fields was the key to the company's long-term success, he worked up to 18 hours a day, pushed his followers to work similar sorts of hours, had little patience for and would publicly disparage those oil rig operators who were behind schedule, and almost fired a manager who gave one of his followers a week off to see the birth of his son back in the United States. As these behaviors continued over time, more and more of his followers either requested transfers or quit to join other companies. Because of these problems with turnover and morale, he was asked to participate in a formal coaching program. Not surprisingly, his 360-degree feedback showed that his boss, peers, and followers found him very difficult to work with or for. These results indicated that he put a premium on getting results, getting ahead, and economic rewards, yet when he was asked to name the things he felt were most important to him as a leader, his priorities were his family, his religion, getting along with others, and developing his followers (Altruism). Obviously, there was a huge gap between what he truly believed in and how he behaved. He felt the company expected him to hold people's feet to the fire and get results no matter what the cost, yet neither the boss nor his peers felt that this was the case. The executive had misconstrued the situation and was exhibiting behaviors that were misaligned with his values.

Although the case above was somewhat extreme, it is not unusual to find leaders acting in ways that are misaligned with their personal values. One way to assess the degree to which leaders are living their lives according to their personal values is by asking what they truly believe in and what they spend their time and money on. For example, you could write down the five things you believe most strongly in (i.e., your top five values), and then review your calendar, daytimer, checkbook, and credit card statements to determine where you spend your time and money. If the two lists are aligned, then you are likely to be living your life according to your values. If not, then you may be living your life according to how others think you should act. And if there is some level of discrepancy between the two lists, what should you do? Of course, some level of discrepancy is likely to occur, as situational demands and constraints can often influence the way leaders behave. On the other hand, large discrepancies between the lists may indicate that you are not living life consistently with your values, and those you interact with may infer that you have a very different set of values than those you personally believe in. A good first step in clarifying this discrepancy is to craft a personal mission statement or a leadership credo, a statement that describes what you truly believe in as a leader.

Examples of different leadership credos for managers across corporate America can be found in Highlight P2.9. There are several aspects of leadership credos worth additional comment. First, leadership credos are personal and are closely linked with a leader's values—a credo should describe what the leader believes in and will (or will not) stand for. Second, it should also describe an ideal state. A leader's behavior may never be perfectly aligned with his or her personal mission statement, but it should be a set of day-to-day behaviors that he or she will strive to achieve. Third, leadership credos should be motivating; leaders should be passionate and enthusiastic about the kind of leader they aspire to be. If the leader does not find his or her personal mission statement to be particularly inspiring, then it is hard to see how followers will be motivated by it. Much of the inspiration of a leadership credo stems from its being personal and values-based. Fourth, personal mission statements should be made public. Leaders need to communicate their values to others, and a good way to do this is to display their leadership credos prominently in their offices. This not only lets others know what you as a leader think is important, it also is a form of public commitment to your leadership credo.

Another key way to build trust is to form strong relationships with others. There is apt to be a high level of mutual trust if leaders and followers share strong relationships; if these relationships are weak, then the level of mutual trust is apt to be low. Techniques for building relationships with peers and superiors have already been described in this section of the text. Perhaps the best way to build relationships with followers is to spend time listening to what they have to say. Because many leaders tend to be action-oriented and get paid to solve (rather than listen to) problems, some leaders overlook the importance of spending time with followers. Yet leaders who take the time to build relationships with followers are much more likely to understand their followers' perspectives of organizational issues, intrinsic motivators, values, level of competence for different tasks, or career aspirations. Leaders armed with this knowledge may be better able to influence and get work done through others. More on building relationships with followers can be found in the Leadership Skills section of Part Three under "Coaching."

Expertise × Trust

Leaders vary tremendously in their levels of both expertise and trust, and these differences have distinct implications for leaders wanting to improve their credibility. Take leaders who fall into the first quadrant of Figure P2.4. These individuals have a high level of trust and a high level of expertise; they would likely be seen by others as highly credible. Individuals falling into the second quadrant might include leaders who have spent little time with followers, who do not follow through with commitments, or who are new to the organization and have had little time to build relationships with co-workers. In all three cases, leaders wanting to improve their credibility should include building relationships with co-workers as key development objectives. Leaders falling into the third quadrant may be new college hires or people joining the company from an entirely different industry. It is unlikely that either type of leader would have the technical competence, organizational or industry knowledge, or time to build relationships with co-workers. These leaders may be in touch with their values and have a personal mission statement, but they will need to share their statement with others and act in a manner consistent with this statement in order to build their credibility. Other development objectives could include building expertise and strong relationships with others. Leaders falling into the fourth quadrant might include those promoted from among peers or transferring from another department within the company. Both sets of leaders may be in touch with their values, have a leadership credo, share strong relationships with co-workers, and have organizational and industry knowledge, but the former may need to develop leadership knowledge or skills and the latter technical competence if they wish to increase their credibility. Finally, it is important to note that leadership credos and development plans also have credibility implications because leaders who do not strive to live up to their ideals or fail to follow through with their developmental commitments are likely to be seen as less trustworthy than those who do.

Sample Leadership Credos

HIGHLIGHT P2.9

As a leader, I . . .

. . . believe in the concept of whole persons and will seek to use the full range of talents and abilities of colleagues whenever possible.

. . . will seek to keep people fully informed.

. . . will more consistently express appreciation to others for a job well done.

. . . will take risks in challenging policies or protocol when they do not permit us to effectively serve our customers.

. . . will selectively choose battles to fight—rather than trying to fight all of the possible battles.

. . . will actively support those providing the most effective direction for our company.

. . . will seek to change the things I can in a positive direction and accept those things I have no chance or opportunity to change.

Source: *Impact Leadership.* Minneapolis: Personnel Decisions International, 1995.

FIGURE P2.4

The credibility matrix.

Source: G. J. Curphy, *Credibility: Building Your Reputation throughout the Organization.* Minneapolis: Personnel Decisions International, 1997.

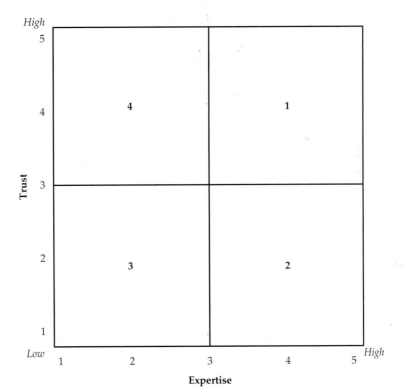

Part Notes

1. Csikszentmihalyi, M. *Flow: The Psychology of Optimal Experience.* New York: Harper & Row, 1990.

2. Bass, B. M. *Bass and Stogdill's Handbook of Leadership.* 3rd ed. New York: Free Press, 1990.

3. Bennis, W. G., and B. Nanus. *Leaders: The Strategies for Taking Charge.* New York: Harper & Row, 1985.

4. Kanter, R. M. *The Change Masters.* New York: Simon & Schuster, 1983.

5. Parks, M. R. "Interpersonal Communication and the Quest for Personal Competence." In *Handbook of Interpersonal Communication.* Eds. M. L. Knapp and G. R. Miller. Beverly Hills, CA: Sage, 1985.

6. Klimoski, R. J., and N. J. Hayes. "Leader Behavior and Subordinate Motivation." *Personnel Psychology* 33 (1980), pp. 543–55.

7. Snyder, R. A., and J. H. Morris. "Organizational Communication and Performance." *Journal of Applied Psychology* 69 (1984), pp. 461–65.

8. Fiechtner, B., and J. J. Krayer. "Variations in Dogmatism and Leader-Supplied Information: Determinants of Perceived Behavior in Task-Oriented Groups." *Group and Organizational Studies* 11 (1986), 403–18.

9. Sanford, A., and S. Garrod. *Understanding Written Language.* New York: John Wiley, 1981.

10. Remland, M. S. "Developing Leadership Skills in Nonverbal Communication: A Situation Perspective." *Journal of Business Communication* 18, no. 3 (1981), pp. 17–29.

11. Luthans, F., and J. K. Larsen. "How Managers Really Communicate." *Human Relations* 39 (1986), pp. 161–78.

12. Sadler, P. J., and G. H. Hofstede. "Leadership Styles: Preferences and Perceptions of Employees of an International Company in Different Countries." *Mens en Onderneming* 26 (1972), pp. 43–63.

13. Davis, B. L., L. W. Hellervik, and J. L. Sheard. *The Successful Manager's Handbook.* 3rd ed. Minneapolis, MN: Personnel Decisions International, 1989.

14. Robbins, S. P. *Organizational Behavior: Concepts, Controversies, and Applications.* Englewood Cliffs, NJ: Prentice Hall, 1986.

15. Gibb, J. R. "Defensive Communication." *Journal of Communication* 13, no. 3 (1961), pp. 141–48.

16. Alberti, R. E., and M. L. Emmons. *Your Perfect Right.* San Luis Obispo, CA: Impact, 1974.

17. Shostrom, E. L. *Man, the Manipulator.* New York: Bantam, 1967.

18. Harvey, J. B. "The Abilene Paradox: The Management of Agreement." *Organizational Dynamics* 3 (1974), pp. 63–80.

19. Benner, P. E. *Stress and Satisfaction on the Job.* New York: Praeger, 1984.

20. McCauley, C. D. "Stress and the Eye of the Beholder." *Issues & Observations* 7, no. 3 (1987), pp. 1–16.

21. Staw, B. M. "Organizational Behavior: A Review and Reformulation of the Field's Outcome Variables." *Annual Review of Psychology* 35 (1984), pp. 627–66.

22. Ivancevich, J. M., D. M. Schweiger, and J. W. Ragan. "Employee Stress, Health, and Attitudes: A Comparison of American, Indian, and Japanese Managers." Paper presented at the Academy of Management Convention, Chicago, 1986.

23. Hogan, R. T., and A. M. Morrison. "The Psychology of Managerial Incompetence." Paper presented at a joint conference of the American Psychological Association–National Institute of Occupational Safety and Health. Washington, DC, October 1991.

24. Shipper, F., and C. L. Wilson. "The Impact of Managerial Behaviors on Group Performance, Stress, and Commitment." In *Impact of Leadership.* Eds. K. E. Clark, M. B. Clark, and D. P. Campbell. Greensboro, NC: Center for Creative Leadership, 1992.

25. McCormick, J., and B. Powell. "Management for the 1990s." *Newsweek,* April 1988, pp. 47–48.

26. Friedman, M., and D. Ulmer. *Treating Type A Behavior—and Your Heart.* New York: Knopf, 1984; Frisch, M. H. "The Emerging Role of the Internal Coach." *Consulting Psychology Journal* 53 (4) (2001), pp. 240–50.

27. Pomerleau, O. F., and J. Rodin. "Behavioral Medicine and Health Psychology." In *Handbook of Psychotherapy and Behavior Change.* 3rd ed. Eds. S. L. Garfield and A. E. Bergin. New York: John Wiley, 1986.

28. Justice, A. "Review of the Effects of Stress on Cancer in Laboratory Animals: Importance of Time of Stress Application and Type of Tumor." *Psychological Bulletin* 98 (1985), pp. 108–38.

29. Latack, J. C. "Coping with Job Stress: Measures and Future Decisions for Scale Development." *Journal of Applied Psychology* 71 (1986), pp. 377–85.

30. Quayle, D. "American Productivity: The Devastating Effect of Alcoholism and Drug Use." *American Psychologist* 38 (1983), pp. 454–58.

31. Jamal, M. "Job Stress and Job Performance Controversy: An Empirical Assessment." *Organizational Behavior and Human Performance* 33 (1984), pp. 1–21.

32. Quayle, D. "American Productivity: The Devastating Effect of Alcoholism and Drug Use." *American Psychologist* 38 (1983), pp. 454–58.

33. Albrecht, K. *Stress and the Manager.* Englewood Cliffs, NJ: Prentice Hall, 1979.

34. Fiedler, F. E. "The Effect and Meaning of Leadership Experience: A Review of Research and a Preliminary Model." In *Impact of Leadership.* Eds. K. E. Clark, M. B. Clark, and D. P. Campbell. Greensboro, NC: Center for Creative Leadership, 1992.

35. Gibson, F. W. "A Taxonomy of Leader Abilities and Their Influence on Group Performance as a Function of Interpersonal Stress." In *Impact of Leadership.* Eds. K. E. Clark, M. B. Clark, and D. P. Campbell. Greensboro, NC: Center for Creative Leadership, 1992.

36. Mulder, M., R. D. de Jong, L. Koppelar, and J. Verhage. "Power, Situation, and Leaders' Effectiveness: An Organizational Study." *Journal of Applied Psychology* 71 (1986), pp. 566–70.

37. Weschler, D. *Weschler Adult Intelligence Scale: Manual.* New York: Psychological Corporation, 1955.

38. Tjosvold, D. "Stress Dosage for Problem Solvers." *Working Smart,* August 1995, p. 5.

39. Wiley, J., and T. Comacho. "Life-Style and Future Health: Evidence from the Alameda County Study." *Preventive Medicine* 9 (1980), pp. 1–21.

40. Berkman, L., and S. L. Syme. "Social Networks, Host Resistance, and Mortality: A Nine-Year Follow-up Study of Alameda County Residents." *American Journal of Epidemiology* 109 (1979), pp. 186–204.

41. Cummings, R. C. "Job Stress and the Buffering Effect of Supervisory Support." *Group and Organizational Studies* 15, no. 1 (1990), pp. 92–104.

42. Jayaratne, S., D. Himle, and W. A. Chess. "Dealing with Work Stress and Strain: Is the Perception of Support More Important than Its Use?" *Journal of Applied Behavioral Science* 24, no. 2 (1988), pp. 34–45.

43. West Point Associates, the Department of Behavior Sciences and Leadership, United States Military Academy. *Leadership in Organizations.* Garden City Park, NY: Avery, 1988.

44. Linville, P. W. "Self-Complexity as a Cognitive Buffer against Stress-Related Illness and Depression." *Journal of Personality and Social Psychology* 52, no. 4 (1987), pp. 663–76.

45. Ellis, A., and R. Harper. *A New Guide to Rational Living.* Englewood Cliffs, NJ: Prentice Hall, 1975.

46. Steinmetz, J., J. Blankenship, L. Brown, D. Hall, and G. Miller. *Managing Stress Before It Manages You.* Palo Alto, CA: Bull, 1980.

47. McKay, M., M. Davis, and P. Fanning. *Thoughts and Feelings: The Art of Cognitive Stress Intervention.* Richmond, CA: New Harbinger, 1981.

48. Yukl, G. *Leadership in Organizations.* 2nd ed. Englewood Cliffs, NJ: Prentice Hall, 1989.

49. Curphy, G. J. "Leadership Transitions and Succession Planning." In *Developing and Implementing Succession Planning Programs.* J. Locke (chair). Symposium conducted at the 19th Annual Conference for the Society of Industrial and Organizational Psychology, Chicago, April 2004.

50. Schmidt, F. L., and J. E. Hunter. "Development of a Causal Model of Job Performance." *Current Directions in Psychological Science* 1, no. 3 (1992), pp. 89–92.

51. Borman, W. C., L. A. White, E. D. Pulakos, and S. A. Oppler. "Models Evaluating the Effects of Rated Ability, Knowledge, Proficiency, Temperament, Awards, and Problem Behavior on Supervisor Ratings." *Journal of Applied Psychology* 76 (1991), pp. 863–72.

52. Hogan, J. "The View from Below." In *The Future of Leadership Selection.* R. T. Hogan (chair). Symposium conducted at the 13th Biennial Psychology in the Department of Defense Conference, United States Air Force Academy, Colorado Springs, CO, 1992.

53. Bugental, D. E. "A Study of Attempted and Successful Social Influence in Small Groups as a Function of Goal-Relevant Skills." *Dissertation Abstracts* 25 (1964), p. 660.

54. Farris, G. F. "Colleagues' Roles and Innovation in Scientific Teams." Working paper No. 552-71. Cambridge, MA: Alfred P. Sloan School of Management, MIT, 1971.

55. Duchon, D., S. G. Green, and T. D. Taber. "Vertical Dyad Linkage: A Longitudinal Assessment of Antecedents, Measures, and Consequences." *Journal of Applied Psychology* 71 (1986), pp. 56–60.

56. Dewhirst, H. D., V. Metts, and R. T. Ladd. "Exploring the Delegation Decision: Managerial Responses to Multiple Contingencies." Paper presented at the Academy of Management Convention, New Orleans, LA, 1987.

57. Leana, C. R. "Power Relinquishment vs. Power Sharing: Theoretical Clarification and Empirical Comparison of Delegation and Participation." *Journal of Applied Psychology* 72 (1987), pp. 228–33.

58. Lowin, A., and J. R. Craig. "The Influence of Level of Performance on Managerial Style: An Experimental Object-Lesson in the Ambiguity of Correlational Data." *Organizational Behavior and Human Performance* 3 (1968), pp. 68–106.

59. Rosen, B., and T. H. Jerdee. "Influence of Subordinate Characteristics on Trust and Use of Participative Decision Strategies in a Management Simulation." *Journal of Applied Psychology* 59 (1977), pp. 9–14.

60. Blau, P. M. "The Hierarchy of Authority in Organizations." *American Journal of Sociology* 73 (1968), pp. 453–67.

61. Howard, A. "College Experiences and Managerial Performance." *Journal of Applied Psychology* 71 (1986), pp. 530–52.

62. Howard, A., and D. W. Bray. "Predictors of Managerial Success over Long Periods of Time." In *Measures of Leadership*. Eds. M. B. Clark and K. E. Clark. West Orange, NJ: Leadership Library of America, 1989.

63. Wexley, K. N., and G. P. Latham. *Developing and Training Human Resources in Organizations*. Glenview, IL: Scott Foresman, 1981.

64. Podsakoff, P. M., W. D. Todor, and R. S. Schuler. "Leadership Expertise as a Moderator of the Effects of Instrumental and Supportive Leader Behaviors." *Journal of Management* 9 (1983), pp. 173–85.

65. Walker, T. G. "Leader Selection and Behavior in Small Political Groups." *Small Group Behavior* 7 (1976), pp. 363–68.

66. Bass, B. M. *Leadership and Performance beyond Expectations*. New York: Free Press, 1985.

67. Penner, D. D., D. M. Malone, T. M. Coughlin, and J. A. Herz. *Satisfaction with U.S. Army Leadership*. Leadership Monograph Series, no. 2. U.S. Army War College, 1973.

68. Avolio, B. J., and B. M. Bass. "Transformational Leadership, Charisma, and Beyond." In *Emerging Leadership Vista*. Ed. J. G. Hunt, B. R. Baliga, and C. A. Schriesheim. Lexington, MA: D. C. Heath, 1988.

69. Curphy, G. J. "An Empirical Examination of Bass' 1985 Theory of Transformational and Transactional Leadership." PhD dissertation, University of Minnesota, 1991.

70. Duchon, D., S. G. Green, and T. D. Taber. "Vertical Dyad Linkage: A Longitudinal Assessment of Antecedents, Measures, and Consequences." *Journal of Applied Psychology* 71 (1986), pp. 56–60.

71. Porter, D. A. "Student Course Critiques: A Case Study in Total Quality in the Classroom." In *Proceedings of the 13th Biennial Psychology in Department of*

Defense Conference. Colorado Springs, CO: U.S. Air Force Academy, 1992, pp. 26–30.

72. Yukl, G. *Leadership in Organizations.* 2nd ed. Englewood Cliffs, NJ: Prentice Hall, 1989.

73. Pulakos, E. D., and K. N. Wexley. "The Relationship among Perceptual Similarity, Sex, and Performance Ratings in Manager-Subordinate Dyads." *Academy of Management Journal* 26 (1983), pp. 129–39.

74. Weiss, H. M. "Subordinate Imitation of Supervisor Behavior: The Role of Modeling in Organizational Socialization." *Organizational Behavior and Human Performance* 19 (1977), pp. 89–105.

75. Gabarro, J. J., and J. P. Kotter. "Managing Your Boss." *Harvard Business Review* 58, no. 1 (1980), pp. 92–100.

76. Kelley, R. E. "In Praise of Followers." *Harvard Business Review* 66, no. 6 (1988), pp. 142–48.

77. Gabarro, J. J., and J. P. Kotter. "Managing Your Boss." *Harvard Business Review* 58, no. 1 (1980), pp. 92–100.

78. Kelley, R. E. "In Praise of Followers." *Harvard Business Review* 66, no. 6 (1988), pp. 142–48.

79. McCall, M. W., Jr., and M. M. Lombardo. "Off the Track: Why and How Successful Executives Get Derailed." Technical Report No. 21. Greensboro, NC: Center for Creative Leadership, 1983.

80. Kouzes, J. M., and B. Z. Posner. *The Leadership Challenge: How to Get Extraordinary Things Done in Organizations.* San Francisco: Jossey-Bass, 1987.

81. Cohen, A. R., and D. L. Bradford. *Influence without Authority.* New York: John Wiley, 1990.

82. Curphy, G. J., A. Baldrica, M. Benson, and R. T. Hogan. Managerial Incompetence. Unpublished manuscript, 2007.

83. Cohen, A. R., and D. L. Bradford. *Influence without Authority.* New York: John Wiley, 1990.

84. Cohen, A. R., and D. L. Bradford. *Influence without Authority.* New York: John Wiley, 1990.

85. Cohen, A. R., and D. L. Bradford. *Influence without Authority.* New York: John Wiley, 1990.

86. Personnel Decisions International. *PROFILOR®* *Certification Workshop Manual.* Minneapolis, MN: Author, 1992.

87. Kouzes, J. M., and B. Z. Posner. *The Credibility Factor.* San Francisco: Jossey-Bass, 1996.

88. Kouzes, J. M., and B. Z. Posner. *The Credibility Factor.* San Francisco: Jossey-Bass, 1996.

Part 3

Focus on the Followers

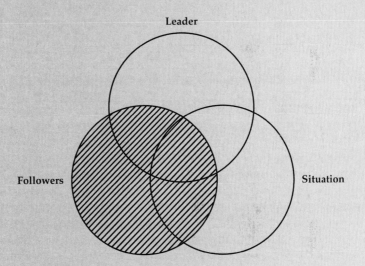

Leader

Followers

Situation

We began Part II with Napoleon's belief that the individual leader is the crucial element of leadership. We begin Part III by qualifying that sentiment. Although the importance of a good leader cannot be denied, followers also play an equally important, if often overlooked, role in the success of any group or organization. It was not, after all, Napoleon by himself who won or lost battles; his soldiers obviously played some part too. In Part III we look at the vital role played by followers in affecting the leadership process.

Chapter 9

Motivation, Satisfaction, and Performance

Introduction

> Polls estimate that if companies could get 3.7 percent more work out of each employee, the equivalent of 18 more minutes of work for each eight-hour shift, the gross domestic product in the U.S. would swell by $355 billion, twice the total GDP of Greece.
>
> *The Gallup Organization*

Why do followers join some teams but not others? How do you get followers to exhibit enough of the critical behaviors needed for the team to succeed? And why are some leaders capable of getting followers to go above and beyond "the call of duty"? The ability to motivate others is a fundamental leadership skill and has strong connections to managerial incompetence as described in Chapter 4. Competent Managers are those who can consistently get followers to engage in the behaviors needed to accomplish team goals; Results Only Managers may be able to do the same thing but for relatively short periods. Cheerleaders and In Name Only Managers seem to lack the ability to get followers to perform the behaviors needed by the team to succeed.

The importance of follower motivation is suggested in findings that most people believe they could give as much as 15 percent or 20 percent more effort at work than they now do with no one, including their own bosses, recognizing any difference. Perhaps even more startling, these workers also believed they could give 15 percent or 20 percent *less* effort with no one noticing any difference. Moreover, variation in work output varies significantly across leaders and followers. The top 15 percent of workers in any particular job may produce 20 to 50 percent more output than the average worker, depending on the complexity of the job. Put another way, the best computer programmers or salesclerks might write up to 50 percent more programs or process 50 percent more customer orders.[1,2] Might better methods of motivating workers lead to higher productivity from *all* the workers? And are more motivated workers happier or more satisfied workers? Does money help to increase productivity and satisfaction or are there other things leaders can do to increase the motivation and satisfaction levels of their followers? For example, the U.S. Army paid $85 million in retention bonuses in 2003 and over $1 billion in bonuses in 2007.[3] Is this money well spent?

Creating highly motivated and satisfied followers depends, most of all, on understanding others. Therefore, whereas motivation is an essential part of leadership, it is appropriate to include it in this part of the book, which focuses on the followers. As an overview, this chapter will address three key areas. First, we will examine the links between leadership, motivation, satisfaction, and performance—four closely related concepts. Second, we will review the major theories and research for motivation and satisfaction. Last, and perhaps most important, we will discuss what leaders can do to enhance the motivation and satisfaction of their followers if they implement these different theories.

Hardly a competent workman can be found in a large establishment who does not devote a considerable amount of his time to studying just how slow he can work and still convince his employer that he is going at a good pace.
Frederick W. Taylor, industrial engineer

Defining Motivation, Satisfaction, and Performance

Motivation, satisfaction, and performance seem clearly related. For example, Colin Powell was the former Chief of Staff of the U.S. Army during the first Gulf War and Secretary of State during the second Gulf War. Powell probably could have pursued a number of different vocations, but was *motivated* to complete ROTC and join the U.S. Army. He was also motivated to put in extra time, energy, and effort in his various positions while in the U.S. Army and was judged or rated by his superiors as being an exceptional performer. His outstanding *performance* as an officer was crucial to his promotion as the head of the Joint Chiefs of Staff during the Reagan and George H. W. Bush administrations and his later appointment as Secretary of State. We could also infer that he was happy or *satisfied* with military life, as he was a career officer in the U.S. Army. Figure 9.1 provides an overview of the general relationships between leadership, motivation, satisfaction, and performance. As we can see, some leadership behaviors, such as building relationships or consideration (Chapter 8), result in more satisfied followers. More satisfied followers are more likely to remain with the company and engage in activities that help others at work (i.e., organizational citizenship behaviors). Other leadership behaviors, such as setting goals, planning, providing feedback, and rewarding good performance (initiating structure from Chapter 8), appear to more directly influence followers to exert higher levels of effort toward the accomplishment of group goals. Research has shown that these follower behaviors result in higher levels of customer satisfaction and loyalty, which in turn lead to better team performance in retail, sales, or restaurant settings.[4-15] And teams with higher levels of performance often achieve more rewards, which further increase follower satisfaction and performance.[16,17] Thus, the leader's ability to motivate followers is vitally important to both the morale and the performance of the work group. However, it is important to understand that the leader's use of good motivational techniques is not the only factor affecting group performance. Selecting the right people for the team (Chapter 4), correctly using power and influence tactics (Chapter 5), being seen as ethical and credible (Chapter 6), possessing many of the bright-side and none of the dark-side personality traits (Chapter 7), and acquiring the necessary resources and developing follower skills (Chapter 8) are other leadership factors affecting a group's ability to accomplish its goals.

> *You have brains in your head. You have feet in your shoes. You can steer yourself in any direction you choose.*
>
> **Dr. Seuss**

Most people probably think of motivation as dealing with choices about what we do and how much effort we put into doing it. Many researchers define **motivation** as anything that provides *direction, intensity,* and *persistence* to behavior.[18-20] Another definition considers the term *motivation* a sort of shorthand to describe choosing an activity or task to engage in, establishing the level of effort to put forth on it, and determining the degree of persistence in it over time.[21] Other researchers define motivation as a behavior probability; it is the likelihood an individual will initiate and continue exhibiting certain behaviors.[22] Like personality traits and types, motivation is not directly observable; it must be inferred from behavior. We would infer that one person would be highly motivated to do well in school if she spent a lot of time studying for exams. She could choose to spend her time and energy on socializing, intramurals, or volunteer work, but because she is spending time outlining readings and reviewing class notes we say she is motivated to do well in school. At work, if one person regularly assembles twice as many MP3 players as any other person in his work group—assuming all have the same abilities, skills, and resources—then we likely would say this first person is more motivated than the others. We use the concept of motivation to explain differences we see among people in the energy and direction of their behavior. Thus, the energy and effort Peter Jackson expended creating the *Lord of the Rings* trilogy or the government of Iran spends developing the country's nuclear capabilities would be examples of the direction, intensity, and persistence components of motivation.

Performance, on the other hand, concerns those behaviors directed toward the organization's mission or goals or the products and services resulting from those behaviors. At work or school we can choose to perform a wide variety of behaviors, but performance would only include those behaviors related to the production of goods or services or obtaining

FIGURE 9.1 Relationships between leadership, job satisfaction, and performance.

Sources: M. A. Huselid, "The Impact of Human Resource Management Practices on Turnover, Productivity, and Corporate Financial Performance." *Academy of Management Journal* 38, no. 4 (1995), pp. 635–72; T. Butorac, *Recruitment and Retention: The Keys to Profitability at Carlson Companies*. Presentation given at Personnel Decisions International, Minneapolis, MN, June 11, 2001; D. J. Koys, "The Effects of Employee Satisfaction, Organizational Citizenship Behavior, and Turnover on Organizational Effectiveness: A Unit-Level, Longitudinal Study." *Personnel Psychology* 54, no. 1 (2001), pp. 101–14; J. Husserl, "Allied's Organizational Life Cycle." *Management Education & Development* 24, no. 3 (1998), p. 8; Sirota Consulting, *Establishing the Linkages between Employee Attitudes, Customer Attitudes, and Bottom-Line Results*. Chicago, IL: Author, 1998; D. S. Pugh, J. Dietz, J. W. Wiley, and S. M. Brooks, "Driving Service Effectiveness through Employee–Customer Linkages." *Academy of Management Executive* 16 (4) (2002), pp. 73–84; B. Schneider, P. J. Hanges, D. B. Smith, & A. N. Salvaggio, "Which Comes First: Employee Attitudes or Organizational, Financial and Market Performance?" *Journal of Applied Psychology* 88 (5) (2003), pp. 836–51.

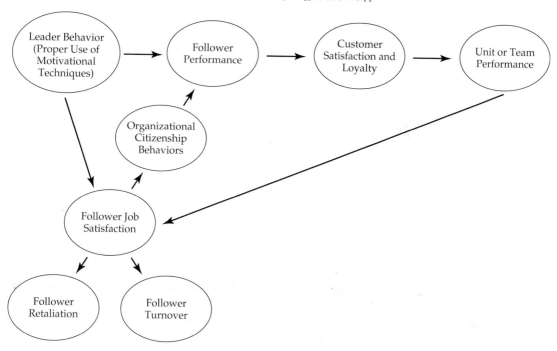

A company is always perfectly designed to produce what it is producing. If it has quality problems, cost problems, or productivity problems, then the behaviors associated with these outcomes are being reinforced. This is not conjecture. This is the cold, hard reality of human behavior.

Anonymous

good grades. Performance differs from **effectiveness,** which generally involves making judgments about the adequacy of behavior with respect to certain criteria such as work-group or organizational goals. Peter Jackson spent seven years creating the three movies in the *Lord of the Rings* series. The behaviors he exhibited in getting the films made would constitute performance; the revenues generated and Academy Awards won by the series would be indicators of his effectiveness as a movie director. However, it is important to understand that performance is affected by more than a follower's motivation. Factors such as intelligence, skill, and the availability of key resources can affect a follower's behavior in accomplishing organizational goals (i.e., performance) independently of that person's level of motivation. *Thus, an adequate level of motivation may be a necessary but insufficient condition of effective performance.*

Job satisfaction is not how *hard* one works or how *well* one works, but rather how much one *likes* a specific kind of job or work activity. Job satisfaction deals with one's attitudes or feelings about the job itself, pay, promotion or educational opportunities, supervision, co-workers, workload, and so on.[11,23–25] Various polls over the past half-century have consistently shown a majority of men and women report liking their jobs.[26–30] Research has also shown that people who are more satisfied with their jobs are more likely to engage in **organizational citizenship behaviors**—behaviors not directly related to one's job that are helpful to others at work. Organizational citizenship behaviors make for a more supportive workplace. Examples might include volunteering to help another employee with a task or project, or filling in for another employee when asked. Happier workers tend to be more helpful workers.[31–36]

Although people generally like the work they do, two related events have caused a downturn in job satisfaction levels among employees in the United States. Over the past 10–15 years, many organizations have downsized, outsourced, or otherwise substantially reduced the number of people on the company payroll. These positions were eliminated to reduce costs and improve profitability but many times they also dramatically increased the workload for the remaining workers (i.e., the same amount of work was being performed by fewer people) and severed the implicit contract between workers and employers (i.e., if workers per-

> *There is one virtue to the 35-hour workweek. It is one of the few French ideals that we don't need to worry about copyrighting. Nobody else wants it.*
>
> **Nicolas Sarkozy, prime minister of France**

Productivity and Satisfaction across the Globe

HIGHLIGHT 9.1

Over the past few years American businesses have downsized considerably, but many have been able to maintain high customer satisfaction and revenue levels, with fewer employees. In terms of the number of hours worked, the average U.S. employee works 137 hours per year more than the typical Japanese employee, 260 hours more per year compared to the average British employee, and 499 hours more than the average French employee. In other words, over the course of a 40-year work career, U.S. employees will work the equivalent of 10 more years than the average French employee. Although American companies are noted for having some of the highest productivity in the world, might there also be a downside to these high levels of productivity?

Research has shown that some of the risks associated with longer workweeks include job dissatisfaction, poorer physical and mental health, and distressed family and social relationships. As long as the U.S. economy is not adding many jobs, many employees seem to prefer those consequences associated with longer work hours than those of being unemployed. But as the economy has heated up and jobs become more readily available, leaders should not be surprised that many of these employees leave for greener pastures.

Sources: J. M. Brett and L. K. Stroh, "Working 61 Plus Hours a Week: Why Do Managers Do It?" *Journal of Applied Psychology* 88 (1) (2003), pp. 67–78; G. J. Curphy, "What We Really Know about Leadership (But Seem Unwilling to Implement)." Presentation given at the Minnesota Professionals for Psychology Applied to Work, Minneapolis, MN, January 2004.

formed at a high level, then employers guaranteed a job for life). The end result is that job dissatisfaction among workers is at an all-time high (see Highlight 9.1). Although people report being satisfied with what they do for a living, the forced overtime, increased workload, and erosion of trust between employers and employees has significantly lowered levels of job satisfaction.[37–41] Although the slowdown in the economy from 2000–2004 helped to reduce the rate of turnover, over the past few years dissatisfied employees have been leaving for other opportunities with the improved economy. Many companies are now finding it very difficult to maintain various indices of organizational effectiveness when many of the best and brightest employees have left the company. Job satisfaction may not have as direct an effect on the accomplishment of organizational goals as motivation or performance, but the indirect effects of reduced organizational citizenship behaviors or increased turnover are so important that leaders can ill afford to ignore them.[12,15,42,43]

> *People don't leave companies, they leave bad bosses.*
> **Beverly Kaye, CEO**

Today many leaders today are facing the dual challenges of having to achieve increasingly difficult unit performance goals while having fewer followers available to do the work. The best leaders and organizations understand that one way to meet these challenges is to recruit, develop, and retain top leadership and technical talent. Savvy companies that spend considerably more time and effort attracting, developing, and retaining the best people often report superior financial results.[9,11,39–41,44–48] For example, many of the organizations appearing in *Fortune* magazine's "The 100 Best Companies To Work For" also do very well when compared to the S&P 500 Index. *The best leaders may well be those who can motivate workers to perform at a high level while maintaining an equally high level of job satisfaction.*

Having now defined motivation, performance, and job satisfaction, we can explore their relationships a bit further. We have already noted how motivation does not always assure good performance. If followers lack the necessary skills or resources to accomplish a group task, then trying to "motivate them more" could be unproductive and even frustrating.[49,50] For example, no high school basketball team is likely to defeat the Los Angeles Lakers, however motivated the players may be. The players on the high school team simply lack the abilities and skills of the Lakers players. Higher motivation will usually only affect performance if followers already have the abilities, skills, and resources to get the job done. Motivating others is an important part of leadership, but not all of it; pep talks and rewards are not always enough.

The relationships between motivation and job satisfaction are more straightforward—as a matter of fact, many theories of motivation are also theories of job satisfaction. The implicit link between satisfaction and motivation is that satisfaction increases when people accomplish a task, particularly when the task requires a lot of effort. It might also seem logical that *performance* must be higher among more satisfied workers, but actually this is not always so.[12,24,51,52] Although satisfaction and performance are correlated at the $r = .3$ level, it is just not true that

Michelle Bachelet

PROFILES IN LEADERSHIP 9.1

Michelle Bachelet was inaugurated as president of Chile in March 2006 and is ranked by *Forbes* as the 17th most powerful female in the world. Bachelet is a surgeon, pediatrician, and epidemiologist with a master's degree in military studies from the Chilean Army War Academy and previous experience as the country's Health and Defense Minister. A moderate socialist who believes in free markets, Bachelet and her government has negotiated a number of bilateral trade agreements with other countries. Her government has also worked to reduce corruption, improve public transportation, resolve border disputes with Peru and Argentina, and reduce the gap between rich and poor (Chile has one of the largest wealth gaps in the world).

Bachelet's father was a Chilean Air Force Brigadier General and she moved a lot while growing up. While in high school her father got a two-year assignment to the Chilean embassy in Washington, D.C. Her family moved back to Chile where she graduated near the top of her high school class and applied to medical school. She had one of the highest scores ever recorded on the medical school entrance examination, but while in medical school Augusto Pinochet came to power and began to purge anyone associated with the previous administration. During this time Bachelet's father was working for the Salvadore Allende government as the head of the Food Distribution Office. He was arrested by Pinochet's forces and interrogated and tortured. He had a heart attack and died while in prison. Shortly thereafter Michelle Bachelet and her mother were also arrested, interrogated, and tortured, but due to family connections were granted exile in Australia. Bachelet then moved to East Germany in order to continue with her medical studies. She remained in East Germany for three years before she was allowed to move back to Chile. Upon return the country's medical establishment refused to honor the course work and medical training Bachelet received in East Germany, so she had to repeat many of the courses she had taken earlier. She graduated near the top of her medical school class and then worked as a doctor helping the children of parents who were tortured or missing during the Pinochet administration's reign.

A fluent speaker of five languages, Bachelet is the first woman to be democratically elected as a head of state in Latin America who was not married to a previous head of state. What do you think motivates Bachelet? How would you measure her performance and effectiveness?

Sources: *The Economist,* March 31, 2007, p. 44; http://en.wikipedia.org/wiki/Michelle_Bachelet.

happy workers are always the most productive ones, nor is it true that unhappy or dissatisfied workers are always the poorest performers. It is entirely possible, for example, for poorly performing workers to be fairly satisfied with their jobs (maybe because they are paid well yet do not have to work very hard, like Homer Simpson in the television show *The Simpsons*). It is also possible for dissatisfied workers to be relatively high performers (they may have a strong work ethic, or they may be trying to improve chances to get out of their current job). Despite the intuitive appeal of believing that satisfied workers usually perform better, it may be that satisfaction has only an indirect effect on performance. Nevertheless, having both satisfied *and* high-performing followers is a goal leaders should usually strive to achieve.

Understanding and Influencing Follower Motivation

Always bear in mind that your resolution to succeed is more important than any other one thing.
Abraham Lincoln, U.S. president

So what do leaders do to "motivate" followers to accomplish group goals? Are all leaders and followers motivated the same way? Is there a universal theory of motivation? In other words, does Osama bin Laden or General David Petraeus, commander of U.S. forces in Iraq, use the same or different techniques to motivate his followers? As seen in Highlight 9.2, organizations spend billions on motivating the troops, but do these interventions actually help to improve job satisfaction, retention, and performance? Research can provide the answers to these questions, and few topics of human behavior have been the subject of so much attention as that of motivation. So much has been written about motivation that a comprehensive review of the subject is beyond the scope of this book. We will, however, survey several major approaches to understanding worker motivation, as well as address the implications of these approaches for follower satisfaction and performance. These motivational theories and approaches provide leadership practitioners with a number of suggestions to get followers to engage in and persist with different behaviors. It is important to understand that some motivational theories are particularly useful in certain situations but are not as applicable in others. Just as a carpenter can successfully build better wooden structures or furniture by having a larger set of tools, so can leadership practitioners solve a greater number of motivational problems among followers by becoming familiar with different motivational theories and approaches. People who have only hammers in their tool kits are more likely to see every problem as a nail needing hammering, and it is not unusual for less effective leaders to call on a very limited number of approaches to any motivational problem. *Leaders who are knowledgeable about different motivational theories are more likely to choose the right theory for a particular follower and situation, and often have higher-performing and more satisfied employees as a result.*

It is important to understand that most performance problems can be attributed to unclear expectations, skill deficits, resource/equipment shortages, or a lack of motivation. Of these underlying causes, leaders seem to have the most difficulty recognizing and rectifying motivation problems. An example might help to illustrate this point. A major airline was having serious problems with the customer service of its flight attendants. Passenger complaints were on the rise and airplane loading (the average number of people per flight) was decreasing. The perceived lack of customer service was beginning to cost the airline market share and revenues; to fix the problem it decided to have all 10,000 flight attendants go through a two-day customer service training program. Unfortunately, passenger complaints only got worse after the training. A thorough investigation of the underlying cause of the problem revealed that flight attendants knew what they were supposed to do, had all of the skills necessary to perform the behaviors, and usually had the resources and equipment necessary to serve customers. The root cause was a lack of motivation to "go the extra mile" for customers. When asked what they found to be the most motivating aspect of being a flight attendant, most stated "time off." In other words the flight attendants were most motivated when they were *not* at work. Given that a strong union represented the flight attendants, how would you go about solving this dilemma? The next section will give you some ideas on how to resolve this and other motivation problems that you may face as a leader.

In this section we will discuss the key aspects of 11 different approaches to understanding motivation in a work or leadership context. We have organized the approaches into four broad categories: need theories, individual difference approaches, cognitive theories, and situational approaches. This categorization seems helpful for explanatory purposes, even though it is admittedly atheoretical. These theories and approaches are listed in Table 9.1. For illustrative purposes we will also discuss how leadership practitioners could apply these approaches to motivate two fictitious followers, Julie and Ling Ling. Julie is a 21-year-old ski lift operator in Banff, Alberta. Her primary job is to ensure that people get on and off her ski lift safely. She also does periodic equipment safety checks and maintains the lift lines and associated areas. Julie works from 7:30 A.M. to 5:00 P.M. five days a week, gets paid a salary, and has a pass that allows her to ski for free whenever she is off work. Ling Ling is a 35-year-old real estate agent in Hong Kong. She works for an agency that locates and rents apartments for people on one- to three-year business assignments for various multinational companies. She works many evenings and weekends showing apartments, and gets paid a salary plus a commission for every apartment she rents. How the 11 approaches could be used to motivate Julie and Ling Ling will be discussed periodically throughout this section.

Organizations Spend Billions on Motivational Programs for Employees, and All They Get Are Burned Feet

HIGHLIGHT 9.2

Organizations are constantly looking for quick fixes to their performance and effectiveness problems. The barriers to team or organizational performance often include a lack of resources and skills, unclear goals, poor performance or accountability standards, or dysfunctional work teams; in other words managerial incompetence plays a key role in many of these barriers. But rather than adopting methods to reduce managerial incompetence, many organizations instead have employees listen to motivational speakers or engage in white-water rafting, bungee jumping, or fire-walking events than take a hard look at their leadership talent. The motivational speaking circuit includes former professional athletes, astronauts, fighter pilots, and military generals, successful and failed business leaders, politicians, psychologists, and consultants. Motivational speaking engagements can be quite lucrative—one of the authors worked with a speaker who gave one speech in Las Vegas at lunch and the same speech that evening in Minneapolis and made $150,000 for the day. The author also has worked with a group of ex-fighter pilots who do half-day "Business Is Combat" seminars for $30,000–$75,000.

Companies think nothing of spending these big bucks in order to motivate employees. For example, the software consulting firm EMC has spent $625,000 to have 5,000 employees walk over burning coals. But do expensive speakers and extreme activities actually help to improve organizational performance? Unfortunately, exhaustive research has shown there is virtually no link between motivational spending and company revenues, profitability, or market share. Perhaps the biggest problem is that employees may find it difficult to see the link between walking over a bed of hot coals or participating in a Business Is Combat mission planning event and making another 20 sales calls every week. The problem is that these events do not address the root cause of many organizational woes, managerial incompetence, but instead covertly shift the burden on "underperforming" employees. Other than bankrolling the motivation industry, these programs do seem to have another benefit. Nine U.S. Air Force recruiters had to go to the emergency room after they received second- and third-degree burns on their feet after one of these "motivational" programs.

Sources: D. Jones, "Firms Spend Billions to Fire Up Workers—With Little Luck," *USA Today,* May 10, 2001, pp. 1–2A; P. G. Chronis, "9 Burn Feet in National Guard Recruiters' Fire Walk," *Denver Post,* December 28, 1998, pp. 1A, 17A; G. J. Curphy and R. T. Hogan, "Managerial Incompetence: Is There a Dead Skunk on the Table?" Working Paper, 2004. G. J. Curphy, M. J. Benson, A. Baldrica, and R. T. Hogan. *Managerial Incompetence.* Unpublished manuscript, 2007.

First rule of survival: Pack your own parachute.

T. L. Hakala

Need Theories

These theories assume people all have basic needs, and leaders can motivate followers by helping them satisfy their needs. One way to get followers to engage and persist with the behaviors needed to accomplish group goals is to appeal to their needs. What underlying needs do flight attendants have, and would they exhibit higher levels of customer service behaviors if leaders satisfied those needs? The two major need theories include Maslow's hierarchy of needs and Alderfer's existence-relatedness-growth (ERG) theory.[53,54] These theories assume that all people share a common set of basic needs; the theories primarily differ in the types of needs that supposedly underlie or drive people's behavior. **Needs** refer to

TABLE 9.1
Eleven Motivational Approaches

Category	Theory or Approach	Major Themes of Characteristics
Need	Maslow's hierarchy of needs	Satisfy needs to change behavior.
	Alderfer's ERG theory	Can satisfy multiple needs simultaneously.
Individual difference	Achievement orientation	Personality trait.
	Values	People are aligned with their personal values.
	Intrinsic motivation	People are more motivated to do some activities than others.
Cognitive	Goal setting	Set goals to change behavior.
	Expectancy theory	Motivate others by clarifying links between behaviors, performance, and rewards.
	Equity theory	People are motivated to reduce inequities between rewards and effort.
	Self-efficacy	One's beliefs about being able to successfully complete a task.
Situational	Operant approach	Change rewards and punishments to change behavior.
	Empowerment	Give people automony and latitude in order to increase their motivation for work.

internal states of tension or arousal, or uncomfortable states of deficiency people are motivated to change. Hunger would be a good example of a need, as people are motivated to eat when they get hungry. Other needs might include the need to live in a safe and secure place, to belong to a group with common interests or social ties, or to do interesting and challenging work. If these needs were not being met, then people would choose to engage in and persist with certain behaviors until they were satisfied. According to these motivational approaches, leadership practitioners can get followers to engage in and persist with certain behaviors by correctly identifying and appeasing their needs.

Maslow's Hierarchy of Needs

According to Maslow, people are motivated by five basic sorts of needs. These include the need to survive physiologically, the need for security, the need for affiliation with other people (i.e., belongingness), the need for self-esteem, and the need for self-actualization. Maslow's conceptualization of needs is usually represented by a triangle with the five levels of needs arranged in a hierarchy called, not surprisingly, the **hierarchy of needs** (see Figure 9.2). According to Maslow, any person's behavior can be understood primarily as the effort directed to satisfy one particular level of need in the

FIGURE 9.2
Maslow's hierarchy of needs.

hierarchy. Which level happens to be motivating a person's behavior at any time depends on whether or not lower needs in the hierarchy have been satisfied. According to Maslow, lower-level needs must be satisfied before the next-higher level becomes salient in motivating behavior.

Maslow believed higher-level needs like those for self-esteem or self-actualization would not become salient (even when unfulfilled) until lower needs were satisfied. Thus, a practical implication of his theory is that leaders may only be successful in motivating follower behavior by taking account of the follower's position on the needs hierarchy. Applying Maslow's hierarchy to Julie, it might be relatively inefficient to try to motivate our ski lift operator by appealing to how much pride she could take in a job well done (i.e., to her self-esteem) if she was underdressed for weather conditions. If her boss wanted Julie to do more, then she should first make sure that Julie's physiological (i.e., clothing) needs were met, that she worked and lived in a secure place, and that she had ample opportunities to socialize with other employees. Only after these lower needs had been met should the boss try to increase Julie's self-esteem. Thus, if leadership practitioners want to use Maslow's hierarchy of needs to motivate employees to work harder, then they need to determine where their followers fall on the needs hierarchy and ensure all lower-order needs are satisfied before appealing to their followers' self-esteem or self-actualization needs. Leadership practitioners should watch for "mismatches" between their motivational efforts and followers' *lowest* (on the hierarchy) unsatisfied needs.

Based on 3 levels of needs

ERG Theory

Alderfer's **existence-relatedness-growth (ERG) theory** is similar to Maslow's hierarchy of needs. In the terms of ERG theory, *existence* needs basically correspond to Maslow's physiological and security needs; *relatedness* needs are like Maslow's social and esteem needs; and *growth* needs are similar to the need for self-actualization. Beyond those similarities, however, are two important differences.

First, Alderfer reported that people sometimes try to satisfy *more than one need at a time*. For example, even though a follower's existence needs may not be entirely satisfied, she may still be motivated to grow as a person. Second, he claimed *frustration of a higher-level need can lead to efforts to satisfy a lower-level need*. In other words, a follower who is continually frustrated in achieving some need might regress and exert effort to satisfy a lower need that has already been satisfied. For example, if Ling Ling had strong relatedness needs but was unable to build friendships with her co-workers, she might regress to satisfying her existence needs. Some of these behaviors might include moving to an upscale neighborhood; buying a more expensive wardrobe, a new sports car, or new stereo equipment; or demanding more pay. Alderfer called this the **frustration regression hypothesis.**

The practical implications for motivating followers using ERG theory are threefold. First, leadership practitioners should identify the degree of need for existence, relatedness, and growth for their followers. Followers having relatively unmet existence or relatedness needs will focus their behaviors on satisfying these needs, and leadership practitioners may be able to help with these endeavors. Second, followers having relatively satisfied existence and relatedness needs are more apt to focus on growth needs. Leadership practitioners can get a lot of motivational "mileage" by helping followers satisfy their growth needs, as these followers are more willing to develop and master new skills, apply skills in new situations, look for more responsibility and independence, and strive to achieve greater personal and organizational challenges. Third, leadership practitioners should also be on the lookout for the frustration regression hypothesis among followers. If followers are repeatedly thwarted in satisfying a need and have shifted their efforts to oversatisfying a lower-level need, then appealing to the need that was thwarted may be relatively fruitless. For instance, trying to motivate Ling Ling to work harder by stating the real estate agency is a team and needs to work together to get results will probably not result in substantial behavioral change for Ling Ling. Instead, the leader may need to work closely with Ling Ling to determine why she has been unable to satisfy her relatedness needs, and coach her on how to build relationships with others in the agency. Only after these relationships are established will the leader be able to motivate Ling Ling to work as a part of a team to get results.

Concluding Thoughts on Need Theories

According to the two need theories, leaders wanting to motivate followers to engage in certain behaviors or exert extra effort should start by determining if their lower-level needs are being satisfied. In most cases it will be difficult for followers to exhibit the behaviors necessary for group success if these lower-level needs are not being met; therefore, leaders should do all they can to help followers meet these needs. Once the lower-level needs are satisfied, leaders can then work to satisfy higher-level needs, which in turn should improve the odds of group success. So how would you apply the need theories to improve the customer service of flight attendants? How would you go about determining the needs of flight attendants, and what kind of program would you implement to improve customer service? Although the two need theories do provide some useful ideas on how to improve customer service, it is important to note that they have several limitations. For one thing, none of the theories makes specific predictions about what an individual will do to satisfy a particular need.[18,54] For example, in Ling Ling's situation she may exert considerable effort to establish new friendships at work, try to make friends outside work, or even spend a lot of money on a new car or stereo equipment (the frustration regression hypothesis). This lack of specificity and predictive power severely limits the practical applicability of the need theories in real-life settings. On the other hand, awareness of the general nature of the various sorts of basic human needs described in these theories seems fundamentally useful to leaders. Leaders will have a difficult time getting followers to maintain various work behaviors by emphasizing good relationships with co-workers or appealing to their sense of pride if the job pays only minimum wage and followers are having a difficult time making ends meet. A person may be reluctant to volunteer for a self-actualizing opportunity in support of a political campaign if such participation may risk that person's financial security. Perhaps the greatest insight provided by these two theories is that leadership practitioners may need to address some basic, fundamental areas before their attempts to get followers to expend more effort on work-related behaviors will be successful.

Individual Differences in Motivation

Some players you pat their butts, other players you kick their butts, and some players you leave alone.

Pete Rose

These approaches assume people differ in key personality traits, work values, and the work they like to do. Leaders can motivate followers by hiring those with the right traits and work values and interests. Is it possible that some people are naturally more "motivated" than others? Do some people automatically put forth a higher level of effort toward group goals simply because of who they are or because they enjoy what they do? Unlike the two need theories that claim all people share some fundamental needs, the individual difference approach to motivation assumes that people vary substantially in their achievement orientation, work values, and intrinsic motivation. This approach to motivation is rather simple. To improve group performance, leaders should select only those followers who possess both the right skills and have a higher level of achievement orientation, have the right work values, or find the work to be intrinsically motivating.

Achievement Orientation

The best job goes to the person who can get it done without passing the buck or coming back with excuses.

Napoleon Hill, author

Atkinson proposed that an individual's tendency to exert effort toward task accomplishment depended partly on the strength of his or her motive to achieve success, or, as Atkinson called it, **achievement orientation**.[56] McClelland further developed Atkinson's ideas and said that individuals with a strong achievement orientation (or in McClelland's terms, a strong *need for achievement*) strived to accomplish socially acceptable endeavors and activities. These individuals also preferred tasks that provided immediate and ample feedback and were moderately difficult (i.e., tasks that required a considerable amount of effort but were accomplishable). Additionally, individuals with a strong need to achieve felt satisfied when they successfully solved work problems or accomplished job tasks. Individuals with a relatively low need to achieve generally preferred easier tasks and did not feel satisfied by solving problems or accomplishing assigned tasks. McClelland maintained that differences in achievement orientation were a primary reason why people differed in the levels of effort they exerted to accomplish assignments, objectives, or goals. Thus, achievement orientation is a bit like "fire in the belly"; people with more achievement orientation are likely to set higher personal and work goals and are more likely to expend the effort needed to accomplish them. People with low levels of achievement motivation tend to set lower personal and work goals, and are less likely to accomplish them.[57]

Achievement orientation is also a component of the Five Factor personality dimension of dependability (see Chapter 7). Like intelligence, dependability has been found to be positively related to performance across virtually all jobs as well as predict success in school, in the military, in blue-collar and retail workers, and in management positions. All things being equal, people with higher levels of achievement orientation are likely to do better in school, pursue postgraduate degrees, get promoted more quickly, and get paid higher salaries and bonuses than their lower-scoring counterparts.[39–41,48,58–67]

Given that individuals with higher achievement orientation scores set high personal goals and put in the time and effort necessary to achieve them, it is hardly surprising that achievement orientation is often a key success factor for people who advance to the highest levels of the organization. For example, achievement orientation appears to be a common success factor underlying the career of Michelle Bachelet, Bob Nardelli, Wu Yi, and Conrad Black (Profiles in Leadership 9.1–9.4). Although

Can Women Have It All?

HIGHLIGHT 9.3

Research has shown that it is very difficult for women to have both a high-powered career and a family. At midlife 30–50 percent of achievement-oriented women do not have children, and those who chose to do so often suffer numerous career setbacks. Because of the media hype of older women having children, many of these high-powered females falsely believe that they can wait until their late 30s and early 40s to start a family. But medical research shows that female fertility rates drop precipitously starting in the mid-30s. What is particularly unfortunate is that high-achieving men do not suffer these same problems; of the 79 percent who want children, 75 percent do in fact have them. And the more successful the male, the more likely they are to have a wife and kids.

Until United States laws provide more liberal support to working parents, it appears that women will need to be more deliberate about their career/family choices. But another potential solution to this dilemma is for women to develop better frameworks for success. Oftentimes high-achieving women (and men, for that matter) only define success in terms of career outcomes. But by doing so, people can never get promoted quickly or high enough. As soon as a person gets promoted from manager to director, they immediately start doing

what is necessary to become a vice president. Over time, many of these people begin to feel that they are on a treadmill, and they get disillusioned and eventually burn out. Nash and Stevenson suggest it might be better to define success as having four components:

- Happiness: Do I enjoy what I am doing?
- Achievement: Am I accomplishing the goals I have set for myself?
- Significance: Am I doing something important?
- Legacy: Will my efforts and achievements endure over time?

People who use these four components to define success will likely avoid climbing the corporate ladder just for the sake of doing so. These individuals may max out the achievement component, but the happiness, significance, and legacy components of success are likely to suffer. By defining success more broadly, men and women should be able to make better choices about the kind of work they want to pursue, where they want to go with their careers, and if and when they want to start a family.

Sources: A. Fels, "Ambition, Gender, and Defining Success." *Harvard Business Review,* April 2004, pp. 50–61; L. Nash and H. Stevenson, "Success That Lasts." *Harvard Business Review,* February 2004, pp. 102–09; S. A. Hewlett, "Executive Women and the Myth of Having It All." *Harvard Business Review,* April 2002, pp. 66–67.

achievement orientation is often associated with higher performance, it is important to note that high achievers can get extremely demoralized when faced with unclear or impossible tasks. Working with elite Army Ranger units, Britt found that these units almost always performed at very high levels and were often very successful. But when given unclear missions with few resources and impossible timelines, these same units could self-destruct very quickly. In these situations the units felt they were being set up to fail, and fail they did. This phenomenon is clearly depicted in the movie *Black Hawk Down,* where Army Ranger units were sent to Mogadishu, Somalia, to capture a Somalian war lord. The important lesson here is that leaders need to give high achievers clear goals and the resources they need to succeed.[68]

So how could a leader apply this knowledge of achievement motivation to improve the performance of Julie, Ling Ling, and the flight attendants? Perhaps the first step would be to ensure the hiring process selected those individuals with higher levels of achievement orientation. Assuming they had higher scores, we would expect Ling Ling to work with her boss to set aggressive goals for renting apartments and then work as many nights and weekends as were needed to achieve them. We might also expect Ling Ling to obtain her MBA from Hong Kong University over the next few years. Julie could also be expected to set high personal and work goals, but she may find that her job limits her ability to pursue these goals. Unlike Ling Ling, who can control the number of nights and weekends she wants to work, Julie has no control over the number of people who ride on her lift. The job itself may limit Julie's ability to fulfill her high level of achievement orientation. As a result, she may pursue other activities, such as becoming an expert skier, joining the ski patrol, doing ski racing, looking for additional responsibilities or opportunities for advancement, or finding another job where she has the opportunity to achieve and get rewarded for her efforts. Because Julie would set and work toward high personal goals, a good boss would work closely with Julie to find work-related ways to capitalize on her achievement orientation. Thus, achievement orientation may be a dual-edged sword. Leadership practitioners may be able to hire a group of highly motivated followers, but they also need to set clear expectations, provide opportunities for followers to set and achieve work-related goals, and provide feedback on progress toward goals. Otherwise followers may find different ways to fulfill their high levels of achievement orientation.

Values

The sins of greed, selfishness, and vanity translate into high Commercial, low Altruism, and high Recognition work values, which are some of the biggest drivers of executives today.

R. T. Hogan, Hogan Assessment Systems

If motivation is all about choosing to engage and persist with particular behaviors, then appealing to followers' work values can be a very powerful motivational strategy.[40,47,69] As described in Chapter 6, values represent a person's most important and enduring beliefs and make up another set of individual difference variables that are related to motivation. In the world of work, some people believe creating high-quality products to be very important, whereas others might believe making money or helping others to be more important. A listing of 10 common work values and suggestions for what leaders can do to motivate followers with specific values can be found in Table 9.2.

It is important to realize that there are no right or wrong work values per se, but followers will be motivated to do activities that are aligned with their personal values and unmotivated to work on those activities they do not believe to be important. Most followers possess two to four key work values, and leaders can motivate followers to engage and persist in certain activities by aligning these activities to followers' underlying values. Just as transformational or charismatic leaders appeal to followers' values as

TABLE 9.2
**Key Work Values
and Motivational
Strategies**

Sources: Adapted from
J. Hogan and R. T. Hogan,
*Motives, Values and
Preferences Inventory Manual.*
Tulsa, OK: Hogan
Assessment Systems, 1996;
G. J. Curphy, *Hogan Assess-
ment Systems Certification
Workshop Training Manual.*
Tulsa, OK: Hogan Assess-
ment Systems, 2003c.

Recognition: Followers with strong Recognition values believe fame, visibility, and publicity are important. Leaders can get followers to engage in and persist with desired behaviors by giving them opportunities for public recognition.
Power: Followers with strong Power values enjoy competition, being seen as influential, and driving hard to make an impact. Leaders can motivate these followers by putting them in jobs where they can achieve, get ahead, and succeed.
Hedonism: Followers with strong Hedonism values are motivated by pleasure, variety, and excitement. Providing these followers with opportunities to take risks, entertain others, and have fun are ways leaders can motivate these individuals.
Altruistic: Leaders can motivate followers with strong Altruism values by giving them opportunities to improve society and help others who are less fortunate.
Affiliation: Followers with strong Affiliation values are motivated if their work allows them to meet new people or work in team environments.
Tradition: These individuals are most motivated when they work in organizations that have strong customs and standards of behavior.
Security: Followers with strong Security values can be motivated to engage in various activities if these activities help create stable, predictable, and risk-free environments.
Commerce: These followers are motivated by financial success. The more they are paid, the more they are motivated to work.
Aesthetics: These followers are most motivated when in environments that place a premium on experimentation, artistic expression, creative problem solving, and quality.
Science: These followers are most motivated when digging deeply into problems, and keeping up to date on technology. They enjoy analyzing data to get at the truth.

an important motivational strategy to drive change (see Chapter 13), so can other leaders align work activities to followers' work values in order to increase satisfaction and performance. The trick is accurately identifying and aligning work activities to followers' work values.

Unfortunately, many leaders do not appear to be very good at accurately assessing followers' work values. When followers are asked to list the things they believe to be most important at work, they describe many of the values found in Table 9.2. But when they are asked to describe what motivates others at work, 75 percent report that money is the best way to motivate others. As such, many leaders appear to suffer from **extrinsic motivational bias** and falsely believe followers are more motivated by money (i.e., Commercial values) rather than by job security, recognition, or helping others. Research has shown that most followers value doing important work (i.e., Power) and being recognized for good performance (i.e., Recognition) over making money, but many people falsely believe that paying followers more is the only path to higher performance.[66,70] Extrinsic motivational bias is a variation of the fundamental attribution error described in Chapter 3, where people are biased to believe that their own success is due to their own efforts and others' success is due to external factors, such as pay.

So how could we apply what we have learned about values to motivate our flight attendants, Ling Ling, and Julie to perform at higher levels? Like achievement orientation, work values develop early in life and are quite difficult to change. So leaders will need to accurately assess what these individuals value and then restructure work so that it is better aligned with their underlying beliefs. In the case of the flight attendants, it appears that these individuals may have stronger Affiliation and Security values. So paying flight attendants more money will probably not help to improve customer service, but leaders might have success by emphasizing how good customer service would help reduce the risk of downsizing if the planes were kept fully loaded with passengers. Because Ling Ling works in sales, she might be more motivated to work harder because part of her compensation is contingent upon performance (i.e., Commercial and Power values). The more apartments she rents, the more commission she gets paid, and the harder she will work. Julie, on the other hand, appears to have stronger Hedonism, Affiliation, and Altruism scores. Her boss might be most successful in motivating Julie to work hard by giving her the opportunity to work with and help others and giving her time off so she can go skiing. These three examples all point out the importance of hiring followers that have values similar to those emphasized in a particular job or restructuring work so that it better fits with followers' work values.

Intrinsic Motivation

Work behavior is motivated by both internal and external factors. In this section, we will focus on the former, although we also will examine how the two factors interact. We use the term **intrinsic motivation** to describe behavior seemingly motivated for its own sake, for the personal satisfaction and increased feelings of competence or control one gets from doing it. In other words, some people are motivated to persist in certain behaviors for the simple reason that they like to do them. As such, intrinsic motivation is closely related to work values, in that people often enjoy doing those activities aligned with their work values. But intrinsic motivation is more specific than work values, as it relates to the specific activities that one enjoys doing. Someone might have strong Altruism values and is intrinsically motivated to teach middle-school students. They may not like to counsel families, draw blood, work in a homeless shelter, and so on, although all of their activities are related to the work value of Altruism. Getting back to our two characters, Julie or Ling Ling might spend a lot of time operating ski lifts or showing apartments, respectively, simply because they enjoy these activities. What is intrinsically motivating for one person, however, may not be for someone else. Hobbies, for example, are almost by definition intrinsically motivating, yet they also reflect the diversity of human

Work Values and Cadet Motivation

HIGHLIGHT 9.4

One of the toughest things for freshmen at a military academy to do is come back to school after winter break. For most freshmen it is the first time they have been home since June and the contrast between civilian and military life is so great that many are tempted to leave military school. The freshmen at the United States Air Force Academy were asked to write a paper on why they returned to the institution after winter break. Read the following paper and determine what work values drive this individual:

Winter Break

So after our sunburns have faded and memories of our winter break have been reduced to pictures we've pinned on our desk boards, and once again we've exchanged t-shirts and swimsuits for flight suits and camouflage, there still remains the question that every cadet in Colorado Springs has asked themselves at some point: Why did we come back? Why, after spending two weeks with our family, could we return to one of the most demanding lifestyles in the country? After listening to our "friends" who are home from State or Ivy League schools chock full of wisdom about how the war in Iraq is unjust and unworldly, why would we return? And after watching the news and reading the papers, which only seem to condemn the military's every mistake and shadow every victory, why would we continue to think it is worth the sacrifice of a normal college life?

Is it because the institution to which we belong is tuition-free? Anyone who claims this has forgotten that we will, by the time we graduate, repay the U.S. taxpayer many times over in blood, sweat, and tears. Is it because the schooling we are receiving is one of the best undergraduate educations in the country? While the quality of the education is second to none, anyone who provides this as a main reason has lost sight of the awesome responsibility that awaits those who are tough enough to graduate and become commissioned officers in the U.S. Air Force.

I come back to the Academy because I want to have the training necessary so that one day I'll have the incredible responsibility of leading the sons and daughters of America in combat. These men and women will never ask about my Academy grade point average; their only concern will be that I have the ability to lead them expertly—I will be humbled to earn their respect.

I come back to the Academy because I want to be the commander who saves lives negotiating with Arab leaders . . . in their own language. I come back to the Academy because, if called upon, I want to be the pilot who flies halfway around the world with three mid-air refuelings to send a bomb from 30,000 feet into a basement housing the enemy . . . through a ventilation shaft two feet wide. For becoming an officer in today's modern Air Force is so much more than just a command; it is being a diplomat, a strategist, a communicator, a moral compass, but always a warrior first . . .

Joseph R. Tomczak
Cadet Fourth Class
United States Air Force Academy

---

tastes for different activities. Stamp collecting may be intrinsically motivating to one person, yet exceedingly boring to many others. The key for leadership practitioners is to identify the activities their followers like to perform (within reason), and increase their job opportunities to do them.

Researchers have consistently reported that individuals often voluntarily put forth effort toward activities they enjoy doing.[71–75] If an individual is already engaged in an intrinsically motivating activity, we might ask what would result if extrinsic rewards were added to the intrinsic reward of just performing the activity. It might seem at first as though the activity would be even further strengthened if external rewards were added to the internal rewards. Sometimes, though, that is not the case. Some research has shown that external rewards or incentives may backfire if they are given to people already intrinsically motivated to perform the tasks. That can result in a *decrease* in the person's intrinsic motivation toward the tasks. Further study of this **overjustification effect** has shown that external rewards can result in a decrease in intrinsic motivation when they are perceived to be "controlling"; however, rewards seen as providing "informational" value (e.g., letting a person know how well he or she is doing) or those that are consistent with societal norms concerning pay and benefits typically do not result in a decrease in intrinsic motivation for the task. After reviewing the results of approximately 100 studies, Eisenberger and Cameron went on to say that the overjustification effect is more of a myth than reality; the number of situations where this occurs is so limited and so easily avoided that it rarely, if ever, happens in the real world. Despite this preponderance of evidence, however, many educators and leaders continue to believe in the notion that rewards reduce the intrinsic motivation of tasks.[76,77]

So how would intrinsic motivation and the overjustification effect work with Julie and Ling Ling? In both cases, the leaders would need to spend time with both individuals to find out what they enjoy doing at work. Not only might the boss learn that Julie really likes to work outdoors, she might also like the social nature of interacting with the crowds waiting in lift lines. This might indicate Julie would particularly enjoy working at the largest and most crowded lifts, something other lift operators may not enjoy so much. Ling Ling might really like sales but hate the paperwork associated with closing leases. Her boss could assign the administrative aspects of Ling Ling's job to an administrative support person, or find other ways (such as using technology) to reduce her administrative workload. Although followers will almost always have to perform activities they may not like, the more a leader aligns her followers' intrinsic interests with their work activities, the more motivated her team is likely to be.

Concluding Thoughts on Individual Differences in Motivation

Because people vary in their achievement orientation, and values, and in the tasks they find intrinsically motivating, one way to ensure that followers will exert the effort needed to accomplish their tasks is to select individuals already high in these motives. Although McClelland has reported successfully training people to be higher in achievement orientation, this can be a relatively expensive and inefficient process; putting more emphasis on selecting the right people for the job in the first place may be a preferable approach for leaders to take.[57]

It is also important to remember that perhaps the most effective way to determine what followers find to be important or intrinsically motivating is to simply ask them what they like to do. However, many leaders either do not have particularly good relationships with their followers or assume they know what motivates them, so they often fail to ask this simple question. While it may not be possible to completely align tasks with followers' intrinsic interests, leaders may be able to reassign or periodically rotate tasks to increase the level of follower motivation. Leaders often assume that jobs and task assignments are static and unchangeable, but most organizations do not care who does the work as long as it gets done. Leaders may be able to get higher-quality work and have more satisfied employees by reassigning work according to values and intrinsic interests. As the head of customer service, how would you use this information about individual differences in motivation to improve the customer service levels of flight attendants?

Cognitive Theories

A good goal is like strenuous exercise—it makes you stretch.

Mary Kay Ashe, CEO

These theories assume leaders can motivate followers by setting goals and bolstering their beliefs about task accomplishment. Another way to get followers to engage and persist with the behaviors associated with the accomplishment of team goals is to persuade them to think differently about their efforts. Rather than appealing to needs or hiring individuals who are naturally more "motivated," the cognitive theories look at whether followers will exert more effort toward group goals when the expectations for performance and the links between the level of effort and desirable outcomes are clear. Should leaders set goals for their teams or simply tell them to do their best? Similarly, should leaders explicitly point out what rewards a group will get if they achieve certain outcomes, or will followers exert more effort if rewards are vague and only loosely tied to performance? The research underlying the cognitive theories provides leadership practitioners with the answers to these two important questions.

Goal Setting

Goal-setting theory has been rated #1 in importance among 73 management theories by organizational behavior scholars.

Ed Locke, University of Maryland

One of the most familiar and easiest formal systems of motivation to use with followers is **goal setting.** From the leader's perspective, it involves helping followers see how a goal might be attained by following a systematic plan to achieve it. According to Locke and Latham, goals are the most powerful determinants of task behaviors. Goals serve to direct attention, mobilize effort, help people develop strategies for goal achievement, and help people continue exerting effort until the goal is reached. That leads, in turn, to even higher goals.[78–80]

Locke and Latham reported that nearly 400 studies involving hundreds of tasks across 40,000 individuals, groups, and organizations in eight different countries have provided consistent support for several aspects of goal setting. First, this research showed goals that were both *specific* and *difficult* resulted in consistently higher effort and performance when contrasted to "do your best" goals. Second, *goal commitment* is critical. Merely

Bob Nardelli

PROFILES IN LEADERSHIP 9.2

Bob Nardelli grew up in Pennsylvania and went to Western Illinois University. After graduating with a BS in Science, Nardelli pursued an MBA at the University of Louisville. Joining General Electric as an entry-level engineer in a manufacturing facility, Nardelli rose through the ranks to eventually become the Senior Vice President of GE's Power Systems division. In 2000 Nardelli was passed over as the successor to Jack Welch and subsequently took over the CEO role at Home Depot. At the time Nardelli took over Home Depot, the company had about 1,000 stories and a strong customer-focused, entrepreneurial culture. The company frowned upon bureaucracy, and store managers had tremendous latitude in the products they opted to sell in their stores. But at the time Home Depot was struggling to keep costs under control and wasn't able to leverage suppliers to the extent it could have, given its huge store network. In addition, the company had grown so quickly that it was difficult to assess how well the company and individual stores were actually performing.

Bob Nardelli went into his new job with a charter of cutting costs, standardizing and streamlining operations, implementing measurement systems to better track store and associate performance, and ultimately making Home Depot attractive to investors by improving stock price. In order to fulfill this mandate, Nardelli let go of a number of seasoned merchandising and operations executives and replaced them with ex-GE types. Although these were laudable goals, one big problem for Nardelli and his new staff was that few if any of these individuals had any big-box retail experience. They did not understand the products or the customers who frequented their stores. As a result, many of Nardelli's initiatives did cut costs and did a better job tracking store and associate performance, but customer service and employee morale suffered tremendously under his watch. The number of associates in the stores during shopping hours was substantially reduced and if customers actually found an associate then more often then not he or she would be in a corner bitching to other associates about the company. If a customer did ask them a question about various home improvement products, they often lacked the knowledge to provide good answers.

Under Nardelli's leadership, the number of stores increased from 1,000 to 2,100, annual revenues increased from $45 billion to $90 billion, and Home Depot became the country's second largest retailer after Wal-Mart. But employee morale and turnover suffered, customer satisfaction was much lower than Lowe's (its biggest competitor), and the stock price remained flat for six years. Despite the lack of improvement in stock price, Nardelli and his top leadership team were among the best compensated executives in the United States. Public outcry over his annual compensation, his ham-fisted interactions with investors and board members, and his failure to improve customer satisfaction and stock price of Home Depot as compared to Lowe's ultimately led to his resignation in early 2007. But Nardelli did not leave empty handed. In many ways he left the company worse off than when he joined, yet the board of directors awarded him $210 million dollars as part of his severance package. Not bad for a leader who at best achieved mixed results. Where do you think achievement motivation, work values, and intrinsic motivation come into play with Home Depot from 2000–2007?

Sources: A. Zimmerman, "Home Depot Tries To Make Nice with Customers." *The Wall Street Journal,* February 20, 2007, p. D1–2; http://en.wikipedia.org/wiki/Robert_Nardelli; http://www.msnbc.msn.com/id/16451112/; http://www. msnbc.msn.com/id/16470818/site/newsweek; http://www.keystonesearch.com/newsletter_q1_2007a.

having goals is not enough. Although follower participation in setting goals is one way to increase commitment, goals set either by leaders unilaterally or through participation with followers can lead to necessary levels of commitment. Commitment to assigned goals was often as high as commitment to goals followers helped to set, provided the leader was perceived to have legitimate authority, expressed confidence in followers, and provided clear standards for performance. Third, followers exerted the greatest effort when goals were accompanied by *feedback*; followers getting goals or feedback alone generally exerted less effort. (See Highlight 9.5 for a practical application of goal-setting theory).

Several other aspects of goal setting are also worth noting. First, goals can be set for any aspect of performance, be it reducing costs, improving the quality of services and products, increasing voter registration, or winning a league championship. Nevertheless, leaders need to ensure that they do not set conflicting goals, as followers can only exert so much effort over a given period of time. Second, determining just how challenging to make goals creates a bit of a dilemma for leaders. Successfully completed goals provide followers with a sense of job satisfaction, and easy goals are more likely to be completed than difficult goals. However, easily attainable goals result in lower levels of effort (and, in turn, performance) than do more difficult goals. Research suggests that leaders might motivate followers most effectively by setting moderately difficult goals, recognizing partial goal accomplishment, and making use of a continuous-improvement philosophy by making goals incrementally more difficult.[81–86]

A leader's implicit and explicit expectations about goal accomplishment can also affect the performance of followers and teams. Research by Dov Eden and his associates in Israel provided fairly consistent support for the Pygmalion and Golem Effects.[87,88] The **Pygmalion Effect** occurs when leaders articulate high expectations for followers; in many cases these expectations alone will lead to higher performing followers and teams. Unfortunately, the **Golem Effect** is also true—leaders who have little faith in their followers' ability to accomplish a goal are rarely disappointed. Thus a leader's expectations for a follower or team have a good chance of becoming a self-fulfilling prophecy (Chapter 3). These results indicate that leaders wanting to improve team performance should set high but achievable goals and express confidence and support that the followers can get the job done.[89,90]

How could leadership practitioners apply goal setting to Julie and Ling Ling in order to increase their motivation levels? Given the research findings just described, Julie and Ling Ling's bosses should work with these two followers to set specific and moderately difficult goals, express confidence that they can achieve their goals, and provide regular feedback on goal progress. Julie and her boss could look at Julie's past performance or

Well-defined goals help organizations avoid the "crisis du jour" mode of operating and give them permission to celebrate success.

Bill Mease, consultant

The Balanced Scorecard

HIGHLIGHT 9.5

A practical method for implementing goal setting in organizational settings involves the creation of Balanced Scorecards. Kaplan and Norton argue that most of the measures typically used to assess organizational performance are too limited in scope. For example, many organizations set goals and periodically review their financial performance, but these indicators suffer from time lags (it may take a month or longer before the financial results of specific organizational activities are available) and say very little about other key organizational performance indicators, such as customer satisfaction, employee turnover, and key internal operational performance. To get around these problems, Kaplan and Norton advocate creating a set of goals and metrics for customers, employees, internal operations, and finance. Customer and employee goals and metrics make up leading indicators, as problems with customer satisfaction and employee turnover often result in subpar operational and financial performance.

Curphy has developed Balanced Scorecards for rural Minnesota hospitals and school districts. For example, hospitals begin this process by going through a comprehensive review of their market demographics, customer trends, financial performance, internal operations (i.e., pharmacy, surgical use, infection rates, radiology and lab use, etc.), and staffing and facility data. Key community and health care leaders then create a new five-year vision for the hospital, and then set strategic priorities in the customer, financial, internal operations, and workforce and facilities categories. These priorities are refined further to create clear, measurable goals with readily available metrics in order to track monthly progress. These Balanced Scorecard goals are then used to drive specific department goals and track hospital performance and have been very effective in helping all hospital employees understand how their efforts contribute to the hospital's overall performance. In several cases hospital performance has dramatically improved as a result of these Balanced Scorecard efforts. A partial example of a typical Balanced Scorecard for one of these rural hospitals is as follows:

- **Customer:** Improve patient satisfaction ratings from 74 to 86 percent by 1 January 2006.
- **Customer:** Increase the number of live births from 12 to 20 per month by 1 January 2006.
- **Financial:** Reduce average accounts payable from 84 to 53 days by 1 January 2006.
- **Financial:** Increase operating margins from 2 to 6 percent by 1 January 2006.
- **Internal Operations:** Increase orthopedic surgeries from 4 to 8 per day by 1 March 2006.
- **Internal Operations:** Reduce patient infection rates from 1 to .5 percent by 1 March 2006.
- **Workforce:** Reduce days needed to hire nurses from 62 to 22 days by 1 March 2006.
- **Workforce:** Reduce employee turnover rates from 27 to 12 percent by 1 March 2006.

A monthly Balanced Scorecard report is included in all employee pay statements and is a key topic of discussion in hospital and department staff meetings. Staff members review goal progress and regularly devise strategies for achieving department and hospital goals. One of the nice things about the Balanced Scorecard is that it helps employees to be proactive and gives them permission to win. In all too many organizations employees work hard but never see how their results contribute to team or organizational performance. Adopting Balanced Scorecards is a way to get around these problems.

Sources: G. J. Curphy, *The Blandin Education Leadership Program.* Grand Rapids, MN: The Blandin Foundation, 2004; R. S. Kaplan and D. P. Norton, "The Balanced Scorecard: Measures That Drive Performance." *Harvard Business Review,* January–February 1992, pp. 71–79; R. S. Kaplan and D. P. Norton, *The Balanced Scorecard.* Boston, MA: Harvard Business School Press, 1996; R. S. Kaplan and D. P. Norton, *The Strategy Focused Organization.* Boston, MA: Harvard Business School Press, 2001.

other lift operators' performance as a baseline, and then set specific and measurable goals around the number of hours worked, the number of people who fall off the lift during a shift, customer satisfaction survey ratings from skiers, the length of lift lines, or the number of complaints from customers. Similarly, Ling Ling and her boss could look at some real estate baseline measures and set goals around the number of apartments rented for the year, the total monetary value of these rentals, the time it takes to close a lease and complete the necessary paperwork, customer complaints, and sales expenses. Note that both Ling Ling and Julie's bosses would need to take care that they do not set conflicting goals. For example, if Julie had a goal only for the number of people who fell off the lift, then she might be more likely to run the lift very slowly, resulting in long lift lines and numerous customer complaints. In a similar vein, bosses need to ensure that individual goals do not conflict with team or organizational goals. Ling Ling's boss would need to make sure that Ling Ling's goals did not interfere with those of the other real estate agents in the firm. If Ling Ling's goals did not specify territorial limits, then she might rent properties in other agents' territories, which in turn might cause a high level of interoffice conflict. Both bosses should also take care to set measurable goals; that way they could provide Julie and Ling Ling with the feedback they need to stay on track. More information on the specific steps of goal setting can be found in Part 4 of this book.

Expectancy Theory

Every substandard organization I have ever seen had low performance standards. If you want superior performance, then you have got to set high standards for your employees.

Norman Schwarzkopf, United States Army

The next cognitive theory is concerned with clarifying the links between what people do and the rewards or outcomes they will obtain. First described by Tolman, **expectancy theory** has been modified for use in work settings.[91–95] It involves two fundamental assumptions: (*a*) motivated performance is the result of conscious choice, and (*b*) people will do what they believe will provide them the highest (or surest) rewards. Thus, expectancy theory is a highly *rational* approach to understanding motivation. It assumes that people act in ways that maximize their expectations of attaining valued outcomes, and that reliable predictions of behavior are possible if the factors that influence those expectations can be quantified. In this model, there are three such factors to be quantified. The first two are probability estimates (expectancies), and the third is a vector sum of predicted positive and negative outcomes. Expectancy theory maintains that leadership practitioners will be able to motivate followers if they understand the process followers use to determine whether certain behaviors will lead to valued rewards.

The first probability estimate is the **effort-to-performance expectancy.** Like all probabilities, it ranges from no chance of the event occurring to absolute certainty of its occurring; or, in decimal form, from 0.0 to 1.0. Here, the follower estimates the likelihood of performing the desired behavior adequately, assuming she puts forth the required effort. The second probability estimate is the **performance-to-outcome expectancy.** In this case, our follower estimates the likelihood of receiving a reward, given that she achieves the desired level of performance. This is a necessary step in the sequence since it is not uncommon for people to actually do good work yet not be rewarded for it (e.g., someone else may be the teacher's pet). Finally, the follower must determine the likely outcomes, assuming that the previous conditions have been met, and determine whether their weighted algebraic sum (**valence**) is sufficiently positive to be worth the time and effort. To put it more simply, expectancy theory says that people will be motivated to do a task if three conditions are met: (1) they can perform the task adequately if they put forth enough effort, (2) they will be rewarded if they do it, and (3) they value the reward (see Figure 9.3).

Applying these three concepts to Ling Ling might be helpful here. With the opening of the Chinese economy, Hong Kong has become a booming real estate rental market. But Ling Ling is focused on renting only upper-end apartments and the number of people who could afford to rent her properties are quite limited. Even though Ling Ling has been working three weekday evenings a week and all day Saturday (showing an average of 12 apartments per week), she is 25 percent behind her sales quota. According to expectancy theory, Ling Ling would first determine if working the additional two weekday evenings a week would enable her to rent more apartments—effort-to-performance expectancy. Second, Ling Ling would have to determine if renting these

FIGURE 9.3

An example of expectancy theory.

additional apartments would be sufficient to reach her sales quota by the end of the year—performance-to-outcome expectancy. Finally, Ling Ling would have to weigh the advantages of reaching her sales quota (sales bonus, job security) relative to the disadvantages (stress, loss of free time, loss of sleep, etc.)—valences. Notice that if Ling Ling did not believe that (a) working additional weekday evenings would help her to rent more apartments, (b) renting these additional apartments would be enough to reach her annual sales quota, or (c) the benefits of reaching her sales quota outweighed the costs, then Ling Ling would choose not to put forth the effort to rent additional apartments. She may feel that the real estate market is in such bad shape or her bonus so low that even if she were to meet her quota, it would not be worth the additional effort. As seen in Figure 9.3, all three components must have a relatively high probability or be favorably weighted in order for Ling Ling to exert further effort in renting additional apartments.

Leadership practitioners using expectancy theory to motivate a follower to do a work project would need to take three steps. First, the leader would have to increase effort-to-performance expectancy by clarifying the links between the follower's level of effort and project completion. To do this, the leader and follower might discuss what the follower would need to do, and the amount of time and resources it would take to complete the project. Second, the leader would need to increase the performance-to-reward expectancy by discussing the positive outcomes to the follower and the organization if the project were completed on time and at cost. This might involve such things as a year-end bonus, increased recognition by upper management, or reduced costs or increased market share for the organization. Finally, the leader would need to clarify all of the potential valences for successfully completing the project. This may not be obvious to the follower, so the leader would need to clearly describe both the pros and the cons but emphasize the positive aspects of the project.

Equity Theory

How am I supposed to feed my family on only $14 million dollars a year?

Latrell Sprewell, professional basketball player

This cognitive approach assumes that people value fairness in leader–follower exchange relationships. Followers are said to be most motivated when they believe that what they put into an activity or a job and what they get out of it are roughly equivalent to what others put into and get out of it. **Equity theory** proposes a very rational model for how followers assess these issues. Followers presumably reach decisions about equitable relationships by assigning values to the four elements in Figure 9.4 and then comparing the two ratios. Regarding the specific elements in each ratio, personal outcomes refer to what one is receiving for one's efforts, such as pay, recognition, job satisfaction, opportunity for advancement, and personal growth. Personal inputs refer to all those things one contributes to an activity or a job, such as time, effort, knowledge, and skills.[96–98]

FIGURE 9.4
Equity theory ratios.

$$\frac{\text{Personal outcomes}}{\text{Personal inputs}} = \frac{\text{Reference group outcomes}}{\text{Reference group inputs}}$$

A key aspect of equity theory is that Figure 9.4 contains *two* ratios. Judgments of equity are always based on a comparison to some reference group. It is the *relationship between the two ratios* that is important in equity theory, not the absolute value of either one's own or another's outcomes or inputs considered by themselves. What matters most is the comparison between one's own ratio and that of a reference group such as one's co-workers or workers holding similar jobs in other organizations. Consider, for example, the story of an investment banker who was making over $1,000,000 per year but was extremely dissatisfied with her pay. The banker stated that, on the one hand, she got paid a "ridiculously high" amount of money for what she did, but on the other hand, she knew investment bankers who were making considerably more than she was. Similarly, Ling Ling may make more money than her peers, but she may also work longer hours, have more skills, and lease more apartments. In other words, although her outcomes are greater, so are her inputs, and thus the ratios may still be equal; there is equity.

In essence, equity theory does not try to evaluate equality of inputs or equality of outcomes. It is concerned with fairness of inputs relative to outcomes. The perception of inequity creates a state of tension and an inherent pressure for change. As long as there is general equality between the two ratios, there is no motivation (at least based on inequity) to change anything, and people are reasonably satisfied. If, however, the ratios are significantly different, a follower will be motivated to take action likely to restore the balance. Exactly what the follower will be motivated to do depends on the direction of the inequality. Adams suggested six ways people might restore balance: (*a*) changing their inputs, (*b*) changing their outcomes, (*c*) altering their self-perceptions, (*d*) altering their perceptions of their reference group, (*e*) changing their reference group, or, if all else fails, (*f*) leaving the situation.[97] Thus, if Julie believed her ratio was lower than her co-workers', she might reduce her level of effort or seek higher pay elsewhere. She could also change her reference group to that of ski lift operators at other resorts, or even quit. Research has shown that perceptions of underpayment generally resulted in actions in support of the model, but perceptions of overpayment did not. Instead of working harder in an overpayment condition (to make their own ratio more equitable), subjects often rationalized that they really deserved the higher pay.[21] An example of how equity theory might affect some salary negotiations is presented in Highlight 9.6.

Leadership, Equity Theory, and Professional Athlete and Executive Salary Demands

HIGHLIGHT 9.6

General managers are responsible for the overall performance of their professional sports teams. They help select players and coaches; negotiate media, player, coach, and stadium contracts; keep team morale at a high level; and take action to ensure the team wins the championship and makes money. One of the most difficult issues general managers deal with is negotiating contracts with players. Players look at their own pay and performance and compare them to that of other athletes in the league. If they feel their compensation is not consistent with that of other players, they usually ask to be traded or for a new contract to be negotiated. These comparisons have led to the $100 million–plus salaries now commanded by marquee players in basketball, football, and baseball. But what happens to team morale, the win–loss record, and financial performance when one or two players make substantially more money than the rest of the team? Research on professional baseball teams over an eight-year period indicated that teams with high pay dispersion levels (i.e., large gaps between the highest and lowest paid starting player) did less well financially and were less likely to win division championships. Researchers surmised that this drop in team performance was due to the high levels of pay dispersion, which eroded team performance and increased inequity for other players on the team. The trick for general managers seems to be to find enough financial rewards to induce higher levels of performance but not create inequity situations for the rest of the team.

Although the effects of equity theory are readily apparent with professional athletes' pay, the same holds true with top executives. Many boards of directors worry that if they do not pay their CEOs and top executives at least on par with those in other companies, they run the risk of executive turnover. But executives who negotiate large signing bonuses and big annual pay packages don't necessarily achieve better results than their lower paid counterparts. As described in Profiles in Leadership 9.2 and 9.4, many executives tout the benefits of pay for performance but appear much more concerned with own pay than their own performance. And you have to wonder if companies with high pay dispersions achieve the same type of results as professional athletic teams with high pay dispersions. The top executives in Japanese companies make 20–30 times more than the average employee; in the United States the top executives make 400 times that of their average employees. With facts like these is it any wonder that workers are less satisfied and more likely to change companies these days?

Sources: M. Bloom, "The Performance Effects of Pay Dispersions on Individuals and Organizations." *Academy of Management Journal* 42, no. 1 (1999), pp. 25–40; J. Lublin, "Boards Tie CEO Pay More Tightly to Performance." *The Wall Street Journal,* February 21, 2006, pp. A1 and A14; L. A. Bebchuk and J. M. Fried, "Pay without Performance: Overview of the Issues." *The Academy of Management Perspectives* 20 (1) (2006), pp. 5–24.

No one can make you feel inferior without your cooperation.
Eleanor Roosevelt, First Lady

Self-Efficacy

So far in this section we have discussed the importance of goals, linking efforts and rewards to goals, and making sure rewards are commensurate with efforts. But we have yet to discuss whether a person's beliefs about whether he or she can or cannot perform certain tasks have any effect on motivation and performance. The last cognitive theory of motivation is self-efficacy, which concerns one's core beliefs about being able to successfully perform a given task.[99] **Positive self-efficacy** is used to note beliefs where people feel confident that they have the power to create desired effects; **negative self-efficacy** is used to note self-debilitating beliefs. Research has shown that people who simply believe they can perform a particular task will often exert considerable effort to get the task accomplished. Conversely, people with negative self-efficacy often give up in the face of difficulty.

Although research has shown that self-efficacy is strongly linked to motivation and performance, it is important to note that self-efficacy varies from one task to the next.[99] A particular follower or team may have positive self-efficacy about one task and negative self-efficacy about others. Because followers' self-efficacy varies from one task to the next, leaders can better motivate followers by finding ways to boost their self-efficacy. Leaders can do this by providing relevant work experience and tying it to training, coaching, encouragement, and support, and ensuring followers get the resources they need to be successful.

So how might we use self-efficacy to increase Julie's level of motivation as a ski lift operator? The first step would be to provide Julie with proper training on how to operate the ski lift equipment. The leader would then want to have Julie practice operating the lift in various emergency situations and give her feedback on how to do it better. Julie will gain positive self-efficacy once she feels comfortable operating the equipment, and the more she operates the equipment, the more self-efficacy she will have. This does not mean that Julie will work harder and put in longer hours, but it does mean that she will be much more likely to persist in the face of difficulties than if she did not know how to operate the equipment.

Ling Ling's supervisor could use a similar approach to help her rent apartments in Hong Kong. Getting Ling Ling proper training, providing coaching support with her early rentals, and being available to provide help with more difficult rentals will help improve Ling Ling's self-efficacy for renting apartments. But as our flight attendant situation aptly points out, having positive self-efficacy may not be enough to keep people motivated to perform certain activities. Many flight attendants have a number of years of experience and plenty of positive self-efficacy for the job. But many also seem inattentive to customers' needs and unwilling to go the extra mile. Self-efficacy seems very important for understanding why people may be unmotivated to do a task, but having positive self-efficacy may be necessary but insufficient to ensure that people engage in those behaviors that result in higher individual or team performance.

In the absence of clearly defined goals we become strangely loyal to performing daily trivia until we ultimately become enslaved by it.

Robert Heinlein,
author

Concluding Thoughts on Cognitive Theories of Motivation

All four of the cognitive theories assume that changing followers' thoughts will help them to engage in particular tasks and activities. Followers will be more inclined to pursue activities that result in the accomplishment of specific goals, that balance perceived inequities, or when they believe they can perform those behaviors needed to accomplish

Goal Setting Theory
Expectancy Theory
Equity Theory
Self Efficacy

goals. Leaders can influence followers' motivational levels by clearly articulating expected outcomes, clarifying the links between efforts and rewards, and providing training, coaching, and feedback to followers as they go about accomplishing tasks.

Perhaps more than the other theories and approaches described in this section, the cognitive theories place a strong premium on leader–follower communication. It is hard to imagine how goal setting, expectancy theory, equity theory, or self-efficacy would work if the leader did not articulate goals, provide ongoing feedback, and continually clarify motivational links with followers. If leader–follower communication is poor, then it is unlikely that leaders will realize the benefits of these four approaches. The research shows that these theories can effectively increase worker motivation; when they fail it often has more to do with how the theory was implemented than with inadequacy of the theory. Thus, leaders with poor interpersonal communication, feedback, and coaching skills might have a difficult time using these theories to increase follower motivation levels.

Is it a problem of bad apples, or is it the barrel?

Kim Clark, Harvard Business School

Situational Approaches

The situational approach assumes leaders can change the situation in order to better motivate followers. So far we have discussed how underlying needs, individual differences in achievement orientation, or goals or performance-to-reward links can affect follower motivation levels. However,

Wu Yi

PROFILES IN LEADERSHIP 9.3

Wu Yi is the Vice Premier and Minister of Health for the People's Republic of China. One of four premiers in charge of running the country, Wu Yi was ranked third on Fortune's list of the most powerful women in the world (after Angela Merkel and Condoleezza Rice). Wu Yi started her career by graduating from the Beijing Petroleum Institute with a degree in petroleum engineering. After school she started as a petroleum technician and eventually achieved the rank of deputy manager at the Beijing Dongfang Hong refinery. A Communist party member, Wu Yi was the Party Secretary at the Beijing Yanshan Petrochemical Corporation before being elected to be the deputy mayor of Beijing in 1988. She held this position during the Tiananmen Square protests and from 1991–1998 moved into positions of ever

increasing responsibility within the Communist party. A protégé of Zhu Rongji, she helped negotiate the country's entry into the World Trade Organization and reorganized the customs service after complaints about intellectual property theft. She also took charge of China's response to the SARS crisis when the previous minister had been fired for covering up the event and is heading up China's delegation in the six-country talks to persuade North Korea to give up its nuclear weapons. Firm and direct in her leadership style, she has been called by some as the "Iron Lady of China." An able diplomat, she has negotiated and signed a number of trade agreements with other Asian countries and she makes frequent inspection visits across the country.

Source: http://en.wikipedia.org/wiki/Wu_Yi; http://www.forbes.com/lists/2006/11/ 06women_Wu-Yi_GGD7.html.

these motivational techniques are mainly follower- or leader-centric; they pertain to certain follower qualities or leader actions. From Chapter 2 we know that leadership is an interaction between the leader, followers, and situation, and the theories of motivation can be categorized using the same framework. The two approaches described in this section show how it is possible to change the situation in order to improve followers' motivation levels. In other words, this research shows that some jobs are more motivating than others and that it is possible to reengineer jobs to improve followers' motivation levels. These two situational approaches to motivation include the operant approach and empowerment.

The Operant Approach

You get what you reinforce, but you do not necessarily get what you pay for.

Fred Luthans, University of Nebraska, and Alexander Stajkovic, University of California, Irvine

One very popular way to change the direction, intensity, or persistence of behavior is through rewards and punishments. It will help at the outset of this discussion of the **operant approach** to define several terms. A **reward** is any consequence that *increases* the likelihood that a particular behavior will be repeated. For example, if Julie gets a cash award for a suggestion to improve customer service at the ski resort, then she will be more likely to forward additional suggestions. **Punishment** is the administration of an aversive stimulus or the withdrawal of something desirable, each of which *decreases* the likelihood a particular behavior will be repeated.[100] Thus, if Ling Ling loses her bonus for not getting her paperwork in on time, then she will be less likely to do so again in the future. Both rewards and punishments can be administered in a contingent or noncontingent manner. **Contingent** rewards or punishments are administered as *consequences of a particular behavior.* Examples might include giving Julie a medal immediately after she wins a skiing race or giving Ling Ling a bonus check for exceeding her sales quota. **Noncontingent** rewards and punishments are not associated with particular behaviors. Monthly paychecks might be examples, if both Julie and Ling Ling receive the same amount of base pay every month whatever their actual effort or output. Finally, behaviors that are not rewarded will eventually be eliminated through the process of **extinction.**

When properly implemented, there is ample evidence to show that the operant approach can be a very effective way to improve follower motivation and performance.[47,101–109] Some of this research has also shown that rewards work better than punishments, particularly if administered in a contingent manner.[102,104,107,110–113] When comparing the relative impact of different types of rewards, Stajkovic and Luthans reported that incentive pay targeted at specific follower behaviors was the most effective, followed by social recognition and performance feedback, for improving follower performance in credit card processing centers.[104] Although Kohn has argued that incentive pay programs do not work, his statements appear to be based on nothing more than his own opinions.[114] The research clearly shows that leaders who properly design and implement contingent reward systems do indeed increase follower productivity and performance.

So how does a leader properly design and implement an operant system for improving followers' motivation and performance levels? Using operant principles properly to improve followers' motivation and hence performance requires several steps. First, *leadership practitioners need to clearly specify what behaviors are important.* This means that Julie's and Ling Ling's leaders will need to specify what they want them to do, how often they should do it, and the level of performance required. Second, *leadership practitioners need to determine if those behaviors are currently being punished, rewarded, or ignored.* Believe it or not, sometimes followers are actually rewarded for behaviors that leaders are trying to extinguish, and punished for behaviors that leaders want to increase. For example, Julie may get considerable positive attention from peers by talking back to her leader or for violating the ski resort dress code. Similarly, Ling Ling may be overly competitive and get promoted ahead of her peers (e.g., by renting apartments in her peers' territories), even when her boss extols the need for cooperation and teamwork. It also may be the case that leaders sometimes just ignore the very behaviors they would like to see strengthened. An example here would be if Julie's boss consistently failed to provide rewards when Julie worked hard to achieve impressive safety and customer service ratings (see Highlight 9.7).

Third, *leadership practitioners need to find out what followers actually find rewarding and punishing.* Leaders should *not* make the mistake of assuming that followers will find the same things rewarding and punishing as they do, nor should they assume that all followers will find the same things to be rewarding and punishing. What may be one follower's punishment may be another follower's reward. For example, Ling Ling may dislike public attention and actually exert less effort after being publicly recognized, yet some of her peers may find public attention to be extremely rewarding. In all likelihood valued rewards will be related to followers' underlying values. Fourth, *leadership practitioners need to be wary of creating perceptions of inequity when administering individually tailored rewards.* A peer may feel that she got the same results as Ling Ling, yet she received a smaller bonus check for the quarter. Leaders can minimize inequities by being clear and consistent with rewards and punishments. Fifth, *leadership practitioners should not limit themselves to administering organizationally sanctioned rewards and punishments.* Oftentimes leaders are limited in the amount of money they can give followers for good performance. However, research has shown that social recognition and performance feedback resulted in significant productivity improvements in followers and these rewards do not cost any money.[103,104] Using a bit of ingenuity, leaders can often come up with an array of potential rewards and punishments that are effective and inexpensive, and do not violate organizational norms or policies. Julie might find driving the snow cat to

The Folly of Rewarding A While Hoping for B

HIGHLIGHT 9.7

Steven Kerr has written a compelling article detailing how many of the reward systems found in government, sports, universities, businesses, medicine, and politics often *compel people to act in a manner contrary to that intended.* For example, voters want politicians to provide the specifics of their programs or platform, yet politicians often get punished for doing so. Some constituency is bound to get hurt or offended whenever the specifics of a program are revealed, which in turn will cost the politician votes. If a politician keeps overall goals vague, more voters are likely to agree with the politician and vote for him or her in the next election. Businesses, like universities and politicians, often utilize inappropriate reward systems. According to Kerr, the following are some of the more common management reward follies:

We hope for . . .	But we often reward . . .
Long-term growth	Quarterly earnings
Teamwork	Individual effort
Commitment to total quality	Shipping on schedule, even with defects
Reporting bad news	Reporting good news, whether it is true or not

Kerr states that managers who complain about unmotivated workers should consider the possibility that their current reward system is incongruent with the performance they desire. And nowhere is this lack of congruence between what companies want and what they reward more visible than with executive compensation. Boards often have to front millions of dollars to new CEOs in order to get them to join the company, and then more often than not provide them with stock options and other forms of compensation in order to retain these individuals even though they consistently fail to hit their numbers. Many corporations talk a good game when it comes to pay for performance, but their actions indicate they are more likely to reward tenure while hoping for improved performance.

Sources: S. Kerr, "On the Folly of Rewarding A, While Hoping for B." *Academy of Management Executive* 9, no. 1 (1995), pp. 7–14; S. Kerr, "Establishing Organizational Goals and Rewards." *Academy of Management Executive* 18, no. 4 (2004), pp. 122–23; S. D. Levitt and S. J. Dubner, *Freakonomics.* New York: HarperCollins Publishers, 2005; L. Bebchuck and J. Fried, *Pay without Performance.* Boston, MA: Harvard University Press, 2004; L. Bebchuck and J. Fried, "Pay without Performance: Overview of the Issues." *The Academy of Management Perspectives* 20 (1) (2006), pp. 5–24; P. Dvorak, "Limits on Executive Pay: Easy to Set, Hard to Keep." *The Wall Street Journal,* April 9, 2007, pp. B1 and B5; J. S. Lublin, "Boards Tie CEO Pay More Tightly to Performance." *The Wall Street Journal,* February 21, 2006, pp. A1 and A4.

Teach me and I will forget, show me and I may remember, involve me and I will understand.
Chinese proverb

be extremely enjoyable, and her boss could use this reward to maintain or increase Julie's motivation levels for operating the ski lift. Finally, because the administration of noncontingent consequences has relatively little impact, *leadership practitioners should administer rewards and punishments in a contingent manner whenever possible.* Highlight 9.7 provides examples of the unintended consequences of implementing an operant approach to boost organizational performance.

Empowerment

Empowerment makes up the other situational approach to motivation. In general, people seem to fall into one of two camps with respect to

I have developed a very agile selective memory across a wide range of nonvalue-added activities.

**Steven Crawley,
human resource
executive**

empowerment. Some people believe empowerment is all about delegation and accountability, a top-down process where senior leaders articulate a vision and specific goals, and hold followers responsible for achieving them. Others believe empowerment is more of a bottom-up approach that focuses on intelligent risk taking, growth, change, trust, and ownership; followers act as entrepreneurs and owners that question rules and make intelligent decisions. Leaders tolerate mistakes and encourage cooperative behavior in this approach to empowerment.[115–119] Needless to say, these two conceptualizations of empowerment have very different implications for leaders and followers. And it is precisely this conceptual confusion which has caused empowerment programs to fail in many organizations.[115] Because of the conceptual confusion surrounding empowerment, companies such as Motorola will not use this term to describe programs that push decision making to lower organizational levels. These companies would rather coin their own terms to describe these programs, thus avoiding the confusion surrounding empowerment.

Is It Possible To Be Effective and Incompetent?

HIGHLIGHT 9.8

To be successful in many organizations requires a high degree of skill and the motivation necessary to get the job done. And many people have all the skills and motivation necessary to perform all aspects of their job, yet at times they may selectively demonstrate incompetence in order to avoid responsibility for a frustrating task. For example, rather than just saying no to a distasteful task, some people avoid responsibility for a task by asking others for help so much that the person being asked eventually assumes responsibility for getting the task accomplished. The person continually bugged for help might find it easier to just get the task done rather than being constantly asked for help in doing it. An example might be learning how to run a copying machine or advanced printer. Some people don't want to take the time to learn how to use the equipment, so when it comes time to make copies they stand around the machine making faces and getting frustrated until someone comes along to help them. And they repeat this behavior every time they need to use the machine, thus getting someone else to actually do the work.

What is interesting about this phenomenon is that many of these individuals are highly effective in the other aspects of their jobs. And when you look at the other things the person is capable of doing, the tasks they find distasteful are clearly within their ability to perform. This phenomenon is quite common in organizational life and is a variation of the leisurely dark-side personality trait described in Chapter 7. Leisurely types are passive-aggressive—they don't like doing anything that doesn't jive with their personal agendas. But rather than just saying no to another's request, they smile and say they will get it done and then do nothing. And when asked why the task didn't get accomplished, it is always someone else's fault. In a similar vein, feigning incompetence helps people avoid those activities that they find frustrating or believe are beneath them. Of course, the easiest way to avoid becoming the victim of someone's attempt to get you to do their work is to either teach them how to do the task or to just say no.

Source: J. Sandberg, "The Art of Showing Pure Incompetence at an Unwanted Task." *The Wall Street Journal,* April 17, 2007, p. B1.

We define empowerment as having two key components. For leaders to truly empower employees, they must delegate leadership and decision making down to the lowest level possible. Employees are often the closest to the problem and have the most information, and as such can often make the best decisions. A classic example was the UPS employee who ordered an extra 737 aircraft to haul presents that had been forgotten in the last-minute Christmas rush. This decision was clearly beyond the employee's level of authority, but UPS praised his initiative for seeing the problem and making the right decision. The second component of empowerment, and the one most often overlooked, is equipping followers with the resources, knowledge, and skills necessary to make good decisions. All too often companies adopt an empowerment program and push decision making down to the employee level, but employees have no experience creating business plans, submitting budgets, dealing with other departments within the company, or directly dealing with customers or vendors. Not surprisingly, ill-equipped employees often make poor, uninformed decisions, and managers in turn are likely to believe that empowerment was not all it was cracked up to be. The same happens with downsizing, as employees are asked to take on additional responsibilities but are provided with little training or support. "Forced" empowerment may lead to some short-term stock gains but tends to be disastrous in the long run. Thus, empowerment has both delegation and developmental components; delegation without development is often perceived as abandonment, and development without delegation can often be perceived as micro-management. Leaders wishing to empower followers must determine what followers are capable of doing, enhance and broaden these capabilities, and give followers commensurate increases in authority and accountability.

The psychological components of empowerment can be examined at both macro and micro levels. There are three macro psychological components underlying empowerment, and these are motivation, learning, and stress. As a concept, empowerment has been around since at least the 1920s, and the vast majority of companies that have implemented empowerment programs have done so to increase employee motivation and, in turn, productivity. As a motivational technique empowerment has a mixed record; often times empowered workers are more productive than unempowered workers, but there are times when this may not be the case. When empowerment does not lead to increased productivity, it may be that senior leaders tend to see empowerment through rose-colored glasses. They hear about the benefits an empowerment program is having in another company, but do not consider the time, effort, and changes needed to create a truly empowered workforce. Relatedly, many empowerment programs are poorly implemented—the program is announced with great fanfare, but little real guidance, training, or support is provided and managers are quick to pull the plug on the program as soon as followers start making poor decisions. Adopting an effective empowerment program takes training, trust, and time, but companies most likely to implement an empowerment program (as a panacea for their poor financial situation) often lack these three attributes.[121] Third, worker productivity and job dissatisfaction in the United States are at an all-time high. Many companies are dealing with high levels of employee burnout, and adding additional responsibilities to already overfilled plates is likely to be counterproductive. As reported by Xie and Johns, some empowerment programs create positions that are just too big for a person to handle effectively, and job burnout is usually the result.[122]

Although the motivational benefits of empowerment are sometimes not realized, the learning and stress reduction benefits of empowerment are more clear-cut. Given that properly designed and implemented empowerment programs include a strong developmental component, one of the key benefits to these programs is that they help employees learn more about their jobs, company, and industry. These knowledge and skill gains increase the intellectual capital of the company and can be a competitive advantage in moving ahead. In addition to the learning benefits, well-designed empowerment programs can actually help to reduce burnout. People can tolerate high levels of stress when they have a high level of control. Given that many employees are putting in longer hours than ever before and work demands are at an all-time high, empowerment can help followers gain some control over their lives and better cope with stress. Although an empowered worker may have the same high work demands as an unempowered worker, the empowered worker will have more choices on how and when to accomplish these demands and as such will suffer from less stress. And because stress is a key component of dysfunctional turnover, giving workers more control over their work demands can reduce turnover and in turn positively impact the company's bottom line.

There are also four micro components of empowerment. These components can be used to determine whether employees are empowered or unempowered, and include self-determination, meaning, competence, and influence.[115,116,123] Empowered employees have a sense of self-determination; they can make choices about what they do, how they do it, and when they need to get it done. Empowered employees also have a strong sense of meaning; they believe what they do is important to them and to the company's success. Empowered employees have a high level of competence in that they know what they are doing and are confident they can get the job done. Finally, empowered employees have an impact on others and believe that they can influence their teams or work units and that co-workers and leaders will listen to their ideas. In summary, empowered employees have latitude to make decisions, are comfortable making these decisions, believe what they do is important, and are seen as influential members of their team. Unempowered employees may have little latitude to make decisions, may feel ill equipped and may not want to make decisions, and may have little impact on their work unit, even if they have good ideas. Most employees probably fall somewhere in between the two extremes of the empowerment continuum, depicted in Figure 9.5.

Concluding Thoughts on Situational Approaches to Motivation

Empowerment and the operant approach make an important point that is often overlooked by other theories of motivation: By changing the situation, leaders can enhance followers' motivation, performance, and satisfaction. Unfortunately, many leaders naively assume it is easier to change an *individual* than it is to change the *situation*, but this is often not the case. It is important to remember that the situation is not always fixed, and followers are not the only variable in the performance equation. Leaders can often see positive changes in followers' motivation levels by restructuring work processes and procedures, which in turn can increase their latitude to make decisions and add more meaning to work. Tying these changes to a well-designed and well-implemented reward system can result in further increases in motivation. However, leaders are likely to encounter some resistance whenever they change the processes, procedures, and rewards for work, even if these changes are for the better. As noted by Peterson and Hicks, doing things the old way is easy, as followers know the expectations for performance and usually have developed the skills needed to achieve results. Followers often find that doing things a new way can be frustrating, as expectations may be unclear and they may not have the requisite skills. Leadership practitioners can help followers work through this initial resistance to new processes and procedures by showing support, providing training and coaching on new skills, and capitalizing on opportunities to reward progress. If the processes, procedures, and rewards are properly designed and administered, then in many cases followers will successfully work through their resistance and, over time, wonder how they ever got work done using the old systems. The successful transition to new work processes and procedures will rest squarely on the shoulders of leaders. So, given the implications of the situational approach to motivation, how could you use empowerment and the operant approach to improve the customer service levels of flight attendants? What information would you need to gather, how would you implement the program, and what would be the potential pitfalls of your program?

Motivation Summary

We hope that after reading this chapter you will have a better understanding of how follower characteristics (needs, intrinsic motivation), leader actions (goal setting), and situational factors (contingent rewards) affect how you and your followers are motivated (and demotivated). Moreover, you should be able to start recognizing situations where some

The Culture of Praise

HIGHLIGHT 9.9

There is no doubt that the generation of people entering the workforce these days has had more positive reinforcement while growing up than any previous generation. As children these individuals got positive strokes in the form of rewards, ribbons, plaques, and certificates for just showing up to athletic events or school activities. For example, one of the authors went to a school assembly for one of his children and watched teachers pass out awards to all 300 students in the elementary school. Some of the awards were for student achievement or citizenship, but many were for "completing your homework for three days in a row" and "having a nice smile." Thirty years ago it was difficult to earn an athletic letter in one or two sports, but some of the athletic jackets of today have 10–15 awards and letters. This culture of praise was intended to boost self-esteem and better prepare students for life after high school, but as described in Highlight 9.7, the use of unconditional praise has had some unintended implications that organizations have had to deal with.

One implication is the people now entering the workforce are much more likely to be self-centered, "narcissistic praise junkies" than the people they are working for. Because of the constant positive reinforcement they received when growing up, a much higher percentage of people in this generation think they are special and should get rewarded for anything and everything that they do. Organizations,

recognizing this need in their youngest employees, are taking some extraordinary steps to boost the self-esteem of (and retain) these individuals. For example, Land's End and Bank of America teach managers how to compliment employees using e-mail, prize packages, and public displays of appreciation. The Scooter Store has a "celebration assistant" whose job is to throw 25 pounds of confetti and pass out 100–500 helium balloons to employees each week. The Container Store, Inc., estimates that one of its 4,000 employees is rewarded every 20 seconds.

But what is the impact of these praise and recognition programs? Company officials argue they would see very high levels of turnover if they did not have these programs in place. But if this younger generation gets constant recognition for just meeting minimum standards, then what happens when they get promoted into supervisory positions? It may well be that this approach to motivating and retaining others may be creating future generations of Cheerleaders—managers who are good at heaping praise and building teams but getting very little accomplished (see Chapter 4). Thus the short-term consequence may be improved retention of young employees, but the long-term consequence may be higher levels of managerial incompetence in these organizations.

Source: J. Zaslow, "The Most Praised Generation Goes to Work." *The Wall Street Journal,* April 20, 2007, pp. W1 and W7.

FIGURE 9.5   The empowerment continuum.

Empowered Employees ⟵————⟶ **Unempowered Employees**

- Self-determined
- Sense of meaning
- High competence
- High influence

- Other-determined
- Not sure if what they do is important
- Low competence
- Low influence

theories provide better insights about problems in motivation levels than others. For example, if we go back to the survival situation described in Chapter 1, then we can see that the need theories (Maslow and Alderfer) provide better explanations for the behavior of the survivors than the job characteristics model or intrinsic motivation. On the other hand, if we think about the reasons we might not be doing well in a particular class, then we may see that we have not set specific goals for our grades or that the links between our efforts and our grades are not very clear. Or if we are working in a bureaucratic organization, then we may see that there are few consequences for either substandard or superior performance; thus, there is little reason to exert any extra effort. Perhaps the best strategy for leaders is to be flexible in the types of interventions they consider to affect follower motivation. That will require, of course, familiarity with the strengths and weaknesses of the different theories and approaches presented here. Just as a carpenter can more effectively build a house by using a variety of tools, a leader can be more effective by using a variety of motivational interventions to resolve work problems.

At this point it is also important to note that one of the most important tools for motivating followers has not been fully addressed in this chapter. As described in Chapter 13, charismatic or transformational leadership is often associated with extraordinarily high levels of follower motivation, yet none of the theories described in this chapter can adequately explain how these leaders can get their followers to do more than they ever thought possible. Perhaps this is due to the fact that the theories in this chapter take a very rational or logical approach to motivation, yet transformational leadership uses emotion as the fuel to drive followers' heightened motivational levels. Just as our needs, thoughts, personality traits, intrinsic interests, and rewards can motivate us to do something different, so can our emotions drive us to engage in and persist with particular activities. A good example here may be political campaigns. Do people volunteer to work for these campaigns because of some underlying need, personal goals, or their intrinsic interests in politics? Although these are potential reasons for some followers, the emotions generated by political campaigns, particularly where the two leading candidates represent different value systems, often seem to provide a better explanation for the large amount of time and effort people contribute. Leadership practitioners should not overlook the interplay between emotions and motivation, and the better able they are to address and capitalize on emotions when introducing change, the more successful they are likely to be.

A final point concerns the relationship between motivation and performance. Many leadership practitioners equate the two, but as we pointed out earlier in this chapter, they are not the same concepts. Getting followers to put in more time, energy, and effort on certain behaviors will not help the team to be more successful if they are the wrong behaviors to begin with. Similarly, followers may not know how and when to exhibit those behaviors associated with performance. Leadership practitioners must clearly identify those behaviors related to performance, coach and train their followers on how and when to exhibit these behaviors, and then use one or more of the theories described in this chapter to get followers to exhibit and persist with those behaviors associated with higher performance levels.

Understanding and Influencing Follower Satisfaction

As stated earlier, job satisfaction concerns one's attitudes about work, and there are several practical reasons why job satisfaction is an important concept for leaders to think about. Research has shown that satisfied workers

Reducing Risk-Taking Behaviors on Offshore Oil Platforms

HIGHLIGHT 9.10

One of the most dangerous jobs in the world is that of an offshore oil-rig employee. These employees often work 12–16 hours a day for two- to four-week shifts operating heavy equipment in very confined spaces. Not only is the work long and hard, but many of these platforms face dangers from high seas, cold weather, icebergs, and even hurricanes. Because of these conditions and the nature of work, many energy companies are very concerned with safety. But what can well managers do to create safe oil platforms? It turns out that using a combination of several motivational techniques may be the best way to reduce oil platform accidents.

To reduce accidents, well managers must first set clear goals and performance expectations for safety. If employees only believe production is important to well managers, then they will do what they think is right to boost productivity and will pay little attention to safety issues. So managers must set the tone for safety by setting safety goals and constantly reminding employees of safety issues. Second, they must hire employees who are motivated to perform safe work behaviors. Well managers should use personality inventories to hire employees with higher dependability scores, as they tend to be risk-averse and are much more rule abiding than those with lower dependability scores.

Third, well managers must ensure that their compensation systems recognize and reward safe behaviors. If the compensation system only rewards productivity, then employees will do what they need to in order to maximize their rewards. The same is true if the compensation system rewards both productivity *and* safety. Using this three-pronged approach will not eliminate all oil-rig accidents, but it will go a long way toward reducing accident rates.

Interestingly enough, these same three techniques work equally well for improving safety performance in other organizations. For example, setting clear safety goals, hiring workers who are more likely to comply with safety rules and less prone to accidents, and rewarding safe behavior can be used to improve the safety performance in power plants, manufacturing and distribution facilities, railroads, long-haul trucking companies, and construction firms. For example, these approaches have been adopted by Waste Management and as a result the company has seen dramatic improvements to its safety record. But the Texas City Refinery incident and leaking pipelines in Alaska indicate that BP has only recently adopted these techniques for use outside of its offshore oil platforms.

Source: R. Gregory, R. T. Hogan, and G. J. Curphy, "Risk-Taking in the Energy Industry." *Well Connected,* 5 (6) (June 2003), pp. 5–7.

*Seventy to ninety
percent of the decisions
not to repeat purchase of
anything are not about
product or price. They
are about dimensions of
service.*

**Barry Gibbons,
Burger King**

are more likely to continue working for an organization.[19,42,43,125–129] Satisfied workers are also more likely to engage in organizational citizenship behaviors, behaviors that go beyond job descriptions and role requirements and help reduce the workload or stress of others in the organization. Dissatisfied workers are more likely to be adversarial in their relations with leadership (e.g., file grievances) and engage in diverse sorts of counterproductive behaviors.[130–138] Dissatisfaction is one of the key reasons people leave organizations and many of the reasons people are satisfied or dissatisfied with work are within the leader's control (see Table 9.3). [43,126–128,139]

Although the total costs of dissatisfaction are difficult to measure, the direct costs of replacing a first-line supervisor or an executive can range from $5,000 to $400,000 per hire, depending on recruiting, relocation, and training fees, and these costs do not include those associated with the productivity lost as a result of unfilled positions.[140] Employee dissatisfaction can also affect revenue and capital available for organizational expansion and upgrades. A survey of major corporations showed that 49 percent switched to another vendor because of poor customer service.[141] Employees are probably not going to provide world-class service if they are unhappy with their job, boss, or company. The inability to retain customers will directly affect revenues and make investors think twice about buying stock in a company. Relatedly, Schellenbarger reported that 35 percent of investor decisions are driven by nonfinancial factors. Number 5 on a list of 39 factors investors weighed before buying stock was the company's ability to attract and retain talent. These findings imply that a company's stock price is driven not only by market share and profitability, but also by service and bench strength considerations. Thus, employee satisfaction (or dissatisfaction) can have a major impact on the organization's bottom line.[142]

Of these outcomes, perhaps employee turnover has the most immediate impact on leadership practitioners. It would be very hard for Julie's or Ling Ling's bosses to achieve results if, respectively, ski resort or real estate personnel were constantly having to be replaced, and the leader was spending an inordinate amount of time recruiting, hiring, and training replacements. Although some level of **functional turnover** is healthy for an organization (i.e., these followers are retiring, did not fit into the organization, or were substandard performers), dysfunctional turnover is not. **Dysfunctional turnover** occurs when the "best and brightest" in an organization become dissatisfied and leave it. Dysfunctional turnover is most likely to occur when downsizing is the response to organizational decline (i.e., increased costs or decreased revenues, market Web share, or earnings). In these situations, dysfunctional turnover may have several devastating effects. First, those individuals in the best position to turn the company around are no longer there. Second, those who remain are even less capable of successfully dealing with the additional workload associated with the downsizings. Compounding this problem is that training budgets also tend to be slashed during downsizings. Third, organizations that downsize have a very difficult time recruiting people with the skills needed to turn the company around. Either competent candidates avoid applying for jobs within the organization because of the uncertainties of job security, or the less competent managers remaining with the company may decide not to hire anyone who could potentially replace them. Because leaders can play an important role in followers' satisfaction levels, and because followers' satisfaction levels can have a substantial impact on various organizational outcomes, it is worth going into the topic in greater detail (see Highlights 9.10 and 9.11).[42,43,129,143,144]

Global, Facet, and Life Satisfaction

There are different ways to look at a person's attitudes about work, but researchers usually collect this data using some type of job satisfaction survey.[39,40,47,128,145,146] Such surveys typically include items such as those found in Table 9.4 and they are usually sent to a representative sample of employees in the organization. Their responses are collected and tabulated, and the results are usually disseminated throughout the organization. Table 9.4 presents examples of three different types of items typically found on a job satisfaction survey. Item 1 is a **global satisfaction** item, which assesses the overall degree to which employees are satisfied with their organization and their job. Items 2 through 7 are **facet satisfaction** items, which assess the degree to which employees are satisfied with different aspects of work, such as pay, benefits, promotion policies, working hours and conditions, and the like. People may be relatively satisfied overall but still dissatisfied with certain aspects of work. For example, a study of junior officers in the United States Army revealed that overall satisfaction among them has been in decline and is beginning to negatively impact reenlistment rates. A higher percentage of junior officers are choosing to leave the Army than ever before; the two primary reasons for this high level of dysfunctional turnover seem to be dissatisfaction with immediate supervisors and top leadership. Many junior officers reported that they were tired of working for career-obsessed supervisors who had a strong tendency to micro-manage and would just as soon throw them under a bus if it would advance their career.[147] And given the multiple tours and tour extensions supporting the conflict in Iraq one suspects that employee dissatisfaction among National Guard and Reserve units is particularly high, which has driven up turnover and made recruitment that much more difficult. For example, retention bonuses for the United States military went from $80 million to $700 million from 2002 to 2006.[148] This decline in global satisfaction is not limited only to the United States Army, as the same phenomenon is happening in many companies today. Much of this decline can be attributed to higher follower expectations, greater follower access to information through technology, economic downturns, organizational downsizings, and incompetent bosses.[40,41] The margin quote at left summarizes what many followers are feeling today.

To reduce job satisfaction from 9 to 8 on the 10 point scale . . . would, for a family with a $65,000 income, have to be matched by an income increase of more than $30,000 a year to leave life satisfaction unchanged . . . Moving from the 50th to the 75th percentile [in job satisfaction] would have a personal income equivalence, for someone of median income, of $17,000 per annum.

Charles Cook, Cook Computing

Would life on a slave ship be much better if the galley master first asked the rowers to help write a mission statement? What employers need to come to terms with is the economic, cultural, and societal benefits of being loyal to their employees. If they don't, eventually their abuses will bite them on the ass.

Daniel Levine, author

TABLE 9.3 **Why People Leave or Stay with Organizations**

Sources: Pace Communication, Inc., *Hemispheres Magazine*, November 1994, p. 155; "Keeping Workers Happy," *USA Today*, February 10, 1998, p. 1B.

Why Do People Leave Organizations?		Why Do People Stay with Organizations?	
Limited recognition and praise	34%	Promises of long-term employment	82%
Compensation	29%	Supports training and education	78%
Limited authority	13%	Hires/keeps hard-working, smart people	76%
Personality conflicts	8%	Encourages fun, collegial relationships	74%
Other	16%	Bases job evaluation on innovation	72%

A Recipe for Success: The Gallup 12

HIGHLIGHT 9.11

More and more organizations are beginning to realize that their overall success depends on how they treat their employees. Hiring good people, setting high goals and performance expectations, providing needed resources, developing new skills, and holding people accountable for results seem to be important ingredients in organizational success. Leaders who use these techniques are likely to have more engaged employees, less turnover, and higher team and organizational level performance. The Gallup Organization has surveyed thousands of companies and has identified 12 key questions that assess employee engagement, which are as follows:

1. I know what is expected from me at work.
2. I have the materials and equipment I need to do my job right.
3. At work, I have the opportunity to do what I do best every day.
4. In the last seven days, I have received recognition and praise for doing good work.
5. My supervisor, or someone at work, seems to care about me as a person.
6. There is someone at work who encourages my development.
7. At work, my opinions seem to count.

8. The mission/purpose of my company makes me feel my job is important.
9. My associates (fellow employees) are committed to doing quality work.
10. I have a best friend at work.
11. In the last six months, someone at work has talked to me about my progress.
12. This past year, I have had the opportunities at work to learn and grow.

Leaders with higher scores on these 12 items consistently have more satisfied employees, lower dysfunctional turnover, and higher team performance. Leaders with lower scores generally have just the opposite results. What is interesting about the Gallup 12 is that many of the items are related to the motivational techniques described earlier in this chapter and are under immediate supervisors' direct control. Oftentimes poor leaders blame followers, the organization, or the situation for poor results or high turnover, when the truth of the matter is that they would more likely pinpoint the source of the problem by looking in the mirror.

Sources: M. Buckingham and C. Coffman, *First, Break All The Rules*. New York: Simon & Schuster, 1999; G. J. Curphy and R. T. Hogan, "Managerial Incompetence: Is There a Dead Skunk on the Table?" Working paper, 2004; G. J. Curphy and R. T. Hogan, "What We Really Know about Leadership (But Seem Unwilling To Implement)." Working paper, 2004.

TABLE 9.4
Typical Items on a Satisfaction Questionnaire

1. Overall, I am satisfied with my job.
2. I feel the workload is about equal for everyone in the organization.
3. My supervisor handles conflict well.
4. My pay and benefits are comparable to those in other organizations.
5. There is a real future for people in this organization if they apply themselves.
6. Exceptional performance is rewarded in this organization.
7. We have a good health care plan in this organization.
8. In general, I am satisfied with my life and where it is going.

These items are often rated on a scale ranging from *strongly disagree* (1) to *strongly agree* (5).

A Recipe for Failure: Abusive Bosses, Workplace Anger, and Violence

HIGHLIGHT 9.12

What did I tell you the first day? Your thoughts are nothing; you are nothing . . . if you were in my toilet bowl I wouldn't bother flushing it. My bath mat means more to me than you . . . you don't like it here, leave!
George Huang, Swimming with Sharks

Workplace anger and violence seem to be on the rise. A recent Gallup survey showed that 25 percent of employees report themselves as being "somewhat angry" at work. One in 20 employees has been assaulted at work, 1 in 6 has been sexually harassed, and 1 in 3 has been the subject of verbal abuse. Workplace homicides are now the second most prevalent reason for death at work, with 709 homicides occurring in 1998. Unfortunately, poor leadership practices appear to be a leading cause of workplace anger, and workers are four times more likely to leave a company if they have an abusive boss. But what can a leader do to control anger and violence in the workplace? First, given that many people are working longer hours than ever before, leaders need to be especially vigilant of follower stress and strain. Second, leaders must be willing to let people take some time off when things start to get out of hand. The work will still be there tomorrow—few people have jobs where things really have to be done at a certain time. Third, never, ever abuse

followers. There are many more of them than there are of you, and they can make your life miserable with various acts of computer sabotage, work slowdowns, and other passive-aggressive acts. More importantly, they are the people who are closest to the customer and do most of the work. If you have a performance problem, counsel the individuals in private and if necessary put them on some kind of performance plan. You could also use some of the development planning and coaching techniques described in Part 3 Leadership Skills section of this text to turn their performance around.

Sources: A. Quigley, "Organizational Consequences of Workplace Aggression." In *Aggression in the Workplace: The Forgotten Problem,* R. T. Hogan and D. K. Sheldon (chairs), symposium conducted at the 14th Annual Conference of the Society of Industrial and Organizational Psychology, Atlanta, GA, May 1999; B. J. Tepper, "Consequences of Abusive Supervision." *Academy of Management Journal* 43, no. 2 (2000), pp. 178–89; D. Hales and R. E. Hales, "Is Work Driving You Mad?" *Parade Magazine,* March 18, 2001, pp. 8–9; G. Strauss, "Workers Hone the Fine Art of Revenge: Acts of Violence, Harassment toward Boss on Rise in Corporate World." *Denver Post,* August 24, 1998, p. 6E; K. L. Zellars, B. J. Tepper, and M. K. Duffy, "Abusive Supervisors and Subordinates' Organizational Citizenship Behavior." *Journal of Applied Psychology* 87 (6), 2002, pp. 1068–76; B. L. Tepper, M. K. Duffy, C. A. Henle, and L. Schurer Lambert, "Procedural Injustice, Victim Precipitation, and Abusive Supervision." *Personnel Psychology* 59 (2006), pp. 101–23.

Leadership practitioners should be aware of several other important findings regarding global and facet satisfaction. The first finding is that people generally tend to be very happy with their vocation or occupation. They may not like the pay, benefits, or their boss, but they do seem to be satisfied with what they do for a living. This finding points out the importance of values and intrinsic motivation, as most people gravitate to tasks or jobs they find interesting and enjoyable. The second finding pertains to the **hierarchy effect.** In general, people with longer tenure or in higher positions tend to have higher global and facet satisfaction ratings than those newer to or lower in the organization.[149] Because people higher in the organization are happier at work, they may not understand or appreciate why people at lower levels are less satisfied. From below, leaders at the top can appear somewhat naive and out of touch. From above, the complaints about morale, pay, or resources are often perceived as whining. One of the authors once worked with a utilities company that had downsized and was suffering from all of the ill effects associated with high levels of dysfunctional turnover. Unfortunately, the executive vice president responsible for attracting and retaining talent and making the company "an employer of choice" stated that he had no idea why employees were complaining and that things would be a lot better if they just quit whining. Because the executive did not understand or appreciate the sources of employee complaints, the programs to improve employee morale completely missed the mark, and the high levels of dysfunctional turnover continued. The hierarchy effect also implies that it will take a considerable amount of top leaders' focus and energy to increase the satisfaction levels of nonmanagement employees—lip service alone is never enough. See Highlight 9.13 for an example of a well-intended but poorly executed corporate attempt at improving employee morale.

Compensation is another facet of job satisfaction that can have important implications for leadership practitioners. As you might expect, the hierarchy effect is alive and well with pay: A survey of 3 million employees reported that 71 percent of senior management, 58 percent of middle management, and only 46 percent of nonmanagers rate their pay as "very good." Of nonmanagers, 33 percent rate their pay as "so-so" and 20 percent rate their pay as "very poor."[150] Given the wage gap between males and females, it may be correct to assume that a disproportionate amount of females can be found in these less satisfied groups. Many of these females may be the highest performers in their positions; therefore, this wage discrepancy, in combination with relatively small annual pay increases over the past few years, may contribute to disproportionately high levels of dysfunctional turnover among females.

People who are happier with their jobs also tend to have higher life satisfaction ratings. **Life satisfaction** concerns one's attitudes about life in general, and Item 8 in Table 9.4 is an example of a typical life satisfaction question. Since leaders are often some of the most influential people in

The Hierarchy Effect and Stupid Corporate Tricks

HIGHLIGHT 9.13

The hierarchy effect can make people at the top oblivious to the frustrations and feelings of those at the bottom of organizations. One example of where the hierarchy effect is alive and well is the airline industry. The major airlines in the United States suffered tremendously after 9/11. Many of the major carriers, such as United, Delta, Northwest, US Airways, and America West had to declare bankruptcy as a result of reduced passenger loads and higher fuel prices. These carriers had to make massive personnel cuts and renegotiate contracts with the pilot, flight attendant, ground crew, and mechanics unions in order to regain financial solvency. Many union employee pensions were tied to airline stock and disappeared when their airline declared bankruptcy. In addition to their pension loss, employees were asked to put in 20 percent more hours while taking 20–30 percent pay cuts. Relationships between labor and management had always been problematic in the airline industry, but employee morale sunk to new lows when these changes were implemented.

But it wasn't as if executives were insensitive to the plight of their employees. One major airline went so far as to create a booklet chock full of tips on how to cope with reduced pay. This booklet was sent to 30,000 employees and contained such helpful ideas as:

- Shop for jewelry at pawn shops.
- Take dates for a free walk in the woods.
- Do not be shy about pulling something you like out of the trash.

With sensitivity such as this, is there any wonder why this airline's customer service, lost baggage, and on-time arrival and departure statistics are in the toilet? This airline is only now recognizing that employees are critical to its long-term success, but their efforts to engage employees have been limited to the cheerleading type events identified in Highlight 9.2. And rather than boosting morale, these mandatory activities have made employees even angrier. It is hard to get fired up to service customers when top management's actions (loss of pension, increased workloads, and pay cuts) speak a whole lot louder than the "concern for employee" messages coming out of these motivational events.

Source: *Minnesota Monthly Magazine.* "Tip No. 102: Avoid Our Overpriced Inflight Snacks," December 2006, p. 81.

their followers' lives, they should never underestimate the impact they have on their followers' overall well-being. Unfortunately, at least some of the increasing violence at home and in the workplace may be exacerbated by poor leadership.[39–41,130,131,135,151,152]

Job satisfaction surveys are used extensively in both public and private institutions. Organizations using these instruments typically administer them every one or two years to assess workers' attitudes about different aspects of work, changes in policies or work procedures, or other initiatives. Such survey results are most useful when they can be compared with those from some **reference group.** The organization's past results can be used as one kind of reference group—are people's ratings of pay, promotion, or overall satisfaction rising or falling over time? Job satisfaction ratings from similar organizations can be another reference group—are satisfaction ratings of leadership and working conditions higher or lower than those in similar organizations?

Figure 9.6 shows the facet and global satisfaction results for approximately 80 employees working at a medium-sized airport in the western United States. Employees completing the survey included the director of aviation and his supervisory staff ($n = 11$), the operations department ($n = 6$), the airfield maintenance department ($n = 15$), the communications department ($n = 6$), the airport facilities staff ($n = 12$), the administration department ($n = 10$), and the custodial staff ($n = 20$). The airport is owned by the city and has seen tremendous growth since the opening of the new terminal. However, less than two years after opening, aircraft emplanements had already reached the level projected for 15 years in the future and had exceeded the capacity of the new terminal. Unfortunately, staffing had remained at the same since the opening and the resulting workload and stress were thought to be adversely affecting morale and job satisfaction. Because of these concerns, the director of aviation decided to do a job satisfaction survey to pinpoint problem areas and develop action plans to resolve them.

Scores above 50 on Figure 9.6 are areas of satisfaction; scores below 50 are areas of dissatisfaction when compared to national norms. Here we see that airport employees are very satisfied with their benefits, are fairly satisfied with the work itself, but are dissatisfied with top leadership, ethics, supervision, feedback, promotion opportunities, and the like. All airport employees got to review these results, and each department discussed the factors underlying the survey results and developed and implemented action plans to address problem areas. Top leadership, in this case the director of aviation, was seen as the biggest source of dissatisfaction by all departments. The director was a genuinely nice person and meant well, but he never articulated his vision for the airport, never explained how employees' actions were related to this mission, failed to set goals for each department, did not provide feedback, never clarified roles or areas of responsibilities for his staff, delegated action items to whomever he happened to see in the hall, often changed his mind with key decisions, and failed to keep his staff informed of airline tenant or city council decisions. In other words, this was an In Name Only Manager from Chapter 4 who could not build a team nor get results. When confronted with this information, the director placed the blame on the rapid growth of the airport and the lack of staffing support from the city (the fundamental attribution error in action again). The city manager then gave the director six months to substantially improve employee satisfaction levels. The director did not take the problem very seriously so, not surprisingly, the survey results six months later were no different for top leadership. The director was subsequently removed from his position because of his failure to improve the morale at the airport.

It is important to point out that rarely is it enough to merely administer surveys. Leaders must also be willing to take action on the basis of survey results, or risk losing credibility and actually increasing job dissatisfaction.

Upon receiving the results of these surveys, leaders with bad results may feel tempted to not share any results with their followers, but this is almost always a mistake. Although the results may not be flattering, the rumors are likely to be much worse than the results themselves. Also, followers will be less than willing to fill out subsequent satisfaction surveys if they see denial of the results and little if any change to the workplace. Furthermore, leaders feeling defensive about such results and tempted to hide them should remember that the bad results may not be a surprise to anyone but themselves; therefore, what's to hide? On a practical level, leaders should never assess employees' attitudes about work unless they are willing to share the results and take action.

Three Theories of Job Satisfaction

All of the theories of motivation described earlier in this chapter provide insight into followers' levels of job satisfaction too. For example, it would be difficult for Julie to be satisfied with her job if she was consistently underdressed for weather conditions, or for Ling Ling to be satisfied if her goals were unclear, she was not provided feedback, or she failed to be rewarded for good performance. Nonetheless, several other theories offer even better explanations for job satisfaction.

Affectivity

Affectivity refers to one's tendency to react to stimuli in a consistent emotional manner. People with a disposition for **negative affectivity** consistently react to changes, events, or situations in a negative manner. They

FIGURE 9.6 Results of a facet satisfaction survey.

Source: D. P. Campbell and S. Hyne, *Manual for the Revised Campbell Organizational Survey.* Minneapolis, MN: National Computing Systems, 1995.

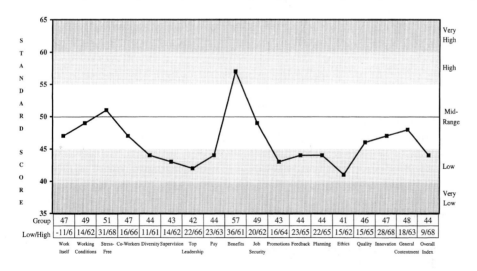

tend to be unhappy with themselves and their lives, and are more likely to focus on the downside or disadvantages of a situation. People with a disposition for **positive affectivity** consistently react to changes, events, or situations in a positive manner. They are happy with their lives, and tend to take an upbeat, optimistic approach when faced with new situations. People with a positive affective disposition tend to see a cup as half full; people with a negative affective disposition are more likely to describe a glass as half empty. These two groups of individuals are thought to attend to, process, and recall information differently, and these differences affect both job satisfaction and satisfaction with life itself. Researchers have found that negative affectivity was related to job dissatisfaction, and positive affectivity to job satisfaction. Of course, such results are hardly surprising—we all know individuals who never seem happy whatever their circumstances, and others who seem to maintain a positive outlook even in the most adverse circumstances.[25,130,153–155]

These findings suggest that leadership initiatives may have little impact on a person's job satisfaction if their affective disposition is either extremely positive or negative. For example, if Ling Ling has a negative affective disposition, she may remain dissatisfied with her pay, working conditions, and so forth, *no matter what her leader does.* This is consistent with the findings of a study of identical twins reared apart and together which discovered that affectivity has a strong genetic component.[153,155,156] Given that leaders can do little to change followers' genetic makeup, these findings again highlight the importance of using good selection procedures when hiring employees. Trying to increase followers' job satisfaction is a reasonable goal, but some followers may be hard (impossible?) to please, no matter what the leader does.

From a leader perspective, affectivity can have several implications in the workplace. First and foremost, one's own affectivity can have a strong influence on followers' morale or satisfaction levels. Say you worked for a leader with negative affectivity. Chances are he or she would find fault in your work, and constantly complain about organizational policies, resources, and so on. The opposite might be true if you worked for someone having positive affectivity. Second, leading a high percentage of followers having either positive or negative affectivity would likely result in very different leadership experiences. The positive group may be much more tolerant and willing to put up with organizational changes; the negative group would likely find fault in any change the leader made. Increasing job satisfaction through affectivity means hiring those with positive affectivity. However, few, if any, selection systems address this important workplace variable. Because negative affectivity may not be assessed or even apparent until a follower has been on the job for a period of time, perhaps the best advice for leadership practitioners is that some followers might well have a permanent chip on their shoulders, and there may be little you can do to change it.

Organizational Fit, Role Ambiguity, and Job Satisfaction

HIGHLIGHT 9.14

The 11 theories of motivation and three of satisfaction provide useful frameworks for understanding why people may or may not be happy at work. But there are two other key causes of job dissatisfaction that do not fit neatly into one of these frameworks. The first has to do with **organizational fit.** Teams and organizations, like individuals, believe some things are important and others to be relatively unimportant. Teams and organizations reinforce different work values, which can easily be seen in organizational decisions, norms, and climate (see Table 9.2). Leaders and followers are attracted to and are most satisfied when their personal work values align with those of the organization. An example might be when both the individual and the organization believe being around others, abiding by societal norms, and making money are important. But people will experience dissatisfaction when there is a mismatch between their personal values and those of the organization. And the greater the mismatch, the higher the dissatisfaction and the greater the retention risk. According to Curphy and Hogan, the degree of fit between personal and organizational values is a leading cause of employee turnover and satisfaction.

Another major cause of job dissatisfaction is role ambiguity. **Role ambiguity** occurs whenever leaders or followers are unclear about what they need to do and how they should do it. Many people come to work to succeed, but all too many leaders set followers up for failure by not providing them with the direction, training, or resources they need to be successful. In these situations followers may exert a high level of effort, but they often times are not working on the right things and as a result get very little accomplished. This sense of frustration quickly turns to dissatisfaction and eventually causes people to look for someplace else to work. An example here is a vice president of human resources who left a position early in his career after he had only been on the job for two weeks. During those first two weeks he had never seen his boss, did not have a desk, and did not even have a phone. The irony of it all was that he was working for a major Canadian phone company. The bottom line is that role ambiguity can have devastating effects but is easily avoidable. Leaders really do not have any good excuses for people leaving because they are uncertain about what they need to do to succeed.

Sources: G. J. Curphy, "What We Really Know about Leadership (But Seem Unwilling To Implement)." Presentation given at the Minnesota Professionals for Psychology Applied to Work, Minneapolis, MN, January 2004; G. J. Curphy and R. T. Hogan, "Managerial Incompetence: Is There a Dead Skunk on the Table?" Working paper, 2004; R. T. Hogan and G. J. Curphy, "Leadership Matters: Values and Dysfunctional Dispositions." Working paper, 2004; G. J. Curphy, A. Baldrica, M. Benson, and R. T. Hogan, *Managerial Incompetence.* Unpublished manuscript, 2007.

If you don't want people to have Mickey Mouse attitudes, then don't give them Mickey Mouse work.

Frederick Herzberg,
researcher

Herzberg's Two-Factor Theory

Herzberg developed the **two-factor theory** from a series of interviews he conducted with accountants and engineers. More specifically, he asked what satisfied them about their work and found that their answers usually could be sorted into five consistent categories. Furthermore, rather than assuming that what dissatisfied people was always just the opposite of what satisfied them, he also specifically asked what *dissatisfied* people about their jobs. Surprisingly, the list of satisfiers and dissatisfiers represented entirely different aspects of work.

Herzberg labeled the factors that led to *satisfaction* at work **motivators,** and he labeled the factors that led to *dissatisfaction* at work **hygiene factors.**

The most common motivators and hygiene factors can be found in Table 9.5. According to the two-factor theory, efforts directed toward improving hygiene factors will not increase followers' motivation or satisfaction. No matter how much leaders improve working conditions, pay, or sick-leave policies, for example, followers *will not* exert any additional effort or persist any longer at a task. For example, followers will probably be no more satisfied to do a dull and boring job merely by being given pleasant office furniture. On the other hand, followers may be asked to work in conditions so poor as to create dissatisfaction, which can distract them from constructive work.[157–159]

Given limited resources on the leader's part, the key to increasing followers' satisfaction levels according to two-factor theory is to just adequately satisfy the hygiene factors while maximizing the motivators for a particular job. It is important for working conditions to be adequate, but it is even more important (for enhancing motivation and satisfaction) to provide plenty of recognition, responsibility, and possibilities for advancement (see Figure 9.7). Although giving followers meaningful work and then recognizing them for their achievement seems straightforward enough, it is interesting to note that these techniques are tremendously underutilized by leaders.[40,47,159] Most leaders prefer to give employees a Kick in the Pants (KITA) to get them to do something rather than appealing to their personal values or give them something meaningful to do. Because of the fear of retaliation, most organizations use positive KITAs, such as employee benefits, to keep employees happy and induce them to remain with the company. But Herzberg argues that KITAs do not drive job satisfaction or motivation, and leaders would be better off restructuring work to make it more meaningful and significant than giving out shirts with company logos or increasing medical co-pays.

The two-factor theory offers leaders ideas about how to, and how not to, bolster followers' satisfaction, but it has received little empirical support beyond Herzberg's own results. In other words, it just may not be an accurate explanation for job satisfaction despite its apparent grounding in data. We present it here in part because it has become such a well-known approach to work motivation and job satisfaction that the present account would appear incomplete if we ignored it. The problem with two-factor theory, however, seems to lie in the very aspect that at first seemed its

TABLE 9.5
Motivators and Hygiene Factors of the Two-Factor Theory

Source: Adapted from F. Herzberg, *Work and the Nature of Men.* Cleveland, OH: World Publishing, 1966.

Hygiene Factors	Motivators
Supervision	Achievement
Working conditions	Recognition
Co-workers	The work itself
Pay	Responsibility
Policies/procedures	Advancement and growth
Job security	

FIGURE 9.7
Herzberg's
two-factor theory.

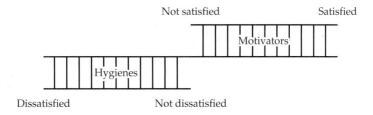

strength: the original data on which it was based. For one thing, as noted earlier, Herzberg developed his theory after interviewing only accountants and engineers, two groups who are hardly representative of workers in other lines of work or activity. Furthermore, his subjects typically attributed job satisfaction to *their* skill or effort, yet blamed their dissatisfaction on circumstances beyond their control. This sounds suspiciously like the fundamental attribution error described earlier in this book. Despite such limitations, the two-factor theory has provided useful insight into what followers find satisfying and dissatisfying about work.

Organizational Justice

Organizational justice is a cognitive approach based on the premise that people who are treated unfairly are less productive, satisfied, and committed to their organizations. Moreover, these individuals are also likely to initiate collective action and engage in various counterproductive work behaviors.[160] According to Trevino, organizational justice is made up of three related components. **Interactional justice** reflects the degree to which people are given information about different reward procedures and are treated with dignity and respect. **Distributive justice** concerns followers' perceptions of whether the level of reward or punishment is commensurate with an individual's performance or infraction. Dissatisfaction occurs when followers believe someone has received too little or too much reward or punishment. Perceptions of **procedural justice** involve the process in which rewards or punishments are administered. If someone is to be punished, then followers will be more satisfied if the person being punished has been given adequate warnings and has had the opportunity to explain his or her actions, and if the punishment has been administered in a timely and consistent manner.[161] Research has shown that these different components of organizational justice are related to satisfaction with the leader, pay, promotion, the job itself, organizational citizenship behaviors, and counterproductive work behaviors (in instances were perceived injustice was taking place).[131,135,137,138,160–167]

So what would leaders need to do if they wish to improve follower satisfaction and reduce turnover using organizational justice theory? The underlying principle for organizational justice is fairness—going back to our earlier characters, do Ling Ling or Julie feel that the process in which rewards or punishments are administered is fair? Are the potential rewards

True patriotism hates injustice in its own land more than anywhere else.

Clarence Darrow, attorney

commensurate with performance? Do Julie and Ling Ling believe the reward system is unbiased? What would the flight attendants have to say about whether they were treated with dignity and respect, whether rewards were commensurate with performance, or whether rewards were administered fairly? Leaders who want to improve job satisfaction using this approach need to ensure that followers answer yes to these three questions. If followers answer no to any of the questions, then leaders need to change the reward and punishment system if they want to improve job satisfaction using organizational justice theory. Brockner notes that fairness in the workplace makes intuitive sense but is woefully lacking in many organizations. All too many managers play favorites, avoid rather than directly deal with uncomfortable situations, or for legal reasons cannot reveal how certain issues were handled.[36] These instances of perceived unfairness contribute to the high levels of managerial incompetence found in many organizations.

Conrad Black

PROFILES IN LEADERSHIP 9.4

In March 2007 Conrad Black began his criminal trial for diverting close to $90,000,000 from his company for his own use. As a child Black grew up in privilege in Montreal, Canada—his father was the president of Canadian Breweries and his mother was the daughter of the founder of Great-West Life Insurance. Upon graduation from high school, Black enrolled at Upper Canada College, where he was expelled for selling stolen exam papers in his first year. He then went to Trinity College School for a year before transferring to and graduating from Thornton Hall. Black then went on to law school for a year, but then dropped out and later completed a master of arts degree in history. He eventually went back to law school and obtained a legal degree.

During and after university, Black got involved in a number of businesses. Most of the businesses involved publishing, where he was taken under the wing of "Bud" McDougald and E. P. Taylor, two prominent Canadian businessmen. Following McDougald's death Black was able to acquire a controlling interest in Argus Corporation, a large Canadian holding company, through a controversial arrangement with McDougald's widow. By

1990 his companies were running over 400 newspapers in North America and he was the 235th richest person in Canada with an estimated wealth of $350,000,000.

In 2001 Black gave up his Canadian citizenship in order to become Baron Black of Crossharbour, a member of the British House of Lords. He hobnobbed with the likes of Henry Kissinger, Margaret Thatcher, and Princess Diana, and split his time between homes in London, New York, Toronto, and Palm Beach. Black reveled in the attention he received as a celebrity on the world scene. But starting in 2003 the U.S. Securities and Exchange Commission began to hear complaints that Black was diverting company funds for personal use. By 2004 the Securities and Exchange Commission had enough information to file suit against him for fraud, racketeering, obstruction of justice, and money laundering. Conrad Black's greed, vanity, and selfishness made him a controversial figure in Canada even before his trial. It will be interesting to see how work values (Commercial, Recognition, and low Altruism) play out in his trial.

Sources: E. Steel and D. Belkin, "O Canada! Black Trial Stirs Interest, Pique Back Home." *The Wall Street Journal,* March 23, 2007, p. B1-2; http://en.wikipedia.org/wiki/Conrad_Black.

Summary

This chapter has reviewed research concerning motivation, satisfaction, and performance. Motivation was defined as anything that provides direction, intensity, and persistence to behavior. Although motivation is an important aspect of performance, performance and motivation are not the same thing. Performance is a broader concept than motivation, as abilities, skills, group norms, and the availability of resources can all affect followers' levels of performance. Job satisfaction is a set of attitudes that people have about work. Although a majority of people are generally satisfied with their jobs, people often have varying levels of satisfaction for different aspects of their jobs, such as pay, working conditions, supervisors, or co-workers.

Many of the approaches to understanding motivation have distinct implications for increasing performance and satisfaction. Therefore, several different theories of motivation were reviewed in this chapter. The first two theories, Maslow's hierarchy of needs and Alderfer's existence-relatedness-growth (ERG) theory, assume that people are motivated to satisfy a universal set of needs. The next three theories examined motivation in terms of individual differences, emphasizing a person's intrinsic motivation to perform a particular task, their personal values, or a person's general level of achievement orientation. The next set of theories, goal setting, equity theory, self-efficacy, and expectancy theory, examined motivation from a cognitive perspective. These theories assume that people make rational, conscious choices about the direction, intensity, and persistence of their behaviors, and generally engage in behaviors that maximize payoffs and minimize costs. The last two theories, empowerment and operant approach, examined motivation from a situational perspective. Leadership practitioners likely will be more effective if they learn to recognize situations where various approaches, or the insights particular to them, may be differentially useful. Just as a carpenter can more effectively build a house by using a variety of tools, a leader can be more effective by using a variety of motivational interventions to enhance work.

Several other theories seem to be more useful for explaining followers' attitudes about work. Some research suggests that individuals vary in the characteristic tenor of their affectivity; some people generally have positive attitudes about work and life whereas others are generally unhappy about work and life. Such differences have a genetic component and may set limits on the extent to which initiatives by leaders will actually impact follower satisfaction. Leaders may also be able to increase satisfaction levels by giving followers more meaningful work and by treating them fairly. Followers (and leaders for that matter) are more likely to have positive attitudes about work if they believe that what they do is important and that the reward and disciplinary systems are fair and just.

Key Terms

motivation, *370*
performance, *370*
effectiveness, *371*
job satisfaction, *372*
organizational
citizenship
behaviors, *372*
needs, *377*
hierarchy of needs,
378
existence-relatedness-
growth (ERG)
theory, *380*
frustration regression
hypothesis, *380*
achievement
orientation, *382*
extrinsic motivational
bias, *385*
intrinsic
motivation, *386*
overjustification
effect, *388*
goal setting, *389*

Pygmalion Effect, *391*
Golem Effect, *391*
expectancy
theory, *393*
effort-to-performance
expectancy, *393*
performance-to-
outcome
expectancy, *394*
valence, *394*
equity theory, *395*
positive
self-efficacy, *398*
negative-self-
efficacy, *398*
operant approach, *400*
reward, *400*
punishment, *400*
contingent, *400*
noncontingent, *400*
extinction, *400*
empowerment, *402*
functional
turnover, *410*

dysfunctional
turnover, *410*
global
satisfaction, *411*
facet satisfaction, *411*
hierarchy effect, *414*
life satisfaction, *414*
reference group, *415*
negative
affectivity, *417*
positive
affectivity, *418*
organizational fit, *419*
role ambiguity, *419*
two-factor theory, *419*
motivators, *419*
hygiene factors, *419*
organizational
justice, *421*
interactional
justice, *421*
distributive
justice, *421*
procedural justice, *421*

Questions

1. Why do you think there are so many different theories or approaches to understanding motivation? Shouldn't it be possible to determine which one is best and just use it? Why or why not?

2. Many good leaders are thought of as good motivators. How would you rate Barack Obama, Hillary Clinton, John Edwards, Rudy Guiliani, Mitt Romney, and John McCain in terms of their ability to motivate others?

3. What is your own view of what motivates people to work hard and perform well?

4. Do you know of any examples where reward systems are inconsistent with desired behavior? How are personal values related to rewards?

5. What do you find personally satisfying or dissatisfying at work or school? For those things you find dissatisfying, how could you make them more satisfying? What theory of job satisfaction best explains your actions?

Activities

1. Earlier in this chapter you were asked how the four types of motivation theories could be used to improve the customer service levels of flight attendants. Break into four groups, and have each group discuss how they would design and implement a motivation program using either a

need, individual difference, cognitive, and situational approach. Each group should then give a 15-minute presentation on their findings. The presentation should include the approach they used, how they would collect any needed additional data, the program design, program implementation, potential barriers to the program, and their evaluation of the effectiveness of their program.

2. Research the trials of Conrad Black (Profiles in Leadership 9.4) and Joe Naccio, the former CEO of Qwest. What verdicts did the jury deliver? What work values do both of these individuals possess?

3. Interview someone in a leadership position on employee satisfaction and retention. Does the organization conduct regular satisfaction surveys? What do the survey results reveal about the organization? Is the organization having any turnover problems? Why or why not?

4. Oftentimes team and organizational values change with changes in leadership, or when an organization is acquired or divested. Interview someone in a leadership position who has been through a merger or a downsizing and determine their level of satisfaction before and after these events.

5. People often leave bosses, not organizations. Interview people with 10–20 years of work experience and ask them to list the reasons why they have left past jobs. How many people left because their bosses demonstrated some characteristics associated with managerial incompetence (Chapter 4) or dark-side personality traits (Chapter 7)?

Minicase

"Initech versus The Coffee Bean"

Consider Peter Gibbons, an employee of the fictional Initech Corporation from the movie *Office Space.* Peter has been asked to meet with efficiency experts (Bob and Bob) to discuss his work environment. One of the Bobs is curious about Peter's tendency toward underperformance and confronts him about his lack of attention to office policies and procedures. It seems Peter has been turning in his TPS reports late and without the company mandated cover sheet:

Peter: You see, Bob, it's not that I'm lazy, it's that I just don't care.

Bob: Don't? Don't care?

Peter: It's a problem of motivation, alright? Now if I work my butt off and Initech ships a few extra units, I don't see another dime, so where's the motivation? And here's another thing, I have eight different bosses right now.

Bob: Eight?

Peter: Eight, Bob. So that means when I make a mistake, I have eight different people coming by to tell me about it. That's my only real motivation, not to be hassled, that and the fear of losing my job. But you know, Bob, that will only make someone work just hard enough not to get fired.

The environment at Initech is an all too familiar one to many office workers. It is an environment in which success is directly proportional to how busy you look, where questioning authority is taboo, and where meticulous attention to paperwork is the only way to get promoted.

Contrast Initech to The Coffee Bean—a chain of gourmet coffee shops. In an effort to boost employee morale and increase productivity, the management team at The Coffee Bean decided to pursue the FISH philosophy. FISH is a management training program that stresses fun in the workplace. It espouses four principles:

Play—"Work that is made fun gets done."

Make Their Day—"When you make someone's day through a small act of kindness or unforgettable engagement, you can turn even routine encounters into special memories."

Be There—"Being there is a great way to practice wholeheartedness and fight burnout."

Choose Your Attitude—"When you learn you have the power to choose your response to what life brings, you can look for the best and find opportunities you never imagined possible."

Stores in The Coffee Bean chain were encouraged to use these principles to make the stores a fun place for employees and customers. The stores have created theme days where employees dress up for themes (NFL day, basketball days, pajama day)—and then give discounts to customers who dress the same. There are also trivia games in which customers who can answer trivia questions get discounts on their coffee purchases: Nancy Feilen, a Coffee Bean store manager, explains: "We tried to come up with something that would help strike up a conversation with guests and engage fun in the stores for team members and guests." In other stores, customers play Coffee Craps. If a customer rolls a seven or an 11, he gets a free drink. Some stores have done Fear Factor Fridays—if the store sells a certain number of drinks, one of the baristas will agree to some act. In one case a barista ate a cricket.

The results? One store increased the average check by 12 percent in six months, turnover has decreased significantly—general managers typically left after 22 months with the chain but now stay an average of 31 months—and the turnover rate for hourly employees dropped to 69 percent from more than 200 percent over a three-year period.

So, where would you rather work?

1. How would you gauge Peter's achievement orientation? What are some of the needs not being met for Peter Gibbons at Initech? What changes might improve Peter's motivation?

2. Would you judge the leaders at Initech as more likely to invoke the Pygmalion or the Golem Effect?

3. What about the environment at The Coffee Bean? Pygmalion or Golem?

4. Why has The Coffee Bean seen such a significant reduction in its turnover?

Sources: http://www.findarticles.com/p/articles/mi_m3190/is_2_38/ai_112248126; http://www.imdb.com/title/tt0151804/quotes; http://www.charthouse.com/home.asp; http://www.gazettenet.com/business/02242003/3706.htm.

Chapter Notes

1. Hunter, J. E., F. L. Schmidt, and M. K. Judiesch. "Individual Differences in Output Variability as a Function of Job Complexity." *Journal of Applied Psychology* 74 (1990), pp. 28–42.

2. Matson, E., and L. Prusak. "The Performance Variability Dilemma." *MIT Sloan Management Review* 45 (1) (2003), pp. 38–44

3. Associated Press. "Democrats Hit Troop Extensions." April 12, 2007. http://www.military.com/NewsContent.

4. Huselid, M. A. "The Impact of Human Resource Practices on Turnover, Productivity, and Corporate Financial Performance." *Academy of Management Journal* 38, no. 4 (1995), pp. 635–72.

5. Sirota Consulting. *Establishing the Linkages between Employee Attitudes, Customer Attitudes, and Bottom-Line Results.* Chicago: Author, 1998.

6. Koys, D. J. "The Effects of Employee Satisfaction, Organizational Citizenship Behavior, and Turnover on Organizational Effectiveness: A Unit-Level, Longitudinal Study." *Personnel Psychology* 54, no. 1 (2001), pp. 101–14.

7. Pugh, S. D., J. Dietz, J. W. Wiley, and S. M. Brooks. "Driving Service Effectiveness Through Employee-Customer Linkages." *Academy of Management Executive* 16 (4) (2002), pp. 73–81.

8. Koene, B. A. S., A. L. W. Vogelaar, and J. L. Soeters. "Leadership Effects on Organizational Climate and Financial Performance: Local Leadership Effect in Chain Organizations." *The Leadership Quarterly* 13 (3) (2002), pp. 193–216.

9. Gelade, G. A., and M. Ivery. "The Impact of Human Resource Management and Work Climate on Organizational Performance." *Personnel Psychology* 56 (2) (2003), pp. 383–404.

10. Carr, J. Z., A. M. Schmidt, J. K. Ford, and R. P. DeShon. "Climate Perceptions Matter: A Meta-analytic Path Analysis Relating Molar Climate, Cognitive and Affective States, and Individual Level Work Outcomes." *Journal of Applied Psychology* 89 (4) (2004), pp. 605–19.

11. Smithey-Fulmer, I., B. Gerhart, and K. S. Scott. "Are the 100 Best Better? An Empirical Investigation of the Relationship between Being a 'Great Place to Work' and Firm Performance." *Personnel Psychology* 56 (4) (2003), pp. 965–93.

12. McFarlin, D. B. "Hard Day's Work: A Boon for Performance but a Bane for Satisfaction?" *Academy of Management Perspectives* 20 (4) (2006), pp. 115–16.

13. Hewlett, S. A., and C. Buck Luce. "Extreme Jobs: The Dangerous Allure of the 70-Hour Work Week." *Harvard Business Review*, December 2006, pp. 48–49.

14. Rode, J. C., M. L. Arthaud-Day, C. H. Mooney, J. P. Near, T. T. Baldwin, W. H. Bommer, and R. S. Rubin. "Life Satisfaction and Student Performance." *Academy of Management Learning & Education* 4 (4) (2005), pp. 421–33.

15. Shaw, J. D., N. Gupta, and J. E. Delery. "Alternative Conceptualizations of the Relationship between Voluntary Turnover and Organizational Performance." *Academy of Management Journal* 48 (5) (2005), pp. 50–68.

16. Kiewitz, C. "Happy Employees and Firm Performance: Have We Been Putting the Cart before the Horse?" *Academy of Management Executive* 18 (2) (2004), pp. 127–29.

17. Schneider, B., P. J. Hanges, D. B. Smith, and A. N. Salvaggio. " Which Comes First: Employee Attitudes or Organizational Financial and Market Performance?" *Journal of Applied Psychology* 88 (5) (2003), pp. 836–51; Schneider, J. "The Cultural Situation as a Condition for the Condition of Fame." *American Sociology Review* 2 (1937), pp. 480–91.

18. Kanfer, R. "Motivation Theory in Industrial and Organizational Psychology." In *Handbook of Industrial and Organizational Psychology.* Vol. 1. Eds. M. D. Dunnette and L. M. Hough. Palo Alto, CA: Consulting Psychologists Press, 1990, pp. 75–170.

19. Locke, E. A., and G. P. Latham. "What Should We Do about Motivation Theory? Six Recommendations for the Twenty-First Century." *Academy of Management Review* 29 (3) (2004) pp. 388–403.

20. Steers, R. M., R. T. Mowday, and D. L. Shapiro. "The Future of Work Motivation Theory." *Academy of Management Review* 29 (3) (2004), pp. 379–87.

21. Campbell, J. P., and R. D. Pritchard. "Motivation Theory in Industrial and Organizational Psychology." In *Handbook for Industrial and Organizational Psychology.* Ed. M. D. Dunnette. Chicago: Rand McNally, 1976, pp. 60–130.

22. Miller, W. R., and S. Rollnick. *Motivational Interviewing: Preparing People to Change Addictive Behavior.* New York: Guilford Press, 1991.

23. Saal, F. E., and P. A. Knight. *Industrial Organizational Psychology: Science and Practice.* Belmont, CA: Brooks/Cole, 1988.

24. Judge, T. A., C. J. Thoresen, J. E. Bono, and G. K. Patton. "The Job Satisfaction–Job Performance Relationship: A Qualitative and Quantitative Review." *Psychological Bulletin* 127 (2001), pp. 376–407.

25. Judge, T. A., and R. Ilies. "Relationship of Personality to Performance Motivation: A Meta-analytic Review." *Journal of Applied Psychology* 87 (4) (2002), pp. 797–807.

26. Campbell, D. P., and S. Hyne. *Manual for the Revised Campbell Organizational Survey.* Minneapolis, MN: National Computer Systems, 1995.

27. Health, Education, and Welfare Task Force. *Work in America.* Cambridge, MA: MIT Press, 1973.

28. Hoppock, R. *Job Satisfaction.* New York: Harper, 1935.

29. Smith, F. J., K. D. Scott, and C. L. Hulin. "Trends in Job-Related Attitudes in Managerial and Professional Employees." *Academy of Management Journal* 20 (1977), pp. 454–60.

30. Staines, G. L., and R. P. Quinn. "American Workers Evaluate the Quality of Their Jobs." *Monthly Labor Review* 102, no. 1 (1979), pp. 3–12.

31. Tepper, B. J., M. K. Duffy, J. Hoobler, and M. D. Ensley. "Moderators of the Relationships between Coworkers' Organizational Citizenship Behaviors and Fellow Employees' Attitudes." *Journal of Applied Psychology* 89 (3) (2004), pp. 455–65.

32. Cropanzano, R., D. E. Rupp, and Z. S. Byrne. "The Relationship of Emotional Exhaustion to Work Attitudes, Job Performance, and Organizational Citizenship Behaviors." *Journal of Applied Psychology* 88 (1) (2003), pp. 160–69.

33. Ilies, R., B. A. Scott, and T. A. Judge. "The Interactive Effects of Personality Traits and Experienced States on the Intraindividual Patterns of Citizenship Behavior." *Academy of Management Journal* 49 (3) (2006), pp. 561–75.

34. Dineen, B. R., R. J. Lewicki, and E. C. Tomlinson. "Supervisory Guidance and Behavioral Integrity: Relationships with Employee Citizenship and Deviant Behavior. *Journal of Applied Psychology* 91 (3) (2006), pp. 622–35.

35. Dalal, R. S. "A Meta-analysis of the Relationship between Organizational Citizenship Behavior and Counterproductive Work Behavior." *Journal of Applied Psychology* 90 (6) (2005), pp. 1241–55.

36. Brockner, J. "Why It's So Hard to Be Fair." *Harvard Business Review*, March 2006, p. 122–30.

37. Mills, V. "Longer Hours, Extra Work." *Orlando Sentinel*, June 16, 1999, p. 3C.

38. Hales, D., and R. E. Hales. "Is Work Driving You Mad?" *Parade Magazine*, March 18, 2001, pp. 8–9.

39. Curphy, G. J. "Comments on the State of Leadership Prediction." In *Predicting Leadership: The Good, The Bad, The Indifferent, and the Unnecessary*. J. P. Campbell and M. J. Benson (chairs). Symposium conducted at the 22nd Annual Conference for the Society of Industrial and Organizational Psychology, New York, April 2007.

40. Curphy, G. J., M. J. Benson, A. Baldrica, and R. T. Hogan. *Managerial Incompetence*. Unpublished manuscript, 2007.

41. Curphy, G. J., and R. T. Hogan. "Managerial Incompetence: Is There a Dead Skunk on the Table?" Working paper, 2004.

42. McElroy, J. C., P. C. Morrow, and S. N. Rude. "Turnover and Organizational Performance: A Comparative Analysis of the Effects of Voluntary, Involuntary, and Reduction-in-Force Turnover." *Journal of Applied Psychology* 86 (6) (2001), pp. 1294–99.

43. Krug, J. A. "Why Do They Keep Leaving?" *Harvard Business Review*, February 2003, pp. 14–15.

44. Charan, R., S. Drotter, and J. Noel. *The Leadership Pipeline: How to Build the Leadership-Powered Company*. San Francisco: Jossey-Bass, 2001.

45. Pfau, B. N., and S. A. Cohen. "Aligning Human Capital Practices and Employee Behavior with Shareholder Value." *Consulting Psychology Journal* 55 (3) (2003), pp. 169–78.

46. Huselid, M. A., R. W. Beatty, and B. E. Becker. "'A Players' or 'A Positions'? The Strategic Logic of Workforce Management." *Harvard Business Review*, December 2005, pp. 110–21.

47. Curphy, G. J., and R. T. Hogan. "What We Really Know about Leadership (But Seem Unwilling To Implement)." Working paper, 2004.

48. Hogan, R. T. *Personality and the Fate of Organizations*. Mahwah, NJ: Lawrence Erlbaum Associates, 2007.

49. Campbell, J. P. "The Cutting Edge of Leadership: An Overview." In *Leadership: The Cutting Edge*. Eds. J. G. Hunt and L. L. Larson. Carbondale: Southern Illinois University Press, 1977.

50. Campbell, J. P. "Training Design for Performance Improvement." In *Productivity in Organizations: New Perspectives from Industrial and Organizational Psychology*. Eds. J. P. Campbell, R. J. Campbell, and Associates. San Francisco: Jossey-Bass, 1988, pp. 177–216.

51. Iaffaldano, M. T., and P. M. Muchinsky. "Job Satisfaction and Job Performance: A Meta-analysis." *Psychological Bulletin* 97 (1985), pp. 251–73.

52. Locke, E. A. and G. P. Latham. "Work Motivation and Satisfaction: Light at the End of the Tunnel." *Psychological Science* 1 (1990), pp. 240–46.

53. Maslow, A. H. *Motivation and Personality*. New York: Harper & Row, 1954.

54. Alderfer, C. P. "An Empirical Test of a New Theory of Human Needs." *Organizational Behavior and Human Performance* 4 (1969), pp. 142–75.

55. Betz, E. L. "Two Tests of Maslow's Theory of Need Fulfillment." *Journal of Vocational Behavior* 24 (1984), pp. 204–20.

56. Atkinson, J. W. "Motivational Determinants of Risk Taking Behavior." *Psychological Review* 64 (1957), pp. 359–72.

57. McClelland, D.C. *Power: The Inner Experience*. New York: Irvington, 1975.

58. Barrick, M. R., and M. K. Mount. "The Big Five Personality Dimensions and Job Performance: A Meta-analysis." *Personal Psychology* 44 (1991), pp. 1–26.

59. Judge, T. A., and R. Ilies. "Relationship of Personality to Performance Motivation: A Meta-analytic Review." *Journal of Applied Psychology* 87 (4) (2002), pp. 797–807.

60. Hogan, R. T. and G. J. Curphy. *Personality and Managerial Competence*. Unpublished manuscript, 2007.

61. Curphy, G. J., and K. D. Osten. *Technical Manual for the Leadership Development Survey*. Technical Report No. 93-14. Colorado Springs, CO: U.S. Air Force Academy, 1993.

62. Curphy, G. J. *Users Guide and Interpretive Report for the Leadership Personality Survey*. Minneapolis, MN: Personnel Decisions International, 1998b.

63. Hogan, R. T., and J. Hogan. *Manual for the Hogan Personality Inventory*. Tulsa, OK: Hogan Assessment Systems, 1992.

64. Nilsen, D. L. *Using Self and Observers' Rating of Personality to Predict Leadership Performance*. Unpublished doctoral dissertation, University of Minnesota, 1995.

65. Hewlett, S. A. "Executive Women and the Myth of Having It All." *Harvard Business Review*, April 2002, pp. 66–67.

66. Curphy, G. J. *Hogan Assessment Systems Certification Workshop Training Manuals*. Tulsa, OK: Hogan Assessment Systems, 2003.

67. R. Gregory, R. T. Hogan, and G. J. Curphy, "Risk-Taking in the Energy Industry." *Well Connected* 5 (6) (June 2003), pp. 5–7.

68. Britt, T. W. "Black Hawk Down at Work." *Harvard Business Review*, January 2003, pp. 16–17.

69. Hogan, J., and R. T. Hogan. *Motives, Values and Preferences Inventory*. Tulsa, OK: Hogan Assessment Systems, 1996.

70. Morse, G. "Why We Misread Motives." *Harvard Business Review*, January 2003, p. 18.

71. Deci, E.L. *Intrinsic Motivation.* New York: Plenum, 1975.

72. Boyatzis, R., A. McKee, and D. Goleman. "Reawakening Your Passion for Work." *Harvard Business Review*, April 2002, pp. 86–96.

73. Brett, J. M., and L. K. Stroh. "Working 61 Plus Hours a Week: Why Do Managers Do It?" *Journal of Applied Psychology* 88 (1) (2003), pp. 67–78.

74. Halbesleben, J. R. B, and W. M. Bowler. "Emotional Exhaustion and Job Performance: The Mediating Role of Motivation." *Journal of Applied Psychology* 92 (1) (2007), pp. 93–106.

75. Levinson, H. "Management by Whose Objectives?" *Harvard Business Review*, January 2003, pp. 107–16.

76. Calder, B. J., and B. M. Staw. "Self-Perception of Intrinsic and Extrinsic Motivation." *Journal of Personality and Social Psychology* 31 (1975), pp. 599–605.

77. Eisenberger, R., and J. Cameron. "Detrimental Effects of Reward: Reality or Myth?" *American Psychologist* 51, no. 11 (1996), pp. 1153–66.

78. Locke, E. A., and G. P. Latham. "Building a Practically Useful Theory of Goal Setting and Task Motivation: A 35-Year Odyssey." *American Psychologist* 57 (9) (2002), pp. 705–18.

79. Locke, E.A. "Goal Setting Theory and Its Applications to the World of Business." *Academy of Management Executive* 18 (4) (2004), pp. 124–25.

80. Latham, G. P. "The Motivational Benefits of Goal Setting." *Academy of Management Executive* 18 (4) (2004), pp. 126–29.

81. Kerr, S., and S. Landauer. "Using Stretch Goals to Promote Organizational Effectiveness and Personal Growth: General Electric and Goldman Sachs." *Academy of Management Executive* 18 (4) (2004), pp. 139–43.

82. Fried, Y., and L Haynes Slowik. "Enriching Goal-Setting Theory with Time: An Integrated Approach." *Academy of Management Review* 29 (3) (2004), pp. 404–22.

83. Locke, E. A. "Linking Goals to Monetary Incentives." *Academy of Management Executive* 18 (4) (2004), pp. 130–33.

84. Eddleston, K. A., D. L. Kidder, and B. E. Litzky. "Who's the Boss? Contending with Competing Expectations from Customers and Management." *Academy of Management Executive* 16 (4) (2002), pp. 85–94.

85. Imai, M. *Kaizen: The Key to Japan's Competitive Success.* New York: Random House, 1986.

86. Van Fleet, D. D., T. O. Peterson, E. W. Van Fleet. "Closing the Performance Feedback Gap with Expert Systems." *Academy of Management Executive* 19 (3) (2005), pp. 35–42.

87. Davidson, O. B., and D. Eden. "Remedial Self-Fulfilling Prophecy: Two Field Experiments to Prevent Golem Effects among Disadvantaged Women." *Journal of Applied Psychology* 83, no. 3 (2000), pp. 386–98.

88. Eden, D., D. Geller, A. Gewirtz, R. Gordon-Terner, I. Inbar, M. Liberman, Y. Pass, I. Salomon-Segev, and M. Shalit. "Implanting Pygmalion Leadership Style through Workshop Training: Seven Field Experiments." *Leadership Quarterly* 11, no. 2 (2000), pp. 171–210.

89. White, S. S., and E. A. Locke. "Problems with the Pygmalion Effect and Some Proposed Solutions." *Leadership Quarterly* 11, no. 3 (2000), pp. 389–416.

90. McNatt, D. B. "Ancient Pygmalion Joins Contemporary Management: A Meta-analysis of the Result." *Journal of Applied Psychology* 83, no. 2 (2000), pp. 314–21.

91. Tolman, E. C. *Purposeful Behavior in Animals and Men.* New York: Appleton-Century-Crofts, 1932.

92. Vroom, V. H. *Work and Motivation.* New York: John Wiley, 1964.

93. Porter, L. W., and E. E. Lawler, III. *Managerial Attitudes and Performance.* Homewood, IL: Dorsey, 1968.

94. Lawler, E. E., III. *Motivation in Work Organizations.* Pacific Grove, CA: Brooks/Cole, 1973.

95. Day, D. D., H. P Sin, and T. T. Chen. "Assessing the Burdens of Leadership: Effects of Formal Leadership Roles on Individual Performance over Time." *Personnel Psychology* 57 (2004), pp. 573–605.

96. Adams, J. S. "Inequity in Social Exchange." In *Advances in Experimental Social Psychology.* Vol. 2. Ed. L. Berkowitz. New York: Academic Press, 1965, pp. 267–96.

97. Adams, J. S. "Toward an Understanding of Inequity." *Journal of Abnormal and Social Psychology* 67 (1963), pp. 422–36.

98. Vecchio, R. P. "Predicting Worker Performance in Inequitable Settings." *Academy of Management Review* 7 (1982), pp. 103–10.

99. Bandura, A., and E. A. Locke. "Negative Self-Efficacy and Goal Effects Revisited." *Journal of Applied Psychology* 88 (1) (2003), pp. 87–99.

100. Arvey, R. D., and J. M. Ivancevich. "Punishment in Organizations: A Review, Propositions, and Research Suggestions." *Academy of Management Review* 5 (1980), pp. 123–32.

101. Curphy, G. J. "What We Really Know about Leadership (But Seem Unwilling to Implement)." Presentation given at the Minnesota Professionals for Psychology Applied to Work, Minneapolis, MN, January 2004.

102. Anderson, L. S. *The Cream of the Corp.* Hastings, MN: Anderson Performance Improvement Company, 2003.

103. Markham, S. E., K. D. Scott, and G. H. McKee. "Recognizing Good Attendance: A Longitudinal Quasi-Experimental Field Study." *Personnel Psychology* 55 (3) (2002), pp. 639–60.

104. Stajkovic, A. D., and F. Luthans. "Differential Effects of Incentive Motivators on Performance." *Academy of Management Journal* 44, no. 3 (2001), pp. 580–90.

105. Luthans, F., and A. D. Stajkovic. "Reinforce for Performance: The Need to Go Beyond Pay and Even Rewards." *Academy of Management Executive* 13, no. 2 (1999), pp. 49–57.

106. Bloom, M., and G. T. Milkovich. "Relationships among Risk, Incentive Pay, and Organizational Performance." *Academy of Management Journal* 41, no. 3 (1998), pp. 283–97.

107. Jenkins, G. D., A. Mitra, N. Gupta, and J. D. Shaw. "Are Financial Incentives Related to Performance? A Meta-analytic Review of Empirical Research." *Journal of Applied Psychology* 83, no. 5 (1998), pp. 777–87.

108. Komacki, J. L., S. Zlotnick, and M. Jensen. "Development of an Operant-based Taxonomy and Observational Index on Supervisory Behavior." *Journal of Applied Psychology* 71 (1986), pp. 260–69.

109. Pritchard, R. D., J. Hollenback, and P. J. DeLeo. "The Effects of Continuous and Partial Schedules of Reinforcement of Effort, Performance, and Satisfaction." *Organizational Behavior and Human Performance* 16 (1976), pp. 205–30.

110. Luthans, F., and R. Kreitner. *Organizational Behavior Modification and Beyond: An Operant and Social Learning Approach.* Glenview, IL: Scott Foresman, 1985.

111. Podsakoff, P. M., and W. D. Todor. "Relationships between Leader Reward and Punishment Behavior and Group Process and Productivity." *Journal of Management* 11 (1985), pp. 55–73.

112. Podsakoff, P. M., W. D. Todor, and R. Skov. "Effects of Leader Contingent and Noncontigent Reward and Punishment Behaviors on Subordinate Performance and Satisfaction." *Academy of Management Journal* 25 (1982), pp. 810–25.

113. Arvey, R. D., G. A. Davis, and S. M. Nelson. "Use of Discipline in an Organization: A Field Study." *Journal of Applied Psychology* 69 (1984), pp. 448–60.

114. Kohn, A. "Why Incentive Plans Cannot Work." *Harvard Business Review*, September–October 1993, pp. 54–63.

115. Quinn, R. E., and G. M. Spreitzer. "The Road to Empowerment: Seven Questions Every Leader Should Consider." *Organizational Dynamics*, Autumn 1997, pp. 37–49.

116. Wagner, S. H., C. P. Parker, and N. D. Christiansen. "Employees That Think and Act like Owners: Effects of Ownership Beliefs and Behaviors on Organizational Effectiveness." *Personnel Psychology* 56 (4) (2003), pp. 847–71.

117. Srivastava, A., K. M. Bartol, and E. A. Locke. "Empowering Leadership in Management Teams: Effects on Knowledge Sharing, Efficacy, and Performance." *Academy of Management Journal* 49 (6) (2006), pp. 1239–51.

118. Seibert, S. E., S. R. Silver, and W. A. Randolph. "Taking Empowerment to the Next Level: A Multiple-Level Model of Empowerment, Performance, and Satisfaction." *Academy of Management Journal* 47 (3) (2004), pp. 332–49.

119. Ahearne, M., J. Mathis, and A. Rapp. "To Empower or Not Empower Your Sales Force? An Empirical Examination of the Influence of Leadership Empowerment Behavior on Customer Satisfaction and Performance." *Journal of Applied Psychology* 90 (5) (2005), pp. 945–55.

120. Combs, J., Y. Liu, A. Hall, and D. Ketchen. "How Much Do High Performance Work Practices Matter? A Meta-analysis of Their Effects on Organizational Performance." *Personnel Psychology* 59 (2006), pp. 502–28.

121. Offermann, L. R. "Leading and Empowering Diverse Followers." In *The Balance of Leadership and Followership.* Eds. E. P. Hollander and L. R. Offerman. Kellogg Leadership Studies Project. College Park: University of Maryland Press, 1997, pp. 31–46.

122. Xie, J. L., and G. Johns. "Job Scope and Stress: Can Job Scope Be Too High?" *Academy of Management Journal* 38, no. 5 (1995), pp. 1288–1309.

123. Spreitzer, G. M. "Psychological Empowerment in the Workplace: Dimensions, Measurement, and Validation." *Academy of Management Journal* 38, no. 5 (1995), pp. 1442–65.

124. Peterson, D. B., and M. D. Hicks. *Leader as Coach: Strategies for Coaching and Developing Others.* Minneapolis, MN: Personnel Decisions International, 1996.

125. Ross, S., and G. J. Curphy. *Foundations of Leadership Executive Overview.* Presentation given to executives at Williams-Sonoma Inc., San Francisco, April 24, 2000.

126. Armour, S. "Bosses Held Liable for Keeping Workers." *USA Today*, April 12, 2000, p. 1B.

127. Sutherland, E. *Bosses Encouraged to Play Nice.* Minneapolis, MN: Personnel Decisions International, 2000.

128. Butorac, T. "Recruitment and Retention: The Keys to Profitability at Carlson Companies." Presentation given at Personnel Decisions International, Minneapolis, MN, June 11, 2001.

129. Rigby, D. "Look Before You Lay Off." *Harvard Business Review*, April 2002, pp. 20–21.

130. Levine, D.S. *Disgruntled: The Darker Side of the World of Work.* New York: Berkley Boulevard Books, 1998.

131. Litzky, B. E., K. E. Eddleston, and D. L. Kidder. "The Good, The Bad, and the Misguided: How Managers Inadvertently Encourage Deviant Behaviors." *Academy of Management Perspectives* 20 (1) (2006), pp. 91–103.

132. Organ, D. W., and K. Ryan. "A Meta-analytic Review of Attitudinal and Dispositional Predictors of Organizational Citizenship Behavior." *Personnel Psychology* 48 (1995), pp. 775–802.

133. Bettencourt, L. A., K. P. Gwinner, and M. L. Meuter. "A Comparison of Attitude, Personality, and Knowledge Predictors of Service-Oriented Organizational Citizenship Behaviors." *Journal of Applied Psychology* 86, no. 1 (2001), pp. 29–41.

134. Mayer, R. C., and M. B. Gavin. "Trust in Management and Performance: Who Minds the Shop While Employees Watch the Boss?" *Academy of Management Journal* 48 (5) (2005), pp. 874–88.

135. Tepper, B. J., M. K. Duffy, C. A. Henle, L. Schurer Lambert. "Procedural Injustice, Victim Precipitation, and Abusive Supervision." *Personnel Psychology* 59 (2006), pp. 101–23.

136. Strauss, G. "Workers Hone the Fine Art of Revenge: Acts of Violence, Harassment toward Boss on Rise in Corporate World." *Denver Post*, August 24, 1998, p. 6E.

137. Colbert, A. E., M. K. Mount, J. K. Harter, L. A. Witt, and M. R. Barrick. "Interactive Effects of Personality and Perceptions of the Work Situation on Workplace Deviance." *Journal of Applied Psychology* 89 (4) (2004), pp. 599–609.

138. Marcus, B., and H. Schuler. "Antecedents of Counterproductive Behavior at Work: A General Perspective." *Journal of Applied Psychology* 89 (1) (2004), pp. 647–60.

139. Tett, R. P., and J. P. Meyer. "Job Satisfaction, Organizational Commitment, Turnover Intention, and Turnover: Path Analyses Based on Meta-analytic Findings." *Personnel Psychology* 46 (1993), pp. 259–93.

140. Curphy, G. J. "In-Depth Assessments, 360-Degree Feedback, and Development: Key Research Results and Recommended Next Steps." Presentation at the Annual Conference for HR Managers at US West Communications, Denver, CO, January 1998.

141. Peters, T. *The Circle of Innovation: You Can't Shrink Your Way to Greatness.* New York: Random House, 1997.

142. Schellenbarger, S. "Investors Seem Attracted to Firms with Happy Employees." *The Wall Street Journal*, March 19, 1997, p. I2.

143. Bedeian, A. G., and A. A. Armenakis. "The Cesspool Syndrome: How Dreck Floats to the Top of Declining Organizations." *Academy of Management Executive* 12, no. 1 (1998), pp. 58–63.

144. Hom, P. W., and A. J. Kinicki. "Towards a Greater Understanding of How Dissatisfaction Drives Employee Turnover." *Academy of Management Journal* 44 (5) (2001), pp. 975–87.

145. Campbell, D. P., G. J. Curphy, and T. Tuggle. *360 Degree Feedback Instruments: Beyond Theory.* Workshop presented at the 10th Annual Conference of the Society for Industrial and Organizational Psychology, Orlando, FL, May 1995.

146. Morrel-Samuels, P. "Getting the Truth into Workplace Surveys." *Harvard Business Review*, February 2002, pp. 111–20.

147. Stone, A. "Army Sees Leaders of the Future Leaving Today." *USA Today*, April 18, 2000, p. 10A.

148. Associated Press. "Military Pay Soars." April 11, 2007. http://military.com/NewsContent.

149. Campbell, D. P., and S. Hyne. *Manual for the Revised Campbell Organizational Survey.* Minneapolis, MN: National Computer Systems, 1995.

150. Kleiman, C. "Survey: Job Satisfaction Can Be Costly to Employers." *Denver Post*, June 22, 1997, p. J-4.

151. Ferlise, W. G. "Violence in the Workplace." *Labor and Employment Newsletter.* Washington, DC: Semmes, Bowen, & Semmes, Winter 1995.

152. Quigley, A. "Organizational Consequences of Workplace Aggression." In *Aggression in the Workplace: The Forgotten Problem.* R. T. Hogan and D. K. Sheldon (chairs). Symposium conducted at the 14th Annual Conference of Industrial and Organizational Psychology, Atlanta, GA, May 1999.

153. Ilies, R., and Judge, T. A. "On the Heritability of Job Satisfaction: The Mediating Role of Personality." *Journal of Applied Psychology* 88 (4) (2003), pp. 750–59.

154. Judge, T. A., J. E. Bono, and E. A. Locke. "Personality and Job Satisfaction: The Mediating Role of Job Characteristics." *Journal of Applied Psychology* 85, no. 2 (2000), pp. 237–49.

155. Judge, T. A., and R. Ilies. "Is Positiveness in Organizations Always Desirable?" *Academy of Management Executive* 18 (4) (2004), pp. 151–55.

156. Arvey, R. D., T. J. Bouchard, Jr., N. L. Segal, and L. M. Abraham. "Job Satisfaction: Environmental and Genetic Components." *Journal of Applied Psychology* 74 (1989), pp. 187–92.

157. Herzberg, F. "The Motivation-Hygiene Concept and Problems of Manpower." *Personnel Administrator* 27 (1964), pp. 3–7.

158. Herzberg, F. *Work and the Nature of Man.* Cleveland, OH: World Publishing, 1966.

159. Herzberg, F. "One More Time: How Do You Motivate Employees?" *Harvard Business Review*, January 2003, pp. 87–96.

160. Sheppard, B. H., R. J. Lewicki, and J. W. Minton. *Organizational Justice: The Search for Fairness in the Workplace.* New York: Lexington Books, 1972.

161. Trevino, L. K. "The Social Effects of Punishment in Organizations: A Justice Perspective." *Academy of Management Review* 17 (1992), pp. 647–76.

162. Siegel, P. A., C. Post, J. Brockner, A. Y. Fishman, and C. Garden. "The Moderating Influence of Procedural Fairness on the Relationship between Work-Life Conflict and Organizational Commitment." *Journal of Applied Psychology* 90 (1) (2005), pp. 13–24.

163. Colquitt, J. A. "On the Dimensionality of Organizational Justice: A Construct Validation of a Measure." *Journal of Applied Psychology* 86, no. 2 (2001), pp. 386–400.

164. Colquitt, J. A., D. E. Conlon, M. J. Wesson, C. O. L. H. Porter, and K. Y. Ng. "Justice at the Millennium: A Meta-analytic Review of 25 Years of Organizational Justice Research." *Journal of Applied Psychology* 86, no. 2 (2001), pp. 425–45.

165. Ambrose, M. L., and R. Cropanzano. "A Longitudinal Analysis of Organizational Fairness: An Examination of Reactions to Tenure and Promotion Decisions." *Journal of Applied Psychology* 88 (2) (2003), pp. 266–75.

166. Tepper, B. J., and E. C. Taylor. "Relationships among Supervisors' and Subordinates' Procedural Justice Perceptions and Organizational Citizenship Behaviors." *Academy of Management Journal* 46 (1) (2003), pp. 97–105.

167. Simons, T., and Q. Roberson. "Why Managers Should Care about Fairness: The Effects of Aggregate Justice Perceptions on Organizational Outcomes." *Journal of Applied Psychology* 88 (3) (2003), pp. 432–43.

Chapter 10

Groups, Teams, and Their Leadership

Introduction

As we have already presented, leaders need to understand some things about themselves. Their skills, abilities, values, motives, and desires are important considerations in determining their leadership style and preferences. Leaders also need to understand, as much as possible, the same characteristics about their followers. But if you could know characteristics about yourself and characteristics about each of your followers, that would still not be enough. This is because groups and teams are different than solely the skills, abilities, values, and motives of those who comprise them. Groups and teams have their own special characteristics.

While much of the leadership literature today is about the individual who fills the leadership role, it is worthwhile noting that a survey of 35 texts on organizational behavior found that, in each one, the chapter on leadership is in the section on group behavior.[1] This should not be terribly surprising since groups (even as small as two people) are essential if leaders are to impact anything beyond their own behavior. What may be surprising is that the concept of groups is sometimes omitted entirely from books on leadership. The **group perspective** looks at how different group characteristics can affect relationships both with the leader and among the followers.

With *teams* and *teamwork* being the buzzwords of the new millennium, it is worth clarifying the difference between groups and teams, although the difference is mostly one of degree. We will begin the chapter with that clarification. The larger distinction, as noted above, is between the characteristics of groups and the characteristics of individuals. We will spend the first half of the chapter discussing some of these factors unique to groups. Given the high interest in organizational teamwork, the latter portion of this chapter will present a model developed to help leaders

We are born for cooperation, as are the feet, the hands, the eyelids, and the upper and lower jaws.
Marcus Aurelius

design, diagnose, and leverage high-impact factors to create the conditions that foster team effectiveness. This chapter will conclude with a section on virtual teams, which are becoming ever more present, if not popular.

Individuals versus Groups versus Teams

As noted previously, there is a significant difference between individual work and group work. But what is the difference between group work and teamwork?

You will learn, in the next section of this chapter, that two identifying characteristics of groups are mutual interaction and reciprocal influence. Members of teams also have mutual interaction and reciprocal influence, but we generally distinguish teams from groups in four other ways. First, team members usually have a stronger sense of identification among themselves than group members do. Often, both team members and outsiders can readily identify who is and who is not on the team (athletic uniforms are one obvious example); identifying members of a group may be more difficult. Second, teams have common goals or tasks; these may range from the development of a new product to an athletic league championship. Group members, on the other hand, may not have the same degree of consensus about goals as team members do. Group members may belong to the group for a variety of personal reasons, and these may clash with the group's stated objectives. (This phenomenon probably happens with teams, too, although perhaps not to the same extent.)

Third, task interdependence typically is greater with teams than with groups. For example, basketball players usually are unable to take a shot unless other team members set picks or pass the ball to them (see Profiles in Leadership 10.1 about Phil Jackson). On the other hand, group members often can contribute to goal accomplishment by working independently; the successful completion of their assigned tasks may not be contingent on other group members. Of course, task interdependence can vary greatly even across teams. Among athletic teams, for example, softball, football, soccer, and hockey teams have a high level of task interdependence, whereas swimming, cross-country, and track teams have substantially lower levels of task interdependence. Fourth, team members often have more differentiated and specialized roles than group members. In the preceding section, we noted that group members often play a variety of roles within the group; however, team members often play a single, or primary, role on a team. Finally, it is important to bear in mind that the distinctions we have been highlighting probably reflect only matters of degree. One might consider teams to be highly specialized groups.

Phil Jackson

PROFILES IN LEADERSHIP 10.1

In the previous section on individual leadership characteristics, it was fairly easy to come up with a leader who typified the particular aspect of leadership we were illustrating. Turns out, it's not quite so easy in this section on teams. If you consider Ginnett's definition of leadership ("The leader's job is to create the conditions for the team to be successful"), then the real team leader might be behind the scenes or, in this case, not even on the court.

Phil Jackson is a basketball coach, but not just any coach. Jackson was the coach of champion Michael Jordan, but ultimately of the championship Chicago Bulls. Certainly, basketball is a team sport and as Michael Jordan and other Bulls found out, having arguably the best player in the sport does not necessarily translate to the best team in the game. In many of the years when Jordan won the individual scoring championship, the Bulls didn't win the championship. Jackson's job as head coach was to transform spectacular individual players into a spectacular team.

Perhaps the best way to get a sense of this challenge and the teamwork Jackson built to win the championship is to extract a few lines from his book, *Sacred Hoops*.

> "The most important part of the (coach's) job takes place on the practice floor, not during the game. After a certain point you have to trust the players to translate into action what they've learned in practice. Using a comprehensive system of basketball makes it easier for me to detach myself in that way. Once the players have mastered the system, a powerful group intelligence emerges that is greater than the coach's ideas or those of any individual on the team. When a team reaches that state, the coach can step back and let the game itself "motivate" the players. You don't have to give them any 'win one for the Gipper' pep talks, you just have to turn them loose and let them immerse themselves in the action."

> "The sign of a great player was not how much *he* scored, but how much he lifted his teammate's performance."

> "You can't beat a good defensive team with one man. It's got to be a team effort."

> "It took a long time for Michael to realize he couldn't do it all by himself. Slowly, however, as the team began to master the nuances of the system, he learned that he could trust his teammates to come through in the clutch. It was the beginning of his transformation from a gifted solo artist into a selfless team player."

> "What appealed to me about the system was that it empowered everybody on the team by making them more involved in the offense, and demanded that they put their individual needs second to those of the group. This is the struggle every leader faces: how to get members of the team who are driven by the quest for individual glory to give themselves over wholeheartedly to the group effort."

Source: P. Jackson, and H. Delehanty. *Sacred Hoops: Spiritual Lessons of a Hardwood Warrior.* New York. Hyperion, 1995.

The Nature of Groups

Perhaps we should begin by defining what a **group** is. A group can be thought of as "two or more persons who are interacting with one another in such a manner that each person influences and is influenced by each other person."[2] Three aspects of this definition are particularly important to the study of leadership. First, this definition incorporates the concept of reciprocal influence between leaders and followers, an idea considerably different from the one-way nature of influence implicit in the dictionary's definition of followers. Second, group members interact and influence each other. Thus, people waiting at a bus stop would not constitute a group, as there generally is neither interaction nor influence between the various individuals. On the other hand, eight people meeting to plan a school bond election would constitute a group, as there probably would be a high level of mutual interaction among the attendees. Third, the definition does not constrain individuals to only one group. Everyone belongs to a number of different groups; an individual could be a member of various service, production, sports, religious, parent, and volunteer groups simultaneously.

It is important to realize that though people belong to many groups, just as they do to many organizations, groups and organizations are not the same thing (groups, of course, can exist within organizations). Organizations can be so large that most members do not know most of the other people in the organization. In such cases there is relatively little inter-member interaction and reciprocal influence. Similarly, organizations typically are just too large and impersonal to have much effect on anyone's feelings, whereas groups are small and immediate enough to impact both feelings and self-image. People often tend to identify more with the groups they belong to than with the organizations they belong to; they are more psychologically "invested" in their groups. Also, certain important psychological needs (e.g., social contact) are better satisfied by groups than by organizations.

Perhaps an example will clarify the distinction between groups and organizations. Consider a church so large that it may fairly be described as an organization: so large that multiple services must be offered on Sunday mornings; so large that dozens of different study classes are offered each week; so large there are numerous different choirs and musical ensembles. In so large a church, the members hardly could be said to interact with or influence each other except on an occasional basis. Such size often presents both advantages and disadvantages to the membership. On the one hand, it makes possible a rich diversity of activities; on the other hand, such size can make the church itself (i.e., the overall organization) seem relatively impersonal. It may be difficult to identify with a large organization other than in name only (e.g., "I belong to First

Presbyterian Church"). In such cases many people identify more with particular groups within the church than with the church itself; it may be easier to *feel* a part of some smaller group such as the high school choir or a weekly study group.

Although groups play a pervasive role in society, in general people spend very little time thinking about the factors that affect group processes and intragroup relationships. Therefore, the rest of this section will describe some group characteristics that can affect both leaders and followers. Much of the research on groups goes well beyond the scope of this chapter (see Gibbard, Hartman, & Mann, 1978; Shaw, 1981; Hackman, 1990), but six concepts are so basic to the group perspective that they deserve our attention.[2,41] These six concepts are group size, stages of group development, roles, norms, communication, and cohesion. Five of them will be addressed in sections below. The sixth, communication, permeates them all.

Group Size

The size of any group has implications for both leaders and followers. First, leader emergence is partly a function of group size. The greater number of people in a large versus a small group will affect the probability that any individual is likely to emerge as leader. Second, as groups become larger, **cliques** are more likely to develop.[3] Cliques are subgroups of individuals who often share the same goals, values, and expectations. Because cliques generally wield more influence than individual members, they are likely to exert considerable influence—positively or negatively—on the larger group. Leaders need to identify and deal with cliques within their groups, as many intragroup conflicts are the results of cliques having different values, goals, and expectations.

Third, group size also can affect a leader's behavioral style. Leaders with a large **span of control** tend to be more directive, spend less time with individual subordinates, and use more impersonal approaches when influencing followers. Leaders with a small span of control tend to display more consideration and use more personal approaches when influencing followers.[4–7] Fourth, group size also affects group effectiveness. Whereas some researchers have suggested the optimal number of workers for any task is between five and seven,[8,9] it probably is wise to avoid such a simple generalization. The answer to the question of appropriate group size seems to be "just big enough to get the job done." Obviously, the larger the group, the more likely it is that it will involve differentiated skills, values, perceptions, and abilities among its members. Also, there certainly will be more "people power" available to do the work as group size increases.

There are, however, limits to the benefits of size. Consider the question, "If it takes 1 person two minutes to dig a 1-cubic-foot hole, how long will it take 20 people to dig the same size hole?" Actually, it probably will take

A committee is an animal with four back legs.
Jean le Carre

the larger group considerably *longer,* especially if they all participate at the same time. Beyond the purely physical limitations of certain tasks, there also may be decreasing returns (on a per capita basis) as group size increases. This is true even when the efforts of all group members are combined on what is called an **additive task.** An additive task is one where the group's output simply involves the combination of individual outputs.[10] Such a case may be illustrated by the number of individuals needed to push a stalled truck from an intersection. One individual probably would not be enough—maybe not even two or three. At some point, though, as group size increases in this additive task, there will be enough combined force to move the truck. However, as the group size increases beyond that needed to move the truck, the individual contribution of each member will appear to decrease. Steiner[11] suggested this may be due to **process loss** resulting from factors such as some members not pushing in the right direction. Process losses can be thought of as the inefficiencies created by more and more people working together.

Group size can affect group effectiveness in a number of other ways. As group size increases, the diminishing returns of larger work groups may be due to **social loafing.**[12] Social loafing refers to the phenomenon of reduced effort by people when they are not individually accountable for their work. Experiments across different sorts of tasks have tended to demonstrate greater effort when every individual's work is monitored than when many individuals' outputs are anonymously pooled into a collective product. Recent evidence, however, suggests the process may be considerably more complicated than initially thought.[13] The performance decrement may be affected more by the level of task complexity or the reward structure (e.g., cooperative versus competitive) than by outcome attribution.

Sometimes, working in the presence of others may actually increase effort or productivity through a phenomenon called **social facilitation.** Social facilitation was first documented in classic experiments at the Hawthorne plant of the Western Electric Company (see Highlight 10.1). However, social facilitation is not limited to research situations. It refers to any time people increase their level of work due to the presence of others. Typically this occurs when the presence of others increases individual accountability for work, in contrast to other occasions when being in a group reinforces individual anonymity and social loafing.[14]

Developmental Stages of Groups

Just as children go through different stages of development, so do groups. Tuckman's[15] review of over 60 studies involving leaderless training, experimental, or therapeutic groups revealed that groups generally went through four distinct stages of development. The first stage, **forming,** was characterized by polite conversation, the gathering of superficial information about fellow members, and low trust. The group's rejection of emerging potential leaders with negative characteristics also took place during the forming

Social Facilitation and the Hawthorne Effect

HIGHLIGHT 10.1

Social facilitation was first documented in experiments conducted at the Hawthorne plant of the Western Electric Company during the late 1920s and early 1930s. These classic studies were originally designed to evaluate the impact of different work environments.[17,18] Among other things, researchers varied the levels of illumination in areas where workers were assembling electrical components and found production increased when lighting was increased.

When lighting was subsequently decreased, however, production again increased. Faced with these rather confusing data, the researchers turned their attention from physical aspects of the work environment to its social aspects. As it turns out, one reason workers' production increased was simply because someone else (in this case, the researchers) had paid attention to them. The term *Hawthorne effect* is still used today to describe an artificial change in behavior due merely to the fact a person or group is being studied.

stage. The second stage, **storming,** usually was marked by intragroup conflict, heightened emotional levels, and status differentiation as remaining contenders struggled to build alliances and fulfill the group's leadership role. The clear emergence of a leader and the development of group norms and cohesiveness were the key indicators of the **norming** stage of group development. Finally, groups reached the **performing** stage when group members played functional, interdependent roles that were focused on the performance of group tasks.

The four stages of group development identified by Tuckman[16] are important for several reasons. First, people are in many more leaderless groups than they may realize. For example, many sports teams, committees, work groups, and clubs start out as leaderless teams. Team or club captains or committee spokespersons are likely to be the emergent leaders from their respective groups. On a larger scale, perhaps even many elected officials initially began their political careers as the emergent leaders of their cliques or groups, and were then able to convince the majority of the remaining members in their constituencies of their viability as candidates.

Another reason it is important to understand stages of group development is the potential relationships between leadership behaviors and group cohesiveness and productivity. Some experts have maintained that leaders need to focus on consideration or group maintenance behaviors during the norming stage to improve group cohesiveness, and on task behaviors during the performing stage in order to improve group productivity.[19,20] They also have suggested that leaders who reverse these behaviors during the norming and performing stages tend to have less cohesive and less productive groups. Thus, being able to recognize stages of group development may enhance the likelihood that one will emerge as a leader as well as increase the cohesiveness and productivity of the group being led.

While Tuckman's model is widely known if for no other reason than its components rhyme with each other, it is not without criticism. Recall that the subjects for Tuckman's research were training, experimental, or therapy groups. None of these particularly represent teams forming to do work in an organizational context. For example, Ginnett observed many surgical teams and never once saw them engage in storming behaviors as they formed. You wouldn't want to be the patient if there was a formation argument between the surgeon, the anesthesiologist, and the scrub nurse about who was going to get to use the scalpel today.

Gersick[21] proposed a better model for teams in organizational settings. In studying **project teams,** she found that teams don't necessarily jump right in and get to work. Rather, they spend most of the first half of the team's life muddling through various ideas and strategies. Then, about midway into the project, the team seems to experience the equivalent of a midlife crisis where there is a flurry of activity and a reexamination of the strategy to see if it will allow them to complete their work. Gersick labeled this process **punctuated equilibrium,** which is obviously quite different from Tuckman's four-stage model.

Group Roles

Group roles are the sets of expected behaviors associated with particular jobs or positions. Most people have multiple roles stemming from the various groups with which they are associated. In addition, it is not uncommon for someone to occupy numerous roles within the same group as situations change. Ginnett[22] found that members of airline crews have varying roles over the course of a day. Although some behaviors were universally associated with certain roles, effective team members on these airline crews generally were more flexible in changing their behavior as other role demands changed. For example, whereas the captain of an airplane is responsible for the overall operation and decision making during a flight, flight attendants often take over responsibility for planning and carrying out the crew's social activities in the evening (i.e., when the flight is over). One captain in the study, however, continued to make *all* the crew's decisions, including their evening social plans; he was inflexible with regard to the role of decision maker. Not coincidentally, he was seen as a less-effective leader—even during the actual flights—than more flexible captains.

Some roles, like positions on athletic teams, have meaning only in relatively specific contexts. Generally speaking, for example, one only plays a lineman's role during football games (admittedly, one might argue that at many schools being an intercollegiate athlete is a role that extends to aspects of student life outside sports). Other roles are more general in nature, including certain common ones that play a part in making any group work—or not work—well. Highlight 10.2 presents a vivid example of how powerful roles can be as determinants of behavior.

The Stanford Prison Experiment

HIGHLIGHT 10.2

A fascinating demonstration of the power of roles occurred when social psychologist Philip Zimbardo and his colleagues[24] created a simulated prison environment at Stanford University. From a larger group of volunteers, two dozen male college students were randomly assigned to be either "prisoners" or "guards." The simulation was quite realistic, with actual cells constructed in the basement of one of the university buildings. The guards wore uniforms, and carried nightsticks and whistles; their eyes were covered by sunglasses. The prisoners were "arrested" at their homes by police cars replete with blazing sirens. They were handcuffed, frisked, blindfolded, and brought to the "jail." They were fingerprinted, given prisoner outfits, and assigned numbers by which they would henceforth be addressed.

It did not take long for the students' normal behavior to be overcome by the roles they were playing. The guards became more and more abusive with their power. They held prisoners accountable for strict adherence to arbitrary rules of prison life (which the guards themselves created), and seemed to enjoy punishing them for even minor infractions. They increasingly seemed to think of the prisoners—truly just other college students—as

bad people. The emotional stress on the prisoners became profound, and just six days into the two-week episode the experiment was halted. This unexpected outcome basically occurred because participants' roles had become their reality. They were not just students role-playing guards and prisoners; to a disconcerting degree they became guards and prisoners.

What should people conclude from the Stanford prison study? At an abstract level, the study dramatically points out how behavior is partly determined by social role. Additionally, it is clear how just being in the role of leader, especially to the extent it is attended by tangible and symbolic manifestations of power, can affect how leaders think and act toward followers. Still another lesson people might draw involves remembering the volunteers all had many different roles in life than those assigned to them in the study, though being a guard or a prisoner was certainly the salient one for a period of time. Whereas everyone has many roles, the salience of one or another often depends on the situation, and a person's behavior changes as his or her role changes in a group.

Source: P. Zimbardo, C. Haney, W. Banks, and D. Jaffe, "The Mind Is a Formidable Jailer: A Pirandellian Prison." *New York Times Magazine,* April 8, 1973, pp. 38–60.

In Chapter 8, leader behavior was characterized initially in terms of two broad functions. One deals with getting the task done (**task role**), and the other with supporting relationships within the work group (**relationship role**). Similarly, roles in groups can be categorized in terms of task and relationship functions (see Highlight 10.3). Many of the roles in Highlight 10.3 are appropriate for followers, not just the official group leader; all of these different roles are part of the leadership process and all contribute to a group's overall effectiveness. Moreover, it is important to recognize that the very distinction between task and relationship roles is somewhat arbitrary. It is sensible enough when looking at the short-term impact of any given behavior, but in another sense relationship roles are task roles. After all, task-oriented behavior may be adequate for accomplishing short-term objectives, but an appropriately cohesive and supportive group increases the potential for long-term effectiveness at future

Task and Relationship Roles in Groups

HIGHLIGHT 10.3

Task Roles

Initiating: Defining the problem, suggesting activities, assigning tasks.

Information Seeking: Asking questions, seeking relevant data or views.

Information Sharing: Providing data, offering opinions.

Summarizing: Reviewing and integrating others' points, checking for common understanding and readiness for action.

Evaluating: Assessing validity of assumptions, quality of information, reasonableness of recommendations.

Guiding: Keeping group on track.

Relationship Roles

Harmonizing: Resolving interpersonal conflicts, reducing tension.

Encouraging: Supporting and praising others, showing appreciation for others' contributions, being warm and friendly.

Gatekeeping: Assuring even participation by all group members, making sure that everyone has a chance to be heard and that no individual dominates.

Source: Adapted from K. D. Benne and P. Sheats, "Functional Roles of Group Members." *Journal of Social Issues* 4 (1948), pp. 41–49.

Dysfunctional Roles

HIGHLIGHT 10.4

Dominating: Monopolizing group time, forcing views on others.

Blocking: Stubbornly obstructing and impeding group work, persistent negativism.

Attacking: Belittling others, creating a hostile or intimidating environment.

Distracting: Engaging in irrelevant behaviors, distracting others' attention.

Source: Adapted from K. D. Benne and P. Sheats, "Functional Roles of Group Members." *Journal of Social Issues* 4 (1948), pp. 41–49.

tasks as well as present tasks. Although the roles in Highlight 10.3 generally contribute to a group's overall effectiveness, several types of problems can occur with group roles that can impede group performance. One type of role problem concerns the **dysfunctional roles,** listed in Highlight 10.4. The common denominator among these roles is how the person's behavior primarily serves selfish or egocentric purposes rather than group purposes.

Another role problem is **role conflict.** Role conflict involves receiving contradictory messages about expected behavior and can in turn adversely affect a person's emotional well-being and performance.[23]

Role conflict can occur in several different ways. Perhaps most common is receiving inconsistent signals about expected behavior from the same person. When the same person sends mixed signals, it is called **intrasender role conflict** ("I need this report back in five minutes, and it had better be perfect"). **Intersender role conflict** occurs when someone receives inconsistent signals from several others about expected behavior. Still another kind of role conflict is based on inconsistencies between different roles a person may have. Professional and family demands, for example, often create role conflicts. **Interrole conflict** occurs when someone is unable to perform all of his roles as well as he would like. A final type occurs when role expectations violate a person's values. This is known as **person–role conflict.**

An example of person–role conflict might be when a store manager encourages a salesperson to mislead customers about the quality of the store's products when this behavior is inconsistent with the salesperson's values and beliefs.

A different sort of role problem is called **role ambiguity.** In role conflict, one receives clear messages about expectations, but the messages are not all congruent. With role ambiguity, the problem is lack of clarity about just what the expectations are.[25,26] There may have been no role expectations established at all, or they may not have been clearly communicated. A person is experiencing role ambiguity if she wonders, "Just what am I supposed to be doing?" It is important for leaders to be able to minimize the degree to which dysfunctional roles, role conflict, and role ambiguity occur in their groups, as these problems have been found to have a negative impact on organizational commitment, job involvement, absenteeism, and satisfaction with co-workers and supervisors.[27]

Group Norms

Norms are the informal rules groups adopt to regulate and regularize group members' behaviors. Although norms are only infrequently written down (see Highlight 10.5) or openly discussed, they nonetheless often have a powerful and consistent influence on behavior.[28] That is because most people are rather good at reading the social cues that inform them about existing norms. For example, most people easily discern the dress code in any new work environment without needing written guidance. People also are apt to notice when a norm is violated, even though they may have been unable to articulate the norm before its violation was apparent. For example, most students have expectations (norms) about creating extra work for other students. Imagine the reaction if a student in some class complained that not enough reading was being assigned each lesson or that the minimum length requirements for the term paper needed to be substantially raised.

Norms do not govern all behaviors, just those a group feels are important. Norms are more likely to be seen as important and apt to be

Putting It In Writing[29]

Rick Reilly

HIGHLIGHT 10.5

Why are sports' unwritten rules unwritten? Get a Xerox machine under these puppies and have a copy on everybody's desk in the morning

After we gave up a touchdown in our first Touch Football/Pulled Groinathon of the year, the guys on the other team sneered and said, "Suckers walk."

"Says who?" asked our left tackle, Cementhead.

"It's an unwritten rule," explained the other side's captain. "Oh, yeah?" said Cementhead. "Show me where." Which is exactly my point. Why are sport's unwritten rules unwritten? Get a Xerox machine under these puppies and have a copy on everybody's desk in the morning.

The coach always sits in the first row on the team bus. If he is out sick or dead, the seat remains empty.

Apologize for a point won on a net cord.

Take two or three pitches if your pitcher just made the second out of the inning.

Never, ever put your finger in someone else's bowling ball.

The starting goalie is always the first player on the ice.

If a line judge makes a bad call in your favor, purposely double-fault the next point.

A manager never drinks at the same bar as his players.

Never knock in the tying run in the ninth inning of an exhibition game. Far better to lose than go extra innings in spring training.

No NBA player attempting a layup in the fourth quarter of a tight game should go unfouled.

In a losing clubhouse you must act as if there has been a death in the family.

Hand the manager the ball when he comes to the mound to take you out.

Never shoot the puck into the net after a whistle blows.

Do not talk to or sit near a pitcher with a no-hitter going. And never bunt to break one up.

A first base coach never stands in the first base coaching box.

Never blow your nose before a fight. (It makes the eyes swell easier later on.)

Stand as far away as possible from a skeet shooter with a perfect score going.

Never walk on a player's putting line, including the two feet on the other side of the cup.

Always clear the inside lane for faster runners.

Never stand behind the pool table pocket your opponent is shooting for.

Never let the interviewee hold the mike.

A catcher may complain to the ump all he wants about balls and strikes, as long as he doesn't turn around and do it face-to-face.

Never hit the quarterback during practice.

Never start the 100 meters in a decathlon into a wind. Trade false starts until the breeze is favorable.

When a soccer player is hurt, the opponents must kick the ball out of play.

Except for Rocky Marciano, the challenger always enters the ring first—and always will.

Throw a handful of salt into the air before your sumo wrestling match begins.

It's true: Suckers walk.

The bus may be delayed by superstars only.

When the coach finally wraps up a long meeting with "Any questions?" nobody better ask one.

Rookies shag balls, whether they are millionaires or not.

Never shoot high on the goalie during warmups.

The back nine is always pressed.

You must admit it when you hit a forehand on the second bounce.

On the playground, offense calls the fouls.

Never write down the score of a bowler who is on a run of strikes.

continued

Continued

Never admit you trapped the ball while trying to make a catch.

No overhead smashes at women in mixed doubles.

The caddie of the last player to putt plants the flag.

NBA refs will take some trash from head coaches but not a word from an assistant.

Never steal with a five-run lead after the seventh inning.

You must alter your course to help a boat in distress.

Boxers never blink during a ref's prefight instructions.

When a receiver drops a pass, go back to him on the next play.

Card games are played in the back of the plane.

Scrubs stand during NBA timeouts.

Winners buy.

Got it, Cementhead?

enforced if they (a) facilitate group survival; (b) simplify, or make more predictable, what behavior is expected of group members; (c) help the group avoid embarrassing interpersonal problems; or (d) express the central values of the group and clarify what is distinctive about the group's identity.[30]

The norms that group members import, such as those listed above, are essentially inward looking. They help the team take care of itself and avoid embarrassing situations caused by inappropriate member behaviors. Hackman[31] recommends that the leader has a responsibility to focus the team outwardly to enhance performance. Specifically, he suggests two core norms be created to enhance performance:

1. Group members should actively scan the environment for opportunities that would require a change in operating strategy to capitalize upon them, and

2. The team should identify the few number of behaviors which team members must always do and those which they should never do to conform to the organization's objectives.

By actively implementing these two norms, the team is forced to examine not only its organizational context but the much larger industry and environmental shells in which it operates. One irony about norms is that an outsider to a group often is able to learn more about norms than an insider. An outsider, not necessarily subject to the norms himself, is more apt to notice them. In fact, the more "foreign" an observer is, the more likely it is the norms will be perceived. If a man is accustomed to wearing a tie to work, he is less likely to notice that men in another organization also wear ties to work, but is *more* likely to note that the men in a third organization typically wear sweaters and sweatshirts around the office.

Group Cohesion

Group cohesion is the glue that keeps a group together. It is the sum of forces that attracts members to a group, provides resistance to leaving it, and motivates them to be active in it. Highly cohesive groups interact with and influence each other more than do less cohesive groups. Furthermore, a highly cohesive group may have lower absenteeism and lower turnover than a less cohesive group, and low absenteeism and turnover often contribute to higher group performance; higher performance can, in turn, contribute to even higher cohesion, thus resulting in an increasingly positive spiral.

However, greater cohesiveness does not always lead to higher performance. A highly cohesive but unskilled team is still an unskilled team, and such teams will often lose to a less cohesive but more skilled one. Additionally, a highly cohesive group may sometimes develop goals that are contrary to the larger organization's goals. For example, members of a highly cohesive research team at a particular college committed themselves to working on a problem that seemed inherently interesting to them. Their nearly zealous commitment to the project, however, effectively kept them from asking, or even allowing others to ask, if the research aligned itself well with the college's stated objectives. Their quite narrow and basic research effort deviated significantly from the college's expressed commitment to emphasize applied research. As a result, the college lost some substantial outside financial support.

Other problems also can occur in highly cohesive groups. Researchers[32,33] have found that some groups can become so cohesive they erect what amount to fences or boundaries between themselves and others. Such overbounding can block the use of outside resources that could make them more effective. Competitive product development teams can become so overbounded (often rationalized by security concerns or inordinate fears of "idea thieves") that they will not ask for help from willing and able staff within their own organizations.

One example of this problem was the failed mission to rescue U.S. embassy personnel held hostage in Iran during the Carter presidency. The rescue itself was a rather complicated mission involving many different sorts of U.S. military forces. Some of these forces included sea-based helicopters. The helicopters and their crews were carried on regular naval vessels, though most sailors on the vessels knew nothing of the secret mission. Senior personnel were so concerned that some sailor might leak information, and thus compromise the mission's secrecy, that maintenance crews aboard the ships were not directed to perform increased levels of maintenance on the helicopters immediately before the critical mission. Even if a helicopter was scheduled for significant maintenance within the next 50 hours of flight time (which would be exceeded in the rescue mission), crews were not told to perform the maintenance. According to knowledgeable sources, this practice did impact the performance of at least one of the failed helicopters, and thus the overall mission.

Symptoms of Groupthink

HIGHLIGHT 10.6

An illusion of invulnerability, which leads to unwarranted optimism and excessive risk taking by the group.

Unquestioned assumption of the group's morality and therefore an absence of reflection on the ethical consequences of group action.

Collective rationalization to discount negative information or warnings.

Stereotypes of the opposition as evil, weak, or stupid.

Self-censorship by group members from expressing ideas that deviate from the group consensus due to doubts about their validity or importance.

An illusion of unanimity such that greater consensus is perceived than really exists.

Direct pressure on dissenting members, which reinforces the norm that disagreement represents disloyalty to the group.

Mindguards, who protect the group from adverse information.

Source: Adapted from I. L. Janis, *Groupthink,* 2nd ed. Boston: Houghton Mifflin, 1982.

Janis[34] discovered still another disadvantage of highly cohesive groups. He found that people in a highly cohesive group often become more concerned with striving for unanimity than in objectively appraising different courses of action. Janis labeled this phenomenon **groupthink** and believed it accounted for a number of historic fiascoes, including Pearl Harbor and the Bay of Pigs invasion. It may have played a role in the *Challenger* disaster, and it also occurs in other cohesive groups ranging from business meetings to air crews, and from therapy groups to school boards.

What is groupthink? Cohesive groups tend to evolve strong informal norms to preserve friendly internal relations. Preserving a comfortable, harmonious group environment becomes a hidden agenda that tends to suppress dissent, conflict, and critical thinking. Unwise decisions may result when concurrence seeking among members overrides their willingness to express or tolerate deviant points of view and think critically. Janis[35] identified a number of symptoms of groupthink, which can be found in Highlight 10.6.

A policy-making or decision-making group displaying most of the symptoms in Highlight 10.6 runs a big risk of being ineffective. It may do a poor job of clarifying objectives, searching for relevant information, evaluating alternatives, assessing risks, and anticipating the need for contingency plans. Janis[36] offered the following suggestions as ways of reducing groupthink and thus of improving the quality of a group's input to policies or decisions. First, leaders should encourage all group members to take on the role of critical evaluator. Everyone in the group needs to appreciate the importance of airing doubts and objections. This includes the leader's willingness to listen to criticisms of his or her own ideas. Second, leaders should create a climate of open inquiry through their own impartiality and objectivity. At the outset, leaders should refrain from stating personal preferences or expectations, which may bias group discussion. Third, the risk of groupthink can be reduced if independent groups are established to make recommendations on the same issue. Fourth, at least one member of the group should be assigned the role of devil's advocate, an assignment that should rotate from meeting to meeting.

One final problem with highly cohesive groups may be what Shephard[37] has called **ollieism.** Ollieism, a variation of groupthink, occurs when illegal actions are taken by overly zealous and loyal subordinates who believe that what they are doing will please their leaders. It derives its name from the actions of Lieutenant-Colonel Oliver North, who among other things admitted he lied to the U.S. Congress about his actions while working on the White House staff during the Iran-Contra affair. Shephard cited the slaying of Thomas à Becket by four of Henry II's knights and the Watergate break-in as other prime examples of ollieism. We will probably see similar examples in the Enron trials. Ollieism differs from groupthink in that the subordinates' illegal actions usually occur without the explicit knowledge or consent of the leader. Nevertheless, Shephard pointed out that, although the examples cited of ollieism were not officially sanctioned, the responsibility for them still falls squarely on the leader. It is the leader's responsibility to create an ethical climate within the group, and leaders who create highly cohesive yet unethical groups must bear the responsibility for the group's actions.

After reading about the uncertain relationships between group cohesion and performance, and the problems with overbounding, groupthink, and ollieism, one might think that cohesiveness should be something to avoid. Nothing, however, could be further from the truth. First of all, problems with overly cohesive groups occur relatively infrequently and, in general, leaders will be better off thinking of ways to create and maintain highly cohesive teams than not developing these teams out of concern for potential groupthink or overbounding situations. Second, perhaps the biggest argument for developing cohesive groups is to consider the alternative—groups with little or no cohesiveness. In the latter groups, followers would generally be dissatisfied with each other and the leader, commitment to accomplishing group and organizational goals may be reduced, intragroup communication may occur less frequently, and interdependent task performance may suffer.[38] Because of the problems associated with groups having low cohesiveness, leadership practitioners need to realize that developing functionally cohesive work groups is a goal they all should strive for.

In summary, the group perspective provides a complementary level of analysis to the individual perspective presented earlier in this chapter. A follower's behavior may be due to his or her values, traits, or experience (i.e., the individual perspective), or this behavior may be due to the followers' roles, the group norms, the group's stage of development, or the group's level of cohesiveness (i.e., the group perspective). Thus, the group perspective can also provide both leaders and followers with a number of explanations of why individuals in groups behave in certain ways. Moreover, the six group characteristics just described can give leaders and followers ideas about (*a*) factors that may be affecting their ability to influence other group members and (*b*) what to do to improve their level of influence in the group.

Teams

With so much attention devoted to teams and teamwork in today's organizations, it is appropriate to spend a fair amount of time examining teams and the factors that impact their effectiveness. After considering some differential measures of team effectiveness, we will look at a comprehensive model of team leadership.

Effective Team Characteristics and Team Building

And yes, teams do vary in their effectiveness. Virtually identical teams can be dramatically different in terms of success or failure (see Highlight 10.7). We must ask, therefore, what makes one team successful and another unsuccessful? Although this is an area only recently studied, exploratory work at the Center for Creative Leadership has tentatively identified several key characteristics for effective team performance (see Highlight 10.8 for an astronaut's perspective on teamwork).

Examples of Effective and Ineffective Teams

HIGHLIGHT 10.7

Most people can readily think up a number of examples of ineffective and effective teamwork. Consider the relative effectiveness of the teams depicted in the following two true stories:

Ineffective Teamwork: After an airline flight crew failed to get a "nose gear down and locked" indicator light to come on while making a landing approach into Miami, all three crew members became involved in trying to change the burned-out indicator bulb in the cockpit. Nobody was flying the airplane and none of them were monitoring the flight of the L-1011 as it descended into the Everglades and crashed.

Effective Teamwork: The crew of a DC-10, after having lost all capability to control the airplane through flight controls as a result of an engine explosion, realized they needed all the help they could get. Captain Al Haynes discovered another experienced captain was traveling in the passenger cabin and invited him to come up to the cabin to help the regular crew out. Miraculously, their combined abilities enabled the crew—using techniques developed on the spot—to control the plane to within a few feet of the ground. Even though there were fatalities, over 100 people survived a nearly hopeless situation.

Women in Leadership: Teamwork from an Astronaut's Perspective

HIGHLIGHT 10.8

Dr. Bonnie J. Dunbar is an American astronaut. She has flown on four space shuttle missions. We asked her to share a few personal reflections about the meaning of teamwork and followership to her as she was growing up, as well as presently in her role in the space program. She wrote this during preparation for her flight in June 1992. She was payload commander for that space shuttle mission.

Above all, the success of a space flight depends upon teamwork: within the crew and between the ground controllers and the crew. Teamwork is a valued attribute among currently selected astronauts.

I was very fortunate as a young girl to have been exposed to that concept by my family. With four children and a multitude of chores to be performed, my mother and father impressed upon us our responsibilities within the family unit. Success of the farm (and our future) depended upon our contribution. As the oldest, I was expected to participate in all chores, including driving the tractor and "round-up" by horseback. There were no distinctions in these responsibilities between my brothers and me. Group experiences within the 4-H organization (showing steers, etc.) and playing on baseball, volleyball, and basketball teams reinforced the pride of sharing success together and consoling each other in defeat.

When I attended college, some of that team experience was missed. By virtue of my gender, I was considered an unwelcome minority by many in the engineering college. Therefore, I was never invited to the study groups or participated in group solution of the homework problems. Still, I found an outlet in group activities by belonging to Angel Flight (co-ed auxiliary to Air Force ROTC—I was elected Commander of 50 my junior year) and by continuing to play co-ed baseball. Ironically, my engineering classmates needed my athletic ability as first baseman on the playing field.

I was also supported by three very important individuals during this time: my father, my mother, and the chairman of the Ceramic Engineering Department, Dr. James I. Mueller. My parents

always encouraged me to pursue my "dreams" and to be the best person I could be. The fact that I was the first in the family to attend college was a source of pride for them. That I subscribed to their principles of hard work, human compassion, and honesty was probably a source of greater pride. They were proud of my selection as an astronaut but my father was more concerned that I not forget how to get manure on my boots.

In my professional life, the closest I have come to real group esprit de corps has come through my association with the Astronaut Office. Perhaps it was due to the concept of "class training," or the similarity of individuals involved, but I consider those I work with as also my closest friends. Our successes are really those of a family team that extends out to the engineers, managers, and administrative support in the Space Shuttle program.

I am now on my third NASA Space Shuttle crew. As Payload Commander I have tried to convey to the noncareer payload specialists on my next flight the importance of being part of the crew . . . that we will share both the successes and the failures of the flight. It has been an interesting experience to assess others' ability to become "part of the team." I have seen what not being part of the team can do, and in a flight environment that can be highly risky. Not being a team member does more than cause internal friction within the crew; it can be hazardous.

So, what does being "part of the team" mean? It doesn't always mean being the smartest or the fastest. It does mean recognizing the big picture goal and the contribution that each individual brings to the whole. It may not mean being the life of the party, but it does mean being able to get along with people and to tread a fine line . . . knowing when to compromise and knowing when to stand firm. And, in an organization such as ours with competitive individuals used to being on top of the hill, it means knowing when to be a Chief and when to be an Indian. In the Astronaut Office, mission specialists rotate through technical jobs and different responsibilities during flights. Sometimes they are Indians instead of Chiefs. Those that perform best and appear to be well-regarded can do each equally well.

The Center for Creative Leadership's research with teams indicated that successful and unsuccessful teams could be differentiated on the basis of eight key characteristics, the first six of which are primarily concerned with task accomplishment.[39] First, effective teams had a *clear mission,* and *high performance standards.* Everyone on the team knew what the team was trying to achieve and how well he or she had to perform in order to achieve the team's mission. Second, leaders of successful teams often *took stock* of their equipment, training facilities and opportunities, and outside resources available to help the team. Leaders of effective teams spent a considerable amount of time *assessing the technical skills* of the team members. After taking stock of available resources and skills, good leaders would work to *secure those resources and equipment* necessary for team effectiveness. Moreover, leaders of effective teams would spend a considerable amount of time *planning* and *organizing* in order to make optimal use of available resources, to select new members with needed technical skills, or to improve needed technical skills of existing members.

The last two characteristics of effective teams were concerned with the group maintenance or interpersonal aspects of teams. Hallam and Campbell's[40] research indicated that *high levels of communication* were often associated with effective teams. These authors believed this level of communication helped team members to stay focused on the mission and to take better advantage of the skills, knowledge, and resources available to the team. High levels of communication also helped to *minimize interpersonal conflicts* on the team, which often drained energy needed for team success and effectiveness. The characteristics of effective teams identified in this research provide leadership practitioners with a number of ideas about how they may be able to increase the effectiveness of their work units or teams.

A different avenue to group and team effectiveness has been to use a normative approach. One example of this technique is described in *Groups That Work (and Those That Don't).*[41] Ginnett[42,43] has developed an expanded model focusing specifically on team leadership, which we will examine in more detail later in this chapter. For now, our concern is with one of the three major leadership functions in Ginnett's model that focuses on team design. The model suggests four components of design of the team itself that help the team get off to a good start, whatever its task. This is important because it is not uncommon to find that a team's failure can be traced to its being set up inappropriately from the very beginning. If a team is to work effectively, the following four variables need to be in place from the beginning.

1. *Task structure:* Does the team know what its task is? Is the task reasonably unambiguous and consistent with the mission of the team? Does the team have a meaningful piece of work, sufficient autonomy to perform it, and access to knowledge of its results?

2. *Group boundaries:* Is the collective membership of the team appropriate for the task to be performed? Are there too few or too many members? Do the members collectively have sufficient knowledge and skills to

perform the work? In addition to task skills, does the team have sufficient maturity and interpersonal skills to be able to work together and resolve conflicts? Is there an appropriate amount of diversity on the team (e.g., members are not so similar that they do not have differing perspectives and experiences, and yet not so diverse that they cannot communicate or relate to one another)?

3. *Norms:* Does the team share an appropriate set of norms for working as a team? Norms can be acquired by the team in three ways: (a) They can be imported from the organization existing outside the team, (b) they can be instituted and reinforced by the leader or leaders of the team, or (c) they can be developed by the team itself as the situation demands. If the team is to have a strategy that works over time, then it must ensure that conflicting norms do not confuse team members. It also needs to regularly scan and review prevailing norms to ensure they support overall objectives.

4. *Authority:* Has the leader established a climate where her authority can be used in a flexible rather than a rigid manner? Has she, at one end of the authority continuum, established sufficient competence to allow the group to comply when conditions demand (such as in emergencies)? Has she also established a climate such that any member of the team feels empowered to provide expert assistance when appropriate? Do team members feel comfortable in questioning the leader on decisions where there are no clear right answers? In short, have conditions been created where authority can shift to appropriately match the demands of the situation?

Many of these team design components may be imported from preexisting conditions in the organization within which the team is forming, from the industry in which the organization operates, or even from the environment in which the industry exists. To help team leaders consider these various levels, Hackman and Ginnett[44,45] developed the concept of **organizational shells** (see Figure 10.1). Notice that the four critical factors for team design (task, boundary, norms, and authority) are necessary for the group to work effectively. In some cases, all the information about one of these critical factors may be input from the industry or organizational shell level. In these cases, the leader need do little else but affirm that condition. In other cases, there may be too little (or even inappropriate) input from the organizational level to allow the team to work effectively. In these cases, the leader needs to modify the factors for team design. Ideally this is done during the formation process—the final shell before the team actually begins work.

These ideas may require a new way of thinking about the relationship between a leader and followers. In many organizational settings, leaders are assigned. Sometimes, however, the people who create conditions for

FIGURE 10.1   Organizational shells.

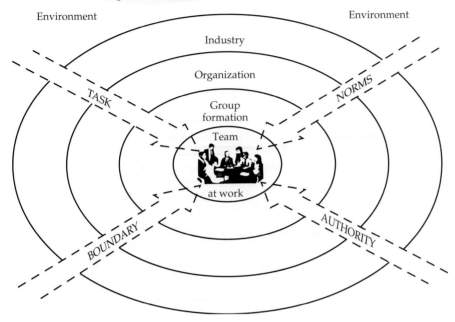

improved group effectiveness are not the designated leaders at all; they may emerge from the ranks of followers. This model has been used to differentiate between effective and ineffective "self-managing work groups"—teams where the followers and leaders were the same people. Moreover, because the model is prescriptive, it also provides a number of suggestions about what ineffective work groups can do to be successful. That same purpose underlies the following model as well.

Ginnett's Team Leadership Model

Since we have emphasized that leadership is a group or team function and have suggested that one measure of leadership effectiveness may be whether the team achieves its objectives, it is reasonable to examine a model specifically designed to help teams perform more effectively: the **Team Leadership Model, or TLM**[46–48] (shortened from earlier versions when it was referred to as the Team Effectiveness Leadership Model). Another way to think of this model is as a mechanism to first identify what a team needs to be effective, and then to point the leader either toward the roadblocks that are hindering the team or toward ways to make the team even more effective than it already is. This approach is similar to McGrath's[49] description of leadership, which suggested that the

FIGURE 10.2

Systems Theory
Applied to Teams.

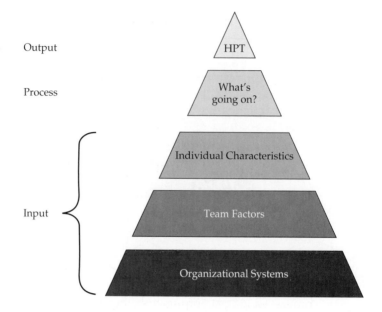

Output — HPT

Process — What's going on?

Input — Individual Characteristics / Team Factors / Organizational Systems

leader's main job is to determine what needs the team is faced with and then take care of them. This approach also will require us to think about leadership not as a function of the leader and his or her characteristics but as a function of the team. As the title of the model suggests, team effectiveness is the underlying driver.

We have mentioned this model of group or team effectiveness briefly before, but now we will explore it in greater detail. The original model for examining the "engine of a group" was developed by Richard Hackman and has been the basis for much research on groups and teams over the last 30 years.[50] The model presented here includes major modifications by Ginnett and represents an example of a leadership model that has been developed primarily using field research. While there have been controlled experimental studies validating portions of the model,[51] the principal development and validation have been completed using actual high-performance teams operating in their own situational context. Examples of the teams studied in this process include commercial and military air crews in actual line flying operations, surgical teams in operating suites, executive teams, product development and manufacturing teams, and teams preparing the Space Shuttle fleet for launch. A complete illustration of the model will be shown later. Because of its complexity, it is easier to understand by starting with a few simpler illustrations.

At the most basic level, this model (see Figure 10.2) resembles a systems theory approach with inputs at the base (i.e., individual, team, and organizational factors), processes or throughputs in the center (i.e., what one can tell about the team by actually observing team members at work),

FIGURE 10.3
Basic TLM outputs:
outcomes of High
Performance Teams.

High **P**erformance **T**eams
3 Components

Outcomes are
acceptable to
stakeholders

Future
capability of the
team improves

GOAL

HPT

Individuals are satisfied

and outputs at the top (i.e., how well the team did in accomplishing its objectives, ideally a High Performance Team). We will examine each of these stages. However, we will proceed through the model in reverse order—looking at outputs first, then the process stage, then inputs.

Outputs

What do we mean by outputs? Quite simply, **outputs** (see Figure 10.3) are the results of the team's work. For example, a football team scores 24 points. A production team produces 24 valves in a day. A tank crew hits 24 targets on an artillery range. Such raw data, however, are insufficient for assessing team effectiveness.

How do we know if a team's output is good? How do we know if a team is effective? Even though it was possible for the three different teams mentioned above to measure some aspect of their work, these measurements are not very helpful in determining their effectiveness, either in an absolute sense or in a relative sense. For comparison and research purposes, it is desirable to have some measures of team effectiveness that can be applied across teams and tasks. Hackman[52] argued that a group is effective if (*a*) the team's productive output (goods, services, decisions) meets the standards of quantity, quality, and timeliness of the people who use it; (*b*) the group process that occurs while the group is performing its task enhances the ability of the members to work as members of a team (either the one they were on or any new teams they may be assigned to) in the future; and (*c*) the group experience enhances the growth and personal well-being of the individuals who compose the team.

Process

It should be obvious why leaders should be concerned with the outputs listed in the preceding section. After all, if a team does not "produce" (output), then it could not be considered effective. But what is process?

And why should a leader care about it? Actually, there are several reasons a leader might want to pay attention to the team's process—how the team goes about its work. Some teams may have such a limited number of products that the leader can ill afford to wait until the product is delivered to assess its acceptability to the client. For example, a team whose task is to build one (and only one) satellite to be launched into orbit will have no second chances. There may be no opportunity to correct any problem once the satellite is launched (or, as was the case with the flawed Hubble Space Telescope, correction can be made only after great expense). Therefore, it may be desirable for the leader of such a team to assess his team's work while it is working rather than after the satellite is launched. Other kinds of teams have such high standards for routine work that there simply are not enough critical indicators in the end product to determine effectiveness from outcome measures. As an example of this situation, a team operating a nuclear power plant is surrounded by so many technical backup systems that it may be difficult to determine team effectiveness by looking at "safe operation" as a measurement criterion. But we have evidence that not all teams in nuclear power plants operate equally well (Chernobyl and Three Mile Island are but two examples). It would seem helpful to be able to assess real teams "in process" rather than learn of team problems only following disastrous outcomes. Even leaders of noncritical teams might like to be able to routinely monitor their teams for evidence of effective or ineffective processes. So it turns out that the way teams go about their work can provide some very useful information to the leader.

Since process assessment is so important, let us focus for a moment on the block containing the four process measures of effectiveness in Figure 10.4.

FIGURE 10.4

TLM diagnosis process: diagnose using the process variables.

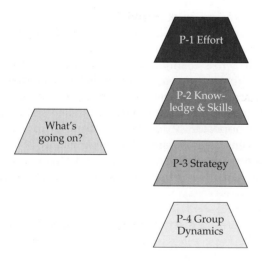

These four **process measures** of effectiveness provide criteria by which we can examine the ways in which teams work. If a team is to perform effectively, it must (a) work hard enough, (b) have sufficient knowledge and skills within the team to perform the task, (c) have an appropriate strategy to accomplish its work (or ways to approach the task at hand), and (d) have constructive and positive group dynamics among its members. The phrase *group dynamics* refers to interactions among team members, including such aspects as how they communicate with others, express feelings toward each other, and deal with conflict with each other, to name but a few of the characteristics. Assessing and improving group process is no trivial matter, as has been documented extensively in a comprehensive view of group process and its assessment by Wheelan.[53]

What should the leader do if she discovers a problem with one of these four process measures? Paradoxically, the answer is not to focus her attention on that process per se. While the four process measures are fairly good diagnostic measures for a team's ultimate effectiveness, they are, unfortunately, not particularly good leverage points for fixing the problem. An analogy from medicine would be a doctor who diagnoses the symptoms of an infection (a fever) but who then treats the symptoms rather than attacking the true underlying cause (a nail in the patient's foot). Similarly at the team level, rather than trying to correct a lack of effort being applied to the task at hand (perhaps a motivation problem), the team leader would be better advised to discover the underlying problem and fix that than to assume that a motivational speech to the team will do the job. This is not to imply that teams cannot benefit from process help. It merely suggests that the leader should ensure that there are no design problems (at the input level) that should be fixed first.

Inputs

In a manufacturing plant, **inputs** are the raw materials that are processed into products for sale. Similarly in team situations, inputs are what is available for teams as they go about their work. However, an important difference between an industrial plant and a team is that for a plant, the inputs are physical resources. Often for team design, we are considering psychological factors. There is a variety of levels of inputs, ranging from the individual level to the environmental level. Some of the inputs provide little opportunity for the leader to have an influence—they are merely givens. Leaders are often put in charge of teams with little or no control over the environment, the industry, or even the organizational conditions. There are other inputs, however, that the leader can directly impact to create the conditions for effective teamwork.

Figure 10.2 shows the multiple levels in the input stage of the model. Note that there are input factors at the individual and organizational levels and that these levels both surround and affect the team design level.

Ask not what your country can do for you. Ask what you can do for your country.

John F. Kennedy

Leadership Prescriptions of the Model

Creation

Following McGrath's[54] view of the leader's role (the leader's main job is to identify and help satisfy team needs), and using the TLM, it is possible to identify constructive approaches for the leader to pursue. As described earlier in this chapter, what leaders do depends on where a team is in its development. Ideally, we should build a team like we build a house or an automobile. We should start with a concept, create a design, engineer it to do what we want it to do, and then manufacture it to meet those specifications. The TLM provides the same linear flow for design of a team. The somewhat more complex version of the TLM model is shown in Figure 10.5 and the leader should, as noted above, begin on the left with the Dream, proceed through all of the Design variables and then pay attention to the Development needs of the team. In this way, she can implement the three critical functions for team leadership: **dream, design, and development.**

FIGURE 10.5 Three functions of leadership.

Dream

Obviously, the team needs to have clear vision. In their book *The Wisdom of Teams*[55] Katzenbach and Smith suggested that this may be the most important single step in teamwork. If the team has a challenging and demanding goal, teamwork may be necessary to accomplish the task. In highly effective work teams, the leader ensures that the team has a clear vision of where they are going. The communication of a vision frequently involves metaphorical language so that team members actually "paint their own picture" of where the team is headed.

Design

The importance of the design function of leadership cannot be overstated. Whether in the start-up of a team or in the midstream assignment of leaders, designing the team is critical. It is also often the most frequently omitted step. Managers have long been trained to detect deviations and correct them. But what if the deviations are not detectable until the output stage? At their best, managers often detect deviations at the process stage and attempt to fix them "right where they are seen." Far too often, little time or attention is focused at the input level. Senior-level leaders may resist changing the organizational systems for a number of reasons, including having a vested interest in maintaining the status quo (whatever it is, it has at least let them rise to their current position!). And while individual team leaders may have little control over the organizational context and systems, they always have the opportunity for making an impact in their own team's design.

Development

If the leader finds that the team has a clear sense of direction and vision, and the input variables at the individual, organizational, and team levels are contributing positively to team effectiveness (i.e., the design portion of the leader's job has been taken care of), then she can turn her attention to the development level. Development is the ongoing work done with the team at the process level to continue to find ways to improve an already well-designed team. Given our individualistic culture, we have identified many teams in organizations that are apparently well designed and supported at the input level, but that have had no training or experience in the concept of teamwork. There are times when effective teamwork is based on very different concepts than effective individual work. For example, for a team to do well, the individuals composing the team must sometimes not maximize their individual effort. Referred to as subsystem nonoptimization, this concept is at first not intuitively obvious to many newly assigned team members. Nevertheless, consider the example of a high school football team that has an extremely fast running back and some very good (but considerably slower) blocking linemen as members of the offense. Often, team members are told they all need to do their absolute best if the team is going to do well. If our running back does his absolute best on a sweep around the end, then he will run as fast as he can. By doing so, he will leave his blocking linemen behind. The team is not likely to gain much yardage on such a play, and the linemen and the running back, who have done their individual best, are apt to learn an important experiential lesson about teamwork. Most important, after several such disastrous plays, all of the team members may be inclined to demonstrate poor team process (lower effort, poor strategy, poor use of knowledge, and poor group dynamics represented by intrateam strife). If we assume that all the input stage variables are satisfactorily in place, ongoing coaching may now be appropriate. The coach would get better results if he worked out a better coordination plan between the running back and the linemen. In this case, the fast running back needs to slow down (i.e., not perform maximally) to give the slower but excellent blockers a chance to do their work. After they have been given a chance to contribute to the play, the running back will have a much better chance to then excel individually, and so will the team as a whole.

As straightforward as this seems, very few leaders get the opportunity to build a team from the ground up. More often the leader is placed into a team that already exists, has most, if not all, of its members assigned, and is in a preexisting organizational context that might not be team friendly. While this situation is more difficult, all is not lost. The TLM also provides a method for diagnosis and identification of key **leverage points** for change.

Diagnosis and Leverage Points

Let us assume that you, as a new leader, have been placed in charge of a poorly performing existing team. After a few days of observation, you have discovered that its members are just not working very hard. They seem to be uninterested in the task, frequently wandering off or not even showing up for scheduled teamwork. By focusing on the Process block of the TLM, (the core or "engine" of the TLM is shown in Figure 10.6, which can be thought of as a four-sided pyramid), we would diagnose this at the process level as a problem of Effort. Note that preceding the term *Effort at the process level* is the label (P-1). Rather than just encouraging them to work harder (or threatening them), we should first look at the Input level to see if there is some underlying problem. But you do not need to examine all 12 Input variables. Since we have already diagnosed a P-1 level process problem, the TLM is designed to focus your attention on the key leverage points to target change. Each face of the pyramid shows the input variables at the Individual, Team, and Organizational levels that most impact the Process variable that one might diagnose. These are referred to as the leverage points for impacting (P-1) Effort. (See the no. 1 face of the pyramid in Figure 10.6.) The individual level (I-1) suggests that we look at the interests and motivations of the individual team members. These are referred to as **individual factors** in the model. If we have built a team to perform a mechanical assembly task, but the individuals assigned

FIGURE 10.6   Team Leadership Model, Robert C. Ginnett, PhD: The four faces of the "engine" of the Team Leadership Model.

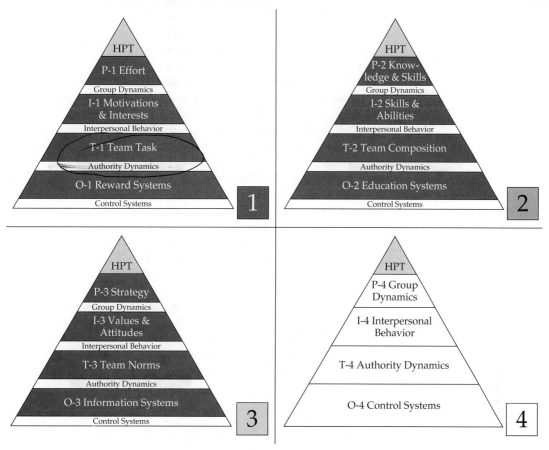

have little or no interest in mechanical work and instead prefer the performing arts, they may have little interest in contributing much effort to the team task. Here, using instruments such as the Campbell Interest and Skills Survey to select personnel may help our team's effort level from an individual perspective.[56]

While it may seem tempting to move to the team-level inputs next, it is important to remember that this model emphasizes the way teams are influenced by both individual and organizational level inputs. Therefore, we will look at the **organizational level** next. At the organizational level (O-1), the model suggests that we should examine the reward system that may be impacting the team. If the individuals have no incentive provided by the organization for putting forth effort, they might not be inclined to work very hard or, perhaps, at all. Similarly, the reward system may be solely structured to reward individual performance. Such a reward structure would be inconsistent with designs for a team task where interdependence and cooperation among members is often an underlying premise. If a professional basketball organization provides rewards for players based only on individual points scored, with no bonuses for team performance (games won or making the playoffs), you can expect little passing, setting picks for teammates, and so on.

Both the individual and organizational level variables contribute to the team's ability to perform the task. But there can also be problems at the **team design** level. Here (T-1), a poorly designed task is hypothesized to be unmotivating. (An approach for designing intrinsically rewarding work based on job characteristics will be discussed in the next chapter.) If a job is meaningless, lacks sufficient autonomy, or provides no knowledge of results, we would not expect to see followers putting forth much effort.

Using the model, we found key leverage points at various levels of the input stage that would impact the way the team went about its work (team process). In the example cited, we diagnosed a process-level problem with effort (P-1), so we examined the 1-level variables at the individual, organizational, and team levels as the most likely location for finding input stage problems. By the way, the concept of leverage point does not imply that only factors at corresponding "numbers" should be considered. For example, a team's effort might be affected by an oppressive and authoritarian leader. As we will discuss next, this "foundation-level variable" can have a tremendous impact on the other variables. Indeed, so powerful is this component, we should examine the process measure of group dynamics (P-4) and its corresponding leverage points in more detail. Consider the following two examples:

> *Surgical team.* A surgical team composed of highly experienced members is involved in a surgical procedure that each member has participated in numerous times before. During one portion of the procedure, the surgeon asks for a particular instrument. The scrub nurse looks across the table at the assistant with a questioning gaze and then hands the surgeon the instrument he requested. Recognizing the instrument he has been handed (and asked for) is not correct for the current procedure, he throws it down on the table and curses at the scrub nurse. All members of the surgical team take a half-step back from the table and all casual conversation stops. No one offers any further voluntary assistance to the surgeon.
>
> *Commercial airline crew.* A commercial airline crew is making a routine approach into an uncrowded airport on a clear day. The captain is flying and has declared a visual approach. His final approach to the runway is not good, which greatly complicates the plane's landing, and the landing is poor. After taxiing to the gate, the captain and his entire crew debrief (discuss) the poor approach, and the team members talk about what they could do individually and collectively to help the captain avoid or improve a poor approach in the future. The captain thanks the members for their help and encourages them to consider how they could implement their suggestions in other situations.

Obviously, the group dynamics are very different in these two cases. In the first example, the surgeon's behavior, coupled with his status, created a condition inappropriate for effective teamwork. The airline captain in the second example, even though not performing the task well, created a team environment where the team was much more likely to perform well in the future. In both of these cases, we would have observed unusual (one negative and one positive) group dynamics while the team was at work. These are examples of the group dynamics at the P-4 level.

Again returning to the model for determining points of leverage, we would check the I-4 variable at the individual level to determine if the team members involved had adequate interpersonal skills to interact appropriately. At the organizational level, the O-4 variable would suggest we check organizational components to determine if there are organizational control systems that inhibit or overly structure the way in which the team can make decisions or control its own fate. Such factors may include organizational design or structure limitations (a subject we will discuss in more detail in Chapter 11), or it may be a rigid computerized control system that specifies every minute detail of the tasks not only of the teams as a whole but of all the individuals composing the team. These excessive controls at the organizational level can inhibit effective teamwork. Finally, at the team design level, the T-4 variable would have us examine authority dynamics created between the leader and the followers. Authority dynamics describe the various ways the team members, including the leader, relate and respond to authority. It is at the team level that the followers have opportunities to relate directly with the team's authority figure, the team leader. The intricacies of how these various authority dynamics can play themselves out in a team's life are more complex than is warranted for this chapter. Suffice it to say that there is a range of authority relationships that can be created, from autocratic to laissez-faire. For a more detailed explanation of this concept, see Ginnett.[57] But even without further description, it should be no surprise that the varied group dynamics observed in the previous two examples were leveraged by the leaders' use of authority in very different ways.

It would be simple if leaders could identify and specify in advance the ideal type of authority for themselves and their teams, and then work toward that objective. However, teams seldom can operate effectively under one fixed type of authority over time. The leader might prefer to use his or her favorite style, and the followers might also have an inherent preference for one type of authority or another; but if the team is to be effective, then the authority dynamics they are operating with should complement the demands of the situation. Since situations often change over time, so should the authority dynamics of the team. This idea is very similar to a point made earlier in the book—that effective leaders tend to use all five sources of leader power.

In research on the behavior of leaders in forming their teams, Ginnett[58] found that highly effective leaders used a variety of authority dynamics in the first few minutes of the team's life. This does not mean that each highly effective leader used a single style that was different from the others' (i.e., other leaders'). It does mean that each one of the effective leaders used a variety of authority styles. At one point in the first meeting of the team, the leader would behave directively, which enabled him to establish his competence and hence his legitimate authority. At another time, he would engage the team in a very participative process and actively seek participation from each member of the team. By modeling a range of authority behaviors in the early stages of the team's life, the effective leaders laid the groundwork for continuing expectations of shifting authority as the situational demands changed.

Concluding Thoughts about Ginnett's Team Leadership Model

It is helpful to point out that not all components of the TLM have been discussed here because of its complexity. For example, we have not discussed **material resources.** Even if a team is well designed, has superior organizational systems supporting its work, and has access to superior-quality ongoing development, without adequate physical resources it is not likely to do well on the output level. Also note that background shells (discussed earlier in this chapter) representing the industry and the environment have *not* been included in this simplified depiction of the TLM. While the team leader may have little opportunity to influence these shells, the shells will certainly have an impact on the team.

Finally, there are several feedback loops which provide information to various levels of the organization. Usually, information is available to the organization as a whole (either formally or informally) about which teams are doing well and which are struggling. Whether leaders have access to this information is largely a function of whether they have created or stifled a safe climate. Feedback at the individual level can influence the perceived efficacy of the individual members of the team,[59,60] while the overall potency of the team is impacted even for tasks that the team has yet to attempt.[61]

Lastly, let us reinforce a limitation noted earlier. For ease of use and guidance, this model has been presented as if it were a machine (e.g., if P-2 breaks, check I-2, O-2, and T-2). As with other models of leadership or other human systems, however, nothing is that simple. There are obviously other variables that impact teams and team effectiveness. There are also complex interactions between the variables described even in this model. But we have considerable evidence that the model can be useful for understanding teams,[62] and, in light of the relationship between teams and leadership, we are now using it as an underlying framework in courses to help leaders more effectively lead their teams.

It has been shown that leaders can influence team effectiveness by (a) insuring the team has a clear sense of purpose and performance expectations; (b) designing or redesigning input stage variables at the individual, organizational, and team design levels; and (c) improving team performance through ongoing coaching at various stages, but particularly while the team is actually performing its task. These "midcourse corrections" should not

*"Well, I guess I did it again, guys? Missed a field
goal in the final seconds. But hey, we're a team,
right? Right, guys? Guys?"*

only improve the team outcomes but also help to avoid many of the team-generated problems that can cause less-than-optimal team performance.[63] Whether the leader gets the luxury of creation or is thrust into the leadership of an existing team, the TLM has been shown to be a useful tool in guiding their behavior. It also is a most effective tool if you believe that the leader's job is to create the conditions for the team to be effective.

Let us integrate the variables from this model into our L–F–S framework (see Figure 10.7). Clearly, there are variables of importance in each of the three arenas. However, in this model the characteristics of the leader play a lesser role because the leader's job is to work on what is not being provided for the team in order for it to perform its task. The focus thus has shifted from the leader to the followers and to the situation.

Virtual Teams

Just as teams and teamwork have become essential to the accomplishment of work in organizations in the present (and as far as we can foresee in the future), so too will be an understanding of teams that are not in a single location. With the movement toward the global marketplace and the resultant globalization of organizations, it is appropriate to briefly consider the difficulties and recommended solutions for leading **geographically dispersed teams (GDTs)** or, as they are more commonly referred to, virtual teams. There is considerable discussion about the labeling of such teams,[64] but for simplicity we will call them **virtual teams** here.

FIGURE 10.7 Factors from the normative model of group effectiveness and the interactional framework.

The marketplace is the globe (see Highlight 10.9). Western corporations are recognizing that growth and development opportunities are often much greater in Russia and other nations of the former Soviet Union, China, Latin America, and Africa than they are in their traditional markets of North America and Europe. But with this realization come new challenges for leading teams that are not only dispersed geographically but are often culturally different as well. Fortunately, information and communication technology is offering some new opportunities, if not solutions, for part of these problems. Early in this millennium, personal computer sales should top 100 million annually, which would be one PC for every 60 people on the planet; more than 60 million people will use cellular phones; and the Internet and World Wide Web are expanding at approximately 100 percent annually.[65] But is the mere opportunity to communicate electronically sufficient to ensure teamwork? Apparently not.

What Is the "Global Population" of Your Classroom?

HIGHLIGHT 10.9

Your authors attended a training session conducted by a major corporation intended for its newly appointed executives. One session was devoted to demonstrating the need for a global perspective in today's environment. To illustrate the key point, the instructor divided the room into unequal groups representing the geographical distribution of the world's population and had each group stand up in turn. As each group stood, she told them the proportion of the global population they represented.

The proportions she used are provided below. You might try it in your classroom—it makes the point dramatically.

Australia and New Zealand	2%
North America	5%
Former Soviet Union	5%
Latin America	7%
Western/Eastern Europe	10%
Africa	12%
Asia	56%

Researchers at the Conference Board[66] reported that there were five major areas that needed to change if global teams were to work. The five listed were senior management leadership, innovative use of communication technology, adoption of an organization design that enhances global operations, the prevalence of trust among team members, and the ability to capture the strengths of diverse cultures, languages, and people.

Armstrong and Cole[67] did in-depth studies of virtual teams and have reported three conclusions that should be considered by leaders of these teams. First, the distance between members of a virtual team is multi-dimensional. "Distance" includes not just geographical distance, but also organizational distance (e.g., different group or department cultures), temporal distance (e.g., different time zones), and differences in national culture. Second, the impact of such distances on the performance of a distributed work group is not directly proportional to objective measures of distance. In fact, Armstrong and Cole suggested that a new measure of distance between group members that reflects the degree of group cohesion and identity, a measure of psychological distance between members, would predict group performance better than geographical distance. Finally, the differences in the effects that distance seems to have on work groups are due at least partially to two intervening variables: (1) integrating practices *within* a virtual team, and (2) integrating practices *between* a virtual team and its larger host organization.

Finally, there are a number of frameworks under development to help leaders work with virtual teams, and there may be specific factors that these frameworks provide which can be useful. However, in our admittedly limited exposure to virtual teams in a pure research sense, a number of our clients have reported the TLM (discussed earlier) has been quite useful in considering the process problems that present themselves and in suggesting appropriate leverage points for intervention.

Leading Virtual Teams: Ten Principles

HIGHLIGHT 10.10

Terence Brake is the president of TMA-Americas and specializes in globalization. He suggests the following guidance for leaders of virtual teams.

Virtual when used in relation to teamwork is an unfortunate term. It implies there is almost teamwork, but not quite. *Virtual* has associations with *nearly, close to,* and *bordering on.* As one wit said, "If you want virtual results, create a virtual team." Alternatively, it is a fortunate term if taken it to imply that greater efforts are needed to achieve real teamwork in virtual teams. What principles can help you do this?

1. **Be proactive.** We often talk of "virtual" teams (VTs) as if they were all of a kind, but each one has its unique challenges. Some have a high level of cultural diversity. Others are more homogeneous. Some use one primary technology for collaboration, while others use a diverse mix. Some are short-lived, targeted on solving an immediate problem. Others are longer-term and strategic. Some cross time zones, and others none. By understanding the most likely challenges to occur, you can take proactive measures and increase team confidence. Confidence is a building block of virtual team performance.

2. **Focus on relationships before tasks.** Early on, team communications should have a significant "getting to know you" component. They should also demonstrate enthusiasm and optimism. Members need to feel valued for who they are, not just what they do. They need to feel engaged and connected. Trust is usually built early on virtual teams, or not at all. Some observers talk of the "virtual paradox"—virtual teams being highly dependent on trust, but not operating under conditions supportive of trust-building. Trust is often built on perceived similarities, but distance makes this process difficult. Chances for misunderstanding are also increased. Goodwill and engagement will solve most problems. Isolation and alienation create problems. Connect, and then collaborate.

3. **Seek clarity and focus early on.** Invest up-front time in clarifying the team's purpose and roles and responsibilities. There is enough uncertainty when working at a distance; it doesn't need to be added to by ambiguity and confusion. Clear purpose and accountabilities support cohesion. Translate purpose and overall accountabilities into specific objectives and tasks so that everyone knows what is expected, by whom, and by when. Virtual teams are highly susceptible to "focus drift" and fragmentation, so keep reminding the team of purpose, objectives, etc.

4. **Create a sense of order and predictability.** In a world wanting us to embrace chaos, "order" and "predictability" might appear unfashionable. But they are critical to the success of virtual teams. Uncertainty creates anxiety, fear, and withdrawal. The result is a demotivated and unproductive team. Use common team tools, templates, and processes; have predetermined times for communicating together; check in with team members regularly without trying to micro-manage; be accessible and an anchor point for the team. Shared expectations are psychological threads connecting separate minds.

5. **Be a cool-headed, objective problem solver.** Problems on virtual teams can appear larger than they actually are; people feeling isolated can lose perspective. Small issues, quickly resolved when working face-to-face, often fester and spread paranoia and distrust. You should establish yourself as someone who is totally fair; you don't play favorites, and you don't overburden some at the expense of others. You also need to be pragmatic. When there is a problem, you keep calm, you engage the team in finding practical solutions, and you communicate often. Panic is a virus that breeds exceptionally well in silent, isolated spaces.

6. **Develop shared operating agreements.** To reduce threats of uncertainty and ambiguity, common methods and processes—operating agreements—need to be established quickly. These agreements provide the team with shared mental models for working together. Typically, operating agreements need to be created in

continued

Continued

areas such as: planning, decision making, communicating, and coordination. A Team Charter acts as a common reference point, and can help orient new team members. Take time during team "meetings" to review how well the operating agreements are working.

7. **Give team members personal attention.** Just as you would on a face-to-face team, allocate time to "meet" with individuals. Find out how he or she is feeling about things. Give each person an opportunity to share personal successes, challenges, needs, and wants. It can be difficult to do this in team "meetings" where the emphasis is on shared tasks and problem solving. Empathize with that person who is on the road, working at home, or in a remote office. Listening, caring, sympathizing, recognizing—they cost little, but benefit everyone.

8. **Respect the challenges of the virtual environment.** I once lived on a boat, and I soon learned to respect the power of nature—the winds, tides, swells, rain, ice, and drought. I had to pay very close attention to these elements or they could sink me, swamp me, or ground me. There is always the temptation to carry over habits from one environment (e.g., land, face-to-face teamwork) into another (e.g., river, working at a distance). We must recognize the differences and adapt. Listening, empathizing, communicating, coordinating, engaging, energizing, and enabling all need to be enhanced.

9. **Recognize the limits of available technologies.** Unless you really have to, don't try and do everything via a virtual team. Sometimes teams are working on projects so complex that no matter how much video- or teleconferencing time they have, it will not be enough. Sometimes it pays dividends to bring people together for a few days. Never assume that because you have been designated a "virtual" team, you must always work in that mode. Focus on cost/benefit over the life of the project. Technology is a tool, and all tools are good for some tasks and not others.

10. **Stay people-focused.** Distance can make faceless abstractions of us all. Never lose sight of the fact that your virtual team members are people, with all that that entails—needs for belonging, meaning, accomplishment, and recognition; feelings of frustration, anger, excitement, boredom, and alienation; political pressures and personal pressures. Think about those features of your physical workplace that enable teams to work well together, e.g., formal meeting rooms, informal spaces, the coffee area, and see what you can do to humanize your virtual workplace, e.g., team pictures and bios, bulletin boards, chat areas.

Applying these virtual team leadership principles will help you avoid *almost* and *close to* teamwork. Virtual teamwork is only going to increase, so many of us need to re-skill ourselves for leading at a distance.

Summary

The group perspective showed that followers' behaviors can be the result of factors somewhat independent of the individual characteristics of followers. Group factors that can affect followers' behaviors include group size, stages of group development, roles, norms, and cohesion. Leadership practitioners should use these concepts to better understand followers' behaviors. Leaders should also use a team perspective for understanding follower behavior and group performance. Leadership practitioners need to bear in mind how a team's sense of identity, common goals or tasks, level of task interdependence, and differentiated roles affect functional and dysfunctional follower behavior. Additionally, because effective teams have several readily identifiable characteristics, leadership practitioners may want to use the suggestions provided by Hackman,[68] Ginnett,[69] or Hallam and Campbell[70] to develop more effective teams.

The Team Leadership Model posited that team effectiveness can best be understood in terms of inputs, processes, and outcomes. The input level consists of the individual characteristics of the followers; the design of the team itself; and various organizational systems that create the context in which the teams will operate. The process level concerns the way in which teams behave while going about their tasks, and the output level concerns whether customers and clients are satisfied with the team's product, whether the team improves and develops as a performing unit, and whether followers are satisfied to be members of the team. By identifying certain process problems in teams, leaders can use the model to diagnose appropriate leverage points for action at the individual, team design, or organizational levels, or for ongoing development at the process level. Leaders concerned with teamwork in organizational settings have found this framework useful in helping them conceptualize factors affecting team effectiveness and identifying targets for change.

Key Terms

group perspective, 437
group, 440
cliques, 441
span of control, 441
additive task, 442
process loss, 442
social loafing, 442
social facilitation, 442
forming, 442
storming, 443
norming, 443
performing, 443
project teams, 444
punctuated equilibrium, 444
group roles, 444
task role, 445

relationship role, 445
dysfunctional roles, 446
role conflict, 446
intrasender role conflict, 447
intersender role conflict, 447
interrole conflict, 447
person-role conflict, 447
role ambiguity, 447
norms, 447
group cohesion, 450
overbounding, 450
groupthink, 451
ollieism, 452
organizational shells, 456

Team Leadership Model (TLM), 457
outputs, 459
process measures, 461
inputs, 461
dream, 462
design, 462
development, 462
leverage point, 464
individual factors, 464
organizational level, 465
team design, 466
material resources, 468
geographically dispersed teams (GDTs), 469
virtual teams, 469

Questions

1. How do the tenets of Ginnett's Team Leadership Model compare with the components of team performance described earlier?

2. Not all group norms are positive or constructive from the leader's perspective. If a group holds counterproductive norms, what should the leader do?

3. On the basis of what you know about global cultures, would people from the U.S., Japan, or Chile be more comfortable with a group or team-based approach to work?

Activity

NASA Exercise: Lost on the Moon

Your spaceship has crash-landed on the dark side of the moon and you are scheduled to rendezvous with the mother ship, which is 200 miles away on the lighted side of the moon. The crash has ruined the ship and destroyed all the equipment except for the 15 items listed below. Your crew's survival depends on reaching the mother ship, so you must choose the most critical items available to take on the 200-mile trip. Your task is to rank-order the 15 items in the order of their importance for your survival. Place a "1" beside the most important item, a "2" beside the second most important item, and so on until you have ranked all 15 items.

_____ Box of matches

_____ Food concentrate

_____ 50 feet of nylon rope

_____ Parachute silk

_____ Solar-powered portable heating unit

_____ Two .45 caliber pistols

_____ One case of dehydrated milk

_____ Two 100-pound tanks of oxygen

_____ Stellar map

_____ Self-inflating life raft

_____ Magnetic compass

_____ Five gallons of water

_____ Signal flares

_____ First-aid kit with hypodermic syringes

_____ Solar-powered FM transmitter/receiver

Your instructor has the "NASA Expert" answers and the instructions for completing the exercise.

Minicase

"Integrating Teams at Hernandez & Associates"

Marco Hernandez is president of Hernandez & Associates Inc., a full-service advertising agency with clients across North America. The company provides a variety of marketing services to support its diverse group of clients. Whether called on to generate a strategic plan, create interactive Web sites, or put together a full-blown media campaign, the team at Hernandez & Associates prides itself on creative solutions to its clients' marketing challenges.

The firm was founded in 1990 with an emphasis in the real estate industry. It quickly expanded its client base to include health care, as well as food and consumer products. Like many small firms, the company grew quickly in the "high-flying" 1990s, but its administrative costs to obtain and service businesses also skyrocketed. And, as with many businesses, the agency's business was greatly affected by the terrorist attacks of September 11 and the economic downturn that followed. Clients' shrinking budgets forced them to scale back their business with Hernandez & Associates and cutbacks in staffing meant clients needed more marketing support services as opposed to full-scale campaigns.

Hernandez & Associates now faced a challenge—to adapt its business to focus on what the clients were asking for. Specifically, clients, with their reduced staffs, were looking for help responding to their customers' requests and looking for ways to make the most of their more limited marketing budgets. Its small, cohesive staff of 20 employees needed to make some changes, and quickly.

As president of Hernandez & Associates, Marco Hernandez knew his team was up for the challenge. He had worked hard to create an environment to support a successful team—he recruited people who had solid agency experience and he consistently communicated the firm's mission to his team. He made sure the team had all the resources it needed to succeed and constantly took stock of these resources. He had built his team as he built his business and knew the group would respond to his leadership. But where to start? Getting the team to understand that growth depended on a shift in how it serviced its clients was not difficult—each of the employees of the small firm had enough contact with the clients that they knew client needs were changing. But making significant changes to the status quo at Hernandez & Associates would be difficult. Group roles had to change—creative folks had to think about how to increase a client's phone inquiries and Web site visits; account people needed a better understanding of the client's desire for more agency leadership. And everyone had to have a better sense of the costs involved. The company as a whole needed a more integrated approach to servicing their clients if they hoped to survive. Marco needed a plan.

1. Like many leaders, Marco has a team in place and does not have the luxury of building a new team from the ground up to adapt to the changing business environment his firm is faced with. Use the TLM to help Marco diagnose the problems faced by the firm and identify leverage points for change.
   a. Consider the major functions of the TLM—input, process, and output. Where do most of the firm's challenges fall?
   b. What are the team's goals for outputs?
2. Identify potential resources for Marco and his team in implementing a strategy to change the way they do business at Hernandez & Associates.

Chapter Notes

1. Ginnett, R. C. "Effectiveness Begins Early: The Leadership Role in the Formation of Intra-Organizational Task Groups." Unpublished manuscript, 1992.

2. Shaw, M. *Group Dynamics: The Psychology of Small Group Dynamics.* 3rd ed. New York: McGraw-Hill, 1981.

3. Yukl, G. A. *Leadership in Organizations.* 1st ed. Englewood Cliffs, NJ: Prentice Hall, 1981.

4. Badin, I. J. "Some Moderator Influences on Relationships between Consideration, Initiating Structure, and Organizational Criteria." *Journal of Applied Psychology* 59 (1974), pp. 380–82.

5. Goodstadt, B. E., and D. Kipnis. "Situational Influences on the Use of Power." *Journal of Applied Psychology* 54 (1970), pp. 201–07.

6. Kipnis, D., S. M. Schmidt, and I. Wilkinson. "Intraorganizational Influence Tactics: Explorations in Getting One's Way." *Journal of Applied Psychology* 65 (1980), pp. 440–52.

7. Udell, J. G. "An Empirical Test of Hypotheses Relating to Span of Control." *Administrative Science Quarterly* 12 (1967), pp. 420–39.

8. Bass, B. M. *Leadership, Psychology, and Organizational Behavior.* New York: Harper, 1960.

9. Indik, B. P. "Organizational Size and Member Participation: Some Empirical Tests of Alternative Explanations." *Human Relations* 18 (1965), pp. 339–50.

10. Steiner, I. D. *Group Process and Productivity.* New York: Academic Press, 1972.

11. Steiner, I. D. *Group Process and Productivity.* New York: Academic Press, 1972.

12. Latane, B., K. Williams, and S. Harkins. "Social Loafing." *Psychology Today* (1979), p. 104.

13. Porter, D. B., M. Bird, and A. Wunder. "Competition, Cooperation, Satisfaction, and the Performance of Complex Tasks among Air Force Cadets." *Current Psychology Research and Reviews* 9, no. 4 (1991), pp. 347–54.

14. Zajonc, R. "Social Facilitation." *Science* 149 (1965), pp. 269–74.

15. Tuckman, B. W. "Developmental Sequence in Small Groups." *Psychological Bulletin* 63 (1965), pp. 384–99.

16. Tuckman, B. W. "Developmental Sequence in Small Groups." *Psychological Bulletin* 63 (1965), pp. 384–99.

17. Mayo, E. *The Human Problems of an Industrial Civilization.* New York: Macmillan, 1933.

18. Roethlisberger, F. J., and W. J. Dickson. *Management and the Worker: An Account of a Research Program Conducted by the Western Electric Company, Hawthorne Works, Chicago.* Cambridge: Harvard University Press, 1939.

19. Stogdill, R. M. "Group Productivity, Drive, and Cohesiveness." *Organizational Behavior and Human Performance* 8 (1972), pp. 26–43.

20. Terborg, J. R., C. H. Castore, and J. A. DeNinno. "A Longitudinal Field Investigation of the Impact of Group Composition on Group Performance and Cohesion." Paper presented at the annual meeting of the Midwestern Psychological Association, Chicago, 1975.

21. Gersick, C. J. G. "Time and Transition in Work Teams: Toward a New Model of Group Development." *Academy of Management Journal* 31 (1988), pp. 9–41.

22. Ginnett, R. C. "Airline Cockpit Crew." In *Groups That Work (and Those That Don't)*. Ed. J. Richard Hackman. San Francisco: Jossey-Bass, 1990.

23. Jamal, M. "Job Stress and Job Performance Controversy: An Empirical Assessment." *Organizational Behavior and Human Performance* 33 (1984), pp. 1–21.

24. Zimbardo, P., C. Haney, W. Banks, and D. Jaffe. "The Mind Is a Formidable Jailer: A Pirandellian Prison." *New York Times Magazine,* April 8, 1973, pp. 38–60.

25. House, R. J., R. S. Schuler, and E. Levanoni. "Role Conflict and Ambiguity Scales: Reality or Artifact?" *Journal of Applied Psychology* 68 (1983), pp. 334–37.

26. Rizzo, J. R., R. J. House, and S. I. Lirtzman. "Role Conflict and Ambiguity in Complex Organizations." *Administrative Science Quarterly* 15 (1970), pp. 150–63.

27. Fisher, C. D., and R. Gitleson. "A Meta-analysis of the Correlates of Role Conflict and Ambiguity." *Journal of Applied Psychology* 68 (1983), pp. 320–33.

28. Hackman, J. R. "Group Influences on Individuals." In *Handbook of Industrial and Organizational Psychology*. Ed. M. D. Dunnette. Chicago: Rand McNally, 1976.

29. Reilly, Rick. *Sports Illustrated* 104 (15) (2006), p. 76.

30. Feldman, D. C. "The Development and Enforcement of Group Norms." *Academy of Management Review,* January 1984, pp. 47–53.

31. Hackman, J. Richard. *Leading Teams—Setting the Stage for Great Performances.* Boston, MA: Harvard Business School Press, 2002.

32. Alderfer, C. P. "Group and Intergroup Relations." In *Improving Life at Work*. Eds. J. R. Hackman and J. L. Suttle, Santa Monica, CA: Goodyear, 1977.

33. Ginnett, R. C. "The Formation Process of Airline Flight Crews." *Proceedings of the Fourth International Symposium on Aviation Psychology*. Columbus, OH, 1987.

34. Janis, I. L. *Groupthink*. 2nd ed. Boston: Houghton Mifflin, 1982.

35. Janis, I. L. *Groupthink*. 2nd ed. Boston: Houghton Mifflin, 1982.

36. Janis, I. L. *Groupthink*. 2nd ed. Boston: Houghton Mifflin, 1982.

37. Shephard, J. E. "Thomas Becket, Ollie North, and You." *Military Review* 71, no. 5 (1991), pp. 20–33.

38. Robbins, S. P. *Organizational Behavior: Concepts, Controversies, and Applications.* Englewood Cliffs, NJ: Prentice Hall, 1986.

39. Hallam, G. L., and D. P. Campbell. "Selecting Team Members? Start with a Theory of Team Effectiveness." Paper presented at the Seventh Annual Meeting of the Society of Industrial/Organizational Psychologists, Montreal, Canada, May 1992.

40. Hallam, G. L., and D. P. Campbell. "Selecting Team Members? Start with a Theory of Team Effectiveness." Paper presented at the Seventh Annual Meeting of the Society of Industrial/Organizational Psychologists, Montreal, Canada, May 1992.

41. Hackman, J. R. *Groups That Work (and Those That Don't)*. San Francisco: Jossey-Bass, 1990.

42. Ginnett, R. C. "Crews as Groups: Their Formation and Their Leadership." In *Cockpit Resource Management*. Eds. E. Wiener, B. Banki, and R. Helmreich. Orlando, FL: Academic Press, 1993.

43. Ginnett, R. C. "Team Effectiveness Leadership Model: Identifying Leverage Points for Change." *Proceedings of the 1996 National Leadership Institute Conference.* College Park, MD: National Leadership Institute, 1996.

44. Hackman, J. R. "Group Level Issues in the Design and Training of Cockpit Crews." In *Proceedings of the NASA/MAC Workshop on Cockpit Resource Management.* Eds. H. H. Orlady and H. C. Foushee. Moffett Field, CA: NASA Ames Research Center, 1986.

45. Ginnett, R. C. "Crews as Groups: Their Formation and Their Leadership." In *Cockpit Resource Management.* Eds. E. Wiener, B. Banki, and R. Helmreich. Orlando, FL: Academic Press, 1993.

46. Ginnett, R. C. "Crews as Groups: Their Formation and Their Leadership." In *Cockpit Resource Management.* Eds. E. Wiener, B. Banki, and R. Helmreich. Orlando, FL: Academic Press, 1993.

47. Ginnett, R. C. "Team Effectiveness Leadership Model: Identifying Leverage Points for Change." *Proceedings of the 1996 National Leadership Institute Conference.* College Park, MD: National Leadership Institute, 1996.

48. Ginnett, R. C. "Team Effectiveness Leadership Model: Design & Diagnosis." 12th Annual International Conference on Work Teams. Dallas, TX, 2001.

49. McGrath, J. E. *Leadership Behavior: Some Requirements for Leadership Training.* Washington, DC: Office of Career Development, U.S. Civil Service Commission, 1964.

50. Hackman, J. R. *Groups That Work (and Those That Don't).* San Francisco: Jossey-Bass, 1990.

51. Smith, K. W., E. Salas, and M. T. Brannick. "Leadership Style as a Predictor of Teamwork Behavior: Setting the Stage by Managing Team Climate." Paper presented at the Ninth Annual Conference of the Society for Industrial and Organizational Psychology, Nashville, TN, 1994.

52. Hackman, J. R. *Groups That Work (and Those That Don't).* San Francisco: Jossey-Bass, 1990.

53. Wheelan, S. A. *Group Processes.* Needham Heights, MA: Allyn & Bacon, 1994.

54. McGrath, J. E. *Leadership Behavior: Some Requirements for Leadership Training.* Washington, DC: Office of Career Development, U.S. Civil Service Commission, 1964.

55. Katzenbach, J. R., and B. K. Smith. *The Wisdom of Teams.* Boston: HarperBusiness, 1994.

56. Campbell, D. P., S. Hyne, and D. L. Nilsen. *Campbell Interests and Skill Survey Manual.* Minneapolis, MN: National Computer Systems, 1992.

57. Ginnett, R. C. "Crews as Groups: Their Formation and Their Leadership." In *Cockpit Resource Management.* Eds. E. Wiener, B. Banki, and R. Helmreich. Orlando, FL: Academic Press, 1993.

58. Ginnett, R. C. "Crews as Groups: Their Formation and Their Leadership." In *Cockpit Resource Management.* Eds. E. Wiener, B. Banki, and R. Helmreich. Orlando, FL: Academic Press, 1993.

59. Bandura, A. "Self-Efficacy: Toward a Unifying Theory of Behavioral Change." *Psychological Review* 84 (1977), pp. 191–215.

60. Lindsley, D. H., D. J. Brass., and J. B. Thomas. " Efficacy-Performance Spirals: A Multilevel Perspective." *Academy of Management Review* 20 (1995), pp. 645–78.

61. Guzzo, R. A., P. R. Yost, R. J. Campbell, and G. P. Shea. "Potency in Teams: Articulating a Construct." *British Journal of Social Psychology* 32 (1993), pp. 87–106.

62. Hackman, J. R. *Groups That Work (and Those That Don't)*. San Francisco: Jossey-Bass, 1990.

63. Steiner, I. D. *Group Process and Productivity.* New York: Academic Press, 1972.

64. Kossler, M., and S. Prestridge. "Geographically Dispersed Teams." *Issues and Observations* 16 (1996), pp. 2–3.

65. Lipnack, J., and J. Stamps. *Virtual Teams: Reaching across Space, Time and Organizations with Technology.* New York: John Wiley, 1997.

66. Conference Board. "Global Management Teams: A Perspective." *HR Executive Review* 4 (1996).

67. Armstrong, D. J., and P. Cole. "Managing Distances and Differences in Geographically Distributed Work Groups." In *Distributed Work.* Eds. P. Hinds and S. Kiesler, Cambridge, MA: MIT Press, 2002, pp. 167–89.

68. Hackman, J. R. *Groups That Work (and Those That Don't)*. San Francisco: Jossey-Bass, 1990.

69. Ginnett, R. C. "Effectiveness Begins Early: The Leadership Role in the Formation of Intra-Organizational Task Groups." Unpublished manuscript, 1992.

70. Hallam, G. L., and D. P. Campbell. "Selecting Team Members? Start with a Theory of Team Effectiveness." Paper presented at the Seventh Annual Meeting of the Society of Industrial/Organizational Psychologists, Montreal, Canada, May 1992.

Part 3

Leadership Skills

In Part Two we presented helpful information on skills which focus on the leader himself or herself. In this section we will cover a number of additional leadership skills which are particularly helpful with regard to the leader's relationship with followers. The skills we address in this section include:

- Providing Constructive Feedback
- Punishment
- Delegating
- Team Building for Work Teams
- Building High Performance Teams: The Rocket Model
- Development Planning
- Coaching
- Empowerment

Providing Constructive Feedback

Make It Helpful
Be Specific
Be Descriptive
Be Timely
Be Flexible
Give Positive as Well as Negative Feedback
Avoid Blame or Embarrassment

Giving constructive feedback involves sharing information or perceptions with another about the nature, quality, or impact of that person's behavior. It can range from giving feedback pertaining specifically to a person's work (i.e., performance feedback) to impressions of how aspects of that person's interpersonal behavior may be pervasively affecting relationships with others. Our use of the term *feedback* here is somewhat different from its use in the systems view of communication (Figure P2.1 in Part Two). In the communication model, the feedback loop begins with actively checking the receiver's *interpretation* of one's own message, and then initiating or modifying subsequent communications as necessary. A simple example of that meaning of feedback might be noting another person's quizzical expression when you try to explain a complicated point, thereby realizing that you'd better say it differently. The skill of giving constructive feedback, however, inherently involves *actively giving feedback to someone else.*

Getting helpful feedback is essential to a subordinate's performance and development. Without feedback, a subordinate will not be able to tell whether she's doing a good job or whether or not her abrasiveness is turning people off and hurting her chances for promotion. And it's not just subordinates who need constructive feedback to learn and grow. Peers may seek feedback from peers, and leaders may seek feedback from subordinates. Besides fostering growth, effective supervisory feedback also plays a major role in building morale.

In many ways, the development of good feedback skills is an outgrowth of developing good communication, listening, and assertiveness skills. Giving good feedback depends on being clear about the purpose of the feedback and on choosing an appropriate context and medium for giving it. Giving good feedback also depends on sending the proper nonverbal signals and trying to detect emotional signals from whoever may be receiving the feedback. In addition, giving good feedback depends on being somewhat assertive in providing it, even when it may be critical of a person's performance or behavior. Although feedback skills are related to communication, listening, and assertiveness skills, they are not the same thing. Someone may have good communication, listening, and assertiveness skills but poor feedback skills. Perhaps this distinction can be made clearer by examining the knowledge, behavior, and evaluative components of feedback skills.

The knowledge component of feedback concerns knowing when, where, and what feedback is to be given. For example, knowing when, where, and how to give positive feedback may be very different from knowing when, where, and how to give negative feedback. The behavioral component of feedback concerns how feedback actually is delivered (as contrasted with knowing how it should be delivered). Good feedback is specific, descriptive, direct, and helpful; poor feedback is often too watered down to be useful to the recipient. Finally, one way to evaluate feedback is to examine whether recipients actually modify their behavior accordingly after receiving it. Of course, this should not be the only way to evaluate feedback skills. Even when feedback is accurate in content and delivered skillfully, a recipient may fail to acknowledge it or do anything about it.

Although most leaders probably believe that feedback is an important skill, research has shown that leaders also believe they give more feedback than their subordinates think they do.[1] There are many reasons leaders may be reluctant to give feedback. Leaders may be reluctant to give positive feedback because of time pressures, doubts about the efficacy of feedback, or lack of feedback skills.[2] Sometimes supervisors are hesitant to use positive feedback because they believe subordinates may see it as politically manipulative, ingratiating, or insincere.[3] Leaders also may give positive feedback infrequently if they rarely leave their desks, if their personal standards are too high, or if they believe good performance is expected and should not be recognized at all.[4] Other reasons may explain the failure to give negative feedback,[5] such as fears of disrupting leader–follower relations[6] or fear of employee retaliation.[7]

Although there are a number of reasons why leaders are hesitant to provide both positive and negative feedback, leaders need to keep in mind that followers, committee members, or team members will perform at a higher level if they are given accurate and frequent feedback. It is difficult to imagine how work-group or team performance could improve without feedback. Positive feedback is necessary to tell followers they should keep doing what they are doing well, and negative feedback is needed to give followers or team members ideas on how to change other behavior to improve their performance. Although accurate and frequent feedback is necessary, there are several other aspects of feedback that everyone can work on to improve their feedback skills, including (a) making sure it's helpful, (b) being direct, (c) being specific, (d) being descriptive, (e) being timely, (f) being flexible, (g) giving both positive and negative feedback, and (h) avoiding blame and embarrassment when giving feedback. Highlight P3.1 gives examples of each of these different aspects of feedback, and the following is a more complete description of ways leaders can improve their feedback skills.

Make It Helpful

The purpose of feedback is to provide others with information they can use to change their behavior. Being clear about the intent and purpose is important because giving feedback sometimes can become emotional for both the person giving it and the person receiving it. If the person giving feedback is in an emotional state (e.g., angry), she may say things that make her temporarily feel better but that only alienate the receiver. In order to be helpful, individuals need to be clear and unemotional when giving feedback, and should give feedback only about behaviors actually under the other person's control.

Tips for Improving Feedback Skills

HIGHLIGHT P3.1

Being Helpful

Do not: "I got better scores when I was going through this program than you just did."

Do: "This seems to be a difficult area for you. What can I do to help you master it better?"

Being Direct

Do not: "It's important that we all speak loud enough to be heard in meetings."

Do: "I had a difficult time hearing you in the meeting because you were speaking in such a soft voice."

Being Specific

Do not: "Since you came to work for us, your work has been good."

Do: "I really like the initiative and resourcefulness you showed in solving our scheduling problem."

Being Descriptive

Do not: "I'm getting tired of your rudeness and disinterest when others are talking."

Do: "You weren't looking at anyone else when they were talking, which gave the impression you were bored. Is that how you were feeling?"

Being Timely

Do not: "Joe, I think I need to tell you about an impression you made on me in the staff meeting last month."

Do: "Joe, do you have a minute? I was confused by something you said in the meeting this morning."

Being Flexible

Do not (while a person is crying, or while they are turning beet-red with clenched teeth in apparent anger): "There's another thing I want to tell you about your presentation yesterday . . . "

Do: When a person's rising defenses or emotionality gets in the way of their really listening, deal with those feelings first, or wait until later to finish your feedback. Do not continue giving information.

People can improve the impact of the feedback they give when it is addressed to a specific individual. A common mistake in giving feedback is addressing it to "people at large" rather than to a specific individual. In this case, the individuals for whom the feedback was intended may not believe the feedback pertained to them. In order to maximize the impact of the feedback, people should try to provide it to specific individuals, not large groups.

Be Specific

Feedback is most helpful when it specifies particular behaviors that are positive or negative. One of the best illustrations of the value of specific feedback is in compositions or term papers written for school. If someone turned in a draft of a paper to the instructor for constructive comments and the instructor's comments about the paper were "Good start, but needs work in several areas," then the person would have a difficult time knowing just what to change or correct. More helpful feedback from the instructor would be specific comments like "This paragraph does not logically follow the preceding one" or "Cite an example here." The same is true of feedback in work situations. The more specifically leaders can point out which behaviors to change, the more clearly they let the other person know what to do.

Be Descriptive

In giving feedback, it is good to stick to the facts as much as possible, being sure to distinguish them from inferences or attributions. A behavior description reports actions that others can see, about which there could be little question or disagreement. Such descriptions must be distinguished from inferences about someone else's feelings, attitudes, character, motives, or traits. It is a behavior description, for example, to say that Sally stood up and walked out of a meeting while someone else was talking. It is an inference, though, to say she walked out because she was angry. However, sometimes it is helpful to describe both the behavior itself and the corresponding impressions when giving feedback. This is particularly true if the feedback giver believes that the other person does not realize how the behavior negatively affects others' impressions.

Another reason to make feedback descriptive is to distinguish it from evaluation. When a person gives feedback based mostly on inferences, he often conveys evaluations of the "goodness" or "badness" of behavior as well. For example, saying "You were too shy" has a more negative connotation than saying "You had little to say." In the former case, the person's behavior was evaluated unfavorably, and by apparently subjective criteria. Yet evaluation is often an intrinsic part of a supervisor's responsibilities, and good performance feedback may necessitate conveying evaluative information to a subordinate. In such cases, leaders are better off providing evaluative feedback when clear criteria for performance have been established. Filley and Pace described criteria that can be used to provide evaluative feedback; some are listed in Highlight P3.2.[8]

An issue related to impressions and evaluative feedback concerns the distinction between job-related (i.e., performance feedback) and more personal or discretionary feedback. Although leaders have a right to expect followers to listen to their performance feedback, that is not necessarily true concerning feedback about other behaviors. It may well be that sharing perceptions of the person's behavior could be very helpful to that person even when the behavior doesn't pertain specifically to his formal responsibilities; in such cases, however, it is the follower's choice whether to hear it or, if he hears it, whether to act on it or not.

Be Timely

Feedback usually is most effective when it is given soon after the behavior occurs. The context and relevant details of more recent events or behaviors

Types of Criteria to Use for Evaluative Feedback

HIGHLIGHT P3.2

1. Compare behavior with others' measured performance. With this method, the subordinate's behavior is compared with that of her peers or co-workers; also called norm-referenced appraisal. For example, a subordinate may be told her counseling load is the lightest of all 10 counselors working at the center.

2. Compare behavior with an accepted standard. An example of this method would be where a counselor was told her workload was substantially below the standard of acceptable performance set at 30 cases per week. This is known as criterion-referenced appraisal.

3. Compare behavior with an a priori goal. With this method, the subordinate must participate in and agree with a goal. This is a form of criterion-referenced appraisal, with the subordinate's "ownership" and acceptance of the goal before the fact critical to the feedback procedure.

4. Compare behavior with past performance.

Source: Adapted from A. C. Filley and L. A. Pace, "Making Judgments Descriptive." In Eds. J. E. Jones and J. W. Pfeiffer. *The 1976 Annual Handbook for Group Facilitators,* La Jolla, CA: University Associates Press, 1976, pp. 128–31.

are more readily available to everyone involved, thus facilitating more descriptive and helpful feedback.

Be Flexible

Although feedback is best when it is timely, sometimes waiting is preferable to giving feedback at the very earliest opportunity. In general, everyone should remember that the primary purpose of feedback is to be helpful. Feedback sessions should be scheduled with that in mind. For example, a subordinate's schedule may preclude conveniently giving him feedback right away, and it may not be appropriate to give him feedback when it will distract him from another more immediate and pressing task. Furthermore, it may not be constructive to give someone else feedback when the person receiving it is in a very emotional state (whether about the behavior in question or other matters entirely). Moreover, it is important to be attentive to the other person's emotional responses while giving feedback and to be ready to adjust one's own behavior accordingly.

A final important part of being flexible is to give feedback in manageable amounts. In giving feedback, one does not need to cover every single point at one time, as doing so would only overload the other person with information. Instead, anyone who needs to give a lot of feedback to someone else may want to spread out the feedback sessions and focus on covering only one or two points in each session.

Give Positive as Well as Negative Feedback

Giving both positive and negative feedback is more helpful than giving only positive or negative feedback alone. Positive feedback tells the other person or the group only what they are doing right, and negative feedback tells the other person or group only what they are doing wrong. Providing both kinds of feedback is best.

Avoid Blame or Embarrassment

Because the purpose of feedback is to give useful information to other people to help them develop, talking to them in a way merely intended (or likely) to demean or make them feel bad is not a helpful part of the development process. Followers tend to be more likely to believe feedback if it comes from leaders who have had the opportunity to observe the behavior and are perceived to be credible, competent, and trustworthy.[9–11] Bass pointed out that followers will continue to seek feedback even if their leaders are not competent or trustworthy—though they will not seek it from their leaders.[12] They will seek it from others they do trust, such as peers or other superiors.

Punishment

Myths Surrounding the Use of Punishment
Punishment, Satisfaction, and Performance
Administering Punishment

In an ideal world, perhaps everyone would be dependable, achievement oriented, and committed to the organization's goals. The fact is, however, that leaders sometimes will need to deal with followers who are openly hostile or insubordinate, create conflicts among co-workers, do not work up to standards, or openly violate important rules or policies. In such cases leaders may need to administer punishment to change the follower's behavior.

Of all of the different aspects of leadership, few are as controversial as punishment. Some of the primary reasons for this controversy stem from myths surrounding the use of punishment, as well as the lack of knowledge regarding the effects of punishment on followers' motivation, satisfaction, and performance. This section is designed to shed light on the punishment controversy by (*a*) addressing several myths about the use of punishment, (*b*) reviewing research findings concerning the relationships between punishment and various organizational variables, and (*c*) providing leadership practitioners with advice on how to properly administer punishment.

Myths Surrounding the Use of Punishment

We should begin by repeating the definition of punishment stated earlier in the book. Punishment is the administration of an aversive event or the withdrawal of a positive event or stimulus, which in turn *decreases* the likelihood a particular behavior will be repeated.[13] Examples of punishment might include verbal reprimands, being moved to a less prestigious office, having pay docked, being fired, being made to run several laps around the athletic field, or losing eligibility for a sport entirely. We should note that, according to this definition, only those aversive events administered on a contingent basis are considered to be forms of punishment; aversive events administered on a noncontingent basis may constitute harsh and abusive treatment but are not punishment. Additionally, punishment appears to be in the eye of the beholder; aversive events that effectively change the direction, intensity, or persistence of one follower's behavior may have no effect on another's.[14] It is even possible that some followers may find the administration of a noxious event or the removal of a positive event to be reinforcing. For example, it is not uncommon for some children to misbehave if that increases the attention they receive from parents, even if the latter's behavior outwardly may seem punishing to others. (To the children, some parental attention of any kind may be preferable to no attention.) Similarly, some followers may see the verbal reprimands and notoriety they receive by being insubordinate or violating company policies as forms of attention. Because these followers enjoy being the center of attention, they may find this notoriety rewarding. From an operant perspective, they may be even more likely to be insubordinate in the future.

We will examine four myths surrounding the use of punishment. Three of these myths were reviewed by Arvey and Ivancevich and included beliefs that the use of punishment resulted in undesirable emotional side effects on the part of the recipient, was unethical and inhumane, and rarely worked anyway (i.e., seldom eliminated the undesirable behavior).[15]

B. F. Skinner's work in behavioral psychology lent support to the idea that punishment was ineffective and caused undesirable side effects. He based his conclusions on the unnatural behaviors manifested by rats and pigeons punished in various conditioning experiments.[16] Despite the dangers of generalizing from the behavior of rats to humans, many people accepted Skinner's contention that punishment was a futile and typically counterproductive tool for controlling human behavior. This was so despite the fact that considerable research regarding the emotional effects of punishment on humans did not support Skinner's claim.[17–19] Parke, for example, suggested that undesirable emotional side effects of punishment might occur only when punishment was administered indiscriminately or was particularly harsh.[20]

With respect to the myth that punishment is unethical or inhumane, it's been suggested that there is an ethical distinction between "future-oriented" and "past-oriented" punishment. Future-oriented punishment, intended to help improve behavior, may be effective in diminishing or eliminating undesirable behavior. Past-oriented punishment, or what we commonly think of as retribution, on the other hand, is simply a payback for past misdeeds. This sort of punishment may be more questionable ethically, especially when it is intended *only* as payback and not, say, as deterrent to others. Moreover, when considering the ethics of administering punishment, one must also consider the ethics of *failing* to administer punishment. The costs of *failing* to punish a potentially harmful behavior, such as unsafe workplace practices, may far outweigh those associated with the punishment itself.[21]

A third myth concerns the efficacy of punishment. Skinner[22] and others claimed that punishment did not result in a permanent behavior change but instead only temporarily suppressed behavior.[23] Evidence to support this claim was found in one study in which incarcerated prisoners had a recidivism rate of 85 percent.[24] However, this high recidivism rate may be due to the fact that criminals may have received punishment primarily for retribution rather than for corrective purposes. Judicious administration of sanctions, combined with advice about how to avoid punishment in the future, may successfully eliminate undesirable behaviors on a more permanent basis.[25] Furthermore, it may be a moot point to argue (as Skinner did) that punishment only temporarily suppresses behavior; so long as sanctions for misdeeds remain in place, their impact on behavior should continue. In that regard, it's relevant to note that the "temporary" effects of punishment on behavior are no different from the "temporary" effects of reinforcement on behavior.

Punishment, Satisfaction, and Performance

It appears that properly administered punishment does not cause undesirable emotional side effects, is not unethical, and may effectively suppress undesirable behavior. However, we also should ask what effect punishment has on followers' satisfaction and performance. Most people probably would predict that leaders who use punishment more frequently will probably have less-satisfied and lower-performing followers. Interestingly, this does not appear to be the case—at least when punishment is used appropriately. Let us look a little more closely at this issue.

Several researchers have looked at whether leaders who administer punishment on a contingent basis also administered rewards on a contingent basis. Generally, researchers have found that there is a moderate positive relationship between leaders' contingent reward behaviors and contingent punishment behaviors.[26–28] There also are consistently strong negative correlations found between leaders' contingent reward and noncontingent punishment behaviors. Thus, leaders meting out rewards on a contingent basis were also more likely to administer punishment only when followers behaved inappropriately or were not performing up to standards.

Keller and Szilagyi maintained that punishment can serve several constructive organizational purposes.[29,30] They said it can help clarify roles and expectations, as well as reduce role ambiguity. Several other authors have found contingent punishment either was unrelated to followers' satisfaction with their supervisor ratings or had a low positive relationship with it.[31,32] In other words, leaders who follow certain rules in administering punishment need not have dissatisfied subordinates. As a matter of fact, judicious and appropriate use of punishment by leaders may result in somewhat *higher* satisfaction of followers overall. These findings make sense when the entire work unit is considered; failing to use punishment when it seems called for in most followers' eyes may lead to perceptions of inequity, which may in turn lead to lower group cohesiveness and satisfaction.[33,34]

With respect to followers' work behaviors, Arvey and Jones reported that punishment has generally been found to reduce absenteeism and tardiness rates.[35] Nevertheless, the evidence about punishment's impact on performance appears mixed. Some authors report a strong positive relationship between punishment and performance,[36-39] whereas others found either no relationship between punishment and performance or a negative one.[40,41]

Despite such mixed findings, there are several points about the relationship between punishment and performance findings still worth noting. First, the level of punishment as well as the manner in which it was administered across studies could have differed dramatically, and these factors could have affected the results. Second, of the studies reporting positive results, Schnake's experiment of the vicarious effects of punishment is by far the most provocative. Schnake hired college students for a temporary job and, after several hours at work, publicly reduced the pay or threatened to reduce the pay of a confederate in the work group. As predicted, the more severe the punishment witnessed (either the threat of reduced pay or the reduction of pay), the higher the subsequent performance of other work-group members.[42]

Although these findings demonstrated that merely witnessing rather than receiving punishment could result in increased performance, these results should be interpreted with some caution. Because most of the individuals in the experiment did not know each other and had only been working together for several hours, there was probably not enough time for group cohesiveness or norms to develop. It is not at all clear whether members of cohesive groups or groups with strong norms would react in the same way if they had observed another group member being punished. Third, one of the studies reporting less favorable punishment–performance results made an important point about the opportunities to punish. It examined the relationships between Little League coaches' behaviors and their teams' win–loss records. They found coaches who punished more often had less-successful teams. These coaches also, however, had less-talented players and therefore had many more opportunities to use punishment. Coaches of successful teams had little if any reason to use punishment. Fourth, many behaviors that do get punished may not have a direct link to job performance. For example, being insubordinate, violating company dress codes, and arriving late to meetings are all punishable behaviors that may not be directly linked to solving work-related problems or producing goods or services.[43]

Finally, almost all these studies implicitly assumed punishment enhanced performance (by correcting problem behaviors), but Curphy and his associates were the only researchers who actually tested this assumption. They collected over 4,500 incidents of documented punishment and performance data from 40 identical organizations over a three-month period. (The punishment and performance data were collected monthly.) They found that low performance led to higher levels of punishment. Moreover, they found that inexperienced leaders administered almost twice as much punishment as experienced leaders. The authors hypothesized that inexperienced leaders used punishment (i.e., relied on their coercive power) more frequently because, by being the newest arrivals to the organization, they lacked knowledge of the organizational norms, rules, and policies (i.e., expert power); had not yet established relationships with followers (i.e., referent power); and were severely limited in the rewards they could provide to followers (i.e., reward power).[44]

In summary, the research evidence shows that punishment can lead to positive organizational outcomes if administered properly. When administered on a contingent basis, it may help increase job satisfaction, may decrease role ambiguity and absenteeism rates, and, depending on the behaviors being punished, may have a positive effect on performance. However, administering intense levels of punishment in a noncontingent or capricious manner can have a devastating effect on the work unit. Group cohesiveness may suffer, followers are likely to become more dissatisfied and less apt to come to work, and they may perform at a lower level in the long term. Thus, learning how to properly administer punishment may be the key to maximizing the benefits associated with its use.

Administering Punishment

Usually, leaders administer punishment in order to rectify some type of behavioral or performance problem at work. However, not every behavior or performance problem is punished, and leaders probably weigh several different factors before deciding whether or not to administer punishment. Green and Mitchell maintained that leaders' decisions concerning punishment depended on whether leaders made internal or external attributions about a subordinate's substandard performance. Leaders making internal attributions were more likely to administer punishment; leaders making external attributions were more likely to blame the substandard performance on situational factors beyond the follower's control.[45]

Attribution theory maintains that leaders weigh three factors when making internal or external attributions about a follower's substandard performance. More specifically, leaders would be more likely to make an internal attribution about a follower's substandard performance (and administer punishment) if the follower had previously completed the task before, if other followers had successfully completed the task, and if the follower had successfully completed other tasks in the past. Moreover, it was found that leaders were biased toward making internal attributions about followers' poor performance (i.e., the fundamental attribution error) and thus more likely to use punishment to modify a follower's behavior.[46,47]

Because leaders are biased toward making internal attributions about followers' substandard performance, leaders can administer punishment more effectively by being aware of this bias and getting as many facts as possible *before* deciding whether or not to administer punishment. Leaders also can improve the manner or skill with which they administer punishment by using certain tips, such as punishment is administered most effectively when it focuses on the act, not the person.[48] Followers probably cannot change their personalities, values, or preferences, but they can change their behaviors. By focusing on specific behaviors, leaders minimize the threat to followers' self-concepts. Also, punishment needs to be consistent across *both* behaviors and leaders; the same actions need to have the same consequences across work groups, or feelings of inequity and favoritism will pervade the organization. One way to increase the consistency in punishment is through the establishment of clearly specified organizational policies and procedures.

Administering punishment properly depends on effective two-way communication between the leader and follower. Leaders need to provide a clear rationale for punishment and indicate the consequences for unacceptable behavior in the future. Finally, leaders need to provide followers with guidance about how to improve. This guidance may entail role-modeling proper behaviors for followers, suggesting followers take additional training courses, or just giving followers accurate feedback about their behavior at work.[49]

Overall, it may be the manner in which punishment is administered, rather than the level of punishment, that has the greatest effect on followers' satisfaction and performance. Leaders need to realize that they may be biased toward administering punishment to rectify followers' substandard performance, and the best way to get around this bias is to collect as much information as possible before deciding whether or not to punish. By collecting the facts, leaders will be better able to focus on the act, not the person; be able to administer a punishment consistent with company policy; provide the rationale for the punishment; and give guidance to followers on how to improve.

A final caution which leaders need to be aware of concerns the reinforcing or rewarding nature of punishment. As stated earlier in the discussion of the operant approach to motivation, behaviors that are rewarded are likely to be repeated. When leaders administer punishment and subsequently see improvement in a follower's behavior, the leader will be rewarded and be more apt to use punishment in the future. Over time, this may lead to an overreliance on punishment and an underemphasis of the other motivational strategies as the means for correcting performance problems. Again, by collecting as much information as possible and by carefully considering the applicability of goal setting, the operant approach, job characteristics theory, and so on, to the problem, leaders may be able to successfully avoid having only one tool in their motivational tool kit.

Delegating

Why Delegating Is Important
Common Reasons for Avoiding Delegation
Principles of Effective Delegation

Although delegation is a relatively simple way for leaders to free themselves of time-consuming chores; provide followers with developmental opportunities; and increase the number of tasks accomplished by the work group, team, or committee, delegation is often an overlooked and underused management option.[50,51] Delegation implies that one has been empowered by one's leader, boss, or coach to take responsibility for completing certain tasks or engaging in certain activities. Delegation gives the responsibility for decisions to those individuals most likely to be affected by or to implement the decision, and delegation is more concerned with autonomy, responsibility, and follower development than with participation. Research has shown that leaders who delegate authority more frequently often have higher-performing businesses,[52] but followers are not necessarily happier when their leaders frequently delegate tasks.[53] Bass maintained that the latter findings were due to subordinates who felt they were (*a*) not delegated the authority needed to accomplish delegated tasks, (*b*) monitored too closely, or (*c*) only delegated tasks leaders did not want to do.[54] Nevertheless, Wilcox showed that leaders who delegated skillfully had more satisfied followers than leaders who did not delegate well.[55] Because leaders who delegate skillfully often have more satisfied and higher-performing work groups, teams, or committees, the following suggestions from Taylor are provided to help leadership practitioners delegate more effectively and successfully. Taylor provided useful ideas about why delegating is important, common reasons for avoiding delegation, and principles of effective delegation.[56]

Why Delegating Is Important

Delegation Frees Time for Other Activities
The essence of leadership is achieving goals through others, not trying to accomplish them by oneself. Learning to think like a leader partly involves developing a frame of mind wherein one thinks in terms of the

whole group's or organization's capabilities and not just one's own. This requires a new frame of reference for many individuals, especially those whose past successes resulted primarily from personal achievement in interpersonally competitive situations. Still, leaders typically have so many different responsibilities, they invariably must delegate some of them to others.

It is not just the mere quantity of work that makes delegation necessary. There is a qualitative aspect, too. Because leaders determine what responsibilities will be delegated, the process is one by which leaders can ensure that their time is allocated most judiciously to meet group needs. The leader's time is a precious commodity that should be invested wisely in those activities for which the leader is uniquely suited or situated to accomplish and that will provide the greatest long-term benefits to the group. What the leader *can* delegate, the leader *should* delegate.

Delegation Develops Followers

Developing subordinates is one of the most important responsibilities any leader has, and delegating significant tasks to them is one of the best ways to support their growth. It does so by providing opportunities for initiative, problem solving, innovation, administration, and decision making. By providing practical experience in a controlled fashion, delegation allows subordinates the best training experience of all: learning by doing.

Delegation Strengthens the Organization

Delegation is an important way to develop individual subordinates, but doing so also strengthens the entire organization. For one thing, an organization that uses delegation skillfully will be a motivating one to work in. Delegation sends an organizational signal that subordinates are trusted and their development is important. Moreover, skillful delegation inherently tends to increase the significance and satisfaction levels of most jobs, thus making subordinates' jobs better. Delegation also can be seen as a way of developing the entire organization, not just the individuals within it. To the extent that a whole organization systematically develops its personnel using delegation, its overall experience level, capability, and vitality increase. Finally, delegation stimulates innovation and generates fresh ideas and new approaches throughout the whole organization.

Common Reasons for Avoiding Delegation

Delegation Takes Too Much Time

Delegation saves time for the leader in the long run, but it costs time for the leader in the short run. It takes time to train a subordinate to perform any new task, so it often really does take less time for a leader to do the task herself than to put in the effort to train someone else to do it. When a task is a recurring or repetitive one, however, the long-term savings will make the additional effort in initial training worth it—both for the leader and for the subordinate.

Delegation Is Risky

It can feel threatening to delegate a significant responsibility to another person because doing so reduces direct personal control over the work one will be judged by.[57] Delegation may be perceived as a career risk by staking one's own reputation on the motivation, skill, and performance of others. It is the essence of leadership, though, that the leader will be evaluated in part by the success of the entire team. Furthermore, delegation need not and should not involve a complete loss of control by the leader over work delegated to others. The leader has a responsibility to set performance expectations, ensure that the task is understood and accepted, provide training, and regularly monitor the status of all delegated tasks and responsibilities.[58]

The Job Will Not Be Done as Well

Often the leader can do many specific tasks or jobs better than anyone else. That is not surprising, as the leader is often the most experienced person in the group. This fact, however, can become an obstacle to delegation. The leader may rationalize not delegating a task to someone else because the follower lacks technical competence and the job would subsequently suffer.[59] However, this may be true only in the short term, and letting subordinates make a few mistakes is a necessary part of their development, just as it was for the leader at an earlier stage in her own development. Few things are likely to be so stifling to an organization as a leader's perfectionistic fear of mistakes. When thinking about delegating tasks to others, leaders should remember what their own skill levels used to be, not what they are now. Leaders should assess subordinates' readiness to handle new responsibilities in terms of the former, not the latter.

The Task Is a Desirable One

A leader may resist delegating tasks that are a source of power or prestige. He may be quite willing to delegate relatively unimportant responsibilities but may balk at the prospect of delegating a significant one having high visibility.[60,61] The greater the importance and visibility of the delegated task, though, the greater will be the potential developmental gains for the subordinate. Furthermore, actions always speak louder than words, and nothing conveys trust more genuinely than a leader's willingness to delegate major responsibilities to subordinates.

Others Are Already Too Busy

A leader may feel guilty about increasing a subordinate's already full workload. It is the leader's responsibility, though, to continually review the relative priority of all the tasks performed across the organization.

Such a review might identify existing activities that could be eliminated, modified, or reassigned. A discussion with the subordinate about her workload and career goals would be a better basis for a decision than an arbitrary and unilateral determination by the leader that the subordinate could not handle more work. The new responsibility could well be something the subordinate wants and needs, and she might also have some helpful ideas about alternative ways to manage her present duties.

Principles of Effective Delegation

Decide What to Delegate

The first step leaders should take when deciding what to delegate is to identify all of their present activities. This should include those functions regularly performed and decisions regularly made. Next, leaders should estimate the actual time spent on these activities. This can be done fairly easily by developing and maintaining a temporary log. After collecting this information, leaders need to assess whether each activity justifies the time they are spending on it. In all likelihood, at least some of the most time-consuming recurring activities should be delegated to others. This process will probably also identify some activities that could be done more efficiently (either by the leader or someone else) and other activities that provide so little benefit they could be eliminated completely.

Decide Whom to Delegate To

There might be one individual whose talent and experience makes her the logical best choice for any assignment. However, leaders must be careful not to overburden someone merely because that individual always happens to be the best worker. Additionally, leaders have a responsibility to balance developmental opportunities among all their followers. Leaders should look for ways to optimize, over a series of assignments, the growth of all subordinates by matching particular opportunities to their respective individual needs, skills, and goals.

Make the Assignment Clear and Specific

As with setting goals, leaders delegating an assignment must be sure the subordinate understands just what the task involves and what is expected of him. Nevertheless, at times leaders provide too brief an explanation of the task to be delegated. A common communication error is overestimating one's own clarity, and in the case of delegation this can happen when the leader already knows the ins and outs of the particular task. Some of the essential steps or potential pitfalls in an assignment that seem self-evident to the leader may not be as obvious to someone who has never done the assignment before. Leaders should welcome questions and provide a complete explanation of the task. The time leaders invest during this initial training will pay dividends later on. When giving an assignment, leaders should ensure that they cover all of the points listed in Highlight P3.3.

Points to Cover When Delegating a Task

HIGHLIGHT P3.3

How does the task relate to organizational goals?

When does the subordinate's responsibility for the task begin?

How has the task been accomplished in the past?

What problems were encountered with the task in the past?

What sources of help are available?

What unusual situations might arise in the future?

What are the limits of the subordinate's authority?

How will the leader monitor the task (e.g., provide feedback)?

Finally, in covering the above points, always convey high confidence and expectations.

Assign an Objective, Not a Procedure

Indicate what is to be accomplished, not *how* the task is to be accomplished. End results are usually more important than the methods. It is helpful to demonstrate procedures that have worked before, but not to specify rigid methods to follow in the future. Leaders should not assume their ways always were and always will be best. Leaders need to be clear about the criteria by which success will be measured, but allowing subordinates to achieve it in their own ways will increase their satisfaction and encourage fresh ideas.

Allow Autonomy, but Monitor Performance

Effective delegation is neither micro-management of everything the subordinate does nor laissez-faire indifference toward the subordinate's performance. Leaders need to give subordinates a degree of autonomy (as well as time, resources, and authority) in carrying out their new responsibilities, and this includes the freedom to make certain kinds of mistakes. An organizational climate where mistakes are punished suppresses initiative and innovation. Furthermore, mistakes are important sources of development. Knowing this, one wise executive reassured a subordinate who expected to be fired for a gigantic mistake by saying, "Why should I fire you when I've just invested $100,000 in your development?"[62]

Once a task has been delegated, even though the subordinate's training and development are continuing, the leader should be cautious about providing too much unsolicited advice or engaging in "rescue" activities. An exception would be when a subordinate's mistake would put significant organizational assets at risk. On the other hand, the leader needs to establish specific procedures for periodically reviewing the subordinate's performance of the delegated task. Leaders need to maintain good records of all the assignments they have delegated, including appropriate milestone and completion dates for each one.

Give Credit, Not Blame

Whenever leaders delegate, they must give subordinates *authority* along with responsibility. In the final analysis, however, leaders always remain fully responsible and accountable for any delegated task. If things should go wrong, then *leaders* should accept responsibility for failure fully and completely and never try to pass blame on to subordinates. On the other hand, if things go well, as they usually will, then leaders should give all the public credit to the subordinates. Also, when providing performance feedback privately to a subordinate, emphasize what went right rather than what went wrong. Leaders should not ignore errors in judgment or implementation, but they need not dwell on them, either. One helpful approach to performance feedback is called the sandwich technique. With this technique, negative feedback is placed in between two "pieces" of positive feedback. It affirms the subordinate's good work, puts the subordinate at least somewhat at ease, and keeps the ratio of positive and negative comments in balance. The idea of a sandwich, however, should not be taken too literally. There is nothing magical about two pieces of positive feedback for one piece of negative feedback. In fact, from the receiver's point of view the balance between positive and negative feedback may seem "about right" when the ratio is considerably higher than 2:1.

In summary, Taylor has provided useful insight about the importance of delegation as well as specific and helpful suggestions for delegating more effectively.

Team Building for Work Teams

Team-Building Interventions
What Does a Team-Building Workshop Involve?
Examples of Interventions

Few activities have become more commonplace in organizations these days than "team-building workshops." One reason for this level of activity is the powerful shift that has occurred in the workplace from a focus primarily on individual work to team-centered work. Unfortunately, however, they do not always achieve their objectives. As noted earlier in this text, it doesn't make sense to hold teams responsible for work if nothing else in the organizational environment changes. Team-building interventions, at the team level, may help team members understand why they are having so much difficulty in achieving team objectives, and even suggest coping strategies for an intolerable situation. They are not, however, very likely to remove root causes of the problem. In order to better understand the importance of looking at teams this way, let's use an example of this kind of erroneous thinking from a quite different context.

Team-Building Interventions

Suppose you have decided that the next car you drive must have outstanding ride and handling characteristics. Some cars you test, such as some huge American-made automobiles, have outstanding ride characteristics, but you are not happy with their handling. They sway and "float" in tight slalom courses. Other cars you test have just the opposite characteristics. They are as tight and as stable as you could hope for in turns and stops, but their ride is so hard that your dental work is in serious jeopardy. But you do find one car that seems to meet your requirements. In fact, a Mercedes-Benz does provide both an extremely comfortable ride and tremendous road handling characteristics in high-performance situations. There is, however, one small problem. The Mercedes costs a lot of money up front—more than you are willing to put into this project. So you arrive at an alternative solution. You find a used Yugo, a little car built in Yugoslavia and no longer imported into the United States, largely because of inferior quality. But it is really cheap, and after purchasing it, you know you will have lots of money left over to beef up the suspension, steering, and braking systems to provide you with the Mercedes-Benz ride you really want.

Ludicrous! Obviously, you are never going to get a Mercedes-Benz ride unless you are willing to put in considerable money and effort *up front* rather than doing little up front and putting all your money into repair work. But that is precisely what many organizations are attempting to do with teams. They do not seem willing to create the conditions necessary for teamwork to occur naturally (a point we will discuss in the section "Team Building at the Top"), but when the teams struggle in a hostile environment, as they invariably will, the leaders seem more than willing to pour tremendous amounts of money into team-building interventions to fix the problem. (And there are lots of team-building consultants out there willing to take their money.) These types of team-building problems are those we would categorize as "top-down."

An equally vexing problem occurs when organizations are committed to teamwork and are willing to change structures and systems to support it, but are not committed to the "bottom-up" work that will be required. This is best illustrated in the rationale for team training shown in Figure P3.1. In our work with organizations, we are frequently asked to help teams that are struggling. In Figure P3.1 we would place these requests at the "TEAM" level, which is the third platform up from the bottom. We believe this type of intervention will work only if the team members have achieved a stable platform from which to work. In this case, that would include the two previous platforms in Figure P3.1. If the foundation is not well established, the solely team-based intervention often leads to intrateam competition or apathy and withdrawal.

As a basis for any work at the team level, individual team members must first be comfortable with themselves. They must be able to answer the questions, "What do I bring to the team?" and "What do *I* need from

FIGURE P3.1 A rationale for individual, interpersonal, team, and organizational training.

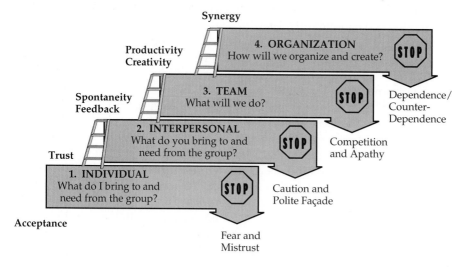

the team?" Not to answer these questions breeds inherent fear and mistrust. When these questions have been answered, team members are then in a position to begin dealing at the interpersonal level, where they may now comfortably ask, "What do *you* bring to the team and what do *you* need from the team?" Not to resolve these issues results in caution in dealing with other members, and interactions at the "polite-façade" level rather than at the level of truth and understanding. If the first- and second-level platforms are in place, a true team-building intervention can be useful. (Incidentally, just because team members have not stabilized themselves at levels 1 and 2 does not mean an intervention can not be conducted. Rather, it means a more extensive intervention will be required than a solely team-based effort.)

What Does a Team-Building Workshop Involve?

There are literally hundreds, if not thousands, of team-building interventions that are being conducted today. There are many good sources, such as the *Team and Organization Development Sourcebook,* which contain team-based activities such as conflict resolution, problem solving, development of norms, trust building, or goal setting, to name but a few. Rather than trying to describe all of these suggestions, however, we will give you a few recommendations that we have found to be useful and then share a few examples of interventions we have used.

At the Center for Creative Leadership, staff are frequently asked to design custom team interventions for mid- to upper-level teams. While we enter these design meetings with no agenda of activities, neither do we enter with a completely blank slate. We believe an intervention at the team level must meet three general requirements to be successful, and at least one activity must be included in the intervention pertaining to each of those three requirements.

The first requirement involves awareness raising. As we noted in our previous chapters, not all cultures are equally prepared or nurtured in the concepts of teamwork. In fact, many of the lessons we think we have learned about teams are incorrect. So we believe we need to dispel such myths and include a healthy dose of team-based research findings about how teams *really* work as a critical element of a workshop. Second, we need some diagnostic, instrument-based feedback so team members can have a reasonably valid map of where they and their teammates now are located. Finally, each intervention must include a practice field, to use Senge's term.[63] Practice is necessary for athletic success, and it is necessary in organizations too. It would be foolish to design a whole new series of plays for a hockey team to implement, talk about them in the locker room, but never actually practice any of them before expecting the team to implement them in a game. Similarly, if you are asking people to change their behaviors in the way they interact to improve teamwork, then it is only fair to provide them with a practice field upon which they can test their new behaviors in a reasonably risk-free, protected environment. This is where experiential exercises can be extremely useful. And it is here that the quality of the team-building facilitator is most critical. Conducting a pencil-and-paper exercise in the classroom does not require the same facilitator skill set as that required to conduct, say, a team-rappelling exercise off the face of a cliff—few facilitators get those requirements wrong and we have seldom discovered problems here. Where we have seen a significant breakdown in facilitator skills is in being able to make the link between the exercise that is conducted and the real world in which the team will be asked to perform. Here facilitators must have not only a good sense of real-time team dynamics, but also a sense of the business in which the team operates. They must help the participants make the links back to team dynamics that occur on the manufacturing floor or in the boardroom, and this seems to be the skill that separates highly effective facilitators from the pack.

Examples of Interventions

Now let us provide a few examples of the range of interventions that can be included in team building. Ginnett conducted an intervention with three interdependent teams from a state youth psychiatric hospital. The teams included members of the administrative services, the professional staff, and the direct care providers. The members of each team were dedicated to their roles in providing high-quality service to the youths under their care, but the three groups experienced great difficulty in working with each other. Extensive diagnosis of the groups revealed two underlying problems. First, each group had a very different vision of what the hospital was or should be. Second, each of the groups defined themselves as "care givers," thus making it very difficult for them to ask others for help since, in their minds, asking for help tended to put them in the role of their patients. We conducted a series of workshops to arrive at a common vision for the hospital, but the second problem required considerably more work. Since the staff members needed to experientially understand that asking for help did not place them in an inherently inferior position, a "Wilderness Experience" was designed where the entire staff was asked to spend four days together in a primitive wilderness environment with difficult hiking, climbing, and mountaineering requirements. By the end of the experience, everyone had found an occasion to ask someone else for help. Even more important, everyone found that actually asking others for help—something they had previously resisted—moved the overall team much higher in its ability to perform. Considerable time was spent each evening linking the lessons of the day with the work in the hospital.[64]

In one of the more interesting programs we've conducted, a team of senior executives spent a week together at a ranch in Colorado. Each morning, the team met for a series of awareness sessions and data feedback sessions. Afternoons were reserved by the chief operating officer for fun and relaxation, with the only requirement being that attendees participate in them as a team or subteams. As facilitators, we actively participated with the teams, and related their team experiences each day to the lessons of the next morning, and to challenges facing the team in its normal work. In interventions like this we have learned that team building can be fun, and that the venues for it are almost limitless. Second, we have learned that being able to observe and process team activity in a real-time mode is critical for team-building facilitators. There is no substitute for firsthand observation as a basis for discerning group dynamics and noting the variety of revealing behaviors that emerge in unstructured team activities.

Building High Performance Teams: The Rocket Model

Mission

Talent

Norms

Buy-In

Power

Morale

Results

Implications of the Rocket Model

As stated throughout this text, leadership is not an individual process. Rather, it involves influencing a group to pursue some type of overarching goal. From Chapter 10 we know that teams vary on a number of important factors, such as group size, norms, development stages, and cohesion. We also know that leaders need to take these factors into consideration when creating and leading teams. The Team Leadership Model in Chapter 10 provides a very comprehensive description of team dynamics and what leaders must do if they want to create high performing teams. What follows is a much simpler and more pragmatic model of team effectiveness. **The Rocket Model of Team Effectiveness** is both a prescriptive and diagnostic model of team building.[65–68] The model is prescriptive in that it tells leaders what steps to take and when to take them when building new teams. The model can also be used as a diagnostic tool for understanding where existing teams are falling short and what leaders need to do to get them back on track.

The Rocket Model is based on extensive research on and experience with teams in the health care, education, retail, manufacturing, service, software, telecommunications, energy, and financial service industries. The model has been used with executive teams at The Home Depot, Waste Management, and the Strategic Health Authority in the United Kingdom; midmanagement teams at Waste Management, Pfizer, and a number of rural hospitals and school districts; and project teams at Qwest Communications and Hewlett-Packard. The model seems to work equally well with different types of teams at different organizational levels in different industries. Leaders in particular like the Rocket Model because of its straightforward and practical approach to team building.

A graphic of the Rocket Model can be found in Figure P3.2. As depicted in the graphic, building a team can be analogous to building a rocket. Just as the booster stage is critical for getting a rocket off the ground, so are the Mission and Talent stages critical for starting a team. Once the Mission and Talent issues have been addressed, leaders will then need to work with team members to sort out team Norms and Buy-In, and so on. Research shows that the teams with the best Results are usually those who report a high level of team functioning on the six other components of the Rocket Model. Teams reporting a high level of functioning in only some of the components usually report mediocre Results, and those with low functioning on all six components usually achieve few if any Results. The following is a more in-depth description of the seven components of the Rocket Model.

Mission

When building a new team, the first thing a leader must do is clarify the team's purpose and goals, set team performance standards, and ensure individual team member goals are aligned with the team's goals. Thus, the **Mission** component of the Rocket Model is concerned with setting a common direction for the team. In some cases the leader works closely with team members to sort out these issues; in other cases the leader makes these determinations; and in other cases the organization may

FIGURE P3.2
The Rocket Model.

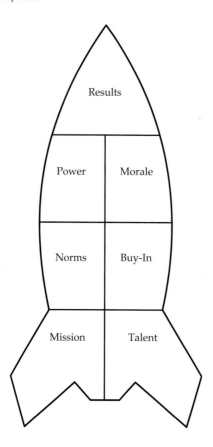

make these decisions. For this component of the model, who makes these decisions is not as important as ensuring that everyone on the team understands what the team is trying to accomplish and how they personally contribute to team success. Teams with this common understanding often experience much lower levels of role ambiguity and conflict.

Of all the components in the Rocket Model, Mission may be the most important component. This is the case because it drives all the other components of the model. The Mission of the team will play a big role in determining the number and skills of people needed to achieve results (Talent), the rules by which the team operates (Norms), and the equipment and budget needed (Power). Because Mission plays such a critical role in team building, leaders of underperforming teams often find it worthwhile to first review the team's purpose, goals, and performance standards when striving to improve team performance.

If we were to apply the Rocket Model to a learning team in a college Leadership course, then the first thing the team should do is clarify what the team wants to accomplish. This might include such things as everyone on the team getting an A on the midterm, final exam, and overall course.

Once the overall Mission and team goals are determined, the learning team would then need to decide who would do what and what the performance standards would be for each team member.

Talent

Teams with too many or too few people or with team members lacking the skills needed to achieve team goals often will report lower Talent scores than teams having the right number of people with the right skills. Selecting the right kind of people and continuously developing those skills needed to achieve team goals are two key leadership activities in this component of the Rocket Model. And the selection and development of Talent is precisely where many teams fall short. Professional athletic and elite military combat teams obsess over hiring decisions and spend countless hours practicing; they actually spend very little time performing. Most other teams seem to do just the opposite in that they do nothing more than throw a group of available people together and expect them to produce. These latter teams do not think through who needs to be on the team, spend little if any time developing needed skills, and never practice.

In the learning team example, Talent would come into play if team leaders selected their teammates on the basis of GPA and how well potential team members got along with others. Once the teams were assembled, team leaders would then determine what skills they still needed to develop and work to ensure the team improved in these areas. Team skills could be developed through coaching, training programs, practice test sessions, and so on. Of course, this scenario assumes the leader gets to pick team members. Many times leaders do not have this luxury. If leaders do not get to pick team members, then it is imperative that they assess and develop those skills needed to accomplish team goals.

Norms

Once team members are selected and have a clear understanding of the team's purpose and goals, leaders then need to address the Norms component of the Rocket Model. Norms are the rules that govern how teams make decisions, conduct meetings, get work done, hold team members accountable for results, and share information. There are several important aspects of norms that are worth noting. First, the decisions the team makes, the way in which it makes decisions, how often and how long the team meets, and so forth, should all be driven by the team's purpose and goals. Second, Norms happen. If the team or team leader is not explicit about setting the rules that govern team behavior, they will simply evolve over time. And when they are not explicitly set, these rules may run counter to the team's purpose and goals. For example, one of the authors was working with a software development team that was responsible for delivering several new products in a six-month time period. The time frame was very aggressive, but one of the team Norms that had evolved was that it was okay for team members to show up late to team meetings, if they even bothered to show up. But the team meetings were very important to the success of the team, as they were the only time the team could discuss problems and coordinate its software development efforts. Team member behavior did not change until an explicit Norm was set for team-meeting participation.

Third, there are many team Norms. These Norms might include where people sit in meetings, what time team members come in to work, what team members wear, the acronyms and terms they use, and so on. But of the domain of possible Norms, those involving decision making, communication, meetings, and accountability seem to be the most important to team functioning. High Performance Teams are very explicit about what decisions the team makes and how it makes those decisions. These teams have also set rules about the confidentiality of team meetings, when team members speak for themselves or speak for the team, and how difficult or controversial topics get raised in team meetings. High Performance Teams also have explicit rules about team meetings and team member accountability. In our learning team example, the team would need to decide how it would prepare for the midterm exam, what the format and quality of the prep material would be, how often and where they would meet to prepare for the exam, what they would do both in and outside of the preparation meetings, and how they would use the results of the midterm exams to adjust their preparations for the final exam. Corporate teams often fail because they do not explicitly set decision making, communication, meeting, and accountability Norms or ask themselves if the rules they have adopted are still working or need to be improved.

Buy-In

Just because team members understand the team's purpose and goals and the rules by which the team operates does not necessarily mean they will automatically be committed to them. Many times team members will do north to south head nods on the team's goals, rules, and action steps in team meetings, but then turn around and do something entirely different after the meetings. This is an example of a team that lacks Buy-In. Teams with high levels of Buy-In have team members who believe in what the team is trying to accomplish and will enthusiastically put forth the effort needed to make the team successful.

There are three basic ways team leaders can build Buy-In. One way to build Buy-In is to develop a compelling team vision or purpose. Many times team members want to be part of something bigger than themselves, and a team can be one venue for fulfilling this need. Whether or not team members will perceive the team to have a compelling vision will depend to a large extent on the degree to which the team's purpose and goals match up to their personal values. Charismatic or transformational leaders (Chapter 13) are particularly adept at creating visions aligned with followers' personal values. A second way to create Buy-In is for the team leader to have a high level of credibility. Leaders with high levels of relevant expertise who share trusting relationships with team members often enjoy high levels of Buy-In. Team members often question the judgment of team leaders who lack relevant expertise, and they question the agendas of team leaders they do not trust. And because people prefer to make choices as opposed to being told what to do, a third way to enhance team Buy-In is to involve team members in the goal, standard, and rule-setting process.

In our learning team example, team Buy-In would likely be enhanced if the team got together and jointly determined its purpose, goals, roles, and rules. Alternatively, the team leader could assemble a group of students who wanted to achieve the same means and believed being part of a team would be the best way to make an A in the class. Team Buy-In might be somewhat lower if the instructor determined the learning team's Mission and Norms. Many teams in the public and private sector world fail because team members do not trust the team leader, believe the team leader to be incompetent, do not see how they personally benefit from being on the team, or were not involved with setting the team's goals.

Power

The Power component of the Rocket Model concerns the decision-making latitude and resources the team has in order to accomplish its goals. Teams reporting high levels of Power have considerable decision-making authority and all of the equipment, time, facilities, and funds needed to accomplish team goals. Teams with low Power often lack the necessary decision-making authority or resources needed to get things done. One of the authors was working with a group of public school administrators who felt they had very little Power to make decisions affecting the school district. The district had had three superintendents over the past four years, and as a result the school board had stepped in to take over the day-to-day operation of the school district.

To improve the Power component of the Rocket Model, team leaders will first need to determine if they have all the decision-making latitude and resources they need to accomplish group goals. If they do not have enough Power, then they will either need to lobby higher-ups to get what they need, devise ways to get team goals accomplished with limited resources, or revise team goals in light of the resource shortfalls. Most teams do not believe they have all the time, resources, or decision-making latitude they need to succeed, but more often than not they have enough of these things to successfully accomplish their goals. Good teams figure out ways to make do with what they have or devise ways to get what they need; dysfunctional teams spend all their time and energy complaining about a perceived lack of resources rather than figuring out ways to achieve team goals. Along these lines, many poor performing teams often make false assumptions or erect barriers that do not really exist. Team leaders will need to challenge these assumptions and break barriers if they are to help the team succeed.

Team Power will play a role in our learning team. In this case, the team leader may need to secure a room or facility to conduct the study sessions, obtain computer resources for team members, or even work with the instructor to see if the members could take group rather than individual exams. The team will also need to determine how much time will be needed to adequately prepare for the examinations and whether all the team members can devote the time needed for the team to succeed. If the team does not have all the resources or time it believes it needs, then the team will either have to find ways to make do with what it has or make a downward revision of the team's goals.

Morale

Just because individual team members understand what the team is trying to accomplish, are committed to achieving team objectives, and understand the rules by which the team gets work done does not necessarily mean team members will all get along with each other. Teams that report high levels of Morale tend to effectively deal with interpersonal conflict and have high levels of morale and cohesion. This does not mean that highly cohesive teams do not experience interpersonal conflict. Instead, teams with high Morale scores have learned how to get conflict out in the open and deal with it in an effective manner. One way leaders can improve Morale is to work with team members to determine the rules for addressing team conflict. On the other hand, some of the best techniques for destroying team Morale are for leaders to either ignore interpersonal conflict or to tell team members to "quit fighting and just get along."

Because of values differences, work load inequities, miscommunication, and differing levels of commitment, it is likely that our learning team will experience some level of interpersonal conflict. If the learning team wanted to improve cohesiveness, then it would have to discuss how members were going to address conflict in the group. These discussions should happen relatively early in the group's formation and team conflict should be a regular topic in team meetings. Interestingly enough, many public and private sector teams report low Morale scores and often take some kind of action to improve team cohesiveness. Usually these actions include sending the team to some sort of team-building program, such as an outdoor learning or high ropes course. In almost all these cases, these interventions have little if any long-term effect on team cohesiveness, the reason being the Morale component of the Rocket Model is often a symptom of a deeper team problem. More often than not, the reason team members are not getting along is due to unclear goals and roles, ill-defined performance standards or accountability norms, a lack of commitment or resources, and so forth. In other words, the reason why team members are fighting has to do with a problem in one or more of the other components of the Rocket Model. Successfully addressing these problem components will not only improve results, they will also have a positive impact on team Morale.

Results

The Mission through Morale components of the Rocket Model describe the "how" of team building. In other words, these components tell team leaders what they specifically need to do if they need to improve team Mission, Norms, and so forth. The Results component of the Rocket model describes the "what" of team building—what did the team actually accomplish? Like Morale, Results are a symptom or an outcome of the other components of the Rocket Model. High performing teams get superior results because they have attended to the other six components of the Rocket Model. Those teams achieving less than optimal results can improve team performance by focusing on those problematic components of the Rocket Model. In our learning team example, if the team received a B on the midterm exam, the team could reexamine its purpose and goals, determine if it had some talent gaps, review its rules to see if they were spending enough time practicing the right things, find another venue or time to study, and so on.

One thing we do know about high performing teams is that they often build executable action plans with clear timelines and accountable parties in order to achieve results. These plans include key milestones and metrics, and good teams regularly review team progress and revise their plans accordingly. Many times these plans include specific action steps to improve team functioning as well as the actions specific team members need to take for the team to achieve results.

Implications of the Rocket Model

As stated at the beginning of this section, the Rocket Model is both prescriptive and diagnostic, and the model works equally well with student-through executive-level teams. When building a new team or determining where an existing team is falling short, leaders should always start with the Mission and Talent components before moving to other parts of the model. Just as a rocket needs a large booster to get off the ground, so do teams need a clear purpose and the right players in order to be successful. Along these lines, the Team Assessment Survey was designed to provide teams with feedback on where they stand with respect to the

FIGURE P3.3

Team assessment results for a dysfunctional health care team.

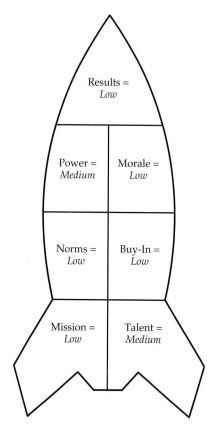

Results = *Low*

Power = *Medium*

Morale = *Low*

Norms = *Low*

Buy-In = *Low*

Mission = *Low*

Talent = *Medium*

seven components of the Rocket Model. Figures P3.3 and P3.4 show the results of two executive level teams. Figure P3.3 is a highly dysfunctional group of executives who led a billion dollar health care organization. Because these executives never learned how to work together as a team, many were let go less than six months after their Team Assessment Survey was completed. Figure P3.4 shows the results for a top executive team running a $6 billion retail organization. This team was more or less hitting on all cylinders; its only real issue was grooming a successor for the soon-to-retire division president.

Second, the components of the Rocket Model roughly correspond to Tuckman's four development stages of groups.[69] According to Tuckman, forming is the first stage teams go through. Team leaders can help teams to successfully work through this stage by focusing on the Mission and Talent components of the Rocket Model. Tuckman maintained that teams then go into the storming stage, during which team leaders should concentrate on the Norms and Buy-In components of the model. Team leaders should focus on Power and Morale in Tuckman's norming phase and the Results component of the Rocket Model in Tuckman's performing stage.

FIGURE P3.4
Team assessment results for a high performing retail team.

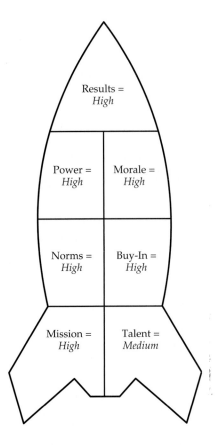

Results =
High

Power =
High

Morale =
High

Norms =
High

Buy-In =
High

Mission =
High

Talent =
Medium

Development Planning

Conducting a GAPS Analysis
Identifying and Prioritizing Development Needs: Gaps of GAPS
Bridging the Gaps: Building a Development Plan
Reflecting on Learnings: Modifying Development Plans
Transfering Learnings to New Environments

Change before you have to.

Jack Welch, former General Electric CEO

Development planning is the systematic process of building knowledge and experience or changing behavior. Two people who have done a considerable amount of cutting-edge research in the development planning process are Peterson and Hicks.[70–72] These two researchers believe development planning consists of five interrelated phases. The first phase of development planning is identifying development needs. Here leadership practitioners identify career goals, assess their abilities in light of career goals, seek feedback about how their behaviors are affecting others, and review the organizational standards pertaining to their career goals. Once this information has been gathered, the second phase consists of analyzing this data to identify and prioritize development needs. The prioritized development needs in turn are used to create a highly focused and achievable development plan, the third phase of this process. To help ensure permanent behavioral change takes place, the plan itself must utilize many of the best-practices techniques described in Chapter 8. Some of these best practices include having a plan that is limited to no more than two or three objectives, that capitalizes on on-the-job activities, and that incorporates multiple sources of feedback. The fourth phase in development planning is periodically reviewing the plan, reflecting on learnings, and modifying or updating the plan as appropriate. As you might expect, the Action-Observation-Reflection (AOR) model, described in Chapter 3, is a key component during this phase of the development planning process. The last phase in development planning is transferring learnings to new environments. Just because a leadership practitioner can successfully delegate activities to his 3-person team may not mean he will effectively delegate tasks or utilize his staff efficiently when he is leading a group of 25 people. In that case, the leader will need to build and expand on the delegation skills he learned when leading a much smaller team. These five phases are well grounded in research—several studies have shown that approximately 75 percent of the leadership practitioners adopting these phases were successful in either changing their behaviors permanently or developing new skills. Because these five phases are so important to the development planning process, the remainder of this section will describe each phase in more detail.[73–75]

Conducting a GAPS Analysis

The first phase in the development planning process is to conduct a GAPS (Goals, Abilities, Perceptions, Standards) analysis. A GAPS analysis helps leadership practitioners to gather and categorize all pertinent development planning information. A sample GAPS analysis for an engineer working in a manufacturing company can be found in Figure P3.5. This individual wants to get promoted to a first-line supervisor position within the next year, and all of the information pertinent to this promotion can be found in her GAPS analysis. The specific steps for conducting a GAPS analysis are as follows:

- *Step 1: Goals.* The first step in a GAPS analysis is to clearly identify what you want to do or where you want to go with your career over the next year or so. This does not necessarily mean moving up or getting promoted to the next level. An alternative career objective might be to master one's current job, as you may have just gotten promoted and advancing to the next level is not as important at the moment. Other career objectives might include taking on more responsibilities in your current position, taking a lateral assignment in another part of the company, taking an

FIGURE P3.5 A sample GAPS analysis.

Sources: D. B. Peterson and M. D. Hicks, *Leader as Coach*. Minneapolis, MN: Personnel Decisions International, 1996; G. J. Curphy, *Career and Development Planning Workshop: Planning for Individual Development*. Minneapolis MN: Personnel Decisions International, 1998.

Goals: Where do you want to go?	Abilities: What can you do now?
Step 1: Career objectives: Career strategies:	*Step 2:* What strengths do you have for your career objectives? *Step 3:* What development needs will you have to overcome?
Standards: What does your boss or the organization expect?	Perceptions: How do others see you?
Step 5: Expectations:	*Step 4:* 360-Degree and Performance Review Results, and feedback from others: • *Boss* • *Peers* • *Direct Reports*

overseas assignment, or even cutting back on job responsibilities to gain more work–life balance. This last career objective may be very appropriate for leaders who are just starting a family or are taking care of loved ones who are suffering from poor health. The two most important aspects of this step in the GAPS analysis are that leadership practitioners will have a lot more energy to work on development needs that are aligned with career goals, and in many cases advancing to the next level may not be a viable or particularly energizing career goal. This latter point may be especially true with organizations that have been recently downsized. Management positions often bear the brunt of downsizing initiatives, resulting in fewer available positions for those wishing to advance.

- *Step 2: Abilities.* People bring a number of strengths and development needs to their career goals. Over the years, you may have developed specialized knowledge or a number of skills that have helped you to be successful in your current and previous jobs. Similarly, you may also have received feedback over the years that there are certain skills you need to develop or behaviors you need to change. Good leaders know themselves—over the years they know which strengths they need to leverage and which skills they need to develop.
- *Step 3: Perceptions.* The perceptions component of the GAPS model concerns how your abilities, skills, and behaviors impact others. What are others saying about your various attributes? What are their reactions to both your strengths and your development needs? A great way of obtaining this information is by asking others for feedback or through performance reviews or 360-degree feedback instruments.
- *Step 4: Standards.* The last step in a GAPS analysis concerns the standards your boss or the organization has for your career objectives. For example, your boss may say that you may need to develop better public speaking, delegation, or coaching skills before you can get promoted. Similarly, the organization may have policies stating that people in certain overseas positions must be proficient in the country's native language, or it may have educational or experience requirements for various jobs.

When completing a GAPS analysis you may discover that you do not have all the information you need. If you do not, then you need to get it before you complete the next step of the development planning process. Only you can decide upon your career objectives, but you can solicit advice from others on whether these objectives are realistic given your abilities, the perceptions of others, and organizational standards. You may find that your one-year objectives are unrealistic given your development needs, organizational standards, or job opportunities. In this case, you may need to either reassess your career goals or consider taking a number of smaller career steps that will ultimately help you achieve your career goal. If you are lacking information about the other quadrants, then you can ask your boss or others whose opinions you value about your abilities, perceptions, or organizational standards. Getting as much up-to-date and pertinent information for your GAPS analysis will help ensure that your development plan is focusing on high-priority objectives.

Identifying and Prioritizing Development Needs: Gaps of GAPS

As seen in Figure P3.6, the Goals and Standards quadrants are future oriented; these quadrants ask where you want to go and what your boss or your organization expects of people in these positions. The Abilities and Perceptions quadrants are focused on the present; what strengths and development needs do you currently have and how are these attributes affecting others? Given what you currently have and where you want to

FIGURE P3.6

A gaps-of-the-GAPS analysis.

Sources: D. B. Peterson and M. D. Hicks, *Leader as Coach.* Minneapolis, MN: Personnel Decisions International, 1996); G. J. Curphy, *The Leadership Development Process Manual.* Minneapolis, MN: Personnel Decisions International, 1998.

Where you want to go

Goals

Standards

←— Gaps? —→

Where you are now

Abilities

Perceptions

Developmental Objectives

Current Position: _____
_____
_____
_____
_____
_____

Next Proposed Position:_____
_____
_____
_____
_____
_____

go, what are the gaps in your GAPS? In other words, after looking at all of the information in your GAPS analysis, what are your biggest development needs? And how should these development needs be prioritized? You need to review the information from the GAPS model, look for underlying themes and patterns, and determine what behaviors, knowledge, experiences, or skills will be the most important to change or develop if you are to accomplish your career goals.

Bridging the Gaps: Building a Development Plan

A gaps-of-the-GAPS analysis helps leadership practitioners identify high-priority development needs, but does not spell out what leaders need to do to overcome these needs. A good development plan is like a road map; it clearly describes the final destination, lays out the steps or interim checkpoints, builds in regular feedback to keep people on track, identifies where additional resources are needed, and builds in reflection time so that people can periodically review progress and determine whether an alternative route is needed. (See Figure 8.8 on page 296 for a sample development plan.) The specific steps for creating a high-impact development plan are as follows:

- *Step 1: Career and Development Objectives.* Your career objective comes directly from the Goals quadrant of the GAPS analysis; it is where you want to be or what you want to be doing in your career a year or so in the future. The development objective comes from your gaps-of-the-GAPS analysis; it should be a high-priority development need pertaining to your career objective. People should be working on no more than two to three development needs at any one time.

- *Step 2: Criteria for Success.* What would it look like if you developed a particular skill, acquired technical expertise, or changed the behavior outlined in your development objective? This can be a difficult step in development planning, particularly with "softer" skills, such as listening, managing conflict, or building relationships with others.

- *Step 3: Action Steps.* The focus in the development plan should be on the specific, on-the-job action steps leadership practitioners will take in order to overcome their development need. However, sometimes it is difficult for leaders to think of the on-the-job action steps to overcome their development needs. Three excellent resources that provide on-the-job action steps for overcoming a variety of development needs are two books, *The Successful Manager's Handbook*[76] and *For Your Improvement*,[77] and the development planning and coaching software *DevelopMentor*.[78] These three resources can be likened to restaurant menus in that they provide leadership practitioners with a wide variety of action steps to overcome just about any development need.

- *Step 4: Whom to Involve and Reassess Dates.* This step in a development plan involves feedback—whom do you need to get it from and how often do you need to get it? This step in the development plan is important as it helps to keep you on track. Are your efforts being noticed? Do people see any improvement? Are there things you need to do differently? Do you need to refocus your efforts?

- *Step 5: Stretch Assignments.* When people reflect on when they have learned the most, they often talk about situations where they felt they were in over their heads. These situations stretched their knowledge and skills and often are seen as extremely beneficial to learning. If you know of a potential assignment, such as a task force, a project management team, or a rotational assignment, that would emphasize the knowledge and skills you need to develop and accelerate your learning, you should include it in your development plan.

- *Step 6: Resources.* Oftentimes people find it useful to read a book, attend a course, or watch a videotaped program to gain foundational knowledge about a particular development need. These methods generally describe the how-to steps for a particular skill or behavior.

- *Step 7: Reflect with a Partner.* In accordance with the action-observation-reflection model of Chapter 3, people should periodically review their learnings and progress with a partner. The identity of the partner is not particularly important, as long as you trust his or her opinion and the partner is familiar with your work situation and development plan.

Reflecting on Learnings: Modifying Development Plans

Just as the development plan is a road map, this phase of development planning helps leaders to see whether the final destination is still the right one, if an alternative route might be better, and whether there is need for more resources or equipment. Reflecting on your learnings with a partner is also a form of public commitment, and people who make public commitments are much more likely to fulfill them. All things considered, in most cases it is probably better to periodically review your progress with your boss. Your boss should not be left in the dark with respect to your development, and periodically reviewing progress with your boss will help ensure there are no surprises at your performance appraisal.

Transfering Learnings to New Environments

The last phase in development planning concerns ongoing development. Your development plan should be a "live" document; it should be changed, modified, or updated as you learn from your experiences, receive feedback, acquire new skills, and overcome targeted development needs. There are basically three ways to transfer learnings to new environments. The first way is to constantly update your development plan. Another way to enhance your learning is to practice your newly acquired skills in a new environment. A final way to hone and refine your skills is to coach others in the development of your newly acquired skills. Moving from the student role to that of a master is an excellent way to reinforce your learnings.

Coaching

Forging a Partnership
Inspiring Commitment: Conducting a GAPS Analysis
Growing Skills: Creating Development and Coaching Plans
Promoting Persistence: Helping Followers Stick to Their Plans
Transferring Skills: Creating a Learning Environment
Concluding Comments

People who are coaches will be the norm. Other people won't get promoted.

Jack Welch, former General Electric CEO

A key success factor in most organizations today is having leaders and followers with the right knowledge and skills. More and more, companies are looking at "bench strength" as a competitive advantage moving into the next century. There are essentially two ways to acquire bench strength; employers can either buy (i.e., hire) the talent they need, or they can build their existing talent through development and coaching programs. Given that many employers face a labor shortage in certain critical positions, many are looking to build their own internal talent.[79] Much of this talent is being developed through informal coaching. As we noted in Chapter 8, most leaders engage in some form of informal coaching. But how good of coaches are they? The authors' conversations with a multitude of leaders indicate that almost every single one was unsure what to do as a coach. Some thought it involved directing their employees on how to do tasks. Others thought it involved counseling employees on personal problems. One stated that his only example of coaching came from his high school football coach, and he wouldn't want to wish that on anyone.

Two thought leaders in this area are Peterson and Hicks,[80] who described coaching as the "process of equipping people with the tools, knowledge, and opportunities they need to develop themselves and become more successful." According to Peterson and Hicks, good coaches orchestrate rather than dictate development. Good coaches help followers clarify career goals, identify and prioritize development needs, create and stick to development plans, and create environments that support learning and coaching. Coaching is really a blend of several different leadership skills. Being a good coach means having well-developed skills, determining where a follower is in the coaching process, and intervening as appropriate. The five steps of coaching provide leaders with both a good road map and a diagnostic model for improving the bench strength of their followers.

Peterson and Hicks pointed out that this model works particularly well for high performers—individuals who tend to benefit the most from, but are often overlooked by, leaders when coaching. We noted in Chapter 9 that high performers produce 20–50 percent more than average employees,[81] so coaching can have a considerable impact on the bottom line if it is targeted at high performers. Further support for the idea that top performers may benefit the most from coaching comes from athletics. If you watched any of the Sydney Olympics in 2000, then you would have seen that many of the world's top athletes had at least one and sometimes two or three coaches. If these world-class athletes feel that coaching can enhance their performance, then it is likely that good coaches can also enhance the performance of any organization's top employees. Although the five-step model also works with poorly performing employees, more appropriate interventions might also include diagnosing performance problems, goal setting, providing rewards and constructive feedback, and punishing these individuals, particularly if informal coaching is not achieving desired results.

Forging a Partnership

The first step in informal coaching involves establishing a relationship built on mutual trust and respect with a follower. If a follower does not trust or respect her leader, then it will be very unlikely that she will pay much attention to his ideas for her development. There are several things leaders can do to forge a partnership with coachees. First, it will be much easier for leaders with high credibility to build strong partnerships with followers than for leaders with low credibility. Therefore, leaders need to determine where they are on the credibility matrix (Figure P2.4 in Part 2), and they may need to take appropriate developmental steps to improve their credibility before their coaching suggestions will have much impact. These developmental steps may include building technical and organizational knowledge as well as building strong relationships with the individuals they want to coach. Having an understanding of the context in which the employee operates can be as important as the relationship the leader shares with the employee. In the "Building Credibility" section in Part 2, we noted that leaders will also need to spend time listening to their coachees; they need to understand coachees' career aspirations, values, intrinsic motivators, view of the organization, and current work situation. Good coaches can put themselves in their coachees' shoes, and can understand how coachees may view issues or opportunities differently than themselves. While forging a partnership, leaders can also provide coachees with realistic career advice, as sometimes coachees have unrealistic estimations of their skills and opportunities. For example, a new graduate from a top MBA program might want to be a partner at a consulting firm after two years with the company, but company policy may dictate that this decision will not be made until she has been with the firm for at least eight years. Her coach should inform her of this policy, and then work with her to map out a series of shorter-term career objectives that would help her become a partner in eight years. If coaches do not know what drives their coachees' behaviors, then another step to forging a partnership is to start asking a lot of questions. This is an excellent opportunity for leaders to practice their listening skills so as to better understand their coachees' career aspirations and intrinsic motivators.

Inspiring Commitment: Conducting a GAPS Analysis

This step in the coaching process is very similar to the GAPS analysis and the gaps-of-the-GAPS analysis, discussed in "Development Planning." The only difference is that these two analyses are now done from the coachee's perspective. Figure P3.7 might help to clarify this difference in perspective. Thus, in the Goals quadrant of the GAPS analysis the leader should write down the coachee's career objectives, and in the Perceptions quadrant the leader would write down how the coachee's behavior is impacting others. It is entirely possible that the leader may not be able to complete all of the quadrants of the GAPS for a coachee. If so, then the leader will need to gather more information before going any further. This

FIGURE P3.7 A GAPS analysis for an employee.

Source: D. B. Peterson, and M. D. Hicks, *Leader as Coach.* Minneapolis, MN: Personnel Decisions International, 1996; G. J. Curphy, *The Leadership Development Process Manual.* Minneapolis, MN: Personnel Decisions International, 1998.

Goals: What does the employee want to do?	Abilities: What can the employee do now?
Step 1: Career objectives: —To become an Engineering Supervisor	*Step 2:* What strengths does the employee have for his or her career objectives? — Understand operational side of the business — Good planning skills — Good job function definition skills — Set clear individual and team goals *Step 3:* What development needs will he or she have to overcome? — Multidirection communication; may need to improve listening skills — May need to improve conflict resolution skills
Standards: What do you or the organization expect?	Perceptions: How do others see the employee?
Step 5: Expectations: • *Boss:* To be promoted, will need to: — Get along better with peers — Develop stronger listening skills	*Step 4:* PPRP and feedback from others: • *Boss* — Good technician — Develops good plans and holds people accountable — More interested in own rather than others' ideas • *Peers* — Can be counted on to get the job done — Can be too set in ways; too argumentative • *Direct Reports* — Has clear goals — Understands technical side of business — Doesn't value our ideas and opinions

information gathering may include discussing career goals and abilities with the coachee, reviewing the coachee's 360-degree feedback results, asking peers about how the coachee comes across or impacts others, or asking human resources about the educational or experience standards relevant to the coachee's career goals. One way to gather additional information is to have both the leader and the coachee complete a GAPS analysis independently, and then get together and discuss areas of agreement and disagreement. This can help ensure that the best information is available for the GAPS analysis and also help to build the partnership between the leader and coachee. During this discussion the leader and coachee should also do a gaps-of-the-GAPS analysis to identify and prioritize development needs. Usually leaders will get more commitment to development needs if coachees feel they had an important role in determining these needs, and a gaps-of-the-GAPS discussion is a way to build buy-in. This discussion can also help ensure that development needs are aligned with career goals.

Growing Skills: Creating Development and Coaching Plans

Once the coachee's development needs are identified and prioritized, coachees will need to build development plans to overcome targeted needs. These plans are identical to those described in the "Development Planning" section. Leaders generally do not build development plans for their coachees. Instead, they may want to go over a sample (or their own) development plan and coach their coachees on the seven steps in building a plan. They can then either jointly build a plan or have the coachee individually build a plan for the leader to review. Providing coachees with an important role in development planning should increase their level of commitment to the plan. Once a draft development plan is created, the leader and coach can then use the development planning checklist in Table P3.1 to review the plan.

TABLE P3.1
Development Plan Checklist

Source: G. J. Curphy, *The Leadership Development Process Manual.* Minneapolis, MN: Personnel Decisions International, 1998.

Objectives:
- One-year career objective identified?
- No more than a total of two or three development goals?
- Areas in which the employee is motivated and committed to change and develop?

Criteria for Success:
- Is the new behavior clearly described?
- Can the behavior be measured or observed?

Action Steps:
- Specific, attainable, and measurable steps?
- Mostly on-the-job activities?
- Includes a variety of types of activities?
- Are activities divided into small, doable steps?

Seek Feedback and Support:
- Involvement of a variety of others?
- Includes requests for management support?
- Are reassess dates realistic?

Stretch Assignments:
- Do the stretch assignments relate to the employee's career objectives?

Resources:
- Uses a variety of books, seminars, and other resources?

Reflect with a Partner:
- Includes periodic reviews of learnings?

In addition to the development plan, leaders will need to build a coaching plan that outlines the actions they will take to support their coachees' development. Some of these actions might include meeting with the coachees on a regular basis to provide developmental feedback, identifying developmental resources or opportunities, or helping coachees reflect on what they have learned. As with development plans, leaders should share their coaching plans so that coachees know what kind of support they will be getting. This will also publicly commit the leaders to the coachees' development, which will make it more likely that they will follow through with the coaching plan.

Promoting Persistence: Helping Followers Stick to Their Plans

Just because development and coaching plans are in place is no guarantee that development will occur. Sometimes coachees build development plans with great enthusiasm, but then never take any further action. This step in the coaching process is designed to help coachees "manage the mundane." An example of managing the mundane might be illustrative. One of the authors successfully completed a triathlon. The most difficult part of this accomplishment was not the event itself, but rather doing all of the training needed to successfully complete the event. Similarly, the inability to stick to a diet or keep a New Year's resolution is primarily due to an inability to manage the mundane; people are initially committed to these goals but have a difficult time sticking to them. The same is true with development planning. Conducting a GAPS analysis and creating a development plan are relatively easy; sticking to the plan is much more difficult. From the leader's perspective, a large part of coaching is helping followers stick to their development plan.

Several development planning steps were specifically designed to promote persistence. For example, ensuring alignment between career and development objectives, getting feedback from multiple sources on a regular basis, and reflecting with a partner can help keep coachees focused on their development. If the leader is a coachee's developmental partner, then reflection sessions can help followers persist with their development. If leaders are not designated as partners in the development plan, then they should commit to meeting regularly with the coachees to discuss progress, what the leaders can do to support development, developmental opportunities, developmental feedback, and so forth.

Leaders can also help to promote persistence by capitalizing on coachable moments. Say a coachee was working on listening skills, and the leader and coach were in a staff meeting together. If the leader provides feedback to the coachee about her listening skills immediately after the staff meeting, then the leader has capitalized on a coachable moment. To capitalize on a coachable moment, leaders must know the followers' developmental objectives, be in situations where they can observe followers practicing their objectives, and then provide immediate feedback on their observations. Few coaches capitalize on coachable moments, but they can go a long way toward promoting persistence in coachees. It is important to note that capitalizing on coachable moments should take little time, often less than two minutes. In the example above, the leader could provide feedback to the coachee during their walk back to the office after the staff meeting.

Transferring Skills: Creating a Learning Environment

To build bench strength, leaders need to create a learning environment so that personal development becomes an ongoing process rather than a one-time event. As Tichy and Cohen[79] aptly point out, the most successful organizations are those that emphasize the learning and teaching process—they focus on constantly creating leaders throughout the company. In reality, leaders have quite a bit of control over the kind of learning environments they want to create for their followers, and there are several interventions they can take to ensure that development becomes an ongoing process. Perhaps the most important intervention is for leaders to role-model development. In that regard, if leaders are not getting regular feedback from followers, then they are probably not doing a good job of role-modeling development. By regularly soliciting feedback from followers, leaders are also likely to create a feedback-rich work environment. Once feedback becomes a group norm, people will be much more willing to help build team member skills, which in turn can have a catalytic effect on group performance. It is important to note that the leader will play a large role in this group norm, because if the leader is feedback averse, it will be difficult to see how this norm will be adopted by followers.

Leaders can also create learning environments by regularly reviewing their followers' development. Perhaps the easiest way to do this is by making leaders and followers development partners; then both parties can provide regular feedback and ongoing support. During these discussions leaders and followers should review and update their development plans to capitalize on new development opportunities or acquire new skills. Leaders and followers can also review coaching plans to see what is and is not working and make the necessary adjustments.

Concluding Comments

Perhaps one of the greatest misperceptions of coaching, and the primary reason why leaders state they do not coach others, is that it takes a lot of time. In reality, nothing could be further from the truth. Leaders are working to build credibility, build relationships with followers, and understand followers' career aspirations and view of the world. Although these do take time, they are also activities leaders should be engaged in even if they are not coaching followers. Doing a GAPS analysis, identifying and prioritizing development needs, helping followers create development plans, and creating coaching plans often takes less than four hours. Although leaders will need to take these steps with all their followers, these four hours can be spread out over a four- to six-week period. As stated earlier, meeting with followers on a regular basis to review development (perhaps monthly) and capitalizing on coachable moments also take little time. Finally, many of the actions outlined in "Transferring Skills: Create a Learning Environment" either take little time or are extensions of actions outlined earlier. The bottom line is that coaching really can take little additional time; it is really more a function of changing how you spend time with followers so that you can maximize their development.

Another note about the coaching model is that good coaches are equally versatile at all five steps of coaching. Some leaders are very good at forging a partnership, but then fail to carry development to the next level by conducting a GAPS analysis or helping followers build a development plan. Other leaders may help followers build a development plan but do not do anything to promote persistence or create a learning environment. Just as leaders need to develop their technical skills, so might they need to assess and in turn develop certain coaching skills. It is also important to remember that coaching is a very dynamic process—good coaches assess where followers are in the coaching process and intervene appropriately. By regularly assessing where they are with followers, they may determine that the relationship with a particular follower is not as strong as they thought, and this lack of relationship is why followers are not sticking to their development plan. In this case, a good coach would go back to forging a partnership with the follower and, once a trusting relationship had been created, go through another GAPS analysis, and so forth.

Finally, it is important to note that people can and do develop skills on their own. Nevertheless, leaders who commit to the five steps of informal coaching outlined above will both create learning organizations and help to raise development to a new level. Given the competitive advantage of companies that have a well-developed and capable workforce, in the future it will be hard to imagine leadership excellence without coaching. Good leaders are those who create successors, and coaching may be the best way to make this happen.

Empowerment

What Is Empowerment?
The Psychological Components of Empowerment
Six Best Practices of Empowerment

Do what you can, where you are at, with what you have.
Theodore Roosevelt

Inside every old company is a new company waiting to be born.
Alvin Toffler

Empowerment has become a very popular concept over the past 10 years. Many companies have embarked on various types of empowerment programs to improve results, yet the success of these programs has been mixed at best. One of the reasons for the mixed results is that empowerment often means different things to different people. This section describes what empowerment is (and is not), as well as some of the psychological constructs underlying empowerment and some of the best practices of empowering others.

What Is Empowerment?

In general, people seem to fall into one of two camps with respect to empowerment. Some people believe empowerment is all about delegation and accountability, a top-down process where senior leaders articulate a vision and specific goals, and hold followers responsible for achieving them. Others believe empowerment is more of a bottom-up approach that focuses on intelligent risk taking, growth, change, trust, and ownership; followers act as entrepreneurs and owners who question rules and make intelligent decisions. Leaders tolerate mistakes and encourage cooperative behavior in this approach to empowerment.[82] Needless to say, these two conceptualizations of empowerment have very different implications for leaders and followers. And it is precisely this conceptual confusion which has caused empowerment programs to fail in many organizations.[83] Because of the conceptual confusion surrounding empowerment, companies such as Motorola will not use this term to describe programs that push decision making to lower organizational levels. These companies would rather coin their own terms to describe these programs, thus avoiding the confusion surrounding empowerment.

We define empowerment as having two key components. For leaders to truly empower employees, they must delegate leadership and decision making down to the lowest level possible. Employees are often the closest to the problem and have the most information, and as such can often make the best decisions. A classic example was the UPS employee who ordered an extra 737 aircraft to haul presents that had been forgotten in the last-minute Christmas rush. This decision was clearly beyond the employee's level of authority, but UPS praised his initiative for seeing the problem and making the right decision. The second component of empowerment, and the one most often overlooked, is equipping followers with the resources, knowledge, and skills necessary to make good decisions. All too often companies adopt an empowerment program and push decision making down to the employee level, but employees have no experience creating business plans, submitting budgets, dealing with other departments within the company, or directly dealing with customers or vendors. Not surprisingly, ill-equipped employees often make poor, uninformed decisions, and managers in turn are likely to believe that empowerment was not all it was cracked up to be. The same happens with downsizing, as employees are asked to take on additional responsibilities but are provided with little training or support. As we stated in Chapter 9, this "forced" empowerment may lead to some short-term stock gains but tends to be disastrous in the long run. Thus, empowerment has both delegation and developmental components; delegation without development is often perceived as abandonment, and development without delegation can often be perceived as micro-management. Leaders wishing to empower followers must determine what followers are capable of doing, enhance and broaden these capabilities, and give followers commensurate increases in authority and accountability.

The Psychological Components of Empowerment

The psychological components of empowerment can be examined at both macro and micro levels. There are three macro psychological components underlying empowerment, and these are motivation, learning, and stress. As a concept, empowerment has been around since at least the 1920s, and the vast majority of companies that have implemented empowerment programs have done so to increase employee motivation and, in turn, productivity. As a motivational technique, however, empowerment has not lived up to its promise; empowered workers may not be any more productive than unempowered workers. There are several reasons why this may be the case. First, senior leaders tend to see empowerment through rose-colored glasses. They hear about the benefits an empowerment program is having in another company, but do not consider the time, effort, and changes needed to create a truly empowered workforce. Relatedly, many empowerment programs are poorly implemented—the program is announced with great fanfare, but little real guidance, training, or support is provided and managers are quick to pull the plug on the program as soon as followers start making poor decisions. Adopting an effective empowerment program takes training, trust, and time, but companies most likely to implement an empowerment program (as a panacea for their poor financial situation) often lack these three attributes.[84] Third, as described in Chapter 9, worker productivity and job dissatisfaction in the United States are at an all-time high. Many companies are dealing with high levels of employee burnout, and adding additional responsibilities to already overfilled plates is likely to be counterproductive. As reported by Xie and Johns, some empowerment programs create positions that are just too big for a person to handle effectively, and job burnout is usually the result.[85]

Although the motivational benefits of empowerment seem questionable, the learning and stress reduction benefits of empowerment seem more clear-cut. Given that properly designed and implemented empowerment programs include a strong developmental component, one of the key benefits to these programs is that they help employees learn more about their jobs, company, and industry. These knowledge and skill gains increase the intellectual capital of the company and can be a competitive advantage in moving ahead. In addition to the learning benefits, well-designed empowerment programs can actually help to reduce burnout. People can tolerate high levels of stress when they have a high level of control. Given that many employees are putting in longer hours than ever before and work demands are at an all-time high, empowerment can help followers gain some control over their lives and better cope with stress. Although an empowered worker may have the same high work demands as an unempowered worker, the empowered worker will have more choices on how and when to accomplish these demands and as such will suffer from less stress. And because stress is a key component of dysfunctional turnover, giving workers more control over their work demands can reduce turnover and in turn positively impact the company's bottom line.

There are also four micro components of empowerment. These components can be used to determine whether employees are empowered or unempowered, and include self-determination, meaning, competence, and influence.[86,87] Empowered employees have a sense of self-determination; they can make choices about what they do, how they do it, and when they need to get it done. Empowered employees also have a strong sense of meaning; they believe what they do is important to them and to the company's success. Empowered employees have a high level of competence in that they know what they are doing and are confident they can get the job done. Finally, empowered employees have an impact on others and believe that they can influence their teams or work units and that co-workers and leaders will listen to their ideas. In summary, empowered employees have latitude to make decisions, are comfortable making these decisions, believe what they do is important, and are seen as influential members of their team. Unempowered employees may have little latitude to make decisions, may feel ill equipped and may not want to make decisions, and may have little impact on their work unit, even if they have good ideas. Most employees probably fall somewhere in between the two extremes of the empowerment continuum, depicted in Figure P3.8. Leaders wanting to create more empowered followers may want to adopt some of the best-practices techniques outlined below.

FIGURE P3.8   The empowerment continuum.

Empowered Employee ⟷ **Unempowered Employees**

Empowered Employee	Unempowered Employees
• Self-determined	• Other-determined
• Sense of meaning	• Not sure if what they do is important
• High competence	• Low competence
• High influence	• Low influence

Six Best Practices of Empowerment

Do We Really Want or Need Empowerment?

Perhaps the first question leaders should ask before adopting an empowerment program is whether the company wants or needs empowerment. Leaders may agree that empowerment is important but may have fundamental differences as to the actions leaders need to take to create an empowered organization. Having a clear initial understanding of just what empowerment is will make the implementation of the program that much easier.

Leaders wanting to adopt an empowerment program must also consider how their own jobs and roles will be affected. They may need to fundamentally change their leadership style to better tolerate employee mistakes, play more of a coaching than directing role, and be willing to be challenged on a regular basis. Because empowered employees have access to considerably more information, they will be much more likely to question past or current decisions, and leaders will need to exert more personal power in order to get decisions adopted. Leaders feeling that this role transition is too much of a stretch will not enthusiastically embrace an empowerment program, making companywide adoption of the program difficult.

Creating a Clear Vision, Goals, and Accountabilities

Once a decision is made to develop and implement an empowerment program, top management must ensure that the company's vision, business strategies, and operational goals are clear and are understood by everyone in the company. It is difficult to ask employees to make wise decisions if they do not know where the company is headed. Employees should know what the company and work unit are trying to accomplish and how these accomplishments will be measured, and they should be given regular feedback on progress. In addition, employees will need to understand how their own goals are related to work-unit and company goals.

Developing Others

Just because employees have a clear understanding of their work goals does not mean they have the knowledge, skills, and resources necessary to get them accomplished. Leaders will need to determine what employees can currently do, what they need to be able to do, and how they will help employees bridge the gaps between current and future capabilities. Perhaps the best way to do this is for leaders to adopt the five steps described in the "Coaching" section. A key component of empowerment is trust, and leaders can build trust by taking the actions prescribed in "Forging a Partnership." Leaders can identify and prioritize development needs through a GAPS analysis, and can work to increase knowledge and skills through development plans, coaching plans, and the actions outlined under "Promoting Persistence" and "Transferring Skills." The five steps of informal coaching give leaders a road map for improving the bench strength of their followers and systematically equipping them to meet the increased challenges of empowerment. Taking these development steps helps with the competence component of empowerment.

Delegating Decision Making to Followers

Once followers are starting to develop the skills, knowledge, and experience necessary to make wise decisions, leaders must systematically increase the degree of latitude and autonomy employees are given to make decisions. Although this sounds fairly straightforward, in practice it can be fairly difficult. Some of the typical mistakes leaders make in this area are pushing followers into decision making too quickly, holding on to decision-making power too long, or taking decision-making power away from followers during a crisis. Other difficulties include the fact that many leaders associate decision making with leadership and may feel personally threatened by delegating decision-making authority to others. This may be particularly true when organizations have recently gone through a downsizing or when the level of trust between leaders and followers is low. Some followers may also feel reluctant to take on increased decision-making responsibility, as their level of skill may be exposed in ways it never had before.[88] Another complication is that some employees may feel that, because they are taking on additional responsibilities, they should be paid more. This is particularly true when empowerment programs are introduced in union environments.

One way to determine how much latitude and authority to provide followers is to use the Situational Leadership® Theory, described in Chapter 12. This model provides a useful heuristic for developing employees and determining when they are ready to take on additional decision-making responsibilities. Another way to effectively delegate decision making to followers is to provide clear boundaries around the decisions they make. For example, employees at the Ritz-Carlton hotels have fixed limits on the amounts employees can spend to satisfy disgruntled guests. As the level of followers' knowledge and experience increases, the scope of the decisions can be increased and their boundaries loosened. Leaders delegating tasks and responsibilities should also follow the tenets of setting goals and delegating described earlier in this section of the text. Because followers will not be very skilled in making wise decisions, leaders will need to be prepared to tolerate followers' mistakes and help them learn from these experiences. The actions outlined under this best practice will help with the self-determination and influence components of empowerment.

Leading by Example

Leaders must be an example of empowerment if they want to successfully empower their employees. An illustration of how a leader could role-model empowerment will be useful. A multimillion-dollar consulting firm, run by one of the authors, was facing an acute labor shortage. Customer requests for additional services created enough work for four new positions. The office had a strong financial track record, and financial analyses provided solid support for the additional positions. Moreover, employee workload was extremely high, and the office was in desperate need of additional help. Armed with these facts, the author submitted job requisitions for the four additional positions to corporate headquarters. But after two months and numerous phone calls to corporate staff, the positions did not seem to be any closer to being approved. The author went ahead and hired the four additional staff, and informed corporate headquarters of his decision once the new personnel were onboard. Although the author took a considerable amount of heat from the COO and the vice president of human resources, the office continued to be financially successful, office morale dramatically improved, and the author sent a clear signal to his staff to seek forgiveness rather than permission.

Quinn and Spreitzer have claimed that it is nearly impossible for unempowered leaders to empower followers.[89] Although there is some truth to this statement, empowerment needs to start somewhere, and it is all too easy for leaders to say that "they" are not allowing us to empower our followers. All too often "they" are the very same people who are making these statements, and it is their own preconceived notions of leadership and misunderstandings of empowerment that are getting in the way. When this occurs, it is all too easy for leaders to waste time finger-pointing and overlook the areas where they *can* empower followers. In the above example the author was not empowered to make these hiring decisions, yet he went ahead and did it anyway. This could have been a career-ending decision for the author, but he weighed the consequences of failing to hire additional help and thought the benefits were greater than the political costs. There is a certain amount of risk taking to leadership, and good leaders are those who themselves take, and allow their followers to take, intelligent risks. Like UPS and the employee who ordered the additional 737, good leaders reward intelligent risk taking and do not punish decisions that were well thought out but failed.

Empowerment Must Be Systemic to Be Successful

Although individual leaders who take initiative can empower their followers, it will be much easier and more effective if senior leadership embraces empowerment as a key business strategy. When reward and performance appraisal systems, selection systems, work processes, training programs, organizational structure, and information systems are strongly aligned with the organization's definition of empowerment, then all these programs will be very successful. On the other hand, merely introducing an empowerment program but failing to make the necessary adjustments in the organizational systems, processes, and structure will likely be a recipe for failure.

Part Notes

1. Greller, M. M. "Evaluation of Feedback Sources as a Function of Role and Organizational Development." *Journal of Applied Psychology* 65 (1980), pp. 24–27.

2. Komacki, J. L. "Why We Don't Reinforce: The Issues." *Journal of Organizational Behavior Management* 4, nos. 3–4 (1982), pp. 97–100.

3. Bass, B. M. *Bass and Stogdill's Handbook of Leadership.* 3rd ed. New York: Free Press, 1990.

4. Deep, S., and L. Sussman. *Smart Moves.* Reading MA: Addison-Wesley, 1990.

5. Larson, J. R., Jr. "Supervisors' Performance Feedback to Subordinates: The Impact of Subordinate Performance Valence and Outcome Dependence." *Organizational Behavior and Human Decision Processes* 37 (1986), pp. 391–408.

6. Harrison, E. L. "Training Supervisors to Discipline Effectively." *Training and Development Journal* 36, no. 11 (1982), pp. 111–13.

7. Parsons, C. K., D. M. Herold, and M. L. Leatherwood. "Turnover during Initial Employment: A Longitudinal Study of the Role of Causal Attributions." *Journal of Applied Psychology* 70 (1985), pp. 337–41.

8. Filley, A. C., and L. A. Pace. "Making Judgments Descriptive." In *The 1976 Annual Handbook for Group Facilitators.* Eds. J. E. Jones and J. W. Pfeiffer. La Jolla, CA: University Associates Press, 1976.

9. Coye, R. W. "Subordinate Responses to Ineffective Leadership." *Dissertation Abstracts International* 43 (6A) (1982), p. 2070.

10. Quaglieri, P. L., and J. P. Carnazza. "Critical Inferences and the Multidimensionality of Feedback." *Canadian Journal of Behavioral Science* 17 (1985), pp. 284–93.

11. Stone, D. L., H. G. Gueutal, and B. MacIntosh. "The Effects of Feedback Sequence and Expertise of Rater of Perceived Feedback Accuracy." *Personal Psychology* 37 (1984), pp. 487–506.

12. Bass, B. M. *Bass and Stogdill's Handbook of Leadership.* 3rd ed. New York: Free Press, 1990.

13. Arvey, R. D., and J. M. Ivancevich. "Punishment in Organizations: A Review, Propositions, and Research Suggestions." *Academy of Management Review* 5 (1980), pp. 123–32.

14. Curphy, G. J., F. W. Gibson, B. W. Asiu, C. P. McCown, and C. Brown. "A Field Study of the Causal Relationships between Organizational Performance, Punishment, and Justice." Working paper, 1992.

15. Arvey, R. D., and J. M. Ivancevich. "Punishment in Organizations: A Review, Propositions, and Research Suggestions." *Academy of Management Review* 5 (1980), pp. 123–32.

16. Skinner, B. F. *The Behavior of Organisms.* New York: Appleton-Century-Crofts, 1938.

17. Kazdin, A. E. *Behavior Modification in Applied Settings.* Homewood, IL: Dorsey, 1975.

18. Johnston, J. M. "Punishment of Human Behavior." *American Psychologist* 27 (1972), pp. 1033–54.

19. Solomon, R. L. "Punishment." *American Psychologist* 19 (1964), pp. 239–53.

20. Parke, R. D. "Some Effects of Punishment on Children's Behavior." In *The Young Child: Reviews of Research.* Vol. 2. Ed. W. W. Hartup. Washington, DC: National Association for the Education of Young Children, 1972.

21. Arvey, R. D., and J. M. Ivancevich. "Punishment in Organizations: A Review, Propositions, and Research Suggestions." *Academy of Management Review* 5 (1980), pp. 123–32.

22. Skinner, B. F. *The Behavior of Organisms.* New York: Appleton-Century-Crofts, 1938.

23. Luthans, F. 1989. *Organizational Behavior.* 5th ed. New York: McGraw-Hill, 1992.

24. Huberman, J. "Discipline without Punishment." *Harvard Business Review,* July–August 1964, p. 62.

25. Arvey, R. D., and J. M. Ivancevich. "Punishment in Organizations: A Review, Propositions, and Research Suggestions." *Academy of Management Review* 5 (1980), pp. 123–32.

26. Arvey, R. D., G. A. Davis, and S. M. Nelson. "Use of Discipline in an Organization: A Field Study." *Journal of Applied Psychology* 69 (1984), pp. 448–60.

27. Podsakoff, P. M., and W. D. Todor. "Relationships between Leader Reward and Punishment Behavior and Group Process and Productivity." *Journal of Management* 11 (1985), pp. 55–73.

28. Strasser, S., R. C. Dailey, and T. S. Bateman. "Attitudinal Moderators and Effects of Leaders' Punitive Behavior." *Psychological Reports* 49 (1981), pp. 695–98.

29. Keller, R. T., and A. D. Szilagyi. "Employee Reactions for Leader Reward Behavior." *Academy of Management Journal* 19 (1976), pp. 619–27.

30. ———. "A Longitudinal Study of Leader Reward Behavior, Subordinate Expectancies, and Satisfaction." *Personnel Psychology* 11 (1978), pp. 119–29.

31. Arvey, R. D., G. A. Davis, and S. M. Nelson. "Use of Discipline in an Organization: A Field Study." *Journal of Applied Psychology* 69 (1984), pp. 448–60.

32. Podsakoff, P. M., W. D. Todor, R. A. Grover, and V. L. Huber. "Situational Moderators of Leader Reward and Punishment Behaviors: Fact or Fiction?" *Organizational Behavior and Human Performance* 34 (1984), pp. 21–63.

33. Curphy, G. J., F. W. Gibson, B. W. Asiu, C. P. McCown, and C. Brown. "A Field Study of the Causal Relationships between Organizational Performance, Punishment, and Justice," Working paper, 1992.

34. Dobbins, G. H., and J. M. Russell. "The Biasing Effects of Subordinate Likeableness on Leaders' Responses to Poor Performance." *Personnel Psychology* 39 (1986), pp. 759–77.

35. Arvey, R. D., and A. P. Jones. "The Use of Discipline in Organizational Settings; A Framework for Future Research." In *Research in Organizational Behavior.* Vol. 7. Eds. L. L. Cummings and B. M. Staw. Greenwich, CT: JAI, 1985, pp. 367–408.

36. Beyer, J. M., and H. M. Trice. "A Field Study in the Use and Perceived Effects of Discipline in Controlling Work Performance." *Academy of Management Journal* 27 (1984), pp. 743–64.

37. Katz, D., N. Maccoby, G. Gurin, and L. G. Floor. *Productivity, Supervision, and Morale Among Railroad Workers.* Ann Arbor, MI: University of Michigan, Survey Research Center, Institute of Social Research, 1951.

38. Podsakoff, P. M., and W. D. Todor. "Relationships between Leader Reward and Punishment Behavior and Group Process and Productivity." *Journal of Management* 11 (1985), pp. 55–73.

39. Schnake, M. E. "Vicarious Punishment in a Work Setting." *Journal of Applied Psychology* 71 (1986), pp. 343–45.

40. Curphy, G. J., F. W. Gibson, B. W. Asiu, C. P. McCown, and C. Brown. "A Field Study of the Causal Relationships between Organizational Performance, Punishment, and Justice." Working paper, 1992.

41. Curtis, B., R. E. Smith, and F. L. Smoll. "Scrutinizing the Skipper: A Study of Behaviors in the Dugout." *Journal of Applied Psychology* 64 (1979), pp. 391–400; Dalton, M. A. "Using 360-Degree Feedback Successfully." *Leadership in Action* 18, no. 1 (1998), pp. 2–11.

42. Schnake, M. E. "Vicarious Punishment in a Work Setting." *Journal of Applied Psychology* 71 (1986), pp. 343–45.

43. Curtis, B., R. E. Smith, and F. L. Smoll. "Scrutinizing the Skipper: A Study of Behaviors in the Dugout." *Journal of Applied Psychology* 64 (1979), pp. 391–400; Dalton, M. A. "Using 360-Degree Feedback Successfully." *Leadership in Action* 18, no. 1 (1998), pp. 2–11.

44. Curphy, G. J., F. W. Gibson, B. W. Asiu, C. P. McCown, and C. Brown. "A Field Study of the Causal Relationships between Organizational Performance, Punishment, and Justice." Working paper, 1992.

45. Green, S. G., and T. R. Mitchell. "Attributional Processes of Leaders in Leader–Member Interactions." *Organizational Behavior and Human Performances* 23 (1979), pp. 429–58.

46. Mitchell, T. R., S. G. Green, and R. E. Wood. "An Attributional Model of Leadership and the Poor Performing Subordinate: Development and Validation." In *Research in Organizational Behavior.* Eds. B. M. Staw and L. L. Cummings. Greenwich, CN: JAI, 1981, pp. 197–234.

47. Mitchell, T. R., and R. E. Wood. "Supervisors' Responses to Subordinate Poor Performance: A Test of an Attributional Model." *Organizational Behavior and Human Performance* 25 (1980), pp. 123–38.

48. Arvey, R. D., and J. M. Ivancevich. "Punishment in Organizations: A Review, Propositions, and Research Suggestions." *Academy of Management Review* 5 (1980), pp. 123–32.

49. Arvey, R. D., and J. M. Ivancevich. "Punishment in Organizations: A Review, Propositions, and Research Suggestions." *Academy of Management Review* 5 (1980), pp. 123–32.

50. Bass, B. M. *Bass and Stogdill's Handbook of Leadership.* 3rd ed. New York: Free Press, 1990.

51. Leana, C. R. "Power Relinquishment vs. Power Sharing: Theoretical Clarification and Empirical Comparison of Delegation and Participation." *Journal of Applied Psychology* 72 (1987), pp. 228–33.

52. Miller, D., and J. M. Toulouse. "Strategy, Structure, CEO Personality and Performance in Small Firms." *American Journal of Small Business*, Winter 1986, pp. 47–62.

53. Stogdill, R. M., and C. L. Shartle. *Methods in the Study of Administrative Performance.* Columbus, OH: Ohio State University, Bureau of Business Research, 1955.

54. Bass, B. M. *Bass and Stogdill's Handbook of Leadership.* 3rd ed. New York: Free Press, 1990.

55. Wilcox, W. H. "Assistant Superintendents' Perceptions of the Effectiveness of the Superintendent, Job Satisfaction, and Satisfaction with the Superintendent's Supervisory Skills." PhD dissertation, University of Missouri, Columbia, 1982.

56. Taylor, H. L. *Delegate: The Key to Successful Management.* New York: Warner Books, 1989.

57. Dewhirst, H. D., V. Metts, and R. T. Ladd. "Exploring the Delegation Decision: Managerial Responses to Multiple Contingencies." Paper presented at the Academy of Management Convention, New Orleans, LA, 1987.

58. Bass B. M. *Bass and Stogdill's Handbook of Leadership.* 3rd ed. New York: Free Press, 1990.

59. Dewhirst, H. D., V. Metts, and R. T. Ladd. "Exploring the Delegation Decision: Managerial Responses to Multiple Contingencies." Paper presented at the Academy of Management Convention, New Orleans, LA, 1987.

60. Bass B. M. *Bass and Stogdill's Handbook of Leadership.* 3rd ed. New York: Free Press, 1990.

61. Dewhirst, H. D., V. Metts, and R. T. Ladd. "Exploring the Delegation Decision: Managerial Responses to Multiple Contingencies." Paper presented at the Academy of Management Convention, New Orleans, LA, 1987.

62. McCall, M. W., Jr., M. M. Lombardo, and A. M. Morrison. *The Lessons of Experience: How Successful Executives Develop on the Job.* Lexington, MA: Lexington Books, 1988.

63. Senge, P. M. *The Fifth Discipline: The Art and Practice of the Learning Organization.* New York: Doubleday/Currency, 1994.

64. Ginnett, R. C. "To the Wilderness and Beyond: The Application of a Model for Transformal Change." *Proceedings of the Ninth Psychology in the Department of Defense Symposium.* Colorado Springs, CO, 1984.

65. Curphy, G. J., and R. T. Hogan. "Managerial Incompetence: Is There a Dead Skunk on the Table?" Working paper, 2004.

66. Curphy, G. J. "A Roadmap for Creating High Performing Teams." Presentation given at the Strategic Staff Meeting of the Mid-Atlantic Division of The Home Depot, Atlantic City, NJ, September 2000.

67. Krile, J. E., G. J. Curphy, and D. R. Lund. *The Community Leadership Handbook.* St Paul, MN: The Fieldstone Alliance, 2006.

68. Curphy, G. J. "Leadership Transitions and Succession Planning." In *Developing and Implementing Succession Planning Programs.* J. Lock (chair). Symposium conducted at the 19th Annual Conference for the Society of Industrial and Organizational Psychology, Chicago April 2004.

69. Tuckman, B. W. "Developmental Sequence in Small Groups." *Psychological Bulletin* 63 (1965), pp. 384–99.

70. Peterson, D. B., and M. D. Hicks. *Professional Coaching: State of the Art, State of the Practice.* Minneapolis, MN: Personnel Decisions International, 1998.

71. Peterson, D. B., and M. D. Hicks. "Coaching across Borders: It's Probably a Long Distance Call." *Development Matters,* no. 9 (1997), pp. 1–4.

72. Peterson, D. B., and M. D. Hicks. *Leader as Coach: Strategies for Coaching and Developing Others.* Minneapolis, MN: Personnel Decisions International, 1996.

73. Hazucha, J. F., S. A. Hezlett, and R. J. Schneider. "The Impact of 360-Degree Feedback on Management Skills Development." *Human Resource Management* 32 (1993), pp. 325–51.

74. Peterson, D. B. "Skill Learning and Behavioral Change in an Individually Tailored Management Coaching and Training Program." Unpublished doctoral dissertation, University of Minnesota, 1993b.

75. Hezlett, S. A., and B. A. Koonce. "Now That I've Been Assessed, What Do I Do? Facilitating Development after Individual Assessments." Paper presented at the IPMA Assessment Council Conference on Public Personnel Assessment, New Orleans, LA, June 1995.

76. Davis, B. L., L. W. Hellervik, and J. L. Sheard. *The Successful Manager's Handbook.* 3rd ed. Minneapolis, MN: Personnel Decisions International, 1989.

77. Lombardo, M. M., and R. W. Eichinger. *For Your Improvement: A Development and Coaching Guide.* Minneapolis, MN: Lominger, 1996.

78. Personnel Decisions International. *DevelopMentor: Assessment, Development, and Coaching Software.* Minneapolis, MN: Personnel Decisions International, 1995.

79. Tichy, N. M., and E. Cohen. *The Leadership Engine: How Winning Companies Build Leaders at Every Level.* New York: HarperCollins, 1997.

80. Peterson, D. B., and M. D. Hicks. *Leader as Coach: Strategies for Coaching and Developing Others.* Minneapolis, MN: Personnel Decisions International, 1996, p. 14.

81. Hunter, J. E., F. L. Schmidt, and M. K. Judiesch. "Individual Differences in Output Variability as a Function of Job Complexity." *Journal of Applied Psychology* 74 (1990), pp. 28–42.

82. Quinn, R. E., and G. M. Spreitzer. "The Road to Empowerment: Seven Questions Every Leader Should Consider." *Organizational Dynamics,* Autumn 1997, pp. 37–49.

83. Quinn, R. E., and G. M. Spreitzer. "The Road to Empowerment: Seven Questions Every Leader Should Consider." *Organizational Dynamics,* Autumn 1997, pp. 37–49.

84. Offermann, L. R. "Leading and Empowering Diverse Followers." In *The Balance of Leadership and Followership.* Eds. E. P. Hollander and L. R. Offerman. Kellogg Leadership Studies Project. College Park: University of Maryland Press, 1997, pp. 31–46.

85. Xie, J. L., and G. Johns. "Job Scope and Stress: Can Job Scope Be Too High?" *Academy of Management Journal* 38, no. 5 (1995), pp. 1288–1309.

86. Quinn, R. E., and G. M. Spreitzer. "The Road to Empowerment: Seven Questions Every Leader Should Consider." *Organizational Dynamics,* Autumn 1997, pp. 37–49.

87. Spreitzer, G. M. "Psychological Empowerment in the Workplace: Dimensions, Measurement, and Validation." *Academy of Management Journal* 38, no. 5 (1995), pp. 1442–65.

88. Offermann, L. R. "Leading and Empowering Diverse Followers." In *The Balance of Leadership and Followership*. Eds. E. P. Hollander and L. R. Offerman. Kellogg Leadership Studies Project. College Park: University of Maryland Press, 1997, pp. 31–46.

89. Quinn, R. E., and G. M. Spreitzer. "The Road to Empowerment: Seven Questions Every Leader Should Consider." *Organizational Dynamics,* Autumn 1997, pp. 37–49.

Focus on the Situation

Part

4

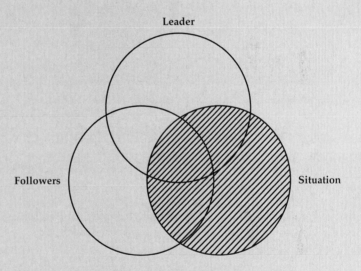

In previous chapters we noted that understanding leaders and followers is much more complicated than many people first think. For example, we examined how leaders' personality characteristics, behaviors, and attitudes affect the leadership process. Similarly, followers' attitudes, experience, personality characteristics, and behaviors, as well as group norms and cohesiveness, also affect the leadership process. Despite the complexities of leaders and followers, however, perhaps no factor in the interactional framework is as complex as the situation. Not only do a variety of task, organizational, and environmental factors affect behavior, but the relative salience or strength of these factors varies dramatically across people. What one person perceives to be the key situational factor affecting his or her behavior may be relatively unimportant to another person.

Moreover, the relative importance of the situational factors also varies over time. Even in the course of a single soccer game, for example, the situation changes constantly: The lead changes, the time remaining in the game changes, weather conditions change, injuries occur, and so on. Given the dynamic nature of situations, it may be a misnomer to speak of "the" situation in reference to leadership.

Because of the complex and dynamic nature of situations and the substantial role perceptions play in the interpretation of situations, no one has been able to develop a comprehensive taxonomy describing all of the situational variables affecting a person's behavior. In all likelihood, no one ever will. Nevertheless, considerable research about situational influences on leadership has been accomplished. Leadership researchers have examined how different task, organizational, and environmental factors affect both leaders' and followers' behavior, though most have examined only the effects of one or two situational variables on leaders' and followers' behavior. For example, a study might have examined the effects of task difficulty on subordinates' performance yet ignored how broader issues, such as organizational policy or structure, might also affect their performance. This is primarily due to the difficulty of studying the effects of organizational and environmental factors on behavior. As you might imagine, many of these factors, such as market conditions or crisis situations, do not easily lend themselves to realistic laboratory experiments where conditions can be controlled and interactions analyzed. Nonetheless, several consistent findings have emerged. We review them in Part 4.

Chapter 11

Characteristics of the Situation

Introduction

April 16, 2007, was a dark day at Virginia Tech, and across the country. On that day, Cho Seung Hui went on a shooting rampage that left 32 students and faculty dead in its wake, and a host of others injured. There is no doubt that Cho was a villain, if not a deranged one, as he created a situation of terror in Norris Hall. But in that same awful situation, heroes were created in Norris Hall. One was Zach Petkewicz.

Zach and his fellow classmates were in a classroom near the one where Cho initiated his massacre. They could hear the initial series of gunshots sounding through the walls and they could hear them getting closer. At first, everyone experienced fear and hid behind whatever they could find for protection. But it occurred to Zach that "there's nothing stopping him from coming in here. We were just sitting ducks." And that's when Zach and others took action.

Zach grabbed a table and shoved it against the door. Seeing his plan, other students joined him, pinning the table against the cinderblock walls around the door frame. And just in time. Cho tried to get into their classroom next. Having tried the door handle and then brute force, Cho emptied a clip of ammunition through the door before giving up and moving on to another room.

Days after the assault, Zach Petkewicz was interviewed by Matt Lauer on NBC's *Today Show*. Lauer asked Zach if he could have predicted, before the shooting, how he would react. The young hero, whose first reaction had been fear, said that's not possible for anyone. "There's no way of telling what I would have done until you're put in that situation."

Zach was right about two things. First, as spoken, it is difficult to predict human behavior, and specifically leadership behavior, unless you consider the situation. Second, we are coming to understand that the situation is one of the most powerful variables in the leadership equation. And that is the topic of this chapter.

Background

In a book designed to introduce students to the subject of leadership, a chapter about "the situation" poses some challenging obstacles and dilemmas. The very breadth of the topic is daunting; it could include almost everything else in the world that has not been covered in the previous chapters! To the typical student who has not yet begun a professional career, pondering the magnitude of variables making up the situation is a formidable request. For one thing, the situation you find yourself in is often seen as completely beyond your control. For example, how many times have you heard someone say, "Hey, I don't make the rules around here. I just follow them." Furthermore, the subject is made more difficult by the fact that most students have limited organizational experience as a frame of reference. So why bother to introduce the material in this chapter? Because the situation we are in often explains far more about what is going on and what kinds of leadership behaviors will be best than any other single variable we have discussed so far!

In this chapter we will try to sort out some of the complexity and magnitude of this admittedly large topic. First, we will review some of the research which has led us to consider these issues. Then, after considering a huge situational change that is now occurring, we will present a model to help in considering key situational variables. Finally, we will take a look forward through one interesting lens. Throughout the chapter, though, our objective will be primarily to increase awareness rather than to prescribe specific courses of leader action.

The appropriateness of a leader's behavior with a group of followers often makes sense only when you look at the situational context in which the behavior occurs. Whereas severely disciplining a follower might seem a poor way to lead, if the follower in question had just committed a safety violation endangering the lives of hundreds of people, then the leader's actions may be exactly right. In a similar fashion, the situation may be the primary reason personality traits, experience, or cognitive abilities are related less consistently to leadership effectiveness than to leadership emergence.[1,2] Most leadership emergence studies have involved leaderless discussion groups, and for the most part the situation is quite similar across such studies. In studies of leadership effectiveness, however, the situation can and does vary dramatically. The personal attributes needed to be an effective leader of a combat unit, chemical research-and-development division, community service organization, or fast-food restaurant may change considerably. Because the situations facing leaders of such groups may be so variable, it is hardly surprising that studies of leader characteristics have yielded inconsistent results when looking at leadership effectiveness across jobs or situations. Thus, the importance of the situation in the leadership process should not be overlooked.

Historically, some leadership researchers emphasized the importance of the situation in the leadership process in response to the Great Man theory of leadership. These researchers maintained that the situation, not someone's traits or abilities, plays the most important role in determining who emerges as a leader.[3–5] As support for the situational viewpoint, these researchers noted that great leaders typically emerged during economic crises, social upheavals, or revolutions; great leaders were generally not associated with periods of relative calm or quiet. For example, Schneider[6] noted that the number of individuals identified as great military leaders in the British armed forces during any time period depended on how many conflicts the country was engaged in—the greater the number of conflicts, the greater the number of great military leaders. Moreover, researchers advocating the situational viewpoint believed leaders were made, not born, and that prior leadership experience helped forge effective leaders.[7] These early situational theories of leadership tended to be very popular in the United States, as they fit more closely with American ideals of equality and meritocracy, and ran counter to the genetic views of leadership that were more popular among European researchers at the time.[8] (The fact that many of these European researchers had aristocratic backgrounds probably had something to do with the popularity of the Great Man theory in Europe.)

More recent leadership theories have explored how situational factors affect leaders' behaviors. In **role theory,** for example, a leader's behavior was said to depend on a leader's perceptions of several critical aspects of the situation: rules and regulations governing the job; role expectations of subordinates, peers, and superiors; the nature of the task; and feedback about subordinates' performance.[9] Role theory clarified how these situational demands and constraints could cause role conflict and role ambiguity.[10] Leaders may experience role conflict when subordinates and superiors have conflicting expectations about a leader's behavior or when company policies contradict how superiors expect tasks to be performed. A leader's ability to successfully resolve such conflicts may well determine leadership effectiveness.[11]

Another effort to incorporate situational variables into leadership theory was Hunt and Osborn's[12] **multiple-influence model.** Hunt and Osborn distinguished between microvariables (e.g., task characteristics) and macrovariables (e.g., the external environment) in the situation. Although most researchers looked at the effects tasks had on leader behaviors, Hunt and Osborn believed macrovariables have a pervasive influence on the ways leaders act. Both role theory and the multiple-influence model highlight a major problem in addressing situational factors, which was noted previously: that situations can vary in countless ways. Because

The way of the superior is threefold, but I am not equal to it. Virtuous, he is free from anxieties; wise, he is free from perplexities; bold, he is free from fear.

Confucius

situations can vary in so many ways, it is helpful for leaders to have an abstract scheme for conceptualizing situations. This would be a step in knowing how to identify what may be most salient or critical to pay attention to in any particular instance.

One of the most basic abstractions is **situational levels.** The idea behind situational levels may best be conveyed with an example. Suppose someone asked you, "How are things going at work?" You might respond by commenting on the specific tasks you perform (e.g., "It is still pretty tough. I am under the gun for getting next year's budget prepared, and I have never done that before."). Or, you might respond by commenting on aspects of the overall organization (e.g., "It is really different. There are so many rules you have to follow. My old company was not like that at all."). Or, you might comment on factors affecting the organization itself (e.g., "I've been really worried about keeping my job—you know how many cutbacks there have been in our whole industry recently."). Each response deals with the situation, but each refers to a very different level of abstraction: the task level, the organizational level, and the environmental level (see Highlight 11.1). Each of these three levels provides a different perspective with which to examine the leadership process (see Figure 11.1).

These three levels certainly do not exhaust all the ways situations vary. Situations also differ in terms of physical variables like noise and temperature levels, workload demands, and the extent to which work groups interact with other groups. Organizations also have unique "corporate cultures," which define a context for leadership. And there are always even broader economic, social, legal, and technological aspects of situations within which the leadership process occurs. What, amid all this situational complexity, should leaders pay attention to? We will try to provide some insights into this question by presenting a model which considers many of these factors.

FIGURE 11.1

An expanded leader–follower–situation model.

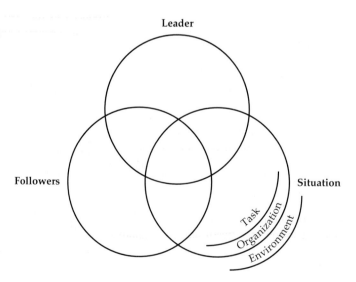

But first, let us consider an environmental aspect of the situation that is changing for virtually all of us as we move into the new millennium.

From the Industrial Age to the Information Age

All of us have grown up in the age of industry, but perhaps in its waning years. Starting just before the American Civil War and continuing up through the last quarter of the 20th century, the industrial age supplanted the age of agriculture. During the industrial age, companies succeeded according to how well they could capture the benefits from "economies of scale and scope."[13] Technology mattered, but mostly to the extent that companies could increase the efficiencies of mass production. Now a new age is emerging, and in this information age many of the fundamental assumptions of the industrial age are becoming obsolete.

Kaplan and Norton[14] described a new set of operating assumptions underlying the information age and contrasted them with their predecessors in the industrial age. They described changes in the following ways companies operate:

Cross Functions. Industrial age organizations gained competitive advantage through specialization of functional skills in areas like manufacturing, distribution, marketing, and technology. This specialization yielded substantial benefits, but over time, also led to enormous inefficiencies and slow response processes. The information age organization operates with integrated business processes that cut across traditional business functions.

Growing Up with The Gap

HIGHLIGHT 11.1

The Gap, Inc., is growing up in the information age. The retail company got its start in 1969 when Don and Doris Fisher opened the first Gap store in San Francisco. The Fishers' goal was to appeal to young consumers and bridge "the generation gap" they saw in most retail stores. Their first store sold jeans only and targeted customers mainly in their 20s. As Gap customers have grown up, so has the brand. In 1983 The Gap acquired Banana Republic mainly for its thriving catalog business and evolved the company from its original travel theme to an upscale alternative to the more casual Gap stores. In 1990 Baby Gap was born, appealing to young parents looking for stylish alternatives for their children. In 1994 Old Navy stores were introduced as the Gap looked for ways to appeal to value-oriented shoppers. Recently, The Gap has announced plans to test a specialty women's retail apparel brand in the United States in the second half of 2005, opening up to 10 stores in two geographic regions. The brand will target women over age 35, offering apparel for a range of occasions in a new specialty retail store environment. From young adult, to career professional, to parent, to cost-conscious family, to aging baby boomer, The Gap has stuck close to its customers and evolved to offer products that would appeal to their changing needs.

Sources: http://www.sfgate.com/cgi-bin/article.cgi?file=/c/a/2004/08/20/BUG8288V9244.DTL&type=printable; http://www.gapinc.com/financmedia/press_releases.htm; http://www.gapinc.com/about/ataglance/milestones.htm.

Links to Customers and Suppliers. Industrial age companies worked with customers and suppliers via arm's-length transactions. Information technology enables today's organizations to integrate supply, production, and delivery processes and to realize enormous improvements in cost, quality, and response time.

 Customer Segmentation. Industrial age companies prospered by offering low-cost but standardized products and services (remember Henry Ford's comment that his customers "can have whatever color they want as long as it is black"). Information age companies must learn to offer customized products and services to diverse customer segments.

Global Scale. Information age companies compete against the best companies throughout the entire world. In fact, the large investments required for new products and services may require customers worldwide to provide adequate returns on those costs.

Innovation. Product life cycles continue to shrink. Competitive advantage in one generation of a product's life is no guarantee of success for future generations of that product. Companies operating in an environment of rapid technological innovation must be masters at anticipating customers' future needs, innovating new products and services, and rapidly deploying new technologies into efficient delivery processes.

Knowledge Workers. Industrial companies created sharp distinctions between an intellectual elite on the one hand (especially managers and engineers), and a direct labor workforce on the other. The latter group performed tasks and processes under direct supervision of white-collar engineers and managers. This typically involved physical rather than mental capabilities. Now, all employees must contribute value by what they know and by the information they can provide.

One needs only to reflect upon Kaplan and Norton's list of changing operating assumptions to recognize that the situation leaders find themselves in today is different from the situation of 20 years ago. What's more, it is probably changing at an ever increasing rate. In a very real sense, the pace of change today is like trying to navigate white-water rapids; things are changing so rapidly it can be difficult to get one's bearings. Therefore, we believe it is helpful to use a model that identifies some of the key elements of the situation in an organizational setting.

The Congruence Model

 Like Ginnett's Team Leadership Model (TLM) described in the previous chapter, the Congruence Model is a systems model with *inputs, processes,* and *outputs.* We will focus on the four factors making up the organizational

FIGURE 11.2   A congruence model.

Source: David Nadler and Michael Tushman, *Competing by Design: The Power of Organizational Architecture.* Copyright © 1997 Oxford University Press. Used by permission of Oxford University Press, Inc.

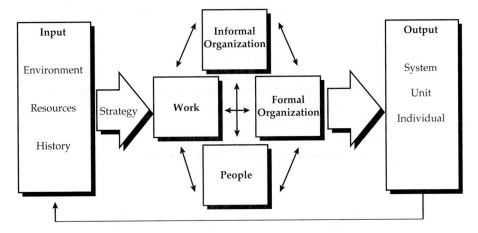

processes in this chapter, but we should briefly discuss the inputs and out-puts first. As can be seen in Figure 11.2, there are three components under inputs: the environment, the resources, and the history. Attention to these components must be kept to a minimum here, but their importance in impacting leaders and followers is nonetheless significant. We already have noted the magnitude of changes resulting from the shift in environment from the industrial age to the information age. Beyond that, *environment* also includes market changes, governmental regulations and laws, competitors, financial institutions, and even changes in weather patterns (consider the impact of *El Niño* in 1998 or the drought in the western United States since 2002). We will return to examine some further ways to specify environmental factors later in the chapter. *Resources* are anything which the organization can use to its benefit, and may include not only material components such as capital or information, but also less tangible components such as perceptions of quality (e.g., Nikon cameras or Mercedes automobiles). *History* of the organization includes not only the recent past that bears upon today's work but also myths about the organization's origin. For example, when taking important visitors on tours of the facilities at a large manufacturing plant, the guides would always stop and point out a series of visitor parking spots located near the executive wing of the building. The guides explained that the first plant manager and his team had decided to do away with executive parking slots by consensus, and that "consensus decision making was still the way everyone worked here"—25 years later.

Outputs are evaluated by the impact on the system as a whole, the unit, and the individual (again, very much like the TLM). At each of these levels, it is appropriate to ask how well the organization met its objectives, how efficient it was at achieving those outcomes, and how well the organization has scanned the horizon for new opportunities and threats. Before moving to the core process variables of the situation in this model, it is necessary to note that strategy is the collective set of business decisions about how to allocate scarce resources to maximize the strengths of the organization, given the external opportunities, while minimizing the organizational weaknesses, given the external threats.

The core of the Congruence Model has four components: the work, the people, the formal organization, and the informal organization. Note that each component relates to the other three. This is a key component of this model and is the basis of its name. Based upon a tenet of systems theory, the components of the model attempt to stay in balance or homeostasis. The better the fit of all the components, the more "congruence" there is between its various elements. Just one implication of this idea is that if a leader wanted to make changes in the outputs of his or her team, the model suggests it would be better to make small but equal changes in all the subsystems than it would be to make a substantial change in only one component. If only one element is changed, the other major components in the model, in trying to achieve homeostasis, would tend to resist and react to pull the "out-of-balance" element back in line.

The Work

At the most fundamental level, the work is "what is to be done" by the organization and its component parts. Given the variety of tasks people perform, it is natural for people to try to order and make sense of them. In thinking back across the many different tasks you have performed, you might categorize them as boring, challenging, dangerous, fun, interesting, and so on. However, labeling tasks is just a reaction to them and does not foster understanding about what aspects of any task may have caused a particular reaction. In looking at tasks, therefore, we want to get beyond subjective reactions to more objective ways of analyzing them.

There are several objective ways to categorize tasks performed by leaders and followers. Tasks can be categorized according to their function, the skills or abilities needed to perform them, the equipment needed to perform them, and so on. As seen in an earlier chapter, tasks also can be described in terms of the characteristics of the job itself: skill variety, task identity, task significance, autonomy, and feedback from the job. We will add to those characteristics two other dimensions: task structure and task interdependence.

Job Characteristics

Skill variety and the next four dimensions of tasks are all components of the job characteristics model[15,16] described in Chapter 9. Skill variety refers to the degree to which a job involves performing a variety of different activities or skills. For example, if an individual attaches the left

The brain is a wonderful organ; it begins working the moment you get up in the morning and does not stop until you get to the office.

Robert Frost

taillight to a car on an automobile assembly line by mechanically screwing in the fasteners, there would be increased work but no increased skill variety if he subsequently stepped over the line to the other side to install the right taillight. Skill variety involves using different skills, whether mechanical, cognitive, or physical. We might also add that there is a qualitative dimension to skill variety. In general, jobs requiring greater skill variety are more enjoyable than those requiring lesser skill variety, but it also matters whether any particular individual personally values the skills she performs.

Although satisfaction may also depend on growth-need strength (the individual's psychological need for personal accomplishment, for learning, and for personal development), typically jobs that require a low variety of skills are repetitive, monotonous, boring, and dissatisfying.[17-19] And like structured tasks, tasks with low levels of skill variety make it easier for leaders to use directive behaviors but, because followers already know how to do the job, also make directive leadership behavior somewhat redundant.[20-23] In such situations, leaders might try to restructure a subordinate's job in order to increase the number of (valued) skills needed. If that is not possible, then high levels of support and consideration for followers are helpful.[24,25]

Task identity refers to the degree to which a situation or task requires completion of a whole unit of work from beginning to end with a visible outcome. For example, if one works on an assembly line where circuit boards for compact disc (CD) players are being produced, and the task is to solder one wire to one electronic component and then pass the circuit board on to the next assembly worker, then this job would lack task identity. At the other extreme, if one assembled an entire CD player, perhaps involving 30 or 40 different tasks, then the perception of task identity would increase dramatically as one could readily see the final results of one's efforts. Furthermore, the job's skill variety (as discussed above) would increase as well.

Task significance is the degree to which a job substantially impacts others' lives. Consider an individual whose task is to insert a bolt into a nut and tighten it down to a certain specification using a torque wrench. If that bolt is one of several that fasten a fender to other parts of an automobile body on an assembly line, then both skill variety and task identity would probably be very low. Moreover, if the assembly person leaves the entire bolt off, it may cause a squeak or a rattle, but probably would not cause the fender to fall off. In such a job, task significance would be quite low as well. However, if the worker tightens the only bolt securing a critical component of a brake assembly on the space shuttle, then skill variety and task identity would be exactly the same as for our fender installer. However, task significance would be substantially higher.

If you want to give a man credit, put it in writing. If you want to give him hell, do it on the phone.

Charles Beacham

Autonomy is the degree to which a job provides an individual with some control over what he does and how he does it. Someone with considerable autonomy would have discretion in scheduling work and deciding the procedures used in accomplishing it. Autonomy often covaries with technical expertise, as workers with considerable expertise will be given more latitude, and those with few skills will be given more instruction and coaching when accomplishing tasks.[26,27]

Moreover, responsibility and job satisfaction often increase when autonomy increases.[28]

The last task component in the job characteristics model is **feedback,** which refers to the degree to which a person accomplishing a task receives information about performance *from performing the task itself.* In this context feedback does not refer to feedback received from supervisors but rather to what is intrinsic to the work activity itself. Driving a car is one example of feedback intrinsic to a task. If you are a skilled driver on a road with a number of twists and turns, then you get all the feedback you need about how well you are accomplishing the task merely by observing how the car responds to the inputs you make. This is feedback from the job itself as opposed to feedback from another person (who in this example would be a classic backseat driver). Extending this example to work or team settings, leaders sometimes may want to redesign tasks so that they (the tasks) provide more intrinsic feedback. Although this does not absolve the leader from giving periodic feedback about performance, it can help to free up some of the leader's time for other work-related activities. Additionally, leaders should understand that followers may eventually become dissatisfied if leaders provide high levels of feedback for tasks that already provide intrinsic feedback.[29-31]

Task Structure

Perhaps the easiest way to explain **task structure** is by using an example demonstrating the difference between a structured and an unstructured task. Assume the task to be accomplished is solving for x given the formula $3x + 2x = 15$. If that problem were given to a group of people who knew the fundamental rules of algebra, then everyone would arrive at the same answer. In this example there is a known procedure for accomplishing the task; there are rules governing how one goes about it; and if people follow those rules, there is one result. These features characterize a *structured task.*

On the other hand, if the task is to resolve a morale problem on a team, committee, or work group, then there may be no clear-cut method for solving it. There are many different ways, perhaps none of which is obvious or necessarily best for approaching a solution. It may even be that different observers would not see the problem in the same way; they may even have quite different ideas of *what morale is.* Solving a morale problem, therefore, exemplifies an *unstructured task.*

People vary in their preferences for, or ability to handle, structured versus unstructured tasks. With the Myers-Briggs Type Indicator (MBTI), for example, perceivers are believed to prefer unstructured situations, whereas judgers prefer activities that are planned and organized.[32] Individuals with high tolerance for stress may handle ambiguous and unstructured tasks more easily than people with low tolerance for stress.[33] Aside from these differences, however, we might ask whether there are any general rules for how leaders should interact with followers as a function of task structure. One consideration here is that while it is *easier* for a leader or coach to give instruction in structured tasks, it is not necessarily the most helpful thing to do.

We can see that by returning to the algebra problem described earlier. If a student had never seen such an algebra problem before, then it would be relatively easy for the teacher to teach the student the rules needed to solve the problem. Once any student has learned the procedure, however, he can solve similar problems on his own. Extending this to other situations, once a subordinate knows or understands a task, a supervisor's continuing instruction (i.e., initiating structure or directive behavior) may provide superfluous information and eventually become irritating.[34,35] Subordinates *need* help when a task is unstructured, when they do not know what the desired outcome looks like, and when they do not know how to achieve it. Anything a supervisor or leader can do to increase subordinates' ability to perform unstructured tasks is likely to increase their performance and job satisfaction.[36] Paradoxically, though, unstructured tasks are by nature somewhat ill defined. Thus, they often are more difficult for leaders themselves to analyze and provide direction in accomplishing. Nonetheless, reducing the degree of ambiguity inherent in an unstructured situation is a leadership behavior usually appreciated by followers.

Task Interdependence

Task interdependence concerns the degree to which tasks require coordination and synchronization in order for work groups or teams to accomplish desired goals. Task interdependence differs from autonomy in that workers or team members may be able to accomplish their tasks in an autonomous fashion, but the products of their efforts must be coordinated in order for the group or team to be successful. Tasks with high levels of interdependence place a premium on leaders' organizing and planning, directing, and communication skills.[37] In one study, for example, coaches exhibiting high levels of initiating-structure behaviors had better-performing teams for sports requiring relatively interdependent effort, such as football, hockey, lacrosse, rugby, basketball, and volleyball; the same leader behaviors were unrelated to team performance for sports requiring relatively independent effort, such as swimming, track, cross-country, golf, and baseball.[38] Like task structure and skill variety, task interdependence can also dictate which leader behaviors will be effective in a particular situation.

In summary, these seven task dimensions provide a variety of ways in which to categorize or describe tasks. For example, ironing a shirt would probably have high task structure, autonomy, task identification, and feedback, and low skill variety, task significance, and task interdependence. On the other hand, building your own home may garner high ratings on all seven dimensions. Still another familiar activity is evaluated on these dimensions in Highlight 11.2. These seven dimensions can provide leaders with insight about how their behavior and work assignments may either help or hinder followers' satisfaction and performance. At the same time, leaders should remember that these dimensions exist somewhat in the eye of the beholder. What one follower perceives as an unstructured task might be seen by another as fairly structured. Finally, as we have emphasized before, leaders should use their communication and listening skills to assure that they understand subordinates' feelings and beliefs about the work they perform.

The People

We can afford to be very brief here since much of the book has already focused on this topic. Still, it is worth repeating that leaders should look at the followers in terms of skills, knowledge, experience, expectations, needs, and preferences. In an increasingly global society, leaders can no longer afford to be parochial in their selection of followers. Compounding the global nature of work is, as noted earlier, the increasing rate of change in the environment. In a stable environment, any species can select a niche and survive for eons. But in a rapidly changing environment, diversity

---

Golf and the Task Factors of the Situation

HIGHLIGHT 11.2

Golf provides a convenient skill for illustrating the seven task factors described in this chapter. Golf provides a reasonable amount of *task structure,* as there are basic rules and procedures for properly hitting woods, long irons, and short irons, and for putting.

Skill variety comes into play because golfers use a variety of skills and talents. These include deciding on a club, the method used to swing the club, how hard to swing it, what kind of equipment to use, where to target the ball, how to compensate for wind, when to putt, and so on.

Because one person does all of the driving, pitching, and putting and is solely responsible for his or her score, a round of golf has a high level of *task identity.*

Task significance may be a little more difficult to appreciate in this example. It may not be there at all unless one is a particularly poor golfer (where he or she endangers the lives of other people) or, in the case of the professional golfer, has a family who depends on his or her performance.

Autonomy is certainly present when playing golf. The golfer gets to decide when to do the "work," how to do it, which clubs to use, and what strategies and tactics to use.

Feedback from the job is also apparent. Shortly after a golfer strikes the ball, she receives feedback on how well her swing worked. Whether it slices, hooks, or goes straight down the fairway is a bit of information that tells the golfer immediately how well her work is being accomplished.

Finally, golf generally lacks *task interdependence.* Golfers are not dependent on the other members in their foursome for their own score.

allows the species to sense and adapt more quickly. The same is true in the leadership world as well. Diversity is no longer merely the politically correct facade of leadership—it is essential to quality and survival in a rapidly changing world.

The Formal Organization

As with tasks, there also are a variety of dimensions for conceptualizing the organizational level of situations. This section will address how level of authority, organizational structure, organizational design, lateral interdependence, and organizational culture affect leaders' and followers' behavior.

Level of Authority

Level of authority concerns one's hierarchical level in an organization. The types of behaviors most critical to leadership effectiveness can change substantially as one moves up an organizational ladder. First-line supervisors, lower-level leaders, and coaches spend a considerable amount of time training followers, resolving work-unit or team-performance problems, scheduling practices or arranging work schedules, and implementing policies. Leaders at higher organizational levels have more autonomy and spend relatively more time setting policies, coordinating activities, and making staffing decisions.[39,40] Moreover, leaders at higher organizational levels often perform a greater variety of activities and are more apt to use participation and delegation.[41,42] A quite different aspect of how level of authority affects leadership is presented in Highlight 11.3.

Organizational Structure

Organizational structure refers to the way an organization's activities are coordinated and controlled, and represents another level of the situation in which leaders and followers must operate. Organizational structure is a conceptual or procedural reality, however, not a physical or tangible one. Typically, it is depicted in the form of a chart that clarifies formal authority relationships and patterns of communication within the organization. Most people take organizational structure for granted and fail to realize that structure is really just a tool for getting things done in organizations. Structure is not an end in itself, and different structures might exist for organizations performing similar work, each having unique advantages and disadvantages. There is nothing sacrosanct or permanent about any structure, and leaders may find that having a basic understanding of organizational structure is not only useful but imperative. Leaders may wish to design a structure to enhance the likelihood of attaining a desired outcome, or they may wish to change a structure to meet future demands. There are a number of ways to describe organizational structures, but perhaps the simplest way is to think of structure in terms of complexity, formalization, and centralization.

A man may speak very well in the House of Commons, and fail very completely in the House of Lords. There are two distinct styles requisite.

Benjamin Disraeli

Despite the dramatic changes in the way people work, the organizations in which they carry out that work have changed much less than might be expected.

**The Economist,
January 21, 2006**

The Glass Ceiling and the Wall

HIGHLIGHT 11.3

While the past 15 years have been marked by increasing movement of women into leadership positions, women still occupy only a tiny percentage of the highest leadership positions. In Fortune 500 companies, for example, less than 5 percent of the corporate officers are women. Researchers at the Center for Creative Leadership embarked on the Executive Woman Project to understand why.[43]

They studied 76 women executives in 25 companies who had reached the general-management level or the one just below it. The average woman executive in the sample was 41 and married. More than half had at least one child, and the vast majority were white.

The researchers expected to find evidence of a "glass ceiling," an invisible barrier that keeps women from progressing higher than a certain level in their organizations *because they are women.* One reason the women in this particular sample were interesting was precisely because they had apparently "broken" the glass ceiling, thus entering the top 1 percent of the workforce. These women had successfully confronted three different sorts of pressure throughout their careers, a greater challenge than their male counterparts faced. One

pressure was that from the job itself, and this was no different for women than for men. A second level of pressure, however, involved being a female executive, with attendant stresses such as being particularly visible, excessively scrutinized, and a role model for other women. A third level of pressure involved the demands of coordinating personal and professional life. It is still most people's expectation that women will take the greater responsibility in a family for managing the household and raising children. And beyond the sheer size of such demands, the roles of women in these two spheres of life are often at odds (e.g., being businesslike and efficient, maybe even tough, at work yet intimate and nurturing at home).

The Center for Creative Leadership researchers described the "lessons for success" of this group of women who had broken through the glass ceiling. They also reported, however, a somewhat unexpected finding. Breaking through the glass ceiling presented women executives with an even tougher obstacle. They "hit a wall" that kept them out of the very top positions. The researchers estimated that only a handful of the women executives in their sample would enter the topmost echelon, called senior management, and that none would become president of their corporation.

Complexity   Horizontal, vertical, and spatial elements make up organizational complexity. Concerning an organizational chart, **horizontal complexity** refers to the number of "boxes" at any particular organizational level. The greater the number of boxes at a given level, the greater the horizontal complexity. Typically, greater horizontal complexity is associated with more specialization within subunits and an increased likelihood for communication breakdowns between subunits. **Vertical complexity** refers to the number of hierarchical levels appearing on an organizational chart. A vertically simple organization may have only two or three levels from the highest person to the lowest. A vertically complex organization, on the other hand, may have 10 or more. Vertical complexity can affect leadership by impacting other factors such as authority dynamics and communication networks. **Spatial complexity** describes geographical dispersion. An organization that has all of its people in one location is typically less spatially complex than an organization that is dispersed around the country or around the world. Obviously, spatial complexity makes it more difficult for leaders to have face-to-face communication with subordinates in geographically separated locations, and to personally administer rewards or provide support and encouragement. Generally, all three of these elements are partly a function of organizational size. Bigger organizations are more likely to have more specialized subunits (horizontal complexity) and a greater number of hierarchical levels (vertical complexity), and to have subunits that are geographically dispersed (spatial complexity).

Formalization   **Formalization** describes the degree of standardization in an organization. Organizations having written job descriptions and standardized operating procedures for each position have a high degree of formalization. The degree of formalization in an organization tends to vary with its size, just as complexity generally increases with size.[44] Formalization also varies with the nature of work performed. Manufacturing organizations, for example, tend to have fairly formalized structures, whereas research-and-development organizations tend to be less formalized. After all, how could there be a detailed job description for developing a nonexistent product or making a scientific discovery?

The degree of formalization in an organization poses both advantages and disadvantages for leaders and followers. Whereas formalizing procedures clarifies methods of operating and interacting, it also may constitute demands and constraints on leaders and followers. Leaders may be constrained in the ways they communicate requests, order supplies, or reward or discipline subordinates.[45] If followers belong to a union, then union rules may dictate work hours, the amount of work accomplished per day, or who will be the first to be laid off.[46] Other aspects of the impact of formalization and other situational variables on leadership are presented in Highlight 11.4.

Centralization   **Centralization** refers to the diffusion of decision making throughout an organization. An organization that allows decisions to be made by only one person is highly centralized. When decision making is dispersed to the lowest levels in the organization, the organization is very decentralized. Advantages of decentralized organizations include increased participation in the decision process and, consequently, greater acceptance and ownership of decision outcomes. These are both desirable outcomes. There are also, however, advantages to centralization, such as uniform policies and procedures (which can increase feelings of equity), and clearer coordination procedures.[47] The task of balancing the degree of centralization necessary to achieve coordination and control, on the one hand, and gaining desirable participation and acceptance, on the other, is an ongoing challenge for the leader.

Are There Substitutes for Leadership?

HIGHLIGHT 11.4

Are leaders always necessary? Or are certain kinds of leader behaviors, at least, sometimes unnecessary? Kerr and Jermier proposed that certain situational or follower characteristics may well effectively neutralize or substitute for leaders' task or relationship behaviors. *Neutralizers* are characteristics that reduce or limit the effectiveness of a leader's behaviors. *Substitutes* are characteristics that make a leader's behaviors redundant or unnecessary.

Kerr and Jermier developed the idea of **substitutes for leadership** after comparing the correlations between leadership behaviors and follower performance and satisfaction with correlations between various situational factors and follower performance and satisfaction. Those subordinate, task, and organizational characteristics having higher correlations with follower performance and satisfaction than the two leadership behaviors were subsequently identified as substitutes or neutralizers. The following are a few examples of the situational factors Kerr and Jermier found to substitute for or neutralize leaders' task or relationship behaviors:

- A subordinate's ability and experience may well substitute for task-oriented leader behavior. A subordinate's indifference toward rewards overall may neutralize a leader's task and relationship behavior.

- Tasks that are routine or structured may substitute for task-oriented leader behavior, as can tasks that provide intrinsic feedback or are intrinsically satisfying.

- High levels of formalization in organizations may substitute for task-oriented leader behavior, and unbending rules and procedures may even neutralize the leader's task behavior. A cohesive work group may provide a substitute for the leader's task and relationship behavior.

Source: S. Kerr and J. M. Jermier, "Substitutes for Leadership: Their Meaning and Measurement." *Organizational Behavior and Human Performance* 22 (1978), pp. 375–403.

Organizational Design

In addition to being classified by their degree of complexity, formalization, and centralization, organizations can also be classified into several different kinds of organizational design. Organizational design can be thought of most easily in the following two questions: (1) How do I want to divide up the work? (2) How do I want the divisions to coordinate their work? Three of the most common kinds of **organizational designs** in the traditional (or industrial age) format include functional, product, and matrix organizations.

Functional Some organizations have their structures designed around certain important and continuing functions. For example, a manufacturing company with a **functional design** might have its organizational chart include one block for manufacturing, one for sales or marketing, one for research and development, and so on (see Figure 11.3). Advantages of functional organizations include efficient use of scarce resources, skill development for technical personnel, centralized decision making and control, and excellent coordination within each functional department. Disadvantages of functional organizations can include poor coordination across departments, slow responses to change, a piling up of decisions at the top of the hierarchy, and narrow or limited views by employees of

FIGURE 11.3   A manufacturing company with a functional design.

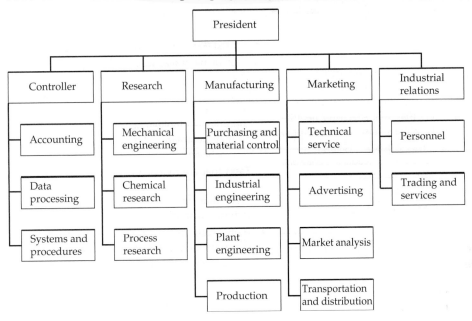

overall organizational goals.[48] In other words, in organizations structured functionally the very commonality within the various functional units can create problems. Functional groups can become so cohesive that they create rigid boundaries and dysfunctional competitiveness between themselves and other groups within the same organization.

Product   In an organization with a **product design,** the blocks on the organizational chart define the various products or services that are delivered ultimately to the consumer. One might consider an automobile organization such as General Motors, where there are the Buick, Chevrolet, Cadillac, Saturn, and Pontiac divisions. These are identifiable products, and employees are assigned to these product groupings. A different product design is represented in Figure 11.4. A product organization design overcomes some of the problems associated with functional organizations, as a product organization has better coordination across functional skills, places a premium on organizational goals rather than functional goals, and has better control over diverse products or services. The disadvantages of product organizations include duplication of resources, less in-depth technical expertise, and weak coordination across different product groupings.

Matrix   The **matrix design** is a combination of the product and functional designs. In this design, both product orientation and functional specialties are maintained (see Figure 11.5). In a matrix organization, there is a product manager for each product and one of his or her tasks is to

FIGURE 11.4   A petroleum company with a product design.

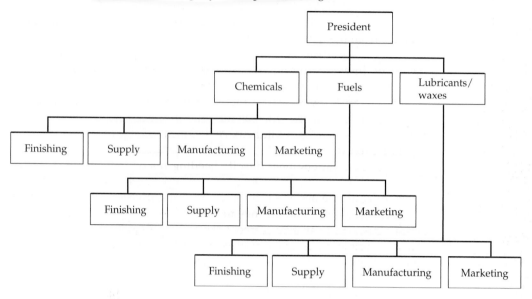

FIGURE 11.5   A manufacturing company with a matrix design.

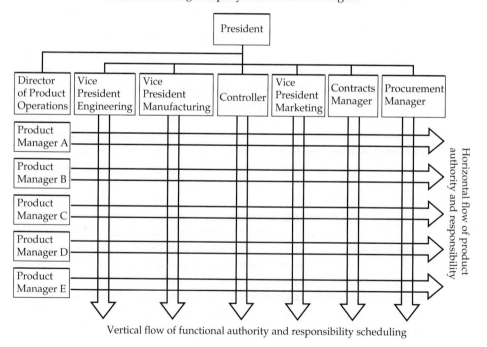

obtain the resources necessary from the functional specialties as requirements demand. If the product will require the services of a computer software engineer, for example, then the product manager must acquire those services from the manager of the engineering function.

The greatest advantage of the matrix is efficient utilization of human resources. Imagine putting together a team to design a new product, and further suppose that a chemical engineer's services are among the team's needs. Also imagine, however, that the chemical engineer is required for only one month's work whereas the total product design phase encompasses a whole year. If our imaginary organization were designed according to a product orientation, the product manager would have to hire a full-time chemical engineer despite needing his or her services for only one month. In a matrix organization, on the other hand, the chemical engineer could be assigned to the engineering division, and the various product managers could arrange to acquire the engineer's time on an as-needed basis. Such an arrangement can create scheduling nightmares, but it also results in more efficient utilization of unusual or scarce resources. Another advantage of the matrix design includes increased lateral communication and coordination.

 The greatest disadvantage of the matrix design is that employees end up working for two bosses. Such a dual-authority structure can create confusion and frustration. In the case above, the chemical engineer may have "professional loyalty" to the engineering group (which would dictate the highest-quality engineering possible) and "profitability loyalty" to the product group (which would dictate the most cost-effective engineering). Our chemical engineer might very well experience conflict over which loyalty to serve first. Additionally, matrix designs can lead to conflict and disagreements over the use of shared resources, and time is lost through frequent meetings to resolve such issues. Thus, administrative costs are high in matrix organizations. Finally, matrix designs can work well only if managers see the big picture and do not adopt narrow functional or product perspectives. In fact, it appears that even the organizations that championed the move to matrix structures are now reconsidering that design. The Dutch electrical giant Philips is but one example of this revised thinking.[49]

Lateral Interdependence

The degree of **lateral interdependence** in an organization can also affect leaders' and followers' behaviors. Lateral interdependence concerns the degree of coordination or synchronization required between organizational units in order to accomplish work-group or organizational goals. Thus, lateral interdependence is similar to task interdependence but at a higher organizational level; lateral interdependence represents the degree to which a leader's work group is affected by the actions or activities of other subunits within the organization.[50,51] For example, a leader of a final assembly unit for personal computers will be very dependent on the activities of the power supply, cabinet, monitor, mother board, floppy drive, and hard drive manufacturing units in order to successfully meet production goals. On the other hand, the leader of a manufacturing unit that makes all of the products used to assemble backpacks has a much lower degree of lateral interdependence. As lateral interdependence increases, leaders usually spend more time building and maintaining contacts in other work units or on public relations activities.[52,53] Moreover, leaders are more likely to use rational persuasion as an influence tactic when the level of lateral interdependence is high.[54,55]

The Informal Organization

One word which sums up the informal organization better than any other is its culture. Although most people probably think of culture in terms of very large social groups, the concept also applies to organizations. **Organizational culture** has been defined as a system of shared backgrounds, norms, values, or beliefs among members of a group,[56] and **organizational climate** concerns members' subjective reactions about the organization.[57,58] These two concepts are distinct in that organizational climate is partly a function of, or reaction to, organizational culture; one's feelings or emotional reactions about an organization are probably affected by the degree to which a person shares the prevailing values, beliefs, and backgrounds of organizational members.[59] If a person does not share the values or beliefs of the majority of members, then in all likelihood this person would have a fairly negative reaction about the organization overall. Thus, organizational climate (and indirectly organizational culture) is related to how well organizational members get along with each other.[60,61] It is also important to note that organizational climate is narrower in scope but highly related to job satisfaction. Generally, organizational climate has more to do with nontask perceptions of work, such as feelings about co-workers or company policies, whereas job satisfaction usually also includes perceptions of workload and the nature of the tasks performed.

Just as there are many cultures across the world, there are a great number of different cultures across organizations. Members of many military organizations have different norms, background experiences, values, and beliefs, for example, from those of the faculty at many colleges. Similarly, the culture of an investment firm is very different from the culture of a research-and-development firm, a freight hauling company, or a college rugby team. Cultural differences can even exist between different organizations within any of these sectors. The culture of the U.S. Air Force is different from the culture of the U.S. Marine Corps, and Yale University has a different culture than the University of Colorado even though they are both fine institutions of higher learning.

TABLE 11.1 **Some Questions That Define Organizational Culture**

Source: Adapted from R. H. Kilmann and M. J. Saxton, *Organizational Cultures: Their Assessment and Change.* San Francisco: Jossey-Bass, 1983.

- What can be talked about or not talked about?
- How do people wield power?
- How does one get ahead or stay out of trouble?
- What are the unwritten rules of the game?
- What are the organization's morality and ethics?
- What stories are told about the organization?

One of the more fascinating aspects of organizational culture is that it often takes an outsider to recognize it; organizational culture becomes so second nature to many organizational members that they are unaware of how it affects their behaviors and perceptions.[62] Despite this transparency to organizational members, a fairly consistent set of dimensions can be used to differentiate between organizational cultures. For example, Kilmann and Saxton[63] stated that organizational cultures can be differentiated based on members' responses to questions like those found in Table 11.1. Another way to understand an organization's culture is in terms of myths and stories, symbols, rituals, and language.[64] A more detailed description of the four key factors identified by Schein can be found in Highlight 11.5.

Here is an example of how stories contribute to organizational culture. A consultant was asked to help a plant that had been having morale and production problems for years. After talking with several individuals at the plant, the consultant believed he had located the problem. It seems everyone he talked to told him about Sam, the plant manager. He was a giant of a man with a terrible temper. He had demolished unacceptable products with a sledgehammer, stood on the plant roof screaming at workers, and done countless other things sure to intimidate everyone around. The consultant decided he needed to talk to this plant manager. When he did so, however, he met a very agreeable person named Paul. Sam, it seems, had been dead for nearly a decade, but his legacy lived on.[65]

It is important for leaders to realize that they can play an active role in changing an organization's culture, not just be influenced by it.[66–69] Leaders can change culture by attending to or ignoring particular issues, problems, or projects. They can modify culture through their reactions to crises, by rewarding new or different kinds of behavior, or by eliminating previous punishments or negative consequences for certain behaviors. Their general personnel policies send messages about the value of employees to the organization (e.g., cutting wages to avoid layoffs). They can use role modeling and self-sacrifice as a way to inspire or motivate

Schein's Four Key Organizational Culture Factors

HIGHLIGHT 11.5

Myths and stories are the tales about the organization that are passed down over time and communicate a story of the organization's underlying values. Virtually any employee of Wal-Mart can tell you stories about Sam Walton and his behavior—how he rode around in his pickup truck, how he greeted people in the stores, and how he tended to "just show up" at different times. The Center for Creative Leadership has stories about its founder, H. Smith Richardson, who as a young man creatively used the mail to sell products. Sometimes stories and myths are transferred between organizations even though the truth may not lie wholly in either one. A story is told in AT&T about one of its founders and how he trudged miles and miles through a blizzard to repair a faulty component so that a woman living by herself in a rural community could get phone service. Interestingly enough, this same story is also told in MCI (now Verizon).

Symbols and artifacts are objects that can be seen and noticed and that describe various aspects of the culture. In almost any building, for example, symbols and artifacts provide information about the organization's culture. For example, an organization may believe in egalitarian principles, and that might be reflected in virtually everyone having the same-size office. Or there can be indications of opulence, which convey a very different message. Even signs might act as symbols or artifacts of underlying cultural values. At one university that believed students should have first priority for facilities, an interesting sign showed up occasionally to reinforce this value. It was not a road sign, but a sign appearing on computer monitors. When the university's main computer was being overused, the computer was programmed to identify nonstudent users, note the overload, and issue a warning to nonstudent users to sign off. This was a clear artifact, or symbol, underlying the priority placed on students at that school.

Rituals are recurring events or activities that reflect important aspects of the underlying culture. An organization may have spectacular sales meetings for its top performers and spouses every two years. This ritual would be an indication of the value placed on high sales and meeting high quotas. Another kind of ritual is the retirement ceremony. Elaborate or modest retirement ceremonies may signal the importance an organization places on its people.

Language concerns the jargon, or idiosyncratic terms, of an organization and can serve several different purposes relevant to culture. First, the mere fact that some know the language and some do not indicates who is in the culture and who is not. Second, language can also provide information about how people within a culture view others. Third, language can be used to help create a culture. A good example of the power of language in creating culture is in the words employees at Disneyland or Walt Disney World use in referring to themselves and park visitors. Employees—all employees, from the costumed Disney characters to popcorn vendors—are told to think of themselves as members of a cast, and never to be out of character. Everything happening at the park is part of the "show," and those who paid admission to enter the park are not mere tourists, but rather "the audience." Virtually everyone who visits the Disney parks is impressed with the consistently friendly behavior of its staff, a reflection of the power of words in creating culture. (Of course, a strict and strongly enforced policy concerning courtesy toward park guests also helps.)

others to work more vigorously or interact with each other differently. Finally, leaders can also change culture by the criteria they use to select or dismiss followers.

Changing an organization's culture, of course, takes time and effort, and sometimes it may be extremely difficult. This is especially true in

John DeLorean and Counterculture at GM

HIGHLIGHT 11.6

One of the more interesting stories about organizational culture and the actions taken to change a culture concerns John DeLorean.[70] DeLorean was a senior executive at GM, an institution with a well-established culture. One of GM's key cultural values was showing deference and respect to authority. For example, subordinates were expected to meet out-of-town superiors at the airport, carry their bags, pay their hotel and meal bills, and chauffeur them around day and night. Additionally, the more senior the executive, the bigger the traveling party would be. Some employees were so eager to please their boss that a group of Chevrolet salespeople had a refrigerator put in the hotel room of a visiting senior executive after they had learned he liked to have a few cold beers and to make a sandwich before going to bed. Unfortunately, the door to the suite was too small to accommodate the refrigerator, so the Chevrolet sales personnel went so far as to hire a crane to bring in and later remove the refrigerator through the windows of the suite. A second core value at GM was communicating invisibly by visible cues. Ideal GM employees dressed identically, had the same office decor and layout, were "team players," and could easily fit in without drawing attention to themselves. The last key cultural value at GM was loyalty to one's boss. Loyalty to one's boss was clearly evident in the ritual of the retirement dinner, where a loyal subordinate was given the task of providing a detailed account of the retiree's steady rise through the corporation, counterpointed with allusions to the retiree's charming wife and family.

DeLorean took a number of actions to change the dominant culture at GM. First, DeLorean liked independence and dissent, and he modeled the behavior he wished others to emulate. He wore suits that stood out, and when appointed to head the Chevrolet division, he immediately changed the office furniture, carpeting, and decor and allowed executives to decorate their offices any way they wanted to "within reasonable limits." Second, because DeLorean believed that subordinates were more productive doing work than catering to superiors, he traveled by himself and did not greet his superiors at the airport, nor did he have his subordinates pick him up. Third, he changed the performance appraisal system within his division. Subordinates were to be rewarded on the basis of objective performance data, not subjective data that indicated a willingness to fit in. Although for a time DeLorean managed to maintain a delicate balance between culture and counterculture, his dissent was eventually met with disfavor, and he left GM to form a company of his own. Nevertheless, DeLorean's story provides several insights about the pervasiveness of organizational culture and the actions a leader might take to change culture.

very large organizations or those with strong cultures (see, for example, Highlight 11.6). New organizations, on the other hand, do not have the traditions, stories or myths, or established rites to the same extent that older companies do, and it may be easier for leaders to change culture in these organizations.

Why would a leader *want* to change an organization's culture? It all should depend on whether the culture is having a positive or a negative impact on various desirable outcomes. We remember one organization with a very "polite" culture, an aspect that seemed very positive at first. There were never any potentially destructive emotional outbursts in the organization, and there was an apparent concern for other individuals' feelings in all interactions. However, a darker side of that culture gradually became apparent. When it was appropriate to give feedback for performance appraisals or employee development, supervisors were hesitant to raise negative aspects of behavior; they interpreted doing so as not being polite. And so the organization continued to be puzzled by employee behavior that tended not to improve; the organization was a victim of its own culture.

Leaders especially need to be sensitive to how their own "brilliant ideas" may adversely impact subtle but important aspects of organizational culture. What may appear to be a major technical innovation (and therefore seemingly desirable) may also be devastating to organizational culture. For example, for hundreds of years in England, coal was mined by teams of three people each. In England, coal is layered in very narrow seams, most only a few feet high. In the past, the only practical means to get the coal out was to send the three-person teams of miners down into the mines to dig coal from the seam and then haul it to the surface on a tram. These mining teams had extremely high levels of group cohesiveness. A technological development called the long-wall method of coal extraction was to upset these close relationships, however. In the long-wall method, workers were arrayed all along an entire seam of coal rather than in distinct teams, and the method should have resulted in higher productivity among the miners. However, the breakdown of the work teams led to unexpected decreases in productivity, much higher levels of worker dissatisfaction, and even disruption of social life among the miners' families. Although the long-wall method was technically superior to the three-person mining team, the leaders of the coal-mining companies failed to consider the cultural consequences of this technological advancement.[71]

After reading these examples, you may be asking whether it is better for leaders to create cultures that emphasize interpersonal relationships or organizational productivity. We can glean some insights into this question by looking at Mitchell's[72] study of two groups of successful organizations. Mitchell compared two different groups of organizational cultures: those of organizations considered well managed, and those of organizations considered well liked by people working in the organization. The former group consisted of the 62 organizations identified in *In Search of Excellence*,[73] and the latter group included firms identified in *The 100 Best Companies to Work for in America*.[74]

Interestingly, there was relatively little overlap between the two lists. According to Mitchell, this lack of overlap was due primarily to differences between task- and relationship-oriented organizational cultures. Cultures in the well-liked organizations emphasized making employees feel they were part of a family, reducing social distance, and making the organization a pleasant one to work in. Cultures in the well-managed organizations, on the other hand, were much more manipulative. Those firms had cultures that valued people not for themselves but as instruments of productivity. Although which type of culture is best for an organization is still under debate, it is important to note that the 62 companies deemed excellently managed by Peters and Waterman did not provide any higher returns on investments than less well-managed firms,[75] and many of these 62 companies and cultures look considerably less excellent today.

An Afterthought on Organizational Issues for Students and Young Leaders
Let us conclude this section by adding an afterthought about what relevance organizational issues may have for students or others at the early stages of their careers, or at lower levels of leadership within their organizations. It is unlikely that such individuals will be asked soon to redesign their organization's structure or change its culture. As noted earlier, this chapter is not intended as a how-to manual for changing culture. On the other hand, it has been our experience that younger colleagues sometimes develop biased impressions of leaders or have unrealistic expectations about decision making in organizations, based on their lack of familiarity with, and appreciation for, the sorts of organizational dynamics discussed in this section. In other words, one of the primary reasons for being familiar with such organizational variables is the context they provide for understanding the leadership process at your own level in the organization. Finally, we have worked with some senior leaders of huge organizations who have been with their company for their entire career. They have often been unable to identify *any* of the dimensions of their culture because they have never seen anything else. In these cases we were amazed by how junior managers were far better at describing the culture of the large organization. While these junior people may have had only five to eight years of total work experience, if that experience had been obtained in several different organizations, they were much better prepared to describe the characteristics of their new large organization's culture than were the senior executives.

Environmental Characteristics

We mentioned the environment earlier in the chapter as an input variable in the Congruence Model. We now return to a slightly more in-depth analysis of environmental characteristics since not attending to environmental characteristics is the root of extinction, both for the organization and for the population at large (see Highlight 11.7). Environmental characteristics concern situational factors outside the task or organization that still affect the leadership process. These include technological, economic, political, social, and legal forces. For example, imagine how changing economic conditions, such as threats of layoffs from a recession, a hostile takeover, or global "off-shoring" would affect leaders' and followers' behavior. These factors often create anxiety and therefore cause an increase in employees' security needs. They also tend to result in decreased training

Workplace Trends

HIGHLIGHT 11.7

1. *Employment Market Turbulence.* More secure employees will stimulate unprecedented churning in the labor marketplace. This turbulence will threaten corporate stability and capacity to serve customers, particularly for employers who took employees for granted in recent years.

2. *Shift to Sellers' Market in Labor.* Employers will face the most severe shortage of skilled labor in history. Corporations will become more aggressive to attract and hold top talent. People will change jobs to find their personal Employer of Choice®.

3. *Fluid International Job Movement.* Economic issues and skilled labor shortages in the United States will move even more jobs to other countries. However, employers will discover that some situations are unsatisfactory and jobs will be returned.

4. *Retirement Will Evaporate.* Traditional retirement will continue its metamorphosis. Retirees will move into jobs in other fields, start their own businesses, and engage in other activities to remain active and productive.

5. *Training and Education Will Accelerate.* Corporate development programs will reach out to new employees and existing staff. Demand for vocational education will grow. Educators will be challenged to make major changes to produce graduates ready to be productive in a faster-moving world.

6. *Leadership Deficit Will Be Crippling.* As employers discover serious inadequacies, leadership development will take on new importance. Up and coming managers will be expected to learn and practice leadership skills before assuming new positions.

7. *Flexible Employment Will Gain Popularity.* As more people work flexible hours, work from home, and use technology to work for employers in distant locations, traditional work arrangements will further erode.

8. *Casual Is Here to Stay.* Despite some movement to return to more formality in the workplace, informality will dominate in clothing, culture, office decor, and workplace structural design.

9. *Advantage of Agility.* Companies will re-create themselves to be more agile, nimble, and responsive to customers and employees. Relationships, resources, knowledge, and speed will become strategic weapons.

10. *Workers Becoming Independent.* More people will become independent contractors, selling their services on a project, contract, or set-term basis. This movement will stimulate emergence of specialized staffing firms and electronic communities to connect workers with employers.

Source: © Copyright 1998–2004 by The Herman Group, Inc.—reproduction for publication is encouraged, with the following attribution: From "The Herman Trend Alert," by Roger Herman and Joyce Gioia, Strategic Business Futurists. (800) 227–3566 or http://www.hermangroup.com. The Herman Trend Alert is a trademark of The Herman Group, Inc.

budgets for workers.[76] Recent changes in the valuation of high-technology and telecommunication stocks cannot be ignored. Political changes also can have substantial impacts on leaders and followers. Just imagine, for example, how leaders' and followers' behaviors are changing in Eastern Europe as the various countries move from communist systems to private ownership of companies even though the changes have not gone smoothly or uniformly. Legal forces affecting Western organizations include those contributing to the growth of new industries (e.g., industrial waste disposal) or to personnel reductions in other industries due to changes in governmental rules and regulations.[77] Finally, technological advances are changing leader–follower relationships. For example, the advent of personal computers, fax machines, and high-speed access lines allows people to work at geographically dispersed locations.

Technology and Uncertainty

Technology affects the leadership process in other ways as well. For example, it might determine what design is best for an organization.[78] In environments of low **technological complexity,** workers play a large role and are able to modify their behavior depending on the situation. In environments of high technological complexity, there is a highly predictable work flow.

Examples of organizations in environments of low technological complexity are printing shops, tailor shops, and cabinetmakers. In each case, the organization is well suited to meeting specific customer orders. One of the authors of this book encountered an organization fitting this mold in trying to find an oak wall unit that would meet his requirements for a stereo system. After much frustrating shopping and finding a number of mass-produced units that would not work, he found a shop that had a variety of different units. Some of these came close to what he needed, but even the closest was not quite right. After listening in detail to the requirements, the owner agreed he didn't have anything on the floor that would work. In the next breath, however, he said, "But if you can draw it, we can build it."

A higher level of technological complexity occurs when mass production is the focus and orders are filled from inventory. An example would be furniture purchased from large warehouse stores. As opposed to the individually crafted wall unit described above, most furniture is not specifically designed and built precisely to meet special customer needs. Instead, manufacturers produce large quantities of various pieces of furniture likely to adequately meet the tastes and needs of most customers.

 The highest level of technological complexity occurs when a continuous process is mechanized from beginning to end. People don't play much of a role in such organizations at all except to monitor the process flow and detect problems. Oil refining operations, chemical production plants, and nuclear power plants are all examples of continuous-process organizations. In such plants, people are merely observing and monitoring the processes and detecting anomalies that need to be corrected.

The significance of such a range of technological complexity is that different kinds of organizational structures or designs are best suited for different technological environments. An organization is most likely to be successful if the structure fits the technology. If the technological environment is one of moderately high complexity (like large furniture-manufacturing companies), a mechanistic or bureaucratic structure to the organization may be most appropriate. On the other hand, if the technological environment is one of low complexity (like the custom cabinetmaker or printer), setting up a rigid, bureaucratic structure will make it difficult for your organization to produce and "flex" as required by the different specific orders.

In addition to technology, the degree of **environmental uncertainty** also affects optimal organizational design. In stable environments where there is little change, a relatively formalized, centralized, and bureaucratic structure may be desirable. In turbulent environments, on the other hand, structures should be flexible enough to adapt to changing conditions.[79] In a similar fashion, flat, highly differentiated, and organic structures are most appropriate for very uncertain environments.[80]

Crises

Another environmental variable that affects the leadership process is the presence or absence of **crises.** Some researchers believe crises play such an important part in charismatic leadership that certain leaders will purposely create crises in order to be perceived as being charismatic.[81–83] Furthermore, the behaviors associated with effective leadership during crises differ from those associated with noncrisis situations. During crises, followers are more likely to look to leaders to identify the problem as well as develop and implement a solution. Thus, work groups facing strong deadlines or crises generally expect their leaders to be more assertive, directive, and decisive.[84] Moreover, leaders are less apt to use participation or consultation during crises.[85,86] These findings make sense when contrasting emergency and nonemergency situations. For example, surgeons spend considerable time consulting with colleagues prior to conducting a difficult surgery. However, surgeons do not have time to consult with other specialists when a patient's heart has just stopped during surgery; the doctor must quickly diagnose the reason for the heart failure and coordinate the efforts of the surgical team for the patient to live. Similarly, coaches often spend considerable time consulting with other coaches and staff members when preparing for games, but during particularly close games they may consult with relatively few members of even their own staffs.

Situational Engineering

One of the most important points this chapter can make concerns the idea of **situational engineering.** Although leaders' and followers' behaviors are affected by a variety of situational factors, all too often leaders and followers completely overlook how changing the situation can help them to change their behavior. Just as a dieter can better stick to a diet by identifying bad eating habits and limiting food cues, so can a leader or follower become more effective by identifying problem areas and restructuring the situation so that these problems become easier to overcome.

Say, for example, a leader attended a leadership development program and received feedback that he did not interact enough with his subordinates. This leader might set a goal and may genuinely make an attempt to increase the level of interaction with his followers. Because his typical day is hectic and he manages a work group with a high level of lateral interdependence, however, situational demands may more or less force him to revert to his old behaviors. This leader would be likely to realize more success if he also restructured the situation in order to facilitate the accomplishment of this goal.

He could, for example, delegate more activities to subordinates. This would give the leader more opportunities to interact with followers (by mutually setting performance goals and monitoring progress), and it would give the leader more time to engage in other activities. Moreover, the leader could project a more approachable and friendly attitude by rearranging office furniture, keeping his door open as much as possible, and building specific times into his daily schedule to "manage by wandering around."[87]

There are a variety of ways in which leaders and followers can change the task, organizational, and environmental factors affecting their behaviors and attitudes. By asking questions and listening effectively, leaders may be able to redesign work using the suggestions from Hackman and Oldham's[88] job characteristics model or Herzberg's[89] two-factor theory in order to improve followers' satisfaction and productivity levels. Similarly, leaders might discover ways to adjust followers' workloads, responsibilities, or levels of task interdependence; rearrange office layouts; establish new or different policies or procedures; or modify reporting relationships

> *I claim not to have controlled events, but confess plainly that events have controlled me.*
> **Abraham Lincoln**

"... Then it's agreed. As a crowd, we'll be subdued in innings one through seven, then suddenly become a factor in innings eight and nine ..."

and appraisal systems.[90] More senior leaders might be able to change the organization itself or work to influence changes in the environment. Perhaps the most important point regarding situational engineering is to get leaders and followers to understand that the situation is not set in concrete, and to think about how they can change the situation in order for everyone to be more satisfied and productive.

One final example may be useful not only to illustrate the powerful impact of the situational variables but also to link this section to our previous discussion of Ginnett's Team Leadership Model, introduced in Chapter 10. You may recall that one of the important inputs in the TLM was the organizational level where we identified four types of systems impacting team process. These systems involved rewards, information, education, and control. In one of the authors' research projects, we were observing a series of work processes performed by teams in a highly centralized and controlled organization. No work was ever performed without specific directions which were generated by a complex computer program. Engineers, who were not in the buildings where the work was performed, would prepare the working procedures, which were then integrated in the computer system and finally printed out for each task. While engineers could change the procedures, the perception of the workers in the processing facility was that the procedures were "like the bible—and equally difficult to change." In one series of work sequences, a team would prepare a sheet of flexible insulation (according to the printed instructions) for installation by the next team. However, when the authors followed the insulation, we found that the first thing the installation team would do was to unfold the flexible sheet and refold it in exactly the opposite manner so that it could be installed. When we asked the preparation team if they were aware that the installation team was having to redo their work, they had no idea that was happening. Even more surprising was that when they did learn of this, both teams decided it was easier to continue their work as described on the computer task sheets than to try to change it! Using the TLM model, we were able to identify at least two systems that were creating problems. First, the interteam information system was inadequate; it should have allowed them to correct inappropriate strategies (e.g., folding it one way only to have that work undone and redone), but it didn't. Of equal impact was the teams' perception of powerlessness because of the oppressive control system in which they operated. Even after problems were discovered, the situation in which the teams operated created conditions that reduced the creative potential of those with direct knowledge of the work flow. Leadership could have changed the way work was done by these teams by improving the information system and modifying the control system. Highlight 11.8 describes one final example of dealing with situations. In this case, a young leader dealt with the stress of being in a new and dangerous situation with a team he'd only just met.

Taking Charge

HIGHLIGHT 11.8

A critical period for any leader often involves those first few moments and days of assuming command. It is a time when first impressions are formed and expectations are set. It is a crucial time for any leader in any situation, but can be a matter of life or death for a young leader in a combat situation. Here are one young officer's first reactions upon arriving in Southeast Asia to command a platoon.

I was alone. That was my first sensation as a leader. The men were going about the morning's business—breaking out C rations, relieving themselves, shaving, brushing their teeth. They moved among each other comfortably, a word here, a smile there. I could hear snatches of conversation: "A good night's sleep . . . " "Only 90 days left." Occasionally a man would nod in my direction, or glance at me for a fleeting moment.

I gathered up my belongings—weapon, web gear, and rucksack—and moved toward the command post. I needed a few minutes to gather my thoughts before I made my debut as a platoon leader. I knew it was going to be a tricky business.

I had assumed that I would have a company commander nearby to give me my orders. But I had not even met him yet; I would not meet him for weeks. The fact was I was totally on my own. What should I do? Whose advice could I ask? The platoon sergeant's? The squad leaders'? In time I would listen to their ideas and incorporate them with my own, but I could hardly begin my tour with "Well what do you think we ought to do, men?" No, I knew that the basic decisions were mine to make.

The first few moments would be crucial. Obviously, I was the object of interest that morning. Everyone was wondering what the new lieutenant would be like, and I would be telling them with my first words, my gestures, my demeanor, my eyes. I would have no grace period in which to learn my way around. This was a life and death environment. If I began with a blunder, my credibility as a leader would be shot, and so might some of the men.

I decided to begin by giving my attention to tactics. In a military environment, everything is determined by tactical considerations. Where you sleep, when you sleep, where you go, what you do, and in whose company you do it—all are dictated by underlying tactical necessities. I would communicate my style of leadership through my tactical instructions.

As I surveyed the soldiers, the nearby village, the distant rice paddies, the heavy undergrowth, the varied terrain, my mind raced back over the years of tactical training I had received. Conscious of the stares of the men, I hoped to appear composed as I fought back the panic of having to decide, both quickly and correctly.

Source: J. M. McDonough, *Platoon Leader.* San Francisco, CA: Presidio Press, 1985, pp. 30–31. Reprinted with permission.

Summary

The situation may well be the most complex factor in the leader–follower–situation framework. Moreover, situations vary not only in complexity but also in strength. Situational factors can play such a pervasive role that they can effectively minimize the effects of personality traits, intelligence, values, and preferences on leaders' and followers' behaviors, attitudes, and relationships. Given the dynamic nature of leadership situations, finding fairly consistent results is a highly encouraging accomplishment for leadership researchers.

As an organizing framework, this chapter introduced the Congruence Model as a way to consider many of the situational factors leaders should consider. In terms of work factors, leaders need to be aware of how task interdependence, task structure, and job characteristics can affect both their own and their followers' behaviors, and how they might change these factors in order to improve followers' satisfaction and performance. Research also has shown that organizational factors, such as lateral interdependence, structure, design, and culture, play major roles in determining why certain communication problems and conflicts might exist, how work is accomplished, and why some people may be more satisfied in the organization than others. The informal organization or the organizational culture can have a profound impact on the way both leaders and followers behave—and may be the least recognizable since it is the water in the bowl where all the fish are swimming. Factors in the environment, such as legal, political, or economic forces, can also affect leaders' and followers' behaviors. Sometimes these may effectively wipe out any changes a leader may make to improve productivity or satisfaction among work-group members.

Finally you might want to try this exercise. Choose two of your most respected heroes, from different fields or vocations, fictional or nonfictional. As an extreme example, you might choose the Dalai Lama (from real life) and Jack Bauer (hero from the hit TV show, *24*). Now, switch the situation in which these two heros operate. Consider the implications of how their personalities would impact their work in these situations and what would still make them effective. These are the kinds of questions we are continuing to ask and research in the 21st century.

Key Terms	role theory, *541*	task	lateral
	multiple-influence	interdependence, *549*	interdependence, *557*
	model, *541*	level of authority, *551*	organizational
	situational levels, *542*	organizational	culture, *558*
	cross functions, *543*	structure, *551*	organizational
	links to customers and	horizontal	climate, *558*
	suppliers, *544*	complexity, *552*	myths and stories, *560*
	customer	vertical complexity, *552*	symbols and
	segmentation, *544*	spatial complexity, *552*	artifacts, *560*
	global scale, *544*	formalization, *553*	rituals, *560*
	innovation, *544*	centralization, *553*	language, *560*
	knowledge workers, *544*	substitutes for	technological
	skill variety, *546*	leadership, *554*	complexity, *565*
	task identity, *547*	organizational	environmental
	task significance, *547*	designs, *554*	uncertainty, *566*
	autonomy, *547*	functional design, *554*	crises, *566*
	feedback, *548*	product design, *555*	situational
	task structure, *548*	matrix design, *555*	engineering, *566*

Questions

1. The term *bureaucratic* has a pejorative connotation to most people. Can you think of any positive aspects of a bureaucracy?

2. Think of a crisis situation you are familiar with involving a group, team, organization, or country, and analyze it in terms of the leader–follower–situation framework. For example, were the followers looking for a certain kind of behavior from the leader? Did the situation demand it? Did the situation, in fact, contribute to a particular leader's emergence?

3. Can you identify reward systems that impact the level of effort students are likely to put forth in team or group projects? Should these reward systems be different than for individual effort projects?

Activity

Your instructor has several exercises available which demonstrate the impact of situational factors on behavior. They are not described here since identifying the situational factors being manipulated in an exercise undercuts the purpose of that exercise.

Minicase

"Innovation at IKEA"

Redecorating and renovating have become *the* international pasttime. In a post 9/11 world facing persistent terrorist alerts, more and more people are opting to stay home and make their homes safe havens. This phenomenon, coupled with lagging economies worldwide, has contributed tremendously to the success of IKEA—the Swedish home furniture giant. In the past 10 years sales for IKEA have tripled, growing from over $4 billion in 1993 to over $12 billion in 2003.

Much of IKEA's success can be attributed to its founder, Ingvar Kamprad. Kamprad used graduation money to start IKEA in the small Swedish village where he was born. He started off selling belt buckles, pens, and watches, whatever residents in the small local village of Agunnaryd needed. Eventually, Kamprad moved on to selling furniture. One day in 1952, while struggling to fit a large table in a small car, one of Kamprad's employees came up with the idea that changed the furniture industry forever—he decided to remove the legs. IKEA's flat-pack and self-assembly methodology was born. It rocketed the company past the competition. "After that [table] followed a whole series of other self-assembled furniture, and by 1956 the concept was more or less systematized," writes Kamprad.

Kamprad is dedicated to maintaining the corporate culture he has helped define over the past 50 years. He is a simple man—his idea of a luxury vacation is riding his bike. He is fiercely cost-conscious and, even though his personal wealth has been estimated in the billions, he refuses to fly first class. He values human interaction above all, and, even though retired, he still visits IKEA stores regularly to keep tabs on what is going on where the business really happens.

The culture at IKEA is a culture closely connected with Kamprad's simple, farm-raised, Swedish roots. It is a culture that strives "to create a better everyday for the many people." IKEA supports this culture by

- hiring co-workers (IKEA prefers the word *co-workers* to "employees") who are supportive and work well in teams;
- expecting co-workers to look for innovative, better ways of doing things in every aspect of their work;
- respecting co-workers and their views;
- establishing mutual objectives and working tirelessly to realize them;
- making cost-consciousness part of everything they do from improving processes for production to purchasing wisely to traveling cost-effectively;
- avoiding complicated solutions—simplicity is a strong part of the IKEA culture;
- leading by example, so IKEA leaders are expected to pitch in when needed and create a good working environment; and
- believing that a diverse workforce strengthens the company overall.

The IKEA culture is one that resonates for many. The buildings are easy to identify—the giant blue and gold warehouses that resemble oversized Swedish flags are hard to miss. Millions of customers browse through the Klippan sofas and Palbo footstools (Nordic names are given to all IKEA products) in the stark, dimly lit warehouses. The surroundings may not be lavish and the service may be mostly self-service, but customers keep going back not just for the bargains, but to experience the IKEA culture as well.

1. Discuss the three input components of the Congruence Model as they apply to the success of IKEA.
2. Consider Schein's four key organizational culture factors as described in Highlight 11.5. What examples can you identify within the IKEA organization that contribute to the company's strong corporate culture?
3. Based on the level of technological complexity and the degree of environmental uncertainty present at IKEA, what type of organizational structure would you expect?

Sources: http://archive.cinweekly.com/content/2004/03/24/0324travelikea.asp; http://www.azcentral. com/home/design/articles/0812ikea12.html; http://strategis.ic.gc.ca/epic/internet/inimr-ri.nsf/en/gr-76894e.html; http://www.geocities.com/TimesSquare/1848/ikea.html; http://www.sustainability.com/news/press-room/JE-teflon-shield-Mar01.asp?popup=1; http://www.benefitnews.com/retire/detail.cfm?id=345.

Chapter Notes

1. Hogan, R. T., and J. Hogan. *Manual for the Hogan Personality Inventory.* Tulsa, OK: Hogan Assessment Systems, 1992.

2. Yukl, G. *Leadership in Organizations.* 2nd ed. Englewood Cliffs, NJ: Prentice Hall, 1989.

3. Murphy, A. J. "A Study of the Leadership Process." *American Sociological Review* 6 (1941), pp. 674–87.

4. Person, H. S. "Leadership as a Response to Environment." *Educational Record Supplement,* no. 6 (1928), pp. 9–21.

5. Spiller, G. "The Dynamics of Greatness." *Sociological Review* 21 (1929), pp. 218–32.

6. Schneider, J. "The Cultural Situation as a Condition for the Condition of Fame." *American Sociology Review* 2 (1937), pp. 480–91.

7. Person, H. S. "Leadership as a Response to Environment." *Educational Record Supplement* no. 6 (1928), pp. 9–21.

8. Bass, B. M. *Bass and Stogdill's Handbook of Leadership.* 3rd ed. New York: Free Press, 1990.

9. Merton, R. K. *Social Theory and Social Structure.* New York: Free Press, 1957.

10. Pfeffer, J., and G. R. Salancik. "Determinants of Supervisory Behavior: A Role Set Analysis." *Human Relations* 28 (1975), pp. 139–54.

11. Tsui, A. "A Role Set Analysis of Managerial Reputation." *Organizational Behavior and Human Performance* 34 (1984), pp. 64–96.

12. Hunt, J. G., and R. N. Osborn. "Toward a Macro-Oriented Model of Leadership: An Odyssey." In *Leadership: Beyond Establishment Views.* Eds. J. G. Hunt, U. Sekaran, and C. A. Schriesheim. Carbondale: Southern Illinois University Press, 1982, pp. 196–221.

13. Chandler, A. D. *Scale and Scope: The Dynamics of Industrial Capitalism.* Cambridge: Harvard University Press, 1990.

14. Kaplan, R. S., and D. P. Norton. *The Balanced Scorecard: Translating Strategy into Action.* Boston: Harvard Business School Press, 1996.

15. Hackman, J. R., and G. R. Oldham. "Motivation through the Design of Work: Test of a Theory." *Organizational Behavior and Human Performance* 16 (1976), pp. 250–79.

16. Hackman, J. R., and G. R. Oldham. *Work Redesign.* Reading, MA: Addison-Wesley, 1980.

17. Bass, B. M. *Bass and Stogdill's Handbook of Leadership.* 3rd ed. New York: Free Press, 1990.

18. Hackman, J. R., and G. R. Oldham. *Work Redesign.* Reading, MA: Addison-Wesley, 1980.

19. House, R. J., and G. Dressler. "The Path-Goal Theory of Leadership: Some Post Hoc and A Priori Tests." In *Contingency Approaches to Leadership.* Eds. J. G. Hunt and L. L. Larson. Carbondale: Southern Illinois University Press, 1974.

20. Howell, J. P., and P. W. Dorfman. "Substitute for Leadership: Test of a Construct." *Academy of Management Journal* 24 (1981), pp. 714–28.

21. Howell, J. P., and P. W. Dorfman. "Leadership and Substitutes for Leadership among Professional and Nonprofessional Workers." *Journal of Applied Behavioral Science* 22 (1986), pp. 29–46.

22. Kerr, S., and J. M. Jermier. "Substitutes for Leadership: Their Meaning and Measurement." *Organizational Behavior and Human Performance* 22 (1978), pp. 375–403.

23. Kipnis, D. "Technology, Power, and Control." *Research in the Sociology of Organizations* 3 (1984a), pp. 125–56.

24. Hackman, J. R., and G. R. Oldham. *Work Redesign.* Reading, MA: Addison-Wesley, 1980.

25. House, R. J., and G. Dressler. "The Path-Goal Theory of Leadership: Some Post Hoc and A Priori Tests." In *Contingency Approaches to Leadership.* Eds. J. G. Hunt and L. L. Larson. Carbondale: Southern Illinois University Press, 1974.

26. Hersey, P., and K. H. Blanchard. *Management of Organizational Behavior: Utilizing Human Resources.* 3rd ed. Englewood Cliffs, NJ: Prentice Hall, 1977.

27. Hersey, P., and K. H. Blanchard. *Management of Organizational Behavior: Utilizing Human Resources.* 4th ed. Englewood Cliffs, NJ: Prentice Hall, 1984.

28. Hackman, J. R., and G. R. Oldham. *Work Redesign.* Reading, MA: Addison-Wesley, 1980.

29. House, R. J., and G. Dressler. "The Path-Goal Theory of Leadership: Some Post Hoc and A Priori Tests." In *Contingency Approaches to Leadership.* Eds. J. G. Hunt and L. L. Larson. Carbondale: Southern Illinois University Press, 1974.

30. Howell, J. P., and P. W. Dorfman. "Substitute for Leadership: Test of a Construct." *Academy of Management Journal* 24 (1981), pp. 714–28.

31. Kerr, S., and J. M. Jermier. "Substitutes for Leadership: Their Meaning and Measurement." *Organizational Behavior and Human Performance* 22 (1978), pp. 375–403.

32. Myers, I. B., and B. H. McCaulley. *Manual: A Guide to the Development and Use of the Myers-Briggs Type Indicator.* Palo Alto, CA: Consulting Psychologists Press, 1985.

33. Bass, B. M. *Bass and Stogdill's Handbook of Leadership.* 3rd ed. New York: Free Press, 1990.

34. Ford, J. D. "Department Context and Formal Structure as Constraints on Leader Behavior." *Academy of Management Journal* 24 (1981), pp. 274–88.

35. Yukl, G. *Leadership in Organizations.* 2nd ed. Englewood Cliffs, NJ: Prentice Hall, 1989.

36. Siegall, M., and L. L. Cummings. "Task Role Ambiguity, Satisfaction, and the Moderating Effect of Task Instruction Source." *Human Relations* 39 (1986), pp. 1017–32.

37. Galbraith, J. *Designing Complex Organizations.* Menlo Park, CA: Addison-Wesley, 1973.

38. Fry, L., W. Kerr, and C. Lee. "Effects of Different Leader Behaviors under Different Levels of Task Interdependence." *Human Relations* 39 (1986), pp. 1067–82.

39. Luthans, F., S. A. Rosenkrantz, and H. W. Hennessey. "What Do Successful Managers Really Do? An Observational Study of Managerial Activities." *Journal of Applied Behavioral Science* 21 (1985), pp. 255–70.

40. Page, R. C., and W. W. Tornow. "Managerial Job Analysis: Are We Any Further Along?" Paper presented at a meeting of the Society of Industrial Organizational Psychology, Atlanta, GA, 1987.

41. Chitayat, G., and I. Venezia. "Determinates of Management Styles in Business and Nonbusiness Organizations." *Journal of Applied Psychology* 69 (1984), pp. 437–47.

42. Kurke, L. B., and H. E. Aldrich. "Mintzberg Was Right! A Replication and Extension of the Nature of Managerial Work." *Management Science* 29 (1983), pp. 975–84.

43. Morrison, A. M., R. P. White, and E. Van Velsor. *Breaking the Glass Ceiling.* Reading, MA: Addison-Wesley, 1987; Morse, G. "Why We Misread Motives." *Harvard Business Review,* January 2003, p. 18.

44. Robbins, S. P. *Organizational Behavior: Concepts, Controversies, and Applications.* Englewood Cliffs, NJ: Prentice Hall, 1986.

45. Podsakoff, P. M. "Determinants of a Supervisor's Use of Rewards and Punishments: A Literature Review and Suggestions for Future Research." *Organizational Behavior and Human Performance* 29 (1982), pp. 58–83.

46. Hammer, T. H., and J. Turk. "Organizational Determinants of Leader Behavior and Authority." *Journal of Applied Psychology* 71 (1987), pp. 674–82.

47. Bass, B. M. *Bass and Stogdill's Handbook of Leadership.* 3rd ed. New York: Free Press, 1990.

48. Austin, J. S., E. J. Conlon, and R. L. Daft. "Organizing for Effectiveness: A Guide to Using Structural Design for Mission Accomplishment." LMDC-TR-84-3-0. Maxwell AFB, AL: Leadership and Management Development Center, Air University, 1986.

49. *The Economist,* January 21, 2006, pp. 3–18.

50. Bass, B. M. *Bass and Stogdill's Handbook of Leadership.* 3rd ed. New York: Free Press, 1990.

51. Sayles, L. *Leadership: What Effective Managers Really Do . . . and How They Do It.* New York: McGraw-Hill, 1979.

52. Hammer, T. H., and J. Turk. "Organizational Determinants of Leader Behavior and Authority." *Journal of Applied Psychology* 71 (1987), pp. 674–82.

53. Kaplan, R. E. "The Warp and Woof of the General Manager's Jobs." In *Facilitating Work Effectiveness.* Eds. B. Schneider and D. Schoorman. Lexington, MA: Lexington Books, 1986.

54. Kanter, R. M. *The Change Masters.* New York: Simon & Schuster, 1983. ———. *Commitment and Community.* Cambridge: Harvard University Press, 1972.

55. Kaplan, R. E. "The Warp and Woof of the General Manager's Jobs." In *Facilitating Work Effectiveness.* Eds. B. Schneider and D. Schoorman. Lexington, MA: Lexington Books, 1986.

56. Schein, E. H. *Organizational Culture and Leadership: A Dynamic View.* San Francisco: Jossey-Bass, 1985.

57. Bass, B. M. *Bass and Stogdill's Handbook of Leadership.* 3rd ed. New York: Free Press, 1990.

58. Kozlowski, S. W. J., and M. L. Doherty. "Integration of Climate and Leadership: Examination of a Neglected Issue." *Journal of Applied Psychology* 74 (1989), pp. 546–53.

59. Schneider, B., P. J. Hanges, D. B. Smith, and A. N. Salvaggio. " Which Comes First: Employee Attitudes or Organizational Financial and Market

Performance?" *Journal of Applied Psychology* 88 (5) (2003), pp. 836–51; Schneider, J. "The Cultural Situation as a Condition for the Condition of Fame." *American Sociology Review* 2 (1937), pp. 480–91.

60. Bass, B. M. *Bass and Stogdill's Handbook of Leadership*. 3rd ed. New York: Free Press, 1990.

61. Kozlowski, S. W. J., and M. L. Doherty. "Integration of Climate and Leadership: Examination of a Neglected Issue." *Journal of Applied Psychology* 74 (1989), pp. 546–53.

62. Bass, B. M. *Bass and Stogdill's Handbook of Leadership*. 3rd ed. New York: Free Press, 1990.

63. Kilmann, R. H., and M. J. Saxton. *Organizational Cultures: Their Assessment and Change*. San Francisco: Jossey-Bass, 1983.

64. Schein, E. H. *Organizational Culture and Leadership: A Dynamic View*. San Francisco: Jossey-Bass, 1985.

65. Dumaine, B. "Creating a New Company Culture." *Fortune*, 1990, pp. 127–131.

66. Bass, B. M. *Leadership and Performance beyond Expectations*. New York: Free Press, 1985.

67. Kouzes, J. M., and B. Z. Posner. *The Leadership Challenge: How to Get Extraordinary Things Done in Organizations*. San Francisco: Jossey-Bass, 1987.

68. Schein, E. H. *Organizational Culture and Leadership: A Dynamic View*. San Francisco: Jossey-Bass, 1985.

69. Tichy, N. M., and M. A. Devanna. *The Transformational Leader*. New York: John Wiley, 1986.

70. Martin, J., and C. Siehl. "Organizational Culture and Counterculture: An Uneasy Symbiosis." *Organizational Dynamics* 11, no. 2 (1983), pp. 52–64.

71. Emery, F. E., and E. L. Trist. "The Causal Texture of Organizational Environments." *Human Relations* 18 (1965), pp. 21–32.

72. Mitchell, T. R. "Review of *In Search of Excellence* versus *The 100 Best Companies to Work for in America*: A Question of Perspective and Values." *Academy of Management Review* 10 (1985), pp. 350–55.

73. Peters, T. J., and R. H. Waterman. *In Search of Excellence*. New York: Harper & Row, 1982.

74. Levering, R., M. Moskowitz, and M. Katz. *The 100 Best Companies to Work for in America*. Reading, MA: Addison-Wesley, 1984.

75. Simpson, W. G., and T. C. Ireland. "Managerial Excellence and Shareholder Returns." *American Association of Individual Investors Journal* 9 (1987), pp. 4–8.

76. Bass, B. M. *Bass and Stogdill's Handbook of Leadership*. 3rd ed. New York: Free Press, 1990.

77. Ungson, G. R., C. James, and B. H. Spicer. "The Effects of Regulatory Agencies on Organizations in Wood Products and High Technology/Electronics Organizations." *Academy of Management Journal* 28 (1985), pp. 426–45.

78. Woodward, J. *Industrial Organization*. London: Oxford University Press, 1965.

79. Burns, T., and G. M. Stalker. *The Management of Innovation*. London: Tavistock, 1961.

80. Lawrence, P. R., and J. W. Lorsch. "Differentiation and Integration in Complex Organizations." *Administrative Science Quarterly* 12 (1967a), pp. 1–47; Lawrence, P. R., and J. W. Lorsch. *Organization and Environment.* Boston: Harvard University Press, 1967b.

81. Bass, B. M. *Leadership and Performance beyond Expectations.* New York: Free Press, 1985.

82. Curphy, G. J. "An Empirical Investigation of Bass' (1985) Theory of Transformational and Transactional Leadership." PhD dissertation, University of Minnesota, 1991a; Curphy, G. J. "Some Closing Remarks about the Use of Self- and Other-Ratings of Personality and Behaviors." In *Multirater Assessment Systems: What We've Learned.* M. D. Dunnette, chair. Symposium conducted at the 99th American Psychological Association Convention, San Francisco, August 1991b.

83. Roberts, N. C., and R. T. Bradley. "Limits of Charisma." In *Charismatic Leadership: The Elusive Factor in Organizational Effectiveness.* Eds. J. A. Conger and R. N. Kanungo. San Francisco: Jossey-Bass, 1988, pp. 253–75.

84. Mulder, M. and A. Stemerding. "Threat, Attraction to Group, and Need for Strong Leadership." *Human Relations* 16 (1963), pp. 317–34.

85. Mulder, M., R. D. de Jong, L. Koppelar, and J. Verhage. "Power, Situation, and Leaders' Effectiveness: An Organizational Study." *Journal of Applied Psychology* 71 (1986), pp. 566–70.

86. Pfeffer, J., and G. R. Salancik. "Determinants of Supervisory Behavior: A Role Set Analysis." *Human Relations* 28 (1975), pp. 139–54.

87. Peters, T. J., and R. H. Waterman. *In Search of Excellence.* New York: Harper & Row, 1982.

88. Hackman, J. R., and G. R. Oldham. *Work Redesign.* Reading, MA: Addison-Wesley, 1980.

89. Herzberg, F. *Work and the Nature of Man.* Cleveland, OH: World Publishing, 1966.

90. Yukl, G. *Leadership in Organizations.* 2nd ed. Englewood Cliffs, NJ: Prentice Hall, 1989.

12

Contingency Theories of Leadership

Introduction

If we were to provide an extremely short summary of the book to this point, we would say leadership is a process that involves aspects, of the leader, the followers, and the situation. In Part 1 we discussed the process aspects, while Part 2 was devoted exclusively to the leader. Part 3 focused on the followers, and in the previous chapter we discussed the situational components of leadership. You may have also noted that as much as we attempted to focus exclusively on the component of interest for the section, there were often overlapping areas in our leader–follower–situation (L-F-S) model. The overlap is true, and our attempts to segregate the concepts were done merely for simplicity. The world of leadership is really a rather complex one where multiple aspects of the L-F-S model will come into play. Leadership is contingent upon the interplay of all three aspects of our model, and these contingencies are the focus of this chapter.

This chapter reviews four of the more well-known contingency theories of leadership. All four address certain aspects of the leader, the followers, and the situation. These four theories also share several other similarities. First, because they are theories rather than someone's personal opinions, these four models have been the focus of a considerable amount of empirical research over the years. Second, these theories implicitly assume that leaders are able to accurately diagnose or assess key aspects of the followers and the leadership situation. Third, with the exception of Fiedler's contingency model,[1] leaders are assumed to be able to act in a flexible manner. In other words, leaders can and should change their behaviors as situational and follower characteristics change. Fourth, a correct match between situational and follower characteristics and leaders' behaviors is assumed to have a positive effect on group or organizational outcomes. Thus, these

It is a capital mistake to theorize before one has data.

Sir Arthur Conan Doyle

theories maintain that leadership effectiveness is maximized when leaders correctly make their behaviors *contingent* on certain situational and follower characteristics. Because of these similarities, Chemers argued that these four theories were more similar than they were different. He said they differed primarily in terms of the types of situational and follower characteristics upon which various leader behaviors should be contingent.

The Normative Decision Model

Obviously, in some situations leaders can delegate decisions to subordinates or should ask subordinates for relevant information before making a decision. In other situations, such as emergencies or crises, leaders may need to make a decision with little, if any, input from subordinates. The level of input subordinates have in the decision-making process can and does vary substantially depending on the issue at hand, followers' level of technical expertise, or the presence or absence of a crisis. Although the level of participation varies due to various leader, follower, and situational factors, Vroom and Yetton maintained that leaders could often improve group performance by using an optimal amount of participation in the decision-making process. Thus, the normative decision model is directed solely at determining how much input subordinates should have in the decision-making process. Precisely because the normative decision model is limited only to decision making and is not a grand, all-encompassing theory, it is a good model with which to begin the chapter.

Levels of Participation

Like the other theories in this chapter, the **normative decision model**[4] was designed to improve some aspects of leadership effectiveness. In this case, Vroom and Yetton explored how various leader, follower, and situational factors affect the degree of subordinates' participation in the decision-making process and, in turn, group performance. To determine which situational and follower factors affect the level of participation and group performance, Vroom and Yetton first investigated the decision-making processes leaders use in group settings. They discovered a continuum of decision-making processes ranging from completely autocratic (labeled "AI") to completely democratic, where all members of the group have equal participation (labeled "GII"). These processes are listed in Highlight 12.1.

Decision Quality and Acceptance

After establishing a continuum of decision processes, Vroom and Yetton[5] established criteria to evaluate the adequacy of the decisions made—criteria they believed would be credible to leaders and equally applicable across the five levels of participation. Although a wide variety of criteria could be used, Vroom and Yetton believed decision quality and

Levels of Participation in the Normative Decision Model

HIGHLIGHT 12.1

Autocratic Processes

AI: The leader solves the problem or makes the decision by him- or herself using the information available at the time.

AII: The leader obtains any necessary information from followers, then decides on a solution to the problem herself. She may or may not tell followers the purpose of her questions or give information about the problem or decision she is working on. The input provided by them is clearly in response to her request for specific information. They do not play a role in the definition of the problem or in generating or evaluating alternative solutions.

Coonsultative Processes

CI: The leader shares the problem with the relevant followers individually, getting their ideas and suggestions without bringing them together as a group. Then he makes a decision. This decision may or may not reflect the followers' influence.

CII: The leader shares the problem with her followers in a group meeting. In this meeting, she obtains their ideas and suggestions. Then she makes the decision, which may or may not reflect the followers' influence.

Group Process

GII: The leader shares the problem with his followers as a group. Together they generate and evaluate alternatives and attempt to reach agreement (consensus) on a solution. The leader's role is much like that of a chairman, coordinating the discussion, keeping it focused on the problem, and making sure that the critical issues are discussed. He can provide the group with information or ideas that he has, but he does not try to "press" them to adopt "his" solution. Moreover, leaders adopting this level of participation are willing to accept and implement any solution that has the support of the entire group.

Source: Adapted from V. H. Vroom and P. W. Yetton, *Leadership and Decision Making.* Pittsburgh, PA: University of Pittsburgh Press, 1973.

decision acceptance were the two most important criteria for judging the adequacy of a decision.

Decision quality means simply that if the decision has a rational or objectively determinable "better or worse" alternative, the leader should select the better alternative. Vroom and Yetton[6] intended quality in their model to apply when the decision could result in an objectively or measurably better outcome for the group or organization. In the for-profit sector, this criterion can be assessed in several ways, but perhaps the easiest to understand is, "Would the decision show up on the balance sheet?" In this case, a high-quality (or, conversely, low-quality) decision would have a direct and measurable impact on the organization's bottom line. In the public sector, one might determine if there was a quality component to a decision by asking, "Will one alternative have a greater cost saving than the other?" or "Does this decision improve services to the client?" Although it may seem that leaders should always choose the alternative with the highest decision quality, this is not always the case. Often, leaders are confronted with equally good (or bad) alternatives. At other times, the issue in question is fairly trivial, rendering the quality of the decision relatively unimportant.

Decision acceptance implies that followers accept the decision as if it were their own and do not merely comply with the decision. Acceptance of the decision outcome by the followers may be critical, particularly if it is the followers who will bear principal responsibility for implementing the decision. With such acceptance, there will be no need for superiors to monitor compliance, which can be a continuing and time-consuming activity (and virtually impossible in some circumstances, such as with a geographically dispersed sales staff).

As with quality, acceptance of a decision is not always critical for implementation. For example, most organizations have an accounting form that employees use to obtain reimbursement for travel expenses. Suppose a company's chief financial officer (CFO) has decided to change the format of the form for reimbursing travel expenses and has had the new forms printed and distributed throughout the company. Further, she has sent out a notice that, effective June 1, the old forms will no longer be accepted for reimbursement—only claims made using the new forms will be processed and paid. Assuming the new form has no gross errors, problems, or omissions, our CFO really has no concern with acceptance as defined here. If people want to be reimbursed for their travel expenses, then they will use the new form. This decision, in essence, implements itself.

On the other hand, leaders sometimes assume that they do not need to worry about acceptance because they have so much power over their followers that overt rejection of a decision is not likely to occur. A corporate CEO is not apt to see a junior accountant stand up and openly challenge the CEO's decision to implement a new policy, even though the young accountant may not "buy into" the new policy at all. Because followers generally do not openly object to the decisions made by leaders with this much power, these leaders often mistakenly assume that their decisions have been accepted and will be fully implemented. This is a rather naive view of what really goes on in organizations. Just because the junior subordinate does not publicly voice his opposition does not mean he will rush right out and wholeheartedly implement the decision. In fact, the junior accountant has a lot more time to destructively undermine the policy than the CEO does to check to ensure it is being carried out to the letter.

The Decision Tree

Having settled on quality and acceptance as the two principal criteria for effective decisions, Vroom and Yetton then developed a normative decision model. (A normative model is one based on what ought to happen rather than describing what does happen.) They also developed a set of questions to protect quality and acceptance by eliminating decision processes that would be wrong or inappropriate. Generally, these questions concern the problem itself, the amount of pertinent information possessed by the leader and followers, and various situational factors.

In order to make it easier for leaders to determine how much participation subordinates should have to optimize decision quality and acceptance,

FIGURE 12.1 Vroom and Yetton's leadership decision tree.

Source: Reprinted from Victor H. Vroom and Philip W. Yetton, *Leadership and Decision Making*, by permission of the University of Pittsburgh Press, © 1973 University of Pittsburgh Press.

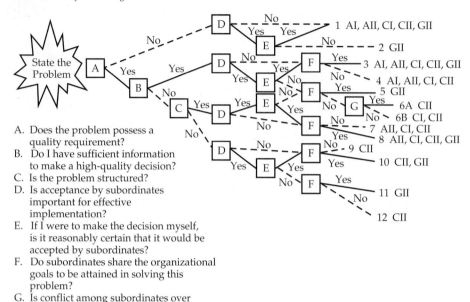

A. Does the problem possess a quality requirement?
B. Do I have sufficient information to make a high-quality decision?
C. Is the problem structured?
D. Is acceptance by subordinates important for effective implementation?
E. If I were to make the decision myself, is it reasonably certain that it would be accepted by subordinates?
F. Do subordinates share the organizational goals to be attained in solving this problem?
G. Is conflict among subordinates over preferred solutions likely?

Vroom and Yetton[7] incorporated these questions into a decision tree (see Figure 12.1). To use the decision tree, one starts at the left by stating the problem and then proceeds through the model from left to right. Every time a box is encountered, the question associated with that box must be answered with either a yes or a no response. Eventually, all paths lead to a set of decision processes that, if used, will lead to a decision that protects both quality and acceptance.

Having reached a set of feasible alternatives that meet the desirable criteria for quality and acceptance among followers, the leader may then wish to consider additional criteria. One very practical consideration is the amount of time available (see Highlight 12.2). If time is critical, then the leader should select the alternative in the feasible set that is farthest to the *left*, again noting that the feasible set is arranged from AI through GII. It generally takes less time to make and implement autocratic decisions than it does to make consultative or group decisions. Nevertheless, it is important to note that the first step is to protect quality and acceptance (by using the model). Only *after* arriving at an appropriate set of outcomes should leaders consider time in the decision-making process. This tenet is sometimes neglected in the workplace by leaders who overemphasize time as a criterion. Obviously, there are some situations where time is absolutely critical, as in life-or-death emergencies. But too often, leaders ask for a decision to be made as if the situation were an emergency when, in reality, they (the leaders, not the situation) are creating the time pressure. Despite such behavior, it is difficult to imagine a leader who would knowingly prefer a fast decision that lacks both quality and acceptance among the implementers to one that is of high quality and acceptable to followers but that takes more time.

Another important consideration is follower development. Again, after quality and acceptance have been considered using the decision tree, and if the leader has determined that time is not a critical element, she may wish to follow a decision process more apt to allow followers to develop their own decision-making skills. This can be achieved by using the decision tree and then selecting the alternative within the feasible set that is farthest to the *right*. As was the case above, the arrangement of processes from AI to GII provides an increasing amount of follower development by moving from autocratic to group decisions.

Finally, if neither time nor follower development is a concern and multiple options are available in the feasible set of alternatives, the leader may select a style that best meets his or her needs. This may be the process with which the leader is most comfortable ("I'm a CII kind of guy"), or it may be a process in which he or she would like to develop more skill.

Concluding Thoughts about the Normative Decision Model

Having looked at this model in some detail, we will now look at it from the perspective of the leader–follower–situation (L-F-S) framework. To do this, we have used the different decision processes and the questions from the decision tree to illustrate different components in the L-F-S framework (see Figure 12.2). Several issues become apparent in this depiction. First, for ease of presentation we have placed each question or factor solely within one circle or another. Nevertheless, one could argue that some of the questions could or should be placed in another part of the model. For example, the question "Do I have sufficient information to make a high-quality decision?" is placed in the leader block. It might be argued, however, that no leader could answer this question without some knowledge of the situation. Strictly speaking, therefore, perhaps this question should be placed in the intersection between the leader and the situation. Nonetheless, in keeping with our theme that leadership involves interactions among all three elements, it seems sufficient at this point to illustrate them in their simplest state.

A second issue also becomes apparent when the normative decision model is viewed through the L-F-S framework. Notice how the Vroom and Yetton[8] model shifts focus away from the leader toward both the situation and, to an even greater degree, the followers. There are no questions about the leader's personality, motivations, values, or attitudes. In fact, the leader's preference is considered only after higher-priority factors

Irrationally held truths may be more harmful than reasoned errors.

Thomas Huxley

FIGURE 12.2 Factors from the normative decision model and the interactional framework.

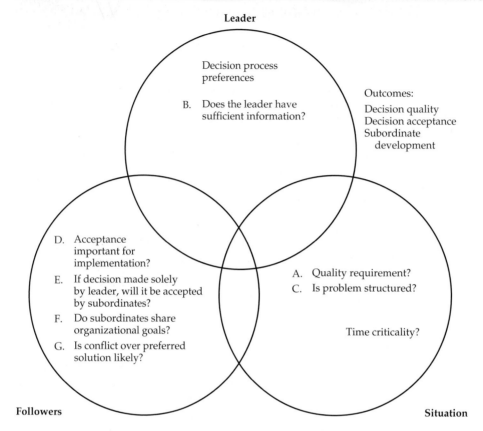

have been considered. The only underlying assumption is that the leader is interested in implementing a high-quality decision (when quality is an issue) that is acceptable to followers (when acceptance is critical to implementation). Given that assumption and a willingness to consider aspects of the situation and aspects of the followers, the leader's behavior can be channeled into more effective decision-making processes.

A third issue is that the L-F-S framework organizes concepts in a familiar conceptual structure. This is an advantage even for a theory with as limited a focus as the normative decision model (i.e., decision making); it will be even more helpful later as we consider more complex theories.

Finally, because the normative decision model is a *leadership theory* rather than Vroom and Yetton's personal opinions, a number of empirical studies have investigated the model's efficacy. Research conducted by Field[9] and Vroom and Jago[10,11] provided strong support for the model, as these studies showed that leaders were much more likely to make effective or successful decisions when they followed its tenets than when they

How Much Time Do I Have?

HIGHLIGHT 12.2

In a world of instant messages that require lightning-fast responses, Steven B. Sample, president of the University of Southern California, is touting the benefits of "artful procrastination." In his course on leadership and his book, *The Contrarian's Guide to Leadership,* a key lesson is never make a decision today that can reasonably be put off to tomorrow:

> With respect to timing, almost all great leaders have understood that making quick decisions is typically counterproductive. I'm not talking about what to have for breakfast or what tie to wear today. President Harry Truman almost personified this concept. When anyone told him they needed a decision, the first thing he would ask is "How much time do I have—a week, 10 seconds, six months?" What he understood was that the

nature of the decision that a leader makes depends to a large extent on how much time he has in which to make it. He also understood that delaying a decision as long as reasonably possible generally leads to the best decisions being made.

Other lessons from Sample include:

- Think gray. Don't form opinions if you don't have to.
- Think free. Move several steps beyond traditional brainstorming.
- Listen first, talk later. And when you listen, do so artfully.
- You can't copy your way to the top.

Sources: http://www.usc.edu/president/book/; http://www.refresher.com/!enescontrarian.html; http://bottomlinesecrets.com/blpnet/article.html?article_id=33302.

ignored them. Nevertheless, although leaders may be more apt to make more effective decisions when using the model, there is no evidence to show that these leaders are more effective overall than leaders not using the model.[12] The latter findings again point out that both the leadership process and leadership effectiveness are complex phenomema; being a good decision maker is not enough to be a good leader (although it certainly helps). Other problems with the model are that it views decision making as taking place at a single point in time,[13] assumes that leaders are equally skilled at using all five decision procedures,[14] and assumes that some of the prescriptions of the model may not be the best for a given situation. For example, the normative decision model prescribes that leaders use a GII decision process if conflict may occur over a decision, but leaders may be more effective if they instead make an AI decision and avoid intragroup conflict.[15] Despite these problems, the normative model is one of the best supported of the four major contingency theories of leadership, and leaders would be wise to consider using the model when making decisions.

The Situational Leadership® Model

It seems fairly obvious that leaders do not interact with all followers in the same manner. For example, a leader may give general guidelines or goals to her highly competent and motivated followers but spend considerable time coaching, directing, and training her unskilled and unmotivated followers. Or leaders may provide relatively little praise and assurances to followers with high self-confidence but high amounts of support to followers with low self-confidence. Although leaders often have different interactional styles when dealing with individual followers, is there an optimum way for leaders to adjust their behavior with different followers and thereby increase their likelihood of success? And if there is, then what factors should the leader base his behavior on—the follower's intelligence? Personality traits? Values? Preferences? Technical competence? A model called **Situational Leadership**® offers answers to these two important leadership questions.

Leader Behaviors

The Situational Leadership® model has evolved over time. Its essential elements first appeared in 1969,[16] with roots in the Ohio State studies, in which the two broad categories of leader behaviors, initiating structure and consideration, were initially identified (see Chapter 8). As Situational Leadership® evolved, so did the labels (but not the content) for the two leadership behavior categories. Initiating structure changed to **task behaviors,** which were defined as the extent to which the leader spells out the responsibilities of an individual or group. Task behaviors include telling people what to do, how to do it, when to do it, and who is to do it. Similarly, consideration changed to **relationship behaviors,** or how much the leader engages in two-way communication. Relationship behaviors include listening, encouraging, facilitating, clarifying, explaining why the task is important, and giving support.

When the behavior of actual leaders was studied, there was little evidence to show these two categories of leader behavior were consistently related to leadership success; the relative effectiveness of these two behavior dimensions often depended on the situation. Hersey's Situational Leadership® model explains why leadership effectiveness varies across these two behavior dimensions and situations. It arrays the two orthogonal dimensions as in the Ohio State studies and then divides each of them into high and low segments (see Figure 12.3). According to the model, depicting the two leadership dimensions this way is useful because certain combinations of task and relationship behaviors may be more effective in some situations than in others.

The real world is a messy place—yet, even a messy place can (should?) be attacked systematically.

Alex Cornell

For example, in some situations high levels of task but low levels of relationship behaviors are effective; in other situations, just the opposite is true. So far, however, we have not considered the key follower or situational characteristics with which these combinations of task and relationship behaviors were most effective. Hersey says that these four combinations of task and relationship behaviors would increase leadership effectiveness if they were made contingent on the readiness level of the individual follower to perform a given task.

FIGURE 12.3
Situational
Leadership®.

Source: Paul Hersey,
Kenneth Blanchard, and
Dewey Johnson, *Management
of Organizational Behavior:
Utilizing Human Resources,*
7th ed. Englewood Cliffs, NJ:
Prentice Hall, 1996, p. 200.
Copyright © 2006. Reprinted
with permission of the
Center for Leadership
Studies, Inc., Escondido, CA
92025. All rights reserved.

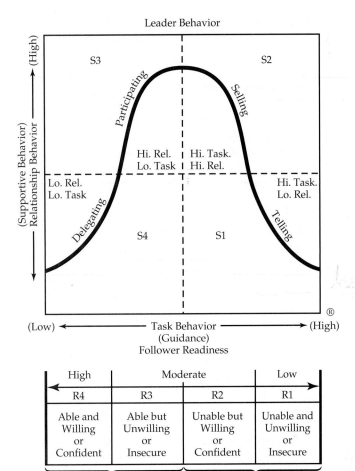

High	Moderate		Low
R4	R3	R2	R1
Able and Willing or Confident	Able but Unwilling or Insecure	Unable but Willing or Confident	Unable and Unwilling or Insecure

Follower Directed | Leader Directed

Follower Readiness

In Situational Leadership®, **follower readiness** refers to a follower's ability and willingness to accomplish a particular task. Readiness is not an assessment of an individual's personality, traits, values, age, and so on. It's not a personal characteristic, but rather how ready an individual is to perform a particular task. Any given follower could be low on readiness to perform one task but high on readiness to perform a different task. An experienced emergency room physician would be high in readiness on tasks like assessing a patient's medical status, but could be relatively low on readiness for facilitating an interdepartmental team meeting to solve an ambiguous and complex problem like developing hospital practices to encourage collaboration across departments.

Prescriptions of the Model

Now that the key contingency factor, follower readiness, has been identified, let us move on to another aspect of the figure—combining follower readiness levels with the four combinations of leader behaviors described earlier. The horizontal bar or arrow in Figure 12.3 depicts follower readiness as increasing from right to left (not in the direction we are used to seeing). There are four segments along this continuum, ranging from R1 (the lowest) to R4 (the highest). Along this continuum, however, the assessment of follower readiness can be fairly subjective. A follower who possesses high levels of readiness would clearly fall in the R4 category, just as a follower unable and unwilling (or *too* insecure) to perform a task would fall in R1.

To complete the model, a curved line is added that represents the leadership behavior that will most likely be effective given a particular level of follower readiness. In order to apply the model, leaders should first assess the readiness level (R1–R4) of the follower relative to the task to be accomplished. Next, a vertical line should be drawn from the center of the readiness level up to the point where it intersects with the curved line in Figure 12.3. The quadrant in which this intersection occurs represents the level of task and relationship behavior that has the best chance of producing successful outcomes. For example, imagine you are a fire chief and have under your command a search-and-rescue team. One of the team members is needed to rescue a backpacker who has fallen in the mountains, and you have selected a particular follower to accomplish the task. What leadership behavior should you exhibit? If this follower has both substantial training and experience in this type of rescue, you would assess his readiness level as R4. A vertical line from R4 would intersect the curved line in the quadrant where both low task and low relationship behaviors by the leader are most apt to be successful. As the leader, you should exhibit a low level of task and relationship behaviors and delegate this task to the follower. On the other hand, you may have a brand-new member of the fire department who still has to learn the ins and outs of firefighting. Because this particular follower has low task readiness (R1), the model maintains that the leader should use a high level of task and a low level of relationship behaviors when initially dealing with this follower.

Hersey suggests one further step leaders may wish to consider. The model described above helps the leader select the most appropriate behavior given the current level of follower readiness. However, there may be cases when the leader would like to see the followers increase their level of readiness for particular tasks by implementing a series of **developmental interventions** to help boost follower readiness levels. The process would begin by first assessing the follower's current level of readiness and then determining the leader behavior that best suits that follower in that task. Instead of using the behavior prescribed by the

A Developmental Intervention Using SLT

HIGHLIGHT 12.3

Dianne is a resident assistant in charge of a number of students in a university dorm. One particular sophomore, Michael, has volunteered to work on projects in the past but never seems to take the initiative to get started on his own. Michael seems to wait until Dianne gives him explicit direction, approval, and encouragement before he will get started. Michael can do a good job, but he seems to be unwilling to start without some convincing that it is all right, and unless Dianne makes explicit what steps are to be taken. Dianne has assessed Michael's readiness level as R2, but she would like to see him develop, both in task readiness and in psychological maturity. The behavior most likely to fit Michael's current readiness level is selling, or high task, high relationship. But Dianne has decided to implement a developmental intervention to help Michael raise his readiness level. Dianne can be most helpful in this intervention by moving up one level to participating, or low task, high relationship. By reducing the amount of task instructions and direction while encouraging Michael to lay out a plan on his own and supporting his steps in the right direction, Dianne is most apt to help Michael become an R3 follower. This does not mean the work will get done most efficiently, however. Just as we saw in the Vroom and Yetton model earlier, if part of the leader's job is development of followers, then time may be a reasonable and necessary trade-off for short-term efficiency.

model, however, the leader would select the next higher leadership behavior. Another way of thinking about this would be for the leader to select the behavior pattern that would fit the follower if that follower were one level higher in readiness. This intervention is designed to help followers in their development, hence its name (see Highlight 12.3, on developmental interventions).

Concluding Thoughts about the Situational Leadership® Model

In Figure 12.4, we can see how the factors in Situational Leadership® fit within the L-F-S framework. In comparison to the Vroom and Yetton model, there are fewer factors to be considered in each of the three elements. The only situational consideration is knowledge of the task, and the only follower factor is readiness. On the other hand, the theory goes well beyond decision making, which was the sole domain of the normative decision model.

Situational Leadership® is usually appealing to students and practitioners because of its commonsense approach as well as the ease of understanding it. Unfortunately, there is little published research to support the predictions of Situational Leadership® in the workplace.[17,18] A great deal of research has been done within organizations that have implemented Situational Leadership®, but most of those findings are not available for public dissemination. Nevertheless, even with these shortcomings, Situational Leadership® is a useful way to get leaders to think about how leadership

FIGURE 12.4 Factors from the Situational Leadership® model and the interactional framework.

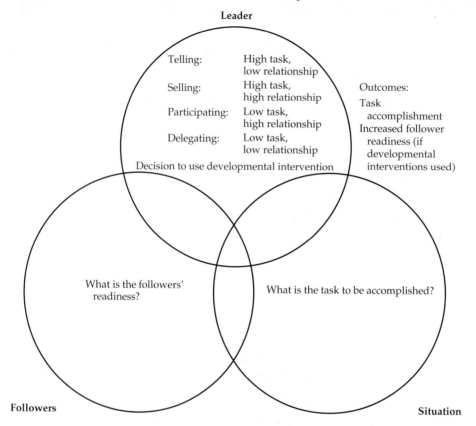

Leader

Telling: High task, low relationship

Selling: High task, high relationship

Participating: Low task, high relationship

Delegating: Low task, low relationship

Decision to use developmental intervention

Outcomes:

Task accomplishment
Increased follower readiness (if developmental interventions used)

What is the followers' readiness?

What is the task to be accomplished?

Followers

Situation

effectiveness may depend somewhat on being flexible with different sub-ordinates, not on acting the same way toward them all.

The Contingency Model

Although leaders may be able to change their behaviors toward individual subordinates, leaders also have dominant behavioral tendencies. Some leaders may be generally more supportive and relationship-oriented, whereas others may be more concerned with task or goal accomplishment. The contingency model[19] recognizes that leaders have these general behavioral tendencies and specifies situations where certain leaders (or behavioral dispositions) may be more effective than others.

Fiedler's[20] **contingency model** of leadership is probably the earliest and most well-known contingency theory, and is often perceived by students to be almost the opposite of SLT. Compared to the contingency model, SLT emphasizes flexibility in leader behaviors, whereas the contingency model maintains that leaders are much more consistent (and consequently less flexible) in their behavior. Situational leadership theory maintains that leaders who *correctly base their behaviors* on follower maturity will be more effective, whereas the contingency model suggests that leader effectiveness is primarily determined by *selecting the right kind of leader for a certain situation or changing the situation* to fit the particular leader's style. Another way to say this is that leadership effectiveness depends on both the leader's style and the favorableness of the leadership situation. Some leaders are better than others in some situations but less effective in other situations. To understand contingency theory, therefore, we need to look first at the critical characteristics of the leader and then at the critical aspects of the situation.

The Least-Preferred-Co-worker Scale

In order to determine a leader's general style or tendency, Fiedler developed an instrument called the **least-preferred-co-worker (LPC) scale.** The scale instructs a leader to think of the single individual with whom he has had the greatest difficulty working (i.e., the least-preferred co-worker) and then to describe that individual in terms of a series of bipolar adjectives (e.g., friendly-unfriendly, boring-interesting, sincere-insincere). Those ratings are then converted into a numerical score.

In thinking about such a procedure, many people assume that the score is determined primarily by the characteristics of whatever particular individual the leader happened to identify as his least-preferred co-worker. In the context of contingency theory, however, it is important to understand that the score is thought to *represent something about the leader, not the specific individual the leader evaluated.*

The current interpretation of these scores is that they identify a leader's motivation hierarchy.[21] Based on their LPC scores, leaders are categorized into two groups: **low-LPC leaders** and **high-LPC leaders.** In terms of their motivation hierarchy, low-LPC leaders are primarily motivated by the task, which means that these leaders primarily gain satisfaction from task accomplishment. Thus, their dominant behavioral tendencies are similar to the initiating structure behavior described in the Ohio State research or the task behavior of SLT. However, if tasks are being accomplished in an acceptable manner, then low-LPC leaders will move to their secondary level of motivation, which is forming and maintaining relationships with followers. Thus, low-LPC leaders will focus on improving their relationships with followers *after* they are assured that assigned tasks are being satisfactorily accomplished. As soon as tasks are no longer being accomplished in an acceptable manner, however, low-LPC leaders will refocus their efforts on task accomplishment and persist with these efforts until task accomplishment is back on track.

In terms of motivation hierarchy, high-LPC leaders are primarily motivated by relationships, which means that these leaders are primarily satisfied

FIGURE 12.5
Motivational hierarchies for low- and high-LPC leaders.

Low-LPC leader motivational hierarchy

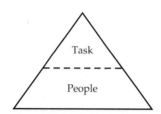

High-LPC leader motivational hierarchy

by establishing and maintaining close interpersonal relationships. Thus, their dominant behavioral tendencies are similar to the consideration behaviors described in the Ohio State research or the relationship behaviors in SLT. If high-LPC leaders have established good relationships with their followers, then they will move to their secondary level of motivation, which is task accomplishment. As soon as leader–follower relations are jeopardized, however, high-LPC leaders will cease working on tasks and refocus their efforts on improving relationships with followers.

You can think of the LPC scale as identifying two different sorts of leaders, with their respective motivational hierarchies depicted in Figure 12.5. Lower-level needs must be satisfied first. Low-LPC leaders will move "up" to satisfying relationship needs when they are assured the task is being satisfactorily accomplished. High-LPC leaders will move "up" to emphasizing task accomplishment when they have established good relationships with their followers.

Because all tests have some level of imprecision, Fiedler[22] suggested that the LPC scale cannot accurately identify the motivation hierarchy for those individuals with certain intermediate scores. Research by Kennedy[23] suggested an alternative view. Kennedy has shown that individuals within the intermediate range of LPC scale scores may more easily or readily switch between being task- or relationship-oriented leaders than those individuals with more extreme scale scores. They may be equally satisfied by working on the task or establishing relationships with followers.

Situational Favorability

The other critical variable in the contingency model is **situational favorability,** which is the amount of control the leader has over the followers. Presumably, the more control a leader has over followers, the more favorable the situation is, at least from the leader's perspective. Fiedler included three subelements in situation favorability. These were leader–member relations, task structure, and position power.

Leader–member relations is the most powerful of the three subelements in determining overall situation favorability. It involves the extent to which relationships between the leader and followers are generally cooperative and friendly or antagonistic and difficult. Leaders who rate leader–member relations as high would feel they had the support of their followers and could rely on their loyalty.

Task structure is second in potency in determining overall situation favorability. Here the leader would objectively determine task structure by assessing whether there were detailed descriptions of work products, standard operating procedures, or objective indicators of how well the task is being accomplished. The more one could answer these questions affirmatively, the higher the structure of the task.

Position power is the weakest of the three elements of situational favorability. Leaders who have titles of authority or rank, the authority to administer rewards and punishments, and the legitimacy to conduct follower performance appraisals have greater position power than leaders who lack them.

The relative weights of these three components, taken together, can be used to create a continuum of situational favorability. When using the contingency model, leaders are first asked to rate items that measure the strength of leader–member relations, the degree of task structure, and their level of position power. These ratings are then weighted and combined to determine an overall level of situational favorability facing the leader.[24] Any particular situation's favorability can then be plotted on a continuum Fiedler divided into octants representing distinctly different levels of situational favorability. The relative weighting scheme for the subelements and how they make up each of the eight octants can be seen in Figure 12.6.

You can see that the octants of situational favorability range from 1 (highly favorable) to 8 (very unfavorable). The highest levels of situational favorability occur when leader–member relations are good, the task

FIGURE 12.6 Contingency model octant structure for determining situational favorability.

Leader–member relations	Good				Poor			
Task structure	Structured		Unstructured		Structured		Unstructured	
Position power	High	Low	High	Low	High	Low	High	Low
Octant	1	2	3	4	5	6	7	8

High ← Overall situation favorability → Low

is structured, and position power is high. The lowest levels of situational favorability occur when there are high levels of leader–member conflict, the task is unstructured or unclear, and the leader does not have the power to reward or punish subordinates. Moreover, the relative weighting of the three subelements can easily be seen by their order of precedence in Figure 12.6, with leader–member relations appearing first, followed by task structure, and then position power. For example, because leader–member relations carry so much weight, it is impossible for leaders with good leader–member relations to have anything worse than moderate situational favorability, regardless of their task structure or position power. In other words, leaders with good leader–member relations will be in a situation that has situational favorability no worse than octant 4; leaders with poor leader–member relations will be facing a leadership situation with situational favorability no better than octant 5.

Prescriptions of the Model

Fiedler and his associates have conducted numerous studies to determine how different leaders (as described by their LPC scores) have performed in different situations (as described in terms of situational favorability). Figure 12.7 describes which type of leader (high or low LPC) Fiedler found to be most effective, given different levels of situation favorability. The solid dark line represents the relative effectiveness of a low-LPC leader, and the dashed line represents the relative effectiveness of a high-LPC leader. It is obvious from the way the two lines cross and recross that there is some interaction between the leader's style and the overall situation favorability. If the situational favorability is moderate (octants 4, 5, 6, or 7), then those groups led by leaders concerned with establishing and maintaining relationships (high-LPC leaders) seem to do best. However, if the situation is either very unfavorable (octant 8) or highly favorable

FIGURE 12.7

Leader effectiveness based on the contingency between leader LPC score and situation favorability.

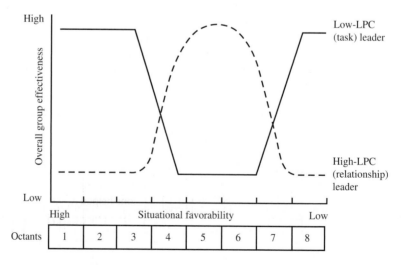

(octants 1, 2, or 3), then those groups led by the task-motivated (low-LPC) leaders seem to do best.

Fiedler suggested that leaders will try to satisfy their primary motivation when faced with unfavorable or moderately favorable situations. This means that low-LPC leaders will concentrate on the task and high-LPC leaders will concentrate on relationships when faced with these two levels of situational favorability. Nevertheless, leaders facing highly favorable situations know that their primary motivations will be satisfied and thus will move to their secondary motivational state. This means that *leaders will behave according to their secondary motivational state only when faced with highly favorable situations* (see Highlight 12.4).

There are several interesting implications of Fiedler's[25] model worthy of additional comment. Because leaders develop their distinctive motivation hierarchies and dominant behavior tendencies through a lifetime of experiences, Fiedler believed these hierarchies and tendencies would be difficult to change through training. Fiedler maintained it was naive to believe that sending someone to a relatively brief leadership training program could substantially alter any leader's personality or typical way of acting in leadership situations; after all, such tendencies had been developed over

High- and Low-LPC Leaders and the Contingency Model

HIGHLIGHT 12.4

Suppose we had two leaders, Tom Low (a low-LPC or task-motivated leader) and Brenda High (a high-LPC or relationship-motivated leader). In unfavorable situations, Tom will be motivated by his primary level and will thus exhibit task behaviors. In similar situations, Brenda will also be motivated by her primary level and as a result will exhibit relationship behaviors. Fiedler found that, in unfavorable situations, task behavior will help the group to be more effective, so Tom's behavior would better match the requirements of the situation. Group effectiveness would not be aided by Brenda's relationship behavior in this situation.

In situations with moderate favorability, both Tom and Brenda are still motivated by their primary motivations, so their behaviors will be precisely the same as described: Tom will exhibit task behaviors and Brenda will exhibit relationship behaviors. Because the situation has changed, however, group effectiveness no longer requires task behavior.

Instead, the combination of situational variables leads to a condition where a leader's relationship behaviors will make the greatest contribution to group effectiveness. Hence, Brenda will be the most effective leader in situations of moderate favorability.

In highly favorable situations, the explanation provided by Fiedler gets more complex. When leaders find themselves in highly favorable situations, they no longer have to be concerned about satisfying their primary motivations. In highly favorable situations, leaders switch to satisfying their secondary motivations. Because Tom's secondary motivation is to establish and maintain relationships, in highly favorable situations he will exhibit relationship behaviors. Similarly, Brenda will also be motivated by her secondary motivation, so she would manifest task behaviors in highly favorable situations. Fiedler believed that leaders who manifested relationship behaviors in highly favorable situations helped groups to be more effective. In this case, Tom is giving the group what they need to be more effective.

many years of experience. Instead of trying to change the leader, Fiedler concluded, training would be more effective if it showed leaders how to recognize and change key situational characteristics to better fit their personal motivational hierarchies and behavioral tendencies. Thus, according to Fiedler, the content of leadership training should emphasize situational engineering rather than behavioral flexibility in leaders. Relatedly, organizations could become more effective if they matched the characteristics of the leader (in this case LPC scores) with the demands of the situation (i.e., situational favorability) than if they tried to change the leader's behavior to fit the situation. These suggestions imply that high- or low-LPC leaders in mismatched situations should either change the situation or move to jobs that better match their motivational hierarchies and behavioral patterns.

Concluding Thoughts about the Contingency Model

Before reviewing the empirical evidence, perhaps we can attain a clearer understanding of the contingency model by examining it through the L-F-S framework. As seen in Figure 12.8, task structure is a function of the

FIGURE 12.8 Factors from Fiedler's contingency theory and the interactional framework.

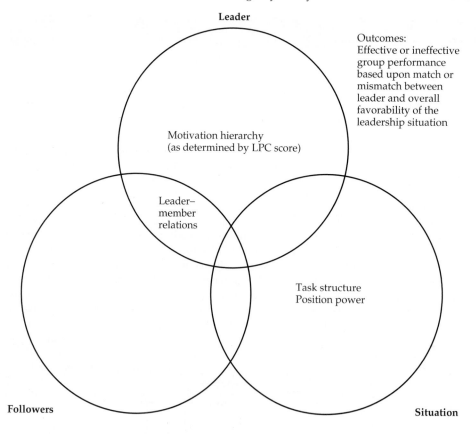

Leader

Motivation hierarchy
(as determined by LPC score)

Outcomes:
Effective or ineffective
group performance
based upon match or
mismatch between
leader and overall
favorability of the
leadership situation

Leader–
member
relations

Task structure
Position power

Followers

Situation

situation and LPC scores are a function of the leader. Because position power is not a characteristic of the leader but of the situation the leader finds him- or herself in, it is included in the situational circle. Leader–member relations is a joint function of the leader and the followers; thus, it best belongs in the overlapping intersection of the leader and follower circles.

As opposed to the dearth of evidence for Hersey and Blanchard's[26,27] situational theory, Fiedler and his fellow researchers have provided considerable evidence that the predictions of the model are empirically valid, particularly in laboratory settings.[28-32] However, a review of the studies conducted in field settings yielded only mixed support for the model.[33] Moreover, researchers have criticized the model for the uncertainties surrounding the meaning of LPC scores,[34-36] the interpretation of situational favorability,[37,38] and the relationships between LPC scores and situational favorability.[39-41] Despite such questions, however, the contingency model has stimulated considerable research and is the most validated of all leadership theories.

The Path-Goal Theory

Perhaps the most sophisticated (and comprehensive) of the four contingency models is path-goal theory. The underlying mechanism of **path-goal theory** deals with expectancy, a cognitive approach to understanding motivation where people calculate effort-to-performance probabilities (If I study for 12 hours, what is the probability I will get an A on the final exam?), performance-to-outcome probabilities (If I get an A on the final, what is the probability of getting an A in the course?), and assigned valences or values to outcome (How much do I value a higher GPA?). Theoretically at least, people were assumed to make these calculations on a rational basis, and the theory could be used to predict what tasks people would put their energies into, given some finite number of options.

Path-goal theory uses the same basic assumptions as expectancy theory. At the most fundamental level, the effective leader will provide or ensure the availability of valued rewards for followers (the "goal") and then help them find the best way of getting there (the "path"). Along the way, the effective leader will help the followers identify and remove roadblocks, and avoid dead ends; the leader will also provide emotional support as needed. These "task" and "relationship" leadership actions essentially involve increasing followers' probability estimates for effort-to-performance and performance-to-reward expectancies. In other words, the leader's actions should strengthen followers' beliefs that if they exert a certain level of effort, then they will be more likely to accomplish a task, and if they accomplish the task, then they will be more likely to achieve some valued outcome.

Although not very complicated in its basic concept, the model added more variables and interactions over time. Evans[42] is credited with the first version of path-goal theory, but we will focus on a later version developed by House and Dressler.[43] Their conceptual scheme is ideally suited to the L-F-S framework because they described three classes of variables, which include leader behaviors, followers, and the situation. We will examine each of these in turn.

Leader Behaviors

The four types of leader behavior in path-goal theory can be seen in Table 12.1. Like SLT, path-goal theory assumes that leaders not only may use varying styles with different subordinates but might very well use differing styles with the same subordinates in different situations. Path-goal theory suggests that, depending on the followers and the situation, these different leader behaviors can increase followers' acceptance of the leader, enhance their level of satisfaction, and raise their expectations

TABLE 12.1
The Four Leader Behaviors of Path-Goal Theory

Directive leadership. These leader behaviors are very similar to the task behaviors from SLT. They include telling the followers what they are expected to do, how to do it, when it is to be done, and how their work fits in with the work of others. This behavior would also include setting schedules, establishing norms, and providing expectations that followers will adhere to established procedure and regulations.

Supportive leadership. Supportive leadership behaviors include having courteous and friendly interactions, expressing genuine concern for the followers' well-being and individual needs, and remaining open and approachable to followers. These behaviors, which are very similar to the relationship behaviors in SLT, also are marked by attention to the competing demands of treating followers equally while recognizing status differentials between the leader and the followers.

Participative leadership. Participative leaders engage in the behaviors that mark the consultative and group behaviors described by Vroom and Yetton.[45] As such, they tend to share work problems with followers; solicit their suggestions, concerns, and recommendations; and weigh these inputs in the decision-making process.

Achievement-oriented leadership. Leaders exhibiting these would be seen as both demanding and supporting in interactions with their followers. In the first place, they would set very challenging goals for group and follower behavior, continually seek ways to improve performance en route, and expect the followers to always perform at their highest levels. But they would support these behaviors by exhibiting a high degree of ongoing confidence that subordinates can put forth the necessary effort; will achieve the desired results; and, even further, will assume even more responsibility in the future.

that effort will result in effective performance, which in turn will lead to valued rewards (see Highlight 12.5).

The Followers

Path-goal theory contains two groups of follower variables. The first relates to the *satisfaction of followers,* and the second relates to the *followers' perception of their own abilities* relative to the task to be accomplished. In terms of followers' satisfaction, path-goal theory suggests that leader behaviors will be acceptable to the followers to the degree followers see the leader's behavior either as an immediate source of satisfaction or as directly instrumental in achieving future satisfaction. In other words, followers will actively support a leader as long as they view the leader's

Shifting Behaviors at Caterpillar

HIGHLIGHT 12.5

James Despain was a leader with a very directive leadership style. He began his career at Caterpillar, Inc., as a young man, sweeping up the factory floor. He followed the lead of others of his generation—the 1950s were a time when leaders were the ultimate authority and words like *participative* and *consultative* were unheard of. Despain worked his way into supervisory positions and finally was named vice president of the track-type tractor division. Despain claims he "spent much of [his] career as a manager focusing on what employees were doing wrong." He focused on the tasks at hand and little else. But in the early 1990s Despain had to face some hard facts: His $1.2 billion division was losing millions of dollars per year, his management team was getting hundreds of grievances from their employees, and morale at the Caterpillar plant was extremely low.

Despain and his leadership group identified the need for a strategic plan to transform the working culture. Key to the plan was to determine a strategy for dealing with employee attitudes and behavior. Despain and his transformation team identified nine behaviors or "Common Values" that they wanted every employee to emulate every day—trust, mutual respect, customer satisfaction, a sense of urgency, teamwork, empowerment, risk taking, continuous

improvement, and commitment. Employee evaluations were then based on the manifestation of these behaviors. Above and beyond those behaviors, top executives and management were expected to lead by example and commit themselves to practice 100 positive leadership traits. Statements such as "I will know every one of my employees by name . . . will recognize their accomplishments with praise . . . will trust my employees to do their work" became the new mantras for those in charge.

Through this process, Despain came to understand that "the most important thing for employees in the workplace is to achieve self-worth." The principal change he was striving to achieve was to make employees accountable for how their jobs got done—for workers that meant stretching a little more every day, to achieve their full potential. For managers it meant shifting away from achieving traditional metrics and toward drawing desired behavior from workers. "And we found that the more we focused on behavior, the better the metrics got." The result: Despain's division cut its breakeven point in half within five years of launching the transformation.

Sources: http://www.tribuneindia.com/2004/20040509/spectrum/book2.htm; http://www.sodexho-usa.com/printer_friendly.htm; http://www.stchas.edu/press/despain.shtml.

actions as a means for increasing their own levels of satisfaction. However, there is only so much a leader can do to increase followers' satisfaction levels, as satisfaction also depends on characteristics of the followers themselves.

A frequently cited example of how followers' characteristics influence the impact of leader behaviors on followers' levels of satisfaction involves the trait of locus of control. People who believe they are "masters of their own ship" are said to have an internal locus of control; people who believe they are (relatively speaking) "pawns of fate" are said to have an external locus of control. Mitchell, Smyser, and Weed[44] found that follower satisfaction was not directly related to the degree of participative behaviors manifested by the leader (i.e., followers with highly participative leaders were not any more satisfied than followers with more autocratic leaders). However, when followers' locus-of-control scores were taken into account, a contingency relationship was discovered. As can be seen in Figure 12.9, internal-locus-of-control followers, who believed outcomes were a result of their own decisions, were much more satisfied with leaders who exhibited participative behaviors than they were with leaders who were directive. Conversely, external-locus-of-control followers were more satisfied with directive leader behaviors than they were with participative leader behaviors.

Followers' perceptions of their own skills and abilities to perform particular tasks can also affect the impact of certain leader behaviors. Followers who believe they are perfectly capable of performing a task are not as apt to be motivated by, or as willing to accept, a directive leader as they would a leader who exhibits participative behaviors. Using the same rationale as for locus of control, one can predict the opposite relationship for followers who do not perceive they have sufficient abilities to perform the task. Once again, the acceptability of the leader and the motivation to

FIGURE 12.9

Interaction between followers' locus of control scores and leader behavior in decision making.

Source: Adapted from T. R. Mitchell, C. M. Smyser, and S. E. Weed, "Locus of Control: Supervision and Work Satisfaction." *Academy of Management Journal* 18 (1975), pp. 623–30.

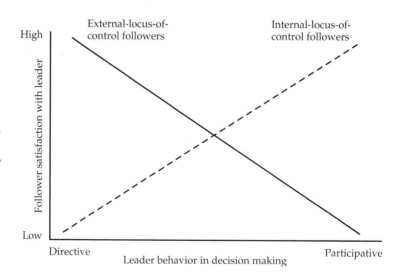

perform are in part determined by followers' characteristics. Thus, path-goal theory suggests that both leader behaviors and follower characteristics are important in determining outcomes.

The Situation

Path-goal theory considers three situational factors that impact or moderate the effects of leader behavior on follower attitudes and behaviors. These include *the task, the formal authority system,* and *the primary work group.* Each of these three factors can influence the leadership situation in one of three ways. These three factors can serve as an independent motivational factor, as a constraint on the behavior of followers (which may be either positive or negative in outcome), or as a reward.

However, it should also be increasingly apparent that these variables can often affect the impact of various leader behaviors. For example, if the task is very structured and routine, the formal authority system has constrained followers' behaviors, and the work group has established clear norms for performance, then leaders would be serving a redundant purpose by manifesting directive or achievement-oriented behaviors. These prescriptions are similar to some of those noted in substitutes for leadership theory,[46] as everything the follower needs to understand the effort-to-performance and performance-to-reward links is provided by the situation. Thus, redundant leader behaviors might be interpreted by followers as either a complete lack of understanding or empathy by the leader, or an attempt by the leader to exert excessive control. Neither of these interpretations is likely to enhance the leader's acceptance by followers or increase their motivation.

Although we have already described how follower characteristics and situational characteristics can impact leader behaviors, path-goal theory also maintains that follower and situational variables can impact each other. In other words, situational variables, such as the task performed, can also impact the influence of followers' skills, abilities, or personality traits on followers' satisfaction. Although this seems to make perfect sense, hopefully you are beginning to see how complicated path-goal theory can be when one starts considering how situational variables, follower characteristics, and leader behaviors interact in the leadership process.

Although people object when a scientific analysis traces their behavior to external conditions and thus deprives them of credit and the chance to be admired, they seldom object when the same analysis absolves them of blame.

B. F. Skinner

Prescriptions of the Theory

In general, path-goal theory maintains that leaders should first assess the situation and select a leadership behavior appropriate to situational demands. By manifesting the appropriate behaviors, leaders can increase followers' effort-to-performance expectancies, performance-to-reward expectancies, or valences of the outcomes. These increased expectancies and valences will improve subordinates' effort levels and the rewards attained, which in turn will increase subordinates' satisfaction and performance levels and the acceptance of their leaders. Perhaps the easiest way to explain this fairly complicated process is through the use of an example. Suppose we have a set of followers who are in a newly created work unit and do not have a clear understanding of the requirements of their positions. In other words, the followers have a reasonably high level of role ambiguity. According to path-goal theory, leaders should exhibit a high degree of directive behaviors in order to reduce the role ambiguity of their followers. The effort-to-performance link will become clearer when leaders tell followers what to do and how to do it in ambiguous situations, which in turn will cause followers to exert higher effort levels. Because role ambiguity is assumed to be unpleasant, these directive leader behaviors and higher effort levels should eventually result in higher satisfaction levels among followers. Figure 12.10 illustrates this process. Similarly, leaders may look at the leadership situation and note that followers' performance levels are not acceptable. The leader may also conclude that the current situation offers few, if any, incentives for increased performance. In this case, the leader may use directive behaviors to increase the value of the rewards (or valence), which in turn will increase followers' effort levels and performance.

Concluding Thoughts about the Path-Goal Theory

Before getting into the research surrounding path-goal theory, you may wish to examine the theory using the L-F-S framework. As seen in Figure 12.11, the components of path-goal theory fit quite nicely into the L-F-S model. The four leader behaviors fit nicely in the leader circle, the characteristics of the followers fit into the follower circle, and the task and the formal authority system fit into the situation circle. Of all the components of path-goal theory, the only "mismatch" with the L-F-S model deals with the primary work

FIGURE 12.10   Examples of applying path-goal theory.

FIGURE 12.11   Factors from path-goal theory and the interactional framework.

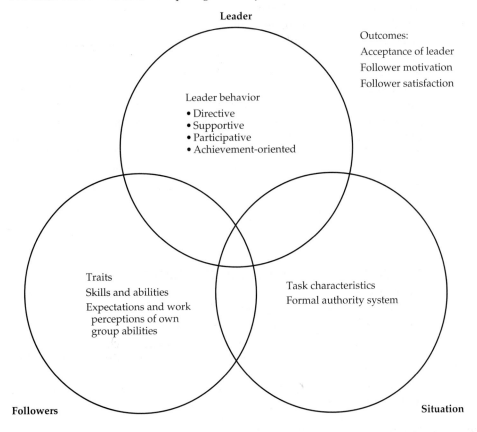

group. The norms, cohesiveness, size, and stage of development of groups is considered to be part of the follower function in the L-F-S model but is part of the situation function in path-goal theory. In that regard, we hasten to note we use the L-F-S framework primarily for heuristic purposes. Ultimately, the concepts described in these four theories are sufficiently complex and ambiguous that there probably is no right answer to any single depiction.

In terms of research, the path-goal theory has received only mixed support to date.[47–50] Although many of these mixed findings may be due to the fact that the path-goal theory excludes many of the variables found to impact the leadership process, that may also be due to problems with the theory. Yukl[51] maintained that most of these criticisms deal with the methodology used to study path-goal theory and the limitations of expectancy theory. Moreover, the path-goal theory assumes that the only way to increase performance is to increase followers' motivation levels. The theory ignores the roles leaders play in selecting talented followers, building their skill levels through training, and redesigning their work.[52]

To act is easy; to think is hard.

Goethe

Nonetheless, path-goal theory is useful for illustrating two points. First, as noted by Yukl,[53] "path-goal theory has already made a contribution to the study of leadership by providing a conceptual framework to guide researchers in identifying potentially relevant situational moderator variables." Path-goal theory also illustrates that, as models become more complicated, they may be more useful to researchers and less appealing to practitioners. Our experience is that pragmatically oriented students and in-place leaders want to take something from a model that is understandable and can be applied in their work situation right away. This does not mean they prefer simplicity to validity—they generally appreciate the complexity of the leadership process. But neither do they want a model that is so complex as to be indecipherable.

Summary

This chapter is designed to provide an overview of four of the more well-known contingency theories of leadership, which include the normative decision model,[54] the Situational Leadership® model, the contingency model,[55] and the path-goal theory.[56] All four models are fairly similar in that they specify that leaders should make their behaviors contingent on certain aspects of the followers or the situation in order to improve leadership effectiveness. In addition, all four theories implicitly assume that leaders can accurately assess key follower and situational factors. However, as the material regarding perception in Chapter 3 shows, it is entirely possible that two leaders in the same situation may reach very different conclusions about followers' levels of knowledge, the strength of leader–follower relationships, the degree of task structure, or the level of role ambiguity being experienced by followers. These differences in perception could lead these two leaders to reach different conclusions about the situation, which may in turn cause them to take very different actions in response to the situation. Furthermore, these actions may be in accordance or in conflict with the prescriptions of any of these four theories. Also, the fact that leaders' perceptions may have caused them to act in a manner not prescribed by a particular model may be an underlying reason why these four theories have reported conflicting findings, particularly in field settings.

Another reason these theories have generally found mixed support in field settings concerns the fact that they are all fairly limited in scope. Many of the factors that affect leader and follower behaviors in work-group, team, or volunteer committee settings are not present in laboratory studies but often play a substantial role in field studies. For example, none of the models take into account how levels of stress, organizational culture and climate, working conditions, technology, economic conditions, or types of organizational design affect the leadership process. Nevertheless, the four contingency theories have been the subject of considerable research, and even if only mixed support for the models has been found, this research has succeeded in adding to our body of knowledge about leadership and has given us a more sophisticated understanding of the leadership process.

Key Terms

normative decision model, *579*
decision quality, *580*
autocratic processes, *580*
consultative processes, *580*
group process, *580*
decision acceptance, *581*
Situational Leadership®, *586*

task behaviors, *586*
relationship behaviors, *586*
follower readiness, *587*
developmental interventions, *588*
contingency model, *590*
least-preferred-co-worker (LPC) scale, *591*
low-LPC leaders, *591*

high-LPC leaders, *591*
situational favorability, *592*
path-goal theory, *597*
directive leadership, *598*
supportive leadership, *598*
participative leadership, *598*
achievement-oriented leadership, *598*

Questions

1. Given the description of the leadership situation facing the airplane crash survivors described in Chapter 1, how would the normative decision model, the situational leadership theory, the contingency model, and the path-goal theory prescribe that a leader should act?

2. Can leaders be flexible in how they interact with others? Do you believe leaders can change their behavior? Their personalities?

3. Think of a leadership situation you are fairly familiar with. Apply each of the theories in this chapter to the situation; which theory best fits the interaction of the leader, followers, and situation in your example? Does any theory allow you to predict a likely or preferred outcome for a current challenge?

Minicase

"Big Changes for a Small Hospital"

As F. Nicholas Jacobs toured the Windber Medical Center facility, he was dismayed by the industrial pink painted walls, the circa 1970 furniture, and the snow leaking through the windows of the conference room. Employees earned 30 percent less than their counterparts in the area, and turnover was steep. As Windber's newest president, Jacobs knew he was the facility's last hope—if he couldn't successfully turn around the aging facility, it would mean closing the doors forever.

Coming to Windber Medical Center in 1997, Jacobs was keenly aware that the hospital could be the next in a series of small hospitals that had fallen victim to a struggling economy. Determined to see that not happen, he began by making connections with the employees of the hospital and the community at large. Jacobs's first step was to interview each of the employees to find out firsthand what they wanted for the Windber community and the medical center. He also looked to members of local community groups like the local library, the Agency on Aging, and local politicians and asked these groups what they wanted from their local medical facility. When Jacobs realized that octogenarians made up a larger percent of the population in Windber, Pennsylvania, than in all of Dade County, Florida, he made it a priority to provide more options to seniors for improving their health and quality of life. He set forth a vision of a medical center that was more of a community center—a center that would allow members of the community to exercise in a state-of-the-art facility while having access to professionals to answer health-related questions. Jacobs realized that keeping people in the community both physically and mentally healthy also meant keeping the hospital financially healthy. He made the center's new preventative-care philosophy clear to the public: "Work out at our hospital so you can stay out of our hospital."

Jacobs's efforts have paid off—in an era when small hospitals are closing left and right, Windber Medical Center is thriving. Under Jacobs's leadership Windber has established an affiliation with the Planetree treatment system, which integrates meditation, massage, music, and other holistic methods into traditional health care. Windber's wellness center, which offers fitness training, yoga, and acupuncture, among other treatments, opened in January 2000 and now generates over $500,000 annually. Gone are the pink walls and dated furniture—replaced with fountains, plants, and modern artwork. Jacobs recruited a former hotel manager to oversee food service. And, despite the dismissal of about 32 employees (those used to a more traditional hospital setting had a tough time in the new environment), the staff has nearly doubled to 450 employees, and pay has improved. Windber has raised more than $50 million in public and private funding and has forged research partnerships with the Walter Reed Army Health System and the University of Pittsburgh, among others. The Windber Research Institute, Windber's heart-disease-reversal program, has treated about 250 patients.

1. Consider the factors from the situational leadership theory outlined in Figure 12.4. Apply these factors to Jacobs and Windber.

2. How do you think Jacobs would score on the least-preferred-co-worker (LPC) scale? Why?

3. Based on the success of Windber, in what range would you guess the overall situational favorability might fall for Jacobs on the continuum illustrated in Figure 12.6?

Sources: http://www.careerjournaleurope.com/columnists/inthelead/20030827-inthelead.html; http://www.haponline.org/ihc/hospitalshealthsystems/models2.asp; http://www.post-gazette.com/pg/04013/260747.stm.

Chapter Notes

1. Fiedler, F. E. "Reflections by an Accidental Theorist." *Leadership Quarterly* 6, no. 4 (1995), pp. 453–61; ———. *A Theory of Leadership Effectiveness.* New York: McGraw-Hill, 1967.

2. Chemers, M. M. "The Social, Organizational, and Cultural Contest of Effective Leadership." In *Leadership: Multidisciplinary Perspectives.* Ed. B. Kellerman. Englewood Cliffs, NJ: Prentice Hall, 1984.

3. Vroom, V. H., and P. W. Yetton. *Leadership and Decision Making.* Pittsburgh, PA: University of Pittsburgh Press, 1973.

4. Vroom, V. H., and P. W. Yetton. *Leadership and Decision Making.* Pittsburgh, PA: University of Pittsburgh Press, 1973.

5. Vroom, V. H., and P. W. Yetton. *Leadership and Decision Making.* Pittsburgh, PA: University of Pittsburgh Press, 1973.

6. Vroom, V. H., and P. W. Yetton. *Leadership and Decision Making.* Pittsburgh, PA: University of Pittsburgh Press, 1973.

7. Vroom, V. H., and P. W. Yetton. *Leadership and Decision Making.* Pittsburgh, PA: University of Pittsburgh Press, 1973.

8. Vroom, V. H., and P. W. Yetton. *Leadership and Decision Making.* Pittsburgh, PA: University of Pittsburgh Press, 1973.

9. Field, R. H. G. "A Test of the Vroom-Yetton Normative Model of Leadership." *Journal of Applied Psychology* 67 (1982), pp. 523–32.

10. Vroom, V. H., and A. G. Jago. "Leadership and Decision Making: A Revised Normative Model." Paper presented at the Academy of Management Convention, Boston, MA, 1974.

11. Vroom, V. H., and A. G. Jago. *The New Theory of Leadership: Managing Participation in Organizations.* Englewood Cliffs, NJ: Prentice Hall, 1988.

12. Miner, J. B. "The Uncertain Future of the Leadership Concept: An Overview." In *Leadership Frontiers.* Eds. J. G. Hunt and L. L. Larson. Kent, OH: Kent State University, 1975.

13. Yukl, G. *Leadership in Organizations.* 2nd ed. Englewood Cliffs, NJ: Prentice Hall, 1989.

14. Yukl, G. A., and D. D. Van Fleet. "Theory and Research on Leadership in Organizations." In *Handbook of Industrial & Organizational Psychology.* Vol. 3. Eds. M. D. Dunnette and L. M. Hough. Palo Alto, CA: Consulting Psychologists Press, 1992, pp. 1–51.

15. Couch, A., and P. W. Yetton. "Manager Behavior, Leadership Style, and Subordinate Performance: An Empirical Extension of the Vroom-Yetton Conflict Rule." *Organizational Behavior and Human Decision Processes* 39 (1987), pp. 384–96.

16. Hersey, P., and K. H. Blanchard. "Life Cycle Theory of Leadership." *Training and Development Journal* 23 (1969), pp. 26–34.

17. Vecchio, R. P. "Situational Leadership Theory: An Examination of a Prescriptive Theory." *Journal of Applied Psychology* 72 (1987), pp. 444–51.

18. Yukl, G. A., and D. D. Van Fleet. "Theory and Research on Leadership in Organizations." In *Handbook of Industrial & Organizational Psychology.* Vol. 3. Eds. M. D. Dunnette and L. M. Hough. Palo Alto, CA: Consulting Psychologists Press, 1992, pp. 1–51.

19. Fiedler, F. E. "Reflections by an Accidental Theorist." *Leadership Quarterly* 6, no. 4 (1995), pp. 453–61. ———. *A Theory of Leadership Effectiveness.* New York: McGraw-Hill, 1967.

20. Fiedler, F. E. "Reflections by an Accidental Theorist." *Leadership Quarterly* 6, no. 4 (1995), pp. 453–61. ———. *A Theory of Leadership Effectiveness.* New York: McGraw-Hill, 1967.

21. Fiedler, F. E. "The Contingency Model and the Dynamics of the Leadership Process." In *Advances in Experimental Social Psychology.* Ed. L. Berkowitz. New York: Academic Press, 1978.

22. Fiedler, F. E. "The Contingency Model and the Dynamics of the Leadership Process." In *Advances in Experimental Social Psychology.* Ed. L. Berkowitz. New York: Academic Press, 1978.

23. Kennedy, J. K. "Middle LPC Leaders and the Contingency Model of Leader Effectiveness." *Organizational Behavior and Human Performance* 30 (1982), pp. 1–14.

24. Fiedler, F. E., and M. M. Chemers. *Improving Leadership Effectiveness: The Leader Match Concept.* 2nd ed. New York: John Wiley, 1982.

25. Fiedler, F. E. "Reflections by an Accidental Theorist." *Leadership Quarterly* 6, no. 4 (1995), pp. 453–61. ———. *A Theory of Leadership Effectiveness.* New York: McGraw-Hill, 1967.

26. Hersey, P., and K. H. Blanchard. "Life Cycle Theory of Leadership." *Training and Development Journal* 23 (1969), pp. 26–34.

27. Hersey, P., and K. H. Blanchard. *Management of Organizational Behavior: Utilizing Human Resources.* 4th ed. Englewood Cliffs, NJ: Prentice Hall, 1982.

28. Fiedler, F. E. "The Contingency Model and the Dynamics of the Leadership Process." In *Advances in Experimental Social Psychology.* Ed. L. Berkowitz. New York: Academic Press, 1978.

29. Fiedler, F. E. "Cognitive Resources and Leadership Performance." *Applied Psychology: An International Review* 44, no. 1 (1995), pp. 5–28.

30. Fiedler, F. E., and M. M. Chemers. *Improving Leadership Effectiveness: The Leader Match Concept.* 2nd ed. New York: John Wiley, 1982.

31. Peters, L. H., D. D. Hartke, and J. T. Pohlmann. "Fielder's Contingency Theory of Leadership: An Application of the Meta-analytic Procedures of Schmidt and Hunter." *Psychological Bulletin* 97 (1985), pp. 274–85.

32. Strube, M. J., and J. E. Garcia. "A Meta-analytic Investigation of Fielder's Contingency Model of Leadership Effectiveness." *Psychological Bulletin* 90 (1981), pp. 307–21.

33. Peters, L. H., D. D. Hartke, and J. T. Pohlmann. "Fielder's Contingency Theory of Leadership: An Application of the Meta-analytic Procedures of Schmidt and Hunter." *Psychological Bulletin* 97 (1985), pp. 274–85.

34. Kennedy, J. K. "Middle LPC Leaders and the Contingency Model of Leader Effectiveness." *Organizational Behavior and Human Performance* 30 (1982), pp. 1–14.

35. Rice, R. W. "Construct Validity of the Least Preferred Co-Worker Score." *Psychological Bulletin* 85 (1978), pp. 1199–1237.

36. Schriesheim, C. A., and S. Kerr. "Theories and Measures of Leadership: A Critical Appraisal of Current and Future Directions." In *Leadership: The Cutting Edge.* Eds. J. G. Hunt and L. L. Larson. Carbondale, IL: Southern Illinois University Press, 1977.

37. Jago, A. G., and J. W. Ragan. "The Trouble with Leader Match Is That It Doesn't Match Fiedler's Contingency Model." *Journal of Applied Psychology* 71 (1986a), pp. 555–59.

38. Jago, A. G., and J. W. Ragan. "Some Assumptions Are More Troubling than Others: Rejoinder to Chemers and Fiedler." *Journal of Applied Psychology* 71 (1986b), pp. 564–65.

39. Jago, A. G., and J. W. Ragan. "The Trouble with Leader Match Is That It Doesn't Match Fiedler's Contingency Model." *Journal of Applied Psychology* 71 (1986a), pp. 555–59.

40. Jago, A. G., and J. W. Ragan. "Some Assumptions Are More Troubling than Others: Rejoinder to Chemers and Fiedler." *Journal of Applied Psychology* 71 (1986b), pp. 564–65.

41. Vecchio, R. P. "Assessing the Validity of Fiedler's Contingency Model of Leadership Effectiveness: A Closer Look at Strube and Garcia." *Psychological Bulletin* 93 (1983), pp. 404–08.

42. Evans, M. G. "The Effects of Supervisory Behavior on the Path-Goal Relationship." *Organizational Behavior and Human Performance* 5 (1970), pp. 277–98.

43. House, R. J., and G. Dressler. "The Path-Goal Theory of Leadership: Some Post Hoc and A Priori Tests." In *Contingency Approaches to Leadership.* Eds. J. G. Hunt and L. L. Larson. Carbondale, IL: Southern Illinois University Press, 1974.

44. Mitchell, T. R., C. M. Smyser, and S. E. Weed. "Locus of Control: Supervision and Work Satisfaction." *Academy of Management Journal* 18 (1975), pp. 623–30.

45. Vroom, V. H., and P. W. Yetton. *Leadership and Decision Making.* Pittsburgh, PA: University of Pittsburgh Press, 1973.

46. Kerr, S., and J. M. Jermier. "Substitutes for Leadership: Their Meaning and Measurement." *Organizational Behavior and Human Performance* 22 (1978), pp. 375–403.

47. Schriesheim, C. A., and A. S. DeNisi. "Task Dimensions as Moderators of the Effects of Instrumental Leadership: A Two Sample Replicated Test of Path-Goal Leadership Theory." *Journal of Applied Psychology* 66 (1981), pp. 589–97.

48. Schriesheim, C. A., and S. Kerr. "Theories and Measures of Leadership: A Critical Appraisal of Current and Future Directions." In *Leadership: The Cutting Edge.* Eds. J. G. Hunt and L. L. Larson. Carbondale, IL: Southern Illinois University Press, 1977.

49. Yukl, G. *Leadership in Organizations.* 2nd ed. Englewood Cliffs, NJ: Prentice Hall, 1989.

50. Schriesheim, C. A., S. L. Castro, X. Zhou, and L. A. DeChurch. "An Investigation of Path-Goal and Transformational Leadership Theory Predictions at the Individual Level of Analysis." *Leadership Quarterly* 17 (2006), pp. 21–38.

51. Yukl, G. *Leadership in Organizations.* 2nd ed. Englewood Cliffs, NJ: Prentice Hall, 1989.

52. Yukl, G. A., and D. D. Van Fleet. "Theory and Research on Leadership in Organizations." In *Handbook of Industrial & Organizational Psychology.* Vol. 3. Eds. M. D. Dunnette and L. M. Hough. Palo Alto, CA: Consulting Psychologists Press, 1992, pp. 1–51.

53. Yukl, G. *Leadership in Organizations.* 2nd ed. Englewood Cliffs, NJ: Prentice Hall, 1989, p. 104.

54. Vroom, V. H., and P. W. Yetton. *Leadership and Decision Making.* Pittsburgh, PA: University of Pittsburgh Press, 1973.

55. Fiedler, F. E. "Reflections by an Accidental Theorist." *Leadership Quarterly* 6, no. 4 (1995), pp. 453–61.

56. House, R. J., and G. Dressler. "The Path-Goal Theory of Leadership: Some Post Hoc and A Priori Tests." In *Contingency Approaches to Leadership.* Ed. J. G. Hunt and L. L. Larson. Carbondale, IL: Southern Illinois University Press, 1974.

Chapter 13

Leadership and Change

Introduction

There is nothing more difficult to take in hand, more perilous to conduct, or more uncertain of success, than to take the lead in the introduction of a new order of things.

Nicolo Machiavelli, writer

Organizations today face a myriad of potential challenges. To be successful they must cope effectively with the implications of new technology, globalization, changing social and political climates, new competitive threats, shifting economic conditions, industry consolidation, swings in consumer preferences, and new performance and legal standards. Think how technology affected Peter Jackson's ability to make the *Lord of the Rings* trilogy or the changes U.S. military had to make as it shifted from stemming the tide of communism to fighting more regionalized conflicts. And how the events of 9/11, the wars in Iraq and Afghanistan, the threats of global terrorism, the emergence of the European Union, the growth of the Chinese and Indian economies, the rising price of oil, and global warming have affected leaders in both the private and public sectors around the world. Leading change is perhaps the most difficult challenge facing any leader, yet it may be that this skill is the best differentiator of managers from leaders and of mediocre from exceptional leaders. The best leaders are those who recognize the situational and follower factors inhibiting or facilitating change, paint a compelling vision of the future, and formulate and execute a plan that moves their vision from a dream to reality.

The scope of any change initiative varies dramatically. Leaders can use goal setting, coaching, mentoring, delegation, or empowerment skills to effectively change the behaviors and skills of individual direct reports. But what would you need to do if you led a pharmaceutical company of 5,000 employees and you had just received FDA approval to introduce a revolutionary new drug into the marketplace? How would you get the research and development, marketing, sales, manufacturing, quality, shipping, customer service, accounting, and information technology departments to work together to ensure a profitable product launch? Or what would you do if you had to reduce company expenses by 40 percent for the next two years, or deal with a recent acquisition of a competitor? Obviously, change on this scale involves more than individual coaching and mentoring. Because this chapter builds on much of the content of the previous chapters, it is fitting that it appears at the end of the text. To successfully lead larger-scale change initiatives, leaders need to attend to the situational and follower factors affecting their group or organization (Chapters 10–12). They then must use their intelligence, problem-solving skills, creativity, and values to sort out what is important and formulate solutions to the challenges facing their group (Chapters 6–8). But solutions in and of themselves are no guarantee for change; leaders must use their power and influence, personality traits, coaching and planning skills, and knowledge of motivational techniques and group dynamics in order to drive change (Chapters 5, 7–10). Finally, leaders can use some of the measures described in Chapter 4 to monitor the progress of their change initiatives (see Highlight 13.1).

As an overview, this chapter begins by revisiting the leadership versus management discussion from Chapters 1 and 2. We then describe a rational approach to organizational change and spell out what leaders can do if they want to be successful with their change efforts. This model also provides a good diagnostic framework for understanding why many change efforts fail. We conclude the chapter with a discussion of an alternative approach to change—charismatic and transformational leadership. The personal magnetism, heroic qualities, and spellbinding powers of these leaders can have unusually strong effects on followers, which often lead to dramatic organizational, political, or societal change. Unlike the rational approach to change, the charismatic and transformational leadership framework places considerable weight on followers' heightened emotional levels to drive organizational change. Much of the leadership research over the past 20 years has helped us to better understand the situational, follower, and leader characteristics needed for charismatic or transformational leadership to occur. The chapter concludes with an overview of these factors and a review of the predominant theory in the field, Bass's Theory of Transformational and Transactional Leadership.[1]

Change in the Waste Industry

HIGHLIGHT 13.1

Even something as mundane as trash disposal can present some significant leadership challenges. One company, Waste Management, acquired over 1,600 smaller waste disposal companies from 1995–2004. All of the acquired companies had their own financial systems, pay scales and benefits, trucks and equipment, and operating procedures. None of the IT or financial systems could "talk" to each other, drivers followed very different operating procedures and had different performance standards and compensation packages, many of the companies were former competitors that now had to collaborate in order to achieve overall company goals, and few if any supervisors had been through any type of leadership training. The board of directors brought in an outsider, Maury Myers from Yellow Freight, to integrate all these acquisitions into a single company. As CEO, Maury's first task was to create a common financial system so that all the company's revenues and expenses could be consolidated into a single financial statement. And given the large number of acquired companies, this in itself was no small task. He also created a system that allowed supervisors and drivers to set goals and measure daily productivity and customer satisfaction rates and introduced other major organizational change initiatives to improve safety and vehicle maintenance, optimize vehicle use, and reduce operating expenses.

The results of these change initiatives have been nothing short of spectacular. Waste Management is now the industry leader in the waste industry, consisting of approximately 50,000 employees that create $1.5 billion in profits on a $12 billion annual revenue stream. Driver productivity, customer satisfaction, and driver safety have improved over 50 percent, and operating expenses have been dramatically

reduced. Maury Myers retired from the CEO role in November 2004 and was replaced by David Steiner, the former CFO.

Since taking the reins at Waste Management David Steiner has been focused on three critical initiatives, which include operational excellence, growth, and rebranding. In terms of operational excellence, the company has implemented a number of company-wide initiatives in order to improve the safety and productivity of employees. Some of these include the Mission for Success Safety program, the Business Process Improvement initiative, and Waste Route, a route optimization program. These programs have helped Waste Management to become the best in the industry in terms of safety and worker productivity. The company is vigorously pursuing a number of organic growth opportunities to generate additional profits, such as capturing landfill gasses to fuel garbage trucks, taking the lead in electronic recycling and disposal, placing power generating windmills at landfills, and developing new waste-to-energy power plants. In terms of rebranding, Waste Management has been repositioning itself with its "Think Green" television, radio, and magazine ads; the use of natural gas-powered trucks; and an aggressive landfill remediation program. It is looking at how it can play a lead role in sustainability, as many companies, such as Wal-Mart, have corporate goals of reducing store waste by 95 percent in the next five years. If these customers dramatically reduce their waste streams, then what will Waste Management have to do in order to remain a good investment for shareholders? Although Waste Management has seen some dramatic changes over the past 10 years, waste stream reduction, alternative energy sources, and global warming may well force Waste Management to undergo even more dramatic changes over the next 10 years.

Leadership and Management: Revisited Again

Earlier in this text we described leadership as "the process of influencing an organized group toward accomplishing its goals." We also differentiated leadership from management, with leadership being more concerned with doing the right thing and management more concerned with doing things right. Bennis[2] stated that leaders inspire and develop others, challenge the status quo, ask what and why questions, and are more apt to take a long-term view. Managers administer programs, control budgets and costs, maintain the status quo, and are more likely to take a short-term view. Building on Bennis's distinctions, one could say that leadership involves changing the way things are, whereas management involves maintaining the current state of affairs. This distinction between leadership and management is more clearly depicted in Table 13.1. Much like a driver uses the gas, brakes, clutch, gears, and steering wheel to control the speed and direction of a car, a manager uses various accounting, information, hiring, performance management, compensation, training, planning, quality, and inventory systems to align the behavior of followers toward the accomplishment of team or organizational goals. If followers are over budget on travel expenses or fail to come to work on time, then managers use various levers in the accounting or performance management system to correct the situation. These systems help followers to behave in both a consistent and an efficient manner. Organizations tend to be more successful when followers exhibit those behaviors most closely aligned with organizational goals. And organizations that need fewer resources to deliver goods and services tend to be more profitable (i.e., efficient) than those needing more resources to do the same thing. There is nothing inherently good or bad with organizational systems, but to some degree the quality of these systems dictates the ease with which a manager can do his or her job.

Although there are several benefits to organizational systems, one of their inherent problems is that they are fairly resistant to change. And well they should be, as they are specifically designed to minimize variability in the way expenses are paid, how software packages are used, the quality of goods and services provided, and so forth. Adding to this resistance is that many people have high security values and have a tendency to fall in love with their systems. Whole bureaucracies and departments are designed to do nothing but support organizational systems. Oftentimes the people working in the accounting, information technology, or quality departments invented the relevant systems used throughout the organization,

TABLE 13.1
Leadership versus Management

Leadership = Change	Management = Control
Vision	Plan
Inspire	Reward
Empower	Direct
Coach	Train
Revenues	Expenses
Forecasts	Budgets
Possibilities	Systems and procedures
Opportunity	Schedule
Synergy	Coordinate

The definition of neurotic management is to continue to do the same thing but expect a different result.

Anonymous

and pride of ownership may get in the way of needed changes. Likewise, the users of these systems may not want to learn new graphics programs, accounting procedures, sales models, lean manufacturing, or six sigma quality processes. Even if current systems are inefficient and dysfunctional, people know how to use them, and with this knowledge comes a certain degree of stability and predictability. Learning new systems and behaviors requires some tolerance for ambiguity and can take a considerable amount of patience, persistence, and hard work. All things being equal, many followers may prefer to have a predictable path rather than risk their success on some uncharted course for the future.[3–13]

So where does leadership come into play in the car analogy? A leader is a person who takes the car down a different road, has a different final destination, or determines whether a car is even the right vehicle. Because technology, globalization, market conditions, consumer preferences, and demographic changes can have big impact on any team or organization, leadership is the key to aligning organizational systems and follower behaviors around a new organizational vision. Whereas managers focus on compliance with existing procedures, leaders take a step back and ask why a system even exists. They create and align systems around a new set of goals for the organization, rather than having existing systems dictate what the organization can and cannot do. Successful leaders are also able to align followers' behaviors with this new vision and systems. But changing followers' behaviors and organizational systems, structure, and goals takes a tremendous amount of skill and effort. You will see that it takes a combination of both leadership and management skills to successfully implement any team or organizational change effort. One of the main reasons for the high base rate of managerial incompetence is that many people in positions of authority struggle with leadership, management, or both sets of skills (see Highlight 13.2). The rest of this chapter describes some of the pertinent research and the steps leadership practitioners must take if they wish to use either the rational or the emotional approach to drive organizational change.

The Rational Approach to Organizational Change

A number of authors have written about organizational change, including O'Toole,[3] Pritchett,[4,23] McNulty,[5] Heifetz and Linsky,[6] Moss Kanter,[7] Krile, Curphy, and Lund,[8] Ostroff,[9] Rock and Schwartz,[10] Kotter,[11] Curphy,[12,13] Burns,[14] Kanter,[15] Bennis and Nanus,[16] Tichy and Devanna,[17] Bridges,[18] Collins and Porras,[19] Treacy and Wiersma,[20] Beer,[21,22] Heifetz and Laurie,[24] and Collins.[25] All of these authors have unique perspectives on leadership and change, but they also share a number of common characteristics. Beer[21,22] has offered a rational and straightforward approach to organizational change that addresses many of the issues

Change in a Rural Community

HIGHLIGHT 13.2

There is no limit to what an organized group can do if it wants to.

George McLean, newspaper editor

Change does not just happen in organizations, it also occurs in communities. Whereas many suburbs are experiencing dramatic growth, most urban and rural communities are experiencing declines in population and business. Some rural communities are working hard to attract new businesses, such as ethanol plants, and build new schools or new community centers; others are organizing to prevent Wal-Mart or other large retailers from building stores in their communities. One of the real success stories of how a community transformed itself is Tupelo, Mississippi. Tupelo is famous for being the birthplace of Elvis Presley; in 1940 it also had the distinction of being the county seat of the poorest county in the poorest state in the country. But Lee County now has a medical center with over 6,000 employees, boasts 18 Fortune 500 manufacturing plants, and has added 1,000 new manufacturing jobs in each of the past 13 years. Tupelo now has a symphony, an art museum, a theater group, an 8,000-seat coliseum, and an outstanding recreational program. Its public schools have won national academic honors and its athletic programs have won several state championships.

So how was Tupelo able to transform from a poor to a vibrant rural community? The town had no natural advantages, such as a harbor or natural resources, which would give it a competitive advantage. It also had no interstate highways, and the closest metropolitan centers were over 100 miles away. The key to Tupelo's success was the ability of the town's citizens to work together. More specifically, the citizens of Tupelo were able to: (1) collaborate effectively in identifying the problems and needs of the community; (2) achieve a working consensus on goals and priorities; (3) agree on ways and means to implement goals and priorities; and (4) collaborate effectively in the agreed actions.

Tupelo's success started when local community members pooled resources to acquire a siring bull. The bull's offspring were used to start local ranches. Farmers shifted from planting cotton to those crops needed to support the ranchers and local populace, and farming and ranching equipment distributors started up local operations. George McLean, the local newspaper publisher, kept the community focused on economic development and helped local entrepreneurs by subsidizing office and warehouse space. With various tax breaks and incentives from local bankers, furniture manufacturers started moving to town. A number of other businesses then sprang up to support the manufacturers, and community leaders made a concerted effort to expand and improve local health care and educational facilities to support the new workforce. Despite the successes to date, Tupelo is now facing even bigger challenges, as many of the local furniture manufacturers are being threatened by low-cost manufacturers in China. But if any community were to succeed in the face of challenge, it would likely be Tupelo. The community seems to have the leaders needed to help citizens fully understand these new challenges and what to do to meet them.

Source: V. L. Grisham, Jr., *Tupelo: The Evolution of a Community.* Dayton, OH: Kettering Foundation Press, 1999.

raised by the other authors. Beer's model also provides a road map for leadership practitioners wanting to implement an organizational change initiative, as well as a diagnostic tool for understanding why change initiatives fail. According to Beer:

$$C = D \times M \times P > R$$

The D in this formula represents followers' **dissatisfaction** with the current status quo. M symbolizes the **model** for change and includes the leader's vision of the future as well as the goals and systems that need to change to support the new vision. P represents **process:** This is concerned with developing and implementing a plan that articulates the who, what, when, where, and how of the change initiative. R stands for **resistance;** people resist change because they fear a loss of identity or social contacts and good change plans address these sources of resistance. Finally the C corresponds to the **amount of change.** Notice that leaders can increase the amount of change by increasing the level of dissatisfaction, increasing the clarity of vision, developing a well-thought-out change plan, or decreasing the amount of resistance in followers. You should also note that the D × M × P is a multiplicative function—increasing dissatisfaction but having no plan will result in little change. Likewise, if followers are content with the status quo, then it may be very difficult for leaders to get followers to change, no matter how compelling their vision or change plan may be. This model maintains that organizational change is a very systematic process and large-scale changes can take months if not years to implement.[21,22] Leadership practitioners who possess a good understanding of the model should be able to do a better job developing change initiatives and diagnosing where their initiatives may be getting stuck. Because change is an important component of leadership, we will go into more detail on each of the components of Beer's model.

Dissatisfaction

Followers' level of satisfaction is an important ingredient in a leader's ability to drive change. Followers who are relatively content are not apt to change; malcontents are much more likely to do something to change the situation. Although employee satisfaction is an important outcome of leadership, leaders who want to change the status quo may need to take action to *decrease* employee satisfaction levels. Follower's emotions are the fuel for organizational change, and change often requires a considerable amount of fuel. The key for leadership practitioners is to increase dissatisfaction (D) to the point where followers are inclined to take action, but not so much that they decide to leave the organization. So what can leaders do to increase follower dissatisfaction levels? Probably the first step is to determine just how satisfied followers are with the current situation. This information can be gleaned from employee satisfaction surveys, grievance records, customer complaints, or conversations with followers. To increase dissatisfaction, leaders can talk about potential competitive, technology, or legal threats or employee concerns about the status quo. They can also capitalize on or even create some type of financial or political crisis, benchmark against other organizations, or substantially increase performance standards. All of these actions can potentially heighten followers' emotional levels; however, leaders must ensure that these emotions are channeled toward the leader's vision for the organization.

Model

There are four key components to the model (M) variable in the change formula, and these include environmental scanning, a vision, the setting of identification of new goals to support the vision, and needed system changes. As discussed earlier, organizations are constantly bombarded with economic, technological, competitive, legal, and social challenges. Good leaders are constantly scanning the external environment to assess the seriousness of these threats. They are also adept at internal scanning; they understand where the organization is doing well and falling short. Thus, keeping up to date on current events, spending time reviewing organizational reports, and taking time to listen to followers' concerns are some of the techniques leaders use to conduct external and internal scans.[3,8,11,12,22,27] This information in turn is used to formulate a vision for the change initiative. What would a new organization look like if it were to successfully counter the gravest external threats, take advantage of new market opportunities, and overcome organizational shortcomings? What would be the purpose of the new organization and why would people want to work in it? A good vision statement should answer these questions. The good news about a vision statement is that it does not have to be a solo effort on the part of the leader. Oftentimes leaders will either solicit followers for ideas or work with a team of followers to craft a vision statement.[8,16,17,28–30] Both of these actions can help to increase followers' commitment to the new vision.

It is important to understand the difference between an organization's vision and goals. Just as the ancient mariners used the stars to navigate, so too should a vision provide guidance for an organization's actions. A vision helps the organization make choices about what it should and should not do, the kind of people it should hire and retain, the rules by which it should operate, and so on.[20,26,28–30] But just as the stars were not the final destination for the ancient mariners, so too is a vision not the final destination for an organization. An organization's goals are the equivalent of the ancient mariner's final destination, and they should spell out specifically what the organization is trying to accomplish and when they will get done.[3,8,19,26,28–31] Depending on the organization, these goals might concern market share, profitability, revenue or customer growth, quality, the implementation of new customer service or information technology systems, the number of patents awarded, school test scores, fund-raising targets, or the reduction of crime rates. Thus, an organization's goals can be externally or internally focused or both, depending on the results of the environmental scan and the vision of the

Without a compelling vision, there is no way for people who lose the most to reconcile their losses.

Bill Mease, Mease & Trudeau

Without a clear vision and an explicit set of goals, all decisions are based on politics.

Pete Ramstad, Toro

An Example of a Vision Statement and Organizational Goals

HIGHLIGHT 13.3

Vision Statement
To be the industry leader in waste-to-energy operating companies.

Selected Organizational Goals

- Increase profitability growth from 5 to 8.5 percent.
- Hold maintenance and repair spending to 2006 levels.
- Maintain 90 percent boiler availability rate across all plants.
- Reduce unscheduled boiler downtime by 29 percent.

- Reduce accounting costs by 12 percent by centralizing the accounting function.
- Achieve zero recordables and zero lost time safety incidents across all plants.
- Implement a metals recovery system across all plants in order to boost recycle revenues by 26 percent.
- Win five new waste-to energy plant operating contracts in 2007.

Source: G. J. Curphy, *The Competitive Advantage Program for Wheelabrator Technologies Incorporated.* North Oaks, MN: Author, 2006.

organization. Highlight 13.3 provides an example of a vision statement and organizational goals for a waste-to-energy power company. (This company burns trash in order to create electricity.)

After determining its goals, the leader will need to determine which systems need to change in order for the organization to fulfill its vision and accomplish its goals. In other words, how do the marketing, sales, manufacturing, quality, human resource, shipping, accounting, or customer service systems need to change if the organization is to succeed? And does the current organizational structure or culture support or interfere with the new vision? Leaders wanting their organizational change initiatives to succeed will need to take a systems thinking approach after setting organizational goals.[27–29,32] A **systems thinking approach** asks leaders to think about the organization as a set of interlocking systems, and explains how changes in one system can have intended and unintended consequences for other parts of the organization. For example, if a company wanted to grow market share and revenues, then it might change the compensation system to motivate salespeople to go after new customers. However, this approach could also cause a number of problems in the manufacturing, quality, shipping, accounting, and customer service departments. Leaders who anticipate these problems make all of the necessary systems changes in order to increase the odds of organizational success. Leaders may need to set goals and put action plans in place for each of these system changes. These actions can be contrasted to **siloed thinking,** where leaders act to optimize their part of the organization at the

FIGURE 13.1   The components of organizational alignment.

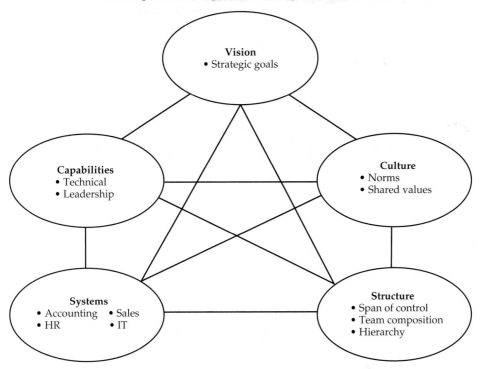

expense of suboptimizing the organization's overall effectiveness.[28,29,32] For example, the vice president of sales could change the sales compensation plan if she believed her sole concern was annual revenues. This belief could be reinforced if her compensation was primarily based on hitting certain revenue targets. If she is a siloed thinker, she would also believe that profitability, quality, or customer service were not her concerns. However, this mode of thinking could ultimately lead to her downfall, as quality and order fulfillment problems may cause customers to leave at a faster rate than new customers are buying products.

Figure 13.1 is a graphic depiction of a systems model for leadership practitioners. All of the components of this model interact with and affect all the other components of the model. Therefore, leaders changing organizational vision or goals will need to think through the commensurate changes in the organization's structure, culture, systems, and leader and follower capabilities. Similarly, changes in the information or hiring systems can affect the organization's capabilities, culture, structure, or ability to meet its goals. One of the keys to successful organizational change is ensuring that all components in Figure 13.1 are in alignment. A common mistake for many leaders is to change the organization's vision, structure, and systems and overlook the organization's culture and leader and follower capabilities. This makes sense in that it is relatively easy to create a new vision statement, organizational chart, or compensation plan. Leaders either discount the importance of organizational culture and capabilities, falsely believe they are easy to change, or believe they are a given because they are so difficult to change. It is possible to change the culture and capabilities of an organization, but it takes considerable time and focused effort. Unfortunately, about 70 percent of change initiatives fail, and the underlying cause for many of these failures is the leader's inability or unwillingness to address these culture and capabilities issues.[6–8,11,22,24,28,29,33–38]

Process

At this point in the change process, the leader may have taken certain steps to increase follower dissatisfaction. She may also have worked with followers to craft a new vision statement, set new team or organizational goals, and determined what organizational systems, capabilities, or structures need to change. In many ways, the D and M components of the change model are the easiest for leadership practitioners to accomplish. The process (P) component of the change model is where the change initiative becomes tangible and actionable because it consists of the development and execution of the **change plan.**[8,12,28–30,39] Good change plans outline the sequence of events, key deliverables, timelines, responsible parties, metrics, and feedback mechanisms needed to achieve the new organizational goals. It may also include the steps needed to increase dissatisfaction and deal with anticipated resistance, an outline of training and resource needs, and a comprehensive communication plan to keep all relevant parties informed.

Depending on the depth and breadth of change, change plans can be fairly detailed and complicated. For example, the waste-to-energy company described earlier could no longer do what it had always done if it were to reach its goals outlined in Highlight 13.3. The company needed new behaviors, metrics, and feedback systems to achieve these goals. The company's change plan was quite extensive and consisted of an overall plan for the company as well as plant-specific goals and change plans. Each of these plans outlined the action steps, responsible parties, metrics, and due dates; progress against the plans was regularly reviewed in monthly plant business and operational reviews. The goals and change plans were constantly adjusted in these meetings to take into account unforeseen barriers, sooner than expected progress, and so on.

Of course the plan itself is only a road map for change. Change will only occur when the action steps outlined in the plan are actually carried out. This is another area where leadership practitioners can run into trouble. One of the reasons why CEOs fail is an inability to execute and it is also one of the reasons why first-line supervisors through executives derail.[38–42] Perhaps the best way to get followers committed to a

Organizational change initiatives will only succeed when the changes are specified down to the individual employee level. Employees need to understand which old attitudes and behaviors are to be discarded and which new ones are to be acquired.

Jerry Jellison,
University of
Southern California

Joel Klein

PROFILES IN LEADERSHIP 13.1

The comment that best summarized the situation as I moved into the Chancellor's role was when somebody told me that the Department of Education was there not to serve the kids, but to serve the employees.

Joel Klein, Chancellor, New York City Department of Education

Prior to moving becoming the Chancellor of the Department of Education in New York City, Joel Klein was the head of the Antitrust Division in the Department of Justice during the Clinton administration and played the role of lead prosecutor during the Microsoft antitrust case. Klein received his BA from Columbia University and his law degree from Harvard. After graduating from Harvard, Klein worked as a clerk for United States Supreme Court Justice Lewis Powell and then went into private practice and specialized in appellate cases. Immediately prior to the Chancellor position, he was the General Counsel for Bertelsmann.

Upon getting elected as the Mayor of New York City, Michael Bloomberg determined that upgrading the public education system was his number one priority. The department was spending approximately 15 billion dollars a year to educate over 1.1 million students, yet only 48 percent were graduating from high school. Because the department was spending nearly twice as much per pupil than other school districts but achieving much lower graduation rates, Bloomberg determined that giving the department more money would not lead to any better results. Bloomberg needed someone who could change the way education was delivered by the department and asked Joel Klein to be the lead change agent for the department.

Upon assuming the Chancellor position, Klein noted that the Department of Education was subdivided into different school districts, with each district having its own school board, administration, teachers, and students. The school districts were run very autonomously and had dramatically different educational goals and curriculums. However, internal politics, favoritism, poor district–community relationships, and a lack of results and accountability seemed to permeate all the districts. One of the first things Klein did was to eliminate the school districts and their boards and create one consolidated board for the Department of Education. The next thing Klein did was to create common reading, writing, and math educational standards and curriculum across all 1,400 schools in the department. Needless to say these changes caused a considerable amount of conflict within the department and became grist for the New York City media. But as dramatic and unpopular as these changes were they were nothing compared to what Klein did next.

The next major change Klein introduced was to create charter schools. These schools were often located within an existing school, but students had to achieve set educational goals and adhere to strict behavioral standards. Teachers and administrators were freed from many of the rules and regulations governing education but had to achieve specific educational goals. Students, teachers, and administrators were held accountable to these goals and standards and would be dismissed from the charter school if they failed to achieve results. Due to the popularity of the program the department now has over 400 charter schools. This program was even more unpopular than those of the earlier changes, with much of the resistance coming from the 80,000 members of the United Federation of Teachers. Yet the department had 3,000 teachers that no one wanted, but because of seniority rules many young and motivated teachers were bumped in order to make room for older and unmotivated teachers. The charter school system eliminated the seniority system and the United Federation of Teachers generated a lot of negative publicity in order to kill the charter school concept. At the time of this writing the public seems to be with the Mayor and the Chancellor, but public opinion could sway the other way if the charter schools stop delivering results that are superior to those of the public schools.

Sources: J. Alter, "Stop Pandering on Education." *Newsweek*, February 12, 2007; G. J. Curphy, *Team 100 Leadership Program for the New York City Department of Education*. North Oaks, MN: Author, 2005; http://en.wikipedia.org/wki/Joel_Klein.

change plan is to have them create it. This way followers become early adopters and know what, why, when, where, who, and how things are to be done. Nevertheless, many times it is impossible for all the followers affected by the change to be involved with the creation of the plan. In these cases follower commitment can be increased if the new expectations for behavior and performance are explicit, the personal benefits of the change initiative are made clear, and followers already have a strong and trusting relationship with their leader.[8,28,29,31] Even after taking all of these steps, leadership practitioners will still need to spend considerable time regularly reviewing progress and holding people accountable for their roles and responsibilities in the change plan. Followers face competing demands for time and effort, and a lack of follow-through will cause many followers to drop the change initiative off of their radar screens. Leaders should also anticipate shifts in followership styles once the change plan is implemented. Exemplary followers may shift to become alienated followers, conformist to passive followers, or passive to alienated followers. Leaders who address these shifts in styles and inappropriate follower behaviors in a swift and consistent manner are more likely to succeed with their change initiatives.

Resistance

So why would followership styles shift as a result of a change initiative? One reason is that it may take some time before the benefits of change are realized. Many times leaders, followers, and other stakeholders assume that performance, productivity, or customer service will immediately improve upon the acquisition of new equipment, systems, behaviors, and so on. However, there is often a temporary drop in performance or productivity as followers learn new systems and skills. This difference between initial expectations and reality is called the **expectation-performance gap** and can be the source of considerable frustration (see Figure 13.2). If not managed properly, it can spark resistance (R), causing followers to revert back to old behaviors and systems to get things done. Leadership practitioners can help followers deal with their frustration by setting realistic expectations, demonstrating a high degree of patience, and ensuring followers gain proficiency with the new systems and skills as quickly as possible. Good change plans address the expectation-performance gap by building in training and coaching programs to improve follower skill levels.[28,29,31,41]

Another reason why followers might resist change is a fear of loss.[4–6,8–10,21,23,24,28,29,35,36] Because of the change, followers are afraid of losing power, close relationships with others, valued rewards, and their sense of identity or, on the other hand, being seen as incompetent. According to Beer,[21] the fear of loss is a predictable and legitimate response to any change initiative, and some of a leader's responses to these fears can be

Everybody resists change, particularly those who have to change the most.

James O'Toole, Aspen Institute

In terms of barriers to change, there is not a single rural community that wouldn't benefit from a few timely deaths.

Jim Krile, The Blandin Foundation

FIGURE 13.2
The expectation-performance gap.

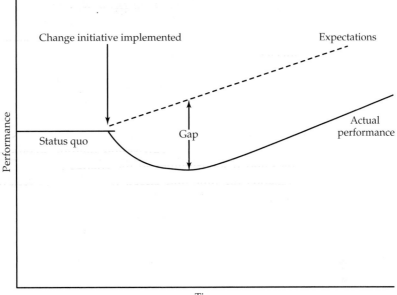

found in Table 13.2. Change initiatives are more likely to be successfully adopted if their change plans identify potential and address these areas of resistance. People also seem to go through some very predictable reactions when confronted with change. An example might help to clarify the typical stages people go through when coping with change. Suppose you were working for a large company that needed to lay off 30 percent of the workforce due to a slowdown in the economy and declining profits. If you were one of the people asked to leave, your first reaction might be shock or surprise. You may not have been aware that market conditions were so soft or that you would be among those affected by the layoff. Next

TABLE 13.2
Common Losses with Change

Loss of:	Possible Leader Actions:
Power	Demonstrate empathy, good listening skills, and new ways to build power.
Competence	Coaching, mentoring, training, peer coaching, job aids, and so forth.
Relationships	Help employees build new relationships before change occurs, or soon thereafter.
Rewards	Design and implement new reward system to support change initiative.
Identity	Demonstrate empathy; emphasize value of new roles.

you would go through an anger stage. You may be angry that you had dedicated many long evenings and weekends to the company and now the company no longer wants your services. After anger comes the rejection stage. In this stage you start to question whether the company really knew what it was doing by letting you go and perhaps rationalize that they will probably be calling you back. In the final stage, acceptance, you realize that the company is not going to ask you back and you start to explore other career options. These four reactions to change—shock, anger, rejection, and acceptance—make up what is known as the **SARA model.**[42] It is important to note that most people go through these four stages whenever they get passed over for a promotion, receive negative feedback on a 360-degree report, get criticized by their boss, and so on.

But what should a leadership practitioner do with the SARA model? Perhaps the first step is to simply recognize the four reactions to change. Second, leaders need to understand that individual followers can take more or less time to work through the four stages. Leaders can, however, accelerate the pace in which followers work though the four stages by maintaining an open door policy, demonstrating empathy, and listening to concerns. Third, it is important to note that people are not likely to take any positive action toward a change initiative until they reach the acceptance stage. This does not mean they are happy with the change; only that they accept the inevitability of the change. Fourth, they also need to understand that where people are in the SARA model often varies according to organization level. Usually the first people to realize that a change initiative needs to be implemented are the organization's top leaders. Like everyone else, they go through the four stages, but they are the first to do so. The next people to hear the news are middle managers, followed by first-line supervisors and individual contributors. These three groups also go through the emotional stages of the SARA model, but do so at different times. These differences in emotional reactions by organizational level are depicted in Figure 13.3. What is interesting in Figure 13.3 is that just when top executives have reached the acceptance stage, first-line supervisors and individual contributors are in the shock or anger stages. By this time top leaders are ready to get on with the implementation of the change initiative and may not understand why the rest of the organization is still struggling. Because they are already at the acceptance stage, top leaders may fail to demonstrate empathy and listening skills, and this may be another reason for the depressed performance depicted in Figure 13.2.

Concluding Comments about the Rational Approach to Organizational Change

The situational, follower, and leader components of the rational approach to organizational change are shown in Figure 13.4. Although organizational vision, goals, and change plans are often a collaborative effort

FIGURE 13.3 Reactions to change.

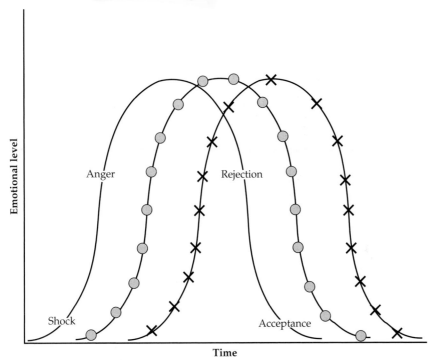

- — Top leaders
- ◯ Middle managers
- ✕ Individual contributors

between the leader and followers, they are the primary responsibility of the leader. Leaders also need to think about the importance of critical mass for driving change.[8,28,29,37] They may be more successful by initially focusing their change efforts on early adopters and those on the fence rather than on those followers who are the most adamant about maintaining the status quo. Once critical mass is reached, the adopters can then exert peer pressure on those followers reluctant to change.[8,22,28,29] This approach also maintains that the leader needs both good leadership and good management skills if a change initiative is to be successful over the long term. Leadership skills are important for determining a new vision for the organization, increasing dissatisfaction, coaching followers on how to do things differently, and overcoming resistance. Management skills are important when setting new goals and creating, implementing, and reviewing progress on change plans. Both sets of skills not only are important components in organizational change but also may play a key

FIGURE 13.4

The rational approach to organization change and the interactional framework.

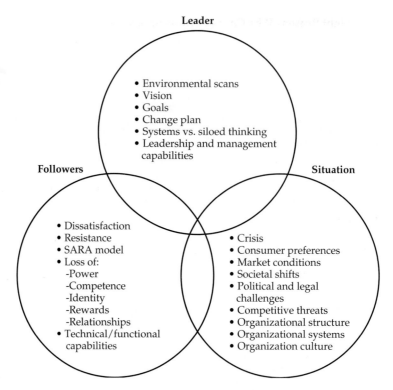

Leader

- Environmental scans
- Vision
- Goals
- Change plan
- Systems vs. siloed thinking
- Leadership and management capabilities

Followers

- Dissatisfaction
- Resistance
- SARA model
- Loss of:
  -Power
  -Competence
  -Identity
  -Rewards
  -Relationships
- Technical/functional capabilities

Situation

- Crisis
- Consumer preferences
- Market conditions
- Societal shifts
- Political and legal challenges
- Competitive threats
- Organizational structure
- Organizational systems
- Organization culture

role in determining whether a new company will succeed or fail. Because of their strong leadership skills, entrepreneurs are often very good at starting up new organizations. Many of these individuals can get people excited about their vision for the new company. However, if entrepreneurs fail to possess or appreciate the importance of management skills, they may not create the systems, policies, and procedures necessary to keep track of shifting consumer preferences, revenues, customer satisfaction, quality, and costs. As a result, these individuals may not have the information they need to make good operational and financial decisions and their companies eventually file for bankruptcy. On the other hand, it is hard to see how planning and execution skills alone will result in the formation of a new company or drive organizational change. It is almost impossible to start up a new company—or for an organization to successfully change—if the person in charge does not have a compelling vision or fails to motivate others to do something different. As seen in Table 13.3, many of the other reasons why organizational change initiatives succeed or fail also have their roots in underdeveloped leadership or management skills.

Although both sets of skills are important, leadership practitioners should recognize that there is a natural tension between leadership and

TABLE 13.3 **Eight Reasons Why Change Efforts Succeed or Fail**

Source: J. P. Kotter, *Leading Change.* Boston: Harvard Business School Press, 1996. Reprinted by permission of Harvard Business School Publishing. Copyright © 1988 by the Harvard Business School Publishing Corporation, all rights reserved.

Succeed	Fail
1. Demonstrate a sense of urgency.	1. Allow too much complacency.
2. Form a strong change coalition.	2. Fail to create a strong change coalition.
3. Envision the future and build strategy.	3. Underestimate the power of vision.
4. Constantly communicate the vision.	4. Undercommunicate the vision by a factor of 10.
5. Remove barriers and align the organization.	5. Permit obstacles to block the vision.
6. Build on early successes.	6. Fail to create short-term wins.
7. Maintain (or increase) the pace of change.	7. Declare victory too soon.
8. Put systems in place to reinforce change.	8. Neglect to anchor changes in the culture.

management skills. In many ways management skills help to maintain the status quo; they help to ensure consistency in behaviors and results. Leadership skills are often used to change the status quo; they help to change the purpose and processes by which an organization gets things done. Leaders who overuse or overemphasize either set of skills are likely to suboptimize team or organizational performance. The first part of this chapter was designed to help leadership practitioners better understand when to use these skills in the change process, and education and experience can help leadership practitioners to improve both sets of skills.

Finally, it is worth noting that the rational approach provides leaders with a systematic process on how to drive change and increased understanding on why change initiatives succeed or fail in their respective organizations. Leadership practitioners can use the $C = D \times M \times P > R$ model as a road map for creating a new vision and goals, changing the products and services their organizations provide, or changing the IT, financial, operations, maintenance, or human resource systems used to support organizational goals. Likewise, leadership practitioners can also use this model as diagnostic to determine where their change initiatives have fallen short—perhaps followers were reasonably satisfied with the status quo, did not buy in to the new vision and goals, critical systems changes were not adequately identified, or change plans were incomplete or were not properly implemented. Given the explanatory power of the model, the rational approach to change provides leaders and leaders to be with a useful heuristic for driving organizational and community change.

An Alternative Approach to Rational Change: Force Field Analysis

HIGHLIGHT 13.4

If you really want to understand something, then try to change it.

Kurt Lewin, researcher

One alternative to Beer's model of organizational change is a technique called **force field analysis** (FFA). An FFA uses vectors to graphically depict the driving forces and the barriers to an organizational change. Stronger forces and barriers are represented by larger vectors; weaker forces and barriers are represented by smaller vectors. An example of an FFA for a rural school district trying to improve third grade student achievement test scores in math can be found below:

Drivers		Barriers
Compelling Vision ⟶	◂———	Budget Reductions
SMART Goals ⟶	◂———	Poor Math Curriculum
Board Support ⟶	◂——	Lack of Parental Involvement
Teacher Buy-In ⟶	◂——	Reduced Number of Teachers
Open Enrollment ⟶	◂—	Increased Class Size
Published Test Results ⟶	◂—	No Mentor Program
		Current State

The first step in an FFA is to graphically depict the current state such as shown above. In many cases the drivers and barriers to change in the current state should more or less balance out, as they represent the current status quo. The second step in an FFA is to formulate strategies to increase the drivers or reduce the barriers to organizational change. (Leaders will often get better results if they focus on reducing barriers rather than increasing the number or size of the drivers for change.) The third and final step in an FFA is to create and implement change plans that outline the steps, accountable parties, and timelines for increasing drivers and reducing the barriers to change.

Source: K. Lewin, "Field Theory and Experiment in Social Psychology: Concepts and Methods." *American Journal of Sociology* 44 (1939) pp. 868–96.

The Emotional Approach to Organizational Change: Charismatic and Transformational Leadership

Although the rational approach provides a straightforward model for organizational change, it seems like many of the large-scale political, societal, or organizational changes were not this formulaic. For example, it is doubtful that Jesus Christ, Muhammad, Joan of Arc, Vladimir Lenin, Adolf Hitler, Mahatma Gandhi, Mao Zedong, Martin Luther King, Jr., the Ayatollah Khomeini, Nelson Mandela, Fidel Castro, Hugo Chávez, or Osama bin Laden followed some change formula or plan, yet these individuals were able to fundamentally change their respective societies. Although these leaders differ in a number of important ways, one distinct characteristic they all

The world of the 1990s and beyond will not belong to "managers" or those who can make numbers dance. The world will belong to passionate, driven leaders—people who not only have enormous amounts of energy but can energize those they lead.

Jack Welch, former CEO of General Electric

share is charisma. Charismatic leaders are passionate, driven individuals who are able to paint a compelling vision of the future. Through this vision they are able to generate high levels of excitement among followers and build particularly strong emotional attachments with them. The combination of a compelling vision, heightened emotional levels, and strong personal attachments often compels followers to put forth greater effort to meet organizational or societal challenges. The enthusiasm and passion generated by charismatic leaders seems to be a dual-edged sword, however. Some charismatic movements can result in positive and relatively peaceful organizational or societal changes; some more recent examples might include the Falun Gong movement in China, Al Gore and the global warming awareness movement, and Louis Farrakhan's Million Man March. On the downside, when this passion is used for selfish or personal gains, history mournfully suggests it can have an equally devastating effect on society. Examples here might include David Koresh of Waco, Texas, infamy, Adolf Hitler, the Serbian leader Slobodan Milosevic, Foday Sankoh of Sierra Leone, or the leader of the Taliban movement in Afghanistan, Muhammed Omar.

So what is it about charismatic leadership that causes followers to get so excited about future possibilities that they may willingly give up their lives for a cause? Even though many people conjure up images of charismatic

Nelson Mandela

PROFILES IN LEADERSHIP 13.2

South Africa was ruled by a white minority government for much of the past 200 years. Although blacks made up over 75 percent of the populace, whites owned most of the property, ran most of the businesses, and controlled virtually all of the country's resources. Moreover, blacks did not have the right to vote and often worked under horrible conditions for little or no wages. Seeing the frustration of his people, Nelson Mandela spent 50 years working to overturn white-minority rule. He started by organizing the African National Congress, a nonviolent organization that protested white rule through work stoppages, strikes, and riots. Several whites were killed in the early riots, and in 1960 the police killed or injured over 250 blacks in Sharpeville. Unrest over the Sharpeville incident caused 95 percent of the black workforce to go on strike for two weeks and in turn the country declared a state of emergency. Mandela then orchestrated acts of sabotage to further pressure the South African government to

change. The organization targeted installations and took special care to ensure no lives were lost in the bombing campaign. Mandela was arrested in 1962 and spent the next 27 years in prison. While in prison he continued to promote civil unrest and majority rule, and his cause eventually gained international recognition. He was offered but turned down a conditional release from prison in 1985. After enormous international and internal pressure, South African President F. W. de Klerk "unbanned" the ANC and unconditionally released Nelson Mandela from prison. Nonetheless, South Africa remained in turmoil and in 1992 four million workers went on strike to protest white rule. Because of this pressure, Mandela forced de Klerk to sign a document outlining multiparty elections. Mandela won the 1994 national election and was the first truly democratically elected leader of the country.

Sources: M. Fatima, *Higher than Hope: The Authorized Biography of Nelson Mandela.* New York: Harper & Row, 1990; S. Clark, *Nelson Mandela Speaks: Forming a Democratic, Nonracist South Africa.* New York: Pathfinder Press, 1993.

individuals when thinking about leadership, the systematic investigation of charismatic leadership is relatively recent. The remainder of this chapter begins with a historical review of the research on charismatic leadership and the leader–follower–situation components of charismatic leadership. We will then review the most popular conceptualization of charisma, Bass's Theory of Transformational and Transactional Leadership. We conclude this chapter by comparing and contrasting the rational and emotional approaches to organizational change.

Charismatic Leadership: A Historical Review

An institution is the lengthened shadow of one man.

Ralph Waldo Emerson, writer

Prior to the mid-1970s charismatic leadership was studied primarily by historians, political scientists, and sociologists. Of this early research, Max Weber arguably wrote the single most important work. Weber was a sociologist interested primarily in how authority, religious, and economic forces affected societies over time. Weber maintained that societies could be categorized into one of three types of authority systems: traditional, legal-rational, and charismatic.[43]

In the **traditional authority system,** the traditions or unwritten laws of the society dictate who has authority and how this authority can be used. The transfer of authority in such systems is based on traditions such as passing power to the first-born son of a king after the king dies. Historical examples would include the monarchies of England from the 1400s to 1600s or the dynasties of China from 3000 BC to the 1700s. Some of the modern-day examples of the traditional authority system include Saudi Arabia, Kuwait, Syria, North Korea, Brunei, and Libya. But these examples should not be limited to countries, as many of the CEOs in privately held companies or publicly traded companies that are controlled by a majority shareholder are often the children or relatives of the previous CEO. Examples include Ford, Marriott, Anheuser-Busch, Cargill, Molson-Coors, Amway, and Carlson Companies (owners of T.G.I. Friday's restaurants and Radisson Hotels). In the **legal-rational authority system** a person possesses authority not because of tradition or birthright, but because of the laws that govern the position occupied. For example, elected officials and most leaders in nonprofit or publicly traded companies are authorized to take certain actions because of the position they occupy. The power is in the position itself, rather than in the person who occupies the position. Thus, Condoleezza Rice can take certain actions not because of who she is or is related to, but because of her role as U.S. Secretary of State.

These two authority systems can be contrasted to the **charismatic authority system,** in which persons derive authority because of their exemplary characteristics. Charismatic leaders are thought to possess superhuman qualities or powers of divine origin that set them apart from ordinary mortals. The locus of authority in this system rests with the individual possessing these unusual qualities; it is not derived from birthright

Kleptocracies and Authority Systems

HIGHLIGHT 13.5

The difference between a kleptocrat and a wise statesman, between a robber baron and a benefactor, is merely one of degree.

Jared Diamond, researcher

In the book *Guns, Germs, and Steel* author Jared Diamond describes the historic, geographic, climatic, technologic, demographic, and economic factors that have caused human societies to emerge, thrive, or disappear. One phenomenon that appears across many groups as they grow to 100 or so people is the emergence of some form of government. Sometimes this government is based around the power of a family (traditional authority); other times it is more formalized (legal-rational authority); and other times it is based on a single leader (charismatic authority). Governments emerge because groups this size begin to recognize that they can solve common problems, such as food, shelter, defense from enemies, etc., by pooling resources rather than working as individuals. Thus members of the group give up certain liberties and resources but gain services they could ill afford on their own. Some people perceive this exchange to be relatively fair; the services they receive seem to offset their costs in terms of taxes, food, etc. But at other times these governments appear to be nothing more than kleptocracies—people pay large tributes to a small group of people at the top but get little in return. Kleptocracies can be found in traditional authority systems; what do British citizens get in return for paying taxes to support having a queen? Kleptocracies can also be found in legal-rational systems; many of the corporate scandals at Enron, WorldCom, Qwest, and United Health were nothing more than executives ripping off employees and shareholders. Charismatic leaders can also head up kleptocracies. At one time Robert Mugabe was seen as a charismatic leader by many of his citizens, but with his two million dollar birthday party, poverty rates at an all-time high, and inflation hovering at 8,000 percent per year it seems like most of the citizens of Zimbabwe are not enjoying the same fruits of success.

Because charismatic leaders are more likely to emerge in a crisis, they may be more likely to appear when citizens believe their fees, taxes, goods, cattle, or people payments are seriously out of whack with the benefits they are getting by keeping their government in place. This is precisely what happened when Mao, Lenin, and Castro led their communist revolutions in China, Russia, and Cuba. More recently this same phenomenon has allowed charismatic leaders to be elected into the Presidential suite in Venezuela and Ecuador. And the (un)fairness of the tax versus service exchange is often used by politicians in the United States to gain votes and get elected into office.

Source: J. Diamond, *Guns, Germs, and Steel: The Fates of Human Societies.* New York: W.W. Norton, 1999.

or laws. According to Weber, charismatic leaders come from the margins of society and emerge as leaders in times of great social crisis. These leaders serve to focus society both on the problem it faces and on the revolutionary solutions proposed by the leader. Thus, charismatic authority systems are usually the result of a revolution against the traditional and legal-rational authority systems. Examples of these revolutions might be the overthrow of the Shah of Iran by the Ayatollah Khomeini, the ousting of the British in India by Mahatma Gandhi, the success of Martin Luther King, Jr., in changing the civil rights laws in the United States, or the economic and social change movements led by Hugo Chavez in Venezuela. Unlike traditional or legal-rational authority systems, charismatic authority systems tend to be short-lived. Charismatic leaders must project an image of success in order for followers to believe they possess superhuman qualities; any failures will cause followers to question the divine qualities of the leader and in turn erode the leader's authority.

A number of historians, political scientists, and sociologists have commented on various aspects of Weber's conceptualization of charismatic authority systems. Of all these comments, however, probably the biggest controversy surrounding Weber's theory concerns the locus of charismatic leadership. Is charisma primarily the result of the situation or social context facing the leader, the leader's extraordinary qualities, or the strong relationships between charismatic leaders and followers? A number of authors argued that charismatic movements could not take place unless the society was in a crisis.[44-46] Along these lines, Friedland, Gerth and Mills, and Kanter argued that, before a leader with extraordinary qualities would be perceived as charismatic, the social situation must be such that followers recognize the relevance of the leader's qualities.[47-49] Others have argued that charismatic leadership is primarily a function of the leader's extraordinary qualities, not the situation. These qualities include having extraordinary powers of vision, the rhetorical skills to communicate this vision, a sense of mission, high self-confidence and intelligence, and setting high expectations for followers.[50,51] Finally, several authors have argued that the litmus test for charismatic leadership does not depend on the leader's qualities or the presence of a crisis, but rather on followers' reactions to their leader. According to this argument, charisma is attributed only to those leaders who can develop particularly strong emotional attachments with followers.[52-56]

 High expectations for Employees

The debate surrounding charismatic leadership shifted dramatically with the publication of James MacGregor Burns's *Leadership.* Burns was a prominent political scientist who had spent a career studying leadership in the national political arena. He believed that leadership could take one of two forms. **Transactional leadership** occurred when leaders and followers were in some type of exchange relationship in order to get needs met. The exchange could be economic, political, or psychological in nature, and examples might include exchanging money for work, votes for political favors, loyalty for consideration, and so forth. Transactional leadership is very common but tends to be transitory, in that there may be no enduring purpose to hold parties together once a transaction is made. Burns also noted that, while this type of leadership could be quite effective, it did not result in organizational or societal change and instead tended to perpetuate and legitimize the status quo.[14]

The second form of leadership is **transformational leadership,** which serves to change the status quo by appealing to followers' values and their sense of higher purpose. Transformational leaders articulate the problems in the current system and have a compelling vision of what a new society or organization could be. This new vision of society is intimately linked to the values of both the leader and the followers; it represents an ideal that is congruent with their value systems. According to Burns, transformational leadership is ultimately a moral exercise in that it serves to raise the standard of human conduct. This implies that the acid test for transformational leadership might be the answer to the question, "Do the changes advocated by the leader advance or hinder the development of the organization or society?" Transformational leaders are also adept at **reframing** issues; they point out how the problems or issues facing followers can be resolved if they fulfill the leader's vision of the future. These leaders also teach followers how to become leaders in their own right and incite them to play active roles in the change movement (see Profiles in Leadership 13.1-13.5).

It is important to note that all transformational leaders are charismatic, but not all charismatic leaders are transformational. Transformational leaders are charismatic because they are able to articulate a compelling vision of the future and form strong emotional attachments with followers. However, this vision and these relationships are aligned with followers' value systems and help them get their needs met. Charismatic leaders who are *not* transformational can convey a vision and form strong emotional bonds with followers, but they do so in order to get their own (i.e., the leader's) needs met. Both charismatic and transformational leaders strive for organizational or societal change; the difference is whether the changes are for the benefit of the leader or the followers. Finally, transformational leaders are always controversial. Charismatic leadership almost inherently raises conflicts over values or definitions of the social "good." Controversy also arises because the people with the most to lose in any existing system will put up the most resistance to a transformational change initiative. The emotional levels of those resisting the transformational leadership movement are often just as great as those who embrace it, and this may be the underlying cause for the violent ends to Martin Luther King, Jr., John F. Kennedy, Mahatma Gandhi, Joan of Arc, and Jesus Christ. Burns stated that transformational leadership always involves conflict and change, and transformational leaders must be willing to embrace conflict, make enemies, exhibit a high level of self-sacrifice, and be thick-skinned and focused in order to perpetuate the cause (see Profiles in Leadership 13.3).[57-63]

Leadership researchers Gary Yukl, Jerry Hunt, and Jay Conger all maintained that the publication of *Leadership* played a key role in renewing interest in the topic of leadership.[64-66] As a result, research over the past 30 years has explored cross-cultural, gender, succession, leader, follower, situational, and performance issues in charismatic or transformational leadership. From these efforts we now know that charismatic or transformational leadership is both common and rare. It is common because it can occur in almost every social stratum across every culture. For example, a high school

Osama bin Laden

PROFILES IN LEADERSHIP 13.3

Osama bin Laden is a member of the prestigious bin Laden family in Saudi Arabia and is the founder of al-Qaeda. Bin Laden was born in Riyadh, Saudi Arabia, and was brought up as a devout Sunni Muslim. He attended the Al-Thager Model School in Jeddah, "the school of the elite," and was exposed to many teachings of the Muslim Brotherhood while growing up. He attended university after his secondary schooling but it is uncertain what he majored in or whether he obtained a degree. At the age of 17 he married his first wife and reportedly has had up to four wives and fathered anywhere between 12 and 24 children. In person he is said to be soft spoken, charming, respectful, and polite. He appears to live a life of discipline, simplicity, and self-sacrifice, preferring that his wealth be used to benefit al-Qaeda rather than improve his personal lifestyle.

Bin Laden first engaged in militant activities in the late 1970s, when he moved to Pakistan to help the mujahideen fight a guerilla war to oust the Soviet Union from Afghanistan. His family connections and wealth helped to fund many of the mujahideen's efforts over the next 10 years. Some of his money and arms may have come from the Central Intelligence Agency, as the United States also wanted to see the Soviet Union get out of Afghanistan.

After Iraq invaded Kuwait in 1990, bin Laden offered to protect Saudi Arabia with 12,000 armed men, but his offer was rebuffed by the Saudi royal family. Shortly thereafter bin Laden publicly denounced the presence of United States troops (infidels) on Saudi soil and wanted all United States bases on the Arab peninsula to be closed. He eventually left Saudi Arabia to take up residence in Sudan, where he established a new base for mujahideen operations. The purpose of his African organization was to propagate Islamist philosophy and recruit new members to the cause. In 1996 bin Laden left Sudan and went to Afghanistan to set a new base of operations, where he forged a close relationship with the leaders of the new Taliban government.

Bin Laden issued fatwas in 1996 and 1998 that stated that Muslims should kill civilians and military personnel from the United States and allied countries until they withdraw support for Israel and withdraw military forces from Islamic countries. It is believed he was either directly involved with or funded the 1992 bombing of the Gold Mihor Hotel in Aden, Yemen; the massacre of German tourists in Luxor, Egypt, in 1997; the 1998 bombings of two United States embassies in Africa; and the World Trade Center and Pentagon bombings on 9/11/2001. He, al-Qaeda, and its splinter movements have been involved with the London subway bombing, the wars in Afghanistan and Iraq, and unrest in the Philippines, Thailand, Indonesia, and Somalia. Given his ability to evade capture and track record, it is likely the world will see more violence from these groups.

It is clear that bin Laden has a following, and that following has grown into the tens of thousands over the past 20 years. These followers are very devoted; some are so committed that they volunteer to be suicide bombers. A much larger group may not play active roles in al-Qaeda but are clearly sympathetic to its cause. But as strong as these followers' feelings are about bin Laden, others are just as intent to see him dead or behind bars.

Source: http://en.wikipedia.org/wiki/Osama_bin_Laden.

student leader in France, a military cadet leader at the United States Naval Academy, a Kenyan community leader, an Indonesian hospital leader, or a Russian business executive could all be perceived as charismatic or transformational leaders. But it is also rare because most people in positions of authority are not perceived to be charismatic or transformational leaders. We also know that females such as Margaret Thatcher, Mary Kay Ash, or

Anita Roddick tend to be perceived as more charismatic than their male counterparts, and that transformational leadership results in higher group performance than transactional leadership.[67–85] Although charismatic or transformational leadership often results in large-scale organizational change and higher organizational performance, there is little evidence that these changes remain permanent in business settings after the leader moves on.[86] In addition, some researchers have found that charismatic or transformational leaders did not result in higher organizational performance, but they did earn higher paychecks for themselves.[86–89] In other words, these leaders were very good at garnering attention, hogging credit, and changing their respective organizations, but many of these changes did not result in higher organizational performance.

As a result of this research, we also have three newer theories of charismatic or transformational leadership. Conger and Kanungo used a stage model to differentiate charismatic from noncharismatic leaders. Charismatic leaders begin by thoroughly assessing the current situation and pinpointing problems with the status quo. They then articulate a vision that represents a change from the status quo. This vision represents a challenge to and is a motivating force for change for followers. The vision must be articulated in such a way that increases dissatisfaction with the status quo and compels followers to take action. In the final stage, leaders build trust in their vision and goals by personal example, risk taking, and their total commitment to the vision.[90] The theory developed by House and his colleagues describes how charismatic leaders achieve higher performance by changing followers' self-concepts. Charismatic leaders are believed to motivate followers by changing their perceptions of work itself, offering an appealing vision of the future, developing a collective identity among followers, and increasing their confidence in getting the job done.[91–93] Avolio and Bass's Theory of Transformational and Transactional Leadership is essentially an extension of Burns's theory. Unlike Burns, who viewed transactional and transformational leadership as the extremes of a single continuum, Avolio and Bass viewed these two concepts as independent leadership dimensions. Thus, leaders can be transformational and transactional, transactional but not transformational, and so on. Transformational leaders are believed to achieve stronger results because they heighten followers' awareness of goals and the means to achieve them, they convince followers to take action for the collective good of the group, and their vision of the future helps followers satisfy higher-order needs. Because Avolio and Bass created a questionnaire to assess a leader's standing on transactional and transformational leadership, this theory is by far the most thoroughly researched and will be discussed in more detail later in this chapter.[94]

What Are the Common Characteristics of Charismatic and Transformational Leadership?

The ultimate measure of a man is not where he stands in moments of comfort and convenience, but where he stands in moments of challenge and controversy.

Martin Luther King, Jr., civil rights leader

Although there are some important differences in the theories offered by Conger and Kanungo, House, and Avolio and Bass, in reality they are far more similar than different. It is also important to note that these researchers either do not differentiate charismatic from transformational leadership, or see charisma as a component of transformational leadership. Therefore, we will use the terms somewhat interchangeably in the next section, although we acknowledge the fundamental difference between these two types of leadership. A review of the common leader, follower, and situational factors from Burns and the three more recent theories can be found in Figure 13.5. Like the past debates surrounding charismatic leadership, modern researchers are divided on whether charismatic leadership is due to the leader's superhuman qualities, a special relationship between leaders and followers, the situation, or some

FIGURE 13.5   Factors pertaining to charismatic leadership and the interactional framework.

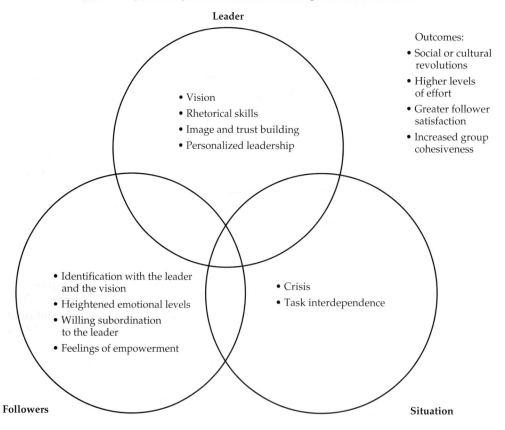

Leader

- Vision
- Rhetorical skills
- Image and trust building
- Personalized leadership

Outcomes:
- Social or cultural revolutions
- Higher levels of effort
- Greater follower satisfaction
- Increased group cohesiveness

- Identification with the leader and the vision
- Heightened emotional levels
- Willing subordination to the leader
- Feelings of empowerment

- Crisis
- Task interdependence

Followers

Situation

combination of these factors. Irrespective of the locus of charismatic leadership, the research does provide overwhelming support for the notion that transformational leaders are effective at large-scale societal or organizational change.

Leader Characteristics

Leadership researchers have spent considerably more time and effort trying to identify the unique characteristics of charismatic leaders than they have exploring follower or situational factors. This is partly because some researchers believe that it is possible to drive higher levels of organizational change or performance through the selection or training of charismatic leaders.[62,67,73,74,79,80,95,96] Although some scholars have argued that the leader's personal qualities are the key to charismatic or transformational leadership, we do not believe the leader's qualities alone result in charismatic leadership.[97,98] We do, however, acknowledge several common threads in the behavior and style of both charismatic and transformational leaders, and these include their vision and values, rhetorical skills, ability to build a particular kind of image in the hearts and minds of their followers, and personalized style of leadership.

Vision

Both transformational and charismatic leaders are inherently future-oriented. They involve helping a group move "from here to there." Charismatic leaders perceive fundamental discrepancies between the way things are and the way things can (or should) be. They recognize the shortcomings of a present order and offer an imaginative **vision** to overcome them. Several aspects of vision are worth elaboration. First, vision is not limited to grand social movements; leaders can use vision to help drive organizational change and performance in any kind or level of organization. Second, both Bennis and Nanus and Tichy and Devanna reported that the leader's vision of the future is often a collaborative effort; the genius of the leader is his or her ability to synthesize seemingly disparate issues and problems and develop a vision that ties all of these concerns together.[16,17,27] Paradoxically, the magic of a leader's vision is often that the more complicated the problem, the more people may be drawn to simplistic solutions. Third, values play a key role in the leader's vision, and serve as a moral compass for aligning the actions of leaders and followers with change initiatives.[57,58,67,93,98–100] As noted previously, this is one way transformational leaders differ from "mere" charismatic leaders: The former builds a vision based on *followers'* values whereas the latter's vision is based solely on his *own* values. Fourth, the leader's vision helps followers interpret events and actions in terms of a common perceptual framework.[99–104] Fifth, Berlew maintained that the vision of the charismatic leader had both a stimulating and a unifying effect on the efforts of

FIGURE 13.6

A leader's vision of the future can align efforts and help groups accomplish more.

Source: Adapted from P. M. Senge, *The Fifth Discipline.* New York: Doubleday, 1990.

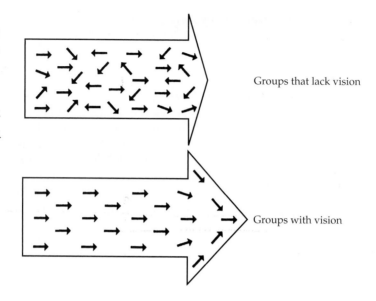

Groups that lack vision

Groups with vision

followers. As seen in Figure 13.6, these effects can help drive greater organizational change and higher performance levels by followers.[105]

Rhetorical Skills

Facts tell, but stories sell.

**Bob Whelan,
NCS Pearson**

In addition to *having* vision, charismatic leaders are gifted in *sharing* their vision. As discussed earlier, charismatic and transformational leaders have superb **rhetorical skills** that heighten followers' emotional levels and inspire them to embrace the vision. As it turns out, both the content of a transformational leader's speeches and the way they are delivered are vitally important. Charismatic leaders make extensive use of metaphors, analogies, and stories rather than abstract and colorless rational discourse to reframe issues and make their points. Moreover, these stories and metaphors can be particularly effective when they invoke potent cultural symbols and elicit strong emotions. Transformational leaders are adept at tailoring their language to particular groups, thereby better engaging them mentally and emotionally. Many transformational or charismatic religious and political leaders effectively use speech techniques like repetition, rhythm, balance, and alliteration to strengthen the impact of their messages.[26,99,100,102,103,107–109] Often the delivery of the speech is even more important than the content itself, as poor delivery can detract from compelling content. Adolf Hitler mastered his delivery techniques so well that his speeches can have a hypnotizing power even to people who do not understand German.[109] Similarly, many people consider Martin Luther King, Jr.'s "I Have a Dream" speech one of the most moving speeches they have ever heard.

"I Have a Dream"

HIGHLIGHT 13.6

This will be the day when all of God's children will be able to sing with new meaning—"my country 'tis of thee, sweet land of liberty, of thee I sing; land where my fathers died, land of the pilgrim's pride; from every mountain side, let freedom ring"—and if America is to be a great nation, this must become true. So let freedom ring from the prodigious hilltops of New Hampshire. Let freedom ring from the mighty mountains of New York. Let freedom ring from the snow-capped Rockies of Colorado. Let freedom ring from the curvaceous slopes of California. But not only that. Let freedom ring from Stone Mountain of Georgia. Let freedom ring from Lookout Mountain of Tennessee. Let freedom ring from every hill and molehill of Mississippi, from every mountainside, let freedom ring. And when we allow freedom to ring, when we let it ring from every village and every hamlet, from every state and every city, we will be able to speed up that day when all of God's children—Black and White men, Jews and Gentiles, Protestants and Catholics—will be able to join hands and to sing in the words of the old Negro spiritual: "Free at last, free at last; thank God Almighty, we are free at last."

Source: Martin Luther King, Jr., "I Have a Dream" speech.

Note his use of different speech techniques and his masterful evocation of patriotic and cultural themes in the excerpt presented in Highlight 13.6.

Image and Trust Building

Setting an example is not the main means of influencing another; it is the only means.
Albert Einstein, physicist

As seen in Profiles in Leadership 13.2 and 12.3, transformational leaders build trust in their leadership and the attainability of their goals through an **image** of seemingly unshakable self-confidence, strength of moral conviction, personal example and self-sacrifice, and unconventional tactics or behavior.[61,91,106,110–115] They are perceived to have unusual insight and ability and act in a manner consistent with their vision and values. Some charismatic leaders even seem to place more importance on creating the *appearance* of success than on success per se.[87,88,91] Whereas transformational leaders **build trust** by showing commitment to followers' needs over self-interest, some charismatic leaders are not beyond taking credit for others' accomplishments or exaggerating their expertise.[106]

Personalized Leadership

Never tell people how to do things. Tell them what to do, and they will surprise you with their ingenuity.
George S. Patton, U.S. Army general

One of the most important aspects of charismatic and transformational leadership is the personal nature of the leader's power. These leaders share strong, personal bonds with followers, even when the leader occupies a formal organizational role.[62,74,86] It is this **personalized leadership** style that seems to be responsible for the feelings of empowerment notable among followers of charismatic or transformational leaders, and it has three important components. First, charismatic leaders are more sensitive to the emotional states of followers.[59,60,62,116] They seem to be more adept at picking up social cues and tailoring their messages accordingly. Second, they also tend to be emotionally expressive, especially through such nonverbal channels as their eye contact, posture, movement, gestures, tone of voice, and facial expressions.[1,26,59,62,117,118] It is partly through their ability to pick up on emotional cues and their nonverbal behaviors that some people are perceived to have a "magnetic" personality. Third, transformational leaders empower followers by building their self-efficacy. They do this by giving followers tasks that lead to successively greater success experiences and heightened self-confidence, encouraging followers to continually upgrade their skills, and creating an environment of heightened expectations and positive emotions.[59,60,90,110,111,119] In terms of personality traits, charismatic leaders possess more surgency and agreeableness and less adjustment (see Chapter 7) than noncharismatic leaders.[62,79,116,120,121]

Political Campaigns and the Attribution of Charisma

HIGHLIGHT 13.7

Political campaigns are a big business in the United States. It is estimated that the 2008 presidential election alone will cost candidates over 1 billion dollars in campaign funds. Most of this money is used for various types of advertisements with the lion's share going to television commercials. These commercials tend to be of two extremes. At one extreme, if the commercial is sponsored by the candidate (or a group that supports the candidate), then it only contains information that paints the candidate in a favorable light. This "positive" spin is intended to leave a favorable impression on the audience so that they vote for the candidate in the upcoming election. At the other extreme, negative attack ads usually consist of half-truths, unflattering photographs, or comments and video clips that are taken out of context and/or modified so that the audience questions the integrity, competence, judgment, and personality of candidates. For example, negative attack ads questioned the integrity, bravery, and legitimacy of 2004 United States presidential candidate John Kerry, a decorated Vietnam War veteran. Curiously enough, the Democratic party did not run negative ads on George W. Bush's Vietnam record, who avoided the Vietnam War by "protecting Texas from Oklahoma" as part of the

Texas Air National Guard. People tend to remember negative attack ads more than those with positive spin, thus candidates have been using them with more and more frequency.

Given the unflattering nature of negative attack ads, one has to wonder if it is possible to perceive political candidates as charismatic leaders. Followers' perceptions are critical in the attribution of charisma, and in the day and age of negative attack ads, unverified blogs, and unflattering video clips and cell phone photos, it may be impossible for anyone wanting to hold an elected office to be seen as charismatic. With technology it is far too easy to catch candidates saying or doing something that destroys their image and trust-building capabilities. On the other hand, positive spin campaigns may help to create the perception of charisma when candidates are anything but charismatic. What does seem true is that technology will give voters more information about candidates than they ever had in the past and that candidates need to be mindful of how anything they say or do can show up on the Internet and national television in just a few hours.

Source: R. E. Riggio, "It's the Leadership, Stupid—An I/O Psychology Perspective on the 2004 U.S. Presidential Election." *The Industrial-Organizational Psychologist* 42 (3) (2005), pp. 21–25.

Follower Characteristics

If charismatic leadership were defined solely by a leader's characteristics, then it would be relatively easy to identify those individuals with good visioning, rhetorical, and impression management skills, and place them in leadership positions. Over time we would expect that a high percentage of followers would embrace and act on the leader's vision. However, a number of leaders appear to possess these attributes, yet are not seen as charismatic. They may be good, competent leaders in their own right, but they seem unable to evoke strong feelings in followers or to get followers to do more than they thought possible. In reality, charisma is probably more a function of the followers' reactions to a leader than of the leader's personal characteristics. If followers do not accept the leader's vision or become emotionally attached to the leader, then the leader simply will not be perceived to be either charismatic or transformational. Thus, **charisma** is in the eyes and heart of the beholder; it is a particularly strong emotional reaction to, identification with, and belief in some leaders by some followers. It is important to note that this definition is value-free—leaders seen as charismatic may or may not share the same values as their followers or meet Burns's criteria for transformational leadership. A recent example of followers' divergent reactions can be seen in regards to U.S. President George W. Bush. Some followers, particularly those in the Republican party, perceive President Bush to be a very charismatic leader. Most Democrats believe he lacks charisma and does not share the same values as the American people, yet he is clearly the same person. Many of the more popular conceptualizations of charisma and charismatic leadership today also define charisma in terms of followers' reactions to the leader.[1,74,90,93,109,111,122,123] Defining charisma as a reaction that followers have toward leaders makes it reasonable to turn our attention to the four unique characteristics of these reactions.

Identification with the Leader and the Vision

Two of the effects associated with charismatic leadership include a strong affection for the leader and a similarity of follower beliefs with those of the leader. These effects describe a sort of bonding or **identification with the leader** personally, and a parallel psychological investment to a goal or activity (a "cause") bigger than oneself. Followers bond with a leader because they see the implementation of the vision as a solution to all of their problems. Followers may be intensely dissatisfied with the status quo but unsuccessful in developing a satisfactory solution on their own. Charismatic leaders capitalize on this dissatisfaction and on the belief that most people want to make a difference in their organizations or society. Followers' identities or self-concepts also become defined in terms of the leader. Being like the leader, or approved by the leader, becomes an important part of one's self-worth.[124–127] Effects like these go

Being attacked by Rush Limbaugh is like being gummed by a newt. It doesn't actually hurt but it leaves you with slimy stuff on your ankle.

Molly Ivins, writer

well beyond what might be expected from the typical contractual or exchange relationships between most supervisors and subordinates.

Heightened Emotional Levels

Charismatic leaders are able to stir followers' feelings, and this **heightened emotional level** results in increased levels of effort and performance.[59,60,62,119,128] Emotions are often the fuel driving large-scale initiatives for change, and charismatic leaders will often do all they can to maintain them, including getting followers to think about their dissatisfaction with the status quo or making impassioned appeals directly to followers. There are several dangers with increasing followers' emotional levels, however. The leader must ensure that followers' emotions are channeled toward the change initiative, otherwise followers will find some other outlet for their feelings and efforts (see Table 13.4). In addition, the people alienated by a charismatic leader and the movement can have emotions just as intense as those of the followers of the vision. This polarizing effect of charismatic leaders may be one reason why they tend to have violent deaths, as those alienated by a charismatic leader are just as likely to act on their emotions as followers within the movement.[129]

Willing Subordination to the Leader

Whereas the preceding factor dealt with followers' emotional and psychological closeness to the leader, **willing subordination to the leader** involves their deference to his or her authority.[126] Charismatic leaders often seem imbued with superhuman qualities. As a result, followers often naturally and willingly submit to the leader's apparent authority and superiority. Followers seem to suspend their critical thinking skills; they have few if any doubts about the intentions or skills of the leader, the correctness of the vision or change initiative, or the actions they need to take in order to achieve the vision.

Feelings of Empowerment

Followers of charismatic leaders are moved to expect more of themselves and they work harder to achieve these higher goals. Charismatic leaders

TABLE 13.4
Followers' Responses to Change

Source: B. Yager. Boise, ID: The Bryan Yager Group, 2003.

Malicious Compliance: This occurs when followers either ignore or actively sabotage change requests.
Compliance: This takes place when followers do no more than abide by the policies and procedures surrounding change requests.
Cooperation: Followers willingly engage in those activities needed to make the change request become reality.
Commitment: Followers embrace change requests as their own and often go the extra mile to make sure work gets done. Charismatic and transformational leaders are very adept at getting followers committed to their vision of the future.

Barack Obama

PROFILES IN LEADERSHIP 13.4

The pundits like to slice and dice our country into Red States and Blue States; Red States for Republicans, Blue States for Democrats. But I've got news for them too. We worship an awesome God in the Blue States, and we don't like federal agents poking around our libraries in the Red States. We coach Little League in the Blue States, and yes, we got some gay friends in the Red States. There are patriots who oppose the war in Iraq and patriots who supported the war in Iraq. We are one people, all of us pledging allegiance to the stars and stripes, all of us defending the United States of America.When we send our young men and women into harm's way, we have a solemn obligation not to fudge the numbers or shade the truth about why they are going, to care for their families while they're gone, to tend to the soldiers upon their return, and to never, ever go to war without enough troops to win the war, secure the peace, and earn the respect of the world.

Barack Obama, United States senator

Barack Obama is currently considered one of the front-runners for the Democratic party nomination for United States President. Born of a Kenyan father and a white mother from Kansas, Obama spent most of his formative years in Hawaii and Indonesia. Upon graduation from high school, Obama attended Columbia University, where he graduated with a BA in political science. He then moved to Chicago and spent three years working for a nonprofit organization that helped local churches provide job training programs. He then went to Harvard Law School, where he was the first black man to be elected class president in the school's 104-year history. He graduated magna cum laude with a JD and moved back to Chicago to work in a law firm.

While in Chicago Obama organized voter registration drives, lectured on constitutional law at the University of Chicago, and got elected to represent the Hyde Park district in the Illinois State Senate. He spent eight years as a state senator before running for United States senator in 2004. While in the United States Senate Obama has sponsored or supported legislation on immigration and election reform, tightening the rules for lobbying and the use of corporate jets for legislator travel, the reduction of greenhouse gasses, the creation of a universal health care program, continuing sanctions against Iran's nuclear enrichment program, and ending the war in Iraq. He gained national prominence with his keynote address at the 2004 Democratic National Convention. A smart, articulate, engaging, and charismatic public speaker, Obama has been able to leverage these assets to become a viable candidate for United States President. Although his early fund-raising efforts have surpassed both his Republican and Democratic rivals, the grind of fund-raising, the primaries, and the 2008 national election will be huge challenges. Over the next year voters will decide whether Obama has the right stuff to be the Democratic Party nominee and the next United States President.

Source: http://en.wikipedia.org/wiki/Barack_Obama.

---

capitalize on the Pygmalion Effect: They set high expectations while boosting the self-confidence of followers by expressing confidence in their abilities and providing ongoing encouragement and support.[78,110,119,130] Somewhat paradoxically, followers feel stronger and more powerful at the same time they willingly subordinate themselves to the charismatic leader. Charismatic leaders are able to make their followers feel more powerful without any diminution or threat to their own status. These **feelings of empowerment,** when combined with heightened emotional levels and a leader's vision of the future, often result in increases in organizational, group, or team performance or significant social change.

Situational Characteristics

Most of the research up to now has focused on identifying the leader attributes associated with charismatic leadership. There is considerably more to learn about the underlying attributes of followers and the situational characteristics of charismatic or transformational leadership.[86,131] Despite this gap in knowledge, many researchers believe that situational factors do play an important role in determining whether a leader will be perceived as charismatic.[77,79,86,88,132] It may be that individuals possessing the qualities of charismatic leaders will be perceived as charismatic *only when confronting certain types of situations.* It may also be that the more favorable the situation is for charismatic leadership, the fewer qualities leaders will need before they are perceived to be charismatic. Because the situation may play an important role in the attribution of charisma, it will be useful to review some of the situational factors believed to affect charismatic leadership.

Crises

Perhaps the most important situational factor associated with charismatic leadership is the presence or absence of a **crisis.** Followers who are content with the status quo are relatively unlikely to perceive a need for a charismatic leader or be willing to devote great effort to fundamentally change an organization or society. On the other hand, a crisis—whether reflected by the failure of traditional social institutions or a corporation's imminent financial failure—often creates a "charisma hunger" in followers; they are looking for a leader to alleviate or resolve their crisis.[134,135] Leaders are given considerably more latitude and autonomy and may temporarily (or sometimes permanently) suspend accepted rules, policies, and procedures in order to pull the organization out of the crisis. Some researchers even believe that some leaders purposely create or manufacture crises to increase followers' acceptance of their vision, the range of actions they can take, and followers' level of effort. Although a crisis situation does not necessarily make every leader look charismatic, such a situation may "set the stage" for particular kinds of leader behaviors to be effective.[77,79,88,97,98,118,133,136]

Task Interdependence and Social Networks

Communication is the currency of leadership.
David Lee, Personal Decisions International

It may be easier for leaders to be seen as charismatic when the tasks performed by their followers require a high level of interdependent rather than independent effort. With **task interdependence,** for example, it may be easier for leaders to be perceived as charismatic when they are leading a software design team rather than a sales team because each individual programmer's code could be affected by the code developed by the other programmers. However, a sales representative with a defined territory will probably not be affected by efforts of the other sales representatives on the team.[76,132,137] In addition to task interdependence, **social networks** can also affect the attribution of charisma. Attributions of charisma will spread more quickly in organizations having well-established social networks, where everybody tends to know everyone else. And more often than not more charismatic leaders have bigger social networks and play a more central role in their networks than leaders seen as less charismatic.[138,139]

Other Situational Characteristics

Several other situational characteristics may help or hinder the emergence of a charismatic leader. Howell and Avolio found that organizations placing a premium on innovation were much more supportive of transformational leadership than those less committed to innovation.[140] Another situational factor that may affect charismatic leadership is outsourcing and organizational downsizing. Many people believe that downsizing has destroyed the implicit contract between employer and employee and left many employees disillusioned with corporate life. On the one hand, because charismatic or transformational leadership is intensely relational in nature, destroying the implicit contract between leaders and followers could greatly diminish the odds of charismatic leadership emergence. On the other hand, this disillusionment has caused many talented managers to leave large organizations to form their own companies. Employees are drawn to these start-up organizations precisely because the company's vision is consistent with their own personal values. But of all the situational variables affecting charismatic leadership, perhaps the most important and overlooked variable is **time.** Charismatic or transformational leadership does not happen overnight. It takes time for leaders to develop and articulate their vision, heighten followers' emotional levels, build trusting relationships with followers, and direct and empower followers to fulfill the vision. It may be that a crisis compresses the amount of time while relatively stable situations lengthen the amount of time needed for charismatic leadership to emerge.

Concluding Thoughts about the Characteristics of Charismatic and Transformational Leadership

Several final points about the characteristics of charismatic leadership need to be made. First, although we defined charisma as a quality attributed to certain leaders based on the relationships they share with followers, charismatic leadership is most fully understood when we also consider how leader and situational factors affect this attribution process. The special relationships charismatic leaders share with followers do not happen by accident; rather, they are often the result of interaction between the leader's qualities, leader and follower values, and the presence of certain situational factors. Second, it seems unlikely that all the characteristics of charismatic leadership need to be present before charisma is attributed to a leader. The bottom line for charisma seems to be the relationships certain leaders share with followers, and there may be a variety of ways in which these relationships can develop. This also implies that charisma may be more of a continuum than an all-or-nothing phenomenon. Some leaders may be able to form particularly strong bonds with a majority of followers, others with a few followers, and still others may get along with most but not form particularly strong bonds with any followers. Third, it does seem that charismatic leadership can happen anywhere—schools, churches, communities, businesses, government organizations, and nations—and does not happen only on the world stage.

Fourth, given that there are a number of ways to develop strong emotional attachments with followers, one important question is whether it is possible to attribute charisma to an individual based solely on his or her position or celebrity status. Some individuals in positions of high public visibility and esteem (e.g., film stars, musicians, athletes, television evangelists, and politicians) can develop (even cultivate) charismatic images among their fans and admirers. In these cases, it is helpful to recognize that charismatic leadership is a two-way street. Not only do followers develop strong emotional bonds with leaders, but leaders also develop strong emotional bonds with followers and are concerned with follower development.[14,78,130] It is difficult to see how the one-way communication channels of radio and television can foster these two-way relationships or enhance follower growth. Thus, although we sometimes view certain individuals as charismatic based on media manipulation and hype, this is not transformational leadership in the truest sense.

So what can leadership practitioners take from this research if they want to use an emotional approach to drive organizational change? They will probably be more successful at driving organizational change if they capitalize on or create a crisis. They also need to be close enough to their followers to determine the sources of discontent and ensure their vision is aligned with followers' values and paints a compelling picture of the future. Leaders must passionately articulate their vision of the future; it is difficult to imagine followers being motivated toward a vision that is unclear or presented by a leader who does not seem to really care about it. Leadership practitioners also need to understand that they alone cannot make the vision a reality; they need their followers' help and support to create organizational or societal changes. Along these lines, they will need to be a role model and coach followers on what they should (and should not) be doing, provide feedback and encouragement, and persuade followers to take on more responsibilities as their skills and self-confidence grow. Finally, leadership practitioners using this approach to organizational change also need to be thick skinned, resilient, and patient (see Highlight 13.8). They will need to cope with the polarization effects of charismatic leadership and understand that it takes time for the effects of this type of leadership to yield results. However, the rewards appear to be well worth the efforts. There appears to be <u>overwhelming evidence that charismatic or transforma-</u><u>tional leaders are more effective than their non-charismatic counter-</u><u>parts,</u> whether they be presidents of the United States,[141] CEOs,[77,81,142] military cadets and officers,[75,76,137,143] college professors,[144] or first-line supervisors and middle-level managers in a variety of public and private sector companies.[74,79,82–85,119,145,146]

Good to Great: An Alternative Framework to the Rational and Emotional Approaches to Organizational Change

HIGHLIGHT 13.8

An alternative conceptualization of organizational change worth noting comes from the book *Good to Great*. Collins and his research team reviewed the financial performance of 1,435 companies that appeared on the Fortune 500 list from 1965–1995. From this list, 11 companies made the leap from being a good to a truly great company—a company that yielded financial returns much higher than those for the overall stock market or industry competitors for at least 15 consecutive years. For example, a dollar invested in these 11 companies in 1965 would have yielded $471 in January 2000, whereas the same dollar invested in the stock market would have returned $56. Collins's research indicates that these 11 companies all followed the same six rules:

1. **Level 5 Leadership:** The *Good to Great* companies were not led by high-profile celebrity leaders, but rather by humble, self-effacing, and reserved individuals who also possessed an incredibly strong drive to succeed.

2. **First Who, Then What:** Before developing a future vision or goals, these leaders first made sure they had the right people with the right skills in the right jobs. Leadership talent management was a key focus of these top companies.

3. **Confront the Brutal Facts (Yet Never Lose Faith):** These leaders met reality head-on—they did not sugarcoat organizational challenges or difficulties. But they also had an unshakable faith in their organizations' ability to meet these challenges.

4. **The Hedgehog Concept:** These companies all focused on being the best in the world at what they did, were deeply passionate about their business, and identified one or two key financial or operational metrics to guide their decision making and day-to-day activities.

5. **A Culture of Discipline:** Companies that had disciplined people did not need hierarchies, bureaucracies, or excessive controls, as the people out in the field knew what they needed to do and made sure it happened.

6. **Technology Accelerators:** All these companies selectively used technology as a means for enhancing business operations, but they were not necessarily leaders in technical innovation.

There were several other surprising findings in Collins's research. First, none of these top performing companies was led by transformational or charismatic leaders. Second, because these top companies were constantly undergoing small but noticeable changes, they did not need to launch major change initiatives or organizational restructuring programs. Third, companies need to abide by all six of these rules to go from good to great; three or four of the six rules were not enough for companies to make the leap to becoming a top performer.

Source: J. Collins, *Good to Great*. New York: Harper-Collins, 2001; J. Collins, "Level 5 Leadership: The Triumph of Humility and Fierce Resolve." *HBR on Point*. Boston, MA: Harvard Business School Press, 2004.

Bass's Theory of Transformational and Transactional Leadership

Much of what we know about the leader, follower, and situational characteristics associated with charismatic or transformational leaders comes from research on Bass's **Theory of Transformational and Transactional Leadership.**[1,111] Bass believed that transformational leaders possessed those leader characteristics described earlier and used perceptions or reactions of subordinates' to determine whether or not a leader was transformational. Thus, transformational leaders possess good visioning, rhetorical, and impression management skills and use them to develop strong emotional bonds with followers. Transformational leaders are believed to be more successful at driving organizational change because of followers' heightened emotional levels and their willingness to work toward the accomplishment of the leader's vision. In contrast, transactional leaders do not possess these leader characteristics, nor are they able to develop strong emotional bonds with followers or inspire followers to do more than followers thought they could. Instead, transactional leaders were believed to motivate followers by setting goals and promising rewards for desired performance.[1,94,110,111,119,121] Avolio and Bass maintained that transactional leadership could have positive effects on follower satisfaction and performance levels, but they also stated that these behaviors were often underutilized because of time constraints, a lack of leader skills, and a disbelief among leaders that rewards could boost performance.[74,94] Bass also maintained that transactional leadership only perpetuates the status quo; a leader's use of rewards does not result in the long-term changes associated with transformational leadership.[111]

Like the "initiating structure" and "consideration" behaviors described in Chapter 8, Bass hypothesized that transformational and transactional leadership comprised two independent leadership dimensions. Thus, individuals could be high transformational but low transactional leaders, low transformational and low transactional leaders, and so on. Bass developed a questionnaire, known as the **Multifactor Leadership Questionnaire (MLQ),** to assess the extent to which leaders exhibited transformational or transactional leadership and the extent to which followers were satisfied with their leader and believed their leader was effective. The MLQ is a 360-degree feedback instrument that assesses five transformational and three transactional factors and a nonleadership factor.[111,147–149] The transformational leadership factors assess the degree to which the leader instills pride in others, displays power and confidence, makes personal sacrifices or champions new possibilities, considers the ethical or moral consequences of decisions, articulates a compelling vision of the future, sets challenging standards, treats followers as individuals, and helps followers understand the problems they face. The three transactional leadership factors assess the extent to which leaders set goals, make rewards contingent on performance, obtain

Duane Lund

PROFILES IN LEADERSHIP 13.5

Although transformational leaders come from all walks of life, one common characteristic they share is their ability to drive change and get things done. One of the best examples of a rural transformational leader is Duane Lund, a retired school superintendent in Staples, Minnesota. In his first year as superintendent of the Staples-Motley school district, Duane lobbied the state legislature and Department of Education to build a new vocational school in the community. Although no new vocational schools had been built in the previous several years, Duane was able to convince key state officials to provide the funding necessary to make this happen. He also helped secure the equipment needed for what would soon be one of the largest machine and allied trades programs in the country. Duane then worked closely with the local Chamber of Commerce and other economic development groups to attract manufacturers that would employ vocational school graduates, and through his efforts more than a dozen such plants sprang up around town.

A tireless promoter of the community, Duane convinced the local railroad to give up some land on a lake just outside of town in order to develop a city park, swimming beach, campground, and athletic fields. An avid writer, Duane has written 36 books and started up and was president of the Community Arts Council for a number of years.

Duane also played a key role in changing the school district–community relationships. He helped pass a bond issue in order to build a new high school auditorium and pool, both of which were made available to community members. He assembled a team of grant writers and secured enough additional funding to keep his class sizes small, his student achievement scores were among the best in the state, and his athletic teams won a number of state championships.

Some of the keys to Duane's success are his ability to create a compelling vision of the future, ability to tell jokes and stories, unbridled optimism and enthusiasm, and genuine down-to-earth charm. All of these qualities help him to get diverse groups working together to get things done. Because of his positive impact on the community, a local foundation has decided to create the "Duane Lund Lifetime Achievement Community Service Award" in his honor, and awards the prize to one person every other year or so for outstanding community service.

necessary resources, provide rewards when performance goals have been met, monitor followers' performance levels, and intervene when problems occur. The MLQ also assesses another factor called laissez-faire leadership, which assesses the extent to which leaders avoid responsibilities, fail to make decisions, are absent when needed, or fail to follow up on requests.

Research Results of Transformational and Transactional Leadership

To date, over 300 studies have used the MLQ to investigate transformational and transactional leadership across a wide variety of situations. These results indicated that transformational leadership can be observed in all countries, institutions, and organizational levels, but it was more prevalent in public institutions and at lower organizational levels.[67,74,75,79,113] In other words, there seemed to be more transformational leaders in the lower levels of the military or other public sector organizations than anywhere else. Second, there is overwhelming evidence that transformational leadership is a significantly better predictor of organizational effectiveness than transactional or laissez-faire leadership. Transformational leaders, whether they are United States presidents, CEOs, school administrators, or plant managers, seem to be more effective at driving organizational change and getting results than transactional leaders. Avolio and Bass also believed that transformational leadership augments performance above and beyond what is associated with transactional leadership.[74] Third, as expected, laissez-faire leadership was negatively correlated with effectiveness.

Given that the MLQ can reliably identify transformational leaders and that these leaders can drive higher levels of organizational change and effectiveness than their transactional counterparts, it seems reasonable to ask whether it is possible to train or select charismatic leaders. Fortunately, researchers have all looked at the effects of transformational leadership training on the performance of military, public sector, and private industry leaders in the United States, Canada, and Israel. Usually these training programs consisted of a one- to five-day initial training session where participants learned about the Theory of Transformational and Transactional Leadership; received MLQ feedback on the extent to which they exhibit transformational, transactional, and laissez-faire leadership; and then went through a series of skill-building exercises and activities to improve their leadership effectiveness. At the end of the initial session, participants were asked to create a development plan to improve specific transformational or transactional leadership skills. Approximately 6 to 24 months after the initial program, participants attended a second training session that also provided a second round of MLQ feedback. The time 1 and time 2 MLQ results allowed researchers to determine quantitatively whether the training program improved the transformational and transactional leadership skills of the participants. These results indicated that improving transactional leadership skills is fairly easy; participants who targeted these skills for improvement reported higher time 2 MLQ scores on the transactional leadership factor. There were also modest gains in the time 2 MLQ transformational leadership factor scores for those participants who targeted these skills in their development plan. Moreover, those areas that were not targeted for improvement saw no commensurate increase in time 2 MLQ scores. Thus, the higher time 2 scores were not due to some general effect, but rather were limited only to those skills that were part of a participant's development plan. These results provided strong evidence that it is possible for leaders to systematically develop their transformational and transactional leadership skills.[67,74,79,80,95,149–151]

An alternative to training leaders to be more transformational is to select leaders with the propensity to be transformational or charismatic in the first place. Several researchers have looked at the importance of childhood experiences, leadership traits, and even genetics in transformational leadership. Zacharatos, Barling, and Kelloway reported that adolescents

TABLE 13.5   Correlations between Five Factor Model Dimensions and Charismatic Leadership Characteristics for 125 Corporate CEOs and Presidents

Source: D. Nilsen, "Using Self and Observers' Ratings for Personality to Predict Leadership Performance." Unpublished doctoral dissertation, University of Minnesota, Minneapolis, 1995.

Personality Dimension	Transformational Leadership Characteristics			
	Visionary Thinking	Empowering Others	Inspiring Trust	High Impact Delivery
Surgency	.32	.33	.16	.47
Dependability	−.08	−.01	.06	−.04
Agreeableness	.02	.52	.48	.35
Adjustment	−.03	.29	.38	.22
Intellectance	.47	.30	.14	.40

who were rated by coaches and peers to be more transformational were also more likely to have parents who were transformational leaders.[152] There is also evidence that certain leadership traits differentiate transformational from transactional leaders. Antonakis and House; Hogan, Curphy, and Hogan; Curphy; Nilsen; House, Spangler, and Woycke; House, Woycke, and Fodor; Ross and Offermann; and Judge and Bono all showed that certain Five Factor Model (FFM) leadership traits (Chapter 7) could be reliably used to identify transformational leaders.[73,116,121,129,153–156] Some of the most compelling evidence comes from Nilsen, who looked at the relationships between FFM personality traits and 125 CEOs. As seen in Table 13.5, not only are the FFM personality dimensions strongly correlated with certain components of transformational leadership, but the pattern of high and low correlations seems to make sense.[155] Given that certain leadership traits are related to transformational leadership, and that leadership traits have a genetic component, then it is not surprising that some researchers also believe that some aspect of transformational leadership is also heritable.[96]

Despite this evidence that it may be possible to select and train transformational leaders, the fact remains that charisma ultimately exists in the eye of the beholder. Thus, there never could be any guarantee that leaders who had the right stuff and were schooled in the appropriate techniques will be seen as charismatic by followers. As discussed earlier, follower and situational variables will play a key role in determining whether leaders are perceived to be transformational and drive organizational change. Certain leaders may get higher transformational leadership scores as a result of a training program, but do they actually heighten followers' emotional levels, get followers to exert extra effort, and as a result achieve greater organizational change or performance after the program? Furthermore, while it may be possible to train some leaders to improve their visioning, impression management, and rhetorical skills, leaders who have relatively low scores on certain personality traits or other individual differences (e.g., intelligence, creativity, surgency, agreeableness, adjustment, and intellectance) may not benefit much from transformational leadership training. Bass,[1] Curphy,[38,76,120] Judge and Bono,[116] and Hogan[153] have all stated that personality is going to have a big effect on whether a leader will be seen as charismatic. Given what we know about individual differences and leadership skills training, it seems likely that a leader's personality will also play a major role in determining whether he or she will benefit from such training.

Finally, several other important comments about the Theory of Transformational and Transactional Leadership are worth noting. First, and perhaps most important, this theory has generated a considerable amount of interest among leadership researchers. This research has helped leadership practitioners to better understand the leader, follower, and situational components of charismatic or transformational leadership, whether transformational leaders are born or made, and so forth. Nevertheless, much of the research is based on surveys and correlational studies; the handful of experiments exploring the effects of transformational and transactional leadership has involved college students, not leadership practitioners.[64,65] Third, this approach to leadership seems to have a strong bias toward people, in that measures such as the MLQ may be more a reflection of socially desirable leadership behaviors than the full range of skills needed by leaders.[121,131,157] For example, it seems likely that business leaders wanting to drive organizational change or performance need to have a good understanding of the industry, business operations, market trends, finance, strategy, and technical/functional knowledge; they also need to effectively cope with stress, negotiate contracts with vendors, demonstrate good planning skills, and develop and monitor key metrics. Yet none of these attributes and skills is directly measured by the MLQ. Relatedly, Beyer, Yukl, and Antonakis and House point out that the primary problem with this theory is that there is only one way to be an effective leader, and that is by demonstrating transformational leadership skills. The contingency theories of leadership no longer matter and situational or follower factors have little impact on leadership effectiveness. In this regard these researchers may be right; leaders probably need to do more than exhibit only transformational leadership skills if they wish to achieve greater organizational change and performance.[64,121,131]

Summary

This chapter began by revisiting the topic of leadership and management. Management skills are important to ensure compliance with existing systems, processes, and procedures; they are used to help preserve the status quo, improve consistency and efficiency, and maintain control. Leadership skills are needed when changes need to be made to existing systems and processes; they are used to create new systems and drive organizational change. The chapter then reviewed two major approaches to organizational change. Although independent lines of research were used to develop the rational and emotional approaches to change, in reality these approaches have several important similarities. With the rational approach, leaders increase follower dissatisfaction by pointing out problems with the status quo, systematically identifying areas of needed change, developing a vision of the future, and developing and implementing a change plan. In the emotional approach, leaders develop and articulate a vision of the future, heighten the emotions of followers, and empower followers to act on their vision. Charismatic leaders are also more likely to emerge during times of uncertainty or crisis, and may actually manufacture a crisis to improve the odds that followers will become committed to their vision of the future. The rational approach puts more emphasis on analytic, planning, and management skills whereas the emotional approach puts more emphasis on leadership skills, leader–follower relationships, and the presence of a crisis to drive organizational change. This chapter described the steps leadership practitioners must take if they wish to drive organizational change. There is ample evidence to suggest that either the rational or the emotional approach can result in organizational change, but the effectiveness of the change may depend on which approach leadership practitioners are most comfortable with and the skill with which they can carry it out.

Key Terms

$C = D \times M \times P > R$, 615
dissatisfaction, 616
model, 616
process, 616
resistance, 616
amount of change, 616
systems thinking approach, 618
siloed thinking, 618
change plan, 620
expectation-performance gap, 622
SARA model, 624
force field analysis (FFA), 628
traditional authority system, 630

legal-rational authority system, 630
charismatic authority system, 630
transactional leadership, 632
transformational leadership, 632
reframing, 633
vision, 637
rhetorical skills, 638
image, 639
build trust, 639
personalized leadership, 639
charisma, 641
identification with the leader, 641

heightened emotional level, 642
willing subordination to the leader, 642
feelings of empowerment, 643
crisis, 644
task interdependence, 644
social networks, 644
time, 645
Theory of Transformational and Transactional Leadership, 648
Multifactor Leadership Questionnaire (MLQ), 648

Questions

1. Are Hillary Clinton, John McCain, or Rudy Guiliani transformational or charismatic leaders? What data would you need to gather to answer this question?

2. Are Vladimir Putin or George W. Bush charismatic or transformational leaders? Would your answers differ if you were a Russian citizen or a member of the Republican party?

3. Research shows that females are seen as more transformational leaders, yet hold relatively few top leadership positions compared to men. Why do you think this is the case? What, if anything, could you do to change this situation?

4. How does the model of community leadership (Chapter 8) compare to the rational and emotional approaches to organizational change?

5. Can leaders possess the dark-side personality traits described in Chapter 7 and still be seen as charismatic?

6. How does charismatic and transformational leadership relate to the four managerial types described at the beginning of Chapter 4?

7. Suppose you wanted to build a new student union at your school. What would you need to do to make this happen it you used a rational versus emotional approach to organizational change?

Activities

1. Break up into teams and identify something that needs to change at your school or at work. Use the rational approach to change ($C = D \times M \times P > R$) to develop a plan for your change initiative.

2. Interview a mid-level leader or executive and ask him or her about the biggest change initiative they were ever a part of. Did they use more of a rational or emotional approach to organizational change, and was the change initiative successful? Why or why not?

3. Create a force field analysis diagram for a change you would like to see happen at your work or school.

Minicase

"Keeping Up with Bill Gates"

Bill Gates inherited intelligence, ambition, and a competitive spirit from his father, a successful Seattle attorney. After graduating from a private prep school in Seattle, he enrolled in Harvard but dropped out to pursue his passion—computer programming. Paul Allen, a friend from prep school, presented Gates with the idea of writing a version of the BASIC computer language for the Altair 8800, one of the first personal computers on the market. Driven by his competitive nature, Gates decided he wanted to be the first to develop a language to make the personal computer accessible for the general public. He and Allen established the

Microsoft Corporation in 1975. Gates's passion and skill were programming—he would work night and day to meet the extremely aggressive deadlines he set for himself and his company. Eventually Gates had to bring in other programmers—he focused on recent college graduates. "We decided that we wanted them to come with clear minds, not polluted by some other approach, to learn the way that we liked to develop software, and to put the kind of energy into it that we thought was key."

In the early days of Microsoft, Gates was in charge of product planning and programming while Allen was in charge of the business side. He motivated his programmers with the claim that whatever deadline was looming, no matter how tight, he could beat it personally if he had to. What eventually developed at Microsoft was a culture in which Gates was king. Everyone working under Gates was made to feel they were lesser programmers who couldn't compete with his skill or drive, so they competed with each other. They worked long hours and tried their best to mirror Gates—his drive, his ambition, his skill. This internal competition motivated the programmers and made Microsoft one of the most successful companies in the computer industry, and one of the most profitable. The corporation has created a tremendous amount of wealth—many of its employees have become millionaires while working at Microsoft, including, of course, Bill Gates, currently one of the richest men in the world. During the 1990s, Bill Gates's net worth grew at an average rate of $34 million per day; that's $200 million per week!

Gates needed a castle for his kingdom and so he built a much-talked-about house on Lake Washington. The house lies mainly underground and looks like a set of separate buildings when viewed from above. The house was conceived as a showcase for Microsoft technology—it took $60 million, seven years of planning and construction, and three generations of computer hardware before it was finally finished. A feature of the house that reveals a lot about its owner is the house's system of electronic badges. These badges let the house computers know where each resident and visitor is in the house. The purpose of the badges is to allow the computer to adjust the climate and music and to match the preferences of people in the house as they move from room to room. What happens when more than one person is in a room? The computer defaults to Gates's personal preferences.

1. Would you classify Bill Gates as a charismatic or transformational leader? Why?
2. Consider followers/employees of Gates. What are some of the unique characteristics of Gates's followers that might identify him as charismatic or transformational?

Sources: http://www.microsoft.com/;
http://news.bbc.co.uk/1/hi/programmes/worlds_most_powerful/3284811.stm;
http://ei.cs.vt.edu/~history/Gates.Mirick.html; http://www.time.com/time/time100/
builder/profile/gates3.html; http://www.pbs.org/cringely/pulpit/pulpit20001123.html.

Chapter Notes

1. Bass, B. M. *Leadership and Performance beyond Expectations.* New York: Free Press, 1985.

2. Bennis, W., and J. Goldsmith. *Learning to Lead.* Reading, MA: Perseus Books, 1997.

3. O'Toole, J. *Leading Change.* San Francisco: Jossey-Bass, 1995.

4. Pritchett, P. *Firing Up Commitment during Organizational Change.* Dallas, TX: Pritchett and Associates, 2001.

5. McNulty, E. "Welcome Aboard (But Don't Change a Thing)." *Harvard Business Review,* October 2002, pp. 32–41.

6. Heifetz, R. A., and M. Linsky. "A Survival Guide for Leaders." *Harvard Business Review,* June 2002, pp. 65–75.

7. Moss Kanter, R. "Leadership and the Psychology of Turnarounds." *Harvard Business Review,* June 2003, pp. 58–64.

8. Krile, J., G. J. Curphy, and D. Lund. *The Community Leadership Handbook: Framing Ideas, Building Relationships and Mobilizing Resources.* St Paul, MN: Fieldstone Alliance, 2005.

9. Ostroff, F. "Change Management in Government." *Harvard Business Review,* May 2006, pp. 141–53.

10. Rock, D., and J. Schwartz. "The Neuroscience of Leadership: Why Organizational Change Hurts." *Strategy + Business* 43 (2006) pp. 71–79.

11. Kotter, J. "Leading Change: Why Transformation Change Efforts Fail." *Harvard Business Review,* January 2007, pp. 96–103.

12. Curphy, G. J. *The Competitive Advantage Program for Wheelabrator Technologies Incorporated.* North Oaks, MN: Author, 2006.

13. Curphy, G. J. *Leadership, Teams, and Change Program for the New York City Leadership Academy.* North Oaks, MN: Author, 2005.

14. Burns, J. M. *Leadership.* New York: Harper & Row, 1978.

15. Kanter, R. M. *The Change Masters.* New York: Simon & Schuster, 1983.

16. Bennis, W. G., and B. Nanus. *Leaders: The Strategies for Taking Charge.* New York: Harper & Row, 1985.

17. Tichy, N. M., and M. A. Devanna. *The Transformational Leader.* New York: John Wiley, 1986.

18. Bridges, W. *Managing Transitions: Making the Most of Change.* Reading, MA: Addison-Wesley, 1991.

19. Collins, J. C., and J. I. Porras. *Built to Last: Successful Habits of Visionary Companies.* Reading, MA: Perseus Books, 1997.

20. Treacy, M., and F. Wiersma. *The Discipline of Market Leaders.* Reading, MA: Perseus Books, 1997.

21. Beer, M. *Leading Change.* Reprint No. 9-488-037. Boston: Harvard Business School Publishing Division, 1988.

22. Beer, M. "Developing Organizational Fitness: Towards a Theory and Practice of Organizational Alignment." Paper presented at the 14th Annual Conference of the Society of Industrial and Organizational Psychology, Atlanta, GA, 1999.

23. Pritchett, P. *The Employee Guide to Mergers and Acquisitions.* Dallas, TX: Pritchett Rummler-Brache, 2002.

24. Heifetz, R. A., and D. L. Laurie. "The Work of Leadership." *Harvard Business Review,* December 2001, pp. 131–40.

25. Collins, J. *Good to Great.* New York: HarperCollins, 2001.

26. Curphy, G. J. *The Role of the Supervisor Program for Andersen Corporation.* North Oaks, MN: Author, 2005.

27. Tichy, N. M., and N. Cardwell. *The Cycle of Leadership: How Great Companies Teach Their Leaders to Win.* New York: HarperBusiness, 2002.

28. Curphy, G. J. *The Blandin Education Leadership Program.* Grand Rapids, MN: The Blandin Foundation, 2003.

29. Ibid.

30. Curphy, G. J. *The High Performing Team Program.* North Oaks, MN: Author, 2004.

31. Curphy, G. J. *The Team Leader Program.* North Oaks, MN: Author, 2004.

32. Senge, P. M. *The Fifth Discipline: The Art and Practice of the Learning Organization.* New York: Doubleday/Currency, 1994.

33. Dickson, M. W., D. B. Smith, M. W. Grojean, and M. G. Ehrhart. "An Organizational Climate regarding Ethics: The Outcome of Leader Values and the Practices That Reflect Them." *Leadership Quarterly* 12, no. 2 (2001), pp. 197–218.

34. Marks, M. L., and P. H. Mirvis. "Making Mergers and Acquisitions Work." *Academy of Management Executive* 15, no. 2 (2001), pp. 80–94.

35. Pritchett, P., and R. Pound. *Smart Moves: A Crash Course on Merger Integration Management.* Pritchett and Associates, 2001.

36. Ruvolo, C. M., and R. C. Bullis. "Essentials of Cultural Change: Lessons Learned the Hard Way." *Consulting Psychology Journal,* 55 (3) (2003), pp. 155–68.

37. Huy, Q. N. "In Praise of Middle Managers." *Harvard Business Review,* September 2001, pp. 72–81.

38. Curphy, G. J., M. J. Benson, A. Baldrica, and R. T. Hogan. *Managerial Incompetence.* Unpublished manuscript, 2007.

39. Bossidy, L., and R. Charan. *Execution: The Discipline of Getting Things Done.* New York: Crown Business Publishing, 2002.

40. Charan, R., and G. Colvin. "Why CEOs Fail." *Fortune,* June 21, 1999, pp. 69–82.

41. Hirschhorn, L. "Campaigning for Change." *Harvard Business Review,* July 2002, pp. 98–106.

42. Kübler-Ross, E. *Living with Death and Dying.* New York: Macmillan, 1981.

43. Weber, M. *The Theory of Social and Economic Organization.* Ed. Talcott Parsons, trans. A. M. Henderson and T. Parsons. New York: Free Press, 1964.

44. Blau, P. M. "Critical Remarks on Weber's Theory of Authority." *American Political Science Review* 57, no. 2 (1963), pp. 305–15.

45. Chinoy, E. *Society.* New York: Random House, 1961.

46. Wolpe, H. "A Critical Analysis of Some Aspects of Charisma." *Sociological Review* 16 (1968), pp. 305–18.

47. Friedland, W. H. "For a Sociological Concept of Charisma." *Social Forces,* no. 1 (1964), pp. 18–26.

48. Gerth, H. H., and C. W. Mills. *Max Weber: Essays in Sociology.* New York: Oxford University Press, 1946.

49. Kanter, R. M. *Commitment and Community.* Cambridge: Harvard University Press, 1972.

50. Tucker, R. C. "The Theory of Charismatic Leadership." *Daedalus* 97 (1968), pp. 731–56.

51. Dow, T. E. "The Theory of Charisma." *Sociological Quarterly* 10 (1969), pp. 306–18.

52. Clark, B. R. "The Organizational Saga in Higher Education." *Administrative Science Quarterly* 17 (1972), pp. 178–84.

53. Deveraux, G. "Charismatic Leadership and Crisis." In *Psychoanalysis and the Social Sciences.* Ed. W. Muensterberger and S. Axelrod. New York: International University Press, 1955.

54. Downton, J. V. *Rebel Leadership: Commitment and Charisma in the Revolutionary Process.* New York: Free Press, 1973.

55. Marcus, J. T. "Transcendence and Charisma." *Western Political Quarterly* 16 (1961), pp. 236–41.

56. Shils, E. "Charisma, Order, and Status." *American Sociological Review* 30 (1965), pp. 199–213.

57. Turner, N., J. Barling, O. Eptiropaki, V. Butcher, and C. Milner. "Transformational Leadership and Moral Reasoning." *Journal of Applied Psychology* 87 (2) (2002), pp. 304–11.

58. Price, T. L. "The Ethics of Authentic Transformational Leadership." *Leadership Quarterly* 14 (1) (2003), pp. 67–82.

59. Rubin, R. S., D. C. Munz, and W. H. Bommer. "Leading from Within: The Effects of Emotion Recognition and Personality on Transformational Leadership Behavior." *Academy of Management Journal* 48 (5), 2005, pp. 845–58.

60. Bono, J. E., and R. Ilies. "Charisma, Positive Emotions, and Mood Contagion." *Leadership Quarterly* 17 (2006), pp. 317–34.

61. Parameshwar, S. "Inventing Higher Purpose through Suffering: The Transformation of the Transformational Leader."*Leadership Quarterly* 17 (2006) pp. 454–74.

62. Greer, M. "The Science of Savoir Faire." *Monitor on Psychology,* January 2005, pp. 28–30.

63. Strange, J. M., and M. D. Mumford. "The Origins of Vision: Effects of Reflection, Models, and Analysis." *Leadership Quarterly* 16 (2005) pp. 121–48.

64. Yukl, G. "An Evaluation of Conceptual Weaknesses in Transformational and Charismatic Leadership Theories." *Leadership Quarterly* 10, no. 2 (1999), pp. 285–306.

65. Hunt, J. G. "Transformational/Charismatic Leadership's Transformation of the Field: An Historical Essay." *Leadership Quarterly,* 10, no. 2 (1999), pp. 129–44.

66. Conger, J. A., and J. G. Hunt. "Charismatic and Transformational Leadership: Taking Stock of the Present and Future." *Leadership Quarterly* 10, no. 2 (1999), pp. 121–28.

67. Bass, B.M. "Two Decades of Research and Development in Transformational Leadership." *European Journal of Work and Organizational Psychology* 8, no. 1 (1999), pp. 9–32.

68. Den Hartog, D. N., R. J. House, P. J. Hanges, S. A. Ruiz-Quintanilla, P. W. Dorfman, and associates. "Culture Specific and Cross-Culturally Generalizable Implicit Leadership Theories: Are Attributes of Charismatic/Transformational Leadership Universally Endorsed?" *Leadership Quarterly* 10, no. 2 (1999), pp. 219–56.

69. Eagly, A. H., and Carli, L. L. "The Female Leadership Advantage: An Evaluation of the Evidence." *Leadership Quarterly* 14 (2003), pp. 807–34.

70. Rosener, J. B. "Ways Women Lead." *Harvard Business Review* 68 (1990), pp. 119–25.

71. Druskat, V. U. "Gender and Leadership Style: Transformational and Transactional Leadership in the Roman Catholic Church." *Leadership Quarterly* 5, no. 1 (1994), pp. 99–120.

72. Bass, B. M., and F. J. Yammarino. *Long-term Forecasting of Transformational Leadership and Its Effects among Naval Officers: Some Preliminary Findings.* Technical Report No. ONR-TR-2. Arlington, VA: Office of Naval Research, 1988.

73. Ross, S. M., and L. R. Offermann. "Transformational Leaders: Measurement of Personality Attributes and Work Group Performance." Paper presented at the Sixth Annual Society of Industrial and Organizational Psychologists Convention, St. Louis, MO, April 1991.

74. Avolio, B. J., and B. M. Bass. *Developing a Full Range of Leadership Potential: Cases on Transactional and Transformational Leadership.* Binghamton: State University of New York at Binghamton, 2000.

75. Bass, B. M. "Thoughts and Plans." In *Cutting Edge: Leadership 2000.* Eds. B. Kellerman and L. R. Matusak. Carbondale, IL: Southern Illinois University Press, 2000, pp. 5–9.

76. Curphy, G. J. "An Empirical Investigation of Bass' (1985) Theory of Transformational and Transactional Leadership." PhD dissertation, University of Minnesota, 1991.

77. Waldman, D. A., G. G. Ramirez, R. J. House, and P. Puranam. "Does Leadership Matter? CEO Leadership Attributes and Profitability under Conditions of Perceived Environmental Uncertainty." *Academy of Management Journal* 44, no. 1 (2001), pp. 134–43.

78. Dvir, T., D. Eden, B. J. Avolio, and B. Shamir. "Impact of Transformational Leadership on Follower Development and Performance: A Field Experiment." *Academy of Management Journal* 45 (4) (2002), pp. 735–44.

79. Bono, J. E. "Transformational Leadership: What We Know and Why You Should Care!" Presentation delivered to the Minnesota Professionals for Psychology Applied to Work, Minneapolis, MN, September 2002.

80. Bass, B. M., B. J. Avolio, D. I. Jung, and Y. Berson. "Predicting Unit Performance by Assessing Transformational and Transactional Leadership." *Journal of Applied Psychology* 88 (2) (2003), pp. 207–18.

81. Waldman, D. A., M. Javidan, and P. Varella. "Charismatic Leadership at the Strategic Level: A New Application of Upper Echelons Theory." *Leadership Quarterly* 15 (3) (2004), pp. 355–80.

82. Judge, T. A., and R. F. Piccolo. "Transformational and Transactional Leadership: A Meta-analytic Test of Their Relative Validity." *Journal of Applied Psychology* 89 (5) (2004), pp. 755–68.

83. Keller, R. T. "Transformational Leadership, Initiating Structure, and Substitutes for Leadership: A Longitudinal Study of Research and Development Project Team Performance." *Journal of Applied Psychology* 91 (1) (2006), pp. 202–10.

84. Whittington, J. L., V. L. Goodwin, and B. Murray. "Transformational Leadership, Goal Difficulty, and Job Design: Independent and Interactive Effects on Employee Outcomes." *Leadership Quarterly* 15 (5) (2004), pp. 593–606.

85. Nemanich, L. A., and R. T. Keller. "Transformational Leadership in an Acquistion: A Field Study of Employees." *Leadership Quarterly* 18 (1) (2007), pp. 49–68.

86. Conger, J. A. "Charismatic and Transformational Leadership in Organizations: An Insider's Perspective on These Developing Streams of Research." *Leadership Quarterly* 10, no. 2 (1999), pp. 145–80.

87. Khurana, R. "The Curse of the Superstar CEO." *Harvard Business Review,* September 2002, pp. 60–67.

88. Tosi, H. L., V. F. Misangyi, A. Fanelli, D. A. Waldman, and F. J. Yammarino. "CEO Charisma, Compensation, and Firm Performance." *Leadership Quarterly,* 15 (3) (2004), pp. 405–20.

89. Agle, B. R., N. J. Nagarajan, J. A. Sonnenfeld, and D. Srinivasan. "Does CEO Charisma Matter? An Empirical Analysis of the Relationships among Organizational Performance, Environmental Uncertainty, and Top Management Team Perceptions of Charisma." *Academy of Management Journal* 49 (1) (2006), pp. 161–74.

90. Conger, J. A., and R. N. Kanungo. *Charismatic Leadership in Organizations.* Thousand Oaks, CA: Sage, 1998.

91. House, R. J. "A 1976 Theory of Charismatic Leadership." In *Leadership: The Cutting Edge.* Eds. J. G. Hunt and L. L. Larson. Carbondale, IL: Southern Illinois University Press, 1977.

92. House, R. J., and B. Shamir. "Toward an Integration of Transformational, Charismatic, and Visionary Theories." In *Leadership Theory and Research Perspective and Directions.* Eds. M. Chemers and R. Ayman. Orlando, FL: Academic Press, 1993, pp. 577–94.

93. Shamir, B., R. J. House, and M. B. Arthur. "The Motivation Effects of Charismatic Leadership: A Self-Concept Based Theory." *Organizational Science* 4 (1993), pp. 577–94.

94. Avolio, B. J., and B. M. Bass. "Transformational Leadership, Charisma, and Beyond." In *Emerging Leadership Vistas.* Eds. J. G. Hunt, B. R. Baliga, and C. A. Schriesheim. Lexington, MA: D. C. Heath, 1988.

95. Towler, A. J. "Effects of Charismatic Influence Training on Attitudes, Behavior, and Performance." *Personnel Psychology* 56 (2), pp. 363–82.

96. Hooijberg, R., and J. Choi. "From Selling Peanuts and Beer in Yankee Stadium to Creating a Theory of Transformational Leadership: An Interview with Bernie Bass." *Leadership Quarterly* 11, no. 2 (2000), pp. 291–300.

97. Boal, K. M., and J. M. Bryson. "Charismatic Leadership: A Phenomenal and Structural Approach." In *Emerging Leadership Vistas*. Eds. J. G. Hunt, B. R. Baliga, H. P. Dachler, and C. A. Schriesheim. Lexington, MA: Heath Company, 1988.

98. Kets de Vries, M. *The Leadership Mystique: A User's Guide for the Human Enterprise*. London: Financial Times/Prentice Hall, 2001.

99. Strange, J. M., and M. D. Mumford. "The Origins of Vision: Charismatic versus Ideological Leadership." *Leadership Quarterly* 13 (4) (2002), pp. 343–78.

100. Mio, J. S., R. E. Riggio, S. Levin, and R. Reese. "Presidential Leadership and Charisma: The Effects of Metaphor." *Leadership Quarterly* 16 (2005), pp. 287–94.

101. Wofford, J. C., and V. L. Goodwin. "A Cognitive Interpretation of Transformational and Transactional Leadership Theories." *Leadership Quarterly* 5 (1994), pp. 161–86.

102. McKee, R. "Storytelling That Moves People: A Conversation with Screenwriting Coach Robert McKee." *Harvard Business Review,* June 2003, pp. 51–57.

103. Palus, C. J., D. M. Horth, A. M. Selvin, and M. L. Pulley. "Exploration for Development: Developing Leaders by Making Shared Sense of Complex Challenges." *Consulting Psychology Journal* 55 (1) (2003), pp. 26–40.

104. Berson, Y., B. Shamir, B. J. Avolio, and M. Popper. "The Relationship between Vision Strength, Leadership Style, and Context." *Leadership Quarterly* 12 (1) (2001), pp. 53–74.

105. Berlew, D. E. "Leadership and Organizational Excitement." In *Organizational Psychology: A Book of Readings*. 2nd ed. Eds. D. A. Kolb, I. M. Rubin, and J. M. McIntyre. Englewood Cliffs, NJ: Prentice Hall, 1974.

106. Conger, J. A. *The Charismatic Leader*. San Francisco: Jossey-Bass, 1989.

107. Shamir, B., M. B. Arthur, and R. J. House. "The Rhetoric of Charismatic Leadership: A Theoretical Extension, a Case Study, and Implications for Research." *Leadership Quarterly* 5 (1994), pp. 25–42.

108. Berson, Y., B. Shamir, B. J. Avolio, and M. Popper. "The Relationship between Vision Strength, Leadership Style, and Context." *Leadership Quarterly* 12 (1) (2001), pp. 53–74.

109. Willner, A. R. *The Spellbinders: Charismatic Political Leadership*. New Haven: Yale University Press, 1984.

110. Bass, B. M., and B. J. Avolio, eds. *Increasing Organizational Effectiveness through Transformational Leadership*. Thousand Oaks, CA: Sage, 1994.

111. Bass, B. M. "Does the Transactional-Transformational Leadership Paradigm Transcend Organizational and National Boundaries?" *American Psychologist* 52, no. 3 (1997), pp. 130–39.

112. Bass, B. M., and P. Steidlmeier. "Ethics, Character, and Authentic Transformational Leadership Behavior." *Leadership Quarterly* 10, no. 2 (1999), pp. 181–218.

113. Sosik, J. J., B. J. Avolio, and D. I. Jung. "Beneath the Mask: Examining the Relationship of Self-Presentation and Impression Management to Charismatic Leadership." *Leadership Quarterly* 13 (3) (2002), pp. 217–42.

114. Pillai, R., E. A. Williams, K. B. Lowe, and D. I. Jung. "Personality, Transformational Leadership, Trust, and the 2000 Presidential Vote." *Leadership Quarterly*, 14 (2) (2003), pp. 161–92.

115. Van Kippenberg, B., and D. van Kippenberg. "Leader Self-Sacrifice and Leadership Effectiveness: The Moderating Role of Leader Prototypicality." *Journal of Applied Psychology* 90 (1) (2005), pp. 25–37.

116. Judge, T. A., and J. E. Bono. "Five-Factor Model of Personality and Transformational Leadership." *Journal of Applied Psychology* 85, no. 5 (2000), pp. 751–65.

117. Den Hartog, D. N., and R. M. Verburg. "Charisma and Rhetoric: Communicative Techniques of International Business Leaders." *Leadership Quarterly* 8, no. 4 (1997), pp. 355–92.

118. Bass, B. M. *Bass and Stogdill's Handbook of Leadership.* 3rd ed. New York: Free Press, 1990.

119. Bono, J. E., and T. A. Judge. "Self-Concordance at Work: Toward Understanding the Motivational Effects of Transformational Leaders." *Academy of Management Journal*, 46 (5) (2003), pp. 554–71.

120. Curphy, G. J. *Hogan Assessment Systems Certification Workshop Training Manuals.* Tulsa, OK: Hogan Assessment Systems, 2003.

121. Antonakis, J., and R. J. House. "On Instrumental Leadership: Beyond Transactions and Transformations." Presentation delivered at the UNL Gallup Leadership Summit, June 2004, Lincoln, Nebraska.

122. Howell, J. M., and P. Frost. "A Laboratory Study of Charismatic Leadership." *Organizational Behavior and Human Decision Processes* 43 (1988), pp. 243–69.

123. Howell, J. M., and B. Shamir. "The Role of Followers in the Charismatic Leadership Process: Relationships and Their Consequences." *Academy of Management Review* 30 (1) (2005), pp. 96–112.

124. Ehrhart, M. G., and K. J. Klein. "Predicting Followers' Preferences for Charismatic Leadership: The Influence of Follower Values and Personality." *Leadership Quarterly* 12, no. 2 (2001), pp. 153–80.

125. Lord, R. G., and D. J. Brown. "Leadership, Values, and Subordinate Self-Concepts." *Leadership Quarterly* 12, no. 2 (2001), pp. 133–52.

126. Kark, R., B. Shamir, and G. Chen. "The Two Faces of Transformational Leadership: Empowerment and Dependency." *Journal of Applied Psychology* 88 (2) (2003), pp. 246–55.

127. Epitopaki, O., and R. Martin. "The Moderating Role of Individual Differences in the Relation between Transformational/Transactional Leadership Perceptions and Organizational Identification." *Leadership Quarterly* 16 (2005), pp. 569–89.

128. Fox, S., and Y. Amichai-Hamburger. "The Power of Emotional Appeals in Promoting Organizational Change Programs." *The Academy of Management Executive* 15 (4) (2001), pp. 84–94.

129. House, R. J., J. Woycke, and E. M. Fodor. "Charismatic and Noncharismatic Leaders: Differences in Behavior and Effectiveness." In *Charismatic Leadership: The Elusive Factor in Organizational Effectiveness.* Eds. J. A. Conger and R. N. Kanungo. San Francisco: Jossey-Bass, 1988, pp. 98–121.

130. Popper, M., and O. Mayseless. "Back to Basics: Applying a Parenting Perspective to Transformational Leadership." *Leadership Quarterly* 14 (1) (2003), pp. 41–66.

131. Beyer, J. M. "Training and Promoting Charisma to Change Organizations." *Leadership Quarterly* 10, no. 2 (1999), pp. 307–30.

132. Lim, B. C., and R. E. Ployhart. "Transformational Leadership: Relations to the Five-Factor Model and Team Performance in Typical and Maximum Contexts." *Journal of Applied Psychology* 89 (4) (2004), pp. 610–21.

133. Hunt, J. G., K. B. Boal, and G. E. Dodge. "The Effects of Visionary and Crisis-Responsive Charisma on Followers: An Experimental Examination of Two Kinds of Charismatic Leadership." *Leadership Quarterly* 10, no. 3 (1999), pp. 423–48.

134. Madsen, D., and P. G. Snow. "The Dispersion of Charisma." *Comparative Political Studies* 16, no. 3 (1983), pp. 337–62.

135. Trice, H. M., and J. M. Beyer. "Charisma and Its Routinization in Two Social Movement Organizations." In *Research in Organizational Behavior.* Vol. 8. Eds. B. M. Staw and L. L. Cummings. Greenwich, CN: JAI Press, 1986.

136. Pawar, B. S., and K. K. Eastman. "The Nature and Implications of Contextual Influences on Transformational Leadership: A Conceptual Examination." *Academy of Management Review* 22, no. 1 (1997), pp. 80–109.

137. Curphy, G. J. "The Effects of Transformational and Transactional Leadership on Organizational Climate, Attrition, and Performance." In *Impact of Leadership.* Eds. K. E. Clark, M. B. Clark, and D. P. Campbell. Greensboro, NC: Center for Creative Leadership, 1992.

138. Pastor, J. C., J. R. Meindl, and M. C. Mayo. "A Network Effects Model of Charismatic Attributions." *The Academy of Management Journal* 45 (2) (2002), pp. 410–20.

139. Bono, J. E., and M. H. Anderson. "The Advice and Influence Networks of Transformational Leaders." *Journal of Applied Psychology* 90 (6), pp. 1301–14.

140. Howell, J. M., and B. J. Avolio. "Transformational Leadership, Transactional Leadership, Focus of Control, and Support for Innovation: Key Predictors of Consolidated Business Unit Performance." *Journal of Applied Psychology* 78 (1993), pp. 243–69.

141. Deluga, R. J. "American Presidential Proactivity, Charismatic Leadership and Rated Performance." *Leadership Quarterly* 9, no. 2 (1998), pp. 265–92.

142. Fanelli, A., and V. F. Misangyi. "Bringing out Charisma: CEO Charisma and External Stakeholders." *Academy of Management Review* 31 (4) (2006), pp. 1049–61.

143. Adams, J., H. T. Prince, D. Instone, and R. W. Rice. "West Point: Critical Incidents of Leadership." *Armed Forces and Society* 10 (1984), pp. 597–611.

144. Labak, A. S. "The Study of Charismatic College Teachers." *Dissertation Abstracts International* 34 (1973), p. 1258B.

145. Shin, S. J., and J. Zhou. "Transformational Leadership, Conservation, and Creativity: Evidence from Korea." *Academy of Management Journal* 46 (6), pp. 703–14.

146. De Hoogh, A. H. B., D. N. Den Hartog, P. L. Koopman, H. Thierry, P. T. Van den Berg, J. G. Van der Weide, and C. P .M. Wilderom. "Leader Motives, Charismatic Leadership, and Subordinates' Work Attitude in the Profit and Voluntary Sector." *Leadership Quarterly* 16 (2005), pp. 17–38.

147. Rafferty, A. E., and M. A. Griffen. "Dimensions of Transformational Leadership: Conceptual and Empirical Extensions." *Leadership Quarterly* 15 (3) (2004), pp. 329–54.

148. Antonakis, J., B. J. Avolio, and N. Sivasubramainiam. "Context and Leadership: An Examination of the Nine Factor Full Range Leadership Theory Using the Multifactor Leadership Questionnaire." *Leadership Quarterly* 15 (2) (2003), pp. 261–95.

149. Bass, B. M., and B. J. Avolio. *The Multifactor Leadership Questionnaire Report.* Palo Alto, CA: Mind Garden, 1996.

150. Frese, M., S. Beimel, and S. Schoenborn. "Action Training for Charismatic Leadership: Two Evaluations of Studies of a Commercial Training Module on Inspirational Communication of a Vision." *Personnel Psychology* 56 (3) (2003), pp. 671–97.

151. Barling, J., C. Loughlin, and E. K. Kelloway. "Development and Test of a Model Linking Safety–Specific Transformational Leadership and Occupational Safety." *Journal of Applied Psychology* 87 (3) (2002), pp. 488–96.

152. Zacharatos, A., J. Barling, and E. K. Kelloway. "Development and Effects of Transformational Leadership in Adolescents." *Leadership Quarterly* 11, no. 2 (2000), pp. 211–26.

153. Hogan, R. T., G. J. Curphy, and J. Hogan. "What Do We Know about Personality: Leadership and Effectiveness?" *American Psychologist* 49 (1994), pp. 493–504.

154. Curphy, G. J. "New Directions in Personality." In *Personality and Organizational Behavior.* R. T. Hogan (chair). Symposium presented at the 104th Annual Meeting of the American Psychological Association, Toronto, Canada, 1996.

155. Nilsen, D. L. *Using Self and Observers' Rating of Personality to Predict Leadership Performance.* Unpublished doctoral dissertation, University of Minnesota, Minneapolis, 1995.

156. House, R. J., W. D. Spangler, and J. Woycke. "Personality and Charisma in the U.S. Presidency: A Psychological Theory of Leadership Effectiveness." *Administrative Science Quarterly* 36 (1991), pp. 364–96.

157. Brown, D. J., and L. M. Keeping. "Elaborating the Role of Transformational Leadership: The Role of Affect." *Leadership Quarterly* 16 (2005), pp. 245–72.

Leadership Skills

In this section we offer some ideas about skills appropriate to the last element of the interactional framework. These skills help leaders facing relatively specific kinds of situations or needs.

- Setting Goals
- Conducting Meetings
- Managing Conflict
- Negotiation
- Problem Solving
- Improving Creativity
- Diagnosing Performance Problems in Individuals, Groups, and Organizations
- Team Building at the Top

Setting Goals

Goals Should Be Specific and Observable
Goals Should Be Attainable But Challenging
Goals Require Commitment
Goals Require Feedback

The Roman philosopher Seneca wrote, "When a man does not know what harbor he is making for, no wind is the right wind." Setting goals and developing plans of action to attain them are important for individuals and for groups. For example, the purpose or goal is often the predominant norm in any group. Once group goals are agreed on, they serve to induce member compliance, act as a criterion for evaluating the leadership potential of group members, and become the criteria for evaluating group performance.[1]

Perhaps the most important step in accomplishing a personal or group goal is stating it right in the first place. The reason many people become frustrated with the outcomes of their New Year's resolutions is not any character flaw on their part (e.g., "I don't have any willpower"), but that their resolutions are so vague or unrealistic they are unlikely to ever lead to demonstrable results. It is possible to keep New Year's resolutions, but one must set them intelligently. In a more general sense, some ways of writing goal statements increase the likelihood that someone will successfully achieve the desired goals. Goals should be specific and observable, attainable and challenging, based on top-to-bottom commitment, and designed to provide feedback to personnel about their progress toward them. The following is a more detailed discussion of each of these points.

Goals Should Be Specific and Observable

As described in Chapter 9, research provides strong support for the idea that specific goals lead to higher levels of effort and performance than general goals. General goals do not work as well because they often do not provide enough information regarding which particular behaviors are to be changed or when a clear end-state has been attained. This may be easiest to see with a personal example.

Assume that a student is not satisfied with her academic performance and wants to do something about it. She might set a very general goal, such as "I will do my best next year" or "I will do better in school next year." At first, such a goal may seem fine; after all, as long as she is motivated to do well, what more would be needed? However, on further thought you can see that "do my best" or "do better" are so ambiguous as to be unhelpful in directing her behavior and ultimately assessing her success. General goals have relatively little impact on energizing and directing immediate behavior, and they make it difficult to assess, in the end, whether someone has attained them or not. A better goal statement for this student would be, for example, to attain a B average or to get no deficient grades this semester. Specific goals like these make it easier to chart one's progress. A more business-oriented example might deal with improving productivity at work. Specific goal statements in this case might include a 20 percent increase in the number of products being produced by the work unit over the next three months or a 40 percent decrease in the number of products being returned by quality control next year.

The idea of having specific goals is closely related to that of having observable goals. It should be clear to everyone when the goal has or has not been reached. It is easy to say your goal is to go on a diet, but a much better goal is "to lose 10 pounds by March." Similarly, it is easy to say the team should do better next season, but a better goal is to say the team will win more than half of next season's games. It is important to note that specific, observable goals are also time limited. Without time limits for accomplishing goals, there would be little urgency associated with them. Neither would there be a finite point at which it is clear a person or group has or has not accomplished the goals. For example, it is better to set a goal of improving the next quarter's sales figures than just improving sales.

Goals Should Be Attainable But Challenging

Some people seem to treat goals as a sort of loyalty oath they must pass, as if it would be a break with one's ideals or be a reflection of insufficient motivation if any but the loftiest goals were set for oneself or one's organization. Yet to be useful, goals must be realistic. The struggling high school student who sets a goal of getting into Harvard may be unrealistic, but it may be realistic to set a goal of getting into the local state university. A civil rights activist may wish to eliminate prejudice completely, but a more attainable goal might be to eliminate racial discrimination in the local housing project over the next five years. A track team is not likely to win every race, but it may be realistic to aim to win the league championship.

The corollary to the preceding point is that goals should also be challenging. If goals merely needed to be attainable, then there would be nothing wrong with setting goals so easy that accomplishing them would be virtually guaranteed. As we have seen previously, setting easy goals does not result in high levels of performance; higher levels of performance come about when goals stretch and inspire people toward doing more than they thought they could. Goals need to be challenging but attainable to get the best out of oneself and others.

Goals Require Commitment

There is nothing magical about having goals; having goals per se does not guarantee success. Unless supported by real human commitment, goal statements are mere words. Organizational goals are most likely to be achieved if there is commitment to them at both the top and the bottom of the organization. Top leadership needs to make clear that it is willing to put its money where its mouth is. When top leadership sets goals, it should provide the resources workers need to achieve the goals and then should reward those who do. Subordinates often become committed to goals simply by seeing the sincere and enthusiastic commitment of top leadership to them. Another way to build subordinate acceptance and commitment to goals is to have subordinates participate in setting the goals in the first place. Research on the effects of goal setting demonstrates that worker acceptance and satisfaction tend to increase when workers are allowed to participate in setting goals.[2,3]

On the other hand, research is less conclusive about whether participation in goal setting actually increases performance or productivity. These mixed findings about participation and performance may be due to various qualities of the group and the leader. In terms of the group, groupthink may cause highly cohesive groups to commit to goals that are unrealistic and unachievable. Group members may not have realistically considered equipment or resource constraints, nor have the technical skills needed to successfully accomplish the goal. In addition, group members may not have any special enthusiasm for accomplishing a goal if the leader is perceived to have little expert power or is unsupportive, curt, or inept.[4-6] However, if leaders are perceived to be competent and supportive, then followers may have as much goal commitment as they would if they had participated in setting the goal. Thus, participation in goal setting often leads to higher levels of commitment and performance if the leader is perceived to be incompetent, but it will not necessarily lead to greater commitment and performance than is achieved when a competent leader assigns a goal. Again, these findings lend credence to the importance of technical competence in leadership effectiveness.

Goals Require Feedback

One of the most effective ways to improve any kind of performance is to provide feedback about how closely a person's behavior matches some criterion, and research shows that performance was much higher when goals were accompanied by feedback than when either goals or feedback were used alone. Goals that are specific, observable, and time limited are conducive to ongoing assessment and performance-based feedback, and leaders and followers should strive to provide and/or seek feedback on a fairly regular basis. Moreover, people should seek feedback from a variety of sources or provide feedback using a variety of criteria. Often, different sources and criteria can paint very different pictures about goal progress, and people can get a better idea of the true level of their progress by examining the information provided and integrating it across the different sources and criteria.

Conducting Meetings

Determine Whether It Is Necessary

List the Objectives

Stick to the Agenda

Provide Pertinent Materials in Advance

Make It Convenient

Encourage Participation

Keep a Record

Meetings are a fact of organizational life. It is difficult to imagine a leader who could (or should) avoid them, particularly when groups, committees, or teams have high levels of task or lateral interdependence. Well-planned and well-led meetings are a valuable mechanism for accomplishing diverse goals and are an important way of exchanging information and keeping open lines of communication within and between work groups or volunteer organizations.[7,8] Although meetings have many advantages, they also cost time and money. The annual cost of meetings in the corporate sector alone may well be in the billions of dollars. Furthermore, unnecessary or inefficient meetings can be frustrating and are often a source of dissatisfaction for participants. Given the investment of time and energy meetings require, leaders have a responsibility to make them as productive as possible. Guth and Shaw[9] provided seven helpful tips for running meetings, which are discussed in the following paragraphs.

Determine Whether It Is Necessary

Perhaps the most important step in conducting a meeting is to take the time to *determine whether or not a meeting is really necessary*. If you are evaluating whether or not to have a meeting, assess what it can accomplish. Have a meeting only if the potential benefits outweigh the costs. As part of this process, get the opinions of the other participants beforehand if that is possible. Moreover, if meetings are regularly scheduled, then you should have significant business to conduct in each meeting. If not, then these meetings should probably be scheduled less frequently.

List the Objectives

Once you have decided that a meeting is necessary, you should then *list your objectives for the meeting and develop a plan for attaining them* in an orderly manner. Prioritize what you hope to accomplish at the meeting. It is often helpful to indicate approximately how much time will be spent on each agenda item. Finally, get the agenda and issues to be covered to the participants well in advance; also let them know who else will be attending.

Stick to the Agenda

Once the meeting gets started, it is important for leaders to *stick to the agenda*. It is easy for groups to get sidetracked by tangential issues or good-natured storytelling. Although you should try to keep a cooperative and comfortable climate in the meeting, it is better to err on the side of being organized and businesslike than being lax and laissez-faire. If items were important enough to put on the agenda, they are important enough to get to in the time allotted for the meeting.

Provide Pertinent Materials in Advance

Besides having an agenda, a meeting is often more effective if leaders also provide the other participants with *pertinent reports or support materials well in advance*. Passing out materials and waiting for people to read them at the meeting itself wastes valuable time. Most people will come prepared, having read relevant material beforehand, if you have given it to them, and almost everyone will resent making a meeting longer than necessary doing work that could and should have been done earlier. In a similar vein, prepare well in advance for any presentations you will make. If you did not provide reports before the meeting, then it is often helpful to provide an outline of your presentation for others to take notes on. Finally, of course, be sure the information you pass out is accurate.

Make It Convenient

Another way to maximize the benefits of meetings is to *pick a time and place as convenient as possible for all participants.* Besides maximizing attendance, this will also keep key participants from being distracted with thoughts of other pressing issues. Similarly, choose a place that is convenient for the participants and suitable for the nature of the meeting. Be sure to consider whether you need such things as a table for the meeting (with seating around it for all participants); a blackboard, an overhead projector, or similar audiovisual aids; coffee or other refreshments; and directions on how to find the meeting place. And start on time; waiting for stragglers is unfair to those who were punctual, and it sends the wrong signal about the seriousness of the meeting. Also plan and announce a time limit on the meeting beforehand and stick to it.

Encourage Participation

Leaders have a responsibility to *encourage participation;* everyone at the meeting should have an opportunity to be heard and should feel some ownership in the meeting's outcome. In some cases, you may need to solicit participation from quieter participants at the meeting, as these members often make valuable contributions to the group when given the chance. Furthermore, ensuring that the quieter members participate will also help you to avoid interpreting someone's quietness as implied consent or agreement. By the same token, you sometimes may need to curtail the participation of more verbal and outspoken participants. You can do this respectfully by merely indicating that the group has a good idea of their position and that it would be useful also to hear from some others. You also help encourage relevant participation by providing interim summaries of the group's discussion.

Keep a Record

During a meeting, the points of discussion and various decisions or actions taken may seem clear to you. However, do not trust your memory to preserve them all. *Take minutes for the record* so you and others can reconstruct what the participants were thinking and why you did or did not take some action. Record decisions and actions to be taken, including *who* will be responsible for doing it and *when* it is supposed to be accomplished. Such records are also very useful for preparing future meeting agendas.

By following the preceding simple steps, both leaders and followers are likely to get much more out of their meetings, as well as appear well organized and effective.

Managing Conflict

What Is Conflict?

Is Conflict Always Bad?

Conflict Resolution Strategies

We read or hear every day in the news about various types of negotiations. Nations often negotiate with each other over land or fishing rights, trade agreements, or diplomatic relations. Land developers often negotiate with city councils for variances on local zoning laws for their projects. Businesses often spend considerable time negotiating employee salaries and fringe benefits with labor unions. In a similar fashion, negotiations go on every day about matters ranging from high school athletic schedules to where a new office copying machine will be located. In one sense, all these negotiations, big or small, are similar. In every case, representatives from different groups meet to resolve some sort of conflict. Conflict is an inevitable fact of life and an inevitable fact of leadership. Researchers have found that first-line supervisors and middle-level managers can spend more than 25 percent of their time dealing with conflict,[10] and resolving conflict has been found to be an important factor in leadership effectiveness.[11] In fact, successfully resolving conflicts is so important that it is a central theme in some of the literature about organizations.[12–14] Moreover, successfully resolving conflicts will become an increasingly important skill as leadership and management practice moves away from authoritarian directives and toward cooperative approaches emphasizing rational persuasion, collaboration, compromise, and solutions of mutual gain.

What Is Conflict?

Conflict occurs when two opposing parties have interests or goals that appear to be incompatible.[15] There are a variety of sources of conflict in team, committee, work-group, and organizational settings. For example, conflict can occur when group or team members (a) have strong differences in values, beliefs, or goals; (b) have high levels of task or lateral interdependence; (c) are competing for scarce resources or rewards; (d) are under high levels of stress; or (e) face uncertain or incompatible demands—that is, role ambiguity and role conflict.[16] Conflict can also occur when leaders act in a manner inconsistent with the vision and goals they have articulated for the organization.[17] Of these factors contributing to the level of conflict within or between groups, teams, or committees, probably the most important source of conflict is the lack of communication between parties.[18] Because many conflicts are the result of misunderstandings and communication breakdowns, leaders can minimize the level of conflict within and between groups by improving their communication and listening skills, as well as spending time networking with others.[19]

Before reviewing specific negotiation tips and conflict resolution strategies, it is necessary to describe several aspects of conflict that can have an impact on the resolution process. First, the size of an issue (bigger issues are more difficult to resolve), the extent to which parties define the problem egocentrically (how much they have personally invested in the problem), and the existence of hidden agendas (unstated but important concerns or objectives) can all affect the conflict resolution process. Second, seeing a conflict situation in win–lose or either/or terms restricts the (perceived) possible outcomes to either total satisfaction or total frustration. A similar but less-extreme variant is to see a situation in zero-sum terms. A zero-sum situation is one in which intermediate degrees of satisfaction are possible (i.e., not either/or), but increases in one party's satisfaction inherently decrease the other party's satisfaction, and vice versa. Still another variant can be when parties perceive a conflict as unresolvable. In such cases neither party gains at the expense of the other, but each continues to perceive the other as an obstacle to satisfaction.[20]

Is Conflict Always Bad?

So far, we have described conflict as an inherently negative aspect of any group, team, committee, or organization. This certainly was the prevailing view of conflict among researchers during the 1930s and 1940s, and it probably also represents the way many people are raised today (i.e., most people have a strong value of minimizing or avoiding conflict). Today, researchers studying group effectiveness have come to a different conclusion. Some level of conflict may be helpful in order to bolster innovation and performance. Conflict that enhances group productivity is viewed as useful, and conflict that hinders group performance is viewed as counter-productive.[21] Various possible positive and negative effects of conflict are listed in Highlight P4.1.

Along these lines, researchers have found that conflict can cause a radical change in political power,[22,23] as well as dramatic changes in organizational structure and design, group cohesiveness, and group or organizational effectiveness.[24,25] Nevertheless, it is important to realize that this current conceptualization of conflict is still somewhat limited in scope. For example, increasing the level of conflict within a group or team may enhance immediate performance but may also have a disastrous effect on organizational climate and turnover. As we noted in Chapter 4, however, leaders may be evaluated in terms of many criteria, only one of which is group performance. Thus, leaders should probably use criteria such as turnover and absenteeism rates and followers' satisfaction or organizational climate ratings in addition to measures of group performance when trying to determine whether conflict is good or bad. Leaders are cautioned against using group performance alone, as these indices may not reveal the overall effects of conflict on the group or team.

although conflict enhances performance, it could be a disaster for the group in the end

So when thinking about what would enhance performance, leaders should also take into account the organizational climate of the group

Possible Effects of Conflict

HIGHLIGHT P4.1

Possible Positive Effects of Conflict	**Possible Negative Effects of Conflict**
Increased effort	Reduced productivity
Feelings get aired	Decreased communication
Better understanding of others	Negative feelings
Impetus for change	Stress
Better decision making	Poorer decision making
Key issues surface	Decreased cooperation
Critical thinking stimulated	Political backstabbing

Conflict Resolution Strategies

In addition to spending time understanding and clarifying positions, separating people from the problem, and focusing on interests, there are five strategies or approaches leaders can use to resolve conflicts. Perhaps the best way to differentiate between these five strategies is to think of conflict resolution in terms of two independent dimensions: cooperativeness/ uncooperativeness and assertiveness/unassertiveness (see Figure P4.1). Parties in conflict do vary in their commitment to satisfy the other's concerns, but they also vary in the extent to which they assertively stand up for their own concerns.[26] Thus, conflict resolution can be understood in terms of how cooperative or uncooperative the parties are and how assertive or unassertive they are.

Using this two-dimension scheme, Thomas[27] described five general approaches to managing conflict:

1. **Competition** reflects a desire to achieve one's own ends at the expense of someone else. This is domination, also known as a win–lose orientation.
2. **Accommodation** reflects a mirror image of competition, entirely giving in to someone else's concerns without making any effort to achieve one's own ends. This is a tactic of appeasement.
3. **Sharing** is an approach that represents a compromise between domination and appeasement. Both parties give up something, yet both parties get something. Both parties are moderately, but incompletely, satisfied.
4. **Collaboration** reflects an effort to fully satisfy both parties. This is a problem-solving approach that requires the integration of each party's concerns.
5. **Avoidance** involves indifference to the concerns of both parties. It reflects a withdrawal from or neglect of any party's interests.

FIGURE P4.1

Five conflict-handling orientations, plotted according to party's desire to satisfy own and other's concerns.

Source: K. W. Thomas, "Conflict and Conflict Management." In *Handbook of Industrial and Organizational Psychology,* ed. M. D. Dunnette, Chicago: Rand McNally, 1976. Reprinted with permission of Marvin D. Dunnette.

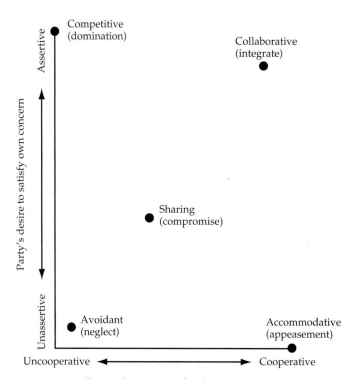

Does one of these approaches seem clearly a better method than the other to you? Each of them does, at least, reflect certain culturally valued modes of behavior.[28] For example, the esteem many people hold for athletic, business, and military heroes reflects our cultural valuation of competition. Valuation of a pragmatic approach to settling problems is reflected in the compromising approach. Cultural values of unselfishness, kindness, and generosity are reflected in accommodation, and even avoidance has roots in philosophies that emphasize caution, diplomacy, and turning away from worldly concerns. These cultural roots to each of the approaches to managing conflict suggest that no single one is likely to be the right one all the time. There probably are circumstances when each of the modes of conflict resolution can be appropriate. Rather than seeking to find some single best approach to managing conflict, it may be wisest to appreciate the relative advantages and disadvantages of all approaches, and the circumstances when each may be most appropriate. A summary of experienced leaders' recommendations for when to use each strategy is presented in Highlight P4.2.

Negotiation

Prepare for the Negotiation
Separate the People from the Problem
Focus on Interests, Not Positions

Negotiation is an approach that may help resolve some conflicts. The following negotiating tips, from Fisher and Ury,[29] include taking the time to prepare for a negotiating session; keeping the people and problems separate; focusing on issues, not positions; and seeking win–win outcomes.

Prepare for the Negotiation

To successfully resolve conflicts, leaders may need to *spend considerable time preparing for a negotiating session.* Leaders should anticipate each side's key concerns and issues, attitudes, possible negotiating strategies, and goals.

Separate the People from the Problem

Fisher and Ury also advised negotiators to *separate the people from the problem.*[30] Because all negotiations involve substantive issues and relationships between negotiators, it is easy for these parts to become entangled. When that happens, parties may inadvertently treat the people *and* the problem as though they were the same. For example, a group of teachers angry that their salary has not been raised for the fourth year in a row may direct their personal bitterness toward the school board president. However, reactions such as these are usually a mistake, as the decision may be out of the other party's hands, and personally attacking the other party often only serves to make the conflict even more difficult to resolve.

There are several things leaders can do to separate the people from the problem. First, leaders should not let their fears color their perceptions of each side's intentions. It is easy to attribute negative qualities to others when one feels threatened. Similarly, it does no good to blame the other side for one's own problems.[31] Even if it is justified, it is still usually counterproductive. Another thing leaders can do to separate the people from the problem is to communicate clearly. Earlier in this text, we suggested techniques for active listening. Those guidelines are especially helpful in negotiating and resolving conflicts.

there doesn't always have to be some one to blame, this usually causes more conflict

Focus on Interests, Not Positions

Another of Fisher and Ury's main points is to *focus on interests, not positions.* Focusing on interests depends on understanding the difference between interests and positions. Here is one example. Say Raoul has had the same reserved seats to the local symphony every season for several years and he was just notified he will no longer get his usual tickets. Feeling irate, he

Situations in Which to Use the Five Approaches to Conflict Management

HIGHLIGHT P4.2

Competing

1. When quick, decisive action is vital—e.g., emergencies.
2. On important issues where unpopular actions need implementing—e.g., cost cutting, enforcing unpopular rules, discipline.
3. On issues vital to company welfare when you know you're right.
4. Against people who take advantage of noncompetitive behavior.

Collaborating

1. To find an integrative solution when both sets of concerns are too important to be compromised.
2. When your objective is to learn.
3. To merge insights from people with different perspectives.
4. To gain commitment by incorporating concerns into a consensus.
5. To work through feelings which have interfered with a relationship.

Compromising

1. When goals are important, but not worth the effort or potential disruption of more assertive modes.
2. When opponents with equal power are committed to mutually exclusive goals.
3. To achieve temporary settlements of complex issues.
4. To arrive at expedient solutions under time pressure.
5. As a backup when collaboration or competition is unsuccessful.

Avoiding

1. When an issue is trivial or more important issues are pressing.
2. When you perceive no chance of satisfying your concerns.
3. When potential disruption outweighs the benefits of resolution.
4. To let people cool down and regain perspective.
5. When gathering information supersedes immediate decision.
6. When others can resolve the conflict more effectively.
7. When issues seem tangential to or symptomatic of other issues.

Accommodating

1. When you find you are wrong—to allow a better position to be heard, to learn, and to show your reasonableness.
2. When issues are more important to others than yourself—to satisfy others and maintain cooperation.
3. To build social credits for later issues.
4. To minimize loss when you are outmatched and losing.
5. When harmony and stability are especially important.
6. To allow subordinates to develop by learning from mistakes.

Source: K. W. Thomas, "Toward Multidimensional Values in Teaching: The Example of Conflict Management." *Academy of Management Review* 2, no. 3 (1977), pp. 484–90. Copyright © 1977 Academy of Management, via Copyright Clearance Center.

goes to the ticket office to complain. One approach he could take would be to demand the same seats he has always had; this would be his *position*. A different approach would be to find alternative seats that are just as satisfactory as his old seats had been; this would be his *interest*. In negotiating,

How to Swim with Sharks

HIGHLIGHT P4.3

It is dangerous to swim with sharks, but not all sharks are found in the water. Some people may behave like sharks, and a best-selling book for executives written a few years ago took its title from that theme. However, an article appeared in the journal *Perspectives in Biology and Medicine* nearly three decades ago claiming to be a translated version of an essay written in France more than a century earlier for sponge divers. The essay notes that while no one wants to swim with sharks, it is an occupational hazard for certain people. For those who must swim with sharks, it can be essential to follow certain rules. See if you think the following rules for interacting with the sharks of the sea serve as useful analogies for interacting with the sharks of everyday life.

Rule 1: Assume any unidentified fish is a shark. Just because a fish may be acting in a docile manner does not mean it is not a shark. The real test is how it will act when blood is in the water.

Rule 2: Don't bleed. Bleeding will prompt even more aggressive behavior and the involvement of even more sharks. Of course, it is not easy to keep from bleeding when injured. Those who cannot do so are advised not to swim with sharks at all.

Rule 3: Confront aggression quickly. Sharks usually give warning before attacking a swimmer. Swimmers should watch for indications an attack is imminent and take prompt counteraction. A blow to the nose is often appropriate since it shows you understand the shark's intentions and will respond in kind. It is particularly dangerous to behave in an ingratiating manner toward sharks. People who once held this erroneous view often can be identified by a missing limb.

Rule 4: Get out of the water if anyone starts bleeding. Previously docile sharks may begin attacking if blood is in the water. Their behavior can become so irrational, even including attacking themselves, that it is safest to remove yourself entirely from the situation.

Rule 5: Create dissension among the attackers. Sharks are self-centered and rarely act in an organized fashion with other sharks. This significantly reduces the risk of swimming with sharks. Every now and then, however, sharks may launch a coordinated attack. The best strategy then is to create internal dissension among them since they already are quite prone to it; often sharks will fight among themselves over trivial or minor things. By the time their internal conflict is settled, sharks often have forgotten about their organized attack.

Rule 6: Never divert a shark attack toward another swimmer. Please observe this final item of swimming etiquette.

Source: V. Cousteau, "How to Swim with Sharks: A Primer." *Perspectives in Biology and Medicine,* Summer 1973, pp. 525–28.

it is much more constructive to satisfy interests than to fight over positions. Furthermore, it is important to focus both on your counterpart's interests (not position) and on your own interests (not position).

Finally, winning a negotiation at your counterpart's expense is likely to be only a short-term gain. Leaders should attempt to work out a resolution by looking at long-term rather than short-term goals, and they should try to build a working relationship that will endure and be mutually trusting and beneficial beyond the present negotiation. Along these lines, leaders should always seek win–win outcomes, which try to satisfy both sides' needs and continuing interests. It often takes creative problem solving to find new options that provide gains for both sides. Realistically, however, not all situations may be conducive to seeking win–win outcomes (see Highlight P4.3).

Problem Solving

Identifying Problems or Opportunities for Improvement

The first step in problem solving is to state the problem so that everyone involved in developing a solution has an informed and common appreciation and understanding of the task. This is a critical stage in problem solving and will take time and probably group discussion. It is dangerous to assume that everyone (or anyone!) knows at the outset what the problem is. A hurried or premature definition of the problem (e.g., as a result of groupthink) may lead to considerable frustration and wasted effort. In counseling and advising, for example, a significant portion of the work with a client is devoted to clarifying the problem. A student may seek help at the school counseling center to improve his study skills because he is spending what seems to be plenty of time studying yet is still doing poorly on examinations. A little discussion, however, may reveal that he is having difficulty concentrating on schoolwork because of problems at home. If the counselor had moved immediately to develop the client's study skills, the real cause of his difficulties would have gone untreated, and the client might have become even more pessimistic about his abilities and the possibility that others could help him. Or consider the case of a police chief who is concerned about the few volunteers willing to serve on a citizen's advisory committee to her department. There are many problems she might identify here, such as citizen apathy or poor publicity concerning the need and importance of the committee. The real problem, however, might be her own reputation for rarely listening to or heeding recommendations made by similar advisory committees in the past. If the chief were to take the time to explore and clarify the problem at the outset, then she *could* discover this important fact and take steps to solve the *real* problem (her own behavior). If, on the other hand, she pressed ahead aggressively, trusting her own appraisal of the problem, then nothing likely would change.

The reason it helps to take time to define a problem carefully is that sometimes people mistake symptoms for causes. In the case of the student, his poor studying was a symptom of another cause (family difficulties), not the cause of his poor grades. In the case of the police chief, lack of citizen participation on the advisory committee was a symptom of a problem, not the problem itself. If a plan addresses a symptom rather than the causes of a problem, the desired results will not be attained. It also is important during this stage to avoid scapegoating or blaming individuals or groups for the problem, which may just engender defensiveness and reduce creative thinking. This is a stage where conflict resolution techniques and negotiating skills can be very important. Finally, the statement of a problem should not imply that any particular solution is the correct one.

As an application of these considerations, let us consider two pairs of problem statements that a teacher might present to his class as a first step in addressing what he considers to be an unsatisfactory situation. These samples of dialogue touch on many aspects of communication, listening, and feedback skills addressed earlier in this book. Here, however, our focus is on differences in defining problems. In each case, the second statement is the one more likely to lead to constructive problem solving.

> **A:** I don't think you care enough about this course. No one is ever prepared. What do I have to do to get you to put in more time on your homework?
>
> **B:** What things are interfering with your doing well in this course?
>
> **A:** Your test grades are too low. I'm going to cancel the field trip unless they improve. Do you have any questions?
>
> **B:** I'm concerned about your test scores. They're lower than I expected them to be, and I'm not sure what's going on. What do you think the problem is?

Another aspect of this first stage of problem solving involves identifying those factors that, when corrected, are likely to have the greatest impact on improving an unsatisfactory situation. Since there are almost always more problems or opportunities for improvement than time or energy to devote to them all, it is crucial to identify those whose solutions offer the greatest potential payoff. A useful concept here is known as the Pareto principle. It states that about 80 percent of the problems in any system are the result of about 20 percent of the causes. In school, for example, most of the discipline problems are caused by a minority of the students. Of all the errors people make on income tax returns, just a few kinds of errors (e.g., forgetting to sign them) account for a disproportionately high percentage of returned forms. We would expect about 20 percent of the total mechanical problems in a city bus fleet to account for about 80 percent of the fleet's downtime. The Pareto principle can be used to focus problem-solving efforts on those causes that have the greatest overall impact.

Analyzing the Causes

Once a problem is identified, the next step is to analyze its causes. Analysis of a problem's causes should precede a search for its solutions. Two helpful tools for identifying the key elements affecting a problem situation are the cause-and-effect diagram (also called the "fishbone" diagram because of its shape, or the Ishikawa diagram after the person who developed it) and

FIGURE P4.2   A cause-and-effect diagram.

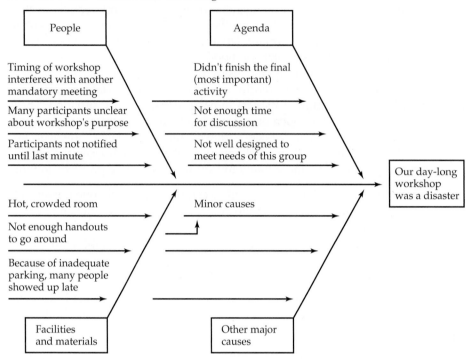

force field analysis. The cause-and-effect diagram uses a graphic approach to depict systematically the root causes of a problem, the relationships between different causes, and potentially a prioritization of which causes are most important (see Figure P4.2).

Force field analysis (see Figure P4.3) also uses a graphic approach, this time to depict the opposing forces that tend to perpetuate a present state of affairs. It is a way of depicting any stable situation in terms of dynamic balance, or equilibrium, between those forces that tend to press toward movement in one direction and those other forces that tend to restrain movement in that direction. So long as the net sum of all those forces is zero, no movement occurs. When a change is desirable, force field analysis can be used to identify the best way to upset the balance between positive and negative forces so that a different equilibrium can be reached.

Developing Alternative Solutions

Several ideas we've examined previously are relevant here (e.g., brainstorming), as is the importance of solutions meeting criteria for quality and acceptance. A procedure called Nominal Group Technique (NGT) is another way

FIGURE P4.3 Force field analysis example: Starting personal exercise program.

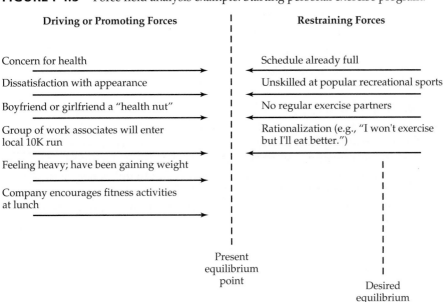

to generate a lot of ideas pertinent to a problem.[32] This procedure is similar to brainstorming in that it is an idea-generating activity conducted in a group setting. With NGT, however, group members write down ideas on individual slips of paper, which are later transferred to a blackboard or flipchart for the entire group to work with.

Selecting and Implementing the Best Solution

The first solution one thinks of is not necessarily the best solution, even if everyone involved finds it acceptable. It is better to select a solution on the basis of established criteria. These include such questions as the following: Have the advantages and disadvantages of all possible solutions been considered? Have all the possible solutions been evaluated in terms of their respective impacts on the whole organization, not just a particular team or department? Is the information needed to make a good decision among the alternatives available?

Assessing the Impact of the Solution

One should not assume that just by going through the preceding steps the actions implemented will solve the problem. The solution's continuing impact must be assessed, preferably in terms of measurable criteria of success that all parties involved can agree on.

Improving Creativity

Seeing Things in New Ways
Using Power Constructively
Forming Diverse Problem-Solving Groups

Seeing Things in New Ways

There are several things leaders can do to increase their own and their followers' creativity. Some of these facilitating factors have already been discussed and include assuring adequate levels of technical expertise, delaying and minimizing the evaluation or judgment of solutions, focusing on the intrinsic motivation of the task, removing unnecessary constraints on followers, and giving followers more latitude in making decisions. One popular technique for stimulating creative thinking in groups is called brainstorming (see Highlight P4.4).

An additional thing leaders can do to enhance creativity is to *see things in new ways,* or to look at problems from as many perspectives as possible.

Steps for Enhancing Creativity through Brainstorming

HIGHLIGHT P4.4

Brainstorming is a technique designed to enhance the creative potential of any group trying to solve a problem. Leaders should use the following rules when conducting a brainstorming session:

1. Groups should consist of five to seven people: Fewer than five limits the number of ideas generated, but more than seven often can make the session unwieldy. It may be more important to carefully decide who should attend a session than how many people should attend.

2. Everybody should be given the chance to contribute. The first phase of brainstorming is idea generation, and members should be encouraged to spontaneously contribute ideas as soon as they get them. The objective in the first phase is quantity, not quality.

3. No criticism is allowed during the idea generation phase. This helps to clearly separate the activities of imaginative thinking and idea production from idea evaluation.

4. Freewheeling and outlandish ideas should be encouraged. With some modification, these ideas may be eventually adopted.

5. "Piggybacking" off others' ideas should be encouraged. Combining ideas or extending others' ideas often results in better solutions.

6. The greater the quantity and variety of ideas, the better. The more ideas generated, the greater the probability a good solution will be found.

7. Ideas should be recorded. Ideally, ideas should be recorded on a blackboard or butcher paper so that members can review all of the ideas generated.

8. After all of the ideas have been generated, each idea should be evaluated in terms of pros and cons, costs and benefits, feasibility, and so on. Choosing the final solution often depends on the results of these analyses.

Source: A. F. Osborn, *Applied Imagination.* New York: Scribner's, 1963.

This is, though, easier said than done. It can be difficult to see novel uses for things we are very familiar with, or to see such in novel ways. Psychologists call this kind of mental block functional fixedness.[33] Creative thinking depends on overcoming the functional fixedness associated with the rigid and stereotyped perceptions we have of the things around us.

One way to see things differently is to think in terms of analogies. Thinking in terms of analogies is a practical extension of Cronbach's definition of creativity—making fresh observations, or seeing one thing as something else.[34] In this case, the active search for analogies is the essence of the problem-solving method. In fact, finding analogies is the foundation of a commercial creative-problem-solving approach called Synectics.[35] An actual example of use of analogies in a Synectics problem-solving group concerned designing a new roofing material that would adjust its color to the season, turning white in the summer to reflect heat and black in the winter to absorb heat. The group's first task was to find an analogy in nature, and it thought of fishes whose colors change to match their surroundings. The mechanism for such changes in fish is the movement of tiny compartments of pigments closer to or farther away from the skin's surface, thus changing its color. After some discussion, the group designed a black roof impregnated with little white plastic balls which would expand when it was hot, making the roof lighter, and contract when it was cold, making the roof darker.[36]

Another way to see things differently is to try putting an idea or problem into a picture rather than into words. Feelings or relationships that have eluded verbal description may come out in a drawing, bringing fresh insights to an issue.

Using Power Constructively

In addition to getting followers to see problems from as many perspectives as possible, a leader can also *use her power constructively to enhance creativity.* As noted earlier, groups may suppress creative thinking by being overly critical or by passing judgment during the solution generation stage. This effect may be even more pronounced when strong authority relationships and status differences are present. Group members may be reluctant to take the risk of raising a "crazy" idea when superiors are present, especially if the leader is generally perceived as unreceptive to new ideas, or they may be reluctant to offer the idea if they believe others in the group will take potshots at it in front of the leader. Leaders who wish to create a favorable climate for fostering creativity need to use their power to encourage the open expression of ideas and to suppress uncooperative or aggressive reactions (overt or covert) between group members. Further, leaders can use their power to encourage creativity by rewarding successes and by not punishing mistakes. Leaders can also use their power to delegate authority and responsibility, relax followers' constraints, and empower followers to take risks. By taking these steps, leaders can help followers to build idiosyncratic credits, which in turn will encourage them to take risks and to be more creative. Along these same lines, the entire climate of an organization can be either more or less conducive to creative thinking, differences that may be due to the use of power within the organization. In an insightful turn of the familiar adage, "Power corrupts," Kanter noted how powerlessness also corrupts.[37] She pointed out how managers who feel powerless in an organization may spend more energy guarding their territory than collaborating with others in productive action. The need to actively support followers' creativity may be especially important for leaders in bureaucratic organizations, as such organizations tend to be so inflexible, formalized, and centralized as to make many people in them feel relatively powerless.

Forming Diverse Problem-Solving Groups

Leaders can enhance creativity by *forming diverse problem-solving groups.* Group members with similar experiences, values, and preferences will be less likely to create a wide variety of solutions and more apt to agree on a solution prematurely than more diverse groups. Thus, selecting people for a group or committee with a variety of experiences, values, and preferences should increase the creativity of the group, although these differences may also increase the level of conflict within the group and make it more difficult for the leader to get consensus on a final solution. One technique for increasing group diversity and, in turn, creativity in problem-solving groups involves the use of the four preference dimensions of the Myers-Briggs Type Indicator (MBTI). Actual evidence to support this specific approach appears scanty,[38] but perhaps preferences only assume significance after certain other conditions for group creativity already have been met. For example, diversity cannot make up for an absence of technical expertise. Although the MBTI dimensions may be useful in selecting diverse groups, this instrument should only be used after ensuring that all potential members have high levels of technical expertise. Choosing members based solely on MBTI preferences ignores the crucial role that technical expertise and intrinsic motivation play in creativity. Another aspect of the relationship between creativity and leadership is described in Highlight P4.5.

Diagnosing Performance Problems in Individuals, Groups, and Organizations

Expectations

Capabilities

Opportunities

Motivation

Concluding Comments on the Diagnostic Model

In many ways leaders will only be as effective as the followers and teams they lead. Along these lines, one of the more difficult issues leaders must deal with is managing individuals or teams that are not performing up to

Managing Creativity

HIGHLIGHT P4.5

R. T. Hogan and J. Morrison (1993) maintained that people who are seen as more creative tend to have several distinguishing personality characteristics. In general, creative people are open to information and experience, have high energy, can be personally assertive and even domineering, react emotionally to events, are impulsive, are more interested in music and art than in hunting and sports, and finally are very motivated to prove themselves (i.e., are concerned with personal adequacy). Thus, creative people tend to be independent, willful, impractical, unconcerned with money, idealistic, and nonconforming. Given that these tendencies may not make them ideal followers, the interesting question raised by Hogan and Morrison is: How does one lead or manage creative individuals? This question becomes even more interesting when considering the qualities of successful leaders or managers. As discussed earlier, successful leaders tend to be intelligent, dominant, conscientious, stable, calm, goal-oriented, outgoing, and somewhat conventional. Thus, one might think that the personalities of creative followers and successful leaders might be the source of considerable conflict and make them natural enemies in organizational settings. Because many organizations depend on creativity to grow and prosper, being able to successfully lead creative individuals may be a crucial aspect of success for these organizations. Given that creative people already possess technical expertise, imaginative thinking skills, and intrinsic motivation, Hogan and Morrison suggested that leaders take the following steps to successfully lead creative followers:

1. *Set goals.* Because creative people value freedom and independence, this step will be best accomplished if leaders use a high level of participation in the goal-setting process. Leaders should ask followers what they can accomplish in a particular time frame.

2. *Provide adequate resources.* Followers will be much more creative if they have the proper equipment to work with, as they can devote their time to resolving the problem rather than spending time finding the equipment to get the job done.

3. *Reduce time pressures, but keep followers on track.* Try to set realistic milestones when setting goals, and make organizational rewards contingent on reaching these milestones. Moreover, leaders need to be well organized to acquire necessary resources and to keep the project on track.

4. *Consider nonmonetary as well as monetary rewards.* Creative people often gain satisfaction from resolving the problem at hand, not from monetary rewards. Thus, feedback should be aimed at enhancing their feelings of personal adequacy. Monetary rewards perceived to be controlling may decrease rather than increase motivation toward the task.

5. *Recognize that creativity is evolutionary, not revolutionary.* Although followers can create truly novel products (such as the Xerox machine), often the key to creativity is continuous product improvement. Making next year's product faster, lighter, cheaper, or more efficient requires minor modifications that can, over time, culminate in major revolutions. Thus, it may be helpful if leaders think of creativity more in terms of small innovations than major breakthroughs.

Source: R. T. Hogan and J. Morrison, "Managing Creativity." In *Create & Be Free: Essays in Honor of Frank Barron,* Ed. A. Montouri, Amsterdam: J. C. Gieben, 1993.

expectations. What makes this issue even more difficult is that, although the lack of performance may be obvious, the reasons for it may not. Leaders who correctly determine why a follower or team is exhibiting suboptimal performance are much more likely to implement an appropriate intervention to fix the problem. Unfortunately, many leaders do not have a model or framework for diagnosing performance problems at work, and

FIGURE P4.4
A model of
performance.

Performance = f(Expectations $\times$ Capabilities $\times$ Opportunities $\times$ Motivation)

as a result many do a poor job of dealing with problem performers. The model in Figure P4.4 provides leaders with a pragmatic framework for understanding why a follower or team may not be performing up to expectations and what the leader can do to improve the situation. This model maintains that performance is a function of expectations, capabilities, opportunities, and motivation and integrates concepts discussed in more detail earlier in this book.

The model is also a modification of earlier models developed by various experts.[39-41] As a multiplicative rather than a compensatory model, a deficit in any one component should result in a substantial decrement in performance that cannot be easily made up by increasing the other components. An example might help to illuminate this point. Recently one of the authors was asked to help the manager of a nuclear power plant fix several safety and operational issues affecting the plant. Apparently many plant personnel did not feel they had to comply with governmental regulations regarding the proper use of safety equipment. An investigation into the problem revealed that the expectations for compliance were clear, everyone had been trained on the proper use of safety equipment, and the equipment was readily available. However, many personnel felt the equipment and procedures were a nuisance and unnecessary. The plant manager's initial attempt to rectify this problem was to run all plant personnel through a three-day nuclear safety training program. Much to the manager's surprise, the training program actually appeared to have a negative impact on safety compliance! This was due to the fact that the underlying issue was not expectations, capabilities, or opportunities but rather motivation. Even if the staff had 30 days of training it still would not have positively affected motivation, which was the underlying barrier to performance. Because there were few if any positive or negative consequences for the staff for properly using the equipment, the problem did not improve until the manager implemented a system of rewards and punishments for safety compliance. A more thorough explanation of the components of the model and what leaders can do to improve performance can be found below.

Expectations

Performance problems often occur because individuals or groups do not understand what they are supposed to do. There are many instances where talented, skilled groups accomplished the wrong objective because of miscommunication or sat idly by while waiting for instructions that never arrived. It is the leader's responsibility for ensuring that followers understand their roles, goals, performance standards, and the key metrics for determining success. More information about goal setting and clarifying team goals and roles can be found in the "Setting Goals" section earlier in this chapter and "Building High Performance Teams" in the Part 3 feedback skills chapter of this text.

Capabilities

Just because followers understand what they are supposed to do does not necessarily mean they can do it. Sometimes followers and teams lack the capabilities needed to achieve a goal or perform above expectations. Abilities and skills are the two components that make up capabilities. Ability is really another name for raw talent, and includes such individual difference variables as athleticism, intelligence, creativity, and personality traits. As such, abilities are characteristics that are relatively difficult to change with training. Because abilities are relatively insensitive to training interventions, sending people who lack the required abilities to more training or motivating them to work harder will have relatively little impact on performance. Instead, the best remedy for this situation is to select those individuals with the abilities needed for performance.

Although followers may have the raw talent needed to perform a task, they still may lack the skills needed to perform at a high level. Such is the case with many athletic teams or musical groups at the beginning of the season or when a work group gets a new set of equipment or responsibility for tasks they have no previous experience with. As discussed in the "Leadership Behavior" chapter (8), skills consist of a well-defined body of knowledge and a set of related behaviors. Unlike abilities, skills are very amenable to training, and leaders with high levels of relevant expertise may coach others in the development of skills, see that they are obtained in other ways on the job, or send their followers to training programs in order to improve followers' skill levels. More information about selecting people with the right abilities can be found in Chapter 4. See Chapters 3 and 9 and the sections on "Building Technical Competence" in the Part 2 leadership skills chapter and on "Coaching" and "Development Planning" in Part 3 feedback skills chapter for more information on building skills.

Opportunities

Performance can also be limited when followers lack the resources needed to get the job done. At other times followers may lack the opportunity to demonstrate acquired skills. Such is the case when passengers are hungry but flight attendants do not have any meals to pass out during the flight. In this situation the flight attendants could have very high levels of customer service goals, capabilities, and motivation but will still not be able to satisfy customer needs. Leaders must ensure that followers and teams have the needed equipment, financial resources, and the opportunities to exhibit their skills if they want to eliminate this constraint on performance.

Motivation

Many performance problems can be attributed to a lack of motivation. The two critical issues here are whether followers or groups choose to perform or exhibit the level of effort necessary to accomplish a task. If this does not occur, then the leader should first try to learn why people are unmotivated. Sometimes the task may involve risks the leader is not aware of. At other times individuals or groups may simply run out of steam to perform the task or there are few consequences for superior or unsatisfactory performance. Leaders have several options to resolve motivation problems in followers and teams. First, they can select followers who have higher levels of achievement or intrinsic motivation for the task. Second, they can set clear goals or do a better job providing feedback about performance. Third, they can reallocate work across the team or redesign the task to improve skill variety, task significance, and task identity. Fourth, they can restructure rewards and punishments so they are more closely linked to performance levels. See the "Motivation, Satisfaction, and Performance" chapter (9) for more information about motivating followers.

Concluding Comments on the Diagnostic Model

In summary, this model provides an integrative framework for many of the topics affecting performance previously reviewed in this text. It reviews some of the factors that affect performance and suggests ideas for rectifying performance problems. It should be emphasized, however, that this model only addresses follower, group, and organizational performance. Leaders need to be mindful that there are other desirable outcomes, too, such as organizational climate and job satisfaction, and that actions to increase performance (especially just in the short term) may adversely impact these other desirable outcomes.

Team Building at the Top

Executive Teams Are Different

Applying Individual Skills and Team Skills

Tripwire Lessons

In certain ways, executive teams are similar to any other teams. For example, just about any group of senior executives that has faced a dire crisis and survived will note that teamwork was essential for its survival. In a nutshell, then, *when teamwork is critical,* all the lessons of the section on "Building High Performance Teams" apply. More specifically, to really be able to benefit from a team-building intervention, individual members must be comfortable with their own strengths and weaknesses and the strengths and weaknesses of their peers. But this raises a question: If all this is true, why do we include a separate section on team building for top teams? Because there are two critical differences between most teams and "teams at the top" that should be addressed.

Executive Teams Are Different

As opposed to other kinds of work teams, not all the work at the executive level requires all (or even any) of the team to be present. An example might help. In our research on teams we studied the air crews that fly the B-1 bomber. These are four-person teams comprising an aircraft commander, a copilot, an offensive systems officer, and a defensive systems officer. While each has individual responsibilities, in every single bombing run we observed, it was absolutely essential that the team work together to accomplish the mission. They had all of the components of a true team (complex and common goal, differentiated skills, interdependence), and no individual acting alone could have achieved success. But this is not always the case for executive teams.

As Katzenbach has observed,[42] many top leadership challenges do not really require teamwork at all. Furthermore, many top leadership challenges that do constitute real team opportunities do not require or warrant full involvement by everyone who is officially on the team. In fact, an official "team at the top" rarely functions as a collective whole involving all the formal members. Thus, the real trick for executive teams is to be able to apply both the technical individual skills that probably got the individuals to the team in the first place and the skills required for high-performance teamwork when a team situation presents itself.

Applying Individual Skills and Team Skills

There are two critical requirements if this is to work. First, one must have the diagnostic skills to discern whether the challenge presenting itself involves an individual situation or a team situation. Then, it requires that leaders "stay the course" when a team situation is present. This means, for example, when pressure for results intensifies, not slipping back into the traditional modes of assigning work to an individual (e.g., one member of that top team), but rather allowing the team to complete the work *as a team*. Again, Katzenbach stated this clearly:

> Some leadership groups, of course, err in the opposite way, by attempting to forge a team around performance opportunities that do not call for a team approach. In fact, the increasing emphasis that team proponents place on "team-based organizations" creates real frustrations as top leadership groups try to rationalize good executive leadership instincts into time-consuming team building that has no performance purpose. Catalyzing real team performances at the top does not mean replacing executive leadership with executive teams; it means being rigorous about the distinction between opportunities that require single-leader efforts and those that require team efforts—and applying the discipline that fits.[43]

To summarize this point, executives do not always need to perform as a team to be effective. But when they do need to perform as a team, the same lessons of team building discussed earlier can be very useful in helping them to enhance their team performance.

The second difference with executive teams is that they have an opportunity to enhance teamwork throughout their organization that few others have. It is our experience that *only the executive team can change organizational systems.* Recall from Chapter 10 we described the Team Leadership Model and mentioned there were four system issues critical to team performance. These systems were all located at the organizational level and consisted of reward systems, education systems, information systems, and control systems. The impact of these systems can be so pervasive across the entire organization that a small change in a system can have monumental impact in the organization. In a sense, then, the executive team has within its control the power to do widespread "team building" in a very different manner than we have discussed to this point. Just consider the impact of changing a compensation system (one element of a reward system) from an individual-based bonus plan to a team-based bonus plan!

Tripwire Lessons

Finally, our experience in working with executives has taught us that leaders at this level have some important lessons to learn about team building at the top. Richard Hackman, in preparing the huge editorial task of having many people produce one coherent book (by his own admission, not necessarily the best of team tasks), assembled the various authors at a conference center. As one of the contributors, one of this text's authors (RCG) recalls a most frustrating task of attempting to put together the simple checklist of steps to ensure a team developed properly. As this arduous process dragged on and tempers flared, it became obvious that "Teamwork for Dummies" was never going to emerge. But something else did start to emerge. It became clear *that some behaviors leaders engaged in could virtually guarantee failure for their teams.* While not the intent, this experience yielded a worthwhile set of lessons. A condensed version of those lessons, labeled "trip wires" by Hackman, concludes our discussion of team building at the top.[44]

Trip Wire 1: Call the Performing Unit a Team But Really Manage Members as Individuals

One way to set up work is to assign specific responsibilities to specific individuals and then choreograph individuals' activities so their products coalesce into a team product. A contrasting strategy is to assign a team responsibility and accountability for an entire piece of work and let members decide among themselves how they will proceed to accomplish the work. While either of these strategies can be effective, a choice must be made between them. A mixed model, in which people are told they are a team but are treated as individual performers with their own specific jobs to do, sends mixed signals to members, is likely to confuse everyone, and in the long run is probably untenable.

To reap the benefits of teamwork, one must actually build a team. Calling a set of people a team or exhorting them to work together is insufficient. Instead, explicit action must be taken to establish the team's boundaries, to define the task as one for which members are collectively responsible and accountable, and to give members the authority to manage both their internal processes and the team's relations with external entities such as clients and co-workers. Once this is done, management behavior and organizational systems gradually can be changed as necessary to support teamwork.

Trip Wire 2: Create an Inappropriate Authority Balance

The exercise of authority creates anxiety, especially when one must balance between assigning a team authority for some parts of the work and withholding it for other parts. Because both managers and team members tend to be uncomfortable in such situations, they may collude to "clarify" them. Sometimes the result is the assignment of virtually all authority to the team—which can result in anarchy or a team that heads off in an inappropriate direction. At other times, managers retain virtually all authority, dictating work procedures in detail to team members and, in the process, losing many of the advantages that can accrue from teamwork. In both cases, the anxieties that accompany a mixed model are reduced, but at significant cost to team effectiveness.

To achieve a good balance of managerial and team authority is difficult. Moreover, merely deciding how much authority will be assigned to the group and how much will be retained by management are insufficient. Equally important are the domains of authority that are assigned and retained. Our findings suggest that managers should be unapologetic and insistent about exercising their authority about *direction*—the end states the team is to pursue—and about *outer-limit constraints* on team behavior—the things the team must always do or never do. At the same time, managers should assign to the team full authority for the means by which it accomplishes its work—and then do whatever they can to ensure that team members understand and accept their responsibility and accountability for deciding how they will execute the work.

Few managerial behaviors are more consequential for the long-term being of teams than those that address the partitioning of authority between managers and teams. It takes skill to accomplish this well, and it is a skill that has emotional and behavioral as well as cognitive components. Just knowing the rules for partitioning authority is insufficient; one also needs some practice in applying those rules in situations where anxieties, including one's own, are likely to be high. Especially challenging for managers are the early stages in the life of a team (when managers often are tempted to give away too much authority) and when the going gets rough (when the temptation is to take authority back too soon). The management of authority relations with task-performing teams is indeed much like walking a balance beam, and our evidence suggests that it takes a good measure of knowledge, skill, and perseverance to keep from falling off.

Trip Wire 3: Assemble a Large Group of People, Tell Them in General Terms What Needs to Be Accomplished, and Let Them "Work Out the Details"

Traditionally, individually focused designs for work are plagued by constraining structures that have built up over the years to monitor and control employee behavior. When groups are used to perform work, such structures tend to be viewed as unnecessary bureaucratic impediments to team functioning. Thus, just as managers sometimes (and mistakenly) attempt to empower teams by relinquishing all authority to them, so do some attempt to get rid of the dysfunctional features of existing organizational structures simply by taking down all the structures they can. Apparently, the hope is that removing structures will release teams and enable members to work together creatively and effectively.

Managers who hold this view often wind up providing teams with less structure than they actually need. Tasks are defined only in vague, general terms. Group composition is unclear or fluid. The limits of the team's authority are kept deliberately fuzzy. The unstated assumption is that there is some magic in the group interaction process and that, by working together, members will evolve any structures that the team actually needs.

It is a false hope; there is no such magic. Indeed, our findings suggest the opposite: Groups that have appropriate structures tend to develop healthy internal processes, whereas groups with insufficient or inappropriate structures tend to have process problems. Worse, coaching and process consultation are unlikely to resolve these problems, precisely because they are rooted in the team structure. For members to learn how to interact well within a flawed or underspecified structure is to swim upstream against a very strong current.

Trip Wire 4: Specify Challenging Team Objectives, but Skimp on Organizational Supports

Even if a work team has clear, engaging direction and an enabling structure, its performance can go sour—or, at least, it can fall below the group's potential—if the team is not well supported. Teams in high-commitment organizations fall victim to this trip wire when given "stretch" objectives but not the wherewithal to accomplish them; high initial enthusiasm soon changes into disillusionment.

It is no small undertaking to provide these supports to teams, especially in organizations designed to support work by individuals. Corporate compensation policy, for example, may make no provision for team bonuses and, indeed, may explicitly prohibit them. Human resource departments may be primed to identify individuals' training needs and provide first-rate courses to fill those needs, but training in team skills may not be available at all. Existing performance appraisal systems, which may be state-of-the-art for measuring individual contributions, are likely to be wholly inappropriate for assessing and rewarding work done by teams. Information systems and control systems may provide managers with the data they need to monitor and control work processes, but they may be neither available nor appropriate for use by work teams. Finally, the material resources required for the work may have been prespecified by those who originally designed it, and there may be no procedure in place for a team to secure the special configuration of resources it needs to execute the particular performance strategy it has developed.

To align existing organizational systems with the needs of teams often requires managers to exercise power and influence upward and laterally in the organization.

An organization set up to provide teams with full support for their work is noticeably different from one whose systems and policies are intended to support and control individual work, and many managers may find the prospect of changing to a group-oriented organization both unsettling and perhaps even vaguely revolutionary.

It is hard to provide good organizational support for task-performing teams, but generally it is worth the trouble. The potential of a well-directed, well-structured, well-supported team is tremendous. Moreover, to stumble over the organizational support trip wire is, perhaps, the saddest of all team failures. When a group is both excited about its work and all set up to execute it superbly, it is especially shattering to fail merely because the organizational supports required cannot be obtained. It is like being all dressed up and ready to go to the prom only to have the car break down en route.

Trip Wire 5: Assume That Members Already Have All the Competence They Need to Work Well as a Team

Once a team is launched and operating under its own steam, managers sometimes assume their work is done. As we have seen, there are indeed some good reasons for giving a team ample room to go about its business in its own way: Inappropriate or poorly timed managerial interventions impaired the work of more than one group in our research. However, a strict, hands-off managerial stance also can limit a team's effectiveness, particularly when members are not already skilled and experienced in teamwork.

Part Notes

1. Bass, B. M. *Bass and Stogdill's Handbook of Leadership.* 3rd ed. New York: Free Press, 1990.

2. Erez, M., P. C. Earley, and C. L. Hulin. "The Impact of Participation on Goal Acceptance and Performance: A Two-Step Model." *Academy of Management Journal* (1985), pp. 359–72.

3. Locke, E. A., G. P. Latham, and M. Erez. "Three-Way Interactive Presentation and Discussion," "A Unique Approach to Resolving Scientific Disputes," and "Designing Crucial Experiments." Papers presented at the Society of Industrial and Organizational Psychology Convention, Atlanta, GA, 1987.

4. House, R. J. "Power in Organizations: A Social Psychological Perspective." Unpublished manuscript, University of Toronto, 1984.

5. Latham, G. P., and T. W. Lee. "Goal Setting." In *Generalizing from Laboratory to Field Settings.* Ed. E. A. Locke. Lexington, MA: Lexington Books, 1986.

6. Locke, E. A., G. P. Latham, and M. Erez. "Three-Way Interactive Presentation and Discussion," "A Unique Approach to Resolving Scientific Disputes," and "Designing Crucial Experiments." Papers presented at the Society of Industrial and Organizational Psychology Convention, Atlanta, GA, 1987.

7. Bass, B. M. *Bass and Stogdill's Handbook of Leadership.* 3rd ed. New York: Free Press, 1990.

8. O'Reilly, C. A. "Supervisors and Peers as Informative Sources, Group Supportiveness, and Individual Decision-Making Performance." *Journal of Applied Psychology* 62 (1977), pp. 632–35.

9. Guth, C. K., and S. S. Shaw. *How to Put on Dynamic Meetings.* Reston, VA: Reston, 1980.

10. Thomas, K. W., and W. H. Schmidt. "A Survey of Managerial Interests with Respect to Conflict." *Academy of Management Journal* 19 (1976), pp. 315–18.

11. Morse, J. J., and F. R. Wagner. "Measuring the Process of Managerial Effectiveness." *Academy of Management Journal* 21 (1978), pp. 23–35.

12. Brown, L. D. *Managing Conflict at Organizational Interfaces.* Reading, MA: Addison-Wesley, 1983.

13. Ouchi, W. G. *How American Business Can Meet the Japanese Challenge.* Reading, MA: Addison-Wesley, 1981.

14. Peters, T. J., and R. H. Waterman. *In Search of Excellence.* New York: Harper & Row, 1982.

15. Robbins, S. P. *Organizational Behavior: Concepts, Controversies, and Applications.* Englewood Cliffs, NJ: Prentice Hall, 1986.

16. Yukl, G. *Leadership in Organizations.* 2nd ed. Englewood Cliffs, NJ: Prentice Hall, 1989.

17. Kets de Vries, M. F. R., and D. Miller. "Managers Can Drive Their Subordinates Mad." In *The Irrational Executive: Psychoanalytic Explorations in Management.* Ed. M. F. R. Kets de Vries. New York: International Universities Press, 1984.

18. Thomas, K. W., and W. H. Schmidt. "A Survey of Managerial Interests with Respect to Conflict." *Academy of Management Journal* 19 (1976), pp. 315–18.

19. Yukl, G. *Leadership in Organizations.* 2nd ed. Englewood Cliffs, NJ: Prentice Hall, 1989.

20. Thomas, K. W. "Conflict and Conflict Management." In *Handbook of Industrial and Organizational Psychology*. Ed. M. D. Dunnette. Chicago: Rand McNally, 1976.

21. Robbins, S. P. *Organizational Behavior: Concepts, Controversies, and Applications*. Englewood Cliffs, NJ: Prentice Hall, 1986.

22. Bass, B.M. *Leadership and Performance beyond Expectations*. New York: Free Press, 1985.

23. Willner, A. R. *The Spellbinders: Charismatic Political Leadership*. New Haven: Yale University Press, 1984.

24. Roberts, N. C., and R. T. Bradley. "Limits of Charisma." In *Charismatic Leadership: The Elusive Factor in Organizational Effectiveness*. Eds. J. A. Conger and R. N. Kanungo. San Francisco: Jossey-Bass, 1988, pp. 253–75.

25. Kanter, R. M. *The Change Masters*. New York: Simon & Schuster, 1983.

26. Thomas, K. W. "Conflict and Conflict Management." In *Handbook of Industrial and Organizational Psychology*. Ed. M. D. Dunnette. Chicago: Rand McNally, 1976.

27. Thomas, K. W. "Conflict and Conflict Management." In *Handbook of Industrial and Organizational Psychology*. Ed. M. D. Dunnette. Chicago: Rand McNally, 1976.

28. Thomas, K. W. "Toward Multidimensional Values in Teaching: The Example of Conflict Management." *Academy of Management Review* 2, no. 3 (1977), pp. 484–90.

29. Fisher, R., and W. Ury. *Getting to Yes*. Boston: Houghton Mifflin, 1981.

30. Fisher, R., and W. Ury. *Getting to Yes*. Boston: Houghton Mifflin, 1981.

31. Blake, R. R., H. A. Shepard, and J. S. Mouton. *Managing Intergroup Conflict in Industry*. Houston, TX: Gulf, 1964.

32. Delbecq, A. L., A. H. Van de Ven, and D. H. Gustafson. *Group Techniques for Program Planning: A Guide to Nominal and Delphi Processes*. Glenview, IL: Scott Foresman, 1975.

33. Duncker, K. "On Problem Solving." *Psychological Monographs* 58, no. 5, 1945.

34. Cronbach, L. J. *Essentials of Psychological Testing*. 4th ed. San Francisco: Harper & Row, 1984.

35. Gordon, W. J. J. *Synectics*. New York: Harper & Row, 1961.

36. Gordon, W. J. J. *Synectics*. New York: Harper & Row, 1961.

37. Kanter, R. M. *The Change Masters*. New York: Simon & Schuster, 1983.

38. Thayer, P. W. "The Myers-Briggs Type Indicator and Enhancing Human Performance." Report prepared for the Committee on Techniques for the Enhancement of Human Performance of the National Academy of Sciences, 1988.

39. Campbell, J. P. "The Cutting Edge of Leadership: An Overview." In *Leadership: The Cutting Edge*. Eds. J. G. Hunt and L. L. Larson. Carbondale, IL: Southern Illinois University Press, 1977.

40. Campbell, J. P., R. A. McCloy, S. H. Oppler, and C. E. Sager. "A Theory of Performance." In *Frontiers in Industrial/Organizational Psychology and Personnel Selection*. Eds. N. Schmitt and W. C. Borman. San Francisco: Jossey-Bass, 1993, pp. 35–70.

41. Boudreau, J. W., and P. Ramstad. *Beyond HR: The New Science of Human Capital.* Boston, MA: Harvard Business School Press, 2007.

42. Katzenbach, J. R. *Teams at the Top.* Boston: Harvard Business School Press, 1998.

43. Ibid.

44. Hackman, J. R. *Groups That Work (and Those That Don't).* San Francisco: Jossey-Bass, 1990.

Subject Index

Note: A Name Index can be found on the book website at www.mhhe.com/hughes6e.